Lamps and Lighting

Lamps and Lighting

Third Edition

A manual of lamps and lighting prepared by members of staff of THORN EMI Lighting Ltd

**General Editors:
M A Cayless and A M Marsden**

Edward Arnold

© Thorn EMI Lighting Ltd 1983

First published in Great Britain in 1966 by
Edward Arnold (Publishers) Ltd, 41 Bedford Square, London WC1B 3DQ

Edward Arnold, 300 North Charles Street, Baltimore, Maryland 21201, USA

Edward Arnold (Australia) Pty Ltd, 80 Waverley Road, Caulfield East, Victoria 3145, Australia

Second edition 1972
Third edition 1983

British Library Cataloguing in Publication Data
Lamps and lighting.—3rd ed.
  1. Lamps   2. Lighting
  I. Cayless, M. A.   II. Marsden, A. M.
  III. Thorn EMI Lighting Ltd
  621.32′2   TH7703

ISBN 0-7131-3487-9

Printed in Great Britain at The Pitman Press, Bath

Preface

The third edition of *Lamps and Lighting* continues the tradition of the two previous editions in finding a series of competent authors from the staff of THORN EMI Lighting Ltd to write a series of chapters to a synopsis designated by the general editors. It is the editors who are responsible for any sins of omission relating to important topics in the field, but the reader may sympathize with their task of trying to include developments of the last decade within a book which had to be no longer than the second edition – their major saving of space has been by some telescoping of topics in lighting applications.

As before, the book begins with some chapters on fundamentals, designed with the needs of students of lighting in mind, before moving on to the book's particular uniqueness and strength – a detailed study of lamps, luminaires, and lighting circuits. The final chapters on lighting are in two parts, covering respectively interior and exterior applications. The whole has been written as a reference source for building services engineers, architects, and specialists in the lighting industry, as well as others with a broader interest in the science and technology of lamps and lighting.

A feature of this edition is the inclusion of absolute spectral power distributions for all the major lamp types in an accurate and strictly comparable format. The absolute radiation output powers are shown as fractions of the input powers, so that the performance of the lamps can be compared. This is a notable technical feat, scarcely possible at the time of the last edition, and the editors are grateful to Dr D O Wharmby who carried out the absolute spectroradiometry and subsequent computer evaluation and plotting of the spectra.

A serious criticism of the second edition was that the references and the general bibliography were inadequate. In this edition the chapter authors have been encouraged to cite references liberally: these have all been collated together alphabetically after the appendices. Suggestions for further general reading are to be found at the end of each individual chapter. The Librarian of the Jules Thorn Lighting Laboratories, Pat Schocktee, is thanked for her meticulous checking and completing of these references and reading suggestions.

The abbreviated organizations used in these references are well known to the professionals, but perhaps the most commonly used should be spelt out here – the British Standards Institution (BSI), the Commission Internationale de l'Éclairage (CIE), the International Electrotechnical Commission (IEC), and the Chartered Institution of Building Services (CIBS). This last body is an institution formed from the amalgamation of the Institution of Heating and Ventilating Engineers with the Illuminating Engineering Society (IES): the hybrid designation CIBS/IES is given to reports produced by the old IES, sometimes reprinted as CIBS Lighting Division documents, but certainly available only from the headquarters of CIBS – Delta House, 222 Balham High Road, London SW12 9BS.

The editors would like to thank the chapter authors for accepting, with varying degrees of reservation, the way their manuscripts have been mutilated or decimated in an attempt to produce a coherent whole of the required size. Individual secretarial help has been provided in various offices of THORN EMI Lighting Ltd, not least in that of one of the editors, for which Natalie Emery is particularly thanked.

Acknowledgements are due to the following for the use of copyright material:

P T Stone for Plate 2.1 (*Ltg. Res. Technol.*, **12,** 146, 1980).

L D Stroebel, H N Todd, and R D Zakin for Figs 2.3, 2.4, and 2.8 (*Visual concepts for photographers* published by Focal Press).

Professor R L Gregory for Figs 2.2 and 2.6 (*Eye and Brain* published by Weidenfeld and Nicholson).

The Electrochemical Society for Fig. 8.2 (*J. Electrochem. Soc.*, **97,** 266, 1950).

The British Broadcasting Company for Fig. 10.10.

The British Standards Institution for Table 16.1 (BS 5841 Part 1: 1980), Table 24.4 and Fig. 24.3 (BS 4533 Part 101: 1981), Table 28.3 (BS 5489 Part 2: 1974), and Fig. 29.1 (BS 1376: 1974).

The Marconi Company Limited for Fig. 17.6b.

CCT Theatre Lighting Limited for Figs 25.1 a, b, and d.

Colortran Limited for Fig. 25.1c.

The Transport and Road Research Laboratory for Fig. 28.1 (Report 929: *The relationship between road lighting quality and accident frequency*, 1980).

La Commission Internationale de l'Éclairage for Table 28.1 (Publication 12.2: *Recommendations for the lighting of roads for motorized traffic*, 1977).

The Chartered Institution of Building Services for many tables and figures in Parts IV and V of the book extracted from its publications – Lighting Research & Technology, Code for Interior Lighting, Lighting Guides, and Technical Reports.

1982   M A Cayless
                                                                             A M Marsden

Contents

Part I
Fundamentals

1 Light

The subject of this book is the modern technology involved in the production and utilization of light. Much of our information about the external world is gained through the visual sense and therefore adequate lighting is of major importance in everyday life. This first chapter begins with a short survey of some of the physical aspects of light and with statements of fundamental laws governing its behaviour, next there is a section on the manner in which the eye responds to stimulation by light, and this is followed by definitions of quantitative measures used for calculations in the lighting field. The final section is devoted to the basic principles governing the design of light controlling devices.

1.1 Electromagnetic radiation and light

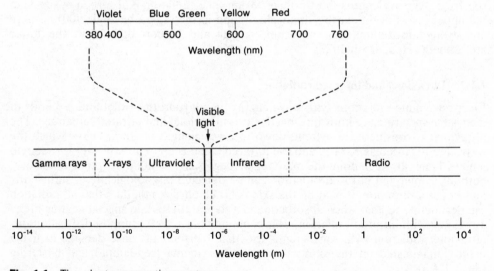

Fig. 1.1 The electromagnetic spectrum

Light is a form of energy that can pass from one material body to another without the need for any material substance in the intervening space. Such energy transfer has come to be called *radiation*, a term which implies that the energy flows out in straight lines in all directions from the source, although in fact straight-line flow does not always occur, particularly when material substance is traversed. Some forms of radiation are known to consist of particles, for example those which are emitted by radioactive materials, and light was at one time thought to consist of a shower of particles, but later it was found by experiments that the behaviour of a light ray could be better described in terms of waves, the ray direction being the direction in which the waves are travelling. About one hundred years ago it became clear that light waves are electromagnetic in character and occupy only a very small part of a huge range of wavelengths that constitute the electromagnetic spectrum (Fig. 1.1). At the long-wave end of this spectrum there are electromagnetic waves used for radio communications, with wavelengths ranging from tens of kilometres down to a few millimetres. At the other end of the electromagnetic spectrum there are X-rays and gamma rays, the latter being emitted during nuclear reactions and having wavelengths which are small even compared with atomic dimensions.

1.1.1 The visible spectrum

The visible portion of the spectrum covers the wavelength range from approximately 380 nm to 780 nm ($1\,nm = 10^{-6}\,mm$) and the eye discriminates between different wavelengths in this range by the sensation of colour. Blue and violet correspond to the short wavelengths and red to the long, yellow and green being in the middle of the visible range of wavelengths. Light consisting of a single wavelength radiation is said to be *monochromatic*, and is not strictly obtainable in practice because all sources produce light covering at least a narrow band of wavelengths. The laser (Sect. 6.4) is the nearest approach to a perfectly monochromatic light source.

Radiation reaching the earth's surface from the sun covers a range of wavelengths from about 290 nm to 1700 nm, which is considerably broader than the visible spectrum. At wavelengths shorter than 290 nm solar radiation is absorbed by ozone in the upper levels of the earth's atmosphere, and in the region beyond 1700 nm there are strong absorptions due to water vapour and carbon dioxide in the lower atmosphere (Henderson 1977).

1.1.2 Ultraviolet and infrared radiation

Electromagnetic radiations with wavelengths just beyond the violet and red ends of the visible spectrum are known respectively as ultraviolet and infrared radiations. The ultraviolet is considered to extend down to a wavelength of 1 nm, below which the waves are regarded as X-rays, and the infrared extends up to an arbitrary wavelength limit of 1 mm, at which point the radio region begins. While not perceptible to the eye, both ultraviolet and infrared radiation can be detected physiologically, if sufficiently intense, as a sensation of heat on the skin. This emphasizes the fact that all radiation can degenerate to heat when absorbed, and also that there is no special heating effect associated with infrared radiation, as is commonly incorrectly supposed. In addition, ultraviolet radiation with wavelengths less than 320 nm can cause damage to living tissues, manifested on the skin as a delayed erythema (reddening) and blistering (Sect. 1.4.3).

1.2 Propagation of light

Light and all other electromagnetic radiations travel through a vacuum in straight lines at the same velocity, which is close to $300\,000\,km\,s^{-1}$. In a material medium, such as air or glass, the velocity of propagation is less than in a vacuum by a factor known as the *refractive index* of the medium.

For any type of wave the velocity v is equal to the product of the wavelength λ and the frequency ν

$$v = \nu\lambda \qquad (1.1)$$

where frequency is defined as the number of waves which pass a fixed point in one second. For example the waves of violet light with a wavelength of 400 nm in vacuum have a frequency of $7{\cdot}5 \times 10^{14}$ Hz, and red light of 750 nm wavelength has a frequency of 4×10^{14} Hz. When waves pass from one medium to another the frequency does not change, but any change in velocity is accompanied by a proportional change in wavelength since by Eq. 1.1 v/λ must be constant. When the wavelength of light is quoted without reference to a medium it is normally taken to be the wavelength in air, which will be only very slightly shorter than that in a vacuum since the refractive index of air is close to unity.

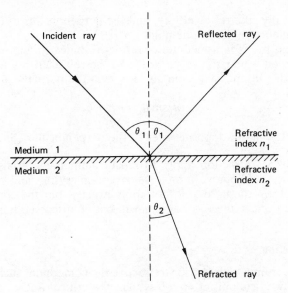

Fig. 1.2   Reflection and refraction at a boundary between two media

At the boundary between two media having different refractive indices incident light waves split into two groups, one is reflected back into the first medium and the other group is refracted into the second medium, as shown by the ray diagram in Fig. 1.2. The directions of the reflected and refracted rays are governed by the laws of geometrical optics, which can be derived from the wave theory of light and are stated in the following two sub-sections.

1.2.1   Laws of specular reflection

At a bounding surface that is smooth compared with the wavelength of the incident light, specular reflection is said to occur. A single incident ray produces a single reflected ray and the following relations hold:

(a)   The incident ray, the reflected ray, and the perpendicular to the bounding surface at the point of incidence all lie in one plane.

(b)   The incident ray and the reflected ray make equal angles with the perpendicular and are on opposite sides of it.

The proportion of light energy which appears in the reflected ray depends, among other things, on the ratio of the refractive indices of the two media and on the angle of incidence, that is the angle between the incident ray and the perpendicular to the surface. As the angle of incidence approaches 90° the proportion of reflected light approaches 100%.

1.2.2   Laws of refraction

Light passing through a smooth boundary surface into the second medium suffers a change of direction according to the following laws:

(a)   The incident ray, the refracted ray, and the perpendicular to the surface at the point of incidence all lie in one plane.
(b)   If the incident ray is in a medium of refractive index n_1 and makes an angle θ_1 with the perpendicular to the surface, and the refracted ray is in a medium of refractive index n_2 and makes an angle θ_2 with the perpendicular, then

$$n_1 \sin \theta_1 = n_2 \sin \theta_2 \tag{1.2}$$

where θ_1 and θ_2 lie on opposite sides of the perpendicular (Snell's law).

The above laws of refraction apply to most common materials, such as glass, transparent plastics, and liquids. In the case of certain crystals and transparent solids which are under strain these laws do not apply exactly, but the complicated effects which are observed under these conditions will not be discussed here (Wood 1967).

1.2.3   Total reflection

When a ray passes from a high to a low refractive index medium, such as from glass to air, a refracted ray exists only if θ_1 is less than the critical angle, which is equal to $\sin^{-1}(n_2/n_1)$. The critical angle corresponds to $\theta_2 = 90°$ in Eq. 1.2 and for glass of refractive index 1·5 has the value 41°49′. If a ray is incident at an angle greater than the critical angle, no refracted ray is present and all of the incident light energy appears in the reflected ray; hence the term total reflection is used for this condition. Total reflection provides a means of obtaining an efficient specular reflector and finds use in prismatic binoculars, reflective signs, and luminaires (Bean and Simons 1968). Another application is known as fibre-optics where light is channelled along transparent rods or fibres, which can be curved if required.

1.2.4   Dispersion

Refractive indices are dependent on the frequency of the light waves, an effect known as dispersion, and for common materials the refractive index increases as the frequency increases. For spectral violet the refraction is therefore greater than for red light. Dispersion effects find application in optical instruments, such as the spectrometer used in the study of lamp spectra, but are usually not significant enough to require taking into account in the design of lighting equipment.

1.2.5   Absorption and scattering

A light ray passing through a perfect vacuum suffers no loss of total energy, although the energy may become more spread out as the ray progresses. In their passage through material media however light rays generally suffer energy losses due to absorption and scattering effects.

Absorption is caused by the conversion of light into some other form of energy, usually heat, but it could be changed into radiation of different wavelength (fluorescence), into electrical energy as in photoelectric cells, or into chemical energy as in the photosynthesis carried out by plants. If the medium is homogeneous the loss in intensity of a parallel beam of light of a particular wavelength as it passes through follows an exponential decay curve of the form

$$i = i_0 \exp(-\alpha x) \tag{1.3}$$

where i_0 is the initial beam intensity, i is the intensity of the beam after travelling a distance x in the medium, and α is the *linear absorption coefficient*, which usually depends on wavelength. For highly transparent materials α is very small, so i does not become appreciably less than i_0 until x is very large. In many materials α is large for all wavelengths, so large that i becomes virtually zero in very short distances; such materials are opaque to light except in very thin layers, for example metals. In some materials α is considerably different for different wavelengths of the visible spectrum; these materials change the spectral distribution of light passing through and form the basis for colour filters.

Under certain conditions the effective absorption coefficient of a medium can be made negative, which means that light passing through it increases in intensity. This is the principle of the laser, a device which can be made to generate a light beam of extremely high intensity. The extra energy required for the light intensification must be supplied to the medium from some suitable source (Sect. 6.4.1).

Scattering occurs in non-homogeneous media and is caused by multiple reflection and refraction at numerous, randomly orientated, boundary surfaces within the medium. Fog and cloud are examples of scattering conditions in air due to the presence of suspended water droplets. Much of the light entering a scattering medium may be scattered back out of it again without much absorption loss. Examples of this are the surfaces of white paper or cloth which consist of densely packed and almost transparent fibres. When light is strongly absorbed at scattering surfaces, such as carbon particles in dark smoke, very little scattered light finds its way out of the medium, which therefore appears black. If the scattering particles absorb selectively in the visible region, a colour is imparted to the medium, for example a paint layer in which coloured pigment particles are suspended in a transparent lacquer and absorb some of the wavelengths from white light, both on its path into the layer and also out of the layer after reflection. Scattering can be wavelength-selective due to a contribution from diffracted light, and this also can impart a colour to a medium. All material media scatter light to some extent because of the molecular structure of matter. Scattering by very small particles, such as molecules, is greater for the shorter wavelengths of light; the blue of the sky is accounted for in this way (McCartney 1976).

1.2.6   Diffuse reflection and transmission; the cosine law

When a light ray meets a surface which has irregularities comparable with or greater than the wavelength of the light there is no longer a single reflected or refracted ray, but the light energy spreads out in all directions from the point of incidence, as in scattering. The light which returns to the medium from which the incident ray emerged is said to be *diffusely reflected*, and that which passes through into the second medium is said to be *diffusely transmitted*. In general the precise angular distribution of the reflected and transmitted light depends on the angle of incidence of the ray to the surface and also on the nature of the surface roughness. With very fine grained surfaces the reflection may be almost specular at angles of incidence approaching 90°.

Uniform diffuser   To enable simple calculations to be made the concept of a uniform diffuser is often used. A uniform diffuse reflector is one in which the reflected light distribution is independent of the angle of the incident light, and the intensity of reflected light in a direction making an angle θ with the perpendicular to the surface is proportional to cos θ. This cosine law can also be applied to uniform diffuse transmission. No real surface completely satisfies the conditions for a uniform diffuser, but some surfaces are good approximations to it, for example a layer of magnesium oxide powder.

1.2.7   Polarization

The electromagnetic waves which make up a light ray have electric fields perpendicular to the direction of propagation. For each wave there is a plane which contains both the field direction and the direction of propagation and this is known as the *plane of polarization* of the wave. Most light sources emit waves which have randomly orientated planes of polarization and the light is said to be *unpolarized*. Certain transparent crystals have the effect of transmitting only those waves whose planes of polarization are orientated in a particular direction and the resultant light is said to be *plane polarized*.

In lighting technology the main interest in polarization of light stems from the fact that when polarized light is reflected from a specular dielectric surface, such as glass, the intensity of the reflected ray depends on the angle of incidence (Sect. 1.2.1) and on the orientation of the plane of polarization. At a particular angle of incidence, known as *Brewster's angle*, the reflected intensity is zero for the polarization plane which contains the incident ray direction and the perpendicular to the surface at the point of incidence. Brewster's angle is equal to the value of θ_1 when $\theta_1 + \theta_2 = 90°$ (Fig. 1.2); from Eq. 1.2 this value is found to be $\tan^{-1}(n_2/n_1)$, which is about 56° for reflection at an air-to-glass interface.

When unpolarized light is incident at Brewster's angle the reflected ray is polarized in the plane perpendicular to the refracted ray (Born and Wolf 1975).

Use can be made of polarization to reduce glare due to light reflected from glossy surfaces, such as polished table tops.

1.2.8   Interference and diffraction

The wave nature of light does not produce any very obvious effects as far as general lighting is concerned, but there are two phenomena which have some technological application, these are known as *interference* and *diffraction*.

Interference is exhibited when a screen is illuminated by two separate but mutually *coherent* sources of light. Mutual coherence means that both sources are radiating light of exactly the same wavelength, and have a constant phase relation (Sect. 6.2). The result of combining the light from both sources is that at some places on the screen the light waves are in phase and add together; at other places the waves are out of phase and cancel each other. Interference between the two sets of waves is normally seen as a pattern of light and dark bands on the screen. In practice mutually coherent sources of light are produced by splitting a beam from a single source, and this is usually achieved by using partially reflecting films on glass. One application of interference in present-day lighting technology is in the *dichroic* filters which are used to reflect or transmit certain selected parts of the spectrum (Sect. 9.2). These also make use of the fact that a beam of light, reflected at normal incidence from the surface of a medium of higher refractive index, suffers a phase change of 180° (Ditchburn 1976).

Diffraction is the bending of light rays round the edges of obstacles. Diffraction effects are generally too small to be noticed by the unaided eye, but are of considerable importance in optical instruments, such as microscopes and telescopes operating at high magnifications. A combination of diffraction and interference occurs with the diffraction grating, a device used in instruments for examining the spectra of light sources.

1.2.9 Quantum phenomena

Although wave theory describes the propagation of light very well, it is not capable of explaining accurately the processes of emission and absorption. Experiments have shown that when light (or any other form of electromagnetic radiation) is emitted or absorbed, discrete amounts of energy called *quanta* are involved. One quantum of light energy is called a *photon* and the energy Q carried by one photon of light is given by Planck's relation

$$Q = hv \tag{1.4}$$

where v is the frequency and h is a constant, known as Planck's constant (Sect. 6.3.1). A photon of visible light carries only a very small amount of energy. At a wavelength of 500 nm, in the blue-green part of the spectrum, a single photon has an energy of 4×10^{-19} J, so a radiant power of 1 W at this wavelength is equivalent to $2 \cdot 5 \times 10^{18}$ photons per second. Using the quantum relation (Eq. 1.4) as a starting-point, Planck in 1901 was able to derive theoretically the continuous spectral distribution of the radiation emitted by a *full radiator* or *black body*, the latter being defined as a body which completely absorbs all radiation falling upon it (Sect. 6.3.1). Incandescent solids, such as tungsten used for lamp filaments, give spectral distributions similar to that of the black body, but with important differences. Discontinuous spectral distributions are observed with electrically excited gases and are also explicable in terms of the quantum theory (Chap. 6).

1.3 Spectral sensitivity of the eye

The sensitivity of the human eye is not uniform over the visible spectrum, but varies with wavelength in the manner shown in Fig. 1.3. The right-hand curve is for the eye in bright viewing conditions (*photopic vision*) and the left-hand curve is for the dark

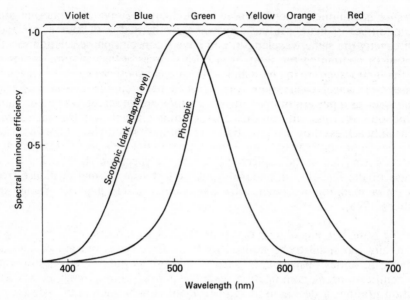

Fig. 1.3 Relative spectral sensitivity of the human eye; the spectral luminous efficiency for the CIE standard observer

adapted eye (*scotopic vision*). Lighting technology is almost entirely concerned with relatively high brightnesses and therefore photopic vision commands greater attention.

1.3.1 Photopic vision

In surroundings where the luminance (Sect. 1.4.6) is generally above about $10 \, cd \, m^{-2}$ vision is entirely mediated by the cone receptors (Sect. 2.1.2) and the visual response is maximum in the yellow-green region of the spectrum, at a wavelength of 555 nm. This response, the right-hand curve in Fig. 1.3, was agreed internationally in 1924 after extensive experimental work requiring subjects to match the brightness of monochromatic stimuli of different wavelengths. With a maximum ordinate of 1·0 this curve is known as $V(\lambda)$, the *spectral luminous efficiency* for photopic vision. It is of fundamental importance in photometric units (Sect. 1.4), colour (Chap. 3), and the measurement of light (Chap. 4), although some reservations are held currently about the short wavelength values.

The normal eye is fully responsive to colour in photopic vision and an indication is given at the top of Fig. 1.3 of the colour names likely to be ascribed to light of different wavelengths. Combining light of different wavelengths gives rise to less strong colours, even to colourlessness or 'achromatic colour'. The eye is unable to analyse the wavelength components in mixed radiation in the way the ear can detect the different frequency components in a musical sound. The colour characteristics of photopic vision are examined in Chap. 3.

1.3.2 Scotopic vision

Scotopic vision comes into operation when the luminance of the surroundings is below $10^{-2} \, cd \, m^{-2}$ and the eye has had time to become dark adapted: up to 30 minutes are required for this. The spectral luminous efficiency curve under these conditions is denoted by $V'(\lambda)$, the left-hand curve of Fig. 1.3, and its peak is at 507 nm which represents a shift toward the blue end of the spectrum compared with $V(\lambda)$.

A peculiar characteristic of scotopic vision is that an object is seen more readily 'out of the corner of the eye' than when it is made the centre of visual observation. The reason for this phenomenon is that at very low luminance levels vision is mediated primarily by the rod receptors (Sect. 2.1.2) which are absent in the central (foveal) region of the retina. Unlike the cone receptors, the rods are insensitive to colour differences, consequently the scotopic view of the world is colourless (Le Grand 1968).

1.3.3   Mesopic vision

As the brightness of a scene is increased, with luminances from about 10^{-2} cd m^{-2} upwards, three effects can be observed in addition to a general increase in luminosity. Firstly, foveal detection becomes as easy as peripheral detection and then easier. Secondly, a sense of colour can be appreciated, feebly at first and then stronger. Thirdly, the relative luminosity of objects of different colours changes: in particular the luminosity of the reds increases more strongly than does that of the blues. This last effect is known as the Purkinje phenomenon and like the other two effects is due to the changing contributions of the rod and cone receptors to vision as the luminance changes in this mesopic range (10^{-2} cd m^{-2} to 10 cd m^{-2}). The overall response to light of different wavelengths lies somewhere between the two curves of Fig. 1.3, moving from the left to the right as the prevailing luminance increases.

1.4   Measures of radiation and light

It is common experience that the amount of detail in a scene that can be perceived by the eye is closely related to the illumination. In order to distinguish fine details, for example to read small print, a relatively high 'level of illumination' is required. To specify the amount of light needed to accomplish a particular task it is therefore necessary to have quantitative measures of illumination and relate them to the power necessary to produce the light. The names and definitions of some of these quantities have changed over the years, but those used here are as set down in the *International Lighting Vocabulary* (CIE 1970).

Some of the quantities are defined in a similar way for radiation and for light; in these cases the same symbol is used, but is distinguished by a subscript 'e' for radiation or 'v' for visible light. The subscript is often omitted when it is clear from the context which one is intended.

1.4.1   Radiant flux and radiant efficiency

Radiant flux Φ_e is equal to the total power in watts of electromagnetic radiation emitted or received. It may include both visible and non-visible components. The radiant efficiency η_e of a source is the ratio of the radiant flux emitted to the power W (watts) consumed by the source

$$\eta_e = \Phi_e/W \qquad (1.5)$$

Spectral radiant flux $\Phi_{e\lambda}$ is the radiant flux per unit wavelength interval, usually taken to be 1 nm, so that $\Phi_{e\lambda}$ is expressed as watts per nanometer $(W\,nm^{-1})$. The total radiant flux Φ_e is found by integrating $\Phi_{e\lambda}$ over the whole spectrum

$$\Phi_e = \int_0^\infty \Phi_{e\lambda}\, d\lambda \tag{1.6}$$

1.4.2   Luminous flux, luminous efficacy, and luminous efficiency

Luminous flux   In the visible wavelength range, namely 380 nm to 780 nm, radiant flux is considered to have associated with it a luminous flux Φ_v, which is a measure of the visual response. The unit of luminous flux is the *lumen* (lm) and is defined in terms of the *candela* (cd) (Sect. 1.4.5). A point source emitting a uniform intensity of 1 cd in all directions emits a total flux of 4π lm. Alternatively the lumen can be defined as the luminous flux associated with a radiant flux of 1/683 W at a wavelength of 555 nm in air; at any other wavelength the associated luminous flux is $V(\lambda)$ lm.

To find the luminous flux $d\Phi_v$ associated with a spectral radiant flux $\Phi_{e\lambda}$ over a wavelength range $d\lambda$ the procedure is as follows. By definition

$$d\Phi_v = 683\, V(\lambda)\, \Phi_{e\lambda}\, d\lambda \tag{1.7}$$

and the total luminous flux Φ_v is found by integrating Eq. 1.7 over the whole of the visible range

$$\Phi_v = 683 \int_{380}^{780} V(\lambda)\, \Phi_{e\lambda}\, d\lambda \tag{1.8}$$

Luminous efficacy   As a measure of the ability of radiation to produce visual sensation the term luminous efficacy of radiation K is used, defined as the quotient of luminous flux in lumens by radiant flux in watts

$$K = \Phi_v / \Phi_e \tag{1.9}$$

For a light source with a total power input W watts the luminous efficacy, denoted by η_v, is given by

$$\eta_v = \Phi_v / W \tag{1.10}$$

where Φ_v is the total light output of the source. η_v is always less than K for the radiation from the source because inevitably some of the input power is dissipated by processes other than radiation. The unit of both K and η_v is the lumen per watt $(lm\,W^{-1})$.

The luminous efficacy of a source can be found experimentally by first measuring the spectral radiant flux from the source and then calculating the luminous flux by integration, as in Eq. 1.8. In practice it is more usual to measure the total luminous flux directly by means of specially corrected photocells and, if it is required, the radiant flux can be measured by means of a power-sensing device, such as a thermopile. Measurements of luminous and radiant flux are known respectively as photometry and radiometry (Chap. 4).

Luminous efficiency   A spectral radiant flux confined entirely to a very narrow wavelength band centred on 555 nm would have a luminous efficacy of 683 lm W^{-1}, denoted by K_m. For any other radiant flux distribution the luminous efficacy K is less than K_m and the ratio K/K_m is known as the luminous efficiency of the radiation, denoted by V.

1.4.3 Ultraviolet and infrared flux

Ultraviolet flux Natural daylight and light from many kinds of artificial source are accompanied by an appreciable amount of ultraviolet radiation. The intensity of ultraviolet radiation is normally measured in standard power units, namely watts for radiant flux and watts per square metre for irradiance. Calculations of ultraviolet irradiance are carried out in a similar fashion to those for illuminance (Sect. 1.4.4).

For convenience of reference the CIE has distinguished three spectral ranges: UV-A from 400 nm to 315 nm, UV-B from 315 nm to 280 nm, and UV-C from 280 nm to 100 nm. In certain fields of application, where a particular property of ultraviolet radiation is of primary interest, some additional units have been introduced.

Erythemal radiation Exposure to ultraviolet radiation of wavelengths shorter than about 320 nm produces an erythema or reddening of the human skin. Although moderate exposure can be used for therapeutic purposes, prolonged exposure can produce painful and even dangerous results. The tissue (conjunctiva) of the eye is particularly sensitive to erythemal radiation, and protective goggles should always be worn if the eyes are likely to be exposed to this radiation (Parrish et al. 1978).

The exact cause of erythema is not known, but it has been shown to be dependent on the wavelength of the radiation. Erythemal efficacy rises to a maximum at a wavelength of 297 nm, declines to a minimum around 270–280 nm, and increases again at shorter wavelengths. Where radiation covering a range of wavelengths is concerned, the erythemal efficacy can be related to the maximum for 297 nm wavelength. For convenience an erythemal unit the *E-viton* is introduced, one E-viton being the radiant flux required to produce the same erythemal effect as $10 \mu W$ of 297 nm radiation. A minimum perceptible erythema is produced on the average untanned white skin by an erythemal flux of 10^4 E-vitons m^{-2} for a period of 2500 s; for 297 nm radiation this corresponds to a *therapeutic dose* of 250 J m^{-2}. The *dose rate*, or irradiance, in this example is 0.1 W m^{-2} or 1 E-viton cm^{-2}, called a *finsen* (Luckiesh 1946).

Bactericidal radiation At wavelengths shorter than 320 nm ultraviolet radiation has a lethal effect on micro-organisms. Bactericidal efficacy is at a maximum at about 260 nm, depending to some extent on the type of organism involved. An electrical discharge in mercury vapour at low pressure produces very intense radiation of wavelength 253·7 nm, close to the maximum for bactericidal efficacy, and this type of source is therefore frequently used for bactericidal (germicidal) purposes. A 'germicidal' unit (GU) of irradiance is sometimes used; it is defined as the irradiance required to produce the same bactericidal effect as 1 W m^{-2} of 253·7 nm radiation (Summer 1962).

Infrared flux The near-infrared part of the spectrum is represented in daylight and in many other sources. For the latter this leads to a loss of luminous efficacy and appears as unwanted heat. As radiant flux it is measured in watts. The wavelength regions of most interest are classified by the CIE as IR-A from 780 nm to $1.4 \mu m$, IR-B from $1.4 \mu m$ to $3 \mu m$, and IR-C from $3 \mu m$ to 1 mm.

1.4.4 Irradiance and illuminance

Irradiance is the radiant flux per unit area falling on a surface; the unit of irradiance is the watt per square metre (W m^{-2}).

Illuminance, denoted by E, is defined similarly to irradiance; the unit is the lumen per square metre ($lm\,m^{-2}$) and is called a *lux* (lx). If an element of area dA is illuminated by a luminous flux dΦ then

$$E = \mathrm{d}\Phi/\mathrm{d}A \qquad\qquad (1.11)$$

In the past the words 'illumination level' or simply 'illumination' have been used with the same meaning as illuminance.

It must be emphasized that illuminance, as defined above, is always with reference to a given plane; for this reason the term planar illuminance is sometimes used. The given plane is usually a horizontal one, but not necessarily so, and if the orientation of the plane is changed then the illuminance may also change.

1.4.5 Intensity

Luminous intensity of a point source   A frequent requirement in lighting engineering is the calculation of the illuminance produced on a surface by a given arrangement of light sources (Chap. 5). The simplest example is the illumination of a plane surface by a single 'point source', which in practice means any source whose dimensions are small compared with its distance from the surface. Referring to Fig. 1.4, a point source S,

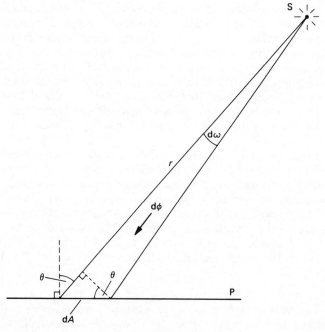

Fig. 1.4   Illumination of a plane surface by a point source

emitting luminous flux in various directions, illuminates a plane surface P. The flux dΦ intercepted by an element of area dA on P is the flux emitted within the solid angle dω subtended at the source by the element dA; it is assumed that no absorption of light occurs in the space between the source and the surface. The quotient dΦ/dω is called the luminous intensity I of the source in the particular direction considered; thus

$$I = \mathrm{d}\Phi/\mathrm{d}\omega \qquad\qquad (1.12)$$

The unit of I is the lumen per steradian (lm sr^{-1}) or *candela* (cd); an earlier term used for this unit was candle-power. Luminous intensity is therefore the luminous flux per steradian emitted in a particular direction. Radiant intensity is similarly defined as radiant flux per steradian. Generally I varies with the direction of the emitted light: in the case where the luminous intensity is the same for all directions the source is said to be uniform. For a uniform point source of luminous intensity 1 cd the total flux emitted is 4π lm; this is the flux emitted by the now obsolete standard candle. At the 16th General Conference on Weights and Measures, Paris 1979, it was decided that:

(a)   The candela is the luminous intensity, in a given direction, of a source emitting monochromatic radiation of frequency 540×10^{12} Hz and whose radiant intensity in this direction is $1/683$ watt per steradian.
(b)   The candela so defined is the base unit applicable to photopic quantities; scotopic quantities to be defined in the mesopic domain.

The frequency of 540×10^{12} Hz corresponds to a wavelength of 555 nm in air and so the above definition of the candela leads to the definition of the lumen given in Sect. 1.4.2.

Inverse square and cosine laws of illumination   The illuminance produced by a point source at a distance r from a plane (Fig. 1.4) is obtained by first eliminating $\mathrm{d}\Phi$ between Eqs 1.11 and 1.12 to give

$$E = I \frac{\mathrm{d}\omega}{\mathrm{d}A} \tag{1.13}$$

Then in Fig. 1.4

$$\mathrm{d}\omega = \frac{\mathrm{d}A \cos \theta}{r^2}$$

and substitution for $\mathrm{d}\omega$ in Eq. 1.13 gives

$$E = \frac{I \cos \theta}{r^2} \tag{1.14}$$

Equation 1.14 expresses the inverse square law and the cosine law of illumination from a point source.

1.4.6   Luminance and radiance

For an extended source, which is not small compared with its distance from the point of observation, the concept of luminous intensity is not directly applicable. An extended source however may be considered to consist of an assemblage of small luminous surface elements of area $\mathrm{d}S$, each of which can be regarded as a point source.

The luminous intensity $\mathrm{d}I$ of each surface element $\mathrm{d}S$, viewed from a particular direction, is proportional to the projected area $\mathrm{d}S'$ in this direction (Fig. 1.5), the constant of proportionality being denoted by L; thus

$$\mathrm{d}I = L \, \mathrm{d}S' \tag{1.15}$$

L is called the *luminance* of the surface and represents the luminous intensity per unit projected area. Luminance is related to the visual sensation of brightness, although the two are not directly equivalent (Sect. 2.2.2). The unit of luminance is the candela per square metre (cd m^{-2}) which can also be expressed as lumens per steradian per square metre ($\text{lm}\,\text{sr}^{-1}\text{m}^{-2}$). The corresponding radiation measure is *radiance L_e*, expressed as watts per steradian per square metre ($\text{W}\,\text{sr}^{-1}\text{m}^{-2}$).

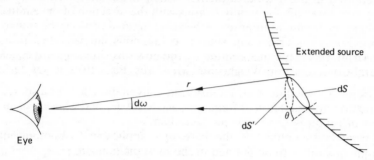

Fig. 1.5 Observation of an extended light source

The concept of luminance can be applied to any surface which is emitting or reflecting light, and can be generalized to include any imaginary surface in space through which light is passing, for example a portion of the sky. It can be shown that the luminance of any such surface in a non-emitting, non-absorbing, and non-scattering medium is constant along a ray passing through the surface (Born and Wolf 1975, pp. 109–121). In less formal terms this statement corresponds to the everyday observation that in clear air the brightness of a surface does not depend on its distance from the observer.

The luminance of an extended source may vary with position on the source and with the direction from which it is viewed and, if these variations are known, the illuminance produced by the source at a given location can be found in principle as follows.

The illuminance dE produced on a plane at distance r from an element of the source having an intensity dI is, from Eq. 1.14, given by

$$dE = dI(\cos\theta)/r^2$$

the angle θ being as shown in Fig. 1.4.

Substitution for dI from Eq. 1.15, and use of the geometrical relation in Fig. 1.5

$$dS' = r^2\,d\omega$$

leads to the equation

$$dE = L\cos\theta\,d\omega$$

which by integration becomes

$$E = \int L\cos\theta\,d\omega \tag{1.16}$$

Equation 1.16 can be used to calculate the illuminance produced by an extended source. In practice the integral is often difficult to evaluate directly, so various specialized methods have been developed to simplify the calculations (Sect. 5.1).

A *uniform diffuse source* is one which has the same luminance over its entire surface for all viewing directions; it is said to obey Lambert's law. A reflecting surface which has this property, and reflects all of the incident light, is called a *perfect diffuse reflector* (Sect. 1.2.6).

Luminance factor   The ratio of the luminance of a reflecting surface to that of a perfect diffuse reflector, identically illuminated, is called the *luminance factor β_v* of the surface. With monochromatic illumination the luminance factor is denoted by $\beta(\lambda)$, to indicate that this quantity may vary with wavelength, and is used in calculations relating to coloured surfaces (Sect. 3.3.1).

1.4.7 Exitance

The luminous exitance M_v at a point on a surface is equal to the total luminous flux emitted per unit area. For an element of area dS emitting a total flux of $d\Phi_v$ (over a solid angle of $2\pi\,sr$)

$$M_v = d\Phi_v/dS \tag{1.17}$$

The corresponding radiation measure is radiant exitance M_e. For a uniform diffuse source (Sect 1.4.6) there is a relation between its luminous exitance and its luminance, namely

$$M_v = \pi L_v \tag{1.18}$$

This is derived by calculating the total luminous flux arriving at a hemispherical surface centred on a plane source assumed to obey Lambert's law (Chap. 5).

1.5 Standard elements for optical control

Practical light sources do not usually give the distribution of light required for a particular lighting application and to overcome this problem various additional elements are needed to deflect, concentrate, or disperse the light as necessary. The basic elements required for this can be broadly grouped into two main categories (a) reflective and (b) transmissive elements.

1.5.1 Reflective elements

Diffusely reflecting surfaces are commonly used for less demanding forms of directional control of light, but for more precise control specular reflectors (mirrors) are required. Mirrors may take several forms, depending on the type of light distribution aimed at, and they form virtual or real images of objects.

Image luminance   An important limitation in any system of mirrors (or lenses) is that the luminance of an image can never be greater than that of the object from which it is formed (Keitz 1971). In practice the image luminance is always less than the object luminance because of inevitable light losses in reflection and transmission.

Plane mirrors   A plane mirror forms a virtual image which appears to be behind its surface. The exact location of the image can be found by ray tracing. In Fig. 1.6a O is a point object; it can be shown geometrically that since the marked angles of reflection and incidence are equal the rays of light will appear to diverge from a (virtual) image I located at a distance behind the mirror equal to the distance that O is in front of it. To locate the image of an object of finite size the images of a number of points on the object can be located, enabling the position of the complete image to be found (Fig. 1.6b). The image may be treated as a normal light source for the purpose of making calculations, bearing in mind that the light appearing to come from the image may be partially obstructed by the source or by the edges of the mirror.

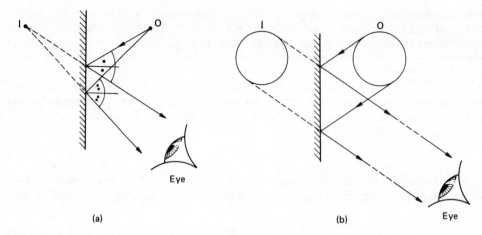

(a)   (b)

Fig. 1.6 Location of an image in a plane mirror

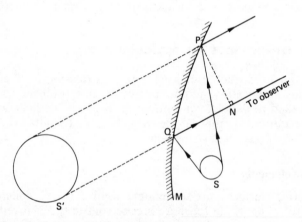

Fig. 1.7 Reflection of a light source in a curved mirror

Curved mirrors A mirror with a curved section can produce one or more virtual or real images; a real image appears to be in front of the mirror surface. Images of either type may be greater or less than the object in size and may be distorted in shape, but this does not affect the limitation on image luminance stated above.

For lighting calculations it may be more convenient to treat the mirror surface, or the mirror aperture, as the source of light rather than an image, since the luminance is the same. In Fig. 1.7 the curved mirror M forms a virtual image S′ of the source S. As seen by a distant observer the mirror appears bright or *flashed* over an area indicated by PQ. If the image has a uniform luminance L then the luminous intensity I in the direction indicated by the rays is given by $I = LA$, where A is the orthogonal projection PN of the image in this direction. The observer's position may be such that not all of the image can be seen, because of obstruction by the mirror edge or by other objects, in which case the area A is reduced and with it the apparent intensity. The maximum intensity is achieved when the mirror is fully flashed and A then corresponds to the orthogonal projection of the unobstructed aperture.

Spherical mirrors   A spherical mirror has the property that rays from a small light source at the centre of curvature are reflected back onto the source (Fig. 1.8a). A small lateral displacement of the source from the centre allows a real image to be formed clear of the source and produces nearly double the luminous intensity for some directions of viewing. If the source is placed at a distance equal to one-half of the radius of curvature from the back of the reflector (Fig. 1.8b), rays from the source that do not deviate more than 10° from the axis of the system are reflected into a substantially parallel beam.

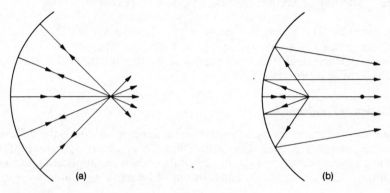

(a)   (b)

Fig. 1.8   Reflection from a spherical or cylindrical mirror

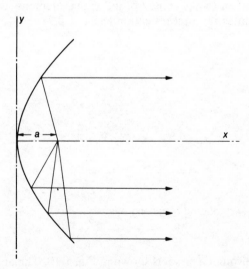

Fig. 1.9   Parallel beam produced by a point source at the focus of a parabolic mirror

Parabolic mirrors   A parabola is a curve defined by the equation $y^2 = 4ax$, and a mirror whose surface is formed by rotation of the parabola about the x axis is commonly referred to as being parabolic. Such a mirror has the property that light from a point source placed at the focus, which is on the axis at a distance a from the mirror surface, is reflected into an accurately parallel beam (Fig. 1.9). This means that the mirror appears fully flashed when viewed from a distant point on the axis. In the more practical case of a small extended source placed at the focus the reflected beam is divergent and the mirror may appear fully flashed over a range of angles off the axis, enabling the intensity to be easily calculated. At greater angles from the axis the mirror is no longer fully flashed and the calculation of beam intensity becomes more complicated (Cotton 1960). Usually the measured intensity is found to be less than that calculated because of imperfections in the mirror shape.

Cylindrical mirrors   For a linear light source a cylindrical mirror with its axis parallel to that of the lamp may be more appropriate, although in this case the beam is fan-shaped. The mirror section may be a circle or a parabola.

Elliptical mirrors   The ellipse is a curve with two foci such that if a point source is placed at one focus all of the rays of light are reflected through the other. This is a useful property when light from a source has to be directed through a small aperture, such as the gate of a projector.

1.5.2   Transmissive elements

A common form of transmissive element used in lighting systems is the diffuser, made of opalescent glass or plastic. For better directional control prisms or lenses are required in a clear material and the design of these calls for application of the laws of refraction (Sect. 1.2.2). Precise calculations must be made for optimum results to be achieved.

Prisms   Prism systems or banks consist of individual elements which deflect light by refraction and sometimes by total reflection (Sect. 1.2.3).

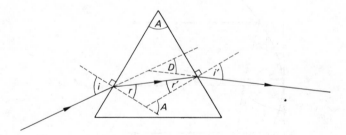

Fig. 1.10   Trace of a ray through a refracting prism

The path of a ray through a prism is shown in Fig. 1.10. The angle D through which the ray is deflected may be calculated from the geometrical relation

$$D = i + i' - A$$

If angles A and i are known then i' may be found from Snell's law (Eq. 1.2) which leads to

$$i' = \sin^{-1}(n \sin r')$$

where

$$r' = A - \sin^{-1}[(\sin i)/n]$$

and n is the refractive index of the prism material, assumed to be in air.

If it is required to determine A from given values of i and D, let

$$E = D + r - i$$

where
$$r = \sin^{-1}[(\sin i)/n]$$

then
$$A = r + \tan^{-1}[(\sin E)/(n - \cos E)]$$

The condition $(i - D + 90°) > A > (i - D - 90°)$ must be satisfied if total reflection is not to occur in the prism. Apart from total reflection, it is important to bear in mind that the proportion of light which is reflected at a surface (Fig. 1.2) increases with angle of incidence. To avoid unacceptable loss at reflections when glass is used the angles i and i' should not exceed 60°. This limits the deviation to about 50° using refraction only; for greater deviations total reflection can be used (Bean and Simons 1968).

Prisms produce virtual images, analogous to those of plane mirrors, and the restriction on image luminance (Sect. 1.5.1) also applies. The projection of the image of a light source onto the prism face defines the flashed area which, when multiplied by the image luminance, gives the effective source intensity.

Lenses Lenses form real and virtual images much as do spherical mirrors, and the image luminance is similarly limited. A simple bi-convex lens with spherical surfaces can give a near-parallel beam of light if a point source is placed at the focus. However, as the collection angle of the lens is made greater by increasing the diameter it is found that rays passing through the periphery of the lens deviate more from true parallelism (spherical aberration). This part of the lens therefore does not appear flashed in the axial direction and there is no gain in beam intensity. Lenses with non-spherical (aspheric) surfaces can be made to overcome this problem.

In optical systems for large sources a simple lens would be very thick, making the system too heavy and costly. The stepped or Fresnel lens is a solution here (Bean and Simons 1968).

Diffusers and controllers Diffusers are made from opal materials and are used to increase the light emitting area of a luminaire in order to decrease its luminance and improve its appearance. To achieve a reasonably even luminance over the surface of a diffuser there must be a sufficient separation between it and the light source, and the diffusing effect of the opal (which usually increases as the transmittance decreases) must be great enough. In a fluorescent luminaire, the diffuser of which is usually extruded, the opal can be reeded to enhance its appearance, or opal sides can be extruded with a clear patterned base to give glare control.

Controllers embody prisms or lenses and are used where more precise optical control than can be obtained by diffusers is required.

Further reading

Hecht E and Zajac A, 1974, *Optics* (Reading, Mass: Addison-Wesley)

Helms R N, 1980, *Illumination engineering for energy efficient luminous environments* (Englewood Cliffs, New Jersey: Prentice-Hall)

IES, 1981, *Lighting handbook*, 6th Edition, 2 volumes (New York: Illuminating Eng. Soc.)

Jenkins F A and White H E, 1965, *Fundamentals of optics*, 4th Edition (New York: McGraw-Hill)

Jolley L B W, Waldram J M and Wilson G H, 1930, *The theory and design of illuminating engineering equipment* (London: Chapman & Hall)

Koller L R, 1965, *Ultraviolet radiation*, 2nd Edition (New York: John Wiley)

Longhurst R S, 1957, *Geometrical and physical optics* (London: Longmans Green & Co)

Moon P, 1961, *The scientific basis of illuminating engineering* (New York: Dover Publications)

Overington I, 1976, *Vision and acquisition* (London: Pentech Press)

Seliger H H and McElroy W D, 1965, *Light: physical and biological action* (New York: Academic Press)

Walsh J W T, 1947, *Textbook of illuminating engineering* (London: Pitman)

Weale R A, 1960, *The eye and its function* (London: Hatton Press)

Wood R W, 1967, *Physical optics* (New York: Dover Publications)

2 Vision

Vision is not instantaneous – it is the end-product of a number of stages of coding and analysis which together give meaning to the changing pattern of ambient luminance and chromaticity. A lighting designer uses his knowledge of these processes to control the luminous environment more effectively.

2.1 The eye as an optical system

The first stage of vision occurs when rays of light enter the eye (Fig. 2.1).

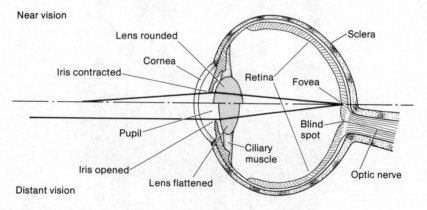

Fig. 2.1 Sectional diagram of the human eye

2.1.1 Optics

As an optical instrument the human eye works like a simple camera. The lens, which projects an inverted image onto the retina, is elastic. Its curvature, and hence its focal length, is controlled by the ciliary muscle; this operation is known as *accommodation*. The aperture of the lens is governed by the iris, which determines the pupil diameter. As in an automatic camera the aperture is enlarged at low illuminances and constricted at high illuminances.

2.1.2 Visual neurons

The retina is the interface between the optical processes and the electrophysiological processes of vision. Anatomically the retina is an outpost of the brain; it is here that the first stages of visual information processing take place. The transmission, analysis, and coding of the retinal image are carried out by a network of nerve cells or *neurons*. These communicate through *nerve impulses*, which are sudden changes in interior electrical potential. An impulse within one cell can have one of two effects on a neighbouring cell: it can *excite* the second cell electrochemically, leading it to produce an impulse of its own, or it can *inhibit* the second cell, making it less likely to respond to impulses from other neighbouring cells. The stronger the initial stimulus, the greater is the frequency of the impulses which it triggers within the communication network.

The visual process is initiated when rays of light, focused by the lens, hit detector cells at the back of the retina, known from their shapes as *rods* and *cones* (Fig. 2.2);

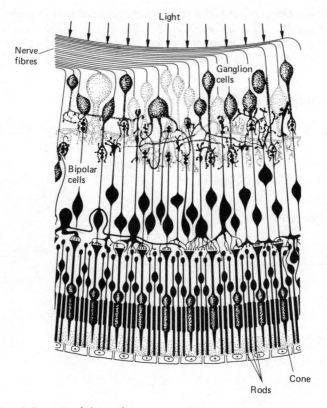

Fig. 2.2   Sectional diagram of the retina

the intervening layers of cells and blood vessels are of course fairly transparent. The rods and cones contain photosensitive pigments which act as transducers, effectively converting light energy into the nerve impulses which initiate the visual process.

Rods are more sensitive than cones; they pick out lower luminances and so play an important role in vision at night. However their response tends to saturate under good lighting conditions so they make little contribution to everyday seeing. A cone may contain any one of three distinct pigments, which respond to light from different, but overlapping, wavelength bands; different colours are distinguished by their differential effects on these three photopigments. The condition of colour blindness is attributed to deficiency in a photopigment or to a defect in the neural network, for example protanopia (red-blindness) suggests the absence of the long-wave photo-pigment.

The centre of the retina, known as the *fovea* (Fig. 2.1), is specially evolved for detailed vision. Here the overlying cells and fibres are pulled to one side, maximizing sensitivity, and fine cone detector cells are packed tight, maximizing visual resolution. The centre of the fovea contains no rods; retinal areas away from the fovea have both rods and cones, the proportion of rods to cones increasing towards the periphery.

2.2 Visual processing

2.2.1 Cybernetics of vision

Our eyes are in continual movement many times a second (Ditchburn 1973). The small ocular tremors set the retinal image in oscillation and the neural network is tuned to detect the consequential local changes in luminance, which play an essential role in vision; without them vision simply fades away. We are therefore more responsive to sharp changes in luminance than to luminance itself (Fig. 2.3). This

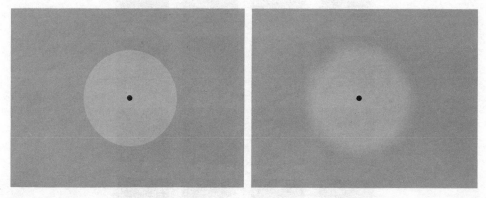

Fig. 2.3 Cover one eye. Focus on the right-hand dot until the light circle vanishes. Repeat for the left-hand dot; this circle will not vanish (Stroebel, Todd, and Zakia: *Visual concepts for photographers*, Focal Press, 1980)

characteristic of vision sharpens our perception of the boundaries of various objects we see around us.

A number of feedback systems combine to optimize visual performance. The main function of the peripheral retina is to detect concentrations of visual information in the retinal image. The requisite aiming signal is conveyed to the muscles controlling the eyeball so as to focus those objects of interest onto the fovea for detailed scrutiny. The two eyes work together, like the twin optics of a rangefinder, for stereoscopic vision. Accommodation matches the focus of the lens to the distance of the object viewed. The pupil dilates at low luminances to admit more light and it contracts at high luminances to reduce spherical and chromatic aberrations.

The concentration of the retinal photopigments is governed by the equilibrium of a reversible photochemical process. Darkness increases the concentration and hence the sensitivity to low luminances. Light reverses this effect, reducing the concentration so that we can discriminate similar proportional differences in luminance at higher levels; see Weber's law (Sect. 2.2.3).

Excitations and inhibitions within the cellular network also have the effect of refining visual performance. They work in two ways (Hurvich and Jameson 1966):

(a)   A high luminance background generally reduces the perceived brightness of an object because the response of surrounding receptors inhibits signals from the retinal image of the object of regard (Fig. 2.4).

Fig. 2.4   The brightness of identical grey squares is affected by the background luminance (Stroebel, Todd, and Zakia: *Visual concepts for photographers*, Focal Press, 1980)

Fig. 2.5   The Hermann grid

In Fig. 2.5 a grey dot appears at the intersections of the white lines, where inhibition is greatest. This effect is known as *simultaneous contrast*.

Lateral inhibition is also at work in Fig. 2.6, but the contrast effect can be strengthened by placing a pencil over the central boundary. This shows that the perception of contrast is not a matter of simple inhibition; form perception is involved, which is also mediated by the neural network. See also Fig. 2.7.

(b)   For certain configurations, especially when finer detail is involved, contrast gives way to *assimilation* (Fig. 2.8). This is presumably because mutual excitation is now stronger than lateral inhibition.

Visual feedback extends to all levels of human activity. Arts, crafts, locomotion, and many other skills depend on oculomotor cybernetics (Gibson 1968). Many, if not all, so-called 'optical illusions' reflect the response of feedback mechanisms to stimuli they were not evolved to cope with.

Fig. 2.6 The Osgood illusion

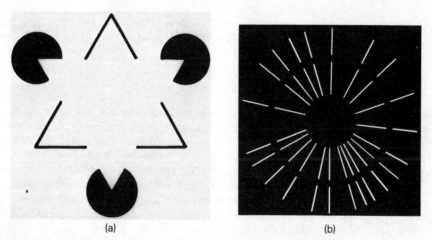

(a)   (b)

Fig. 2.7 (a) the Kaniza illusion: the illusory triangle is best seen peripherally and under dim light. (b) the illusory circle and ring seem blacker than their background

Poor lighting can unbalance these finely tuned control systems, especially by starving them of the visual cues required for accommodation and convergence. The sight of a bare incandescent or high pressure discharge lamp causes a local dilution of retinal photopigments; regeneration is then accompanied by complementary after-images until photochemical equilibrium is restored. Over-bright light sources produce other disturbances; a haze appears around their retinal image, which impairs the visibility of nearby objects, and lateral inhibition makes such objects look darker. These effects are known as *disability glare*. Excessive brightness causes the pupillary

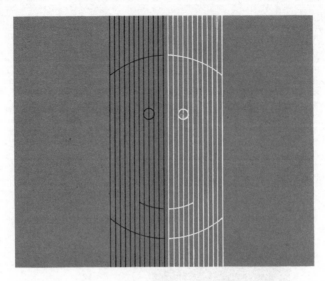

Fig. 2.8 Assimilation – the grey background is uniform in reflectance, but superimposed black lines darken it and white lines lighten it. Lateral inhibition would produce the opposite effect (Fig. 2.4) (Stroebel, Todd, and Zakia: *Visual concepts for photographers*, Focal Press, 1980)

muscles to close the pupil more tightly. The resulting muscular fatigue causes instability in the pupil itself, and is believed to be partly responsible for *discomfort glare.*

2.2.2   Apparent brightness

It is clear that the apparent brightness of a surface depends not only on its own luminance, but also on the luminance of its surroundings and, in a complex manner, on the shapes, sizes, and positions of the various surfaces that make up our visual environment. Luminance can be measured; the corresponding visual impression of brightness is, in principle, harder to quantify. Nevertheless it is useful, for engineering purposes, to have a method of expressing and comparing, however roughly, the perceived brightness of various surfaces under alternative lighting systems.

The *magnitude estimation* procedure (Stevens 1975) offers such a method. Observers are simply asked to choose a single number which best expresses how bright a given object looks. If a second object looks twice as bright as the first its apparent brightness will naturally be double the first number. By correlating numerous estimates of apparent brightness with measurements of luminance Marsden (1970) found that it is possible to express the apparent brightness B of a given surface as a simple function of the three variables L, the luminance of the surface in cd m^{-2}, L_{max}, the luminance of the brightest non-luminescent surface in the room, and B_{max}, the estimated apparent brightness of the brightest non-luminescent surface in the room, as

$$B/B_{max} = (L/L_{max})^{0.58} \qquad (2.1)$$

In a given room therefore the apparent brightness of the various surfaces is roughly proportional to the 0·6 power of their luminance. However, the brightest surface, to which all others are related in Eq. 2.1, is an exception. Its apparent brightness B_{max} is related to its luminance L_{max} by the expression

$$B_{max} = \text{constant} \times L_{max}^{0.37} \qquad (2.2)$$

By combining Eqs 2.1 and 2.2 we can write an expression for the apparent brightness B of any surface as a function of luminance

$$B = \text{constant} \times L^{0.58}/L_{max}^{0.21} \qquad (2.3)$$

These equations have important implications for lighting design. Consider the effect of a change in overall illuminance from E_1 lux to E_2 lux. This will alter both L and L_{max} in the ratio E_2/E_1. From Eq. 2.3 the ratio of the new apparent brightness B_2 to the old value B_1 will be given by the expression

$$B_2/B_1 = (E_2/E_1)^{0.37} \qquad (2.4)$$

Next consider changing the reflectance of a single surface from ρ_1 to ρ_2. This leaves L_{max} and hence B_{max} unchanged, but alters L in the ratio ρ_2/ρ_1. From Eq. 2.1 we see that the ratio of the new apparent brightness B_2 to the old value B_1 is now

$$B_2/B_1 = (\rho_2/\rho_1)^{0.58} \qquad (2.5)$$

Comparing Eq. 2.4 with Eq. 2.5 we see that a change in reflectance has much more effect on the apparent brightness of the surface concerned than does a proportional change in overall illuminance. To double the apparent brightness we must increase the reflectance by a factor of 3·3, i.e. $2^{1/0.58}$, or increase the illuminance by a factor of 6·5, i.e. $2^{1/0.37}$ – roughly twice as much.

2.2.3 Laws of contrast

The luminance contrast C between a task detail, such as a printed dot of luminance L_t and its background L_b, is defined by the expression

$$C = \left| \frac{L_t - L_b}{L_b} \right| \qquad (2.6)$$

If its contrast C is too small the detail will be invisible, so the laws which govern minimum perceptible contrasts (sometimes referred to as *threshold* contrasts) are important in lighting engineering.

The earliest law, *Weber's law*, asserts that the smallest detectable luminance step $|L_t - L_b|$ is proportional to L_b, i.e. the minimum perceptible contrast C is independent of L_b, and is therefore unaffected by changes in illuminance. Weber's law must obviously fail when L_b is very low, otherwise we could see in the dark. Even under good lighting visual discrimination tends to improve when illuminance increases. Indeed much of the skill of a lighting designer consists in getting the better of Weber's law. Nevertheless Weber's law retains some credibility as a useful approximation over quite a wide range of lighting conditions, which is an impressive testimony to the stability and effectiveness of the various ocular feedback mechanisms; it can also be generalized to suprathreshold conditions. This means that equal *proportional* differences of luminance should look equally noticeable.

The minimum detectable contrast C depends also on the *size* of the task detail. For very tiny objects, subtending less than 6 minutes of arc at the eye (about 0·5 mm at a reading distance of 300 mm), vision is limited by diffraction and optical imperfections within the eye. Since the retinal images of such minute objects are virtually indistinguishable the threshold contrast must be inversely proportional to the projected area A of the detail, for a given viewing distance. This relationship is known as *Ricco's law*

$$\text{detectability} = f(CA) \tag{2.7}$$

For objects large enough to be resolved and distinguished Ricco's law breaks down and the integrative properties of the neural network come into play. For angular subtenses between about 2° and 20° the threshold contrast is inversely proportional to the square root of the projected area A, for a given viewing distance. This relationship is known as *Piper's law*

$$\text{detectability} = f(C\sqrt{A}) \tag{2.8}$$

Like Weber's law, both Ricco's law and Piper's law are applicable also to suprathreshold viewing, i.e. to the conspicuity of objects which are clearly visible. For very large surfaces, subtending more than 20°, perceptibility is independent of area and depends almost entirely on contrast.

The detectability of a flashing light is governed by the *Blondel–Rey law*

$$E_e \doteq Et/(a + t) \tag{2.9}$$

where E = average illuminance at the eye during a flash,
$\quad E_e$ = illuminance from equally detectable steady signal,
$\quad t$ = duration of flash in seconds,
$\quad a$ = 0·2 s for achromatic light.

For very brief flashes Eq. 2.9 becomes

$$E_e = Et/a \tag{2.10}$$

This relationship, which is known as *Bloch's law* or the *Bunsen–Roscoe law*, tells us that the visibility of brief flashes of light is determined by the product of illuminance and duration.

The laws of contrast have many implications for lighting engineers. Weber's law, implying that equal ratios of luminance should be equally visible, justifies the use of daylight factors (Sect. 20.2.1) and illuminance ratios (see Sect. 2.4.3 below) as lighting criteria.

It is also interesting to observe how wattage ratings for different lamps have evolved into approximate geometric series as Weber's law would predict. Take for example the GLS incandescent lamp range

40 W, 60 W, 75 W (used only occasionally), 100 W, 150 W, 200 W, 300 W, 500 W

Ricco's law (Eq. 2.7) shows that area and contrast contribute equally to the visibility of a very fine detail. An increase in contrast is only half as effective as a proportional increase in its linear dimensions. Clearly then the best way to improve the visibility of a very intricate task may be to use a magnifying glass or some other optical aid. An increase in luminance contrast must be much greater to be equally effective. At high illuminance Weber's law tells us that any further rise in illuminance will have very little effect on perceived contrast, but at low illuminance, when Weber's law is unreliable, an increase in illuminance should improve visual performance (see Sect. 2.3.1).

For tasks of normal size Piper's law (Eq. 2.8) will prevail. The size of the target now makes less difference to its visibility; contrast becomes more important. Optical aids are no longer appropriate. Adequate illuminance is still required, but is again subject to the law of diminishing returns.

A

How is this excitation produced? In practically all types of lamp, the applied electric field is used to accelerate electrons which then collide with atoms, producing excitation which subsequently radiates spontaneously, often after a series of intermediate transitions. In the great majority of cases the kinetic energy of the accelerated electrons is randomised, or 'thermalised' by repeated

B

How is this excitation produced? In practically all types of lamp, the applied electric field is used to accelerate electrons which then collide with atoms, producing excitation which subsequently radiates spontaneously, often after a series of intermediate transitions. In the great majority of cases the kinetic energy of the accelerated electrons is randomised, or 'thermalised' by repeated

C

How is this excitation produced? In practically all types of lamp, the applied electric field is used to accelerate electrons which then collide with atoms, producing excitation which subsequently radiates spontaneously, often after a series of intermediate transitions. In the great majority of cases the kinetic energy of the accelerated electrons is randomised, or 'thermalised' by repeated

D

How is this excitation produced? In practically all types of lamp, the applied electric field is used to accelerate electrons which then collide with atoms, producing excitation which subsequently radiates spontaneously, often after a series of intermediate transitions. In the great majority of cases the kinetic energy of the accelerated electrons is randomised, or 'thermalised' by repeated

E

How is this excitation produced? In practically all types of lamp, the applied electric field is used to accelerate electrons which then collide with atoms, producing excitation which subsequently radiates spontaneously, often after a series of intermediate transitions. In the great majority of cases the kinetic energy of the accelerated electrons is randomised, or 'thermalised' by repeated

F

How is this excitation produced? In practically all types of lamp, the applied electric field is used to accelerate electrons which then collide with atoms, producing excitation which subsequently radiates spontaneously, often after a series of intermediate transitions. In the great majority of cases the kinetic energy of the accelerated electrons is randomised, or 'thermalised' by repeated

G

How is this excitation produced? In practically all types of lamp, the applied electric field is used to accelerate electrons which then collide with atoms, producing excitation which subsequently radiates spontaneously, often after a series of intermediate transitions. In the great majority of cases the kinetic energy of the accelerated electrons is randomised, or 'thermalised' by repeated

Plate 2.1 The effect of a visibility meter; contrast is varied, but the background luminance remains constant.

2.3   Lighting for results

There is no single optimum illuminance for a given activity, for under favourable lighting conditions near-threshold vision continues to improve with illuminance up to very high lighting levels. However, since the prescription of illuminance is often the starting-point for lighting design, much debate rightly centres on the way in which lighting can influence visual performance.

2.3.1   The CIE framework

The Commission Internationale de L'Éclairage (CIE) has sponsored an ambitious programme of studies into this question, under the inspiration of Professor H R Blackwell (CIE 1972b, 1981a). As the work develops the theoretical framework becomes increasingly complex; the interim account which follows mentions only a few of the many new concepts that have emerged.

To compare various different tasks on a common basis Blackwell and his collaborators have evolved a family of *visibility meters*, Fig. 2.9 (Blackwell 1970).

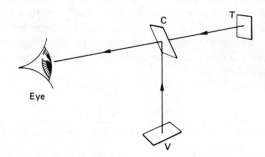

Fig. 2.9   A visibility meter – component C blends direct light from the task T with veiling light V; the background luminance is unchanged

The essential function of such a meter is to place a calibrated translucent optical mist between the task and the observer, who adjusts the transmittance of the mist so that the task is just, but only just, identifiable. The instrument is so constructed that the overall luminance of the task background is unaffected by the presence or absence of the mist; this ensures that the mist does not affect those ocular feedback mechanisms which depend on the general luminance of the surroundings. Plate 2.1 gives an impression of the view through a visibility meter; contrast is varied, background luminance remains constant.

The *visibility level* (VL) of the task is the ratio of the actual task luminance contrast C to the threshold contrast $\tilde{C}$ at which it is just visible through the optical mist.

$$VL = C/\tilde{C} \qquad (2.11)$$

A visibility level of unity, written $VL1$, would represent threshold visibility. Consider the visibility of a proof-reading task, such as that in Plate 2.1. Suppose that the original print has a contrast of 0·84 and that proof-reading is just, but only just, impossible at a contrast $\tilde{C}$ of 0·12. The visibility level (VL) equals the ratio of C to $\tilde{C}$, which in this case is 0·84/0·12 = 7·0.

It is obvious from an inspection of Plate 2.1 that an increase in visibility level close to threshold ($VL1$) is worth more than a similar increment at a higher visibility level, so a lighting engineer normally wants to avoid low visibility levels. The visibility level depends on several variables:

(a)   The task itself. An improvement in contrast or angular size will increase the visibility level.

(b)   The background luminance L_b. For a given task an increase in L_b would involve increasing the illuminance. The effect of this is discussed below.

(c)   Few, if any, visual tasks are perfectly matt. Pencil and ball-point lines are distinctly shiny. They will mirror light from a badly-placed luminaire straight into an observer's eye, impairing the contrast between the task and its background and hence reducing the visibility level. See Fig. 2.10.

(d)   Disability glare, discussed above (see Sect. 2.2.1), may also reduce the visibility level of a given task.

(e)   A glance away from the visual task may set in train the various ocular feedback processes. Their balance will be restored, but not instantly, when attention is redirected to the task. Meanwhile the visibility level of the task will be temporarily reduced.

The effect on the visibility level of the last two processes – disability glare and temporary impairment – are generally ignored, if only because there is no generally-agreed procedure for taking them into account. To compare against a common baseline the effects of different lighting systems in producing glossy reflections with a given task Blackwell defines a *reference lighting* condition, namely a uniform hemisphere of unpolarized light.

The *contrast rendering factor* (*CRF*) can be defined as

$$CRF = \frac{\text{visibility level of task } (VL)}{\text{visibility level under reference lighting conditions } (VL_{\text{ref}})} \qquad (2.12)$$

Both the visibility levels in Eq. 2.12 may be determined by means of a visibility meter. Alternatively one can use the simple *CRF* indicator recently developed at the Jules Thorn Laboratory, Enfield (Lynes 1982).

One may now summarize some important features of the CIE framework which have emerged up to this point. On the credit side it is logically structured, it is commendably free from theoretical commitment, and it does not rest on ex-perimentally determined laws of contrast. The one debatable assumption, that tasks of high visibility level are more legible than tasks of low visibility level, is certainly true for exacting tasks, but recent evidence suggests that it may cease to be true for large targets or for luminance contrasts approaching 1·0. To the extent that this assumption is false, the use of the visibility meter must be wrong. On the debit side it is undeniably complex, possibly too complex for general acceptance even among lighting engineers. In addition it depends on the use of a visibility meter, and such instruments are seldom available outside research laboratories. Blackwell himself (CIE 1972b, 1981a) recommends the use of a more indirect, but experimentally sounder, method of determining visibility levels, to eliminate differences between one observer and the next. It involves comparing the visibility of the task with that of a standard target; the ramifications of the technique are of little interest to lighting engineers.

The one vital factor omitted from this brief survey of the CIE framework is unfortunately also the most contentious: the effect of illuminance on the visibility level. To allow for this it has been necessary to agree internationally on an experimentally determined law of contrast. This is illustrated in Fig. 2.11, which

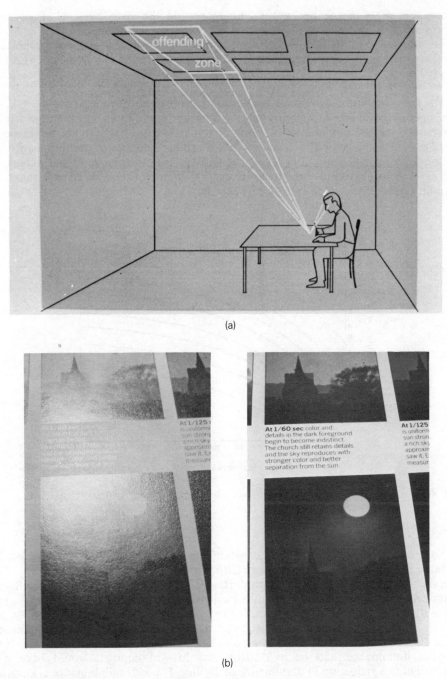

(a)

(b)

Fig. 2.10 Visibility, glare, and contrast: (a) light from the offending zone is mirrored into the reader's eyes, reducing legibility, and (b) left: low *CRF*; right: high *CRF*

shows the effect of the background luminance on the visibility level. Each curve represents a different task, the lower ones being the hardest to see.

To use Fig. 2.11 to find the effect of illuminance we first express the abscissa, showing the background luminance L_b (cd m^{-2}), in terms of illuminance E (lux)

$$E = \pi L_b / \beta_b \tag{2.13}$$

where β_b is the luminance factor of the task background (Sect. 1.4.6).

Consider a task whose visibility level at a background luminance of 1 cd m^{-2} is 2·1. Increasing the illuminance by a factor of ten raises the background luminance to 10 cd m^{-2} and the visibility level to 5·0. Further increments of illuminance will continue to raise the visibility level, but will be less effective at higher values. An increase in background brightness from 1000 cd m^{-2} to 10000 cd m^{-2} raises the visibility level of the same task from 12 to only 13.

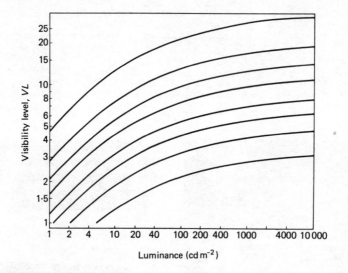

Fig. 2.11   Blackwell's law of contrast

Next consider the effect of shine within the task itself, Fig. 2.10. Suppose this reduces the contrast rendering factor (*CRF*) from 1·0 to 0·8. According to Eq. 2.12, the visibility level (*VL*) will fall in proportion to the *CRF*. This has the same effect as a reduction in illuminance. Thus at a background luminance of 1000 cd m^{-2} and a visibility level of 9 a fall in *CRF* from 1·0 to 0·8 reduces the visibility level to 9 × 0·8, or 7·2. From Fig. 2.11 this has the same effect as a reduction of background luminance from 1000 cd m^{-2} to 259 cd m^{-2}, i.e. a reduction in illuminance of about 4 to 1. If the original illuminance had been 1150 lux, the loss of contrast would have been equivalent to a reduction in illuminance to 288 lux. The latter illuminance is known as the *equivalent reference illuminance* (*ERI*) or, in the more commonly used terminology of the Illuminating Engineering Society (IES) of North America, as the *equivalent sphere illuminance* (*ESI*).

The *ESI* or *ERI* is defined as the illuminance which would produce, under reference lighting conditions, the same visibility as is found in the existing lighting installation.

In effect the equivalent sphere illuminance tells us the combined effect of task illuminance E and contrast rendering factor *CRF*.

Instead of using Fig. 2.11 the *ESI* can be estimated using the following rule of thumb for a background luminance between $20\,\text{cd}\,\text{m}^{-2}$ and $200\,\text{cd}\,\text{m}^{-2}$ or, for a white background, a task illuminance E between about 100 lux and 1000 lux (Fischer 1981)

$$ESI = E \times CRF^5 \tag{2.14}$$

An alternative figure of merit, the *lighting effectiveness factor* (*LEF*), is the ratio of the equivalent sphere illuminance to the task illuminance

$$LEF = ESI/E \tag{2.15}$$

or

$$LEF = CRF^5 \tag{2.16}$$

approximately.

The latest developments of the CIE framework take into account the effects of age and the additional load imposed on the visual feedback mechanisms by tasks which require rapid searching in directions remote from the visual axis.

The intention of the CIE framework was threefold:

(a) To prescribe illuminances, task by task, perhaps on the basis of a common visibility level.
(b) To compare the effectiveness of alternative lighting systems for a given task.
(c) To provide reliable performance data for cost-benefit studies.

Figure 2.11 is perhaps the weakest link in a very long chain of reasoning and experiment. The shapes of the curves seem to be affected by the size of the task, the age of the observer, and the extent to which searching or scanning are involved. While it may become possible to take these effects into account, the trend of opinion within the UK has been to avoid too much reliance on concepts which depend on Fig. 2.11, such as *ESI* and *LEF*, but to accept the *CRF* as an index of lighting quality and the visibility meter as a useful tool for comparing alternative lighting systems (Boyce 1978).

2.3.2 Field studies

For some generations the Holy Grail of lighting research has been to formulate a law linking an increase in illuminance with a consequential increase in productivity. Laboratory studies have yielded the CIE framework, but if the signposts are now more numerous the goal is no nearer. The direct approach – measuring output before and after relighting a factory – is also beset with difficulties. Many reports, mostly of an anecdotal nature, are in circulation; not unnaturally a drastic increase in productivity is more likely to be publicized than would be a negative outcome. The most serious study in this field, which opened a new phase in industrial sociology, was carried out by Mayo, in the Hawthorne Works of the Western Electric Company, Chicago, during the nineteen-twenties. Two groups of employees were chosen: a control group who worked under the same lighting through the experiment and a test group for whom the illuminance was increased. As had been anticipated, the output in the latter group improved, but, unexpectedly, the output from the control group also increased. The investigators then reduced the illuminance for the test group, whose output increased once more. Subsequent experiments on a smaller group of workers, extending over a period of five years, studied the effects of piece-work, work-breaks, and a shorter working week, and finally reverted to the conditions at the start of the experiment, when output broke all previous records. Details of the investigation may be found in text books of industrial psychology (Brown 1970); the chief conclusion was that production depended much more on the workers' satisfaction with each other and with their job than on their physical environment. Where better lighting leads to higher output this is more likely to be due to improved morale than to the operation of the laws of contrast.

The Hawthorne experiment also has methodological implications: the very fact that investigators seem to be taking an interest in a person may raise his self-esteem and hence his attitude to the job he is doing, and this 'Hawthorne effect' is the despair of any researcher seeking to elucidate the influence of lighting on performance or productivity outside the artificial environment of the laboratory.

These conclusions do not deliver the Holy Grail, but they do have very positive implications for illuminating engineering. Precisely because it is more visible than the other building services the lighting of a work-place must express an employer's pride in his premises and concern for his employees. The intangible benefits that go with good lighting may thus be out of all proportion to utilitarian parameters, such as illuminance. The converse is also true. Employees who feel disgruntled may well be predisposed to complain of 'eyestrain' and to blame the lighting. 'Trouble-shooting' in these circumstances places a special responsibility on the lighting engineer. Whatever the social context it should always be assumed that visual factors are at least partly at fault. Sympathetic attention to lighting or to decorations will then be doubly beneficial, and the remainder of this chapter deals with those aspects of lighting quality which affect our well-being rather than our visual performance.

2.4   Modes of appearance

The retinal image is an inverted picture of the ambient luminances. So is the image on the back of a camera. Here, however, the resemblance ends since the purpose of vision is recognition and decision rather than detection. The ocular system with its feedback mechanisms evolved to translate luminance signals into information about the environment. The outcome may seem paradoxical, as in Fig. 2.12a where the panel near the window has a slightly higher luminance than has the panel of higher reflectance on the same wall, but actually looks darker. This can be at least partly ascribed to the effects of lateral inhibition and small eye movements; abrupt changes in luminance, e.g. at the edges of the two panels, will affect the apparent brightness more strongly than will gradual changes in luminance, e.g. the lighting gradient across the wall. But, whatever the explanation, the phenomenon itself should not surprise us. In the recognition of objects around us, information about reflectance is worth far more than is information about illuminance. The visual sense has therefore evolved to select the former at the expense of the latter.

The apparent brightness of the two panels in Fig. 2.12a can be manipulated by excluding their environment. This can be achieved by viewing a real interior through a *reduction tube* (a blackened tube with a small aperture). As Fig. 2.12b shows, the apparent brightness of the two panels now depends solely on their luminance, for a change in illuminance is now indistinguishable from a change in reflectance.

Once the reduction tube is removed two stimuli having the same luminance may well look quite different in apparent brightness and in other respects too. A solid will look solid, a liquid will look liquid, and so forth. A number of different *modes of*

Fig. 2.12 (a) a daylit interior and (b) the panels removed from their background

appearance in which light or colour can be experienced may be identified; the following are particularly relevant (Judd 1961):

(a) The *surface mode*, in which the stimulus is perceived as the coloured surface of an object.

(b) The *volume mode*, in which colour is seen in depth behind the surface, as in a coloured transparent medium. (The surface mode and the volume mode are sometimes grouped together, as the *object mode*.)

(c) The *illuminant mode*, in which light and colour are perceived as emerging from a self-luminous body, such as a fluorescent lamp.

(d)   The *aperture mode*, typified by the view through a reduction tube, or by a uniform expanse of blue sky, where the source of light or colour is unidentifiable for lack of visible information.

(e)   The *illumination mode*, in which attention is focused on the composition of the incident light.

The mode of appearance does not describe the object itself, only the way in which we experience it. A given object will not always appear in the same mode. For example an extinguished fluorescent lamp would normally be seen in the surface mode, with a definite reflectance; once switched on it would appear in the illuminant mode and its surface characteristics, such as its reflectance, would be impossible to identify. Viewed through a reduction tube even its self-luminous nature would be unverifiable; it would be seen in the aperture mode.

It is helpful to identify the perceptual cues on which the modes depend. Thus we perceive in the surface mode when our eyes can focus on the surface itself, distinguishing the tiny gradations of luminance which we have learned to interpret as texture, sheen, convexity, etc. Other cues are afforded by the sharp transition of luminance and colour which typifies the edge of an object, and by the relative luminance of object and background; if the object is much brighter than its background it tends to appear in the illuminant mode. We perceive it in the volume mode when the stimulus contains cues for spatial depth, and in the aperture mode when all spatial cues are removed.

2.4.1   The illuminant mode

Stimuli perceived in the aperture mode can differ in shape, size, brightness, colour, and transparency, but not in surface properties, such as roughness or sheen, which would indicate the nature and location of the stimulus; light from a luminescent body seems to emanate from a volume rather than from a surface. When this is not so, for example in the case of a dim luminous ceiling, the mode of appearance becomes uncertain; this condition is avoided in good lighting practice.

Many plants and other organisms, including man, are attracted by bright lights. This pull is termed the *phototropic effect*. It is exploited by lighting engineers to guide drivers and pedestrians at night, 'beacon lighting', or to attract shoppers from one department in a shop to the next. Unfortunately the phototropic effect may occur where it is not wanted; its distracting effect is one cause of discomfort glare.

Discomfort glare cannot be measured directly, but for engineering purposes it is sufficient to quantify the relative effects of its principal physical determinants, namely: the source luminance L_s (cd m^{-2}) in the direction of the observer, the background luminance L_b (cd m^{-2}), and the solid angle ω (steradians) subtended at the eye by the source (Hopkinson 1963).

The laws of contrast and of apparent brightness yield the necessary information. For most practical light sources Piper's law applies and so Eq. 2.8 may be rewritten as

$$\text{conspicuity of source} = f(L_s \vee \omega) \tag{2.17}$$

Since Eq. 2.1 defines a ratio scale of apparent brightness we may assume that the conspicuity of the distracting source depends on the ratio of the apparent brightness B_s of the source to the apparent brightness B_b of the general background.

From Eq. 2.4 B_b is proportional to $L_b^{0.37}$ and from Eq. 2.1 B_s is proportional to $L_s^{0.58}$.

Incorporating these factors in Eq. 2.17 and normalizing, as is customary, the exponent of L_b we obtain

$$\text{conspicuity} = f\left(\frac{L_s^{1.6}\omega^{0.8}}{L_b}\right) \tag{2.18}$$

Equation 2.18 enables us to predict what change in the background luminance L_b would buffer a given change in the source luminance L_s and/or in the solid angle ω subtended by the source. If multiple sources are involved they will all share the same value of L_b, which is why the exponent of L_b was normalized. Their combined effect is obtained by calculating the bracketed term in Eq. 2.18 separately for each source and then summing the results.

The *Glare Index* of a lighting installation is actually defined by the Building Research Station formula (cf. Sect. 5.5.1)

$$\text{glare index} = 10\log_{10}\left[\frac{0.239}{L_b}\sum L_s^{1.6}\omega^{0.8}p\right] \tag{2.19}$$

The glare index is usually calculated for the least comfortable viewpoint in a room, the summation being carried out for all the luminaires visible from that point.

p is an empirical index which, for a fixed viewing direction, shows the effect of removing a glare source from the direct line of sight. The logarithmic scale and the constants were chosen, by analogy with the decibel system in acoustics, so that one unit of glare index is the smallest interval that can be detected under laboratory conditions. Six units of glare index are the interval between the classical experimental criteria of discomfort – 'perceptible', 'acceptable', 'uncomfortable', and 'intolerable'.

2.4.2 The object mode

The object mode of appearance, sometimes known as the located mode, embraces the surface mode and the volume mode. Stimuli perceived in this mode can differ in shape, size, lightness, colour, transparency, gloss, texture, sheen, and lustre. Thus the object mode is inherently richer in visual information; greys, browns, olive-greens, and navy-blues are not found in any of the non-located modes.

The perceived lightness of an object is related to its reflectance or, in the case of a translucent body, its transmittance. It is remarkable the extent to which this lightness continues to look more-or-less the same even when the incident lighting changes in illuminance and in direction. A dimly-lit sheet of paper will have a lower luminance than will a sunlit lump of coal, but the former will look white and the latter black. This tendency of illuminated objects to keep their perceived lightness relatively unchanged through quite large changes in the quality and concentration of the incident light is known as *brightness constancy* (Hurvich and Jameson 1966).

Brightness constancy is an unfortunate expression on two counts. 'Lightness' or 'whiteness' would be better words than 'brightness' to describe the characteristic concerned, and the term 'constancy' suggests, wrongly, that changes in lighting have no effect whatsoever on the appearance of an object. In fact constancy is never complete. Although we can, to a large extent, distinguish changes in illuminance from changes in reflectance, as in Fig. 2.12, we are also conscious that the apparent brightness of an illuminated surface does increase when the illuminance is raised. Brightness constancy is thus the perceptual counterpart of Eqs 2.4 and 2.5. It also accords with Weber's law, i.e. perceived contrast seems unaffected by changes in illuminance.

Brightness constancy is an essential characteristic of the object mode, and conditions which tend to reduce the degree of constancy also tend to change the appearance of an illuminated scene from the object mode towards the aperture mode of appearance. The following check-list contains a number of precepts for maintaining brightness constancy (Lynes 1971):

(a)   Avoid sharp shadows or highlights.
(b)   Illuminance should be adequate.
(c)   Colour rendering should be good.
(d)   Disability glare should be minimized.
(e)   On poorly-lit surfaces colours of high chroma or high reflectance should be used.
(f)   Sources of light should be obvious.
(g)   A variety of hues should be visible.
(h)   Natural organic materials with characteristic colours and textures should be present.
(i)   Glossy areas should be kept small.
(j)   Small white areas should be well scattered around the visual field.
(k)   Surface textures should be well revealed.

It need not surprise us that this check-list harmonizes well with accepted lighting practice, since departure from these precepts would reduce the visual information available in the environment. Clearly there are many situations in which the maintenance of brightness constancy can be regarded as a criterion of good lighting, but there are also plenty of exceptions. Where dramatic lighting is required, brightness constancy is undesirable. Floodlighting, for example, is most effective when constancy breaks down, when the illuminated objects lose their surface qualities and even appear in the illuminant mode.

2.4.3   The illumination mode

The illumination mode of appearance is experienced when we observe the qualities of the incident lighting as distinct from the characteristics of the object illuminated. The illumination mode is thus a concomitant of the object mode. Unless object and illumination can be distinguished separately, brightness constancy can no longer exist and the mode of appearance degenerates towards the aperture mode.

The illumination mode is the most subtle of the modes of appearance because it is generally far less obvious than the object mode with which it coexists. Stimuli perceived in the illumination mode differ in brightness and colour, but do not necessarily have shape or size. The illumination mode is experienced most distinctly in the presence of sharp shadow: in extreme form, in the splashes of coloured light in a discotheque. In Fig. 2.12a the gradual change of luminance along the wall actually exceeds the difference of luminance between the panels and their respective backgrounds. The play of light along the wall is perceived in the illumination mode, and is barely noticed. The panels appear in the object mode, and stand out clearly. The shadow cast by the filing cabinet is quite visible, but the darkening is still seen in the illumination mode, as a diminution in lighting, not as a change in surface reflectance. Under uniform omnidirectional lighting conditions illuminance as such is virtually imperceptible; the ocular feedback mechanisms all tend to mitigate its effects. This is the dilemma of illuminating engineering; illuminance is the medium for lighting design, but it is also the least conspicuous of the available lighting parameters.

A severe reduction in illuminance affects what we see both in the illumination mode and in the object mode. Textures are harder to see because acuity falls; brightness constancy vanishes as cues to the object mode are eliminated. We talk of 'patches' of light, but 'pools' of darkness. Colours tend to look less vivid, and take on a colder cast. Contrast discrimination also suffers, but the reduction in contrast is not evenly distributed over the whole reflectance range. White and near-white surfaces retain their contrast, while the distinction between dark-grey and black surfaces is reduced. Under very low lighting the visual field becomes polarized into white highlights standing out from an apparently featureless dark background which no longer appears in the object mode. This has been called the *white-dog effect*: white dogs having been found unaccountably conspicuous under war-time blackout conditions.

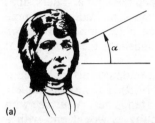

(a)

(b)

(c)

Fig. 2.13 Direction of illumination: (a) the angle α should be preferably between 15° and 45° to the horizontal, (b) $\alpha = 90°$, i.e. light coming straight down, and (c) $\alpha = 30°$

A transition from brighter to dimmer illuminance occurs every time directional lighting strikes a solid object. The gradations of illuminance reveal the sculptural form. This lighting effect is associated with the prevailing *illumination vector* (Sect. 5.1.3). The perceived direction of the *flow of light* coincides with the direction of the vector, and experiments have shown that most people prefer it to have a distinct sideways component. The ideal direction – difficult to reconcile with the need to limit glare – would be between 15° and 45° from the horizontal (Fig. 2.13) and, in plan, between 45° and 135° from the observer's direction of view.

The perceived strength of modelling depends on the viewing direction and also on the *vector/scalar ratio*; this is the ratio of the illumination vector magnitude to the scalar illuminance (Sect. 5.1.4, Cuttle 1971). If the vector direction is substantially downwards, which is normally the case at about eye-level in an office lit evenly from overhead, a vector/scalar ratio between 1·2 and 1·8 has been recommended. These figures apply when the occupants are sitting close enough for a quiet chat. In more formal situations, for example a teacher facing a class, higher vector/scalar ratios would be more appropriate.

Very low illuminances affect the perception of modelling in a paradoxical manner. The white-dog effect enhances the perceived contrast between the light and dark sides of the object, making the modelling look harsher. At the same time the whole environment seems to lose the solidity which belongs to the object mode. Although contrast apparently increases, sculptural qualities are diminished; the environment seems flatter, like a picture post-card.

The ability of a lighting system to reveal the texture of a sculpted surface depends on the angle of incidence of the illumination vector (Lynes 1979). The more obliquely the vector strikes the surface, the more strongly its texture stands out. A surface with large-scale texture does not need such asymmetrical lighting as would one with a tighter surface rhythm.

The spatial impression of a room provides another instance of interaction between the illumination mode and the object mode. Any brightly-lit surface will appear to recede from the observer, so a high overall illuminance makes an interior look more spacious. The perceived proportions and even the character of a room may be manipulated by changing the relative illuminances of ceiling, walls, and working plane. Thus a room with a bright ceiling and dark walls will seem taller and hence more formal. A room with brighter walls will seem friendlier, and also larger in plan.

The CIBS/IES Code for Interior Lighting (CIBS 1977a) imposes additional constraints on surface illuminances in working interiors. The ratio of the ceiling illuminance to the horizontal illuminance on the table-top or work-bench should lie between 0·3 and 0·9. If the ceiling/task ratio is below 0·3 brightness constancy on the ceiling may be impaired. If the illuminance of the ceiling is greater than the task illuminance its phototropic effect may distract occupants from the task in hand.

The Code also sets limits to the ratio of the wall illuminance to the horizontal illuminance on the working plane. This wall/task illuminance ratio should lie between 0·5 and 0·8; brightly-illuminated walls make a room look pleasant, but the necessary sideways intensity from the luminaires may raise the glare index to unacceptable levels (Jay 1968).

2.5   Pointers for lighting design

The lighting criteria that have emerged in this chapter fall under two headings:

(a)   Those concerned with the performance of a visual task, e.g. task illuminance, contrast rendering factor, etc.

(b)   Those concerned with the general appearance of a space and its contents, e.g. glare index, illuminance ratios, vector/scalar ratios, etc.

The skill of a lighting designer consists in assessing the relative importance of the various criteria, and in responding creatively to their often-conflicting demands. The CIBS/IES Lighting Code, and similar documents published outside the UK, do not and should not remove the obligation to exercise judgement. Their function is to provide a standard against which alternative proposals may be compared. The fact that the Code requires a standard service illuminance of 500 lux for a general office simply means that this level accords with good current practice. If one wants an office to look brighter than this one must prescribe a higher level, perhaps 1000 lux. If one chooses to accept a dimmer environment one can prescribe a lower level, perhaps 300 lux; anything less would start to fall short of reasonable expectations. As we have seen, there is no single 'right' illuminance for a given task. The CIBS/IES Lighting Code can be no more than a summary of the contemporary professional consensus; this is why its recommendations may vary, from one edition to the next, often in response to recent advances in visual research.

Similarly an experienced designer will not be inhibited by tables of limiting glare indices, recommended daylight factors, illuminance ratios, vector/scalar ratios, etc. Except in the dullest interiors these should not be taken as a point-of-departure. Creative lighting design is a question of priorities. A good lighting engineer will determine afresh for each project what character the lighted space should express. Photometric criteria then take their rightful place as tools for defining and achieving the appropriate pattern of light and shade.

Further reading

Boyce P R, 1981, *Human factors in lighting* (London: Applied Science)

Carterette E C and Friedman M P (Eds), 1975, *Handbook of perception*, **5**, *Seeing* (New York: Academic Press)

Cornsweet T N, 1970, *Visual perception* (New York: Academic Press)

de Boer J B and Fischer D, 1978, *Interior Lighting* (Holland: Philips Technical Library)

Gazzaniga M S and Blakemore C (Eds), 1975, *Handbook of psychobiology* (New York: Academic Press)

Gregory R L, 1974, *Concepts and mechanisms of perception* (London: Duckworth)

Hopkinson R G, 1963, *Architectural physics: lighting* (London: HMSO)

Jameson D and Hurvich L M, 1972, *Visual psychophysics* (Berlin: Springer)

Lynes J A (Ed), 1978, *Developments in lighting*, **1** (London: Applied Science)

3 Colour

The complicated mechanism of vision has been discussed in Chapter 2 and mention made of the fact that each wavelength of light gives rise to a certain sensation of colour. The components involved in the process of perception, i.e. the light source, the object viewed, the eye, and the brain, all affect the final sensation which consequently will be altered by a change in any of the components. These effects are complicated enough when dealing with black and white signals, but when colour is introduced the position becomes highly complex. In this chapter some of the experimental facts of colour and the way in which they have been used as a basis for colour measurement are described. It must be admitted that colorimetry, although a convenient and necessary technique for communication between users of colour in many fields of work, is nevertheless built on a very simplified physical expression of the behaviour of the human eye and brain, and therefore cannot be expected to agree with all subjective observations.

3.1 The nature of colour

3.1.1 Historical experiments

Discussion of the subject of colour, particularly as evinced by the rainbow, has interested philosophers and scientists for many centuries, but it is only in the last three hundred years that theories demonstrating the true relationship between the wavelength of light and sensation of colour have been developed.

In his famous experiments Newton demonstrated that a beam of white light, obtained in his case from sunlight, could be dispersed by means of a prism into a spectrum. He identified seven distinct hues in the spectrum, but observed that they merged into each other 'so that there appeared as many degrees of colours, as there were sorts of rays differing in refrangibility'. At the same time he recognized the subjective nature of colour as shown by the following quotation from his book on 'Opticks'. 'The rays to speak properly are not coloured. In them there is nothing else than a certain power and disposition to stir up a sensation of this or that colour.' The nature of surface colours was also studied by Newton; thus 'colours in the object are nothing but a disposition to reflect this or that sort of rays more copiously than the rest'.

Two other important facts that Newton discovered were that the properties of the rays, or wavelengths, were not altered by refraction or reflection and that the separate wavelengths could be recombined to give 'the same white light as before'. He also showed that colours produced by mixing separate wavelengths could give the same visual effect as an intermediate wavelength, but emphasized that their spectral compositions would be different.

In these experiments Newton laid the foundation of the modern science of colorimetry. Although he failed to produce white light by a mixture of two or three 'primaries', the laws of three-colour mixing were well established by 1860 when Maxwell commenced his work on the quantities of red, green, and blue light necessary to match the colours of different spectral wavelengths. Primaries are now known as matching or reference colour stimuli. In this chapter square brackets are used to distinguish them from other stimuli.

3.1.2   The experimental basis of trichromatism

The two fundamental experimental facts of colorimetry are (a) that any colour of light can be exactly imitated (or matched to visual observation) by a combination of not more than three suitable primary radiations, sometimes with the necessary use of a negative amount of one or two of the primaries, and (b) that additive relations in colour mixture are found to hold over a wide range of observing conditions. Different sets of primaries can be used as reference colour stimuli, but the ones usually chosen are red, green, and blue. These basic principles may be formulated as follows, supposing that the matching stimuli are red, green, and blue and the stimulus to be matched is (C).

$$c(C) \equiv R[R] + G[G] + B[B] \tag{3.1}$$

where [R], [G], and [B] represent the reference colour stimuli and have no numerical value, and the terms c, R, G, and B represent the amounts of the stimuli. The equivalent sign ($\equiv$) means that a match exists between (C) and the mixture of [R], [G], and [B] in respect of colour appearance only and not of spectral distribution.

Suppose two test colours denoted by (C_1) and (C_2) are mixed to produce (C_3), then

$$c_3(C_3) \equiv c_1(C_1) + c_2(C_2) \equiv R_3[R] + G_3[G] + B_3[B]$$

and, if additivity holds, it would be expected that

$$R_3 = R_1 + R_2$$
$$G_3 = G_1 + G_2$$
$$B_3 = B_1 + B_2$$

Certain assumptions have to be made for such a system of colorimetry to be widely applicable. They are that (a) most eyes have nearly the same colour response, (b) the match holds over a wide range of luminance and visual adaptation, and (c) the viewing conditions under which the test colour is compared with the mixture of the reference colour stimuli will not affect the match.

It is known that a certain number of people suffer from some degree of defective colour vision (Sect. 2.1.2) and such observers may use different amounts of the reference colour stimuli compared with normal observers when matching certain colours. Normal observers also exhibit appreciable differences of colour vision, but the practical consequences of these variations have been reduced by the adoption of the CIE Standard Observer data.

As described in Sect. 2.2.1, the mechanism of the eye adjusts automatically to the prevailing luminance and this process is known as adaptation. In a similar way the eye is affected by changes in the colour of the illumination and this effect is called chromatic adaptation (Sect. 3.5.3). It has been found that a colour match is not disturbed by adaptation to white, coloured, or varying quantities of light, provided that the areas of the retina being used for matching are not affected differently in respect of adaptation.

The effects of viewing conditions on a colour match are complicated since the colour-matching properties of the eye vary with field size because of the variation over the retina of the number of rods and cones (Sect. 2.1.2) and consequently a match made with the centre of the eye will not necessarily hold for peripheral vision. If there is identity of spectral power distribution between the test and matching stimuli, the match will hold for all viewing and luminance conditions, but this is not usually the case where a visual colorimeter uses three reference colour stimuli. More reference colour stimuli are needed if the match is to hold for differing conditions and five would probably be sufficient to satisfy these requirements (Palmer 1972).

Experimental evidence to date shows that these laws of additivity hold reasonably well for a viewing field of 2° angular subtense at the eye, at any rate for most practical purposes. This means that it is possible to build a visual trichromatic colorimeter in which a test colour is matched by an additive mixture of three reference colour stimuli, ideally narrow spectral bands of red, green, and blue light. White can be obtained by mixing appropriate amounts of the three reference colour stimuli and adjustments of these amounts yield colours intermediate between white and the reference colour stimuli. The test colours are then specified in terms of the amounts of the reference colour stimuli necessary for a match.

An interesting feature of a system of colorimetry designed in this way is that the actual sensation produced by the test colour is not defined; only the amounts of three known reference colour stimuli which cause the same visual sensation as that of the test colour are quoted. For a colour match the quantities of light in Eq. 3.1 must be equal and so

$$c = R + G + B \tag{3.2}$$

Division of Eq. 3.1 by Eq. 3.2 gives

$$1 \cdot 0(C) \equiv r[R] + g[G] + b[B] \tag{3.3}$$

where

$$r = \frac{R}{R + G + B} \qquad G = \frac{G}{R + G + B} \qquad b = \frac{B}{R + G + B} \tag{3.4}$$

and hence

$$r + g + b = 1 \tag{3.5}$$

Equations 3.1 and 3.3 are trichromatic equations, R, G, and B are the tristimulus values, and r, g, and b are the chromaticity coordinates of (C) which can be plotted on a two-dimensional chart known as a colour triangle or chromaticity diagram (Fig. 3.1).

The method of mixing three stimuli is shown geometrically in Fig. 3.1 with different sets of reference colour stimuli at the corners of the triangles. The stimuli can be real light sources, for example very narrow spectral bands [R], [G], and [B] or sources, such as [X], [Y], and [Z], which are not physically realizable. By the laws of additivity, the point representing a new colour formed by mixing two stimuli, for example by mixing reference colour stimuli [G] and [B], lies on the straight line joining [G] and [B], and the position of the new point can be determined using a simple calculation from the amounts of [G] and [B] used in the mixture. Extending this idea to mixtures of [R], [G], and [B], it will be seen that all colours situated within the triangle [RGB] can be produced by suitable mixtures of the three reference colour stimuli. Suppose, however, that the point (Q) represents a light source. It lies outside the [RGB] triangle and therefore cannot be obtained by mixing positive amounts of [R], [G], and [B]. If a small amount of [R], the stimulus of complementary wavelength, is added to

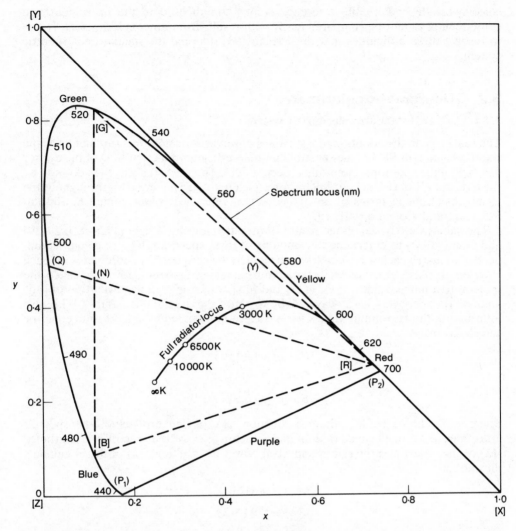

Fig. 3.1 CIE 1931 (*x, y*) chromaticity diagram illustrating different sets of reference stimuli

(Q) (this process is known as desaturation), the colour (N) can be obtained and (N) can be matched by a mixture of [G] and [B]. Thus (Q) has been matched by positive amounts of [G] and [B] and a negative amount of [R].

It is an experimental fact that single spectral wavelengths cannot be matched by additive amounts of any real red, green, and blue reference colour stimuli, but if the desaturation technique is used their colours can be matched and they lie on the curved line $(P_1)[B](Q)[G][R](P_2)$, which is called the spectrum locus. All real colours are contained within the area bounded by the spectrum locus and the chord $(P_1)(P_2)$, where purples are located. A considerable number of real colours lie outside any practicable [RGB] triangle, which results in their formulation in terms of negative amounts of other real colours. This is an unsatisfactory situation in practical colorimetry. Another difficulty is that the coordinates obtained from a particular colorimeter depend on the reference colour stimuli used in the instrument and consequently cannot be compared easily with results from other colorimeters. It was to resolve these difficulties that the CIE in 1931 adopted the standard colorimetric system.

3.2   Trichromatic colorimetry

3.2.1   CIE 1931 standard colorimetric system

The first stage in the adoption of a standard observer for colour measurement was the standardization in 1924 of the spectral luminous efficiency function $V(\lambda)$ of the eye for a 2° field under photopic conditions (Sect. 1.3.1). The next step was the adoption by the CIE in 1931 of colour coordinates for wavelengths at 5 nm intervals throughout the visible spectrum in terms of an agreed set of reference colour stimuli at 700 nm, 546·1 nm, and 435·8 nm (CIE 1971).

The values were based on the results of investigations by Wright (1928–9, 1929–30) and Guild (1932) to determine the amounts of three spectral reference colour stimuli needed to match each wavelength which yielded the chromaticity coordinates for each wavelength. Also specified were the colour-matching functions, formerly called the spectral tristimulus values, $\bar{r}(\lambda)$, $\bar{g}(\lambda)$, and $\bar{b}(\lambda)$, which give the contribution of unit amount of energy at each wavelength towards the tristimulus values. With this information the tristimulus values for a surface illuminated by a light source can be calculated from

$$R = \int \varphi(\lambda)\,\bar{r}(\lambda)\,d\lambda$$

$$G = \int \varphi(\lambda)\,\bar{g}(\lambda)\,d\lambda \qquad\qquad (3.6)$$

$$B = \int \varphi(\lambda)\,\bar{b}(\lambda)\,d\lambda$$

where the relative colour stimulus function $\varphi(\lambda)$ is the product of the spectral reflectance $\rho(\lambda)$, or the spectral luminance factor $\beta(\lambda)$, or the spectral transmittance $\tau(\lambda)$ of the object and the relative spectral power distribution $S(\lambda)$ of the illuminant; thus either

$$\varphi(\lambda) = \rho(\lambda)\,S(\lambda)$$

or $$\varphi(\lambda) = \beta(\lambda)\,S(\lambda) \qquad\qquad (3.7)$$

or $$\varphi(\lambda) = \tau(\lambda)\,S(\lambda)$$

The chromaticity coordinates can then be obtained using Eq. 3.4.

The final part of the system was the selection of a set of reference colour stimuli that were independent of any real stimuli. The reference colour stimuli chosen, [X], [Y], and [Z], were those indicated in Fig. 3.1 and were not physically realizable since they lay outside the location of real colours. Tables of the colour coordinates, x, y, and z (Fig. 3.1) and colour-matching functions, $\bar{x}(\lambda)$, $\bar{y}(\lambda)$, and $\bar{z}(\lambda)$ (Fig. 3.2) were given for wavelengths at 5 nm intervals from 380 nm to 780 nm. In 1971 values at 1 nm intervals were interpolated and the range extended to 360 nm and 830 nm.

The system satisfies the following requirements:

(a)   All numerical quantities used in chromaticity calculations are positive and thus all real colours have positive chromaticity coordinates.

(b)   The $\bar{y}(\lambda)$ curve is identical with $V(\lambda)$ and therefore Y is the exclusive measure of luminance.

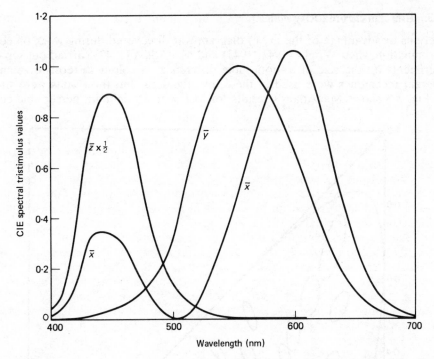

Fig. 3.2 CIE 1931 colour-matching functions for a centrally viewed field of angular subtense between 1° and 4°

(c) The primaries were also chosen to give the most convenient shape to the spectrum locus on the [XYZ] triangle and this resulted in the [Z] axis being coincident with the spectrum locus between about 630 nm and 770 nm and very close to it from 580 nm to 630 nm (Fig. 3.1).

(d) The units of [X], [Y], and [Z] were chosen such that the computed colour of the equi-energy illuminant occupies the centre of the [XYZ] triangle. This theoretical illuminant has a distribution of constant power per unit wavelength interval throughout the visible spectrum (illuminant S_E in Fig. 3.6).

The calculation of chromaticity coordinates x, y, and z is described in Sect. 3.2.4. Plate 3.1 gives a general indication of the location of colours within the [XYZ] triangle.

3.2.2 CIE 1964 supplementary standard colorimetric system

The 2° data standardized in 1931 applies to a field of view with an angular subtense between 1° and 4°. More recently, demand for a system applicable to large-field viewing resulted in the adoption by the CIE in 1964 of colour-matching functions, $\bar{x}_{10}(\lambda)$, $\bar{y}_{10}(\lambda)$, and $\bar{z}_{10}(\lambda)$, for a 10° field, based on the work of Stiles and Burch (1959) and Speranskaya (1959). Sizeable differences exist between the 2° and 10° data. Many colour-matching and viewing situations use 2° fields, but the 10° data is recommended for those applications where the field size is greater than 4° (CIE 1971).

3.2.3   Uniform chromaticity scales

A serious disadvantage of the (x, y) diagram was discovered during work on colour discrimination when Wright (1941, 1943) and MacAdam (1942) carried out separate experiments on the size of a 'noticeable difference' in colour in terms of x and y. Different techniques were used in these investigations, but the results were similar and Fig. 3.3 shows MacAdam's results for loci of ten 'minimum perceptible colour

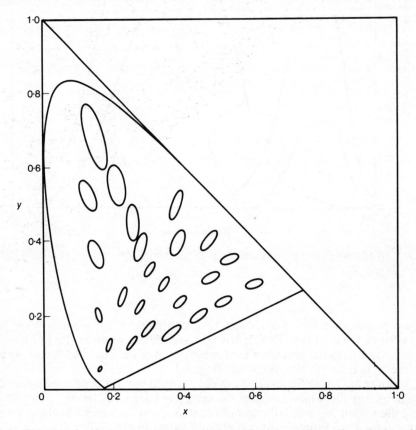

Fig. 3.3   CIE 1931 (x, y) chromaticity diagram with MacAdam ellipses (ten times enlarged)

differences' (m.p.c.d.) plotted on the (x, y) diagram. (Although usually so named, these are really differences of 10 times the standard deviation in colour-matching under the conditions used.) It will be seen that the size of the m.p.c.d. varies with its position on the diagram and the direction in which the difference occurs – an ellipse represents equal visual steps in colour away from the centre point in any direction. This means that the (x, y) diagram is not uniform, i.e. equal steps in x and y do not represent visually equal colour differences, and this is a serious disadvantage when measuring colour differences and specifying colour tolerances.

CIE 1960 uniform-chromaticity-scale (UCS) diagram   Various projections of the (x, y) diagram have been developed in an attempt to find a more uniform system, but none of them has been completely satisfactory, probably due to the fact that most of

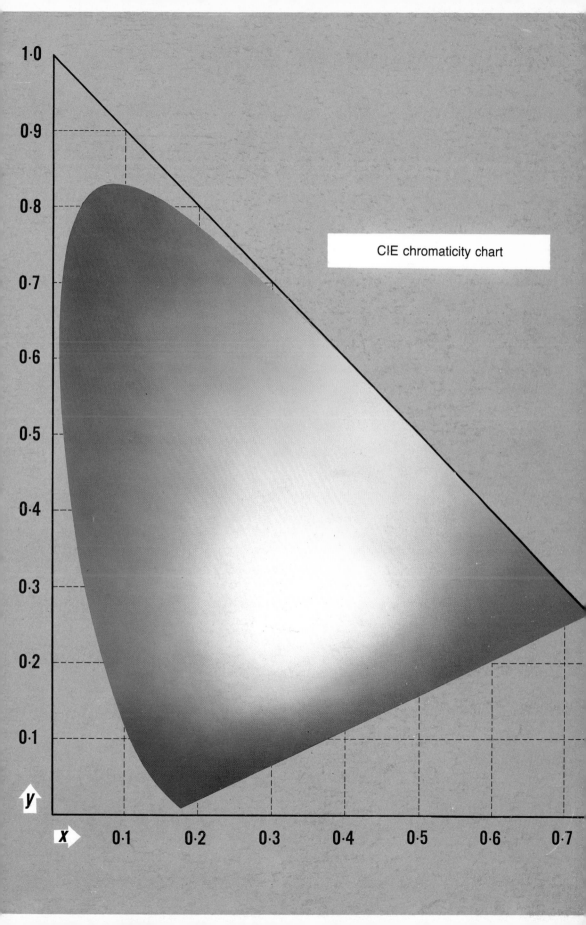

CIE chromaticity chart

Plate 3.2 Model of Munsell system, reflected in mirror

them involve linear transformations of the data. In 1960 the CIE recommended a transformation developed by MacAdam (1937) which improved the uniformity so that in the centre of the diagram near the full radiator locus (Sect. 3.2.5) at 6500 K the m.p.c.d. locus is almost a circle. The coordinates in this system can be obtained by using the following equations.

$$u = \frac{4X}{X + 15Y + 3Z} = \frac{4x}{-2x + 12y + 3}$$

$$v = \frac{6Y}{X + 15Y + 3Z} = \frac{6y}{-2x + 12y + 3}$$

(3.8)

CIE 1976 uniform-chromaticity-scale diagram   Following the extension of the 1960 UCS diagram to three dimensions in 1964 (Sect. 3.4.1), various workers found that

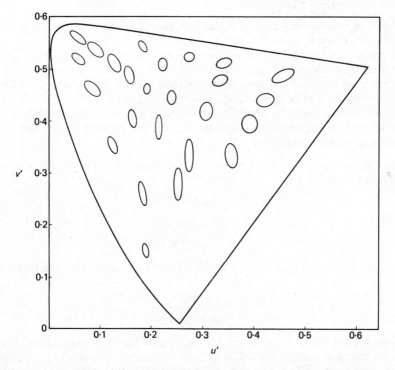

Fig. 3.4   CIE 1976 uniform-chromaticity-scale diagram with MacAdam ellipses (ten times enlarged)

the new recommendations did not produce the expected improvements in their evaluations of small colour differences. The result was that two new colour spaces were recommended for trial by the CIE (Sect. 3.4.1, CIE 1978a), one of which supersedes the 1960 system and incorporates a chromaticity diagram that is a linear transformation of the CIE 1931 (x, y) diagram. This means that straight lines in the (x, y) diagram remain straight after the transformation and this is important when coloured lights are mixed additively. The main difference between the 1960 and 1976

UCS diagrams is that the v scale is expanded in the 1976 system and the transforms are

$$u' = u = \frac{4X}{X + 15Y + 3Z} = \frac{4x}{-2x + 12y + 3}$$

$$v' = 1 \cdot 5v = \frac{9Y}{X + 15Y + 3Z} = \frac{9y}{-2x + 12y + 3}$$

(3.9)

The 1976 UCS (u', v') diagram is shown in Fig. 3.4 where the ratios of the major to minor axes of the 10 m.p.c.d. ellipses are more uniform than on the (x, y) diagram (Fig. 3.3).

3.2.4   Specification of colour

Colorimetry   The determination of the colour of an object in terms of x and y may be performed by four different methods:

(a)   By visual colorimetry in which the test colour is matched by three (or more) lights of known hue, but of arbitrary spectral composition.
(b)   By photocells used to measure several parts of the spectrum of the test colour isolated by coloured filters.
(c)   By measurement of the complete spectrum of the light emitted, reflected, or transmitted by the object in energy (or power) units $\varphi(\lambda)$.
(d)   By calculation from the spectral power distribution of the illuminant $S(\lambda)$ and the spectral reflectance $\rho(\lambda)$, spectral luminance factor $\beta(\lambda)$, or spectral transmittance $\tau(\lambda)$ of the object.

The tristimulus values X, Y, and Z can be calculated from the spectral power data using equations similar to Eq. 3.6, namely

$$X = k \int \varphi(\lambda) \, \bar{x}(\lambda) \, d\lambda$$
$$Y = k \int \varphi(\lambda) \, \bar{y}(\lambda) \, d\lambda$$
$$Z = k \int \varphi(\lambda) \, \bar{z}(\lambda) \, d\lambda$$

(3.10)

where $\varphi(\lambda)$ is defined as in Eq. 3.7 and the constant k is a normalizing factor defined as

$$k = \frac{100}{\int S(\lambda) \, \bar{y}(\lambda) \, d\lambda}$$

Y calculated from Eq. 3.10 is called the luminance factor of the colour. Use of the factor k means that a perfectly diffusing white material, whose $\beta(\lambda) = 1$ throughout the visible spectrum, has a luminance factor of 100. Integration limits include the whole visible spectrum. The chromaticity coordinates x, y, and z may be calculated as before (Eq. 3.4), but using X, Y, and Z in place of R, G, and B.

The luminous flux emitted by a source can also be calculated from Eq. 3.10 if $S(\lambda)$ is known in absolute units since $\bar{y}(\lambda) = V(\lambda)$.

$$\Phi_v = K_m \int S(\lambda) \, \bar{y}(\lambda) \, d\lambda$$

(3.11)

where K_m is the maximum luminous efficacy of radiation and is equal to 683 lm W^{-1}.

In general only two of the chromaticity coordinates, usually x and y, are quoted since

$$x + y + z = 1$$

(3.12)

Very roughly *x* is associated with redness, *y* with greenness, and *z* with blueness. It will be seen from Fig. 3.1 that an additive mixture of red and green gives yellow, green and blue produce blue-green (cyan), and purple (magenta) results from blue and red.

Dominant wavelength An alternative method of specifying a colour using the chromaticity diagram is in terms of dominant wavelength and purity. The concept is used less now than previously, but it still has some merit since it gives a rough correlation with the subjective attributes of hue and saturation. The most saturated colours that exist are those of the spectrum wavelengths and as the colour moves towards the centre of the diagram it becomes less saturated. All the colours that lie on the straight line joining the white point to the spectrum locus are assumed to have the same hue and the monochromatic stimulus is known as the dominant wavelength of that hue. For colours on the purple side of the white point the dominant wavelength is that of the complementary wavelength.

Purity Purity is a measure of the saturation of a colour and is determined from the proportions of the white and monochromatic sources that are needed in an additive match of the test colour. These proportions can be calculated in different ways yielding either the excitation purity or the colorimetric purity (CIE 1971).

3.2.5 The Planckian (full) radiator

It is well known that most bodies when heated to sufficiently high temperatures emit red light and as the temperature increases the emitted light becomes whiter. The complete unifying principle that explains the phenomenon of thermal radiation was given by Planck in 1901 and is described in Sect. 6.3.1. The spectral power distribution curves for full radiators (or black bodies) at various temperatures are shown in Fig. 6.2. The colour coordinates calculated from such curves, when plotted on a chromaticity diagram, lie on a smooth curve called the full radiator locus (Figs 3.1 and 3.5).

Correlated colour temperature If a light source has a chromaticity on the full radiator locus it is said to have the same colour temperature as that particular full radiator, even though their spectral power distributions may differ. A source not on the full radiator locus can be described by its correlated colour temperature, i.e. the temperature of the full radiator whose perceived colour most closely resembles that of the source. The recommended method of determining the correlated colour temperature of a source is by finding the colour temperature of the point of intersection of the full radiator locus with the isotemperature line containing the chromaticity of the source. An isotemperature line is one on which all the chromaticities have the same correlated colour temperature and is currently a normal to the full radiator locus when plotted on a (u, v) or $(u', \frac{2}{3}v')$ chromaticity diagram, Fig. 3.5 (CIE 1970).

Correlated colour temperature is a theoretical concept with limited experimental evidence to justify the isotemperature lines (Grum et al. 1978). It has some significance for sources with chromaticities on or close to the full radiator locus, such as phases of natural daylight, but it has been much abused in the case of non-incandescent sources with chromaticities well away from the full radiator locus.

3.2.6 Standard illuminants and sources

In 1931 the CIE recognized the necessity for specifying internationally some standard sources, particularly for calibration purposes in the colorimetry of surface colours.

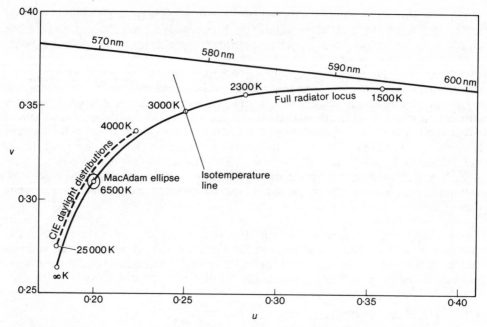

Fig. 3.5 CIE (*u*, *v*) chromaticity diagram with full radiator locus, isotemperature line, and the locus of the CIE daylight illuminants

Three lamp or lamp and filter combinations were chosen. More recently, the CIE decided to specify standard illuminants, not necessarily realizable in practice, in terms of their spectral power distributions (CIE 1971) and, where possible, it recommended practical sources to realize them.

CIE standard illuminant A   The fact that the spectral power distribution for an incandescent lamp conforms closely to that of a full radiator makes such a lamp an immediate choice for Source A, S_A (CIE 1971). The colour temperature is 2856 K and the spectral power distribution is shown in Fig. 3.6. In practice this colour temperature is achieved by operating a gas-filled (non-halogen) tungsten lamp at an applied voltage less than the nominal value. Since the spectral emissivity is not constant over the visible spectrum, the spectral power distribution of a full radiator at 2856 K is achieved by a tungsten lamp at a real temperature of approximately 2790 K, but the lamp is said to have a colour temperature of 2856 K.

CIE standard illuminants B and C   For practical sources at temperatures higher than that a tungsten filament can achieve the CIE specified that S_A should be used in conjunction with liquid filters to produce sources at colour temperatures (on the present scale) of approximately 4874 K and 6774 K, S_B and S_C respectively. An appendix to the 1931 resolution contained the spectral power distributions for these sources, Fig. 3.6 (CIE 1971). Unfortunately the liquid filters were difficult to prepare and maintain and the sources were of no use where large-area illumination was required.

CIE standard daylight illuminants   The best known and most widely used light source is natural daylight and, variable though it is in intensity and spectral composition, it is

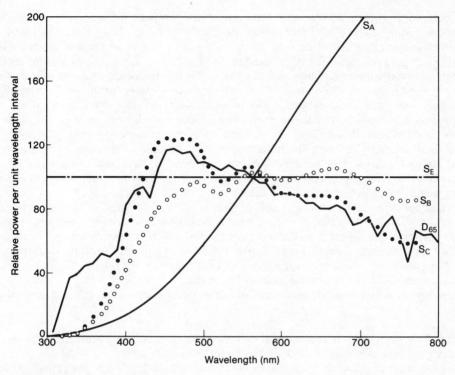

Fig. 3.6 Spectral power distribution curves for the CIE standard illuminants A, B, C, and D_{65} and the equi-energy illuminant

a readily-accepted standard for showing how objects 'ought' to look, north skylight especially being much used for visual colour-matching purposes. In 1967 the CIE recommended a daylight distribution at 6500 K as a standard illuminant, D_{65} (Fig. 3.6) together with a method for obtaining the spectral power distributions for daylight at other colour temperatures in the range 4000 K to 25 000 K (CIE 1971). These distributions were based on several hundred measurements of natural skylight by Henderson and Hodgkiss, Condit and Grum, and Budde (Judd 1964). The locus of the chromaticities fell on the green side of the full radiator locus (Fig. 3.5). It has proved impossible so far to produce sources which imitate very closely the standard daylight illuminants, though reasonable approximations can be obtained for less exacting requirements than those of colorimetry. The CIE has recently published a method for assessing how closely a daylight source simulates a particular standard daylight illuminant (CIE 1981b).

3.3 Surface colours

3.3.1 Reflection and transmission

Single surfaces Colour considerations so far in this chapter have concentrated on light sources as this approach is essential for establishing the principles of colour measurement. A more common problem is the evaluation of the colour of light either reflected from or transmitted by an illuminated sample. Restricting the discussion to reflection from diffusely reflecting surfaces, since the same considerations apply to transmission, certain wavelengths are more strongly reflected from a coloured surface than are others, and the object is colloquially called by the hue of the most strongly reflected wavelengths. Thus the colour of the surface is mainly produced by subtracting wavelengths from the incident light, and it is important to remember that the perceived colour depends on both the spectral reflectance of the object and the spectral emission of the source. This can easily be demonstrated by illuminating a range of coloured samples with a low pressure sodium lamp when most colours will appear to be brown, black, or grey. The colour coordinates of a sample can be calculated as described in Sect. 3.2.4, but they do not completely define the colour as it is also necessary to know the luminance factor Y. This is particularly important for surface colours as it is possible for two samples to have the same chromaticity coordinates, but to look completely different because their luminance factors are not the same, for example yellow and brown.

In general pigments and dyes reflect over a fairly wide band of wavelengths and, consequently, it is impossible to obtain saturated colours where the spectrum locus on the chromaticity diagram is curved because the colour depends on the integrated effect over the wavelength range that is reflected. Thus only saturated yellows and reds are obtainable since the spectrum locus is straight in this region. Moreover, there is a theoretical limit to the luminance factor that a coloured surface can have for a given chromaticity and, in practice, only saturated yellows and reds approach these limits.

Multiple reflections   When a beam of light falls on a coloured surface some of the wavelengths are absorbed and, if the reflected beam falls on a similarly coloured surface, more of the same wavelengths will be absorbed. Each time the reflected beam is incident on the coloured surface the absorption will be repeated and this means that the perceived saturation of a colour increases with multiple reflections of the light from it. This explains the effect that the walls of a room are often noticeably more saturated in colour than a small sample of the colour seen separately.

3.3.2   Colour contrast

Another effect that can cause large changes in the appearance of coloured surfaces is that of contrast between an object and its neighbour. Any colour tends to induce a complementary colour in its neighbour whether this is neutral or coloured and so existing hue or lightness differences between neighbouring colours will tend to increase. This has a practical significance as it tends to make objects more conspicuous against their backgrounds. Some of these contrast effects can be quite striking, especially if a pattern is involved when the magnitudes of the apparent colour shifts become functions of the pattern size and detail. The effect may be partially explained by the fatiguing of receptors, the rapid involuntary movements which the eye makes continuously, and interactions between nerve impulses, but other factors in the eye and brain are also involved and the full explanation of all the phenomena of contrast has not yet been found.

3.3.3   Fluorescent pigments and dyes

In recent years a noticeable improvement in the brightness (luminosity) and saturation of surface colours has occurred with the development of fluorescent pigments and dyes. These materials absorb energy mainly in the long-wave ultraviolet or blue regions of the spectrum and convert it to light. The emission bands are fairly narrow and are superimposed on the reflection spectrum that the sample would have in the absence of fluorescence. Similar materials emitting violet or blue light are used as fluorescent whitening agents to overcome the natural yellowness of most 'white' materials (CIBA–GEIGY 1973).

3.3.4   Subtractive colour mixture

It has been shown that the perceived colour of a surface is produced by a subtractive process and therefore, if two colorants, i.e. pigments or dyes, are mixed, the resultant colour cannot be predicted by the principles of additive mixtures of lights (Sect. 3.1.2). Subtractive mixing can be illustrated by considering a mixture of blue and yellow pigments. Examination of their reflectance curves (Fig. 3.7) shows that the

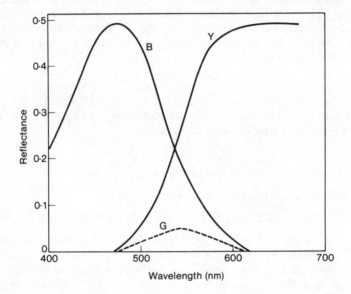

Fig. 3.7 Spectral reflectance curves for blue and yellow coloured pigments and their subtractive mixture

only region of the spectrum reflected by both pigments is the green. Hence a mixture of blue and yellow pigments produces green whereas the addition of blue and yellow lights yields white. The reflectance curve for a mixture of pigments or dyes is obtained by multiplying together the curves for the individual components. In the example quoted the low reflectance of the mixture is noticeable.

The most useful subtractive primaries are those which when mixed together produce the widest range of other colours; they also yield black when mixed in the correct proportions. They are cyan, magenta, and yellow which are the complementaries of the additive primaries red, green, and blue. In a subtractive mixture magenta and yellow give red, yellow and cyan produce green, and blue results from cyan and magenta. Colour printing and photography rely on these relations and the Lovibond method of colour measurement uses subtractive effects on white light by means of calibrated glasses coloured red, yellow, and blue.

3.4   Colour spaces and colour solids

It is estimated that there are at least 10 million colours that are detectably different, so for practical purposes it is essential that these should be arranged in a logical manner, usually in a three-dimensional colour space. That part of colour space occupied by surface colours is called a colour solid and a colour atlas is a collection of colour samples arranged in a specified manner.

3.4.1   Colour spaces and colour difference equations

CIE 1964 uniform colour space and colour difference equation   The complete specification of a surface colour under a given illuminant comprises its chromaticity coordinates and luminance factor, Y (Sects 3.2.3 and 3.3.1). In 1964 the CIE decided to extend the CIE 1960 UCS system (Sect. 3.2.3) to colour space, but it was not satisfactory to use the luminance factor for the third dimension as the size of the discrimination steps in this parameter varies considerably. Instead, another function for lightness, W^*, was defined by

$$W^* = 25Y^{1/3} - 17 \tag{3.13}$$

where $100 \geqslant Y \geqslant 1$. It was decided to place the achromatic (white) point at the centre of the colour space and the chromaticity coordinates u_n and v_n are usually those of the illuminant. Two more variables were defined by

$$U^* = 13W^*(u - u_n)$$
$$V^* = 13W^*(v - v_n) \tag{3.14}$$

The colour difference between two samples is given by

$$\Delta E = [(\Delta U^*)^2 + (\Delta V^*)^2 + (\Delta W^*)^2]^{1/2} \tag{3.15}$$

and, in practice, a unit of ΔE is approximately equal to five times the smallest difference that can just be detected under the best experimental conditions.

The CIE 1964 uniform colour space was not widely accepted in industry as many workers found that the calculated values of ΔE did not correlate very well with subjective judgements of small colour differences. However it was adopted by the CIE for the method of assessing the colour rendering properties of light sources (Sect. 3.5.1).

CIE 1976 ($L^*u^*v^*$) colour space (CIELUV)   One difficulty with the 1964 UCS space is that W^* only equals 99·04 when $Y = 100$ and in 1976 a revised colour space was recommended by the CIE (CIE 1978a) in which a modified function for lightness, L^*, was specified and $L^* = 100$ when $Y = Y_n = 100$.

$$L^* = 116[Y/Y_n]^{1/3} - 16 \tag{3.16}$$

where $Y/Y_n > 0·008\,856$. Y_n is the luminance factor of the achromatic (white) stimulus. The other two variables are

$$u^* = 13L^*(u' - u'_n)$$
$$v^* = 13L^*(v' - v'_n) \tag{3.17}$$

where u' and v' are obtained from Eq. 3.9 and u'_n and v'_n are the chromaticity coordinates of the white point or illuminant.

CIE 1976 (L*a*b*) colour space (CIELAB) An alternative colour space to CIELUV was also recommended by the CIE in 1976 (CIE 1978a) for those people in industries concerned with colorant mixtures, for example textiles and dyestuffs, who favoured existing colour difference equations based on a cube-root type of formula (McDonald 1982a, b). The quantities are defined by L^* from Eq. 3.16 and

$$a^* = 500[(X/X_n)^{1/3} - (Y/Y_n)^{1/3}]$$
$$b^* = 200[(Y/Y_n)^{1/3} - (Z/Z_n)^{1/3}]$$

(3.18)

where X/X_n, Y/Y_n, and Z/Z_n are all greater than 0·008 856. X, Y, and Z and X_n, Y_n, and Z_n are the tristimulus values of the sample and the white point respectively.

An (a^*, b^*) diagram can be plotted, but it is not a projective transformation of the CIE 1931 (x, y) diagram and hence straight lines in the latter diagram generally produce curved lines when transformed into the CIELAB diagram.

CIE 1976 colour difference equations The colour difference between two samples is calculated from

$$\Delta E_{uv}^* = [(\Delta L^*)^2 + (\Delta u^*)^2 + (\Delta v^*)^2]^{1/2} \qquad (3.19)$$

or $\qquad \Delta E_{ab}^* = [(\Delta L^*)^2 + (\Delta a^*)^2 + (\Delta b^*)^2]^{1/2} \qquad (3.20)$

The magnitude of a colour difference calculated from Eq. 3.19 compared with that from Eq. 3.15 is hardly affected by the change from W^* to L^*, but the replacement of v by v' does have an effect since $v' = 1·5v$.

Using subjective terms, a colour difference between two samples is composed of differences in hue ΔH^*, lightness ΔL^*, and chroma ΔC^*. A colour difference equation can therefore be written as

$$\Delta E^* = [(\Delta H^*)^2 + (\Delta L^*)^2 + (\Delta C^*)^2]^{1/2} \qquad (3.21)$$

The quantity C^* was defined in 1976 by the CIE (CIE 1978a) as

$$C_{uv}^* = (u^{*2} + v^{*2})^{1/2}$$

and $\qquad C_{ab}^* = (a^{*2} + b^{*2})^{1/2}$

ΔC^*, ΔL^*, and ΔE^* can all be obtained from the measured colour parameters and hence it is possible to calculate ΔH^* from Eq. 3.21.

3.4.2 Colour solids and atlases

Munsell system of colour notation Many colour solids and colour atlases based on different methods of arranging the samples have been developed. The best known is that due to Munsell (Nickerson 1976) in which the central vertical axis, called the *Value* (lightness) scale, ranges from white at the top to black at the bottom with nine equally spaced shades of grey in between. The saturated colours are arranged on the equator of the solid into 10 *Hues*, B, BG, G, GY, Y, YR, R, RP, P, and PB, each of which is divided into 10 steps. The saturation, or *Chroma*, of the colour increases, also by visually equal steps, as it moves away from the central axis (Plate 3.2). A colour is specified by a combination of three numbers, for example 5YR 6/8 where 5YR is the Hue, the Value is 6, and the Chroma is 8. In practice the Munsell solid is not a sphere because it is not possible to produce saturated greens and blues with lightnesses as high as those for yellows and reds. The complete system contains approximately 1000 samples which are intended to be viewed under daylight. Their spectral luminance factors are known, making it possible to calculate the chromaticities for any illumination.

Munsell's ideal was that the visual difference between adjacent samples at any position in the solid should be the same, but this was not achieved. The system has the advantage that it is well known and used internationally and hence provides a means of communication between users.

BS 5252: 1976 Framework for colour co-ordination for building purposes   Another system used widely in the building industry in the UK is BS 5252 (BSI 1976e). It was produced in order to facilitate colour co-ordination where combinations of various materials and finishes are required for interior and exterior applications, but it was not intended to replace the Munsell system. The colours are arranged systematically using the concepts of *hue*, *greyness*, and *weight* and the framework contains about 240 colours. Greyness gives an estimate of the colourfulness of the sample and the amount of grey decreases as the saturation of the colour increases. It does not correspond to Munsell Chroma since the rate of change of greyness varies for different levels of Munsell Value and for different hues. The term weight refers to how light or dark the colour appears to be and for achromatic colours, i.e. those in which no hue can be perceived, the scale goes from near-white to near-black, with a series of light to dark greys in between. Weight is similar, but not exactly equivalent, to Munsell Value. BS standards for specific finishes, e.g. BS 4900 (BSI 1976b) – *Specifications for vitreous enamel colours for building purposes*, select a number of colours from BS 5252 that are appropriate to the particular material. (See also BSI 1976c, d and 1981d.)

3.5   Colour rendering

During the last three decades the availability of a wide range of different lamps has shown the possible variations in the appearances of coloured surfaces due to different light sources. In general it is unpractical to assess the colour rendering properties of light sources by direct observations and an objective system of measurement is required. Various methods have been studied based on different approaches, but most methods require comparison of the test source with a suitable reference illuminant.

3.5.1   CIE method of measuring colour rendering properties of light sources

The CIE method (CIE 1974) is based on the change of chromaticity of a surface colour that occurs when the test source is replaced by a reference illuminant. The problem of chromatic adaptation (Sect. 3.5.3) makes it difficult to compare two sources having very different chromaticities and hence it is necessary to select a standard with a correlated colour temperature as close as possible to that of the test source.

Reference standards   At colour temperatures below 3500 K, full radiators are the obvious choice for reference standards as these are simulated by incandescent lamps. The standardization by the CIE in 1967 (CIE 1971) of the daylight illuminants provided a series of standards for colour temperature higher than 5000 K. The intermediate region between 3500 K and 5000 K presented difficulties because no familiar natural source exists in this region so it was decided to adopt full radiators up to 5000 K.

Test colour samples It was necessary to specify a standard series of surface colours and the CIE selected a representative set of eight Munsell samples that covered the hue circle and had medium Value and Chroma. A supplementary set of four saturated colours and two representing skin tone and foliage were also chosen.

CIE special colour rendering index R_i The chromaticity shift ΔE_i for a test colour sample in the CIE 1964 UCS system (Sect. 3.4.1) caused by the replacement of the test source by the appropriate reference illuminant is determined. The chromaticities of the test source and reference illuminant are not usually exactly the same, causing different states of adaptation for the two illuminants. A correction for this is made using a von Kries type of transformation (Sect. 3.5.3) and the corrected chromaticities used for determining ΔE_i. The CIE special colour rendering index is then obtained from

$$R_i = 100 - 4 \cdot 6 \Delta E_i$$

where the factor 4·6 changes the scale so that a warm white fluorescent lamp has a general colour rendering index of 50. When a colour rendering index is quoted, the reference standard should be indicated, e.g. $R_i = 73$ (3000 K). Samples other than those specified by the CIE can be used to produce a special colour rendering index provided that their descriptions are given with the index.

CIE general colour rendering index R_a The special index refers to only one particular sample and in order to obtain information about the general colour rendering properties of a source it is necessary to assess a number of samples. The CIE general colour rendering index is the mean of the special colour rendering indices for the recommended set of eight samples.

Any system that describes the colour rendering properties of a source by a single number is bound to restrict the amount of information available. Equivalence of the CIE general index for two lamps will not guarantee interchangeability since the same mean may result from very different sets of special indices. The uncertainty regarding the correction for adaptation makes comparison of sources with dissimilar chromaticities difficult and leads to inaccuracies in the indices for lamps that are some distance in chromaticity from the full radiator locus.

3.5.2 Metamerism

Light source metamerism In describing the principles of additive colour mixtures (Sect. 3.1.2) it was shown that a colour (N) (Fig. 3.1) can be matched by a mixture of [G] and [B] or (Q) and [R]. These two mixtures have the same chromaticity, but since their spectral power distributions are different they possess different colour rendering properties and are said to be metameric. Normally such an extreme degree of metamerism is not shown by practical light sources, but a pair of metameric lamps that can be produced fairly readily consists of a low pressure sodium lamp and an incandescent lamp with an appropriate yellow filter.

Surface colour metamerism Metamerism occurs more frequently for surface colours than for light sources. A pair of samples may match under one illuminant, but differ under a second illuminant whose spectral power distribution is different from that of the first one. The degree of metamerism that is shown by a pair of samples can vary widely as it depends on the difference between the combined effects of the spectral reflectances of the samples and the spectral emissions of the illuminants. The phenomenon often poses serious problems in manufacturing industries where it may be desired to produce the same colour in articles having different substrates necessarily containing different colorants.

Observer metamerism   A third form of metamerism is that due to differences between the colour vision of individual observers.

Metamerism index   The CIE recommended (CIE 1972a) that the currently recom-mended colour difference equations (Sect. 3.4.1) should be used for computing a metamerism index for a change in illuminant, a correction being made if the two samples fail to match exactly under the reference conditions.

3.5.3   Chromatic adaptation

If the eye is exposed to a saturated colour, the colour channel that is most highly stimulated will become fatigued and the perceived sensation will move towards the complementary colour of the fatiguing stimulus. For example, suppose a white surface stimulates equal responses in the red, green, and blue channels. If the eye is then fatigued by exposure to green light, the white surface on re-examination will appear pink. Coloured after-images are also related to this effect.

The process of chromatic adaptation is the reason why large changes caused by the colour rendering properties of different light sources are often accepted without comment. For example, a side-by-side comparison of 6500 K natural daylight with a similar level of illumination from a 2800 K incandescent lamp reveals marked differences in the appearances of coloured samples, yet these changes are accepted quite readily when the sources are viewed successively, the eye adapting in turn to the blueness of daylight and the yellowness of incandescent light. It might be said that the eye and its associated functions in the brain are always trying to maintain a state of colour constancy in the field of view.

The objective assessment of the colour rendering properties of lamps is complicated by this constancy effect as no completely satisfactory method of making an allowance mathematically for chromatic adaptation has yet been developed. The current correction is based on the work of von Kries (von Kries 1902). He suggested that chromatic adaptation effects could be explained by assuming that the shapes of the spectral sensitivity curves for the three types of visual mechanism did not change with the colour of the adapting stimulus, but that the magnitude of the responses of the receptors relative to one another altered in inverse proportion to the strength of the activation by the illuminant. Thus, if the reference colour stimuli used for the chromaticity system could be ones which would stimulate a single type of receptor, the von Kries coefficient law states that the tristimulus values R, G, and B of colours under one condition of adaptation would have fixed ratios to the corresponding tristimulus values R', G', and B' for visually equivalent colours under another condition of adaptation. That is

$$R' = a_r R$$
$$G' = a_g G$$
$$B' = a_b B$$

The relative values of the coefficients a_r, a_g, and a_b can be determined from the tristimulus values of the two adapting illuminants and it is thus possible to predict the chromaticity of a visually equivalent colour to the test colour under a different state of adaptation.

Many subjective experiments on chromatic adaptation have been carried out (MacAdam 1956, Bartleson 1979a, b) and the predictions using von Kries type transformations do not agree very closely with the experimental results, but no alternative type of transformation has been accepted yet by the CIE.

3.5.4   Visual clarity

In the mid 1960s the introduction into general lighting situations of de luxe type fluorescent lamps (Sect. 11.3.3) with very good red colour rendering gave rise to anecdotal evidence from lighting engineers that such installations appeared to be brighter than measurements indicated that they should be. Controlled laboratory experiments by a number of workers showed that the illuminance for a de luxe lamp was between 10 and 25% lower than that for a high efficacy lamp when similar interiors lit by the two lamp types were compared for equality of visual satisfaction (Bellchambers and Godby 1972, Boyce and Lynes 1976). This effect was called 'visual clarity', but the term was not defined when the original experiments were carried out. There is now some confusion between those workers using the term in the sense of 'clearness of vision' and those using it for the more indefinite concept of 'satisfaction'. This confusion does not help towards an explanation of the effect, which is not fully understood at present. It is certainly caused partly by the way in which the visual mechanism deals with contrasts in perceived colour and brightness, but there may also be other factors involved.

Further reading

Grum F and Bartleson C J (Eds), 1980, *Optical radiation measurements*, **2,** *Colour measurement* (London: Academic Press)

Grum F and Becherer R (Eds), 1979, *Optical radiation measurements*, **1,** *Radiometry* (London: Academic Press)

Halstead M B, 1978, *Color 77, Proc. 3rd AIC Congress*, 97–127: Colour rendering: past, present and future (Bristol: Adam Hilger)

Henderson S T, 1977, *Daylight and its spectrum*, 2nd Edition (Bristol: Adam Hilger)

Hunt R W G, 1975, *The reproduction of colour in photography, printing and television*, 3rd Edition (Kings Langley, Herts: Fountain Press)

Hunter R S, 1975, *The measurement of appearance* (New York: John Wiley & Sons)

Judd D B and Wyszecki G, 1975, *Color in business, science and industry*, 3rd Edition (New York: John Wiley & Sons)

Wright W D, 1971, *The measurement of colour*, 4th Edition (London: Adam Hilger)

Wyszecki G and Stiles W S, 1967, *Color science* (New York: John Wiley & Sons)

4 Measurements

The measurement of light and colour poses special problems in that, unlike purely physical measurements, it is concerned with the psychophysical response to the band of wavelengths which is perceived by the eye as light. The eye is incapable of measurement and can only judge equality, so it is necessary to arrange any instrument using the eye as a detector on this principle. Until forty years ago all photometry was performed visually, but since then with the development of suitable photocells and $V(\lambda)$ correcting filters nearly all photometry is now made with physical photometers as the photocell and $V(\lambda)$ filter are called. For vision research and some standardizing by national laboratories, however, visual methods are still used. Essentially, physical photometers perform a radiometric measurement which is converted into a photometric one by means of filters or calculation. One point that must be stated is that the luminance incident on the photocell must be in the photopic range, otherwise the measurement will not give the same response as visual methods.

4.1 Standards and detectors

4.1.1 Standards

The realization and provision of primary standards are the concern of national standards laboratories, in this country, the National Physical Laboratory (NPL). These set up their own standard of spectral power distribution which is then maintained in the form of sets of electric lamps. These lamps are specially constructed or chosen to be very stable and reproducible and these lamps are then used as working standards.

In most countries, for the visible and infrared regions of the spectrum, this standard was a full radiator operating at the melting point of platinum and assumed to have a spectral distribution as predicted by Planck's equation, but recently the synchrotron has come into use as a standard in the ultraviolet portion of the spectrum. Conveniently there is an overlap in the spectral ranges of the two standards: the full radiator could go down to 250 nm and the synchrotron can go up as far as 400 nm. The two standards can be used as a check on each other because they are based on different theories. Deuterium lamps form secondary standards for the ultraviolet and are calibrated from the synchrotron. From the full radiator source lamps can be calibrated in terms of colour temperature, luminous intensity, and luminous flux. For the calibration of spectroradiometers (Sect. 4.2.1) tungsten halogen incandescent lamps are calibrated in terms of spectral irradiance over the wavelength range 250–2600 nm. This range covers the ultraviolet to the infrared. Below 250 nm radiation is absorbed by the oxygen in the atmosphere and equipment for measuring in this part of the spectrum should be flushed with nitrogen or evacuated.

For making photometric measurements the substandard supplied by the standardizing laboratory should be used to calibrate a set of working standards for day-to-day measurements. Periodically these working standards should be checked against the substandards. When measurements of high precision are required two standards should be used, one at the beginning of the measurements and one at the end, and the mean result taken. For luminous flux measurements a laboratory should have a series of calibrated lamps covering the sizes and types measured including tungsten, fluorescent, high and low pressure sodium, and high pressure mercury lamps. For use with photoelectric colorimeters and for checking the calibrations of spectroradiometers chromaticity standards are also required. Lamps which are to be used as standards should be of high quality and be aged to improve their stability.

4.1.2 Radiation detectors

Radiation detectors are devices that convert radiation into an electrical signal. The two main groups are thermoelectric detectors and photoelectric detectors.

Thermoelectric detectors Those most frequently used are thermocouples, thermopiles, and bolometers. A thermocouple or thermopile converts thermal energy into electrical energy by means of the Seebeck effect. A thermocouple consists of a circuit of two dissimilar metals or semiconductors. One of the junctions is blackened and absorbs the radiation to be measured whereas the other junction is screened and remains cool. The current generated is proportional to the temperature difference between the two junctions and proportional to the flux absorbed. A thermocouple employs one junction whereas a thermopile consists of a number of thermocouples connected together in series with all the blackened junctions grouped together to make a target. Essentially a bolometer consists of two small thin ribbons of blackened metal forming two arms of a Wheatstone bridge. One of the ribbons is exposed to radiation and becomes heated changing its resistance and upsetting the balance of the bridge; the other ribbon is screened from the radiation.

The most important feature of all these detectors is that their spectral sensitivity is independent of wavelength, provided a suitable black material is used. The receiver elements can be mounted in evacuated envelopes to make them more sensitive and less susceptible to air currents. Thermoelectric detectors are not as sensitive as photoelectric detectors and are more suitable for use in laboratories.

Photoelectric detectors In these the incident radiation produces its effects directly and not by way of the heat generated. Dependent on the effect produced, there are three broad classes of photoelectric detectors: photoemissive, photovoltaic, and photoconductive cells.

Photoemissive cells In this type of cell electrons emitted from a photocathode by the action of the incident radiation are transferred to an anode maintained at a positive potential by an external voltage. A current proportional to the radiant intensity flows. There are three main types: vacuum, gas-filled, and the photomultiplier. Of these only the first and last are used in photometry since, although an increased current is obtained from a gas-filled cell, the performance is greatly affected by gas pressure and the applied voltage.

Vacuum types are used because they are very stable over long periods of time and the current for a given quantity of radiation is practically independent of the applied voltage. It is customary to place a very high resistance in series with the cell and measure the voltage drop across the resistance due to the incident radiation, amplified with one of the many suitable circuits available.

The photomultiplier uses intermediate electrodes, dynodes, each at a fixed potential above the next, typically 100 V. The number of stages is normally between 6 and 13; the greater the number the greater will be the amplification. It is customary to connect a resistor chain to a high voltage supply to obtain the dynode voltages and, because the amplification is dependent on the applied voltage, it is important that the voltage be adjustable and highly stabilized. Sensitivities greater than 200 A lm^{-1} can be obtained whereas vacuum photocells achieve only up to 35 μA lm^{-1}. This enormous increase makes photomultipliers very useful for spectroradiometry, where small quantities of power are to be measured in very narrow spectral bands. It is desirable to measure the current caused by incident radiation, and a convenient method is to use a high gain operational amplifier circuit designed to present zero resistance to the input and convert the current to a voltage.

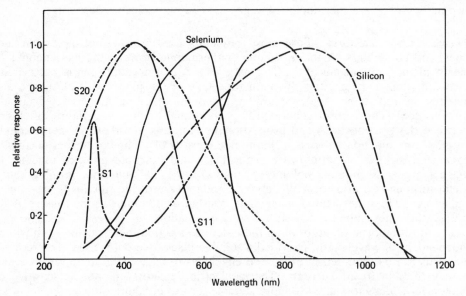

Fig. 4.1 The relative spectral response of selenium and silicon photocells and three photocathode materials S1, S11, and S20, where S1 = AgOCs, S11 = Cs$_3$SbO, and S20 = Na$_2$KSbCs

Photovoltaic cells   In these the incident radiation causes the transfer of electrons across a rectifying boundary, producing a current in an external circuit. Unlike the photoemissive cell, no external voltage is required. Selenium and silicon are the materials most commonly used for making photovoltaic cells. Silicon cells are more linear than selenium cells. However, selenium cells are spectrally close to the $V(\lambda)$ curve.

Photovoltaic cells are only linear when operating into a low resistance circuit, and their output is great enough (500 μA lm^{-1}) to operate a microammeter directly, but the best results are obtained when operating into a short-circuit. This can be achieved by using an operational current amplifier, the output of which can then be used to drive a relatively insensitive voltmeter.

Photoconductive cells In these the absorption of radiation leads to a change in the conductance of the device. A number of materials can be used for making photoconductive cells, such as cadmium sulphide, which has peak response at 600 nm, and lead sulphide and lead selenide, which have peak responses in the near-infrared. Silicon photocells may also be used in the photoconductive mode. Photoconductive cells have fast response and are sensitive, but are not as linear as photoemissive cells and can suffer from hysteresis effects.

Unlike thermoelectric detectors, all photoelectric detectors vary in response with wavelength. Figure 4.1 shows the spectral response of various materials used for making photocells. If measurements are required over a wide wavelength range more than one detector will be required, or a thermoelectric one may be used at reduced sensitivity. All types of photocell are to some extent temperature-sensitive in their response and the majority suffer from fatigue to varying degrees. Silicon cells have the major advantage of being relatively free from fatigue. For use in a physical photometer a photocell should have a response as close to the $V(\lambda)$ curve as possible. This can be achieved by the use of glass or liquid filters. Some excellent glass Dressler-type filters have been developed for correcting silicon photocells in particular.

One general point should be made: in using photocells it is essential that all of the radiation-sensitive area is exposed to the radiation to be measured. Failure to observe this can lead to substantial errors in measurement, since in most cases these areas are not uniformly sensitive.

4.2 Spectral measurements and colorimetry

4.2.1 Spectral measurements

Spectral measurements are fundamental to the study of light sources because the analysis of the spectral power data can provide photometric and colorimetric quantities as well as information on the colour rendering properties of the light source. The instrument required to perform these measurements is known as a spectroradiometer. This consists of a monochromator of some type and a photodetector and some means of converting the output readings into relative spectral power values.

The function of the monochromator is to disperse the homogeneous radiation from the light source into a spectrum with provision for isolating discrete bands of energy with known bandwidth. Basically a monochromator consists of an entrance slit, collimating device, dispersing element, and an exit slit. The dispersing element may be a prism, diffraction grating, circular interference filter, or a set of discrete interference filters. Interference filters are used in the simpler instruments. There are advantages and disadvantages to prisms and gratings. With prisms the dispersive power is wavelength-dependent, with the greatest dispersion at low wavelengths; thus with a fixed slit width the bandwidth changes through the spectrum. Diffraction gratings have the advantage of linear dispersion, but suffer from the problem of overlapping orders; however this can be overcome with filtering. In addition gratings are capable of better resolution of the spectra than are prisms.

With a single monochromator there is the problem of stray light due to unwanted reflections in the instrument. One way to overcome this problem is to use two monochromators in series. The two instruments have to be coupled in exact synchronism, but only a small fraction of the incident power is transmitted through the double instrument.

For accurate repeatable results it is necessary to irradiate the optical system and the photocathode of the photocell uniformly. This can be accomplished by irradiating a pressed barium sulphate plate with the radiation, thus diffusing it, and mounting the plate so that the entrance slit is uniformly irradiated.

Calibration of the instrument of whatever type is carried out by taking measurements on a suitably calibrated lamp of known spectral power distribution under the same conditions as the test lamp. For each point measured in the spectrum the ratio of the measured current from the detector for the test lamp and the calibrating source is multiplied by the known spectral power distribution of the standard source giving the spectral power distribution of the unknown lamp at that point.

This spectral power distribution will be in terms of relative power. For some purposes the spectral power distribution is required in absolute terms. A factor F by which the relative values are multiplied can be calculated if the luminous flux of the test lamp is known:

$$F \sum_{380}^{780} S(\lambda) \, V(\lambda) = \Phi/K_m$$

where $S(\lambda)$ = relative power,
$V(\lambda)$ = spectral luminous efficiency function,
Φ = luminous flux,
K_m = theoretical maximum conversion efficacy of electrical power into light $(683 \, \text{lm W}^{-1})$.

Methods of performing spectral measurements are discussed in a CIE document to be published in the near future. A common method of performing spectral power distribution measurements is to take readings of the spectrum at 5 nm intervals with an instrument bandwidth of 5 nm over the wavelength range required. A 5 nm bandwidth is a compromise giving reasonable resolution of the spectrum while keeping down the number of readings to be taken. There are occasions when a higher resolution of the spectrum is required and this method cannot then be used.

The measurements and subsequent calculation required may be performed entirely manually or the equipment may be automated and the calculation performed by an off-line computer. However, with the availability of powerful small computers, the whole process can now be computer controlled and the calculations performed on-line.

There is a wide range of suitable monochromators available, some physically quite small, which with a suitable photocell can form the basis of a spectroradiometer. With suitable auxiliary lenses, a telespectroradiometer can be made which enables measurements to be made at a distance.

The spectral power distribution of a lamp is the first step in calculating a number of important parameters of a light source. The relative spectral power distribution is suitable for calculating the chromaticity coordinates and the CIE colour rendering index R_a. The absolute spectral powers in the ultraviolet, visible, and infrared are required for producing an energy balance which is of use in understanding lamp behaviour.

4.2.2   Colorimeters

Spectroradiometry is the definitive method for measuring the chromaticity of light sources, but for many purposes, such as quality control, some simpler, more rapid method is required.

A simple and inexpensive colorimeter can be constructed by using three photo-detectors which have the spectral responses of the CIE distribution coefficients (Sects 3.2.1 and 3.2.4). This can be achieved by the use of filters over the photocells. If the measurements are made on a light source the photocurrents from the three cells will be in proportion to the tristimulus values X, Y, and Z from which the chromaticity coordinates x, y, and z may be calculated.

The $\bar{x}$ distribution coefficient is very difficult to represent because of the subsidiary peak in the blue part of the spectrum. One way to overcome this is to add a proportion of the $\bar{z}$ signal to the $\bar{x}$, or to use two photocell and filter combinations to represent the $\bar{x}$ response. Even if this is done the quality of the correction is still not good enough for tristimulus colorimeters, as they are called, to be used for measuring the chromaticity of light sources. The results obtained by such an instrument can be greatly improved if the instrument is calibrated with a light source of known chromaticity and correction factors then calculated, but the calibrating source must have a spectral power distribution very similar to that of the lamp being measured.

If very great care is taken in correcting the photocell responses using multiple cells and partial filtering, very good correction can be achieved, and this has been done for silicon photocells. Colorimeters can be constructed which have excellent correction and can be used without a calibrating source. These instruments also give a continuous digital readout of the chromaticity coordinates, but are very expensive (Geutler 1974).

Another way to produce good correction is the mask and dispersion system. It has a lens and prism or grating system to disperse the light incident on the slit into a spectrum, in the plane of which are masks cut to profiles which combine the shape of the distribution coefficients and the spectral response of the photocell, which measures the integral light transmitted through the masks. The larger the spectrum produced the better the masks can be cut (Winch 1951). This system is capable of high accuracy and is used in a colorimeter developed by the NPL.

In addition to measuring the chromaticity of light sources it is also necessary to measure the chromaticity of surface colours. The chromaticity of a surface colour is dependent on the spectral composition of the light sources under which it is viewed (Sects 3.3 and 3.2.1). One way is by measuring the spectral reflectance curve of the sample and then multiplying this, wavelength by wavelength, by the source spectral distribution and then calculating the chromaticity coordinates in the normal way.

Instruments that measure spectral reflectance are called spectrophotometers. Optically they are similar to spectroradiometers. The light from a suitable source is dispersed and then directed onto either the sample or a white standard surface. This is accomplished by splitting the dispersed beam into two equal components or deflecting the beam alternately onto the two surfaces. From the ratio of the readings the reflectance can be calculated at each wavelength through the spectrum. A suitable white surface is pressed barium sulphate. The input optics and the arrangement of the sample and how it is illuminated are very important to make meaningful measurements.

If the material being measured scatters the light it is necessary to collect the reflected light in a small integrating sphere. Spectrophotometers may also be arranged to measure spectral transmittance. The chromaticity of a transparent material may be determined by measuring the spectral transmittance of the material and calculating the chromaticity of the material when illuminated by a standard source. The illumination and collection geometry preferred in spectrophotometry are discussed in a CIE publication (CIE 1977c).

4.3   Illuminance and luminance

4.3.1   Illuminance meters

In lighting engineering it is often necessary to make measurements on lighting installations in the field and portable illuminance meters are used for this purpose. They usually consist of a photocell on a lead and some form of meter by which the illuminance readings may be taken. In the simpler instruments the photocell is a selenium one, but these are being replaced by silicon cells which have superior properties.

If the photocell is not $V(\lambda)$ corrected the manufacturer will supply factors by which the reading must be multiplied to give the correct value, providing that the colour of the illuminant is known. If the response of a photocell to illumination incident normally is $I(0)$, when this same illumination is incident at some other angle θ, the ideal response $I(\theta)$ would be $I(\theta) = I(0)\cos\theta$. Real photocells do not have this response because of the reflective properties of their surfaces and the error increases as θ is increased. This error can be greatly reduced if a disc or dome of diffusing material is placed over the photocell; this is known as cosine correction. Good cosine and $V(\lambda)$ correction do, however, reduce the sensitivity of the photocell. Another reason for needing good colour and cosine correction is that when measuring the illuminance in an actual installation the light from the lamps can be reflected from coloured walls which will change the colour of the light and, under these conditions, some light will be incident at large angles to the photocell surface.

4.3.2   Luminance meters

It is often necessary in lighting design and laboratory practice to be able to measure the luminance of a source or surface, and luminance meters have been developed for this purpose. In using them it is desirable to be able to view the area being measured through the meter. Sometimes the area is small and also has to be viewed from a distance, so luminance meters contain a lens and an optical system, and some form of diaphragm to isolate the area being measured.

The principle on which they operate is of measuring the illuminance produced on the surface of a photocell by the image of the surface being measured. The illuminance on the photocell due to this image is proportional to the luminance L of the surface being measured and the aperture of the lens. The flux on the lens surface is LSA/d^2 where S is the area of the surface, A is the area of the lens, and d is the distance from the surface to the lens. The flux falling on the photocell is $\tau LSA/d^2$ where τ is the transmission of the lens. The area of the image of the surface is Sv^2/d^2 where v is the distance from the lens to the photocell. Therefore the illuminance is given by $\tau LA/v^2$ which is independent of the surface area being measured and the distance from it. The illuminance can be measured with a calibrated photocell that has good $V(\lambda)$ correction. Practical luminance meters have reflex viewing systems and are able to measure angular areas of 1°. More complex instruments can measure angular areas of $1'$ to 3°.

4.4   Photometry

4.4.1   Photometric bench methods

A photometric bench is a device on which equipment under test and a measuring head may be arranged to be on the same axis and at a known distance apart. The measuring head is a photocell which can be calibrated and thus used to calibrate other devices. Luminance, illuminance, and intensity can all be measured on the bench. When making measurements on sources of different spectral distributions a photocell with very good $V(\lambda)$ correction is needed.

The bench makes use of the inverse square and cosine laws and it is necessary that the distance and angles be measured to a high degree of accuracy. For example, a photometric accuracy of 1% requires the distance to be measured to 0.5%. The bench must be of rigid construction and situated in a dark room or at least be screened by heavy curtains which reach the floor. To reduce unwanted reflections from the walls they should be finished in matt black paint.

Screens are needed along the bench to stop stray light from falling onto the photocell, they can be made from light sheet metal with various sized apertures in them and should be finished in matt black. The $V(\lambda)$ corrected photocell should be mounted in a black box with baffles in front of the photocell to define the angle required. If proper attention is not paid to the screening there can be large errors in the measurements.

Intensity measurements   A suitable calibrated lamp is arranged on the bench correctly aligned with the photometer head, which is mounted at the end of the bench. Two methods are available: in the first the $V(\lambda)$ corrected photocell is kept a fixed distance from the lamp and the photocurrent R_s for the standard lamp is noted. The test lamp is then substituted for the standard lamp and the photocurrent R_t for the test lamp is noted. If the luminous intensity of the standard lamp is I_s then that of the test lamp I_t is given by

$$I_t = I_s R_t / R_s$$

In the second method the distances d_s and d_t are adjusted until an identical photocurrent is obtained in each case. The luminous intensities are then in the ratio of the distances squared.

$$I_t = I_s (d_t / d_s)^2$$

This method has the advantage of not depending on the linearity of the photocell and is suitable where there is a large difference in the intensities being measured. The first method is suitable for use with silicon cells which are very linear.

Luminance measurements   The luminous intensity can be measured as above and the luminance found by dividing the value obtained by the projected area of the surface in the given direction. It is often convenient to place an aperture of known size in front of the surface, particularly if there is a variation in luminance across it, in which case the luminance distribution and a mean value can be determined.

Calibration of photocells and illuminance meters   A photometric bench provides a convenient means for testing the calibration of illuminance meters and determining the relationship between the illuminance and photocurrent for photocells and their associated equipment. The object in both cases is to arrange the photocell on the bench and align it with a substandard lamp. Then the distance between the lamp and cell is varied and the readings of the photocurrent noted. It may be necessary to use a series of different standard lamps because the illuminance can vary from 0.2 lux for an emergency lighting meter up to, say, $10\,000$ lux. If a suitable angle-measuring head is used the photocell can be mounted on it and the cosine response tested by measuring the photocurrent at various angles and comparing it with values obtained at normal incidence multiplied by the cosine of the angle. The procedure for checking the calibration of illuminance meters is given in BS 667 (BSI 1968).

4.4.2   Flux measurements

Luminous flux is one of the most important properties of a lamp designed for lighting purposes. Fundamentally, luminous flux is measured by a goniophotometer which by a series of measurements determines the mean luminous intensity of the lamp in all directions in space. By definition this value multiplied by 4π gives the luminous flux. It is assumed that the goniophotometer has a photocell with perfect $V(\lambda)$ correction. For comparative measurements an integrating photometer can be used to determine the flux from a lamp by comparing it with that of a standard lamp of known flux.

Integrating sphere   In the integrating sphere use is made of the fact that the illuminance received at any position on the surface from another part of the surface is independent of the position of the two points.

Consider a sphere of radius r with a light source L at its centre. The surface of the sphere is coated with a diffusing material of reflectivity ρ (Fig. 4.2a). P is a point on

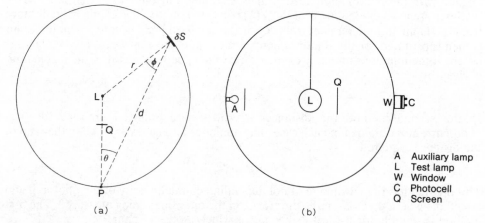

A   Auxiliary lamp
L   Test lamp
W   Window
C   Photocell
Q   Screen

(a)   (b)

Fig. 4.2   (a) the integrating sphere and (b) the integrating photometer

the inner surface and is shielded from direct light by a baffle Q. Let P receive light reflected from the whole of the sphere surface.

The illuminance δE at P due to an element of the surface S at distance d is

$$\delta E = \frac{L\delta S \cos\theta \cos\varphi}{d^2} \tag{4.1}$$

using Eq. 1.14 where

$$\delta I = L\,\delta S \cos\varphi$$

for the element δS of luminance L.

From the geometry of the sphere $\theta = \varphi$ and $d = 2r\cos\varphi$. Therefore

$$\delta E = L\,\delta S / 4r^2 \tag{4.2}$$

δE is independent of θ, showing that the illuminance received at any position on the surface of the sphere from another part of the surface is independent of their relative positions. Hence the inter-reflected illuminance E must be constant over the surface of the sphere.

Let Φ be the total flux striking the interior of the sphere from a light source placed within it. Then

$$\Phi = \Phi_D + \Phi_I \qquad (4.3)$$

where Φ_D is the direct flux from the source and Φ_I is the inter-reflected flux.

The reflectance ρ is the ratio of the reflected flux to incident flux.

$$\Phi_I = \rho\Phi \qquad (4.4)$$

So eliminating Φ from Eq. 4.3 we obtain

$$\Phi_I = \rho\Phi_D/(1-\rho) \qquad (4.5)$$

The inter-reflected illuminance E, which is constant over the sphere surface, is given by the expression

$$E = \Phi_I/S = \rho\Phi_D/S(1-\rho) \qquad (4.6)$$

where S is the surface area of the sphere.

Figure 4.2b shows a typical integrating photometer. The illuminance E may be measured with a $V(\lambda)$ corrected photocell. Equation 4.6 cannot be used as it stands to measure the luminous flux produced by a lamp by measuring the illuminance E at the window W because the presence of the source causes errors due to absorption and the properties of real sphere paints are far from ideal.

Substitution Some of these problems may be overcome or minimized by using the 'substitution' method. In this a lamp of known luminous flux is placed inside the integrating sphere and the illuminance of the wall measured. The test lamp is then put into the sphere in place of the standard lamp and the illuminance measured. If the two lamps are physically identical, except for their luminous flux outputs, then from the ratio of the illuminance readings the flux of the test lamp can be calculated. In this arrangement both the standard and test lamps absorb the same amount of radiation. If the test and standard lamps are physically different it is necessary to measure the ratio of self-absorption. This can be achieved by placing an auxiliary lamp A close to the sphere wall and baffled to prevent light falling directly onto the photocell or the test lamp L. A reading is taken with the auxiliary lamp, after which the standard lamp is placed in its normal position in the centre of the integrator, but unlit, and a further reading is taken. Let the ratio of these readings be R_s. This procedure is then repeated with the test lamp in place of the standard lamp. Let this ratio be R_t. The ratio R_s/R_t is used to correct the readings taken in the normal way.

The *light output ratio* (*LOR*), which is the ratio of the flux emitted by the lamps in a luminaire to the flux emitted by the bare lamps, can be measured in a similar way. In this case the readings are taken of the lamp or lamps and repeated with the lamps in the luminaire. The light output ratio is given by the readings corrected for self-absorption ratio as described and calculated above.

Instead of using a photocell to measure the illuminance at the window it is possible to use a spectroradiometer (Sect. 4.2.1) and integrate over the visible spectrum to give complete $V(\lambda)$ correction. It is used to measure the ratio of the luminance of the sphere window for the test and standard lamps. This method is now recommended by the CIE, but so far it has not proved as good as conventional substitution photometry (McSparron et al. 1970). The poor results are due to a lack of experience in the use of spectroradiometry for this type of measurement. An advantage is that from one measurement the luminous flux, colour, and colour rendering parameters can all be calculated.

To obtain the best accuracy integrating photometers should be as large as possible commensurate with acceptable sensitivity and handling. Very large photometers pose problems of accommodation, access, and repainting.

4.4.3   Distribution photometry

The aim of distribution photometry is to discover how the luminous intensity varies round a luminaire in order to plot the data in a suitable form for lighting engineers to use. The type of equipment needed for testing street lanterns and indoor luminaires is the same – a polar photometer. Floodlighting luminaires and airfield signal luminaires need special apparatus with a long light path – a goniophotometer.

The difference in the type of measurements made with the two pieces of apparatus is that the polar photometer makes measurements of the luminous intensity on a sphere surrounding the luminaire, whereas the goniophotometer measures over a relatively small angular area. Also a goniophotometer measures in small angular increments, but essentially both instruments measure the variation in luminous intensity with angle around the luminaire.

Polar photometer   A simple polar photometer consists of a photocell, mounted on the end of an arm or on a curved track, which is capable of being rotated about the luminaire to give measurements of the luminous intensity at known angles. The luminaire is firmly attached to a rotatable platform, enabling readings at any angle of azimuth to be taken. It is very important that only light that is to be measured reaches the photocell. The exclusion of extraneous light is achieved by the use of baffles on the front of the photocell housing; these are arranged so that the field of view is restricted as far as possible to the cone of light coming from the luminaire. It is essential that the whole of the sensitive surface of the photocell is illuminated by the light from the whole of the luminaire. Thus the photocell has a field of view beyond that required. This can be reduced by extending the baffled area as far as possible from the photocell. The photocell can respond to light from beyond the luminaire, so that parts of the apparatus and the walls should be blackened. For meaningful measurements to be made the optical path length should be at least five times the largest dimension of the luminaire being tested, so that the inverse square law can apply with reasonable accuracy. Another requirement is that the luminaire should operate in its designed position. The light output of fluorescent lamps in particular is temperature-sensitive, being maximum at an ambient temperature of 25 °C. When such lamps are in a luminaire they are usually much hotter than this and consequently there is a fall in light output. If the luminaire is rotated about its axis or mounted in other than the designed position the heat can escape and so increase the light output. Similarly low pressure sodium lamps cannot be rotated because the liquid sodium in them runs and changes the light output.

The basic requirements for a polar photometer may be met in a variety of different ways, depending on the equipment available and the space for the photometer. In order to reduce the size of the instrument it is possible to lengthen the optical path by use of a mirror. A polar photometer which meets all the above requirements is shown in Fig. 4.3. In this instrument the photocell is mounted in a baffled box on the rotating arm that holds the mirror. The luminaire is mounted on a gantry which can be raised and lowered for access. Its position is adjusted so that its light centre is at the centre of rotation of the mirror.

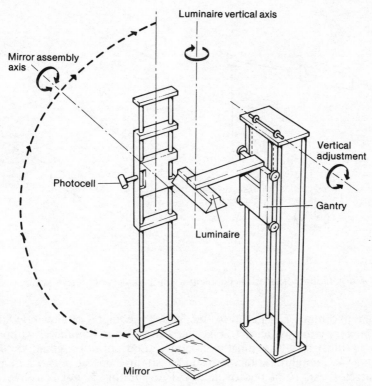

Fig. 4.3 A polar photometer

Measurements of luminous intensity are made by taking readings of the photocurrent at the required angles. The intervals in elevation and azimuth at which readings are taken depend on the type of luminaire and are given in the relevant BS and CIE documents (BSI 1975a, CIE 1973a, CIE 1973c). Taking the measurements is time consuming and it is better that the equipment be automated. The mirror arm and luminaire are driven by electric motors and the angular position indicated by shaft encoders. By the use of suitable circuitry these can be made to trigger the measuring equipment to take a reading. The readings may be stored on paper or magnetic tape which can be processed on a computer with a program to do the calculations required.

As described the readings only give relative luminous intensity and have to be calibrated in some way. Usually polar curves and other intensity diagrams are calibrated in terms of the nominal output of the lamp used rather than the actual output of the test lamp, or the intensity may be expressed in candelas per 1000 lumens.

Goniophotometer Floodlights, projectors, automobile headlights, and other concentrating beams have to be tested at much greater distances than do indoor luminaires. The detector should be far enough away so that it 'sees' the whole of the reflector flashed with light (Sect. 1.5.1). For normal floodlighting luminaires as used in stadium lighting 33 m is sufficient, but by international agreement automobile headlamps are tested at 25 m. One consequence of the long path length is that the photocell has to be fixed and the luminaire rotated.

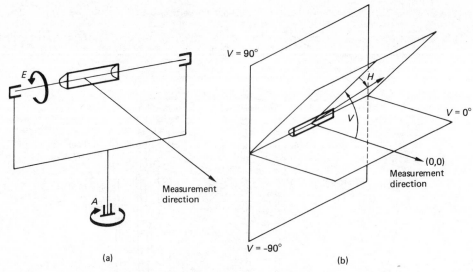

Fig. 4.4   (a) a goniophotometer for floodlights. (b) the *V–H* coordinate system

The goniophotometer required for measuring the angles of elevation and azimuth needs to be very strongly made to take the weight of the luminaires without sagging. Figure 4.4a illustrates the most commonly used form of goniophotometer for floodlights. The luminaire holder turns in elevation *E* and also moves in azimuth *A*.

The detector can be a photovoltaic cell or, if this is not sensitive enough, a photomultiplier. It is convenient to arrange for the readout of the photocell to be at the same position as the goniophotometer so that only one person is needed to take the readings and work the goniophotometer. The equipment can be computer controlled so that the readings are taken at predetermined intervals and the goniophotometer turned by electric motors controlled by the computer.

The measurements are carried out in a darkened room with the luminaire mounted on the goniophotometer. In order to obtain the necessary path length it is sometimes convenient to locate the detector at the end of a light-tight tunnel which can pass through adjoining rooms. There should be baffles fixed to the wall of the tunnel to reduce the amount of stray light. The photometry of floodlights is discussed in a CIE publication (CIE 1979a).

4.4.4   Data presentation

Having measured the variation in luminous intensity of a luminaire some thought must be given to presenting the data obtained in the most useful form. Some information can be conveyed in only one number, such as the luminous flux emitted by a lamp or the light output ratio of a luminaire. One obvious way of presenting data is in the form of a table of values giving the intensity for every 10° in azimuth and 10° in elevation. Such a table does not have the immediate impact that a diagram has, although it can be more precise.

Coordinate systems   In making the measurement of luminous intensity no consideration has been given to the type of coordinate system to be used for presenting the data. Indoor and street lighting luminaires are generally measured in their normal operating position and the coordinate system should take account of this by having the reference point directly below the luminaire.

The system most commonly used and recommended by the CIE (CIE 1973c) is the $C-\gamma$ coordinate system (Fig. 4.5). The angle C represents planes in azimuth and γ

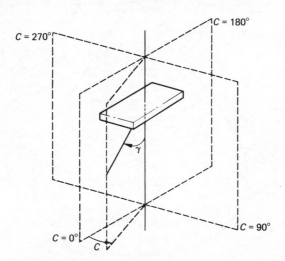

Fig. 4.5 The $C-\gamma$ coordinate system

represents planes in elevation. The axis of the system passes through the centre of the luminaire. γ angles are measured from the nadir.

For use with floodlighting luminaires the most widely used system is the $V-H$ one (Fig. 4.4b). V angles are those measured of a plane through the axis of the luminaire and H angles are those measured in that plane. The reference position of this system is the position $V = 0$, $H = 0$; thus when floodlights are measured they are horizontal, but when used in an installation they can be used at quite large angles to the horizontal and so the reference direction will be at this angle also.

Distribution of luminous intensity This must be considered the primary photometric specification for a luminaire. Since it is variable in three dimensions, it is necessary to select aspects of the distribution from which the whole can be assessed.

Many luminaires, particularly those with small incandescent sources, have an axis of symmetry; this implies that the intensity distribution in any plane containing that axis is the same. One *polar curve*, a polar coordinate graph showing the luminous intensity in any axial plane as a function of angle, is adequate to describe the intensity distribution for such a luminaire. Polar curves for two axially-symmetrical luminaires are shown in Fig. 4.6: luminaire A emits all its light downwards in a cone subtending about 70°, whereas luminaire B emits much of its light in near-horizontal directions.

It would appear from the curves that luminaire A emits more luminous flux than does luminaire B, but this is not the case. Luminaire A has certainly a higher maximum intensity, but the solid angle subtended by the beam is very much less than the solid angle subtended by the horizontal beam of luminaire B. This misleading impression is one disadvantage of the polar curve method of presenting an intensity distribution; a second disadvantage is the lack of precision when the intensity is changing very rapidly with angle, at 35° in luminaire A for example.

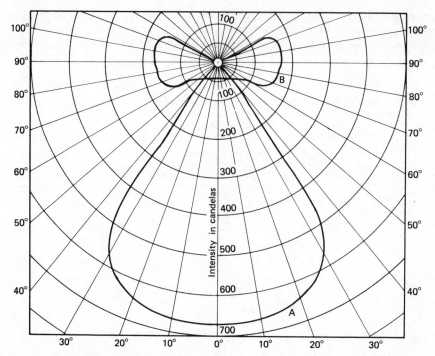

Fig. 4.6   Vertical plane polar intensity curves

Despite these disadvantages the polar curve is the most common method of presenting intensity distributions for general lighting luminaires. For luminaires with concentrating beams, such as spotlights emitting all their luminous flux within a few degrees of solid angle, cartesian coordinates are preferred because of the need for more precision than a polar curve allows.

Interior luminaires for fluorescent lamps do not have an axially-symmetrical intensity distribution, but there is not the dramatic difference in the shape of the distribution for different vertical planes found in street lighting and floodlighting luminaires. It is common practice to produce for fluorescent luminaires polar curves in the vertical plane containing the axis of the luminaire and the vertical plane at right angles to this, known as axial and transverse polar curves: in the C–γ coordinate system these would be the planes $C = 90°$ and $C = 0°$ respectively (Fig. 4.5).

For luminaires which have no symmetry in their intensity distribution the usual method of representing tables of intensity values is an *isocandela diagram*, like that in Fig. 4.7, which shows the complete distribution of the luminaire in one hemisphere. A spherical surface surrounding the luminaire is plotted on a plane, as in maps of the world, and lines are drawn joining points of equal luminous intensity – isocandela contours (cf. height contours on a map). Although it is not essential, it is useful to use a form of projection such that equal areas on the sphere surrounding the luminaire are represented by equal areas on the projection, a characteristic of most mapping projections currently used. A sinusoidal equal-area projection (Sanson's net) was formerly used for isocandela diagrams, but the equal-area zenithal projection shown in Fig. 4.7 is now preferred, particularly for street lighting applications, because on this projection the edges of a straight road appear as straight lines instead of curves (Sect. 5.2.6). The coordinate system used is the C–γ one (Fig. 4.5). Degrees C along

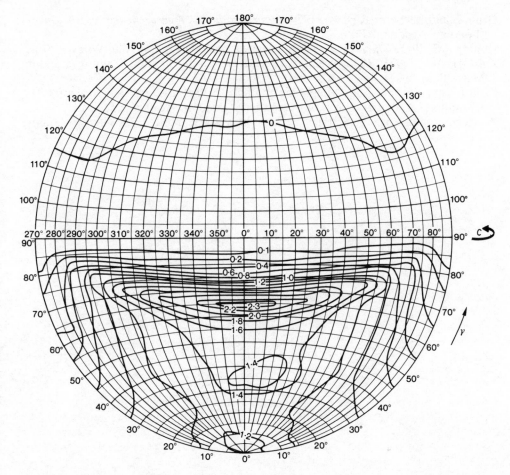

Fig. 4.7 Equal-area zenithal projection with isocandela contours

the equator are azimuths from the road direction: $C = 0°$ is along the direction of the road, $C = 90°$ is directly across the road, and $C = 270°$ is directly away from the road. Degrees γ round the circumference give angles from the downward vertical, so $\gamma = 0°$ is directly down from the luminaire. Isocandela diagrams do not produce the misleading impression regarding flux given by polar curves. They have the disadvantage that they do not lend themselves to accurate interpolation between the contours.

Further reading

Bean A R and Simons R H, 1968, *Lighting fittings performance and design* (Oxford: Pergamon)

CIE, 1970, Publication No. 18 (E–1.2): *Principles of light measurement*

CIE, 1973, Publication No. 25 (TC–1.2): *Procedures for the measurement of luminous flux of discharge lamps and for their calibration as working standards*

CIE, 1979, Publication No. 44 (TC–2.3): *Absolute methods of reflectance measurement*

Grum F and Becherer R (Eds), 1979, *Optical radiation measurements*, **1,** *Radiometry* (London: Academic Press)
Hunter R S, 1975, *The measurement of appearance* (New York: John Wiley & Sons)
Keitz H A E, 1971, *Light calculations and measurements*, 2nd Edition (London: Macmillan)
Landsberg H E and Van Mieghem J (Eds), 1970, *Advances in geophysics*, **14,** Drummond A J (Ed), *Precision radiometry* (London: Academic Press)
Wyszecki G and Stiles W S, 1967, *Color science* (New York: John Wiley & Sons)

5 Lighting calculations

In Chap. 4 methods of taking photometric measurements on luminaires have been described. In this chapter the calculations used for converting the raw data so obtained into forms useful for planning lighting schemes, both interior and exterior, are explained.

5.1 Illuminance calculations

The inverse square law of illumination (Sect. 1.4.5) is only strictly applicable to point sources of light. For practical purposes it can be applied directly to large diffusing sources, provided that r (Eq. 1.14) is more than five times the largest dimension of the source. For shorter distances the source may be split into small elements and the contribution from each of these to the illuminance at a point summed, either by calculus or by numerical integration.

5.1.1 Linear sources

In Fig. 5.1 AB represents a linear source of length l. The illuminance is required on P in the plane CD which is parallel to the source. APEB is an axial plane, that is, it passes through the axis of the source. It is at an angle θ to the vertical and makes an angle φ with the normal PN to the plane CD.

Consider an element δx at S, distance x from A. ST lies in the axial plane and is normal to the axis of the source. Let $I(\alpha, \theta)$ be the intensity of the source AB in the direction parallel to SP.

The illuminance δE at P on the plane CD due to the element δx of the source is then given by

$$\delta E = \frac{\delta x}{l} I(\alpha, \theta) \frac{\cos \alpha \cos \varphi}{(x/\sin \alpha)^2} \tag{5.1}$$

Since

$$AP = \frac{h}{\cos \theta} = \frac{x}{\tan \alpha}$$

$$x = h \tan \alpha \sec \theta$$

and

$$\delta x = h \sec^2 \alpha \sec \theta \, \delta \alpha$$

Substitution of these for x and δx in Eq. 5.1 gives

$$\delta E = \frac{I(\alpha, \theta)}{lh} \cos \theta \cos \varphi \cos \alpha \, \delta \alpha$$

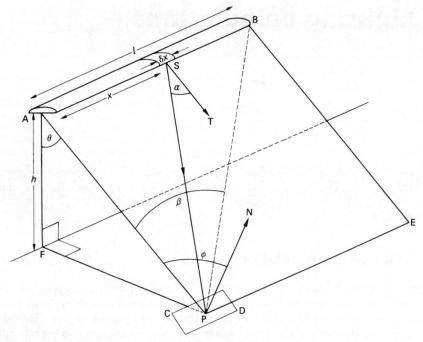

Fig. 5.1 Illuminance from a linear source

For the whole length of the source

$$E = \frac{I(0, \theta)}{lh} \cos \theta \cos \varphi \int_0^\beta \frac{I(\alpha, \theta)}{I(0, \theta)} \cos \alpha \, d\alpha \tag{5.2}$$

The integral is known as the *parallel plane aspect factor*. It is a function of the shape of the intensity distribution in the axial plane inclined at θ to the horizontal and the angle β (the aspect angle) subtended by the luminaire at P, which must be opposite one end of the luminaire, as in Fig. 5.1.

It is found that for most practical fluorescent luminaires the shape of the intensity distribution is similar in any axial plane. Thus for a given luminaire the aspect factor is independent of θ; it varies only with β. It may therefore be denoted by $AF(\beta)$.

Where the shape of the axial distribution can be expressed mathematically, $AF(\beta)$ can be found by integration. For a uniform diffuser, for which $I(\alpha)$ equals $I(0) \cos \alpha$

$$AF(\beta) = \int_0^\beta \cos^2 \alpha \, d\alpha$$
$$= (\beta + \sin \beta \cos \beta) \tag{5.3}$$

This procedure can be used for other theoretical distributions which give a good match to practical distributions (CIBS 1968), for example

$$\frac{I(\alpha)}{I(0)} = \tfrac{1}{2}(\cos \alpha + \cos^2 \alpha), \cos^2 \alpha, \cos^3 \alpha, \text{ and } \cos^4 \alpha$$

A method more related to practice is to use numerical integration. This can be done by dividing the axial curve into a number of equiangular zones.

To determine the illuminance produced at a point opposite the end of a luminaire on a plane parallel to the luminaire (CD in Fig. 5.1) the aspect angle β is determined and the value of $AF(\beta)$ is entered in Eq. 5.2

$$E = \frac{I(0, \theta)}{lh} \cos \theta \cos \varphi \, AF(\beta) \tag{5.4}$$

Should the point concerned not be opposite the end of the luminaire, the principle of superposition is applied. If it is opposite a point on the luminaire then the illuminance due to the left- and right-hand parts of the luminaire are added; if it is beyond the luminaire then the illuminance due to a luminaire of extended length is reduced by the illuminance due to the imagined extension.

The same method is used for calculating the illuminance on a plane perpendicular to the axis of the luminaire (AFP in Fig. 5.1). The analysis followed above applies with $\sin \alpha$ replacing $\cos \alpha \cos \varphi$ in Eq. 5.1, resulting in a final expression for the illuminance at P

$$E = \frac{I(0, \theta)}{lh} \cos \theta \int_0^\beta \frac{I(\alpha, \theta)}{I(0, \theta)} \sin \alpha \, d\alpha \tag{5.5}$$

The integral expression is now the *perpendicular plane aspect factor af(β)*, again substantially independent of θ in most practical situations. Thus

$$E = \frac{I(0, \theta)}{lh} \cos \theta \, af(\beta) \tag{5.6}$$

determines the illuminance on a plane perpendicular to a linear luminaire.

It is interesting to note that the illuminance due to a long linear source is, of course, inversely proportional to its distance from the measurement point, as opposed to the square of the distance for a small source.

5.1.2 Area sources

Dividing up area sources into elemental areas and integrating usually leads to cumbersome integrals. An easier approach is the unit hemisphere method, which can however only be applied to uniform diffusers.

In Fig. 5.2 the illuminance E from an elementary source area δA of uniform luminance L is required at P on the plane ABCD. H is a hemisphere of unit radius on ABCD. Let δA subtend a solid angle $\delta\omega$ at P. The area which the cone encloses on the hemisphere of unit radius is equal to $\delta\omega$. The projection of this onto ABCD is $\cos \theta \, \delta\omega$. This area multiplied by the luminance L equals the illuminance E at P (Eq. 1.16). By summation this argument can be applied to a large source, so it is possible to say that the total illuminance at P is the product of the source luminance and the area of intersection on the hemisphere projected on the base of the hemisphere.

The method of application may be demonstrated by using it to find the illuminance from a disc source.

In Fig. 5.3 the illuminance is required at P from the uniformly diffusing disc of radius r, at a height h above P. The radius of the cap enclosed on the unit hemisphere by the cone from the disc to P is $r/\sqrt{(h^2 + r^2)}$, which is also the radius of the projection of the cap onto the base of the hemisphere. It follows that the illuminance at P is $\pi L r^2/(h^2 + r^2)$, or $\pi L \sin^2 \theta$ in terms of θ marked on Fig. 5.3.

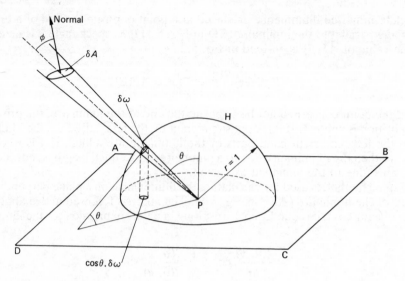

Fig. 5.2   Unit hemisphere method

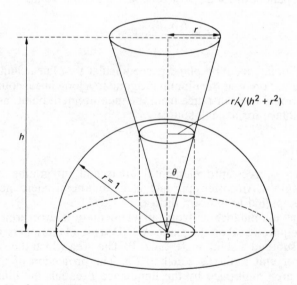

Fig. 5.3   Illuminance from a disc source

The illuminance from an infinitely large source (which is a uniform diffuser) can be found by making θ equal to 90°, giving the result πL. Other applications are given in Bean and Simons (1968).

5.1.3   The illumination vector

The expression for the illuminance E on a plane surface produced by a point source, $I \cos \theta / d^2$ (Eq. 1.14), shows that E can be regarded as the component of a vector of magnitude I/d^2 (Gershun 1936). The component is in the direction of the perpendicular into the plane on which the value of E is required, and the vector is directed away from the point source and towards the plane (Fig. 5.4). The correct value of E is given only if θ is not greater than 90°, that is E is calculated on the side of the plane which is facing the source, otherwise a negative figure for illuminance is obtained because $\cos \theta$ is negative if θ lies between 90° and 180°.

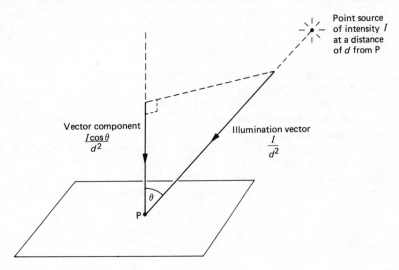

Fig. 5.4 Illumination vector due to a single point source

If there are many point sources, each source can be thought of as producing an illumination vector, and these can be combined into a single resultant vector. The resultant vector can be used to calculate the illuminance on a plane, but only if all the sources lie on the same side of the plane. If the latter restriction is ignored then the vector method of calculation gives the difference in illuminance on opposite sides of the plane.

If the illumination vector at a point in space is zero, it does not necessarily mean that there is no light at that point, but only that the illuminances on both sides of a plane placed there are equal for all orientations of the plane; an example of this would be a point midway between two point sources of equal luminous intensity.

5.1.4 Non-planar illuminance

So far in this chapter only illuminance on planes has been considered. There are two measures of non-planar illuminance which are found to be useful as correlates of the subjective impression of the lighting quality; these are *mean spherical illuminance* (Hewitt et al. 1965) and *mean cylindrical illuminance* (Lynes et al. 1966) (see Sect. 2.4.3).

Mean spherical illuminance is the mean illuminance over an infinitely small sphere placed at the point of interest and, because the measure is independent of direction, it is sometimes called *scalar illuminance*.

Calculation of scalar illuminance proceeds by considering a point source of luminous intensity I at a distance d from a small sphere of radius r. The sphere intercepts the same luminous flux as would a disc of radius r, which is therefore $\pi r^2 I/d^2$. The mean illuminance E_s on the surface of the sphere is hence given by

$$E_s = (\pi r^2 I/d^2)/4\pi r^2$$
$$= I/4d^2 \tag{5.7}$$

For an extended source of luminance L this becomes

$$E_s = \tfrac{1}{4}\int L \, d\omega$$

or for a uniform diffuser

$$E_s = \tfrac{1}{4}L\omega$$

where ω is the solid angle subtended by the whole source.

Mean cylindrical illuminance is the mean illuminance over an infinitely small cylinder placed at the point of interest, usually with the axis of the cylinder vertical. In contrast to mean spherical illuminance, mean cylindrical illuminance depends on the direction of the incident light.

Calculation proceeds in a manner similar to that of scalar illuminance except that the flux intercepted by the cylinder depends on the angle ψ between the axis of the cylinder and the incident rays of light (Fig. 5.5). Then, if the radius of the cylinder is r and its height is l, its projected area in the direction of the incident light is $2rl\sin\psi$.

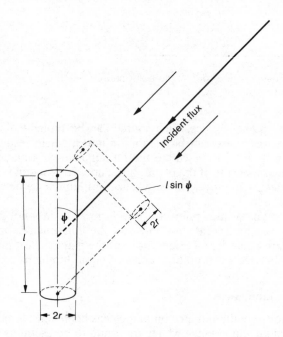

Fig. 5.5   Cylindrical illuminance

If I is the intensity of the source and d its distance from the cylinder, the flux intercepted by the cylinder is given by $2rl \sin \psi I/d^2$. This divided by the surface area $2\pi rl$ of the cylinder gives the mean cylindrical illuminance

$$E_c = (I \sin \psi)/\pi d^2$$

For an extended source of luminance L this becomes

$$E_c = \frac{1}{\pi} \int L \sin \psi \, d\omega$$

$$= \frac{L}{\pi} \int \sin \psi \, d\omega$$

for a uniform diffuser, the integration being taken over the whole source.

5.2 Derivation of luminous flux from luminous intensity

Distribution photometry described in Chap. 4 enables the luminous intensity I of a lamp or luminaire to be measured in all directions. From these data it is often necessary to find the total luminous flux Φ emitted by the luminaire or the flux that falls on a surface. Generally, the most convenient equation for this purpose follows from integrating Eq. 1.12.

$$\Phi = \int I \, d\omega \tag{5.8}$$

For practical light distributions, in which intensity cannot usually be expressed as a simple mathematical function of angle, numerical methods of integration are used.

A second, less useful, equation is obtained by integrating Eq. 1.11.

$$\Phi = \int E \, dA \tag{5.9}$$

where E is the illuminance over an element of the surface area A.

5.2.1 Zonal factor method

This is the most commonly used method for finding the total flux, and the flux in the lower and upper hemispheres, from a source. It makes use of Eq. 5.8.

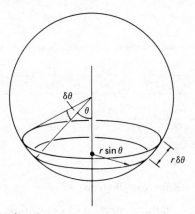

Fig. 5.6 Calculation of zone factors

Consider a sphere enclosing the source, which is at its centre as in Fig. 5.6. The solid angle used is that subtended at the centre of the sphere by the part of the sphere lying between two lines of latitude subtending angles of θ_1 and θ_2 measured from the downward vertical. Now solid angle is equal to the area of the zone divided by the square of the radius r. Thus for an elementary zone at an angle of θ subtending an angle of $\delta\theta$ the solid angle is

$$\delta\omega = \frac{2\pi r \sin \theta \, r \, \delta\theta}{r^2} = 2\pi \sin \theta \, \delta\theta \qquad (5.10)$$

For the zone extending from θ_1 to θ_2

$$\omega = 2\pi \int_{\theta_1}^{\theta_2} \sin \theta \, d\theta = 2\pi(\cos \theta_1 - \cos \theta_2) \qquad (5.11)$$

The value of this is called the zone factor and for convenience it is usual to divide the sphere into zones subtending equal angles of elevation θ at the centre of the sphere. The total for a sphere is 4π.

To find the flux in a zone the zone factor is multiplied by the average intensity I in the directions of the zone. For a luminaire nominally symmetrical about its vertical axis this can be found from the average of intensities at $\frac{1}{2}(\theta_1 + \theta_2)$ in elevation taken at intervals of 45° in azimuth. For linear luminaires, e.g. for fluorescent lamps, the interval is reduced to 30° in azimuth. Once the flux in each of the zones from $\theta = 0°$ to 180° has been found, the total and lower and upper hemispherical flux values can be obtained by summation.

5.2.2   Russell angles

Instead of taking zones subtending equal angles of elevation, zones are taken which subtend equal solid angles to overcome the inconvenience of having to multiply the zonal intensities by different zone factors. In each of the equi-solid angle zones the intensity is measured at an angle of elevation, the Russell angle, such that the corresponding line of latitude divides the zone into two zones of equal solid angle. Intensities measured by this method can be averaged and multiplied by 4π to find the total flux. Russell angles may be determined by using Eq. 5.11. They are given for 10 and 20 increments in Table 5.1.

Table 5.1   Russell angles for determining total luminaire flux

20 angles (°)																		
18·2	31·8	41·4	49·5	56·6	63·3	69·5	75·5	81·4	87·1	92·9	98·6	104·5	110·5	116·7	123·4	130·5	138·6	148·2	161·8

10 angles (°)									
25·8	45·6	60·0	72·5	84·3	95·7	107·5	120·0	134·4	154·2

5.2.3   Graphical method – Rousseau diagram

The Rousseau diagram is a graphical method of determining zonal and total flux from an average polar curve in the vertical plane, obtained in the same way as for the zonal factor method.

The polar curve PQRS shown on the left of Fig. 5.7 is enclosed by a semicircle of radius OA = r and is projected to the right so that A′O′B′ corresponds to AOB and the distances A′P′, O′Q′, XR′, etc. are made equal to OP, OQ, OR, etc. (that is, values of I_θ). A small sector OR of the polar curve subtending $\delta\theta$ at O, when projected

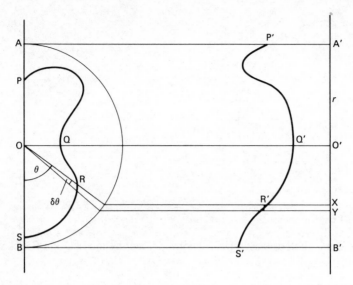

Fig. 5.7 Rousseau diagram for determining flux from a polar intensity curve

as shown on the Rousseau diagram, gives an intercept XY on AO′B′. The area of the element R′XY is

$$I_\theta \, r \sin \theta \, \delta\theta$$

and the total area of the figure P′Q′S′B′A′ is

$$\text{area} = \int_0^\pi I_\theta \, r \sin \theta \, d\theta$$

However the total flux from an axially-symmetric luminaire is, using Eq. 5.10,

$$\Phi = \int I_\theta \, d\omega = 2\pi \int_0^\pi I_\theta \sin \theta \, d\theta = \frac{2\pi}{r} \times \text{area} \qquad (5.12)$$

Since A′B′ = 2r, the mean height of the curve S′P′ is area/2r, so the flux is

$$\Phi = 4\pi \times \text{mean height} \qquad (5.13)$$

This mean height may be determined graphically by any convenient method, such as counting squares or planimeter, or by dividing A′B′ into 10 or 20 equal intervals and averaging.

The use of the Rousseau diagram may be illustrated by finding the flux emitted by a uniform diffuser (Fig. 5.8).

Since $I_\theta = I_0 \cos \theta$, in this case, its polar curve is a semicircle, so ORS is a right angle. R′X = OR = OS cos θ and O′X = OB cos θ, giving R′X/O′X = OS/OB. Since this is a constant, R′O′ must have a constant slope and S′O′ must therefore be a straight line. Since S′B′ = I_0, the mean height of the triangle over A′B′ is $I_0/4$. Therefore

$$\Phi = 4\pi \times \text{mean height} = \pi I_0$$

the same result as obtained by direct integration. Dividing by area gives the relation between exitance and luminance of a uniformly diffusing source (Eq. 1.18)

$$M = \pi L$$

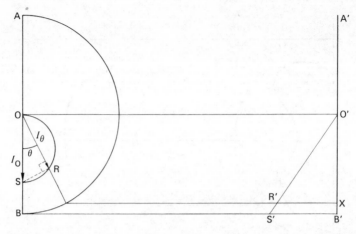

Fig. 5.8   Determination of flux from a uniform diffuser by the use of a Rousseau diagram

This is an important relation and may be used to find the intensity I normal to the surface of a uniformly diffusing cylinder, such as a fluorescent tube, when its lumen output Φ is known. Let the length of the tube be l and its radius be r. Then the luminance equals the quotient intensity/projected area, that is

$$L = \frac{I}{2rl} \qquad (5.14)$$

The lumen output per unit surface area, exitance, is given by

$$M = \frac{\Phi}{2\pi rl}$$

so from Eq. 1.18

$$L = \frac{\Phi}{2\pi^2 rl} \qquad (5.15)$$

Therefore

$$I = \Phi/\pi^2 \qquad (5.16)$$

For rough calculations the intensity in candelas of a fluorescent tube normal to its surface may be taken as one-tenth of its lumen output.

5.2.4   Isocandela diagram on equal-area zenithal projection

The total or hemispherical flux can be deduced from an isocandela diagram (Sect. 4.4.4), provided that this is on an equal-area projection (Figs 4.7, 5.10a), that is, the areas on the projection must be proportional to the corresponding areas on the surface of a sphere. The average intensity is determined by measuring the areas between pairs of contours, multiplying each area by the average intensity of the two contours, summing the result, dividing by the area of the diagram, and multiplying by 4π.

5.2.5   Direct flux on horizontal working plane

In a room the horizontal working (or reference) plane is taken to be 0·85 m above the floor. The direct flux on this is required in the calculation of utilization factors (Sect. 5.3.3). One method of calculating the direct flux is by determining the illuminances at a number of equally spaced points, averaging, and multiplying by the area. This is not the most convenient method, however, particularly where the flux from a complete installation is required. Instead the zonal multiplier method is used.

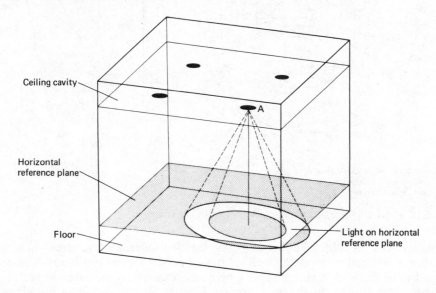

Fig. 5.9   Determination of zonal multiplier

A zonal multiplier (ZM) gives the fraction of flux in a zone, typically of 10° subtense, that reaches the horizontal working plane from all the luminaires in an installation (Fig. 5.9). For the *single* luminaire A in Fig. 5.9 (assumed to be a point source and symmetrical about the vertical) it is the solid angle subtended by the unshaded portion of the ring divided by the solid angle subtended by the complete ring. It follows that

flux reaching horizontal working plane = zonal flux × ZM

These flux values are summed up for all the zones in the lower hemisphere of the luminaires to give the total flux reaching the working plane. When this is divided by the lower hemispherical flux from all the luminaires the result is known as the direct ratio (*DR*). Division by the total bare lamp flux gives the distribution factor, which is used in the calculation of utilization factors (Sect. 5.3.3). Zonal multipliers are published in a CIBS technical memorandum (CIBS 1980b).

5.2.6   Direct flux on road surfaces

Isocandela diagrams on the equal-area zenithal projection are usually available for street lanterns and these may be used to find the flux falling on a road surface (Fig. 5.10). It is a property of the zenithal projection that a kerb line projected onto the web appears as a radius inclined at the angle of elevation which the kerb line subtends at

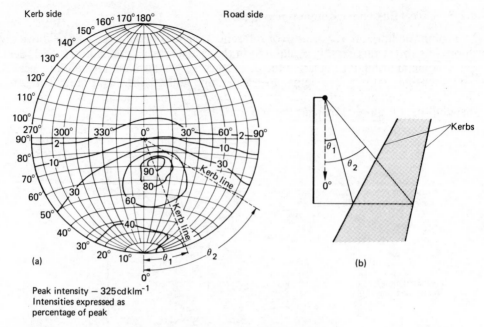

Peak intensity – 325 cd klm^{-1}
Intensities expressed as
percentage of peak

Fig. 5.10   Kerb lines superimposed on an isocandela diagram

the lantern (Fig. 5.10b). The flux falling on the road surface is therefore equal to the flux on the diagram between the inclined radii representing the two kerbs. This can be found by the method of summing flux between contours as indicated in Sect. 5.2.4. The total flux falling on the road surface is twice this value, for a bisymmetrical lantern, as the isocandela diagram only represents the flux emitted from one side of the lantern. When this total flux is expressed as a fraction of the bare lamp flux it is known as the utilization factor (*UF*) (Sect. 28.3.3).

5.2.7   Floodlighting – isocandela diagram

It is not usually convenient to use the equal-area zenithal web for representing the light distribution from floodlights. This is because many of these have narrow beams, which could not be represented in accurate detail on such a diagram. Instead a rectangular grid is used (Fig. 26.5) and the angular scales chosen to suit the extent of the light distribution. As mentioned in Sect. 4.4.4, the angular coordinate system used is the *V–H* one, so the angles on the ordinate and abscissa are labelled as vertical and horizontal respectively to distinguish them from azimuth and elevation of the *C–γ* system (Figs 4.4b and 4.5). The way in which a direction of a point P is specified in these two systems is compared in Fig. 5.11.

The method of calculating the flux in each one of the rectangles enclosed by vertical and horizontal grid lines in an isocandela diagram can be derived when it is remembered that the *V–H* system is equivalent to the *C–γ* system rotated so that the poles are east and west instead of north and south, and that *V* and *H* are measured from the centre of the diagram. It follows from Eq. 5.11 that the solid angle subtended by the zone between two horizontal angles H_1 and H_2 is $2\pi(\sin H_2 - \sin H_1)$. If the vertical angular increment between two lines in a rectangle is *V* (degrees) then the solid angle subtended by the rectangle is $\pi V(\sin H_2 - \sin H_1)/180$ steradians.

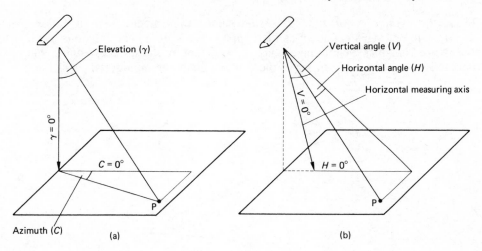

Fig. 5.11 Comparison of (a) the azimuth–elevation and (b) the vertical–horizontal angular coordinate systems

The flux in a rectangle can be found by multiplying this solid angle by the average intensity in the rectangle. The flux in the beam down to one-tenth peak intensity is found by putting in the one-tenth peak intensity isocandela line and summing all the flux in the rectangles so enclosed. An appropriate allowance should be made for rectangles that are only partially enclosed.

The flux falling on an area can be found by the method described in Sect. 26.3.2.

5.3 Flux transfer and inter-reflection

5.3.1 Flux transfer

In an illuminated room each surface receives light reflected from any other surface on a line of sight, and the calculation of these effects is an important one in determining the total effect of a luminaire. The simplest theoretical case is that of a point source in an integrating sphere (Sect. 4.4.2), but a room offers a much more complicated problem.

In Fig. 5.12 suppose the surfaces A_1 and A_2 are uniformly diffusing and have luminances of L_1 and L_2 respectively. Consider the light from an element of area δA_1 in A_1 directed towards δA_2 in A_2 at a distance d, the normals to the elements being NN. The luminous intensity of δA_1 is $L_1 \delta A_1 \cos \theta$ and the resulting illuminance at δA_2 is $L_1 \delta A_1 \cos \theta_1 \cos \theta_2 / d^2$.

The flux falling on δA_2 is $\delta \Phi_2 = L_1 \delta A_1 \delta A_2 \cos \theta_1 \cos \theta_2 / d^2$. If M_1 is the luminous exitance of A_1 $(= \pi L_1)$ then

$$\frac{\delta \Phi_2}{M_1} = \frac{\delta A_1 \, \delta A_2 \cos \theta_1 \cos \theta_2}{\pi d^2}$$

Hence the total flux received by A_2 from A_1 is given by

$$\frac{\Phi_2}{M_1} = \int \int \frac{\cos \theta_1 \cos \theta_2}{\pi d^2} \, dA_1 \, dA_2 \tag{5.17}$$

From the symmetry of the expression under the integral sign it follows that $\Phi_2/M_1 = \Phi_1/M_2$. This is known as the reciprocity theorem. The fractions Φ_2/M_1 and Φ_1/M_2 are known as the mutual exchange coefficient for the surfaces 1 and 2. They are denoted by g_{21} or g_{12}, the order of the coefficients being immaterial.

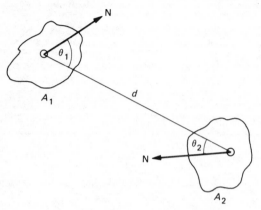

Fig. 5.12   Flux transfer between surfaces

Another useful term is the form factor (Phillips and Prokhovnik 1960). For two surfaces, 1 and 2, this is defined as the proportion of flux leaving 1 that is received by 2. The symbol is f_{12} and it should be noted that the suffices are in the same order as the flow of light. f_{12} may be expressed in terms of E_1 and M_2 and in terms of f_{21} as follows.

$$f_{12} = \frac{A_2 E_2}{A_1 M_1} \tag{5.18}$$

By the reciprocity theorem

$$\frac{A_2 E_2}{M_1} = \frac{A_1 E_1}{M_2}$$

where E_2 and E_1 are the illuminances received by surfaces 2 and 1 respectively, so

$$f_{12} = \frac{E_1}{M_2} \qquad \left(\text{or } \frac{A_2}{A_1} f_{21}\right) \tag{5.19}$$

That is, f_{12} is equal to the ratio of the illuminance on surface 1 to the exitance of surface 2, in which case the suffices are in the reverse order to the flow of the light.

Form factors can be deduced from the mutual exchange coefficient, evaluated from Eq. 5.17. Once the form factor for a pair of surfaces in a room is known the others can be obtained quite easily. For example, if 3 denotes the walls, 1 and 2 the floor and ceiling, and f_{12} is known then

$$f_{13} = f_{23} = 1 - f_{12}$$

From Eq. 5.19 it follows that

$$f_{31} = \frac{\text{area of ceiling}}{\text{area of walls}} f_{13}$$

and

$$f_{33} = 1 - 2f_{31}$$

5.3.2 Inter-reflection

The series of flux transfers between various surfaces of an enclosed space is known as inter-reflection. The process results in the illuminances being greater than would have been predicted from the direct illuminances provided by a luminaire in the space.

The final illuminances $E_1, E_2, \ldots, E_n$ in a space made up of n surfaces (allowing for inter-reflection) can be determined using form factors, assuming that the initial illuminances (due to direct light on the surfaces) $E_{01}, E_{02}, \ldots, E_{0n}$ are known. In addition the reflectance ρ of each surface must be known. This is defined as the flux emitted by the surface divided by the flux received by it. Hence, for example, the flux emitted from a surface of area A receiving an illuminance E would be ρEA.

The total flux reaching surface 1 is equal to the directly incident flux $E_{01}A_1$ plus the flux received from all the surfaces. Hence

$$E_1 A_1 = E_{01} A_1 + f_{11} A_1 E_1 \rho_1 + f_{21} A_2 E_2 \rho_2 + \ldots + f_{n1} A_n E_n \rho_n \tag{5.20}$$

Similarly for surface 2

$$E_2 A_2 = E_{02} A_2 + f_{12} A_1 E_1 \rho_1 + f_{22} A_2 E_2 \rho_2 + \ldots + f_{n2} A_n E_n \rho_n \tag{5.21}$$

and so on for the other surfaces.

The solution of these n simultaneous equations for the final illuminances can be obtained by means of matrix algebra (Phillips and Prokhovnik 1960) or by using any standard numerical method.

5.3.3 Utilization factors for interiors

The utilization factor $UF(S)$ for a surface S is the ratio of the total flux received by S to the total lamp flux of the installation. Utilization factors are used to calculate the number of luminaires needed to provide a given illuminance on a surface. Their derivation has already been mentioned in Sect. 5.2.6 in relation to road surfaces. In interiors their calculation is more complicated because inter-reflected light has to be taken into account (CIBS 1980b). *UF*s vary according to the light distribution of the luminaire, the geometry of the room, the layout of the luminaires, and the reflectance of the reflecting surfaces.

Certain simplifications and conventions are adopted in their calculation:

(a) The space (or ceiling cavity) above the luminaires, when these are suspended, is replaced by a plane C at the level of the luminaires having the effective reflectance of the ceiling cavity (Fig. 5.9). Similarly, the space (or floor cavity) below the horizontal reference or working plane, usually taken as being 0·85 m above the floor, is replaced by a plane F having the effective reflectance of the floor cavity.

(b) The rooms are square in plan. In practice rooms are rectangular in plan. Provided that the breadth is not greater than four times the width, a rectangular room can be equated to a square room for calculating utilization factors. For this purpose the room index is used. This is twice the plan area divided by the area of W, the part of the walls lying between C and F.

(c) All the room surfaces are uniform diffusers.

(d) All four walls have the same reflectance.

(e) The layout of the luminaires, which are assumed to be all the same, is on a square grid with the luminaires spaced from the walls at one-half the spacing between the luminaires.

(f) The luminaires are assumed to be point sources, symmetrical about the vertical axis. Real luminaires are frequently large and frequently asymmetrical: these departures from the assumed conditions do not generally give rise to significant errors in practice.

The calculation of *UF*s from zonal flux data can be divided into three distinct parts: (a) determination of spacing to mounting height ratio, (b) calculation of the fraction of bare lamp flux reaching F, C, and W, and (c) calculation of the inter-reflected flux.

Spacing to mounting height ratio The luminaires have to be suitably spaced to achieve the desired uniformity of illuminance (ratio of minimum to average) on the working plane. The standard of uniformity adopted for this is 0·8, recommended by the CIBS (1977a).

The spacing is expressed in terms of the spacing to mounting height ratio (*SHR*), the height being measured from the working plane to the luminaires. Standard tables of *UF*s are based on the nominal spacing to mounting height (*SHR NOM*), which is the maximum *SHR* in the series 0·75, 1·00, 1·25, etc. at which the uniformity of illuminance is not less than 0·8.

Once again, to simplify presentation and calculation of the data, certain conventions are adopted in the calculation of *SHR NOM*. Inter-reflections are ignored. This underestimates uniformity since the inter-reflected light is spread more evenly than is the direct light, and hence this errs on the side of safety. Also a layout of only 16 luminaires is considered (Fig. 5.13). This is justified on the grounds that adding more

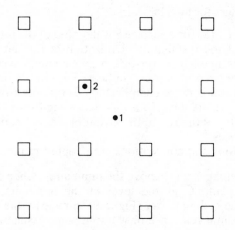

Fig. 5.13 Layout of luminaires for determining uniformity of illuminance

rows of luminaires does not affect the uniformity of illuminance over the area delimited by the four central luminaires. A uniformity (minimum to *average*) of 0·8 is normally achieved over the central area if the ratio of the minimum to the *maximum* illuminance is greater than 0·7.

These illuminances can be found by using one of the methods already described. Generally the minimum value $E(1)$ occurs at position 1 in Fig. 5.13 and the maximum value $E(2)$ at position 2. Obviously use can be made of this to further simplify the calculation. The ratio $E(1)/E(2)$ is known as the mid-point ratio.

Flux reaching F, C, and W   The next stage is the calculation of the fraction of bare lamp flux reaching F, C, and W, that is, the distribution factors for these, $DF(F)$, $DF(C)$, and $DF(W)$. The calculation of $DF(F)$ was outlined in Sect. 5.2.5 and zonal multipliers appropriate to the *SHR NOM* are used. Then $DF(W)$ is the light output ratio down minus $DF(F)$ and $DF(C)$ is the light output ratio up, since all the upward light falls on surface C.

Inter-reflected flux   The inter-reflected component of the flux falling on the room surfaces is allowed for by using transfer factors (*TF*). The transfer factor for the walls to the horizontal reference plane $TF(W, F)$, for example, is the ratio of the total flux falling on the floor cavity, as a result of the flux illuminating the walls, to the direct flux on the walls. Similar definitions apply to other pairs of surfaces. They are a function of the reflectances of the room surfaces and the geometry of the room.

Transfer factors are calculated by using the inter-reflection equations in Sect. 5.3.2 (for three surfaces). It should be noted however that, since transfer factors are expressed as ratios of total flux emitted by and received by surfaces, terms such as E_1A_1, $E_{01}A_1$, A_2E_2, etc. can each be replaced by single symbols for flux. Values of *TF* for pairs of surfaces which are different are less than unity for the reflectances used in practical rooms. However, where the surfaces are the same, as in $TF(F, F)$ and $TF(W, W)$, the *TF* has a value equal to or greater than unity since the incident flux includes the direct flux as well as the inter-reflected flux.

Utilization factors for the horizontal reference plane $UF(F)$ can now be calculated from the equation

$$UF(F) = DF(F)\,TF(F, F) + DF(C)\,TF(C, F) + DF(W)\,TF(W, F) \qquad (5.22)$$

Similar expressions can be derived for $UF(W)$ and $UF(C)$.

Tables of $UF(F)$ are generally calculated for a range of room indices and surface reflectances covering most practical situations. The CIBS standard format is shown in Table 21.3, which also includes a table of glare indices.

5.4   Luminance calculations

5.4.1   Interiors

To find the luminance distribution in an interior utilization factors $UF(F)$, $UF(C)$, and $UF(W)$ for the floor cavity, ceiling cavity, and walls respectively are used to determine the illuminance on these surfaces. The illuminance values (in lux) are multiplied by the respective reflectance of the surface and divided by π to yield the luminance (in cd m^{-2}).

When it is desired to select a luminaire to give a particular luminance distribution in a room, Eqs 5.20, 5.21, etc. can be used to find the direct illuminances. From these values the flux required on the room surfaces can be determined and a luminaire chosen with a suitable light distribution. The solution of these equations does not present any problem since the final illuminances E_1, E_2, and E_3 can be found by dividing the required luminances by the respective reflectances, so the initial illuminances E_{01}, E_{02}, and E_{03} can be found by direct substitution without the need to solve the equations simultaneously.

5.4.2   Road surfaces

In a lighted street objects are seen in silhouette against the bright road surface. It is therefore important to know the luminance of the road surface (CIE 1976a).

It cannot be assumed that the road surface behaves even approximately as a uniform diffuser because it is very rough and irregular. Hence reflectance cannot be used in calculating the luminance of a road surface, but the luminance coefficient, which takes into account the geometry of the incident and reflected rays, has to be used instead. The luminance coefficient q is defined as the ratio of the luminance L of a surface in the direction of observation to the illuminance E of the surface, that is, q equals L/E.

The luminance coefficient generally depends on the three angles α, β, and γ in Fig. 5.14. However these can be reduced to two by making the simplifying assumption that

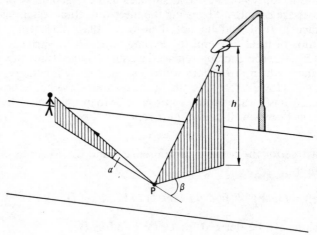

Fig. 5.14   Determination of luminance on a road surface

the stretch of road lying between 60 m and 160 m ahead of the driver is of most importance as regards the driver's vision. For this area α varies from 0·5° to 1·5°, over which angle it has been found experimentally that the luminance coefficient does not vary significantly. To obtain a representative result luminance coefficients are measured at an angle α of 1°.

In Fig. 5.14 consider the luminance L at P. Let I be the intensity from the light source at height h towards P. Then

$$L = qE$$
$$= qI \cos^3 \gamma / h^2 \qquad \text{or} \qquad I(q \cos^3 \gamma)/h^2 \qquad (5.23)$$

The quantity in brackets is known as the reduced luminance coefficient r. This is more convenient to use than the luminance coefficient q since it incorporates the $\cos^3 \gamma$ factor. Tables of r for a range of values of β and γ have been prepared for a variety of road surfaces (Sect. 28.3.2).

For dry surfaces a classification system has been developed in which surfaces are classified according to their average luminance coefficient Q_0 and a factor S_1 which takes into account the specular reflecting properties of the road. There is also a classification system for wet roads. This uses Q_0 measured for the surface dry, and a modified specular reflection factor measured in the wet surface.

Average luminance over the road surface can be found from luminance yield curves (Fig. 28.5). Luminance yield η_L is defined by

$$\eta_L = \frac{LSW}{FQ_0} \tag{5.24}$$

where L = average luminance of the road $(\mathrm{cd\,m^{-2}})$,
$\quad S$ = spacing between lanterns,
$\quad W$ = width of road (m),
$\quad F$ = bare lamp flux (lm),
$\quad Q_0$ = average luminance coefficient.

η_L is found by computing a luminance grid from 60 m to 160 m from the observer and finding the average luminance of longitudinal strips of the road. The above formula is then applied. η_L varies with the position of the observer relative to the kerb, the mounting height of the lanterns, the road surface, and the light distribution of the lanterns. Generally η_L curves are given for three observer positions as in Fig. 28.5. In practice the luminance yield curves are used to find the spacing S needed to provide a given average luminance L. This can be found by rearranging the formula for η_L.

5.5 Discomfort glare

5.5.1 Direct calculation (glare index method)

In the UK the formula used for predicting glare from an interior installation is, as quoted in Sect. 2.4.1,

$$\text{glare index} = 10\log_{10}\left[\frac{0.239}{L_b}\sum L_s^{1.6}\omega^{0.8}p\right]$$

the summation being performed for all the luminaires in the field of view.

L_s, the luminance of the luminaire in $\mathrm{cd\,m^{-2}}$ in the direction of the observer's eye, is evaluated by dividing the intensity of the luminaire by its projected area, both being taken in the direction of the observer's eye. ω, the solid angle subtended by the luminaire at the observer's eye, is found by dividing the projected area of the luminaire in the direction of the observer's eye by the square of its distance from the observer. L_b, the background luminance in $\mathrm{cd\,m^{-2}}$, is numerically equal to the illuminance in lux, divided by π, on a plane at the observer's eye normal to the line of sight. This illuminance is found by using utilization factors for the wall $UF(\mathrm{W})$. p, the position factor, takes into account the decrease in glare sensation as a luminaire is moved out of the line of sight.

In the evaluation of this formula according to CIBS (1967b) certain conventions are adopted to standardize data. Glare indices are worked out for two positions of the observer in a rectangular room. These are at the vertical mid-line of a long wall and a short wall. The line of sight is horizontal and directed to the mid-line of the opposite wall. Eye height is 1·2 m (this is for a seated person) and the height of the plane of the luminaires above eye level is 3·05 m.

5.5.2   BZ method

Tables of glare indices for individual luminaires (Table 21.3) provide the easiest way of determining the glare index for an installation. Where these are not available the British Zonal classification (BZ classification) can be used instead. In this 10 standard distributions (Fig. 5.15), known as BZ1 to BZ10, have been selected; calculations

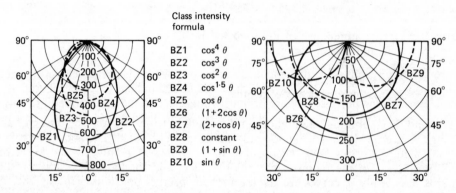

Fig. 5.15   British Zonal classification of luminaires showing theoretical intensity distributions used

have been made to show how the direct ratio of these varies with room index. To classify a luminaire direct ratios are found for the same range of room indices and compared with those for the BZ distribution. The luminaire is then classified at each room index by the BZ distribution having the direct ratio closest to that of the luminaire.

In CIBS (1967b) tables of initial glare indices are given for the range of BZ classifications from 1 to 10.

Further reading

Bean A R and Simons R H, 1968, *Lighting fittings and design* (Oxford: Pergamon)

Keitz H A E, 1971, *Light calculations and measurements*, 2nd Edition (London: Macmillan)

Moon P, 1961, *The scientific basis of illuminating engineering* (New York: Dover Publications)

Walsh J W T, 1958, *Photometry*, 3rd Edition (London: Constable & Co)

Zijl H, 1951, *Manual for the engineer on large size perfect diffusers* (Eindhoven: Philips Technical Library)

6 Production of radiation

There are many physical and chemical processes which generate electromagnetic radiation, but only those processes which are exploited in lamps are described here in detail. For lighting purposes we are primarily interested in the production of radiation in the visible region, i.e. at wavelengths between 380 nm and 780 nm; however ultraviolet and infrared radiation are important, both in their own right and because they can be converted efficiently to visible. The physical principles underlying the production of radiation are described in this chapter, whilst succeeding chapters show how these principles are employed in practical lamps. Even though lasers are not used for illumination purposes, their principles of operation and applications are described briefly.

6.1   Sources of radiation

Many different forms of energy can be converted into visible radiation; the processes are generally distinguished by the source of the input energy. Some of them are defined below.

Incandescence   Solids and liquids emit visible radiation when they are heated to temperatures above about 1000 K. The intensity increases and the appearance becomes whiter as the temperature increases.

Electric discharges   When an electric current is passed through a gas the atoms and molecules emit radiation whose spectrum is characteristic of the elements present.

Electroluminescence   Light is generated when electric current is passed through certain solids, such as semiconductor or phosphor materials.

Photoluminescence   Radiation at one wavelength is absorbed, usually by a solid, and re-emitted at a different wavelength. When the re-emitted radiation is visible the phenomenon may be termed either *fluorescence* or *phosphorescence* (or simply *luminescence*).

Cathodoluminescence   Light is generated when phosphors are bombarded with electrons.

Chemiluminescence   Light is sometimes generated during chemical reactions, without necessarily generating heat.

Thermoluminescence   Light is generated by heating certain solids; the material glows more brightly than is predicted by the laws governing incandescence, but only for a limited period of time.

6.2   Generation of radiation

The laws of classical physics predict that electromagnetic radiation is generated when charged particles accelerate or decelerate. This radiation, which is known as *Bremsstrahlung* (literally 'braking radiation', Beiser 1967), figures only in xenon lamps, and it is not considered in any detail.

Consider an atom as consisting of a positively charged nucleus immersed in a cloud of negatively charged electrons. Quantum physics asserts that the outermost electron in an atom may take only a number of discrete energies (the electron is said to be in a particular energy level); normally the electron resides in the lowest energy level, otherwise known as the ground state. When the electron absorbs energy it is excited and jumps into a level of higher energy; eventually it is de-excited and falls back to the ground state. The difference in energy between the levels is dissipated by the emission of a burst of radiant energy, known as a *photon*. This process is by far the most important source of radiation in lamps.

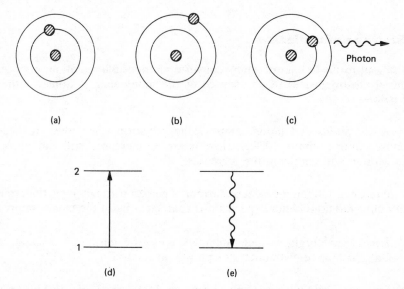

Fig. 6.1   Excitation and spontaneous emission of radiation

The sequence of excitation and de-excitation is shown schematically in Fig. 6.1. In Fig. 6.1a the outer electron of the atom is shown in an orbit corresponding to the ground state (or lowest energy state); in (b) sufficient energy has been communicated to the electron to induce it to jump to an orbit corresponding to an excited state (or a higher energy level; see also (d)). In (c) and (e) the electron spontaneously falls back to the ground state, and a photon is emitted. The frequency v of the light radiated is given by *Planck's relation* (Richtmyer et al. 1969).

$$Q = hv \tag{6.1}$$

where Q is the difference in energy between the levels and h is a fundamental constant $(6 \cdot 626\,176 \times 10^{-34}\,\text{J s})$, known as Planck's constant.

The discussion so far has related to isolated atoms which generate photons of a single wavelength. In reality atoms are never completely isolated and interactions between atoms cause the energy levels to be perturbed slightly; consequently the corresponding photon wavelength is also changed. Therefore the excited atoms in a real material generate a spectral line which has a finite width and which is said to be *broadened* by the atomic interactions (Thorne 1974, Sobel'man 1964).

These ideas can be extended to include the case of a gas molecule, where the outermost electrons are shared between the constituent atoms. Energy levels appropriate to vibrations and rotations of the polyatomic molecules must now be included; these energy levels are much more numerous and closely spaced than those of a single atom, with the result that a molecular spectrum is smeared to such an extent that it approaches a continuum (Beiser 1967).

An excited atom may relax to the ground state and generate a photon either *spontaneously* or because it is *stimulated* to do so by another photon. The phases of photons which result from spontaneous transitions are unrelated, and the light is *incoherent* (Lipson and Lipson 1969). This random superposition of waves can be likened to the waves on a choppy sea. In the case where an atomic transition is stimulated, the stimulating and the generated photons have the same phase; this light is said to be *coherent*.

Spontaneous and stimulated transitions occur together, but under normal circumstances the spontaneous transitions far out-number the stimulated transitions. In a LASER (an acronym for Light Amplification by the Stimulated Emission of Radiation) this situation is reversed (Sect. 6.4.1). Coherent waves are rather like the standing waves set up in a rope which has one end fixed and the other end moved at the right frequency and phase. The operation and some of the multitudinous applications of lasers are described in Sect. 6.4.

6.3   Production of incoherent radiation

6.3.1   Incandescence

Thermal radiation   When a body is heated to a high temperature its constituent atoms become excited by numerous interactions and energy is radiated in a continuous spectrum. The continuous spectrum arises because the energy levels of the electrons in solids are broadened to the point of merging into a continuous band. The process is complex and almost defies analysis; however thermodynamics has been successful in describing the macroscopic properties of a perfect *black body* (also known as a *full radiator*) (Zemansky 1957). By definition a black body completely absorbs all radiation falling on it, provided that it is held at a constant temperature. Only a few materials, such as carbon black and platinum black, approach this ideal in practice. In the laboratory a black body is simulated by a carefully shaped cavity, whose walls are formed from a highly absorbing material. The radiation from an aperture in the heated cavity is used to determine temperature and to calibrate certain radiation standards (Sect. 4.1.1).

By taking the bold step of postulating that energy is transferred in discrete quanta Planck derived his celebrated law (Born 1957) defining the spectral distribution of thermal radiation.

$$M_{e\lambda}^{th} = \frac{c_1}{\lambda^5[\exp(c_2/\lambda T) - 1]} \tag{6.2}$$

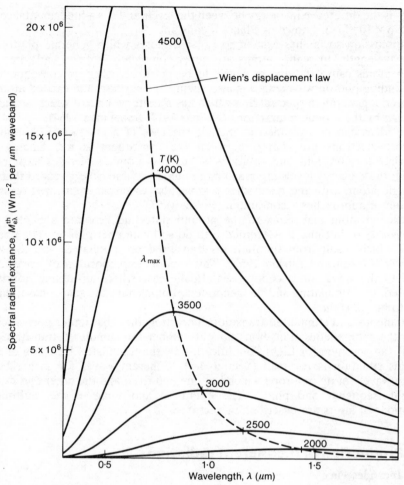

Fig. 6.2   Black body radiation according to Planck's law

where c_1 and c_2 are constants ($3\cdot741\,82 \times 10^{-16}\,\mathrm{W\,m^2}$ and $1\cdot438\,76 \times 10^{-2}\,\mathrm{m\,K}$ respectively), λ is the wavelength in m, T is the temperature in K, and $M_{e\lambda}^{th}$ is the spectral radiant exitance (formerly called the spectral radiant emittance) of a black body in $\mathrm{W\,m^{-3}}$. The spectral radiant exitance of a black body is plotted in Fig. 6.2 as a function of wavelength and at different temperatures. Radiation of this form is called thermal radiation or black body radiation.

The maximum radiant exitance increases rapidly with temperature, and the wavelength at maximum power is inversely proportional to the temperature T. The latter observation is known as *Wien's displacement law*.

$$\lambda_{max}\,T = c_3 \tag{6.3}$$

where c_3 is $2\cdot8978 \times 10^{-3}\,\mathrm{m\,K}$ (Fig. 6.2). This law corresponds to the observation that a heated body first glows red, then yellow, and then bluish.

The total radiant exitance of a black body surface is found by integrating Eq. 6.2 over all wavelengths. The result is a surprisingly simple relation, known as the *Stefan–Boltzmann law*.

$$M_e^{th} = \sigma T^4 \tag{6.4}$$

where M_e^{th} is the radiant exitance in $W\,m^{-2}$ and σ is the Stefan–Boltzmann constant $(5\cdot670\,32 \times 10^{-8}\,W\,m^{-2}\,K^{-4})$. A black body radiates uniformly in all directions. Siegel and Howell (1972) give a more detailed description of thermal radiation.

Selective radiators   In practice the above analysis must be modified to allow for the fact that most materials do not approach the absorption/emission characteristics of a black body. The emissivity is defined as a measure of how well a body radiates energy as compared with a black body; its value lies between zero and one. The emissivity $\varepsilon(\lambda)$ is a function of wavelength and is defined as

$$M_{e\lambda} = \varepsilon(\lambda)\,M_{e\lambda}^{th} \tag{6.5}$$

where $M_{e\lambda}^{th}$ and $M_{e\lambda}$ are the spectral radiant exitance of a black body and a non-black body respectively, at the same temperature. The emissivity is normally measured experimentally at a direction normal to the surface, and as a function of wavelength (Svet 1965).

Furthermore, *Kirchhoff's law* for a thermal radiator states that the emissivity equals the absorptivity $\alpha(\lambda)$ which is defined as the fraction of the incident radiation absorbed by the surface.

$$\varepsilon(\lambda) = \alpha(\lambda) \tag{6.6}$$

for a surface at a uniform temperature. The emissivity and the absorptivity of a black body are both equal to one. A *grey body* is defined as one which has an emissivity which is less than one and is independent of wavelength.

The above discussion indicates that materials which are appropriate for use as incandescent filaments must be able to withstand high temperatures (i.e. greater than 2000 K) and have a selective emissivity which favours the visible. Tungsten wire satisfies both these conditions and it is a commonly used filament material. The filament is operated at temperatures approaching the melting point of tungsten, and the consequent evaporation of tungsten not only blackens the bulb, but also thins the filament, so forming hot spots. The introduction of halogens to the bulb mitigates these effects by preventing the deposition of evaporated tungsten on the bulb by a regenerative chemical cycle (Chap. 10).

The poor efficiency of incandescent lamps is attributed to the large proportion of thermal radiation which lies in the infrared. Various attempts have been made to reclaim this wasted energy. The most attractive technique would be to coat the bulb with a layer which selectively reflects the infrared radiation back onto the filament. So far, a commercial lamp based on this principle has not been developed.

Heat and light units, which are widely used for livestock, make full use of the infrared radiation generated by a Nernst filament. The Nernst filament is an extruded rod of zirconia and yttria which is electrically heated to between 1700 K and 2000 K. In this case the emissivity is high in the infrared, although this filament was originally used as a source of visible light.

Enhanced radiation   Radiation from chemical sources can exceed the thermal radiation because of the excitation of the constituent atoms during chemical reactions. This can occur in the body of a flame, say, or at some surface immersed in it, such as incandescent particles of soot (Siegel and Howell 1972). Recombination and de-excitation occur more readily at surfaces than elsewhere, so the surface glows more brightly than expected. The *gas mantle* is another example of this behaviour. It is formed from rare-earth oxides, which have the advantage of radiating selectively in the visible; additional radiation is formed by chemical interactions at the surface, which burns away slowly. A similar effect occurs in the *limelight*, in which calcium oxide is heated by a coal gas or hydrogen flame. A more modern example is the photographer's flash bulb, in which aluminium or zirconium shreds are burned rapidly under controlled conditions (Chap. 16).

6.3.2   General features of gas discharges

In order to understand the production of light by gas discharges it is first necessary to consider the mechanism of electrical conduction. In a solid conductor the current is carried by electrons moving through a regular lattice of atoms or ions, which are immobile apart from thermal vibrations. Metallic conductors contain approximately equal numbers of electrons and fixed atoms or ions, hence the electrical conductivity is high. The only direct effects of the passage of an electric current through a metal are heating and the production of a magnetic field around the conductor. Light is only emitted if the conductor is heated to incandescence.

By contrast there are normally no free electrons in a gas and conduction can only take place if the gas atoms are ionized to produce electrons and positive ions. The flow of electricity through a gas is called a *discharge*. The electric field causes the electrons to drift towards the anode and the positive ions to drift towards the cathode (Fig. 6.3).

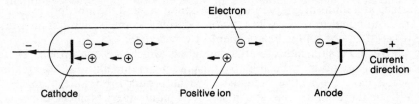

Fig. 6.3   Electric discharge through a tube of ionized gas

The total current through the tube is thus the sum of the electron and ion currents. Ions are several thousand times heavier than electrons and much less mobile; the ion current is usually only 0·1 to 1% of the total current (von Engel 1965, Cobine 1958).

6.3.3   Low pressure discharges

Consider a discharge tube a few centimetres in diameter and a metre or so in length containing one or more gases at a total pressure of approximately one-hundredth of an atmosphere: a fluorescent lamp discharge is a typical example. With currents no larger than an ampere or two, there is negligible heating of the gas and we speak of a low pressure discharge. Under these conditions ionization is principally produced by electron impact (von Engel 1965).

Ionization by electron impact   When a free electron collides with a neutral gas atom one of three things may happen:

(a)   The electron may rebound with only a small loss in energy: an elastic collision.
(b)   The atom may be excited, as illustrated in Fig. 6.1, with the electron sustaining a corresponding loss of kinetic energy.
(c)   The atom may be ionized, releasing one of its own electrons completely. The incident electron again loses kinetic energy.

The relative probability of these processes depends on the energy of the colliding electron. Electron energies are usually expressed in electron volts (eV), 1 eV being the energy gained by an electron accelerated through a potential difference of one volt ($1 \text{ eV} = 1 \cdot 602 \times 10^{-19}$ J). The ionizing energy for mercury is $10 \cdot 4$ eV and for argon is $15 \cdot 7$ eV so that, in a mixture of mercury vapour and argon, mercury is preferentially ionized.

Thus in a fluorescent lamp discharge, which contains mercury and argon, most of the ions are mercury ions produced by collisions of mercury atoms with the more energetic electrons in the discharge. Very few have sufficient energy to ionize or even excite argon, so most electron collisions with argon atoms are elastic collisions, which have the effect of slightly heating the gas.

Positive column and plasma The large uniform region of the discharge between the electrodes is called the positive column. This consists of a mixture of gas atoms, ions, and electrons, all moving largely at random. The heavier particles form a gas at a temperature only slightly above the surroundings of the tube (typically 10 °C to 30 °C above, but sometimes a few hundred °C). The electrons require much more energy to cause ionization, however, and typically have energies corresponding to an *electron temperature* of 10 000 K to 20 000 K: this additional energy is derived from their acceleration by the electric field as they drift, with many collisions, in the direction of the anode.

The concept of electron temperature plays an important role in the treatment of low pressure discharges. It implies that the electrons behave substantially as a separate gas from the heavier particles, with an energy distribution corresponding to that of the atoms of a gas in thermodynamic equilibrium at a much higher temperature. This is termed the electron temperature T_e and implies a Maxwellian distribution of energies. At $T_e = 7737$ K the mean energy of the electrons is 1 eV, but there are a few electrons at many times this energy which produce excitation and ionization. Electrons with a non-Maxwellian distribution of energies are often represented as having an 'effective electron temperature' as an approximation, but this is not usually very satisfactory.

Most of the electrons are themselves the result of the ionization process, and throughout the positive column electrons and ions are present in almost exactly equal numbers. This equality is accentuated by the electrostatic attraction of the ions and electrons to each other, so that throughout the positive column there is practically no net space charge. Such a region of charge neutrality is called a *plasma*. The electron number density at any point is equal to the ion number density, and either is normally termed the *plasma density*.

As well as drifting towards the electrodes, the electrons and ions drift radially towards the wall, where they recombine to form neutral atoms. To preserve charge neutrality they must do this in equal numbers, so the wall acquires a small negative potential (a few volts) which slows down the faster-moving electrons. This type of neutral charge drift is termed *ambipolar diffusion* and is one of the sources of loss of energy in the discharge (Cobine 1958).

Electrical characteristics For the discharge to operate in a steady condition the rate of ionization must exactly balance the rate of loss of electrons and ions by ambipolar diffusion to the walls. The longitudinal electric field must therefore have such a value that the electrons acquire just enough energy, or electron temperature, to maintain this balance. The electrical conductivity of the discharge is proportional to the electron density, or plasma density, which increases with the discharge current. There is therefore no simple relationship between voltage and current, such as Ohm's law, and the voltage–current relationship, or electrical characteristic of the discharge, is very complex and dependent on all the constituents of the discharge and conditions of operation. The increase in conductivity with current is normally so great that the voltage required to maintain the current falls as the current rises, and the discharge has a 'falling characteristic': the volt–ampere curve has a negative slope. Consequently most discharges are not current-limiting and for stable operation from a constant voltage supply must include a current-limiting device, such as a resistor or, for a.c. operation, an inductor, a capacitor, or some combination which minimizes power loss (Sect. 18.1.2). Voltage and current waveforms in a.c. circuits depart substantially from the sinusoidal form and simple r.m.s. relationships are not valid.

Electrodes and starting   Since the electron current is much larger than the ion current, the cathode has the important function of supplying the electrons necessary to maintain the discharge; the anode is much less important, being mainly a receiver of the charged particles to complete the circuit.

Most lamps have hot cathodes which are heated either by a circulating current provided by the control gear, by the passage of the discharge current itself, or by bombardment by positive ions from the neighbouring region of the discharge called the *negative glow*. These provide electrons by thermionic emission, assisted by photoelectric emission, field emission, and several other processes. Some form of electron emissive material is usually coated on the electrode, which is of a light construction and is easily heated (Chap. 7).

A few lamps have cold cathodes: these are larger in area and operate as 'glow discharge' cathodes. A voltage drop of 100–200 V, known as the *cathode fall*, separates the cathode from a surrounding *cathode glow*; this provides a copious supply of ions which are accelerated to the cathode to produce secondary electrons on impact which in turn produce more ions. The cathode fall in hot cathode discharges is only about 10 V.

The electrodes play an important role in starting the discharge. On initially applying a voltage across the tube there is practically no ionization and the gas behaves as an insulator. Once a few ions or electrons are present a sufficiently high voltage accelerates these to provide more by electron impact ionization, and breakdown is achieved by a cumulative process or 'avalanche'. The initial electrons may be left from a previous discharge, provided by radioactive materials in the gas or on the tube, or from natural radioactivity, but suitable cathodes supply electrons at a very early stage in the breakdown process by field emission, photoelectric emission, or thermionic emission, greatly reducing the excess voltage needed to strike the discharge. If the electrodes are preheated or if some arrangement, such as an adjacent auxiliary electrode, is provided the voltage required is further reduced.

The control gear for the discharge has therefore not only to provide a stable limited-current supply for the steady operation of the discharge, but must also provide an excess voltage for striking as well as supplies for preheating electrodes, or auxiliary electrodes, as required (Chap. 18).

This striking voltage is often reduced by using what is known as a *Penning mixture* in place of a single inert gas. A small proportion of another gas is added which has an ionization energy slightly lower than the excitation energy of the main gas. Ions are then readily produced by electrons first exciting the major constituent which in turn ionizes the minor constituent by transferring its excitation energy on collision. Typical examples are 99%Ne–1%Ar (excitation and ionization energies 16·5 eV and 15·7 eV respectively) and Ar–Hg mixtures (11·6 eV and 10·4 eV respectively).

Production of radiation   Most of the radiation from the majority of discharge lamps is from the uniform positive column. The energetic electrons which produce the ionization also produce excitation of the gas atoms, which subsequently radiate at their characteristic frequencies: at low pressure these usually produce a discrete line spectrum. Normally many energy levels are excited: Fig. 6.4 shows just a few of the excitation and radiating transitions of importance in lamps containing mercury vapour. More comprehensive information is given by Kenty (1950).

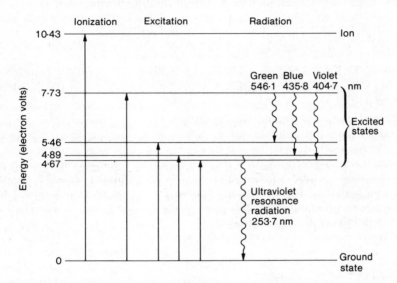

Fig. 6.4   Simplified transition diagram for mercury

The lowest excited state which can radiate produces what is called *resonance radiation*. This is important in low pressure discharges because it is usually very efficiently generated. In the case of mercury, ultraviolet resonance radiation at 253·7 nm is the principal source of radiation for exciting the phosphor on the wall of a fluorescent lamp, as well as being one of the principal sources available of short-wave ultraviolet radiation. Mercury also has another resonance line at 185·0 nm, but this is of less importance in the present context. Certain states, such as those at 4·67 eV and 5·46 eV in mercury, cannot radiate: these are called *metastable states*. In the case of sodium the resonance radiation is in the yellow region at 589·3 nm (2·10 eV) near the wavelength for maximal visual response; hence the importance of the low pressure sodium vapour discharge. Much basic information on these topics is given by Mitchell and Zemansky (1934).

One of the most important aspects of discharge lamp design is to ensure that as much as possible of the input power is directed into transitions producing the wavelengths desired. For example, by suitable choice of conditions, well over 50% of the input power to a fluorescent lamp type discharge can be radiated at 253·7 nm. However, by raising the pressure and operating at a higher gas temperature, this can be almost entirely suppressed, and the power radiated from the other transitions which give visible radiation (Fig. 6.4). Cayless (1963) gives a fuller treatment of this discharge.

One of the characteristics of resonance radiation is that it is easily absorbed by other atoms in the ground state (compare Kirchhoff's law, Sect. 6.3.1, a form of which applies in this case also). Consequently it cannot reach the walls of the discharge tube without being repeatedly absorbed and re-emitted. This phenomenon is known as *resonance radiation imprisonment*, which in addition to limiting the efficiency of low pressure discharges becomes increasingly important in determining the spectrum emitted by high pressure discharges.

Most practical discharge lamps contain one or more of the inert gases helium, neon, argon, or krypton in addition to the metal vapour which produces the radiation. This gas, often called a buffer gas, performs the following functions:

(a)   It reduces ion losses to the wall by ambipolar diffusion.
(b)   It controls the mobility of the electrons, and hence the electrical conductivity.
(c)   It provides easier breakdown at a lower striking voltage.
(d)   It prolongs the life of the electrodes by reducing sputtering and evaporation.
(e)   In the case of fluorescent lamps it forms some protection of the phosphor from mercury ions.

However the inert gas dissipates energy from the electrons by elastic collisions in the form of heat. This is least when the gas is heavy, so argon is used, for example, in fluorescent lamps to give maximum reduction of ion losses to the walls with minimum elastic collision losses. In sodium lamps however the tube must be heated to some 600 K to provide an adequate vapour pressure of sodium, hence a relatively high pressure of neon is used to provide sufficient heat in this way. If sufficient thermal insulation can be provided in the form of vacuum jackets or infrared reflecting layers (Chap. 12) the neon pressure can be reduced to give a high efficiency of radiation production.

6.3.4   High pressure discharges

Comparison with low pressure discharges   If we start with a low pressure discharge and gradually raise the pressure to a few atmospheres, two principal changes occur:

(a)   The gas temperature is gradually increased by energy transfer by the increasing number of collisions (mainly elastic collisions) with the energetic electrons, and the mean electron energy, or electron temperature, is gradually decreased accordingly, until both are practically equal at some intermediate temperature, typically 4000 K to 6000 K. At these temperatures significant numbers of electrons have sufficient thermal energy to ionize the gas.
(b)   The high temperature becomes localized at the centre of the discharge; there being a temperature gradient towards the walls, which are much cooler.

This situation is represented schematically in Fig. 6.5. More detailed treatments are given by Elenbaas (1951) and Lochte-Holtgreven (1968).

The analysis of a high pressure discharge is greatly simplified by the assumption of local thermodynamic equilibrium. A system is said to be in *thermodynamic equilibrium* provided that (a) there are no unbalanced forces in its interior (mechanical equilibrium), (b) the chemical composition of the system does not change, and (c) the temperature is constant and uniform. Taken as a whole, a high pressure discharge does not approach these conditions because of temperature gradients and because energy is lost via radiation. However, collisions between electrons and gas atoms are sufficiently frequent for the gas and electron temperatures to be similar, and for the approximation that the plasma is *locally* in thermodynamic equilibrium to be valid (Griem 1964). This assumption of *local thermodynamic equilibrium* (LTE) allows us

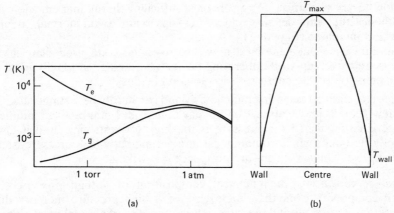

Fig. 6.5 Temperatures in a high pressure discharge (schematically): (a) transition from low to high pressure (T_e = electron temperature, T_g = gas temperature) and (b) radial temperature distribution in a high pressure discharge

to make some important simplifications in determining the properties of high pressure discharges, and these will be described later.

The wall becomes much less important at high pressures, and not altogether essential: discharges can operate between two electrodes without any restraining wall, and are then referred to as arcs. There is no essential difference between an arc and a high pressure constricted discharge in a tube, which also is frequently called an arc. There is however a strong tendency to instability: the arc may either bow (as its name implies) or writhe around, making it useless as a stable light source. A constraining wall or electrodes which are not too far apart are the principal means of preventing this, and we speak of wall-stabilized and electrode-stabilized arcs. Magnetic fields are also used sometimes. The longer types of lamp are usually wall-stabilized and the shorter, compact source types are usually electrode-stabilized. There are also other factors necessary for good stability, the achievement of which is one of the major problems facing the lamp designer.

Like low pressure discharges, high pressure discharges generally have a falling characteristic, i.e. a volt–ampere curve of negative slope over much of their range of operation. In some cases this levels off, and may actually rise again at high currents, especially if the vapour density continues to rise as the power is increased, as in the case of some types of mercury lamp. Nevertheless, they are inherently unstable characteristics and a current-limiting device, such as a choke or high reactance transformer, is still necessary to ensure stable operation at the required power.

Electrodes and starting   The electrodes are more robust in construction than in a low pressure discharge, and are invariably self-heated by ion bombardment. Electron emission is essentially thermionic, with a cathode fall of only a few volts. In discharges containing a vaporizable material, such as mercury, sodium, or metal halides, and an inert gas, only the gas (and a trace of mercury, when present) is available for ionization on first striking. Three phases may be distinguished in establishing the discharge:

(a)   Initial breakdown of the rare gas, as in a low pressure discharge. The discharge then operates as a glow discharge, with a high cathode fall, until the cathode has been sufficiently heated.

(b) Glow to arc transition. When there is sufficient thermionic emission from the cathode, the cathode fall suddenly collapses and (with normal circuitry) the current increases (Fig. 18.1).

(c) Run-up. The heat generated now vaporizes the condensed material and the pressure builds up to its operating value. The voltage gradually increases and the emission of the characteristic radiation begins.

Sometimes (a) and (b) occur instantaneously and can hardly be distinguished; in other cases a few seconds may elapse. Run-up may take from 1 minute to 15 minutes. If the discharge is extinguished the pressure is too high for restriking until it has cooled sufficiently. In lamps which contain a gas at a permanently high pressure, such as the xenon lamp, very high voltages are necessary for striking.

Chemical composition The chemical composition of a high pressure discharge varies in complexity from the simple case of a high pressure mercury discharge, which contains a rare gas and mercury only, to the case of a metal halide lamp, which contains a rare gas, mercury, and the halides of a number of elements.

Elements are conveniently introduced to the arc tube as one or more of their halides, because the vapour pressure of the halide is normally greater than that of the element, sodium being a notable exception. The use of halides has two important disadvantages. Firstly, the lamp chemistry becomes very complex; the chemical compounds may segregate so that the lower part of a vertically-operated lamp is rich in elements, such as sodium and the rare earths, whilst the top of the lamp reverts to a high pressure mercury discharge. Secondly, the highly reactive halogens may attack the electrodes or the envelope causing premature failure. However, an important advantage is that the halide molecules present in the outer parts of the arc tube may generate a weak continuum background spectrum, which is beneficial to the colour rendering properties of the lamp.

The equilibrium composition of complex chemical systems is determined by finding the composition which has the lowest thermochemical energy (van Zeggeren and Storey 1970). This composition varies throughout the volume of the plasma.

Ionization Ionization occurs in all high pressure discharges. In LTE the number densities of (singly ionized) ions n_i and electrons n_e (in m^{-3}) are given by *Saha's equation* (Lochte-Holtgreven 1968)

$$\frac{n_e n_i}{n_g} = 4 \cdot 83 \times 10^{21} \frac{U_i}{U_g} T^{3/2} \exp\left(-\frac{E_i}{kT}\right) \qquad (6.7)$$

where E_i is the ionization energy, k is Boltzmann's constant ($8 \cdot 617\,35 \times 10^{-5}\,eV\,K^{-1}$), U_i and U_g are two small numbers called the partition functions of the ion and atom respectively, and n_g is the number density of atoms in the ground state. In a plasma the number densities of the electrons and ions are the same if all the ions are only singly ionized.

Production of radiation The atoms in the hot core of the discharge are excited by collisions with electrons and radiation is generated on de-excitation, mainly by spontaneous transitions. When conditions of LTE are satisfied the number density of atoms excited to any state r is completely determined by *Boltzmann's equation* (Lochte-Holtgreven 1968)

$$\frac{n_r}{n_g} = \frac{g_r}{g_g} \exp\left(-\frac{E_r}{kT}\right) \qquad (6.8)$$

where n_g and n_r are the number densities of atoms in the ground state and excited state respectively, E_r is the energy difference between the excited and ground states, and g_r and g_g are known small integers called the statistical weights of the states.

The excited atoms radiate exactly as in the case of low pressure discharges: as the pressure is increased, the wavelength of the lines becomes less precise, i.e. the lines become increasingly broadened. Collisions between emitting atoms and other gas atoms or electrons cause random perturbations of the energy levels, resulting in line broadening and frequently also a shift in the position of the line.

Collisions between emitting atoms and the buffer gas atoms (van der Waals interaction) both shift the line centre and broaden it asymmetrically, i.e. the line extends further towards the red end of the spectrum than to the blue end (Griem 1964). In the hot core of the discharge, where the number densities of the electrons and ions are substantial, interaction with electric fields during collisions between emitting atoms and charged particles (Stark interactions) broadens the lines symmetrically and shifts the line centre (Lochte-Holtgreven 1968).

The radiation generated by transitions from an excited state to the ground state is known as resonance radiation. These spectral lines are subject to a special kind of broadening called resonance broadening, which occurs during collisions between excited and ground state atoms of the same type (Griem 1964); the line width increases linearly with the number density of the atoms. The yellow sodium D-lines and mercury 253·7 nm line are important examples of resonance lines. These primary line broadening mechanisms give rise to widths of the order of a few ångströms.

Detailed treatments of radiation transfer in gases are given by Armstrong and Nicholls (1972) and Chandrasekhar (1960). Under conditions of LTE the radiation emission coefficient approaches the product of the Planck function (Eq. 6.2) and the plasma absorption coefficient (a form of Kirchhoff's law, Griem 1964). A de-excitation process with a high transition probability must correspond to an excitation process with a similarly high absorption probability; in practical terms strong spectral lines are always self-absorbed in a high pressure discharge. In a high pressure sodium lamp the high number density of sodium atoms near the arc tube wall gives rise to considerable self-absorption. The result is a self-reversed spectral line, in which the radiation near the line centre is absorbed almost completely. This effect is clearly shown in the high pressure sodium lamp spectrum (Chap. 13), which has a dark centre between two bright wings. The width of this self-reversed line is about 100 ångströms, i.e. it is much broader than expected for the primary broadening mechanisms. The width is attributable to repeated absorption and re-emission processes; this phenomenon is termed secondary broadening. It is similar to the radiation trapping described in Sect. 6.3.3, but it is intensified by the high pressure. The line appears to be broad because the centre of the line is completely removed by self-absorption, and only the wide base of the absorption line escapes (see, for example, de Groot and van Vliet 1975). Sodium radiation generated in a metal halide lamp experiences much less self-absorption because of the low sodium number density near the wall, resulting in correspondingly narrower spectral lines.

The spectrum, and thereby the colour rendering and colour temperature, of the lamp can be tailored by the addition of a variety of elements, each of which has its own characteristic spectrum. The transition elements which generate a multitude of feeble lines, especially in the blue region of the spectrum, are commonly used. Continuous molecular spectra are important, but are relatively weak because molecules only exist in cool parts of the plasma. Various models for evaluating these discharges have been devised (see, for example, Eardley et al. 1979).

At higher pressures the broadened lines merge together and form *continuum* radiation. Where there are self-reversed lines involved, these show as dark lines or bands against the background continuum (as in the case of the Fraunhofer lines in the sun's spectrum). Continua can also arise from transitions involving free electrons and ions. In the limit, at the highest pressures and greatest currents, the radiation tends towards black body radiation of the same type as that emitted from solids, and the discharge is effectively an incandescent gas. Since the temperature can be much greater than that of any solid, a much greater radiant intensity can be obtained from a discharge. Note that even when these conditions are not reached the maximum intensity at any wavelength cannot exceed that of a black body at the temperature of the discharge, and is normally well below that corresponding to the maximum temperature of the discharge in most sources at moderate pressure. There is therefore an absolute limit to the intensity which can be obtained at any given discharge temperature.

In the case of low pressure discharges it is the electron temperature which establishes this limit; since this can be very high, the spectral intensity of a given line can also be very high, but since the lines are narrow, the total intensity from any transition is usually less than in a corresponding high pressure discharge.

6.3.5 Luminescence

Luminescence is the emission of light from a body in excess of its thermal radiation at the same temperature, or the temperature of the exciting source. It is characteristic of luminescence that the exciting source is often non-thermal in nature (as, for example, the energetic electrons in cathode-ray tubes) and it is therefore not limited by the same thermodynamic consideration as all the processes described so far.

Frequently luminescent materials are near room temperature when operating. The alternative term *fluorescence* is sometimes applied to an instantaneous rise or decay of emission, in contrast to the visibly slow decay of *phosphorescence* occurring after the excitation process.

Physical principles   Figure 6.6 shows idealized energy level schemes for electrons in fluorescent, phosphorescent, cathodoluminescent, and thermoluminescent materials.

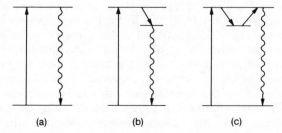

(a)   (b)   (c)

Fig. 6.6 Simplified representation of (a) luminescence, (b) luminescence with relaxation, and (c) luminescence with trapping

The simplest possible case is shown in Fig. 6.6a, where an electron is excited by some non-thermal means, such as the absorption of a photon or a collision with another electron. A photon is emitted when the electron returns to the ground state. The energy, or (by Eq. 6.1) the frequency, of the incoming photon or electron need only be greater than the energy gap, whereas the wavelength of the emitted photon is defined by the energy gap. The active electrons are normally bound to impurity atoms, which are distributed randomly and thinly throughout a host crystal lattice (Curie 1963). Therefore these active electrons experience a spread of crystal electric fields, which results in a broadening of the emitted spectrum.

In fluorescence there may be an intermediate and non-radiative transition (relaxation), as shown in Fig. 6.6b, before the radiative transition generates a photon of longer wavelength than might have been expected. The energy level system for phosphorescence is slightly more complex (Fig. 6.6c); it includes a metastable state, which by definition will not allow a direct transition to the ground state. The electron falls from its excited state onto a level called an electron trap. There it remains until it is induced by receiving energy to return to the excited state. The electron may fall to the ground state, with the emission of a photon. In thermoluminescent materials the energy required to stimulate the transition is supplied by heating.

Actual luminescent materials have much more complicated systems of energy levels and intermediate transitions than those shown in Fig. 6.6 (Goldberg 1966). The levels may relate to single atoms or molecules, or they may be broad energy bands, which extend throughout the material. Emission may take place at the same atom or centre as excitation, or the energy may be transferred to another region first. In zinc sulphide, for example, and similar materials, the upper level is a conduction band through which the excited electrons may pass from one region to another before dropping to a lower level and radiating: these materials therefore behave as a type of semiconductor. In ionic materials energy can be transferred from one centre to another by a quantum process known as *resonance transfer* (no radiation is involved in this, see Dexter 1953). Thus, in the halophosphates used in fluorescent lamps, excitation occurs in antimony ions: some of this is radiated from the same site, after relaxation, giving a blue radiation, but a proportion is transferred by this process to manganese ions a short distance away, subsequently producing an orange radiation. In this case the manganese is considered to be the *activator*, while the antimony is called the primary activator or *sensitizer* (Sect. 8.3.1).

Fluorescence, phosphorescence, thermoluminescence, and cathodoluminescence (the list is not exhaustive) are all closely related; only the means of excitation and the path of de-excitation differ. In Sect. 8.3 luminescence is classified in terms of the method by which energy is supplied.

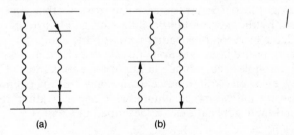

Fig. 6.7 Stokes' law: (a) conventional phosphor obeying Stokes' law and (b) anti-Stokes phosphor

The most important of these for our purpose is excitation by electromagnetic radiation. This is governed by an important relation known as Stokes' law (Goldberg 1966), which states that the wavelength of the emitted radiation is longer than that of the absorbed radiation. This is illustrated by Fig. 6.7a: evidently the energy of the emitted radiation must be less than that absorbed. All the phosphors used in fluorescent and discharge lamps for converting ultraviolet to visible light (Chap. 8), or for detecting X-rays or gamma rays (Chap. 17), obey Stokes' law.

Recently, however, certain types of phosphor have been developed which convert infrared into visible radiation. This is only possible if two or more quanta of the exciting radiation are absorbed for each emitted quantum, for example as in Fig. 6.7b. These clearly violate Stokes' law, and are called anti-Stokes phosphors, or two-quantum phosphors (Chap. 8). Since a double absorption is required they are only efficient under very intense incident radiation, and have mainly been of interest in semiconductor electroluminescence, discussed below.

6.3.6   Electroluminescence

Electroluminescence is the direct conversion of electrical energy into light, without any intermediate process such as heating. The two main mechanisms by which this is achieved are (a) the recombination of current carriers in certain semiconductors (Williams and Hall 1978, Thornton 1967) and (b) via the excitation of luminescent centres in phosphors (Thornton 1967, Curie 1963).

In pure form semiconductor materials have very high (intrinsic) resistivities. However the addition of small quantities of certain impurities can decrease the resistivity dramatically; some impurities (called donors) induce n-type conductivity, in which the current is carried by negatively charged electrons, whilst other impurities (called acceptors) induce p-type conductivity, in which the current is carried by positively charged holes. The electron levels in semiconductors are broadened so much that they form two bands: the valence and conduction bands. An electron in the conduction band can recombine with a hole in the valence band, and the generated photon has a wavelength which corresponds to the energy difference between the valence and conduction bands. Thus semiconductor lamps, Light Emitting Diodes (LEDs), produce monochromatic light whose colour can be changed by varying the band gap. This is an inherent property of the material. The classic treatment of the physics of semiconductors is given by Smith (1964).

Electroluminescence in phosphors is still not completely understood. Luminescence can be achieved in single crystals or powders which are doped with suitable activators by exciting them with either an a.c. or a d.c. field. There are two main explanations of this type of electroluminescence. The first is that electrons which have been accelerated by the electric field collide with and ionize an activator atom; the ion is then available to recombine radiatively with the energetic free electrons. The second is that electrons are injected into material which is naturally p-type (or vice versa); the electrons and holes recombine via impurity centres (Sect. 17.1.1).

Both types of electroluminescence are low current phenomena, so that they find application as indicators or luminescent panels, rather than as illuminants. The devices and their applications are described in Chap. 17.

6.4   Production of coherent radiation

6.4.1   Principles of laser operation

A laser is a device which generates coherent radiation (Sect. 6.2) in a well-defined narrow pencil of light, instead of radiating in all directions. The radiation has a very small spread of wavelengths, i.e. it is highly monochromatic.

Photons can be generated when electrons fall from an excited level to a lower level. Normally, most of these transitions occur spontaneously and only a small minority are stimulated by photons (Sect. 6.2). However, if the populations of the atomic energy levels can be inverted, i.e. with more electrons in the upper level than in the lower level, then the majority of transitions may be stimulated by photons. A generated photon travels in the same direction and has the same phase as the stimulating photon. The process avalanches since the number of photons doubles at each stage: hence we have an *amplifier* which is called a *laser*.

Physically, lasers consist of a volume of material containing suitable atoms, placed between a pair of partially transmitting mirrors which form a resonant cavity. The material can be a solid, a liquid, or a gas. A means of exciting the atoms to the point of inverting the population must be provided before lasing occurs. This might be achieved, for example, by irradiating the material with an intense flash of light or by a suitable form of discharge. Provided that the gain in the bulk of the material is greater than the losses in the cavity, the device will act as a laser and produce a beam of radiation, which is extremely intense, has a well-defined wavelength, and is spatially coherent. For a more detailed description see, for example, Corney (1977).

6.4.2 Available laser sources

Lasers have been produced from many materials; only some of the more important ones are described here.

Single crystal lasers In 1960 the first laser was demonstrated using a ruby rod which produced red coherent radiation. The ends of the ruby crystal were polished and coated with a reflecting film to form a resonant cavity and the chromium ion was pumped into the excited state by irradiating the ruby with a xenon flash tube. The performance of ruby lasers is impressive: pulses of about 10^{11} W lasting for 10^{-8} s have been produced (Lipson and Lipson 1969).

Lasers have been made from many other crystals: in particular neodymium-doped yttrium–aluminium garnet, which lases at 1·064 microns. Some glasses can also be used.

Gas lasers The majority of gas lasers operate through excitation by collisions with electrons in a discharge. The *helium–neon* laser is a popular low power laser in the red (632·8 nm). The pressures of helium and neon are typically a few thousandths and ten-thousandths of an atmosphere respectively. The neon atoms are responsible for the laser action. Power levels of tens of milliwatts are typical (Cherrington 1979). The *argon ion laser* generates lines at 488 nm and 514·5 nm; d.c. powers of 100 W can be achieved, with pulsed outputs of the order of tens of kilowatts (Cherrington 1979). The *carbon dioxide laser* generates continuous infrared power of the order of a hundred kilowatts at a wavelength of 10·6 microns. The efficiency of the system is enhanced by the addition of helium and nitrogen to give efficiencies of between 10 and 15% (Cherrington 1979).

Semiconductor lasers Semiconductor lasers resemble light emitting diodes (Sect. 6.3.6), and operate in both pulsed and d.c. modes in the visible and infrared. Since the output can be modulated easily, semiconductor lasers are used for wide-band communications in spite of their low power (Gooch 1969, Williams and Hall 1978).

Dye lasers Certain fluorescent dyes exhibit laser action when dissolved in an appropriate solvent. The dye is pumped either by another laser or by a xenon flash tube (Lengyel 1971, Snavely 1969). The laser operates at room temperature with an efficiency of about 10%. Different dyes are chosen to give different wavelengths throughout the visible region: the wavelength distribution in a particular case depends on the solvent and the dye concentrations. Dye lasers are important because their emission can be tuned throughout the visible region.

6.4.3   Applications of lasers

The principal features distinguishing laser radiation from ordinary radiation are, in brief, that it is much more intense, directional, monochromatic, and coherent. High intensity pulses of extremely short duration (10^{-11} s) can also be produced. These properties indicate its main applications and potential applications, of which there are so many that only a few can be mentioned.

The high degree of parallelism obtainable provides applications in surveying and optical alignment and, when pulsed, in ranging and tracking rockets, missiles, and other military objects. Lenses or mirrors can focus the radiation into a very small area, providing localized sources of energy, or heat for melting, welding, drilling, etc., where special precision, special atmospheres, or special materials are involved. Lasers are used in lamp making for cutting glass and welding metal electrodes. Other areas are micromachining and certain medical applications, such as retinal surgery on the eye. Extreme applications of this type are the focusing of giant pulses to produce very high temperatures, with a view to triggering thermonuclear devices, and for various military purposes.

There are many scientific applications in very high speed photography, spectroscopy, and plasma diagnostics; also in the field of non-linear optics, including frequency multiplication (for example the generation of ultraviolet radiation from red light), and frequency mixing (the generation of sum and difference frequencies): these are phenomena which only occur at extremely high radiation densities. Laser radiation has revolutionized optical interferometry, leading to much greater flexibility and refinement. Applications include precision mensuration of lengths, determination of translational and rotational velocities, and determination of refractive index variations.

A related development is holography in which objects illuminated by coherent light are recorded as transformed images called holograms (Butters 1971, Fincham and Freeman 1980, Stitch 1979). These contain much more information than a conventional image, such as a photograph. For example the three-dimensional properties of the object are included, and different views can be reconstructed from the same hologram by varying the viewing arrangement, again using coherent light. One important engineering application is to the study of small deformations arising, for example, from wear or thermal changes. The spatial structure of moving particles, as in smoke, or convection currents, as in lamps, can be studied by holography (Ostrovsky et al. 1980). Holograms are used for data storage: a high density of information can be achieved, but it is difficult to alter the data. A further application in the computer industry is the use of lasers in high speed, high quality printers.

The coherent nature of laser radiation has led to much consideration of its possibilities in communications. The high frequencies available indicate enormous potential for the transmission of information via optical fibres and in space; terrestrial communication is hampered by scattering in rain and fog.

Further reading

Beiser A, 1967, *Concepts of modern physics* (New York: McGraw-Hill, Kogakusha)
Cobine J D, 1958, *Gaseous Conductors* (New York: Dover Publications)
Hoyaux M F, 1968, *Arc physics* (Berlin: Springer-Verlag)
Lipson S G and Lipson H, 1969, *Optical physics* (Cambridge: The University Press)
Waymouth J R, 1971, *Electric discharge lamps* (Cambridge, Mass: MIT Press)
Williams E W and Hall R, 1978, *Luminescence and the light emitting diode* (Oxford: Pergamon)

Part II
Lamps

7 Lamp materials

The performance of lamps is often critically dependent on the behaviour of the materials of construction and several instances exist where technical innovations have had to await the development of suitable materials. Material behaviour and exploitation are governed by the inter-relationship between the physical, structural, and compositional properties and so it is these material parameters that demand attention during the development, manufacture, and operation of lamps.

Materials used in lamps have to perform many diverse functions under a variety of conditions and so it is perhaps not surprising that a wide range of materials are utilized in lamp engineering. In this chapter the four main groups of materials, namely glasses, ceramics, metals, and gases, are discussed in terms of their manufacture, properties, and applications.

7.1 Glasses

The term glass refers to a range of non-crystalline inorganic materials with widely differing compositions and properties. The vast majority of commercially produced glasses can however be divided into three main groups: soda-lime silicate, lead-alkali silicate, and borosilicate glasses. The type most commonly used in the lamp industry is soda-lime silicate glass, since with only minor variations in batch composition it is used as the envelope material for general incandescent, fluorescent, and low wattage discharge lamps.

Relatively cheap raw materials are fed continuously into one end of a large tank furnace at a rate which balances that at which the molten glass is delivered to machines at the other end. The properties of the glass are designed to provide the optimum viscosity–temperature characteristics to enable components to be made on high speed machines at maximum efficiency. In the high speed manufacture of incandescent lamp bulbs on the Corning ribbon machine (Tooley 1971) a preshaped, horizontal ribbon of glass travels between two endless belts, the top belt consisting of a series of blowing heads and the bottom belt consisting of a corresponding series of moulds. As the belts and the glass ribbon travel on, the glass is blown into the moulds which have been sprayed with water and are rotating. The steam cushion formed between the glass and the mould leaves the bulb with a polished surface whilst the rotation eliminates mould seams. The shaped bulb is finally cracked from the ribbon and dropped on to an annealing conveyor. This process produces up to 60 000 bulbs per hour per machine, depending on bulb size. If pearl bulbs are required, the interior of the bulb is treated, subsequent to the annealing process, with an etching fluid comprising mainly hydrofluoric acid and then washed and dried.

Tubing for fluorescent lamp envelopes is continuously drawn from the same type of furnace using either the Danner or the Vello process (Hawkins 1965). In the Danner process glass flows from the furnace at a controlled rate on to the top of an inclined, rotating, hollow refractory mandrel. Air is blown down the centre of the mandrel as tubing is drawn from the bottom by a drawing machine, which may be 50 m distant. The glass tube, as it solidifies, is supported between the mandrel and the drawing machine by a series of shaped carbon rollers placed at regular intervals. The size of tubing drawn depends on the diameter of the mandrel, draw speed, amount of blowing air, glass temperature, and cooling rate.

The internal glass components of fluorescent and general incandescent lamps, and also many types of small incandescent lamp bulbs, particularly for wedge base type lamps (Sect. 9.4), are made from lead-alkali silicate glass. Lead glass, as it is termed, is preferred to soda-lime glass because of its higher electrical resistivity, which prevents electrolysis occurring in the pinch seal. The glass seals readily to soda-lime envelopes and has a somewhat lower softening point and longer working temperature range than does soda-lime glass, all factors which assist in lamp making. The standard lead glass used in lamp making contains about 30% by weight of lead oxide. In recent years however, because of the high cost and the introduction of more stringent health and safety regulations concerning the handling of lead compounds, there has been an increase in the use of glasses containing 20–22% lead oxide. These have similar working characteristics to standard lead glass and, although they have a lower electrical resistivity, it is adequate for the majority of lamp applications.

For lamps in which the operating temperature is too high for soda-lime glass, such as envelopes for conventional projector and high wattage discharge lamps, borosilicate glass is used. In addition to its ability to withstand higher operating temperatures, it also has a much lower thermal expansion coefficient and thus withstands greater changes in temperature. This leads to its use in sealed beam and other specialized types of lamps which may be subjected to sudden temperature variations. Lead and borosilicate glasses are usually melted in a similar way to soda-lime glasses, although often on a smaller scale.

Where even higher service temperatures are required aluminosilicate glass is used. This is the most refractory conventional glass used in the lamp industry. Its thermal shock resistance is however inferior to that of most borosilicate glasses. It is produced in relatively small quantities, although it is now being used increasingly for the envelopes of small low wattage tungsten halogen lamps (Sect. 10.2.2). Glasses for this application are essentially free from alkalis and are usually of the alkaline-earth aluminosilicate type.

A glass having a small and very specialized application in the lamp industry is sodium resistant glass (Sect. 12.2.1). The powerful reducing properties of hot alkaline vapours produce rapid blackening in normal silicate glasses by reduction, and this can be eliminated by using glasses which contain little or no silica or other readily reducible oxides.

Of the two basic compositions shown in Table 7.1, the glass containing silica stains slowly throughout life, whereas the silica-free glass does not discolour but physically absorbs ionized argon which eventually prevents the lamp from starting. The choice of glass for the lamp is therefore something of a compromise and it is the silica-containing glass that is used. Unfortunately, all these aluminoborate glasses are readily attacked by atmospheric moisture and are expensive and difficult to work. To produce a durable, economic material suitable for lamp fabrication 'ply-tubing' is manufactured by flashing a thin layer (about 100 μm) of the sodium resistant glass onto the inside of a tube of standard soda-lime glass.

In the development of more compact and powerful light sources conventional glasses became inadequate and led to the use of transparent silica as an envelope

Table 7.1 Composition and physical properties of materials for lamp envelopes

Nominal composition (weight %)	Soda-lime silicate	Lead-alkali silicate (i)	Lead-alkali silicate (ii)	Boro-silicate (tungsten sealing)	Alumino-silicate (molybdenum sealing)	Alumino-borate (sodium resistant)	Alumino-borate (sodium resistant)	Vycor	Vitreous silica	Ceramic alumina
SiO_2	73	57	64	75	63	8		96	100	
Na_2O	16	5	8	4		14	2			
K_2O	1	7	6	2			8			
CaO	5				9	6				
MgO	4									
Al_2O_3	1	1	2	1	16	24	26			99.9
PbO		30	20							
B_2O_3				18	12	48	22	3		
BaO							42			
Property										
Expansion coefficient (per °C × 10^{-7})	92	91	93	37	43	83	91	8	5	80/86[1]
Melting point (°C)										2050
Softening point (°C)	700	630	640	770	1020			~1530	1580	
Annealing point (°C)	520	430	440	520	800			~1020	1190	
Log_{10} of d.c. resistivity at 250 °C	6.5	9.3	8.5	8.6	12.6			~10	11.7	11.3[2]

Notes:
Expansion coefficients are for the range 50 °C to 300 °C.
Softening point corresponds to a dynamic viscosity of $10^{6.6}$ Ns m^{-2}.
Annealing point corresponds to a dynamic viscosity of 10^{12} Ns m^{-2}.
(1) for 25 °C to 800 °C and 25 °C to 1200 °C respectively.
(2) at 500 °C.

material. This material is essentially pure silicon dioxide having only a few parts per million (p.p.m.) of other metals and hydroxyl, that is OH^- groups, present as impurities. It is colloquially known as 'quartz' in the lamp industry, although it is vitreous, not crystalline.

Two main processes are used for manufacturing tubing for lamp making. The vacuum melting process uses particles of natural quartz which are first sorted, acid washed, crushed, and screened and then melted in a carbon mould in a vacuum furnace to produce a thick walled, bubble-free, tubular ingot. After cooling, the carbon is removed and the ingot is ground to size using diamond tools. It is then placed in a second furnace which is fitted with a mandrel and an orifice in the base. The ingot is reheated in a reducing atmosphere of forming gas (about 90% N_2 and 10% H_2) and tubing is drawn through the orifice. This method produces extremely high quality tubing which is virtually free from airlines and has a low hydroxyl content of about 4 p.p.m. It is however expensive, so in order to reduce costs a continuous single stage process has been developed. Quartz particles, which have been washed and sorted, are fed into a furnace and melted in a refractory metal crucible in an atmosphere of forming gas. The feed rate is controlled to maintain a constant level of melt as tubing is drawn through the base, as in the second stage of the vacuum process. The tubing contains many airlines caused by entrapped furnace gases and is of inferior optical quality to vacuum fused material. Its hydroxyl content is around 50 p.p.m.

This process has recently been dramatically improved by replacing the forming gas atmosphere in the crucible with a mixture of helium and hydrogen (Antezak et al. 1973). Since both gases diffuse rapidly and are readily soluble in fused silica, there are fewer airlines and the optical quality of the tubing is much improved. The hydroxyl content remains about the same, but by baking the tubing at around 1000 °C for a few hours this level can be reduced to less than 10 p.p.m. if the furnace atmosphere is air, or to essentially zero if baked in vacuo. This baked material is thus a viable alternative to vacuum melted silica and is being increasingly used over a wide range of lamp types. Furthermore, because of increasing costs and supply difficulties associated with the use of natural quartz crystal, manufacturers are making increasing use of purified quartz sands as the raw material in both processes.

The main advantages of fused silica are its transparency, resistance to thermal shock, and high operating temperature (up to 900 °C). The hydroxyl content is extremely important as far as envelope materials for tungsten halogen and metal halide lamps are concerned. In many applications a level of below 10 p.p.m. is required and in certain critical designs the aim is to obtain a zero hydroxyl level.

An alternative to fused silica for certain tungsten halogen lamps is the material Vycor†. It starts as a borosilicate glass and as such can be worked and shaped using standard equipment to normal working tolerances. A heat-treatment schedule then induces separation into two phases, the main one consisting almost entirely of silica. An acid leaching process removes the other phase leaving behind a porous body, consisting of silica plus a small amount of alkali borates. High temperature firing consolidates the structure and results in the article shrinking about 35% by volume (Volf 1961). The amount of shrinkage can be predicted precisely and thus an article having a good dimensional control allied with good optical quality can be achieved. However, the presence of a significant amount of boric oxide in the final material limits its use for lamp envelopes.

† 'Vycor' is a registered trade mark of Corning Glass Works, Corning, New York.

7.2 Ceramics

7.2.1 Optical ceramics

The incompatibility of glasses containing silica with alkali metal vapours at high temperatures and pressures has led to a demand for lamp envelope materials resistant to chemical attack under these conditions, particularly for the construction of high pressure sodium lamps. Modern developments in ceramic technology have made it possible to produce polycrystalline metal oxide bodies of almost theoretical densities. The essentially pore-free nature of articles produced from these materials means that they are able to transmit a large proportion of any visible light incident upon them and this property, together with their intrinsic refractoriness, makes them valuable materials in the construction of high temperature arc tubes (Parrott 1974). Oxides which may be produced in translucent or transparent form include alumina, common spinel, magnesia, beryllia, zirconia, thoria, yttria, and various rare-earth oxides.

At present, by far the most commonly used material is alumina. In addition to its occurrence in various ores, alumina is found naturally in comparatively pure form as corundum and the gemstones sapphire and ruby. It crystallizes into two distinct forms. The poorly defined cubic gamma alumina is stable only below about 1000 °C, whilst above this temperature the stable alpha alumina is formed. Alpha alumina is one of the most stable of all compounds, being practically insoluble in strong mineral acids and resistant to attack by most metals (including sodium) and dry halogens; some reaction does occur with alkalis at high temperatures. It has a melting point of 2050 °C and displays an adequate resistance to thermal shock. Alumina powder is normally relatively coarse and contains sodium, silicon, iron, and calcium as major impurities. Powders of the highest purity are obtained by decomposition of purified organic or inorganic precursors, such as ammonium alum, and may have sub-micron particle diameters, according to the calcination technique. Such sub-micron powders typically contain up to 40 p.p.m. each of sodium and silicon, 20 p.p.m. iron, and 10 p.p.m. calcium as the main impurities, these levels being tolerable for the production of sintered alumina of high translucency. Sodium impurities are progressively injurious leading to exaggerated grain-growth, entrapment of pores, and hence loss of translucency during sintering. On sintering, silicon in any appreciable quantity diffuses to grain boundaries and would be readily attacked by the sodium in a high pressure lamp, leading to early failure.

The process of sintering alumina to translucency (Coble 1957) involves the inclusion of a small quantity of a grain-growth inhibiting agent, such as magnesia, which on sintering segregates at the boundaries of the alumina grains, reducing their high temperature mobility. Diffusion path lengths of gases entrapped in closed pores within the alumina grains are thus minimized, allowing the gases and atomic vacancies (missing atoms) to diffuse away to grain boundaries during sintering (Kingery et al. 1976). Since gases are then able to escape readily from the sintering body along grain boundaries, a polycrystalline mass of almost theoretical density results. In addition, if the alumina is sintered in an atmosphere of hydrogen, the gas is able to diffuse readily through the alumina lattice. Hence the contents of any pores isolated from grain boundaries are also able to escape during sintering, leading to a finished body of the highest density ($3980 \, kg \, m^{-3}$).

Polycrystalline translucent alumina (PCA) tubes may be fabricated by normal ceramic methods. The starting powder is prepared by thoroughly admixing the grain-growth regulating agents and a small amount of organic binder with pure alumina powder; it is then isostatically pressed to a tubular shape in automatic machinery. After presintering the pressed shapes at 1100 °C in air to increase their strength and remove the binder, the tubes are sintered usually in a hydrogen atmosphere or in vacuo at a temperature of about 1800 °C for a few hours. The densification process which occurs during sintering is used to make the 'monolithic' end seal in which alumina end plugs having a higher pressed density than the tubing are inserted into the ends of the tubes prior to sintering. The density of the plugs is optimized so that on sintering good contact is maintained as the tube shrinks over the plug, allowing grain-growth to occur across the interface and the production of a hermetic seal in this region. This type of end construction is used extensively in the manufacture of SON lamps (Chap. 13).

Ceramic alumina made by this process is translucent because of the essential absence of porosity (Peelan 1976). Figure 7.1 compares the pore-free microstructure

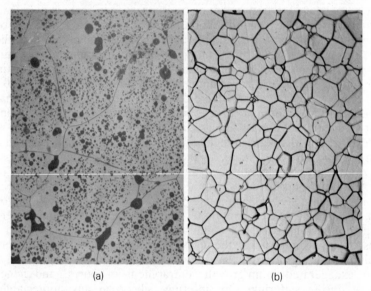

(a)   (b)

Fig. 7.1   (a) porous microstructure of a conventional impervious ceramic and (b) pore-free microstructure of translucent polycrystalline alumina. × 200

of dense polycrystalline alumina with that of a conventional impervious ceramic. The mean grain diameter of the dense alumina is of the order of 40 μm. Although the straight-line transmission or transparency in the visible region of a parallel-sided piece of material 1 mm thick is only about 15%, the integrated transmission through a tube of 1 mm wall thickness exceeds 90%.

A fully transparent form of alumina in tubular form, grown directly from molten alumina to the finished dimensions, has been produced (Tyco Labs 1970). These tubes are essentially pure single crystal sapphire and, although the material displays excellent thermal and chemical properties and good transparency, the total integrated transmission of visible light through a tube is not much greater than that of a polycrystalline tube. Furthermore, its anisotropic thermal expansion makes it extremely difficult to make reliable, long lasting seals to this material.

The other oxides mentioned are at present of little practical importance, although some recent work (Rhodes 1978) on yttria containing amounts of either lanthana or alumina as a sintering aid has shown it can be fabricated into suitable shapes and sintered to produce a material with good optical and thermal properties.

7.2.2 Cermets

One of the major limitations of refractory oxide ceramics is their lack of ductility. This imposes severe limitations on the design of structural components and, although the strength of ceramic materials can be markedly improved by reducing the grain size and level of porosity, catastrophic failure usually occurs once the fracture stress is exceeded. An increase in toughness can be achieved by the incorporation of one or more ductile phases in the ceramic matrix, but the amount and geometrical disposition of the second phase profoundly affects the strengthening and toughening of the brittle matrix composites.

A cermet may be defined as a ceramic material containing a proportion of metal as a separate phase, for example an alumina ceramic containing tungsten or molybdenum. Such material may either be an insulator or an electrical conductor, depending on the relative proportions of the oxide and the metal and on the particle size and distribution of the metal in the sintered material.

A cermet has been developed (Evans et al. 1976) in which a low volume fraction (less than 0·2) of refractory metal is used to thinly coat alumina granules and produce a continuous conductive network extending through the cermet. This electrically conducting material has a thermal expansion coefficient closely matching that of alumina, which leads to its use as an end closure material for sintered alumina arc tubes in high pressure sodium and metal halide lamps (Sects 13.2.2 and 15.6).

7.2.3 Conventional ceramics

Although the term conventional ceramics covers materials having widely different compositions and properties, the most common types consist mainly of alumina and silica in varying proportions. These materials are opaque and generally impervious, although they contain varying amounts of internal porosity and they are selected for their mechanical, electrical, and thermal properties. These ceramics are most commonly used as bases and end caps for lamps and as such they need to have good mechanical strength and thermal shock resistance, be good electrical insulators over a range of temperatures, and be resistant to attack by atmospheric moisture, etc.

The traditional electrically insulating ceramic material is electrical porcelain, which is a mixture of clay (hydrous aluminium silicate), feldspar (alkali-aluminosilicates), and flint (silica). This material however has a rather high loss factor (power factor × dielectric constant), its resistance to thermal shock is only fair, and its electrical resistivity decreases rapidly with increasing temperature. These shortcomings have led to porcelain being largely superseded by steatite materials, which consist mainly of talc (hydrous magnesium silicate) and clay, plus small amounts of alkali or alkaline-earth oxides. Steatites are cheap and easy to produce by automatic machines and can be produced in a wide range of shapes to suit individual lamp designs.

7.3 Metals

7.3.1 Filament materials

As explained in Chap. 6, the total radiant energy emitted by an incandescent body increases with temperature, as does the radiation within the visible region of the wavelength spectrum. Radiation from incandescent light sources is usually below that of the perfect black body radiator and their emissivity (Sect. 6.3.1) can vary with the wavelength of the radiation, as shown by the curves in Fig. 7.2, and also to some

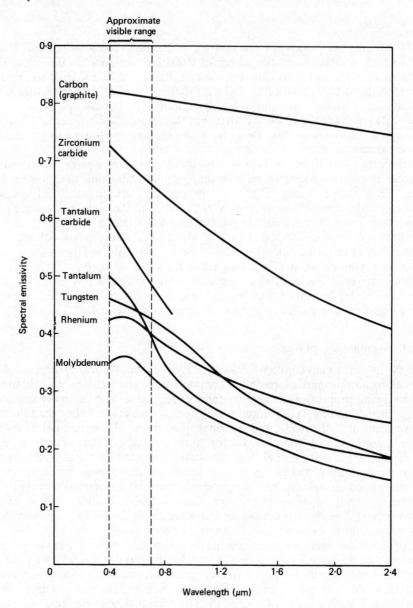

Fig. 7.2   Spectral emissivity of various materials at 2000 K

extent with temperature. It can be seen that for carbon the emissivity is almost independent of wavelength, but in contrast the other materials have a higher emissivity in the visible range than in the infrared, and are thus attractive as lamp filament materials.

To achieve a high efficiency a filament material must therefore be capable of operating at as high a temperature as is consistent with satisfactory performance and at the same time act as a selective radiator. Other desirable properties include low vapour pressure, adequate strength and ductility, and microstructural stability.

Unfortunately, no single material exists that satisfies all the diverse requirements and so some compromise has to be made.

The first practical lamps made by Swan and Edison in 1879 contained carbon filaments, but, unfortunately, the high melting point (3600 °C) of this element could not be fully exploited as the high evaporation rate caused excessive darkening of the lamp bulb. Platinum (m.p. 1772 °C) and osmium (m.p. 3027 °C) were also tried as filaments, but a lack of thermal stability and high costs precluded their use on a commercial basis. Tantalum (m.p. 3000 °C) was used quite extensively in the early lamps, but from 1911 this metal was replaced by tungsten following the development of a process for making ductile tungsten in wire form (Coolidge 1909). Considerable effort has been applied to the development of filament materials possessing greater thermal stability and more favourable emissive properties, but so far no material has emerged that is likely to supersede tungsten in the forseeable future.

Tungsten used for filament manufacture is extracted from ores containing the minerals scheelite, $CaWO_4$, and wolframite $(FeMn)WO_4$. The ore concentrates are chemically treated to produce pure tungsten trioxide, WO_3, from which the metallic powder is obtained by a high temperature reduction with hydrogen. The powder is subsequently pressed into bars and the tungsten densified by sintering at temperatures approaching 3000 °C. Further densification occurs during fabrication into rods by hot rolling and swaging operations, after which the tungsten is progressively drawn into wire of the required diameter. Throughout, strict control has to be maintained over the level of impurities since quite small quantities of elements such as carbon, nitrogen, oxygen, iron, and nickel can adversely affect the mechanical properties of the metal or promote adverse chemical interactions between the filament and the gases used in halogen lamps (Chap. 10).

In the shaping of coiled filaments the tungsten wire is helically wound on either an iron or molybdenum mandrel, while in coiled coil configurations the primary coil is wound again on to a second but larger mandrel. The coiled wires are then heat-treated to remove internal stresses and the mandrels removed by preferential dissolution in hydrochloric or nitro-sulphuric acids. Extreme accuracy in coil geometry and dimensions is essential since the performance of a filament is very sensitive to parameters such as wire diameter, pitch, and the coil length and diameter.

The microstructure of a metal often has a controlling influence on its engineering properties and this is particularly so in the case of the production and operation of tungsten lamp filaments. In the as-drawn condition tungsten wire possesses a fibrous grain structure (Fig. 7.3a) and it is essential that this particular property is retained during coiling since only in this microstructural state does the tungsten wire possess sufficient strength and ductility to accommodate the stresses and strains imposed during the shaping of the coil. However, in order to attain adequate strength at high temperatures it is necessary to replace the fibrous grains by grains of a much larger size. This is achieved when the tungsten is heated above its recrystallization temperature and the distorted fibrous grains are replaced by larger strain-free grains. As the microstructural properties of the recrystallized tungsten have an important effect upon the high temperature strength and dimensional stability of a lamp filament, the recrystallization behaviour is subject to close metallurgical control.

Pure tungsten is not suitable for filament applications since after recrystallization the grains do not attain the size and shape which are essential to the development of adequate high temperature strength. Individual grain boundaries tend to completely transverse the wire diameter, an alignment which promotes grain boundary shearing and 'offsetting'. This offsetting causes a localized reduction in the wire section and ultimately leads to overheating and a fusion failure of the wire.

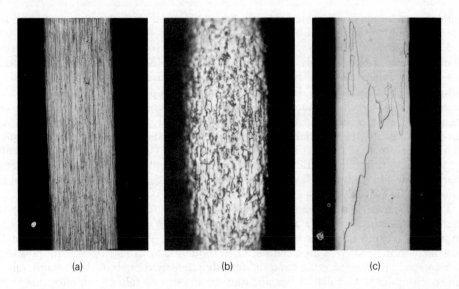

(a)   (b)   (c)

Fig. 7.3 Microstructure of tungsten wires: (a) after drawing, (b) recrystallized wire doped with thoria, and (c) recrystallized wire doped with alkali silicate. × 200

The production of microstructures that are thermally stable and creep-resistant at filament operating temperatures (2200–3100 °C) is achieved through the use of small quantities of additives which are blended into the tungsten trioxide powder prior to hydrogen reduction. An oxide additive, such as thoria, is sometimes used when the need exists for tungsten filaments with a particular combination of physical and mechanical properties. However, the most widely used additives include a combination of potassium silicate and alumina, sometimes referred to as 'AKS' dopants.

The oxide dopants produce a recrystallized structure containing elongated and thermally stable grains which increase the filament resistance to mechanical shock, distortion, and grain boundary offsetting (Fig. 7.3b).

The AKS dopants (total concentration 100–150 p.p.m.) produce even larger grains with axially-aligned boundaries (Fig. 7.3c). Such a grain morphology is a prerequisite to the production of filaments with the greatest strength and sag resistance. It has now been established (Moon and Koo 1971) that the action of the combined dopants is to create linear arrays of very small voids, 5–100 nm in diameter, which preferentially control the movement of the grain boundaries during recrystallization. These dopant-induced voids can be readily observed by transmission electron microscopy (Fig. 7.4). The linearity, size, and spacing of the voids are critical structural parameters and are sensitively influenced by the chemical nature of the dopants, impurities, the oxide reduction and sintering schedules, and the thermomechanical treatments applied during wire and filament production.

Most incandescent lamp filaments are now made from AKS tungsten and only in special cases is use made of thoriated wire (0·5–3·0% ThO_2) or tungsten with 3–5% rhenium. Thoriated wire may be used for filaments subject to vibrational and impact loading and the tungsten–rhenium wire in cases where a particular combination of high strength and ductility is essential. However, the high cost of rhenium severely restricts the use of the alloy wire.

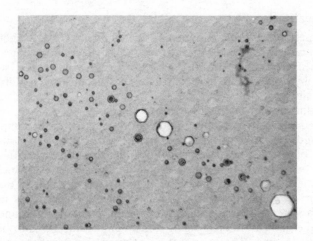

Fig. 7.4 Transmission electron micrograph showing arrays of voids in doped tungsten wire. × 50 000

7.3.2 Electrodes

The normal function of electrodes is to conduct electrical power into a discharge lamp and provide a copious supply of electrons to maintain the discharge. The electrode material must be a good emitter of electrons and also be capable of operating at high temperatures (1000–2500 °C) since only then can the necessary electron emission densities be attained. The electrode must have a low evaporation rate, not only to maintain its own life, but also to avoid excessive contamination of the lamp atmosphere. In addition, it must resist attack by substances in the ionized state and possess adequate mechanical strength and resistance to sputtering. Few materials fulfil these requirements and only tungsten and, to a lesser extent, tantalum have found commercial importance.

Tungsten is a copious emitter of electrons at temperatures over 2000 °C, but such high operating temperatures impose restrictions on lamp design and life. However, electron emission is considerably enhanced and operating temperatures accordingly reduced by coating the electrodes with one or more alkaline-earth oxides, e.g. barium oxide and strontium oxide. Alternately, a fine dispersion of thoria (0·5–3·0%) may be incorporated into the tungsten such that the thorium can readily diffuse to the electrode surface and increase emission. Thoriated tungsten electrodes are used in high wattage lamps where an emitter coating would be sputtered off and also in metal halide lamps where the halogen would react with alkaline-earth oxides to form involatile solids. In contrast, both thorium and tungsten react with the halogen to give a metal-halogen transport cycle in which the metal vapours can be redeposited on to the incandescent electrodes.

Occasionally, materials other than tungsten are used as electrodes. For example, in miniature low pressure discharge lamps the anode is of nickel whereas in some neon lamps, such as is used in advertising signs, the electrodes are of pure iron and unheated (cold cathodes).

7.3.3   Getter materials

During lamp operation some components, such as filaments and electrodes, achieve very high temperatures and as a consequence their behaviour becomes quite sensitive to the gaseous environment. Interaction with contaminant gases, such as oxygen, water vapour, hydrogen, and hydrocarbons, can occur very readily, often to the detriment of lamp performance, and so it is essential that such gases are either removed or reduced to an ineffective level.

Materials used to remove gaseous impurities retained after the lamp bulbs or tubes have been sealed are known as getters. The gettering action exploits the ability of certain solids, often metals, to react with and also retain specific gases through absorption, adsorption, occlusion, or chemical reaction. Getters, which often require some form of thermal activation, may be incorporated in lamps in the form of wire, sheet, or as surface deposits on selected components. The metals most commonly used include barium, tantalum, titanium, niobium, and zirconium and some of their binary alloys, the choice of getter being dependent on the gases to be removed and also on the type of lamp. The temperature of maximum sorption or interaction will vary with the getter material and so the location of the getter and the method of thermal activation are important.

One non-metallic getter that deserves mention because of its extensive and long-continued use is red phosphorus, which is very effective in removing traces of oxygen and moisture from the inert gases commonly used in lamps.

Getters are essentially of two types: flash getters and bulk getters. Flash getters are applied to selected components as thin deposits or films and the active metal is evaporated by rapid heating or flashing after seal-off. Phosphorus, barium, and magnesium are examples of flash getters. Bulk getters are often used in the form of wires, structural members, or semi-porous deposits which absorb gas when at elevated temperatures and often remain effective throughout the life of the lamp. Tantalum, titanium, zirconium, and certain aluminium–zirconium alloys are examples of commonly used bulk getters. Much information on getter materials is contained in Dushman (1949) and Kohl (1972).

7.3.4   Miscellaneous uses of metals

Metallic materials perform a wide variety of functions in both the manufacture and operation of lamps. Properties which may be taken advantage of include melting point, vapour pressure, mechanical strength, ductility, formability, corrosion resistance, solderability, thermal expansion and conduction, electrical resistivity, gaseous sorption and desorption, microstructural stability, electron emission, and emissivity.

For those lamp components that have to operate at elevated temperatures, such as filament supports, use is often made of the refractory metals tungsten, molybdenum, and tantalum. Both tungsten and molybdenum possess high mechanical strength, but their relatively poor resistance to oxidation above about 400 °C necessitates strict control of the lamp processing and service environments. To avoid the adverse effects of metal–oxide interactions much use is made of environments containing hydrogen, nitrogen, and certain inert gases. This is particularly important in forming processes which can only be conducted at high temperatures and above the ductile-to-brittle transitions which characterize many of the refractory metals.

Much use is also made of both pure nickel and the various nickel alloys since they combine good mechanical strength with good resistance to corrosion, low vapour pressure, reasonable electrical conductivity, and ease of fabrication and joining. Nickel, when alloyed with metals such as copper, iron, chromium, and manganese, is used as mechanical supports, lead wires, glass-sealing alloys, fuse wires, and bimetallic strips. Copper or one of its alloys is to be found in almost every lamp construction. Pure copper is much used as an electrical lead wire, but alloys containing beryllium, chromium, or oxide dispersions may be used where it is necessary to combine high strength with electrical conductivity. Brass containing 65% copper and 35% zinc is widely used in the making of lamp caps, but increasing use is being made of aluminium, purely on account of lower costs. Aluminium, in the form of coatings vapour-deposited on to bulb wall surfaces, is also used to create light reflecting surfaces in spot lamps. Niobium is important in the construction of high pressure sodium lamps (Sect. 13.2.2).

Numerous metals are used in the vapour state to produce particular radiation bands in the spectra of discharge lamps: these include calcium, gallium, holmium, indium, iron, magnesium, mercury, scandium, sodium, thallium, thorium, thulium, and tin. In photoflash lamps a continuous spectrum of white light is produced by the ignition of zirconium foil.

Considerable use is made of composite metals so that specific properties of more than one metal may be exploited simultaneously and often to economic advantage. For example, nickel-coated iron and platinum-coated molybdenum permit dual advantage to be taken of the relatively high strength, low-cost iron and molybdenum and the corrosion-resistant but more costly nickel and platinum. A particularly important composite wire is that known as Dumet wire (Sect. 7.4). Another form of composite is the bimetallic strip used in flashing lamps and starter switches where thermally controlled deflections are obtained by exploiting differences in the thermal expansion coefficients of nickel and nickel–iron alloys.

The various metals and alloys used in lamp manufacture have to be combined to complete structures with high-integrity joints. It is sufficient to state here that numerous metals and alloys are used to join components by welding, brazing, soldering, and reaction bonding.

7.4 Glass–metal seals

One of the major factors affecting the choice of vitreous material for a particular application is its ability to seal hermetically to other materials, particularly metals (Partridge 1949, Volf 1961).

The properties required of a glass to produce an ideal, stress-free seal to a metal are as follows:

(a) Its thermal expansion coefficient should match that of the metal over a wide range of temperature and particularly from the annealing temperature to room temperature.
(b) It must be readily workable in the sealing region.
(c) It must exhibit satisfactory chemical resistance to atmospheric attack.
(d) Its electrical resistivity, dielectric constant, and dielectric loss must be satisfactory.
(e) It must be perfectly homogeneous and its properties must not fluctuate from batch to batch.

Where requirement (a) is met, a matched seal between the glass and metal is produced. Matched seals can be made between certain soda-lime and lead-alkali silicate glasses and alloys, such as 50% nickel–iron, nickel–iron–chromium–cobalt, and iron–chromium.

These combinations are little used however since a porous oxide layer tends to build up on the alloy surface during sealing, resulting in a tendency to leakage. In order to overcome this difficulty in sealing unprotected nickel–iron alloys Dumet alloy is used almost exclusively throughout the industry for sealing to lead-alkali silicate glass. Dumet is a composite material consisting of a central core of 42–58% nickel–iron alloy sheathed with copper which constitutes about 25% by weight of the complete wire. The surface of the wire is coated with sodium borate which prevents the formation of spongy cuprous oxide during sealing and also enables the wire to be more easily 'wetted' by the glass. As a result of its composite structure, the thermal expansion coefficient of the wire is different in the axial and radial directions. In the radial direction it matches that of the glass, whilst in the axial direction it is less than that of the glass. Consequently, to avoid dangerous axial tensile stress in the glass the seal is not completely annealed, but cooled at a rate such that, at room temperature, it exhibits axial compressive stress. The stress is limited by keeping the wire diameter below 0·8 mm.

Matched seals can be made successfully between certain of the borosilicate and aluminosilicate glasses and nickel–iron–cobalt alloys and the refractory metals, tungsten and molybdenum. In many respects the two refractory metals behave in a similar manner, but molybdenum is often preferred for use in seals because it is less expensive, has greater ductility, and a lower brittle-to-ductile transition temperature. Since both metals oxidize readily precautions must be taken to avoid excessive oxidation during sealing, such as sleeving the wire with a thin coating of glass before it is sealed to the glass component proper.

A sleeving process is also carried out prior to sealing Dumet alloy into the ply-glass used for low pressure sodium vapour lamps. In this case the wires are sleeved with a glass of high electrical resistivity in order to prevent electrolysis occurring in the pinch during lamp operation. This glass must seal satisfactorily to the Dumet alloy and its expansion coefficient should preferably not exceed that of the soda-lime silicate base glass.

A major problem exists when making seals between metals and fused silica or Vycor. This is because the thermal expansion coefficients of these materials are so low that there is no suitable metal with an expansion coefficient remotely matching them. The technique adopted in making seals to these materials is to use a length of feather-edged molybdenum foil about 0·025 mm thick and pinch-seal it into the vitreous material. The foil in this form is sufficiently ductile to deform and so prevent fracture of the seal under the tensile stresses produced (Chaps 10 and 16).

Special glasses have been developed for sealing niobium metal to alumina ceramic (Burgraaf and Van Velzen 1969). Calcium aluminate glasses in which the minor constituents are magnesia, baria, and sometimes boric oxide are commonly used in this application. This type of seal is particularly important in high pressure sodium lamps where the glass has to withstand the corrosive action of sodium vapour at temperatures up to about 800 °C, as well as be compatible with the other components of the seal over this wide temperature range.

Capping cements are required to provide a reliable mechanical joint between materials with widely different thermal expansion characteristics over a wide temperature range after many thousands of hours. The material used for fixing metal caps onto glass bulbs consists of about 90% marble dust filler plus phenolic, natural, and silicone resins. For fixing ceramic caps onto fused silica-bodied lamps a much more refractory cement is used and this consists essentially of silica powder mixed with an inorganic binder, such as sodium silicate.

7.5 Gases

The principal gases used in lamps are found as naturally occurring constituents of air from which they are separated by fractional distillation. They are often used to control a variety of physical and chemical processes, while in some cases the production of light exploits some specific property of the gas itself.

The chemical activity of many lamp materials is often much increased by the high temperatures they achieve during lamp operation. Phenomena such as oxidation and corrosion must be strictly controlled if serious degradation of the constructional materials is to be avoided. This control is normally achieved by ensuring that the operational environment consists of an inert or non-reacting gas: argon and nitrogen are often used for such purposes.

Physical processes, such as evaporation and sputtering, often shorten the life of such critical components as filaments and electrodes. Process reaction rates can be significantly reduced when the gaseous environment is made both chemically inert and relatively dense. In general, increases in the gas pressure and density increase the frequency of atomic collisions and reduce surface temperatures, so making the escape of atoms from the surface more difficult. Evaporation and sputtering are accordingly reduced. Argon is much used for this purpose, although in some incandescent lamps the denser gas krypton is used to reduce thermal conduction and to further suppress filament evaporation and so extend lamp life.

Use is often made of the arc quenching properties of the nitrogen molecule to prevent destructive arcs forming between components which are at different electrical potentials within lamps. Gas fillings often consist of nitrogen or mixtures of nitrogen with the inert gases argon and krypton.

In gas discharge lamps use is made of monomolecular gas fillings, such as argon, neon, helium, and xenon, since they help initiate an electrical discharge and then act as a form of buffer in the main discharge (Sect. 6.3.3).

Other examples of the chemical function of gases are to be found in the halogen lamps. Reactive gases, such as hydrogen iodide (HI), hydrogen bromide (HBr), tribromomethane ($CHBr_3$), dibromomethane (CH_2Br_2), bromomethane (Ch_3Br), and nitrogen trifluoride (NF_3), are used in halogen lamps to generate tungsten transport cycles. They simultaneously inhibit tungsten deposition on the inner wall of the bulb and promote the return of the evaporated metal to the filament or to those surfaces within the lamp which have little influence on the production of light and its transmission through the bulb walls (Chap. 10).

Due to the high operating temperatures some of the critical components in lamps are very sensitive to the presence of quite small quantities of specific gases, particularly those with oxidizing or carburizing potentials. Examples of such gases are oxygen, carbon monoxide and dioxide, hydrocarbons, and water vapour. These gases are among the more common contaminants and their activity in lamps is minimized by degassing treatments and, after sealing off, through the action of getters. Only a few parts per million of total gas impurities can be tolerated in most lamp fillings.

Further reading

Adams O, 1978, *Ltg. Res. Technol.*, **10**, 83–93: Use of glass in electric lamps

Coaton J R, 1975, *The Metallurgist and Materials Technologist*, **7**, 510–514: Lamp materials

Hampel C A, 1961, *Rare metals handbook*, 2nd Edition (London: Chapman & Hall)

Kingery W D, Bowen H K and Uhlmann D R, 1976, *Introduction to ceramics* (New York: Wiley)

Kohl W H, 1967, *Handbook of materials and techniques for vacuum devices* (New York: Reinhold)

McMillan P W, 1979, *Glass-ceramics*, 2nd Edition (London: Academic Press)

Partridge J H, 1949, *Glass-to-metal seals* (Sheffield: Soc. of Glass Technology)

Rawson H, 1980, *Properties and applications of glass*, **3,** *Glass Science and Technology* (Amsterdam: Elsevier)

Smithells C J, 1976, *Metals reference book*, 5th Edition (London: Butterworth)

Tooley F V, 1971, *Handbook of glass manufacture*, Volumes 1 and 2 (New York: Ogden Publishing Co)

van Vlack L, 1970, *Materials science for engineers* (Massachusetts: Addison-Wesley)

Volf M B, 1961, *Technical glasses* (London: Pitman)

Wyatt O H and Dew-Hughes D, 1974, *Metals, ceramics and polymers: introduction to the structure and properties of engineering materials* (Cambridge: The University Press)

Yih S W H and Wang C T, 1979, *Tungsten: sources, metallurgy, properties and applications* (New York: Plenum Press)

8 Phosphors

Historically, the term phosphorescence originates from the element phosphorus whose ability to glow in the dark was of great interest to the alchemists in the 17th and 18th Centuries. Derived from this is the term phosphor which is now widely used to describe materials, usually solids, which have the ability to luminesce. By coincidence many of the important phosphors used today are phosphorus compounds, such as the phosphates, but whereas the luminescence of these compounds is brought about by the ability of the material to absorb one form of energy and re-emit part of it as visible light, in the case of the element phosphorus the glow is due to a chemical reaction which takes place when the element undergoes oxidation. The term *fluorescence* is a general one covering many types of light emitting phenomena, but is usually restricted to describe very fast processes, as distinct from the slower processes of *phosphorescence*. It is more usual nowadays to use the term *luminescence* for all similar processes of light emission.

8.1 Methods of excitation

In order to differentiate between various types of luminescence a prefix is often used: in this way the glow of phosphorus is described as *chemiluminescence*, the luminescence caused by bombarding a phosphor with cathode rays is *cathodoluminescence*, and that excited by electromagnetic radiation is *photoluminescence*. The feeble light emission from certain living organisms, such as fireflies, glow-worms, and marine plankton, is classed as *bioluminescence* – which is a form of chemiluminescence. Similarly, there are other forms of luminescence bearing the prefixes *electro-*, *tribo-*, *thermo-*, etc., where the stimulating or exciting energy is an electric field, frictional energy, heat, etc.

8.1.1 Excitation by electromagnetic radiation

Certain materials have the ability to absorb one or more forms of electromagnetic radiation, such as infrared, visible light, ultraviolet, X-rays, or gamma rays, and re-emit at least part of the absorbed energy as light. The emitted light is normally at a longer wavelength than that of the radiation absorbed (Stokes' law). The energy which is absorbed and produces the emission is called the *excitation*; energy which is absorbed and is not effective in producing luminescence is dissipated as heat within the material. A convenient way of exciting phosphors is by the use of the ultraviolet radiation which is produced in certain gas discharges. If an electrical discharge takes place in a low pressure of mercury vapour and argon, 50% or more of the energy applied to the discharge is converted into ultraviolet radiation at wavelengths of 253·7 nm and 185·0 nm. By using selected phosphors to convert this ultraviolet into visible light an efficient conversion of electrical energy into white light is obtained, and this is the basis of the fluorescent lamp. During the past thirty-five years the efficacy of generating white light in this way has risen to over 90 lm W^{-1}: this is higher than for any light source which generates light by increasing the temperature of a solid to incandescence.

High pressure arcs in mercury, although producing a high proportion of visible light, also emit some ultraviolet and different types of luminescent material can be used to convert this into a more useful form.

X-rays and gamma rays from radioactive materials are very short wavelength radiation, and they excite many materials to luminescence. Their great penetrating power reduces the amount of energy which can actually be absorbed by a luminescent screen of reasonable thickness so that light outputs are small, but are often very useful for indicating purposes, for example in radiology.

Under very high excitation and precisely controlled optical conditions certain crystalline phosphors, which have a line emission under normal conditions, can be made to emit the same wavelength in a very powerful narrow beam of coherent light: this is laser action and is not usually considered as fluorescence, although this is largely a question of definition (Sect. 6.4).

Infrared radiation, normally of little interest because of its spectral location, is emitted by some semiconductors when excited by an electric field. Certain special phosphors can convert this infrared radiation into useful visible light and are sometimes used for this purpose with light emitting diodes. Such materials are known as *anti-Stokes phosphors*, *two-quantum phosphors*, or *up-converters* and are usually compounds containing high concentrations of rare-earth elements. A more exciting application for phosphors of this type would be to convert the infrared emission from incandescent filament lamps into useful visible light because about 90% of the radiation appears in this form, but no suitable materials have yet been found.

8.1.2   Excitation by charged particles

Particles of high energy, such as protons and alpha and beta particles, are useful in the excitation of some phosphors, and at one time the effect was used in some luminous paints where a radioactive material was mixed with a phosphor. A more recent application is for beta-lamps which consist of sealed glass tubes or bulbs containing radioactive tritium or krypton 85: these produce beta particles which excite a phosphor coated onto the inside wall of the glass vessel. They find application for illuminating telephone dials, marine compasses, marker buoys, and in other situations where a maintenance-free life of many years is required.

Beams of electrons are used to excite the phosphor screens in cathode-ray tubes which are used as display devices and in particular for television pictures. In contrast to radioactive sources where the energy of the particles is extremely high, but unalterable, and the incident density of radiation is normally very small, the usual cathode-ray source transfers more useful energy to a luminescent material. This is because many more particles, but of smaller individual energy, are involved, and this results in an acceptable light yield and less deterioration of the luminescent material. The efficacy of a 'black-and-white' cathode-ray tube screen for television reception is of the order of 40 lm W^{-1} when the bulb is of clear glass. Phosphors with a very short afterglow (or fast decay) are necessary in cathode-ray tubes used for television or display purposes, but in tubes used for radar some phosphorescence or persistence of emission may be desirable to provide a longer viewing time: this is achieved by using different phosphors.

8.1.3   Excitation by electric field

Electroluminescence can be used to produce useful light levels for indicators and signs, but is not suitable for general lighting purposes (Chap. 17). In these electro-luminescent devices, which are similar in construction to capacitors, special phosphors are used and appear to be capable of locally enhancing the electric field applied to them. The increased field strength can then excite electrons in the phosphor crystal to levels of energy from which they can make transitions which generate light. This is similar to the mechanism of light emission from a phosphor excited by ultraviolet radiation, but the manner of producing the free electrons is different and the efficacy of an electroluminescent panel is only of the order of $0.5\,\text{lm W}^{-1}$. The recombination of charge barriers at a p–n junction is the cause of the light emitted from silicon carbide when subjected to a powerful electric field; other binary compounds have now proved much more efficient in producing light in this way (Chap. 17).

8.2   Solid luminescent materials

8.2.1   Chemical composition

Although there are many interesting cases of luminescence in gases and liquids, only solid materials are of practical value for lighting purposes. The first known solid luminescent materials were those which showed the emission of light after exposure to daylight or sunlight: these were sulphides of the alkaline-earth metals. The artificial production of these materials was naturally very primitive and it was not until suitable ultraviolet sources and methods of experiment were available that any rational advances could be made. It was then realized that a number of naturally occurring minerals are fluorescent and that by synthesizing them in a purer state, but with the same crystalline form, efficient phosphors could be obtained. Later, a multitude of phosphors in various crystal forms were synthesized, often having no known mineral counterpart or perhaps only a non-fluorescent one. A recognizable crystal structure is an almost indispensable property of solid inorganic phosphors.

A feature common to a great many phosphors is the presence of small quantities of foreign elements incorporated in the material and these are essential to the develop-ment of luminescence. These foreign elements are called *activators* and one of particularly wide application is manganese; some of the rare-earth elements are also outstanding as activators. In some cases the presence in the host material of one activator, called the primary activator, sensitizes the material to the effects of a second activator which by itself is ineffective: in these circumstances the primary activator is known as the *sensitizer*. Apart from phosphors with one or two activators, some useful materials, the so-called self-activated phosphors, require no foreign element at all for activation. There are many phosphors of this type, such as calcium and magnesium tungstates, barium titanium phosphate, magnesium titanium borate, and certain vanadates and molybdates. In this class of material the activator is not a foreign cation replacing a cation of the matrix, but is a complex anion forming an integral part of the matrix. Whereas the fluorescence of many activated phosphors can be varied by compositional changes, the emission from self-activated phosphors, such as barium titanium phosphate, is a wide band of constant shape and position which cannot be usefully changed without causing a marked reduction in the brightness of the phosphor.

Although the presence of certain specific foreign elements may be essential as activators, the presence of other elements may be very detrimental and even minute traces can completely quench or 'kill' the fluorescence. Impurities of this type are often referred to as *killers* and their presence has to be rigorously avoided during the preparation of phosphors. In fact the successful technology of phosphor preparation depends largely on carefully controlling the purity of the material and the preparation process.

Historically, the mineral willemite, which is a zinc orthosilicate containing a trace of manganese, is important because it is sometimes found naturally in a fluorescent form which can convert short wavelength ultraviolet radiation into green light. This was one of the materials used by Crookes in his original work on discharge tubes. Synthetic zinc silicate containing a carefully controlled amount of manganese is obviously a more reliable source than are random mineral specimens. During the latter half of the 1930s it was found (McKeag and Randall 1936, Leverenz 1936) that by incorporating small amounts of beryllium compounds into zinc silicate during the preparation, a range of fluorescent colours varying from green through yellow to yellow-orange and even pink could be obtained. These manganese-activated zinc beryllium silicates were at one time very important for fluorescent lamp production.

In general, phosphors for discharge lamps are almost exclusively oxygen-containing materials, such as silicates, phosphates, tungstates, aluminates, vanadates, etc. Although certain of these are also used for cathode-ray tubes, some binary materials, such as sulphides and fluorides, are also very important in these latter applications, but these same phosphors are not suitable for use in lamps. In fact very few luminescent materials are equally efficient under a number of different types of excitation and, in general, each phosphor needs to be adapted in composition or structure to the particular type of excitation for which it is required.

X-rays were originally made visible for medical diagnostic purposes by using screens of luminescent barium platinocyanide: these were subsequently replaced by screens of zinc cadmium sulphide. The photographic action of X-rays is increased by the use of phosphor screens in contact with the film and rare-earth phosphors are now important for X-ray intensifying screens for this purpose.

Luminescent properties are not confined to inorganic solid materials, thus organic luminescent materials are familiar in the 'Day-Glo' type of poster paints. Some of these consist of organic dyestuffs, such as rhodamine, deposited on synthetic plastics of a particle size suitable for making into a paint and operate by virtue of the violet and ultraviolet radiations present in natural daylight. Colourless organic dyes which show a blue fluorescence under ultraviolet are used as fluorescent brighteners in detergents and for white textiles and paper: their faint violet or blue fluorescence offsets the slightly yellowish colour of the fabric and so produces a 'brighter white'. Similar materials are also used for providing secret markings in papers and cards, but none of these organic materials are sufficiently stable to be used in lamps.

8.2.2   Emission

Whereas the fluorescence of unrestricted atoms (in gases) consists of sharp spectral lines, the mutual interference which occurs in liquids, and still more in crystalline solids, usually causes a widening of what are fundamentally lines into bands. Some of these are evidently broadened lines, others are so wide that they cover the whole of the visible spectrum. The widest bands arise from self-activated phosphors and the widest known single emission band is probably that of barium titanium phosphate (Fig. 8.1a), which extends from the ultraviolet to infrared with a peak in the blue-green (Henderson and Ranby 1951). Figure 8.1b shows the contrasting narrow emission band of a manganese-activated phosphor.

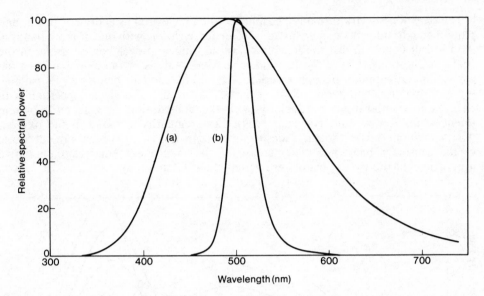

Fig. 8.1 Spectral emission curves of (a) barium titanium phosphate and (b) manganese-activated magnesium gallate; both curves normalized at peak emission

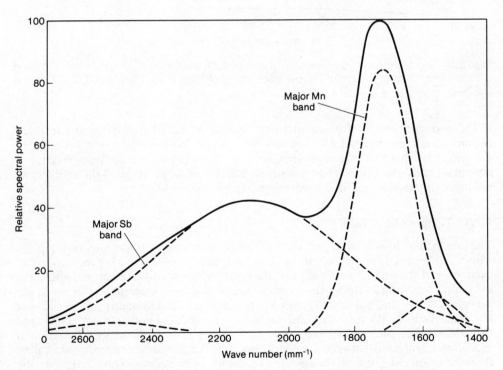

Fig. 8.2 Gaussian analysis of the fluorescent emission from a calcium halophosphate (Sb, Mn) phosphor

The emission spectra of many phosphors, when measured as energy or power and plotted on a frequency or wave number scale, agree closely with one or more bands in the form of Gaussian distribution functions, and this approach can be useful in the study of phosphors (Fig. 8.2). By Gaussian band analysis of the emission from the zinc cadmium sulphide phosphor series, several independent bands can be isolated for each material and these show regular shifts through the visible spectrum with changes in composition, particularly with the substitution of zinc by cadmium (Henderson, Ranby, and Halstead 1959). Less regularity is found in the oxygen-dominated materials, although if sensitization occurs it is easy to observe the decrease of the sensitizer band and the increase of the manganese band as the relative proportions of the two activators are varied (Figs 8.2 and 8.3).

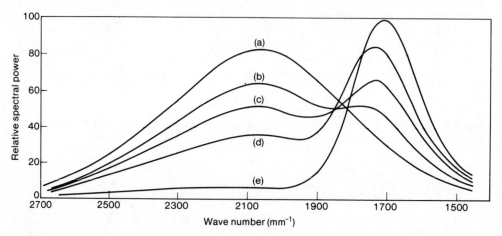

Fig. 8.3 Spectral power distributions of halophosphates with a 3:1 ratio of F:Cl and different Mn contents. Atoms of Mn per three atoms of P: (a) 0, (b) 0·025, (c) 0·05, (d) 0·1, and (e) 0·4

The emission bands of phosphors may appear in the ultraviolet or the infrared regions of the spectrum. Little use has been found for infrared luminescence, but ultraviolet is valuable for special purposes, e.g. 'black light' from fluorescent tubes or mercury lamps for display and theatrical effects, in artificial daylight sources, in photocopying lamps, medical applications, and for sun-beds.

8.2.3 Temperature effects

The emission of light from a phosphor depends on electronic transitions taking place within the material brought about by the absorption of energy during the process of excitation. If the light emitting process depends on transitions of electrons within the ions of the activator, without the intervention of free or 'conductivity' electrons, the processes of rise and fall of light emission are exponential and nearly independent of the temperature. To this class belong most of the oxygen-dominated lamp and cathode-ray tube phosphors, with decay times varying from less than a millionth of a second to a few hundredths of a second: cerium and manganese are typical activators in these respective speed groups. However, if free electrons are involved, the processes are greatly accelerated by a rise of temperature, and of this class sulphides are typical examples. Their normal phosphorescent decay, which may last for hours or even days, especially when activated by copper, can be dramatically reduced by heating. It is quite usual to find several independent decays with different time constants in the same phosphor.

For a given excitation most phosphors have a maximum output of light at a particular temperature and for commercially useful materials this should be at or near room temperature. As the temperature rises the efficiency falls to zero with the increasing atomic vibrations in the crystal absorbing more and more of the input power. This temperature quenching varies greatly in detail (Fig. 8.4): some phosphors, such as calcium tungstate, lose all their luminescence at about 150 °C, whereas others, such as certain aluminates activated by chromium, are still increasing in brightness up to 500 °C. Temperature resistance is necessary in phosphors used with mercury lamps since they may be operating in the region of 300 °C.

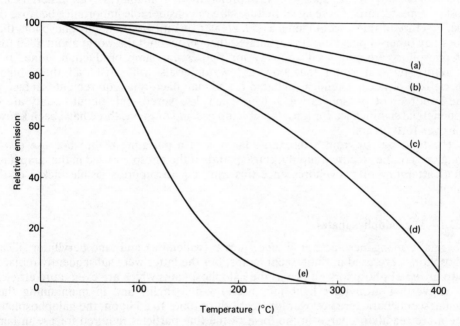

Fig. 8.4 Effect of temperature on the intensity of fluorescence of the following phosphors excited by 253·7 nm ultraviolet radiation: (a) magnesium aluminate (Ce, Tb), (b) yttrium oxide (Eu), (c) calcium halophosphate (Sb, Mn) (3500 K), (d) zinc silicate (Mn), and (e) magnesium tungstate

8.3   Phosphors for fluorescent lamps

The fluorescent lamp has been an established light source for so many years that it is possible to describe in detail the properties which a useful fluorescent lamp phosphor must possess:

(a)   It should be a non-toxic inorganic material of a sufficiently stable nature that it will withstand both processing and operating conditions.
(b)   It must have a strong optical absorption band in the short ultraviolet region to absorb the 253·7 nm and 185·0 nm radiation with consequent fluorescence.

(c)   It must have a minimum optical absorption in the visible part of the spectrum, i.e. it should have no appreciable body colour.

(d)   In most cases it must fluoresce in the required part of the visible spectrum with as little emission as possible in the near-ultraviolet and infrared regions.

(e)   The optical absorption and fluorescence characteristics should be at a maximum at the normal operating temperature of the lamp, i.e. between 40 °C and 50 °C.

(f)   The material must be capable of being prepared in a finely divided form or broken down to fine particles without loss of fluorescent efficiency.

(g)   It must retain its fluorescent characteristics over long periods of operation in a lamp.

Although these are some of the more important general properties required of a lamp phosphor dictated by the conditions of its use, there are still the equally important practical considerations, such as ease of preparation, availability of raw materials, and cost of manufacture. These latter features are of considerable importance because the manufacture of fluorescent lamps uses a greater quantity of inorganic phosphors than does any other application: it is estimated that throughout the world about 8000 tons of phosphors are produced annually for fluorescent lamp production alone. It is therefore not surprising that only a few materials will satisfy all these highly specialized physical, chemical, economic, and manufacturing requirements; in fact, of the hundreds of phosphors which have been discovered, only about twenty are of commercial significance for fluorescent lamp use and of these, three have been known for over forty years.

The light output from a discharge lamp is of a pulsating nature because of the frequency of the electrical supply, consequently if the phosphor used in the lamp has a short afterglow or phosphorescence this can help to suppress visible flicker of the lamp.

8.3.1   The halophosphates

Originally manganese-activated zinc silicate (willemite) and zinc beryllium silicate phosphors were used in fluorescent lamps, but the latter were subsequently replaced by a group of phosphors known as the halophosphates which are even more efficient in converting ultraviolet light into useful visible light, and in maintaining their luminescent characteristics over long periods of time. In addition, the halophosphates are more readily prepared in the form of the fine particles required for use in lamp coatings and have no known toxic properties. Although they were discovered in 1942 (McKeag and Ranby 1942), their wide scale use did not commence until about 1948 and since then increases in light output of fluorescent lamps containing halophosphates have been almost continuous, due to gradual improvements in their manufacture (Fig. 8.5). Thus the 1200 mm 40 W White lamp has shown a fairly steady increase totalling about 60% in its initial efficacy in the past thirty years, and a still greater percentage increase after some thousands of hours' life due to improved maintenance.

The halophosphates are alkaline-earth halogen-containing phosphates of the hexagonal apatite crystal structure with antimony and manganese activators: the alkaline-earth metal is usually calcium, but strontium may be substituted in part. The colour of the fluorescence can be controlled by changing the ratio of fluorine to chlorine retained in the matrix and by adjusting the concentration of manganese.

The halophosphates absorb strongly in the ultraviolet and are effectively excited by the mercury lines at 253·7 nm and 185·0 nm, but not by the long wavelength mercury lines near 365 nm. The excitation curve for the simplest of the halophosphates,

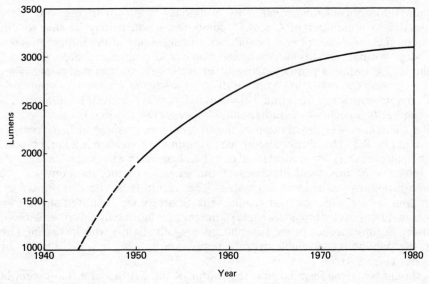

Fig. 8.5 Lumen output progress of 1200 mm 40 W White fluorescent lamps coated with halophosphate phosphors

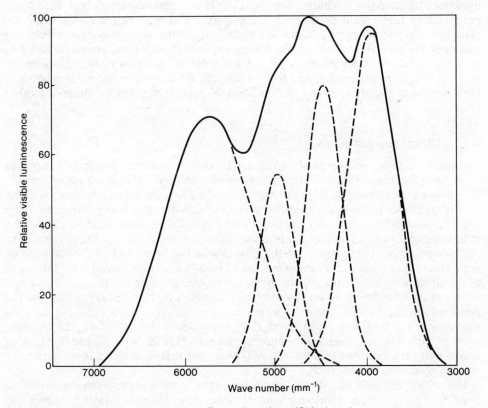

Fig. 8.6 Excitation curve for calcium fluorophosphate (Sb) phosphor

calcium fluorophosphate activated by antimony, is shown in Fig. 8.6. It can be analysed into a number of Gaussian components which may be due to different activator sites or different energy states of the antimony in the lattice.

Under normal conditions manganese-activated halophosphates do not show luminescence unless a primary activator or sensitizer, such as antimony, is present. This is because the excitation band for divalent manganese is too far in the ultraviolet and energy transfer is required between the primary activator antimony and the manganese: this occurs by a radiationless process (Dexter 1953).

The spectral power distribution of the fluorescence of some of these phosphors is shown in Fig. 8.3. The blue emission due to antimony activation is a fairly broad band: when manganese is incorporated a new band appears at longer wavelengths and the intensity of this band increases at the expense of the antimony band as the concentration of manganese increases. The result is a complex emission band extending over a wide spectral region. The fluorescence is shifted slightly towards longer wavelengths by replacing some of the matrix fluorine by chlorine. Although the intensity of fluorescence of the halophosphates falls slightly with increasing temperature, the stability is reasonable over the temperature region in which a lamp normally operates (Fig. 8.4).

It should be borne in mind that the colour of the light from a fluorescent lamp is decided by both the phosphor emission and the visible emission from the mercury discharge so that, although the spectral energy distribution of many phosphors is a smooth curve, superimposed on this in the case of the fluorescent lamp are the strong lines from the mercury discharge, see Fig. 11.7. It is a remarkable fact that the colours produced by fluorescent lamps with halophosphate phosphors are so conveniently placed within the range of acceptable 'whites'. It is however not always possible or economically best to obtain the exact colour required by using one phosphor alone. It is normal practice in manufacture to use a number of halophosphate phosphors of more or less constant colour, and then obtain the final colour required in a lamp by blending them together, or by the addition of relatively small quantities of other phosphors.

8.3.2   Other lamp phosphors

There are a number of phosphors which can be used in mixtures with halophosphates or alone in fluorescent lamps. The general properties required of these phosphors are the same as those previously discussed. The emission must be in a suitable spectral region and the phosphors must be compatible with one another during lamp manufacture and not show any marked difference in light output during use. It is also of advantage if there is no great difference in the physical density of the phosphors so that when they are being applied to the glass tube in the form of a liquid suspension no separation takes place, otherwise there could be a colour difference from end to end of the finished lamp. Of these phosphors, the most important are given in Table 8.1.

One reason for the need for a variety of phosphors is the comparative lack of red emission in the halophosphates, which as a result are highly efficient in light production, but less so in colour rendering properties. Calcium silicate, the alkaline-earth phosphates, and magnesium fluorogermanate have all been used at one time or another to provide this desirable red radiation, but it is now more usual to use red yttrium oxide for this purpose.

However, for some situations the requirement to save energy can outweigh the need for good colour rendering and so one type of energy-saving fluorescent lamp which has been developed utilizes a mixture of very efficient halophosphate

Table 8.1 Some of the more important lamp phosphors

Matrix	Composition	Activator(s)	Emission
Zinc silicate	Zn_2SiO_4	Mn	Green
Calcium silicate	$CaSiO_3$	Pb, Mn	Pink
Calcium halophosphates	$Ca_5(PO_4)_3(F, Cl)$	Sb, Mn	Blue to pink
Strontium magnesium phosphate	$(Sr, Mg)_3(PO_4)_2$	Sn	Pinkish white
Barium titanium phosphate	$Ba_4Ti(PO_4)_4$	—	Blue-white
Calcium tungstate	$CaWO_4$	—	Deep blue
Magnesium tungstate	$MgWO_4$	—	Pale blue
Magnesium gallate	$MgGa_2O_4$	Mn	Blue-green
Magnesium fluorogermanate	$Mg_4GeO_6.MgF_2$	Mn	Deep red
Magnesium fluoroarsenate	$Mg_6As_2O_{11}.MgF_2$	Mn	Deep red
Yttrium oxide	Y_2O_3	Eu	Red
Yttrium vanadate	YVO_4	Eu	Red
Magnesium aluminate	$RMgAl_{11}O_{19}$	R = Ce, Tb	Green
Barium magnesium aluminate	$BaMg_2Al_{16}O_{27}$	Eu	Blue

phosphors. In these lamps a high brightness yellow calcium fluorophosphate phosphor is mixed with a blue-emitting halophosphate, which is often the strontium halophosphate, and the resulting lamp, although deficient in the red end of the spectrum, produces a near-white light at a high efficiency and therefore these lamps can be described as energy-saving. This approach has received fairly wide acceptance in the USA, but has not proved as popular in European markets, where a greater importance is attached to the quality of a lighting system.

8.3.3 Narrow band phosphors

Although the halophosphates are the most widely used and most important of the lamp phosphors, there is always continuous research to try to find new or better materials. A new replacement phosphor providing a near-white colour would need to be brighter than the halophosphates, have a better maintenance of light output in use, or be cheaper to prepare: no material with these characteristics has been found. Alternatively, if there were a number of bright phosphors whose emissions consisted of sharp narrow bands in different parts of the spectrum, these could be used together in a fluorescent lamp to give a high light output of better colour than can be obtained with conventional halophosphates because allowance could be made for the colour distortions produced by the mercury lines.

One possibility which was considered in this direction was the use of blends of europium-activated alkaline-earth silicate phosphors. These materials were discovered before the halophosphates and some emit in fairly narrow emission bands in different parts of the spectrum, but not in the red. By the time a suitable red phosphor was available this approach had been abandoned in favour of the *triphosphor* approach (Sect. 11.3.3). It can be shown that by using a mixture of near-monochromatic red, green, and blue lights to produce a 'white' light then good colour rendering with high efficiency can be obtained (Thornton 1971). In terms of fluorescent lamps this means that if efficient phosphors with very narrow emission bands in the red, green, and blue were available then mixtures of these could be used to produce more efficient fluorescent lamps with higher colour rendering indices than can be obtained with conventional phosphors which have wide emission bands. In practical terms the narrow band phosphors should emit strongly between 455 nm and 485 nm for the blue phosphor, between 525 nm and 560 nm for the green phosphor, and between 595 nm and 620 nm for the red phosphor.

The yttrium oxide (Eu) phosphor (Table 8.1) is a highly efficient red phosphor whose main emission is a narrow band peaking at 611 nm and consequently satisfies the conditions required for the red phosphor in this triphosphor approach (Fig. 8.7).

Zinc silicate phosphor (Table 8.1) is a very bright green phosphor with a fairly narrow emission band which peaks at 525 nm, so this might satisfy the conditions required for the green phosphor. Alternatively, magnesium aluminate activated by cerium and terbium has a very strong narrow emission band in the green with a peak at 545 nm (Fig. 8.7).

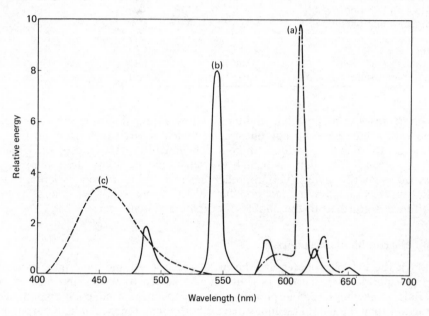

Fig. 8.7 Spectral emission curves of (a) red yttrium oxide (Eu), (b) green magnesium aluminate (Ce, Tb), and (c) blue barium magnesium aluminate (Eu)

A number of blue phosphors are known which have a maximum in their emission spectra close to the required wavelength and one which has proved useful is barium magnesium aluminate activated by europium, this has a peak at 450 nm (Fig. 8.7).

By using blends of these red, green, and blue phosphors 'white' fluorescent lamps can be produced which are highly efficient and have high colour rendering indices R_a, e.g. up to an R_a of 84; for comparison a standard White fluorescent lamp has an R_a of 56 (Verstegen 1974).

When three phosphors are used together in this way it is essential that the maintenance of light output during the life of the lamp should be nearly the same for all three phosphor components, otherwise the colour of the lamp will change during use. The green zinc silicate phosphor has a poor maintenance compared with the red phosphor, whereas magnesium aluminate (Ce, Tb) is relatively good, so that in practice triphosphor lamps usually employ red yttrium oxide, green magnesium aluminate, and blue barium magnesium aluminate. Each of these phosphors is much more expensive – up to 50 times more – than conventional halophosphates because not only are expensive rare-earth compounds required for their preparation, but also the temperatures to which they are heated during their preparations are much higher than are usually employed for most lamp phosphors.

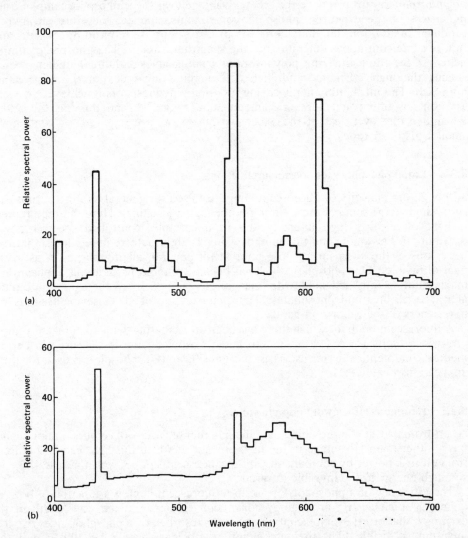

Fig. 8.8 Spectral emission curves of lamps coated with (a) a triphosphor blend and (b) a single halophosphate; both of which are used for Cool White fluorescent lamps

Now, although white fluorescent lamps produced by using these three phosphors are more efficient than those using conventional halophosphates, and are therefore of importance because of the need to conserve energy, their expensive nature adds substantially to the manufacturing cost of a triphosphor lamp. Also, although such a triphosphor lamp gives a higher colour rendering index measurement R_a, such measurements do not allow for certain colour distortions known as metamerism (Sect. 3.5.2), which in this instance can occur because of the discontinuous nature of the emission spectrum from the lamp (Fig. 8.8).

In practice these problems can be partially overcome by coating the fluorescent tube first with a thin layer of a conventional halophosphate phosphor and then with a thin layer of the triphosphor blend (Sect. 11.3.3). Such lamps are conveniently termed *polyphosphor* lamps and have the great advantage over the triphosphor lamp of using much less of the expensive phosphor components, and are therefore cheaper to produce. In addition, the metameric colour distortions are reduced by the introduction of some continuous emission into the spectrum from the halophosphate component. At the same time the polyphosphor coating gives a fluorescent lamp which retains the high efficiency and high colour rendering index of the triphosphor approach. The maximum energy-saving by using polyphosphors is achieved by using krypton gas filling and narrow diameter tubes, e.g. T8, and this has the added advantage that even less of the expensive phosphors are required for coating the smaller diameter tubes.

8.3.4   Lamp phosphors for special applications

Although the majority of fluorescent lamps are used for general lighting purposes, a surprisingly large number are used in photocopying machines. Here the requirement is light of a fairly high intensity and of a carefully controlled spectral power distribution. Phosphors emitting in narrow bands are usually required and sometimes in regions of the spectrum of little interest for general lighting purposes, as in the near-ultraviolet. One phosphor which has become of importance in this application is magnesium gallate activated with manganese (Fig. 8.1b), others are europium-activated silicates and phosphates. The characteristic of all these materials is the narrowness of their emission bands.

A fluorescent lamp for which there has been an increasing demand in recent years is one which emits UVA for use in sun beds; a similar lamp is also used in certain medical treatments, e.g. for psoriasis; barium silicate (Pb) phosphor is used for these applications (Table 8.1).

8.3.5   Luminous efficacy of lamp phosphors

Apart from its value in providing light in an immense variety of colours, luminescence has another main advantage in the high efficacy at which this light can be obtained from electric power by comparison with incandescent sources which necessarily emit so much energy in the invisible infrared.

The efficiency of a phosphor for use in a fluorescent lamp is a function of both its quantum efficiency η_{qe} and energy conversion efficiency at the wavelength of the exciting radiation. If every excitation quantum absorbed by a phosphor gives rise to a quantum of visible light then its quantum efficiency would be 100%, and this condition is nearly attained in some circumstances. Now Planck's relation (Sect. 6.2) shows that quantum energy is inversely proportional to wavelength, and since by Stokes' law (Sect. 8.1.1) the wavelength λ_{em} of a fluorescent emission is greater than that of the excitation λ_{ex}, then the energy $h\nu_{em}$ of the emitted visible quantum from a phosphor must be less than that of the absorbed exciting quantum $h\nu_{ex}$ and so the efficiency of energy conversion is less than 100%: the difference in energy being lost as heat. The total efficiency η of a phosphor can therefore be expressed by

$$\eta = \eta_{qe}\frac{h\nu_{em}}{h\nu_{ex}} = \eta_{qe}\frac{\lambda_{ex}}{\lambda_{em}}$$

and for a high efficiency a phosphor should have both a high quantum efficiency and a high energy conversion efficiency.

An interesting example where the quantum efficiency is high, but the efficiency of energy conversion is low, is provided by the use of green-emitting zinc silicate phosphor in a neon discharge tube. Such tubes were used in the past to provide an amber coloured 'neon' sign. The peak of the phosphor emission is at 525·0 nm and the luminescence is excited by the ultraviolet of the neon discharge at 73·8 nm. Even if the quantum efficiency is 100%, the conversion of energy from this short wavelength of ultraviolet to the green emission cannot be greater than the wavelength ratio, i.e. one-seventh, and therefore the luminous efficacy of these tubes was low.

The highest possible efficacy of a light source is 680 lm W^{-1} for monochromatic yellow-green light of wavelength 555 nm; the corresponding value for a reasonable white with a wide spectral distribution is about 250 lm W^{-1}. In practice yields approaching 100 lm W^{-1} can be obtained by the fluorescence process in a tubular low pressure lamp with a white emission. This should be compared with moderate sized incandescent lamps which give only 12 lm W^{-1}. It must be emphasized that with the fluorescent lamp the current-limiting control, which is not required with an incandescent lamp, dissipates appreciable power and lowers the overall efficacy.

Although the power dissipated at any one point in the phosphor layer of a fluorescent lamp is fairly low, exposure of the phosphor continues for many thousands of hours in an atmosphere which is not chemically inert and so a gradual loss of brightness occurs. Methods of phosphor manufacture leading to more complete chemical combination and methods of lamp manufacture leading to tubes less contaminated by traces of air, water, and other foreign materials have greatly improved the situation, although the chemical and physical reactions responsible for phosphor deterioration are still not fully understood. Physical absorption of the mercury on the surface layer of the phosphor grains and in the glass plays a large part, and different compositions of glass are also significant because of the migration of sodium from the glass into the phosphor, with damaging effects on the maintenance. There is still a need to improve the performance, especially for lamps with power loadings above the normal ratings because under these conditions phosphor deterioration can be accelerated.

8.4 Phosphors for colour corrected discharge lamps

Improvement of the colour of mercury lamps has been an aim of lamp manufacturers for many years. The considerable amount of ultraviolet emission near 365 nm from these lamps can be converted by fluorescence into visible light, given suitable phosphors excited by this wavelength. The first to be used in this way, coated inside the outer envelope of the lamp, were zinc cadmium sulphides. To minimize the serious fall in emission which occurs in the case of sulphide phosphors at elevated temperatures the envelopes had to be large and were 'isothermally' shaped. A phosphor capable of operating at high temperatures eliminates the need for such a large outer envelope and the first improvements in this direction were obtained by using either magnesium fluoroarsenate or magnesium fluorogermanate; both these phosphors are activated by manganese and emit deep red light. However, when yttrium vanadate activated by europium became available in quantity for colour television tubes, its valuable qualities for the correction of mercury lamp spectra were recognized (Levine and Palilla 1966). It has a better temperature resistance than have magnesium fluoroarsenate and magnesium fluorogermanate and its emission in the

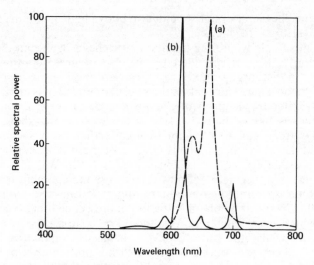

Fig. 8.9 Spectral emission curves of (a) magnesium fluorogermanate and (b) yttrium vanadate; both curves normalized at peak emission

red is at somewhat shorter wavelengths which produces greater lumen output (Fig. 8.9). The spectral power distribution of a colour corrected mercury lamp using yttrium vanadate is shown in Fig. 14.7b.

The mercury lamp could be still further improved by additional phosphors compatible with the vanadate but emitting narrow bands in the blue and orange regions of the spectrum. Such materials have not yet been found, but would probably be activated by rare earths. Although the phosphor in a mercury lamp is not exposed to the discharge itself, as in a fluorescent lamp, some materials deteriorate by photolysis under these conditions so the phosphors used have to be carefully prepared and treated.

Phosphors are also used in some other types of discharge lamps, e.g. metal halide discharge lamps, where the purpose is similar to that in mercury lamps: that is, the phosphor emission only supplements the main light emitting process of the halide discharge.

Further reading

Burrus H L, 1972, *Lamp phosphors* (London: Mills & Boon Ltd)

Butler K H, 1980, *Fluorescent lamp phosphors technology and theory* (University Park and London: Pennsylvania State University Press)

Ryan F M, 1981, *J. Luminescence*, **24/25**, Part II, 827–834: Changing requirements of fluorescent lamp phosphors

9 Incandescent lamps

The filament lamp, whose centenary is now past, has undergone many changes and improvements in design and manufacture to bring it to its present performance and convenience as a light source. In spite of more efficient competing types of source, it still accounts for a greater number made annually than any other kind of lamp. In the home it is still scarcely challenged, offering low installation and replacement cost and flexibility of use. Whilst offices, factories, public buildings, shops, and vehicles steadily adopt more and more fluorescent and other discharge lamps, the incandescent lamp still seems to have an unlimited future. In this chapter the present state of the tungsten lamp is discussed, omitting developments in the tungsten halogen field which are treated in Chap. 10.

9.1 General lighting service lamps

Incandescent lamps emit visible light as well as radiating infrared energy as a result of the heating effect (first noticeable at 500 °C) of an electric current flowing through a filament wire. Tungsten is particularly suitable for use as a filament material as a result of its high melting point and relatively low rate of evaporation at high temperatures. The filament wire is coiled to shorten the overall length and to reduce thermal loss.

Construction   Figure 9.1 illustrates a standard type of general lighting service (GLS) incandescent lamp with a coiled coil tungsten filament A. The filament is supported at intermediate points by molybdenum wires B and the electrical connections to the filament are made through clamps on the end of nickel or nickel-plated wires C, which form part of a sub-assembly comprising usually three or more components. The inner wire C is welded to a section of Dumet wire D (Sect. 7.4). The lower end of the Dumet is connected to a protective fuse E, which is usually a small diameter copper–nickel alloy wire. This fuse can be encapsulated in a glass sleeve F filled with minute glass balls (ballotini) which have arc quenching properties, otherwise two unfilled fuses are required to provide suitably long arc paths. The connection between the fuse and the soldered external contact is made by the lead wire G, which is led through an eyelet in the cap and electrically connected by solder at the contacts H. The exhaust tube K is kept open in the glass pinch J to allow the air to be pumped from the bulb L after sealing, and for the introduction of the final filling gas. The metal lamp cap M is fixed to the bulb by a heat-curing cement N. The lamp cap is usually fabricated from either aluminium or brass with an opaque glass insulator.

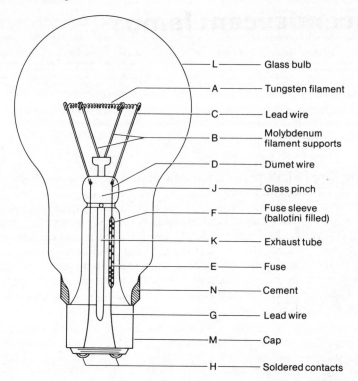

L	Glass bulb
A	Tungsten filament
C	Lead wire
B	Molybdenum filament supports
D	Dumet wire
J	Glass pinch
F	Fuse sleeve (ballotini filled)
K	Exhaust tube
E	Fuse
N	Cement
G	Lead wire
M	Cap
H	Soldered contacts

Fig. 9.1   Construction of a GLS lamp

Filaments   The design of incandescent filaments is dictated to a large degree by the required operating parameters. The length of wire in the filament is primarily a function of the operating voltage and the wire diameter is determined by the operating current. These characteristics are modified somewhat by the running temperature which is in turn a function of the required life. The length of the wound coil is determined by (a) the control of mandrel to wire diameter ratio which is necessary to give the filament adequate stiffness and (b) the desire to make a coil as short as possible in order to reduce thermal loss from the filament. An extension of this principle is the use of secondary coiling (coiled coil) which has the effect of reducing the finished coil length on a 40 W GLS lamp from 50 mm to 25 mm, so raising the filament efficacy by 20% for the same life. It should be recognized however that while the coiled coil filament, with its greater light output, is perfectly suitable for normal domestic applications, it does not have the same robust characteristics as the single coil design recommended for any installations which have an environment of shock or vibration.

A further range of heavy duty lamps is produced for service where high levels of vibration and shock are unavoidable. Improved lamp characteristics for such conditions can be achieved by making filaments of small mandrel to wire ratios and by the inclusion of more intermediate filament supports. On certain types, particularly lamps for operation at low filament temperatures, improved vibration resistance can be achieved by the use of special grades of tungsten, with either rhenium or thoria additives which produce a more suitable metallurgical structure for this application (Sect. 7.3.1).

Bulbs The bulbs of GLS lamps are predominantly the long-established pear-shaped bulbs or the mushroom-shaped bulbs introduced in the late 1950s. The high speed manufacturing equipment on which these bulbs are made (Sect. 7.1) is unsuitable for frequent changes in bulb dimensions, and economic advantages result from the reduction in the variety of shapes and sizes which has occurred over the past few years. At present the pear- and mushroom-shaped varieties of 40 W, 60 W, and 100 W coiled coil lamps are all made in a 60 mm diameter bulb. The minimum dimensions of a finished lamp are also limited by the acceptance by lamp manufacturers of a series of maximum levels for cap temperature rise during use. This, coupled with the fact that there is now a requirement for luminaires to be marked with the maximum acceptable wattage, should reduce problems of overheating by the use of higher wattage lamps than those for which luminaires are designed.

Gas filling The proportion of the radiation from a filament which gives visible light increases sharply with temperature (Sect. 9.5, Coaton 1969), so it is advantageous to operate the filament at the highest possible temperature. In a vacuum this is limited by the evaporation rate of tungsten. This can be greatly reduced by filling the bulb with an inert gas, so that the temperature can be raised without the life becoming too short, and the radiation efficacy thus increased. The disadvantage is that the gas conducts heat away from the filament, which reduces the overall lamp efficacy.

There is clearly a balance between these two factors, which can be evaluated for each type of lamp (Coaton 1969). Generally, vacuum is advantageous for lower power lamps and gas filling for higher power lamps. The changeover occurs at about 15 W for mains voltage lamps and at about 3 W for miniature lamps, such as torch bulbs.

The heat loss to the gas can be determined using the 'Langmuir sheath model' (Langmuir 1962). This assumes that the viscous, low density gas layer immediately surrounding an incandescent surface is free from convection currents, and heat flow from the filament is by conduction and radiation only. Outside this layer convection becomes the chief means by which heat is transferred to the bulb wall. Calculation of the power loss, tungsten evaporation rate, and effect on efficacy using the model are dealt with in detail by Coaton (1969, 1970b, 1971). The causes of ultimate filament failure are reviewed by Fisher et al. (1975).

Generally, household lamps are filled to just below 1 atm pressure (Sect. 9.4.1) with 90% argon and 10% nitrogen, but lamps containing the heavier, less conductive, inert gas krypton with nitrogen give a higher efficacy for the same life (Sect. 7.5). The nitrogen is necessary to prevent arcing between the ends of the hot filament, which would be likely to occur at mains voltage if the pure inert gas were used.

The majority of GLS lamps in the UK offer 1000 h life. This life was determined by calculations to evaluate the conditions for the minimum cost per unit of light, including the cost of lamps, power, and lamp replacement. Where the cost of lamp replacement is high, manufacturers offer 2000 h life lamps with reduced light output. Sect. 21.2 discusses the factors affecting lighting economics.

9.2 Special purpose lamps

9.2.1 Decorative lamps

The incandescent filament lamp is, in its simplest form, purely a functional light source, but the fact that an integral part of the lamp is a bulb fashioned from glass enables the designer to adapt and modify this envelope in order to give the product some aesthetic appeal.

One of the earliest attempts at decoration was the internal etching of the pear-shaped bulb to produce the 'pearl' lamp (Sect. 7.1). Internal coatings and finishes are now commonly applied to lamps of standard ratings, for example finely divided silica or titania on mushroom-shaped bulbs, where virtual obscuration of the filament and reduction of glare can be achieved with a light output loss as low as 4%. Coloured lamps are produced either by internally or externally coating the surface of the bulb with pigments. Lamps coloured by the external application of a silicate suspension are especially suited, by virtue of their resistance to thermal shock, for use out of doors. It is necessary to ensure that the heating effect of the colour coatings neither raises the bulb wall to temperatures which release impurities nor raises the cap region to unacceptable temperature levels. Transparent coloured lacquers find use on lamps for electric fires. Perhaps the commonest form of decorative bulb is the candle lamp, which is produced in some quantity with either a smooth shape or in a twisted form. The finish may be clear, white, or frosted. In more recent years other lamps have been marketed which combine the roles of light source and decorative luminaire by virtue of their bulb shapes. They are usually of larger dimensions than conventional lamps. The 'striplight' range of incandescent filament lamps is another form which finds extensive domestic use. These lamps comprise a long tubular bulb of glass, either clear or white-coated, fitted with a small cap carrying an electrical connection point at either end of the bulb. A lamp has been produced with a film of silicone-rubber applied to the outside of the bulb which holds together the glass fragments in the event of breakage in food preparation establishments, hospitals, garages, etc. The coating also makes the bulb resistant to breakage from thermal shock, as by water falling on a lit lamp.

9.2.2   Directional beams

A further range of special purpose lamps is made with directional beam properties for use in display and associated applications. These lamps are constructed with the filament at the focal point of a paraboloid, blown or pressed to form an integral part of the bulb surface and coated with a highly reflective material, usually vacuum-deposited aluminium. As the atmosphere within the bulb is inert, the condition of this coating is maintained throughout the life of the lamp. Lamps in this category range from the 12 V 50 W screw cap types designed for use with a transformer and having a particularly high intensity, low divergence beam, to the 150 W reflector display lamps (Fig. 9.2a) which operate from mains voltage and are designed to produce the beam characteristic shown (Fig. 9.2b). A narrow, sharply-defined beam can also be produced using a bowl or crown silvered lamp with a purpose-made separate parabolic reflector (Fig. 9.3). Externally-applied colours extend the use of these types in both continuous and intermittent operational use.

9.2.3   Sealed beam lamps

A separate range of lamps of this type is made in the sealed beam (or pressed glass) construction (Fig. 9.4). The manufacturing process for these lamps ensures that the filament is positioned relative to the reflector with a high degree of accuracy and this, together with the improved reflector profiles possible with this design, enables higher performance beam characteristics to be achieved. The sealed beam lamp is made in separate spotlight and floodlight designs and these are intended for a rather longer life

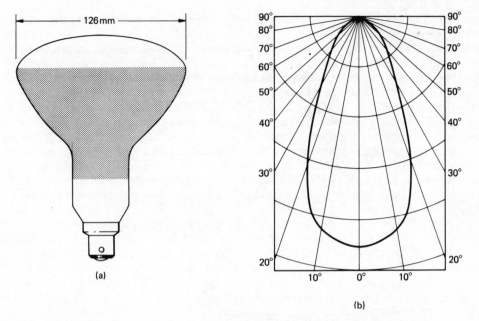

Fig. 9.2 (a) 150 W reflector display lamp and (b) its polar intensity distribution

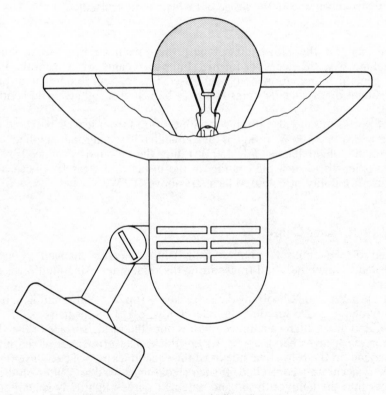

Fig. 9.3 Crown silvered lamp and separate parabolic reflector

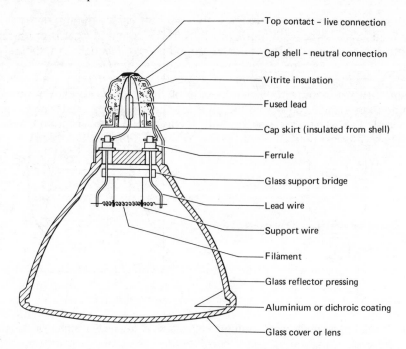

Fig. 9.4   Construction of a 150 W sealed beam lamp (spot or flood)

than is normal for the blown glass type. Apart from applications in studio and photographic work, the necessity for high intensity beams arises from the increased levels of general illumination now being used in shops and commercial premises, where highlighting of specific items can only be achieved by powerful spotlights or floodlights.

Sealed beam lamps are also produced with coloured front lenses to extend the field for these lamps. A 100 W rating is available having externally-applied coloured lacquers on floodlight lenses. For 150 W rating the colour is produced by using a stained glass lens or a dichroic coating on the inside of a clear lens because of the temperature instability of coloured lacquers above 100 W.

9.2.4   Dichroic-coated lamps

The colour of the emitted radiation from lamps may be changed by selectively reflecting some wavebands and transmitting the remainder using multilayer interference filters.

Many transparent non-absorbing dielectric layers (up to 23) alternating in refractive index from high, e.g. 2·3 for zinc sulphide, to low, e.g. 1·38 for magnesium fluoride, are evaporated under high vacuum conditions onto the inside surface of the glass lens or reflector, each layer being about 0·1 μm thick. The properties of the multilayer coating depend on the refractive index and the exact thickness of each layer and these must be very accurately controlled. If such a coating is used as a filter on the lens to reflect back into the lamp both red and blue light, green light only is emitted by the lamp. If a red lamp is desired then the filter is designed to reflect blue and green light.

Such filters are called dichroic coatings. By a suitable choice of filter, any colour may be obtained. Since practically no light is absorbed, coloured light is produced more efficiently by interference filters than by stained glass or lacquers. Another advantage is their ability to operate at higher temperatures than is possible with coloured lacquers, so they are used for reflector lamps rated above 100 W.

The majority of the infrared component in the beam may be removed by the use of a suitable interference coating on the reflector surface which reflects more than 95% of the visible light striking it, but transmits the infrared radiation into the light fitting. These lamps producing 'cold' light find many applications, including cine projectors, the illumination of refrigerated food displays, and operating theatre lamps.

9.3   Automobile and miniature lamps

9.3.1   Headlights

The design of headlights is dictated by international regulations and throughout Europe legislation has been harmonized to allow standardized types of headlight beam distribution and the use of a limited number of standardized lamp types, either under a United Nations Agreement (ECE 1958a) with an 'E' approval mark, or under a directly related European Community Council Directive (EEC 1976) with an 'e' approval mark. In the UK it is also permitted to use certain sealed beam headlights with an American type of beam pattern, conforming to BS AU40 (BSI 1966b, c). However, most cars in the UK use a European approved dipped beam pattern which is distinguishable by its sharp cut-off, horizontal on the off-side of the vehicle and rising at 15 degrees towards the near-side kerb. The European regulations specify the illumination of various points and areas on a screen placed 25 m in front of the headlight, both on dipped beam and main beam and allow either a sealed beam construction or a unit using standardized replaceable lamps.

Sealed beam headlights are hermetically sealed units with either bare filaments or complete tungsten halogen lamp capsules accurately positioned in aluminized, pressed glass reflectors, sealed usually by melting together the rims of the reflector and the glass front lens. The whole unit is then filled with a dry inert gas. Sealed beam units have the advantages that the beam pattern is adjusted to meet the regulations during manufacture, and that the reflector is totally protected from degradation by outside moisture and dust. However, the difficulty of melting the rims together evenly limits the outline shapes that can be mass produced, thus restricting the freedom of the automobile stylists.

Replaceable lamp headlights consist of an aluminized, metal or high temperature plastic reflector joined to a front lens, usually made of glass. The reflector has a seating ring which positions the flange of a standardized lamp type which can have one or two filaments and an inert gas or halogen filling. The twin filament lamps have an accurately positioned, cup-shaped shield partly surrounding the dipped filament in order to produce the sharp cut-off of the European beam (see halogen H4 lamps, Sect. 10.3.3). The advantages of this type of headlight are a cheaper replacement lamp and that the whole unit can be styled to suit the car design. However, it has been found almost impossible to prevent the headlight from 'breathing' when the gas inside the unit is alternately heated and cooled, leading to the ingress of dust and water vapour, resulting in condensation in cold weather and gradual deterioration of performance.

9.3.2 Auxiliary lamps

The lamps used for side lights, turn indicators, tail lights, brake lights, and fog lights have also been made the subject of European standardization, drastically reducing the number of ratings and types being used.

9.3.3 Panel lamps

The traditional system of panel illumination in automobiles was by use of lamps fitted with either miniature Edison screw or miniature bayonet caps. Electrical contact to the lamps was made by wiring which terminated at the sockets, but this required a great deal of assembly time and increased the cost. The introduction of wedge base lamps allowed the use of printed circuit techniques and so made substantial reductions in assembly time and cost.

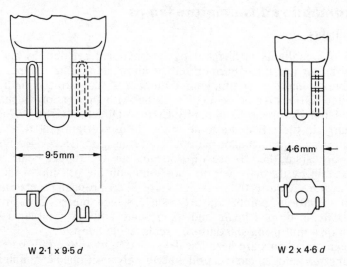

W 2·1 x 9·5 *d*   W 2 x 4·6 *d*

Fig. 9.5 Wedge base designs

The wedge base lamp is made without the usual metal cap and is retained in place by a specially designed socket with spring contacts locating in grooves moulded into the base of the bulb (Fig. 9.5). Electrical contact is achieved by means of hairpin-shaped lead wires from the lamp which are pressed between contacts in the socket and the glass of the base. The lamp has the advantage of simple assembly and in use offers improved resistance to shock and vibration. There are gas-filled types for external use on vehicles and vacuum types for panel applications.

9.3.4 Sub-miniature lamps

Perhaps the most extensive use of sub-miniature lamps, usually lamps with less than 6 mm bulb diameter, is to be found in aircraft applications. This results from the necessity to conserve space and weight, and these requirements led to the development of special lamp types. Figure 9.6a shows a typical aircraft panel indicator lamp made in a 5·6 mm diameter bulb with a midget flange cap. As the lighting system in aircraft is usually 28 V, the relatively long filament needs two intermediate filament supports in order to withstand the rigorous vibration conditions of service. In some instances voltage controls are introduced into the circuits and 6 V and 12 V filaments are also produced for this application.

The need to conserve space is however not exclusive to aircraft and increasing use is being made of sub-miniature wedge base lamps. An international standard has been established for a 5 mm diameter wedge base design (Fig. 9.6b) and a 12 V 1·2 W version is now being used extensively in automobile panel illumination where the

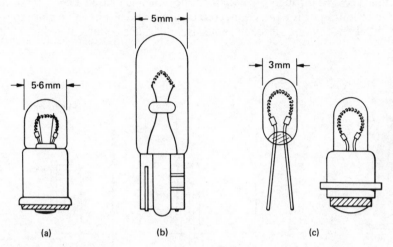

Fig. 9.6 (a) aircraft panel indicator lamp, (b) 5 mm diameter wedge base lamp, and (c) 3 mm diameter sub-miniature lamp

compact dimensions offer new design possibilities. At the lower end of the sub-miniature lamp scale is a range of lamps in bulbs of 3 mm diameter and less (Fig. 9.6c). These lamps are often used in installations where replacement would be exceedingly difficult and for this reason the lamps are often designed to have indefinitely long life by virtue of low filament operating temperatures. Even smaller lamps have also been produced for incorporation in medical apparatus.

9.3.5 Miners' lamps

For many years now it has been standard practice to manufacture special high performance lamps for use in mines. The basic requirement is for the miner to have a light beam of adequate intensity which will last for the duration of a shift and can be operated from a battery small and light enough not to hinder his manual operations. These considerations led to a range of krypton-filled lamps which yielded a 25% increase in light output for the same life and current rating as an argon-filled version.

9.4 Manufacturing methods

9.4.1 Sealing techniques

There are three methods of construction used in the standard ranges of incandescent lamps: drop-seal, butt-seal, and pinch-seal. As a rough guide, the drop-seal technique is used on lamps rated in excess of 10 W and the butt-seal technique on ratings below this level. Because of the potential for high speed manufacture and automation, the pinch-seal technique is also used for capped lamps up to 21 W; uncapped versions are commonly called wedge base lamps.

Drop-seal construction   Lamps of the drop-seal type are produced by sealing an inner sub-assembly comprising a flare tube, exhaust tube, lead wires, support wires where appropriate, and filament into a preformed bulb (Fig. 9.7). After sealing the hot lamps are evacuated through the exhaust tube which is held in a compression head on an indexing rotating turret and connected by pipes and a split valve plate to a series of vacuum pumps. Pumping on each index is sometimes followed by inert gas flushes

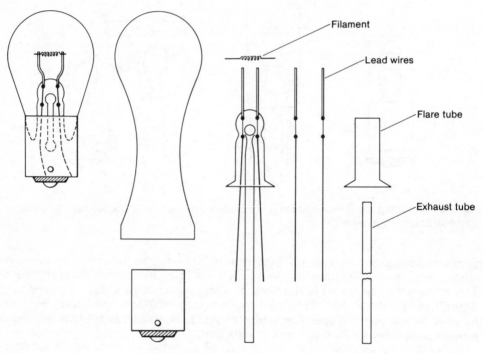

Fig. 9.7 Components of drop-seal lamp

between pumping stages until the position on the machine at which the filling gas is introduced is reached. The pressure of the filling gas is normally just below one atmosphere so that, in the last position, where the exhaust tube is sealed off (tipping-off), the internal pressure of the gas does not blow out the molten glass.

The lamp cap on GLS lamps is normally of the bayonet type in the UK or the screw type in Europe and the USA. It is fixed to the bulb by a heat-curing cement. The lead wires from the inner assembly are normally soldered to the two eyelets at the base of the bayonet caps, but are sometimes welded to the contact points on screw caps.

In order to improve the atmosphere within the bulb it is common practice to include, on the lamp assembly, gettering materials which take up residual oxygen and hydrogen. Red phosphorus suspensions applied to the filament and zirconium–aluminium mixtures applied to the lead wires are typical examples of the getters used (Sect. 7.3.3). The initial lighting of a filament is often a critical operation in order to produce the optimum gettering effect and to promote the necessary recrystallization of the tungsten filament wire to overcome sagging tendencies. It is customary to use a protective impedance in series with the lamp to avoid damage due to possible arcing.

Butt-seal construction The bulbs for this type of lamp are often produced from tubing held on rotating machines. The lowermost end of the tubing is progressively melted and blown into an external mould. After shaping the bulbs are cracked off to produce the shape shown on the left in Fig. 9.8.

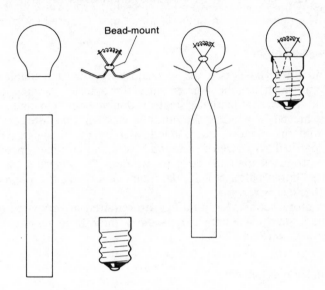

Fig. 9.8 Components of butt-seal lamp

The inner sub-assembly of this type of lamp is known as a bead-mount. This comprises two lengths of Dumet wire held by a bead of sintered glass and shaped into a form which seats on the open end of the bulb neck. At the other end it is splayed out and hooked around the tails of the filament, normally produced on a retractable mandrel coiling head on the bead-mount machine.

Assembly of this type of lamp is achieved by inserting the bead-mount into the neck of the bulb and sealing on a length of tubing of approximately the same diameter as the bulb neck. At a later stage this tubing is constricted above the area of the seal to facilitate the subsequent tipping-off process. The processes of exhaust and gas-filling are largely as described for the drop-seal technique.

Pinch-seal construction The bulbs are produced in the same way as for butt-seal lamps. The inner mount assembly is also produced as for butt-seal mounts, but it is customary to use nickel-plated Dumet in order to reduce oxidation which may cause contact problems where the lead wires themselves form the external contacts (Figs 9.5 and 9.6).

The lamp assembly is made by separately holding the exhaust tube, the bead-mount, and the bulb together in position while the neck of the bulb is heated until the base shape can be impressed upon it. Exhausting, gas-filling where appropriate, and tipping-off follow the methods already described.

9.4.2   High speed GLS manufacture

In order to keep down manufacturing costs it is necessary to use automated equipment operating at high speeds. One such type of equipment manufactures GLS lamps at a speed approaching 5000 lamps per hour. Mounts, or completed internal lamp assemblies, are produced by a linear (non-rotary) machine operating on a duplex indexing system whereby each process stage is duplicated, thus doubling the production rate. The rotary sealing, exhaust machine, and capper are also operated on the duplex principle.

9.4.3   Filaments and bulbs

In order to reduce thermal losses and to dispose the tungsten filament wire (Sect. 7.3.1) in a form which can be conveniently fitted inside a lamp envelope it is customary to coil the wire into either a single or double helix. On mains voltage lamps this is usually achieved by winding the tungsten wire on a mandrel of either steel or molybdenum, and the mandrel is removed later by dissolving in acid. On lower voltage lamps, particularly those of 12 V and below, modern high speed manufacturing equipment produces filament coils by winding the tungsten on a retractable mandrel which withdraws after coiling; the filament is then cut off and automatically transferred to the lead wires.

Bulbs for the more popular lamp ratings are required in very large quantities and are normally made on a machine which produces them from a continuous ribbon of molten soda-lime glass (Sect. 7.1).

9.4.4   Caps and capping cement

The caps used on incandescent lamps fall into three main groups:

Bayonet caps have barrel diameters up to 22 mm and are fitted into sockets by pushing inwards against contacts and engaged by rotating.

Screw caps are available in diameters up to 40 mm. Electrical contact is made when the contact in the base engages with the corresponding socket contact. The shell of the cap makes the other connection.

Prefocus caps are used on lamps where close control of filament position is essential as in projectors or headlights.

Caps, and also the bases for wedge base lamps, are standardized in IEC 161 (IEC 1969). The relevant British Specifications are BS 52 (BSI 1963), BS 5042 (BSI 1978), and BS 841 (BSI 1966a).

Capping cements are usually mixtures of a thermo-setting resin and an inert inorganic filler. Some cements will operate satisfactorily at temperatures up to 210 °C.

9.4.5   Quality and safety controls

In the manufacture of all the above lamp types it is essential that great attention is paid to the maintenance of material quality, filament characteristics, gas purity, pump effectiveness, temperature settings, and all relevant processing schedules. To produce lamps of good quality frequent checks of filament rating, exhaust quality, and dimensional control ensure consistent performance. Statistical sampling techniques to monitor all specification requirements for physical, electrical, and photometric characteristics are essential. Reliable photometric methods and the use of life test voltages stabilized to about 0·5% are necessary. Particularly on high voltage lamps, such as GLS types, it is usual to operate additional controls with high overload voltage tests which can produce extra information on lamp quality. It should perhaps be noted that high overload voltage testing can lead to very misleading results unless correctly interpreted, owing to the fact that the lamp loadings and operating temperatures are substantially changed from normal. If any contaminants are present in lamps, the relationship between voltage and life is altered.

Test conditions are laid down in IEC 64 (IEC 1973), BS 161 (BSI 1976a), BS 555 (BSI 1962), and BS 941 (BSI 1970) where details are given of selection, inspection, photometry, and life testing. Burning position, switching, light output, maintenance through life, and cap adhesion are also considered in these.

For GLS lamps additional comprehensive controls are imposed on materials and all stages of manufacture to ensure the safety of lamps for domestic and similar general lighting purposes. Conditions of compliance are laid down in BS 5971 (BSI 1980a).

9.4.6 Environmental testing

The service environments of many lamps impose special conditions of high temperature, humidity, or vibration. Appropriate test equipment has been and is still being developed to simulate such service conditions in order that the performance of lamps may be assessed in the laboratory.

The effect of high humidity on capping cement adhesion is usually tested in a special cabinet which cycles humidity and temperature conditions, e.g. a temperature of 60 °C at a relative humidity of 99% for a period of 16 h followed by cooling to room temperature over 8 h.

There has been a tendency in the past to specify arbitrary tests for lamp resistance to shock and vibration. More recently, however, much greater emphasis has been placed on the necessity for accurate reproduction of the service environment so that lamps may be tested under strictly comparable conditions.

9.5 Working characteristics

The operating requirements of incandescent lamps in service lead to a great diversity of specifications in terms of life, light output, and wattage. For example an automobile headlight is required to project a high intensity beam of light and to last about 100 operating hours, whereas a panel indicator lamp is required to produce a relatively low illuminance to facilitate night-time instrument reading, to consume as little power as possible, and to operate virtually for the life of the vehicle. These two conflicting requirements result in the filament of the non-halogen automobile headlight operating at a temperature of 2800 K, while that of the panel lamp is of the order of 2400 K. The operating temperature of the filament has a direct influence on the evaporation rate and therefore on the life. If the voltage, current, and either life or output of a lamp are specified then the complete operating characteristics of the lamp are fixed. The influence of temperature on life can be transformed into a function of applied voltage. The relationship is that for moderate changes in voltage (say ±25%) the lamp life is inversely proportional to the nth power of the voltage, where $n = 13$

for vacuum lamps, 14 for gas-filled GLS lamps, and 11·2 for headlamps. This shows that for an increase of only 5% in operating voltage the lamp life is halved; it would of course be doubled by a 5% decrease. Thus photoflood lamps, which are overloaded in order to increase light output and efficacy, have as a result a very short life.

The dependence on voltage of other GLS lamp parameters may be described in similar terms. The exponents vary according to lamp type, but representative values may be quoted. The current is directly proportional to the square root of the voltage, the efficacy to the square, and the luminous flux to the power 3·6.

The effect of frequent switching on life is quite marked on lamps designed to operate at high efficacy levels, such as in projectors. Lamps of lower efficacy and longer life are less sensitive to intermittent operation.

The ordinary 100 W GLS coiled coil gas-filled lamp has an efficacy of 12·6 lm W^{-1}. This varies with type and rating (see Appendix I), being rather lower for single coil types and rather higher for higher power lamps. This low efficacy is because 75% of the input power is radiated in the infrared, even though the filament is to some extent a selective radiator (Sect. 6.3.1, De Vos 1954). A further 19% is lost as conducted and convected heat, and 0·25% in the ultraviolet, only 5·75% emerging as visible light. Various schemes for reducing the energy lost as infrared radiation (Studer and Cusano 1953, Brett et al. 1981) have so far not proved practical on any scale. The one proved method of improving the efficacy is to operate at a higher filament temperature, and this is made possible by the tungsten halogen principle, which is the subject of the next chapter.

One consequence of this high proportion of infrared radiation is that the incandescent lamp is very suitable for heating applications requiring a high infrared intensity. The higher power tungsten halogen lamps provide a similar spectral power distribution (Fig. 15.5e) at slightly shorter wavelengths.

Further reading

Coaton J R, 1969, *Ltg. Res. Technol.*, **1,** 98–103: The optimum operating gas pressure for incandescent tungsten filament lamps
Horacsek O, 1980, *IEE Proc.*, **127,** Part A, 134–141: Properties and failure modes of incandescent tungsten filaments
Philips, 1975, *Philips Tech. Rev.*, **35,** 295–306: Research on incandescent lamps

10 Tungsten halogen lamps

Progress since the invention of the incandescent light source, just over one hundred years ago, has taken place with the quest for longer lamp lives and increased efficacy from carbon wire to single coil tungsten and onto coiled coil constructions, all giving considerable gains, not to mention the cost-effectiveness of using the gains attributable to the use of rare and more expensive inert gases. Patents published as long ago as 1881 (Scribner 1881) indicated that an advantageous chemical reaction between a halogen and tungsten within a lamp envelope could take place. However, due to many constraints, it was not feasible to utilize this phenomenon until around 1959, when it was discovered how to make a halogen cycle work in a practical lamp using iodine (Zubler and Mosby 1959).

This chapter outlines the present state of the art which has resulted in a whole new range of lamps considerably extending the use of the incandescent lamp principle.

10.1 The regenerative cycle

The conventional incandescent gas-filled lamp loses filament material by evaporation, much of it being deposited onto the bulb wall. When a halogen is added to the filling gas, and if certain temperature and design conditions are established, a reversible chemical reaction occurs between tungsten and the halogen. In the simplest terms tungsten is evaporated from the incandescent filament and some portion of this diffuses towards the bulb wall. Within a specific zone between the filament and the bulb wall, where temperature conditions are favourable, the tungsten combines with the halogen. The tungsten halogen molecules diffuse towards the filament where they dissociate, the tungsten being deposited back onto the filament, while the halogen is available for a further reaction cycle.

In order to understand this cycle let us consider in more detail an incandescent filament positioned along the axis of a closed tube containing an inert gas and a halogen (Fig. 10.1). The filament would normally operate at a temperature between 2350 °C and 3150 °C, the temperature being dependent on the desired life and applied voltage. Between the filament and the bulb wall there is a temperature gradient through the inert filling gas. This gradient can be divided into three zones, extending radially from filament to bulb wall with limiting temperatures dividing them. Within the zone or layer immediately surrounding the filament there are no reactions, the inert filling gas, tungsten, and halogen atoms being present as separate components. The next outward zone sees a reaction between these components so that a combination of the halogen and tungsten atoms to form tungsten halides takes place, with dissociation taking place at the higher temperature side of this zone. Beyond the lower temperature side of this zone to the bulb wall there is no thermal dissociation, but a continuing combination of halogen atoms takes place to complete the formation

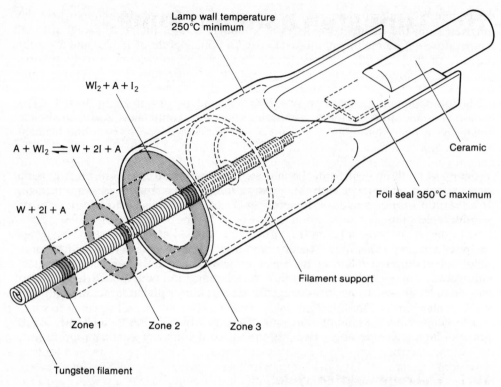

Fig. 10.1   Simplified mechanism of the iodine regenerative cycle

of the tungsten halides. These tungsten halides diffuse towards the filament, being circulated in the convection current, where they again dissociate into the halogen and tungsten. Unfortunately, the regenerated tungsten is not in most cases deposited directly back onto the filament, but is liberated in the inner zone where the tungsten vapour density is enhanced and the solid is deposited onto the filament. In the cases of the iodine and bromine cycles it does not settle on the hot spots from where it was originally evaporated, but on the cooler sections of the filament nearer the supports and tails.

All halogens are theoretically capable of supporting a regenerative cycle in a tungsten halogen filament lamp, the main difference between them being the temperature at which the various reactions in the cycle may take place. In addition, the extent to which they react with components and impurities, especially oxygen and hydrogen, within the lamp also determines their usefulness. Good reviews are given of halogen regenerative cycles by Coaton (1970a) and Dettingmeijer et al. (1975).

10.2   Design and construction

10.2.1   Choice of halogen

Tungsten iodine lamps   Of all the tungsten halogen lamps, the iodine lamp was the first to become commercially available. This was mainly because the temperatures required to maintain the regenerative cycle were well suited to many practical lamp designs: in particular to lamps which have a life in excess of 1000 hours where the tungsten from the filament vaporizes at a moderate rate. Iodine is a solid at room temperature with a melting point of 113·6 °C, a boiling point of 183 °C, and a vapour pressure of 49·3 Pa at 25 °C. It is dried by sublimation in vacuum over phosphorus pentoxide to reduce the moisture content to a sufficiently low level for lamp use.

The predominant reaction is $W + 2I \rightleftharpoons WI_2$ and occurs at about 1000 °C. The operating temperatures in the case of iodine and iodine compounds, such as hydrogen iodide, have been determined, and for a successful regenerative cycle the filament must run at a minimum temperature of 1700 °C with the bulb wall at least 250 °C. The quantity of iodine required is variable and dependent on the amount of tungsten to be regenerated, this in turn being related to filament temperature and overall lamp loading. The greater the proportion of iodine vapour in a lamp, the greater is the light loss due to absorption by the characteristic pink vapour: this could be up to 5% in practical lamp designs.

Tungsten bromine lamps The tungsten bromine cycle is very similar to the iodine cycle. The reaction in this case involves the formation of WBr_2 or higher bromides, and requires a temperature of about 1500 °C. Bromine is far more reactive than iodine and one of its disadvantages is that a small excess of the elemental form causes erosion of the cooler parts of the filament below 1500 °C. This has been overcome to some extent by the introduction of compounds, such as HBr, CH_2Br_2, and CH_3Br, which dissociate in the zone close to the filament, releasing sufficient bromine to react with the evaporated tungsten. Most of the excess bromine remains in compound form as HBr until, during life, some hydrogen diffuses through the bulb, leaving excess bromine which attacks the filament. Therefore, bromine lamps are restricted to a short life of under 1000 hours and, where the rate of evaporation of tungsten is greater than in the case of iodine lamps, with filament temperatures higher than 2800 °C. Bromine is a liquid at room temperature with a melting point of −7·3 °C, a boiling point of 58·2 °C, and a vapour pressure of 30 800 Pa at 25 °C. A major advantage of these bromine compounds is that they can be introduced in gaseous form at room temperature, thus simplifying the manufacturing process. Bromine in the quantities used gives practically no light absorption and therefore there is a gain in efficacy over iodine. The regenerative cycle also operates over a somewhat wider range of bulb temperatures, approximately 200 °C to 1100 °C.

Gettering of bromine lamps Langmuir (1913) discovered that small traces of water vapour could produce blackening of the bulb wall by the formation of oxides on the hot tungsten filament, diffusion to the bulb wall, and reduction of the oxides on the wall by residues of hydrogen. In addition, transport of tungsten can be produced along the filament if there is a temperature gradient along the coil and between the coil supports (Geszti and Gaal 1974). In the case of halogen lamps traces of oxygen, hydrogen, and water are frequently present. These traces cause various transport cycles of the tungsten if they are not carefully regulated, with reactions involving WO_2, WO_2Br_2, and other compounds (Coaton 1970a). These cycles occur in the vicinity of the temperature gradient in the filament, and may lead to early lamp failure due to thinning of the filament wire. It appears that the direction of the tungsten transport along the temperature gradient varies according to the gas present. Excess oxygen in the lamp produces transport of tungsten up the temperature gradient from the supports to the hotter filament, whereas water causes transport in the opposite direction towards the support, building up dendritic growths in the form of spikes.

A recent innovation has been the introduction of the halogen together with phosphorus as a getter for oxygen and water vapour, in the form of bromophosphon-itrile $(PNBr_2)_n$ (Rees 1970). In this way bromine can be added as trimeric and tetrameric bromophosphonitrile, which are chemically inert solids of low vapour pressure. The melting points and vapour pressures of $(PNBr_2)_3$ and $(PNBr_2)_4$ are 192 °C and 202 °C and 10^{-4} Pa and 5×10^{-8} Pa respectively at room temperature. Thus it is now possible to administer into the lamp in solution an exact amount of a combination of phosphorus getter and halogen. This does not dissociate until the filament is lighted on ageing, after which the accurately controlled amount of bromine carries out its function in the halogen cycle and phosphorus takes up the unwanted gases, thus achieving a longer and more controlled life, with less variation within a batch of lamps.

Tungsten fluorine lamps   Further research has been directed to extend the life of the tungsten halogen lamp and to produce a truly regenerative cycle, depositing tungsten onto the hottest parts of the filaments, thereby reducing the rate of formation of hot spots. The possibility of this self-healing tungsten fluorine cycle has been known for several years (Schröder 1964), but there are three major technological difficulties which have so far prevented the development of a successful practical lamp:

(a)   At temperatures above 400 °C fluorine and/or tungsten fluorides rapidly react with the fused silica bulb which ties up the fluorine and leads to rapid bulb blackening and short filament life.

(b)   The quantity of fluorine required to establish a self-healing cycle is very small, around 40 micrograms for a lamp of 1 cm³ volume, and must be dispersed with an accuracy better than ±0·15%.

(c)   The tungsten lead-in wire, or filament legs, are attacked by fluorine, which gradually erodes them away.

However, some limited success to date has been achieved by introducing a protective, fluoride resistant, inorganic, glassy coating based on a system of Al_2O_3, TiO_2, and P_2O_5 on the bulb wall, by dosing the lamp with a fluorinated polymer dissolved in a solvent, a method which is accurate to within ±0·15%, and by providing substantial tungsten supports which produce a tungsten reservoir condition, but eventually erode the supports away (Fitzpatrick and Rees 1979). This is the main mode of failure currently being experienced. There is no doubt that we will one day see an advantage in fluorine, which may be by the development of a chemical buffer to combine with the free fluorine in the cool region and release it close to the filament.

10.2.2   Bulb and seal

The majority of lamps manufactured to date have utilized bulbs made from pure fused silica or similar materials with a silica content of greater than 96%, such as Vycor (Sect. 7.1). This is the ideal material for lamps which have to operate at a high bulb wall temperature and are subjected to violent thermal shocks on switching. Successful results, it should be noted, are also being achieved using a high melting point glass, such as an aluminosilicate (Sect. 7.1). This has augmented the design facility and has usefully extended the tungsten halogen lamp range where, for economic reasons, a lower wattage lamp or large volume high wattage lamp is compatible with the particular application. However, in the silica or Vycor product the low expansion properties of the material require a different form of hermetic seal because there are no metals capable of matching this low expansion and high temperature sealing characteristic. The technique therefore is to use very thin molybdenum foil (Sect. 7.4) which has the capability of producing a seal (even though not matching in expansion) and has sufficient electrical conductivity, but which does impose limitations with regard to lamp design to be discussed later in the chapter.

A suitable lamp design using aluminosilicate glass has major advantages at the seal point in that glass compositions have been formulated to produce a matching seal, thus some of the complexities of lamp manufacture have been removed.

10.2.3   Filament and supports

The filaments of tungsten halogen lamps not only operate at higher temperatures, but they also are often more closely wound to give greater luminous flux per unit area. Being in extremely small bulbs, they must remain quite rigid, without sag, throughout life. A further demand is that the wire must be free from trace contaminants, such as nickel and iron, which would combine to form unwanted halides and condense on the bulb wall taking the halogen out of the cycle. This means that the tungsten wire has to be specially controlled from the powder stage throughout the processing. After it is coiled, the wire structure of the filament is still fibrous and the filament is then held rigidly on a tungsten mandrel in a vacuum or hydrogen atmosphere and heated to about 2400 °C (Sect. 7.3.1). During this operation, the fibrous material is converted to a crystalline state; the crystals must interlock to prevent slip which would cause sagging of the filament (Fig. 10.2).

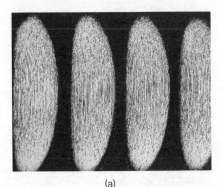
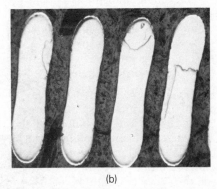

(a)   (b)

Fig. 10.2   Micrographs of cross-sections of coiled tungsten filaments: (a) before and (b) after temperature treatment. × 217

The supports holding the filament are normally made from tungsten. In some designs molybdenum supports are being used, but these lamps have a life of only a few hundred hours. If the design of the filament is complicated, having many limbs, then a silica bridge holding the various filament support wires can also be incorporated. As every lamp must have two conductor leads, the designs include double ended linear lamps where there is one seal at each end and single ended lamps with both seals at one end. The double ended lamps are mainly used for floodlighting and general illumination purposes, whereas the single ended lamps have more compact filaments and are used in conjunction with precise optics.

10.2.4   Advantages of the tungsten halogen lamp

The improved efficacy and life of the tungsten halogen lamp over a conventional incandescent lamp do not, in fact, arise from the redeposition of tungsten onto the filament, but because the regenerative cycle prevents the accumulation of the tungsten on the bulb wall. This not only gives virtually 100% lumen maintenance throughout life, but it also permits change in the geometry and a radical reduction in the size of the lamp, which in turn enable the lamp to operate at an increased gas pressure and hence at an increased density. This increase in gas density suppresses evaporation of tungsten from the filament. Thus there is an increase in the intrinsic quality of the lamp, to be used as higher efficacy or longer life, depending on the required application. The volume of a tungsten halogen lamp is very much less than that of the equivalent conventional lamp. For example a 500 W tungsten halogen lamp is only 1% of the volume of its conventional counterpart (Fig. 10.3). The resulting

Fig. 10.3   Comparative sizes of 500 W GLS and 500 W tungsten halogen lamps

compact source can be used extremely efficiently in optical systems, producing improved control of the light directional characteristics.

The respective diameters of the filament and of the lamp bulb are important design factors. Not only must the minimum temperature conditions be satisfied, but also the bulb diameter should be designed so that there is virtually no gas convection which could cause heat losses and lower efficacy. Langmuir's 'sheath theory' shows that this absence of convection may apply to designs used in tungsten halogen lamps and this is one reason for their increased efficacy over the conventional lamp when the sheath diameter exceeds the lamp diameter (Sect. 9.1). The evaporation rate of the filaments is determined by the size and density of the surrounding gas molecules. Gases normally used are nitrogen, argon, or krypton, depending on the lamp design; as a general rule, nitrogen would be used for high voltages and krypton at low voltages. These factors are determined by the ionization potential of the gas and its molecular weight and structure.

The theoretical maximum efficacy of tungsten at its melting point of 3410 °C is about 53 lm W^{-1}. In practice such a temperature cannot be achieved as there are losses at the filament ends, resulting in uneven temperature, and other heat losses through the gas filling. As a result, the maximum efficacy of a lamp with a substantial filament carrying 10 A is about 40 lm W^{-1}, but the life would only be a few hours. By their design advantages, tungsten halogen lamps have efficacies up to 50% higher than those of conventional lamps. Depending on the life required in the particular application, the efficacy varies from 15 lm W^{-1} to 35 lm W^{-1} with corresponding filament temperatures of 2400 °C to 3250 °C.

One further feature of the lamp worthy of mention is its larger emission of ultraviolet radiation than is the case for the ordinary tungsten lamp. This is due to the higher filament temperature in conjunction with the use of a silica bulb which transmits radiation in the ultraviolet region. Usually, the ultraviolet radiation is reduced to harmless proportions by a glass housing or shield. Lamps designed using the hard glass envelope suppress the ultraviolet radiation.

10.3   Lamps for various applications

The tungsten halogen lamp has a number of distinct performance and design merits over the conventional lamp. These include its near 100% lumen maintenance throughout life, its increased life or efficacy, with a filament of higher luminance, and its small, strong bulb with robust internal construction allowing luminaires and optics to be miniaturized and made less expensive, as the following applications show.

10.3.1   Floodlighting

Floodlighting requires long life lamps, i.e. lives in excess of 2000 hours. They are designed for mains voltage in tubular bulbs with diameters ranging from 8 mm to 10 mm and lengths from 80 mm to 330 mm for 100 W to 2 kW. There is a standardized end contact, designated R7S, used across this range, a fuse being incorporated in this cap where necessary.

Limitations have been reached with the conventional support arrangement (Fig. 10.4) due to excessive cooling of the lamp support enmeshed in the coil. This effectively produces a thermal gradient causing tungsten erosion, as previously described. A new design has emerged which overcomes these limitations whereby the support is independently suspended from an auxiliary silica rod within the lamp envelope, Fig. 10.5 (Halberstadt et al. 1980). The physical dimensions of the support and method of attachment allow the filament to operate through the supporting coils without substantial loss in temperature. This unique design enables gains in terms of efficacy and/or life and has extended the range to lower wattages hitherto unachievable.

Typical applications for the higher wattages are for garage forecourt security lighting and general floodlighting where a low installation cost is a necessity. The lower wattages are being used similarly, but have extended tungsten halogen floodlighting into the areas of domestic security and shop and exhibition lighting. A direct replacement lamp range for GLS luminaires, where a more effective lamp is

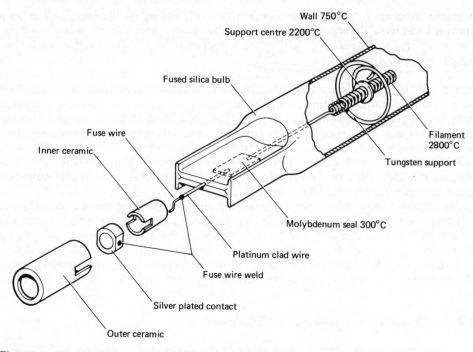

Fig. 10.4 Exploded view of end section of linear lamp and cap assembly

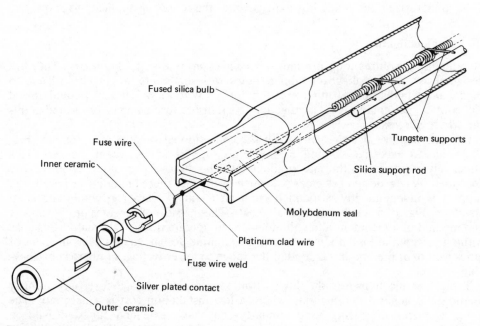

Fig. 10.5 Exploded view of independently suspended coil supports reducing losses due to thermal gradients

required in terms of overall performance, is available by the use of a linear lamp encapsulated within an outer glass envelope.

10.3.2 Projector and photographic lamps

Projector lamps are designed to have compact filaments and are used in conjunction with an optical system to concentrate the beam through a film gate and give maximum light on a screen. This is obtained by operating the filament at the highest possible temperature compatible with an economic life, which is normally of the order of 50 hours. Voltage control can have a great influence on the life of these lamps which operate not far below the melting point of tungsten. Lamps operating below 30 V can utilize flat mandrel or coiled coil filaments: the low voltage heavier current produces a more compact source and can be run at significantly higher temperatures, whereas mains voltage lamps have coiled coil, monoplane, or biplane filament constructions.

There are several film sizes for cine and still projection and these include 8 mm and 16 mm cine and a variety of slide, microfilm, microfiche, and overhead projectors. More recently, low voltage lamps have been developed which are used in conjunction with an ellipsoidal dichroic ('cold light') mirror (Sect. 9.2). These lamps give maximum light intensity on the film plane at the gate of the projector (Fig. 10.6), and limit by as much as 60% the unwanted infrared radiation which is transmitted rearwards through the mirror.

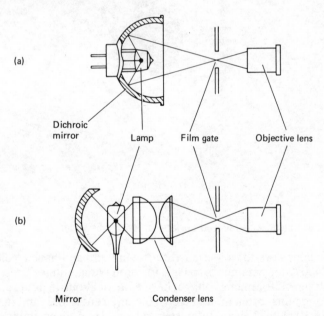

Fig. 10.6 Comparison of super 8 mm cine optical system: (a) using a lamp integrated with the dichroic ellipsoidal mirror and (b) using a single ended halogen lamp with condenser beam

A new and interesting addition to the integral mirror lamp range is the introduction of the faceted mirror lamp, which was specifically introduced for microfiche. The design intention of this concept is to achieve a uniformity of light distribution across the film gate. A specular mirror achieves a high light intensity at the screen centre with noticeable 'fall-off' at the edges. A diffuse reflector minimizes this effect, but by reducing the peak intensity and boosting the edge values. A faceted reflector, still specular, redirects the filament images uniformly across the film aperture, giving a high distribution whilst still retaining the light intensity (Fig. 10.7).

Fig. 10.7 Specular mirror with faceted surface on a 12 V 50 W lamp

Photographic lamps are those designed for taking film and have a colour temperature of either 3400 K for amateur or 3200 K for professional films. Those operating at 3400 K, when designed for mains voltage, have a life of about 15 hours and are used in 'Sun-Gun' lighting units, often mounted on a bar adjacent to the camera. For example one 15 hour life 1000 W U-shaped tungsten halogen lamp gives equivalent illumination to seven 275 W reflector photoflood lamps which have a life of only 4 hours (Fig. 10.8).

10.3.3   Automobile lamps

The higher efficacy, compactness of filament, and reduced bulb size of tungsten halogen lamps have created new possibilities for automobile lighting. Four lamps which have been internationally standardized (ECE 1958b) are finding increasing use

Fig. 10.8 'Sun-gun' lighting unit incorporating 1000 W U-shaped lamp

in spotlight, foglight, and headlight applications. Three of these are single filament 12 V 55 W rated lamps, designated H1, H2, and H3. The H1 and H2 both have axial filaments and, to satisfy other designers' requirements, the H3 has a transverse filament of similar rating. Their simple design, incorporating a fixed prefocus cap which accurately aligns the filament in relation to a prefocus ring, has enabled these to be the first tungsten halogen lamps to be produced on automatic equipment. The H4 lamp is a twin filament lamp with one filament for the driving beam and the other producing the meeting beam. A shield is incorporated around this latter filament which, in conjunction with a specially designed front lens, gives an assymetric beam of light. This produces a sharp cut-off with no upward light on the off-side of the road, which eliminates glare for the oncoming driver and intensifies the beam onto the kerb to produce adequate visibility when passing other vehicles. Early developments showed that tungsten from the cold filament suffered chemical reaction, resulting in transport of this tungsten to the hot filament. There are alternatives for the successful design of a twin filament lamp. Either (a) both filaments operate in close proximity in order that the cold filament is at a sufficiently high temperature from radiation or conduction to prevent chemical attack or (b) the cold filament is substantially isolated from the running filament, being in an area of the bulb where there is insufficient free bromine to cause erosion. The latter design has been utilized in the H4 lamp (Fig. 10.9).

It should be borne in mind that these lamps, with their very precise approval and conformity specifications, have been designed for the European market where the practice is for headlight and fog/spot lights to be made by appropriate hardware

Fig. 10.9 H4 twin filament lamp showing shield and frame construction together with fixed prefocus caps

manufacturers, having glass lenses sealed to metal or plastic reflectors of a multiplicity of shapes and sizes, but all ultimately conforming to give a beam pattern with a standard lamp within the specification as laid down in the regulation. Hence the reflectors all contain an accurately positioned seating plane to accept the focusing ring as positioned with respect to the filaments on each lamp. This has enabled European cars to adopt a stylish 'front end', sometimes giving aerodynamic advantages, but certainly lowering the line of sight from a driver's eye over the front of the vehicle. Other lighting schemes subject to legislation have retained sealed beam lamps, which are hermetically sealed glass reflectors and lens units and, although the use of a halogen inner bulb or capsule is permitted, there are real problems in economically producing complex shapes in glass similar to those now in use in Europe.

10.3.4 Studio lamps

Studio lamps range from 500 W to 10 kW and their requirements are somewhat different from those discussed so far. In addition to the high power, they are used in luminaires where the operating temperature is very high and a constant colour temperature of 3200 K is specified to match the colour film or TV camera. The useful life of a non-halogen lamp in this sphere of activity is determined not by filament failure, but by the degree of blackening, which reduces light output and produces blistering in spite of the large bulb size used. The use of a halogen cycle is particularly relevant to this class of lamp and high efficacies with no blackening or blistering are obtained within relatively small lamp dimensions. The usual format is a single ended lamp with a flat grid filament which suits the optics of the typical studio Fresnel luminaire. However, a parallel range of lamps for theatre applications in profile spotlights, having slightly different optical requirements, and some biplane or axial coiled coil alternatives are available and may have advantages in some luminaire designs.

. A small range of twin filament designs is available for TV studio use. The filaments may have differing wattages, e.g. 1·25 kW + 2·50 kW, to allow use of either filament or both, i.e. three different power levels which, by operating from a dimmer circuit, can give a 6:1 variation in light level from a single luminaire within the colour variability that is acceptable to a TV camera. The luminaire may also be designed to give the normal spot/flood arrangement from one end and, by rotation of the optics, a soft light from the other, thus enabling almost any lighting requirement to be met from the one unit. A typical studio would use a grid saturated with such units to avoid the expensive time loss involved in 'rigging' lighting units for each production (Fig. 10.10).

Fig. 10.10 The BBC Cardiff studio using 180 Kahouteck lanterns with twin filament lamps, as inset photograph

Most studio and theatre lamps now use silica envelopes, and this permits the size to be reduced to a limit defined often by the filament size. The stronger shape thus enables a high pressure filling which leads to a longer life as filament evaporation rate is reduced. The use of silica in these high current lamps has meant considerable development of the pinch-seal construction techniques referred to in Sect. 10.2.2 to the extent that seals capable of carrying 100 A (120 V 10 kW) are now developed. Protection of the external leads by platinum coating and the sealing foil ends by a subsidiary low melting point glass is necessary to give survival at the elevated temperatures encountered in some luminaires and operation up to 500 °C at this point is not unusual.

Further reading

Coaton J R, 1970, *IEE Proc.*, **117,** 1953–1959: Modern tungsten halogen lamp technology
Coaton J R and Fitzpatrick J R, 1980, *IEE Proc.*, **127,** Part A, 142–148: Tungsten halogen lamps and regenerative mechanisms
Rees J M, 1970, *Ltg. Res. Technol.*, **2,** 257–260: Bromophosphonitrile lamps

11 Fluorescent lamps

Fluorescent lamps have now been commercially available for forty years and yet they are still the most widely used and most successful of all the discharge lamps. They have always been an efficient source of converting electrical energy into light, but with the ever-increasing cost of energy recent years have seen the introduction of energy-saving fluorescent lamps which are even more efficient. Even so, they are still not fully accepted as a domestic light source except possibly in the kitchen and bathroom. Very recently, smaller lamps have been produced of many different shapes which will, it is hoped, have major applications in the home.

11.1 Design

11.1.1 Principles

The theory of low pressure discharges has been discussed within Sect. 6.3.3, so how does it apply for a fluorescent lamp?

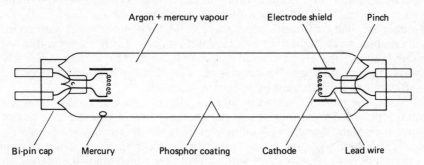

Fig. 11.1 Construction of a fluorescent lamp

A standard lamp construction is as shown in Fig. 11.1. It consists of a soda-lime glass tube with its inside coated with a fluorescent powder. Tungsten wire electrodes coated with a thermionic emitter are sealed into each end and electrode shields are often placed around the electrodes, especially in the more highly loaded lamps, to reduce black marks forming at the ends of the tube due to evaporation of the emitter from the electrode which is thus deposited onto the shield. The shields also reduce flicker. The finished lamp is filled with an inert gas, such as argon, to a pressure of 200 Pa to 660 Pa (1·5 torr to 5 torr).

A small droplet of mercury is introduced into the tube and it is this mercury which is used in the discharge to create light. More recently, because mercury is poisonous, other forms of mercury dosing have been used which also control more accurately the amount of mercury in each lamp. These include encapsulating controlled doses in glass or metal phials, which are usually welded to the lead wires and then broken using radio frequency heating to release the mercury after the lamp is completed, or else using combined mercury dispensing/getter strips as electrode shields, which again are heated after the lamp is completed to release the mercury and also getter any gaseous impurities in the lamp. At lamp operating temperatures the mercury pressure is only 1·3 Pa and at this pressure most of the radiation emitted from the mercury arc occurs in the ultraviolet at 253·7 nm, a resonance line, plus small additions of other ultraviolet lines, and only about 10% in the visible region. Without the phosphor coating present on the tube, the lamp efficacy is only 6 lm W^{-1}, about half that of an incandescent lamp.

In order to improve the efficacy the 253·7 nm ultraviolet radiation has to be converted into visible light and this is the function of the phosphor on the inside of the tube (Chap. 8). Its effect is to increase the efficacy to about 80 lm W^{-1}, six times the efficacy of an incandescent lamp.

The spectrum of the standard white fluorescent lamp is shown in Fig. 11.7a. The sharp peaks are the mercury lines and the background continuum is due to the phosphor on the inside of the tube. Changing the type of phosphor used changes the shape of the background continuum and hence the colour of the lamp, as in the other spectra shown in Fig. 11.7.

The inert gas filling, such as argon, krypton, neon, or combinations of these gases, does not contribute to the radiation, but performs a number of functions (Sect. 6.3.3) including aiding starting, since at room temperature the vapour pressure of mercury is very low. The gas pressure used has to be controlled at the correct value. If it is too high it makes lamp starting difficult and causes a loss in lamp lumen output, but improves lamp life and lumen maintenance and decreases end-darkening. If it is too low it reduces lamp life and lumen maintenance and increases end-darkening, but improves lamp starting and lumen output. A compromise is therefore used which gives adequate lamp life and good starting. Although the inert gas contributes virtually nothing to the light output of the lamp, it does consume energy due to elastic collisions between the electrons and the gas. If we therefore change the gas from argon-based to krypton-based, a heavier gas, these energy losses are reduced and the lamp efficacy can be increased by approximately 5%.

Decreasing the tube diameter also has the effect of making the arc more efficient and therefore, providing other design parameters can still be met, such as optimum cool spot temperature and wall loading, further gains in efficacy are possible.

Since it is a discharge lamp it has a negative coefficient of resistance in operation and it therefore has to be operated with control gear which limits the current through the lamp (Sect. 18.1.2). This control gear, or associated equipment, such as a starter switch, also has to heat the electrodes to provide thermionic emission of electrons to start the discharge (Sect. 18.3).

11.1.2 Lamps and electrodes

Lamps   A number of basic requirements have to be met when designing a fluorescent lamp for operation on mains voltage. These include performance properties, such as lumen output and efficacy, life, colour and colour rendering, lamp wattage and voltage, lamp starting and stability, and design parameters, such as wall loading, cool spot temperature for optimum mercury pressure, and hence light output, gas-fill mix and pressure, electrode design, and optimum phosphor coating thickness. As well as all these considerations, the lamp has to remain alight and be stable over a wide range of operating conditions, such as changes in ambient temperature, supply voltage, and ballast tolerances. Lamps in common use today range in length from 150 mm to 2400 mm and in diameter from 11 mm to 38 mm. Their wattages range in size from 4 W to 125 W.

Electrodes   Many different forms of electrodes exist for fluorescent lamps. Examples are (a) a tungsten wire which has been coiled and this primary coiling coiled again (the 'coiled coil'), (b) a braid made from eight tungsten wires to form a tube and then coiled (the 'braided electrode'), (c) a 'triple coil' made by overwinding a tungsten wire with a very fine wire and then coiling the composite wire twice as in (a), or (d) a 'stick electrode' made as (c), but only coiling the composite wire once. These are the major designs in use today, but other variations do exist.

The electrode is filled with an emissive material consisting mainly of carbonates of barium, strontium, and calcium which are decomposed to the oxides during lamp manufacture. The design must be such that the electrode, under all conditions, is at a high enough temperature to produce sufficient electron emission, but not so high that excessive evaporation of emitter is obtained. Also it must hold the maximum amount of emitter in order to give long life.

Fluorescent lamps were originally designed for use in switch-start circuits, in which the preheat current passed through the electrodes on starting was controlled by a choke (Sect. 18.3.1). The electrodes were therefore made of comparatively high resistance (the 8 V electrode) in order to obtain long life. When circuits using transformers to preheat the electrodes were introduced in the UK, the transformers were designed to match the electrode, and were connected across the lamp in order to reduce the electrode voltage when the lamp struck. In the USA the standard voltages of 110 V to 125 V necessitated the use of step-up transformers and it was found convenient to put the electrode heating windings on the same core, with the result that the electrode voltage was not reduced when the lamp struck. The low resistance or 3·5 V electrode was therefore introduced using the triple coil construction to maintain adequate lamp life. In some countries both high and low resistance electrodes are at present available in some sizes of lamps. The lamps are only interchangeable in circuits (switch-start and semi-resonant-start) in which the electrode heating current and not the voltage is controlled. Electronic-starting devices are now being used more frequently for starting fluorescent lamps and since these usually control the current they are also suitable for both high and low resistance electrodes.

The striking voltage of fluorescent lamps is at a minimum at about 20 °C, rising on either side of this value, most steeply below 5 °C and above 60 °C, although the starter switch and type of ballast influence it. Lamps are specially made for use in low ambient temperatures by reducing the argon filling pressure, but this has the disadvantage of reducing the lamp life.

11.1.3   Lamp types – standard and slimline

The different fluorescent lamp types available are as shown in Table 11.1 and in the past the majority of these have been based on the 38 mm diameter tube.

Standard lamps   These are coated with a transparent water-repellant silicone coating which prevents the formation of a continuous film of water on the glass (type MCFE/U). On starterless circuits (Sects 18.3.3 and 18.3.4) the starting voltage of the lamp is partially dependent on the electrical resistance of the glass surface and is at a minimum when the resistance is either very low or very high: the coating brings about

Table 11.1   Types of fluorescent lamp

British type reference	Other reference	Lamp description	Application
MCFE/U	Standard TL	Standard fluorescent lamp with transparent silicone varnish water-repellant on outside of glass tube. HR electrodes. This includes the new slimline 26 mm tubes	Switch-start, resonant-start, quickstart circuits, electronic starters
MCFA/U	Metal strip type	Fluorescent lamp with metal starting strip fitted to outside of tube and connected to both metal lamp caps. HR electrodes	Resonant-start and quickstart circuits when metal strip is earthed
MCFB/U	TL-X or TL-S	Fluorescent lamp with internal metal starting strip fitted with special single contact caps. IS electrodes	Division 2 luminaires on instant-start circuits
MCFR/U	Reflector TL-F	Fluorescent lamp with internal reflector. HR electrodes	As MCFE/U
Amalgam	TL-H	Fluorescent amalgam. HR electrodes	Hot surrounding temperatures on switch-start, resonant-start, or quickstart circuits
Rapid-start	RS	Fluorescent lamp. LR electrodes	Rapid-start circuits
Instant-start		American type instant-start lamp with special single contact cap. IS electrodes. Often referred to as slimline lamps in the USA	Instant-start circuits
Circular	Circline or TL-E	Circular tube. Usually with LR electrodes	Switch-start or rapid-start circuits
Low temperature	TL-B	Special MCFE/U lamp for low temperature starting	Switch-start circuits
	TL-M	External metal strip connected to one electrode via a 2 MΩ resistor. LR electrodes	Mainly resonant-start circuits

Notes:
HR electrode (high resistance) requires preheat at 6·5–10 V which falls after the lamp has started.
LR electrode (low resistance) requires preheat at 3·5 V which is maintained after the lamp has started.
IS electrode is designed to withstand cold starting without preheat.

this latter condition. The former condition is satisfied in the MCFA/U lamp which has a metal strip fitted to the outside of the lamp tube and connected to each cap. The strip is earthed through one of the lamp caps.

The MCFB/U lamp has an internal high resistance strip connected to one electrode. When a voltage is applied, a glow discharge takes place between the unconnected end of the strip and the electrode nearest to it. There is then sufficient ionization to start the discharge between the two electrodes. These lamps may be operated on a choke ballast or tungsten lamp resistor. Special lamp caps are fitted to prevent exposure to full mains voltage if one end of the lamp is inserted in the holder and the pins at the other end are touched while the mains switch is on.

The TL-M lamp has an external conducting strip connected to one electrode through a $2\,\text{M}\Omega$ resistor in the cap. The lamp is not earthed, but the high resistor value makes it safe if the strip is touched. This lamp is used in a starterless circuit and gives reliable starting at lower ambient temperatures.

The MCFR/U, amalgam, and circular lamps are described in Sect. 11.4. Miniature lamps are standard types except for their low ratings (4 W, 6 W, 8 W, and 13 W), narrow bulbs (16 mm), and miniature bipin caps. They have poor overall efficacy owing to high control gear losses, but are convenient in some applications (Sects 21.4 and 23.3.2).

Instant-start lamps, which are commonly used in the USA, have single contact bases and are coated on the outside with a transparent silicone material. They are available in the slimmer 26 mm as well as the standard 38 mm diameter tube. These lamps operate on similar circuits to the normal bipin instant-start lamps.

Slimline lamps These are the 26 mm diameter tubes that are now beginning to become the standard diameter tube in Europe. 26 mm diameter lamps had been in use for over twenty years before interest in them increased (Vrenken 1978), but during the early 1980s their range has been greatly extended by filling these lamps with a krypton-based inert gas. The effect of this is to reduce the lamp wattage by 10% when these lamps are interchanged for 38 mm diameter lamps of the same length. The need for these energy-saving lamps of higher efficacy has been accelerated by the rapidly increasing cost of energy which now accounts for 66% of the annual running cost of a standard fluorescent lamp.

Simply changing from argon to krypton gas in a 38 mm tube only gives energy savings if the lamps are operated on constant current circuitry, so that the reduction in lamp volts caused by lower arc losses results in lower lamp watts. 38 mm diameter energy-saving lamps do exist, such as the 2400 mm 100 W lamps in the UK or the Supersaver/Wattmiser lamps in the USA. However, a 26 mm tube containing the krypton gas mix gives the same lamp voltage as a 38 mm tube of the same length containing argon, so the lamps will operate at the same current. The energy saving comes from a reduction in lamp power factor, causing a reduction of 10% in lamp wattage.

Currently these energy-saving 26 mm diameter tubes are available as 600 mm 18 W, 1200 mm 36 W, 1500 mm 58 W, and 1800 mm 70 W lamps. They are also available with either the existing phosphor coatings, such as warm white, white, and cool white, or else using the new narrow band phosphors (Sect. 8.3.3) when high efficacy and high colour rendering index are required (Vrenken 1976, Thornton 1971). The colour of these new lamps is normally quoted in terms of rounded-off colour temperature, that is warm white becomes 3000 K, white 3500 K, and cool white or daylight 4000 K. (The actual colour temperatures are 3000 K, 3400 K, and 4100 K respectively.)

11.2   Manufacture

11.2.1   Phosphor coating

The phosphor, which may be a single material or a blend of several (Sect. 8.3), is made into a suspension in either an organic solvent or a water-based system with an appropriate binder. This process is carefully controlled so that the phosphor is dispersed with the minimum amount of damage to the phosphor particles as this reduces the conversion efficiency of the phosphor. Glass tubes are thoroughly washed in hot, demineralized water and dried and coated with phosphor suspension, either by allowing suspension delivered from a coating gun to run down the inside of the tubes or by blowing the suspension up the tube from a stock tank by compressed air. In both cases the excess suspension is allowed to drain back into the stock tank.

The tubes are allowed to dry in a temperature- and humidity-controlled room under conditions to give as even a coating of phosphor, from end to end, as possible. It is important to control the amount of phosphor on the tube: too little results in low light output due to some of the ultraviolet radiation not being converted into visible light, while with too much phosphor the same result is obtained due to light absorption in the coating. The amount of phosphor in the tube is controlled by measurements of the phosphor weight and the optical density of the coating; adjustments are made in the relative density and viscosity of the phosphor suspension to give the optimum conditions. The dried phosphor-coated tubes are baked to remove the binder, and phosphor is removed from the ends to allow the cathode assemblies to be sealed into them, as small amounts of phosphor in the seals can give rise to cracks in the glass.

In certain cases more than one coating may be applied to the lamp. A good example of this is the new 26 mm energy-saving lamp which uses the new narrow band phosphors to achieve good colour rendering and high efficacy. These phosphors are about 50 times as expensive as conventional halophosphates, so it would cost £1 to coat a 1500 mm 26 mm tube as a single layer. Since most of the light is generated in the phosphor nearest the discharge, a layer of the cheaper halophosphate is first coated onto the tube and this is then covered with a layer of the expensive phosphor. The total amount used is about the same, but the amount of expensive phosphor has been reduced by at least 50%.

11.2.2   Lamp processing

The electrode assemblies are made on automatic units by a series of operations which soften the glass of the flare and seal in the lead wires and exhaust tubes. The nickel or alternative metal ends of the leads are bent to shape and the electrode positioned and clamped. Finally, the electrode is dipped in the suspension of emissive material and allowed to dry. If necessary, electrode shields are added automatically on the same machine after the emitter coating has been completed.

The electrode assemblies (Fig. 11.2) are sealed into the ends of the tubes either singly or at both ends simultaneously and the tube is then pumped. Two processes are in common use. One method is to pump all the air from the tube and refill it with argon to the required pressure of 200 Pa to 660 Pa, depending on the lamp type and rating. The second and most commonly used method involves passing argon into the horizontal tube at one end after pumping out most of the air; the mixture of argon and remaining air is continuously removed from the other end. During this phase the electrodes are heated by controlled currents to convert the alkaline-earth carbonates of the emitter to oxides, the resulting carbon oxides being removed by the argon flow

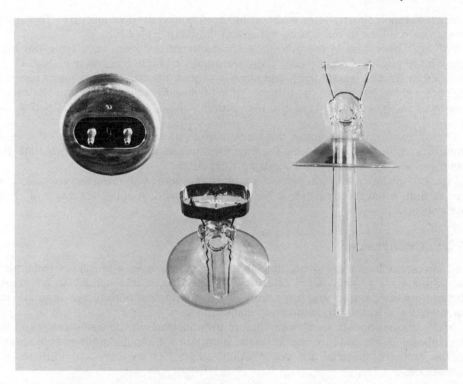

Fig. 11.2 Fluorescent lamp cap and electrode assembly, showing position of shield, when fitted

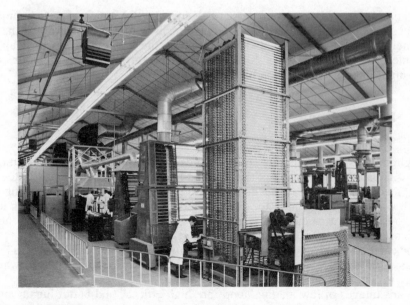

Fig. 11.3 Typical fluorescent lamp manufacturing unit

which is stopped shortly after addition of the required drop of mercury. The argon pressure is reduced to the correct value and the lamp sealed off.

The next operation is the automatic threading of the lead wires from the tube through the pins of the lamp cap. Caps are usually of bipin construction (Fig. 11.2), specified in BS 1875 (BSI 1952), and already coated internally with a basing cement; the ends are baked to cure the cement, which is usually a phenolic resin. The excess lengths of the wires are cut off and then either welded, soldered, or crimped to the pins.

The operation of the lamp at this stage is often unstable due to traces of gaseous impurities in it, and is aged by running for some minutes during which time the impurities are 'cleaned up' and the lamp is stabilized.

Figure 11.3 shows a typical view of a largely automatic unit using this process. This type of unit, often referred to as a horizontal unit, produces lamps at a rate of about one a second.

11.2.3   Quality control

As fluorescent lamps are made at high speed and have very long lives (making it impossible to test every batch of lamps before sale), it is necessary to have very efficient quality controls and inspection. These are applied both to the lamp making equipment and to the product during manufacture.

All lamp components are checked before use, for example dimensional tests on the glass tubes and performance checks on the phosphor for lumen output and colour and on the emissive material for composition, impurities content, and particle size distribution.

Quality controls during lamp manufacture are aimed at checking those conditions which are known to influence the final performance, namely light output and life. They include such inspections as the amount of phosphor on the glass tube, the amount of emissive material on the cathodes, and the gas pressure to which lamps are filled.

Selections of lamps taken from those ready for despatch are checked for compliance with BS 1853 (BSI 1979a). The tests specified include adequate marking of the lamp, its dimensions, cap adhesion and insulation of the cap pins from the cap shell, attachment of the lead wires to the cap pins, starting voltage, colour, colour rendering, lumen output, lumen maintenance, and life.

11.3   Performance

11.3.1   Light output

The light output of a fluorescent lamp depends on the lamp loading, or the amount of power dissipated per unit area of the tube, and the type of phosphor used. Regarding power loading, lamps may be divided into three groups: the low loading group operating at about $280\,W\,m^{-2}$, for example the 1200 mm 40 W lamp, the high loading group operating at about $400\,W\,m^{-2}$, for example the 1800 mm 85 W, and the American very high output group operating at about $740\,W\,m^{-2}$.

If the current in a given lamp is increased, it follows that the lamp voltage is lowered by reason of the negative volt–ampere characteristic of the discharge, while the wattage is increased and with it the lumen output.

The advantages of low loading lamps are high efficacy and better lumen maintenance against which must be set the higher lumen output per unit length of the high loading types, even though they suffer losses in efficacy due to increased mercury vapour pressure and electrode losses.

The other major factor that affects lumen output is the type of phosphor used. In the past it has always been the case that the better the colour rendering of the lamp the lower is its light output. For example 1500 mm cool white tubes give approximately 50% more light than do their equivalent rated natural tube, but have a colour rendering index of 57 compared to 85. The new narrow band phosphors (Sect. 8.3.3) are approximately 10% more efficient than the normal halophosphates used for white, warm white, and cool white tubes, but they have a similar colour rendering index to the natural tube. These new high temperature phosphors in 26 mm energy-saving tubes enable lamp efficacies of 95 lm W^{-1} to be achieved.

A fluorescent lamp has its highest light output as soon as it reaches working temperature after switching on, but in the first 100 h of its life the light output falls by 2 to 4% and thereafter at a slower rate until at 2000 h it has fallen by only a further 5 to 10%, depending on the lamp rating and phosphor mixture. This fall-off of lumen output through life is worse for the De luxe colours and is also dependent on wall loading, being lower as the lamp loading decreases. Impurities in the lamp, such as water vapour, can seriously affect maintenance.

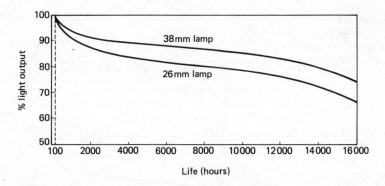

Fig. 11.4 Typical lumen maintenance curves for 38 mm and 26 mm halophosphate lamps

Typical lumen maintenance curves for 38 mm and 26 mm halophosphate-coated tubes are shown in Fig. 11.4. (The 100% light output figure refers to its 100 h value.) 26 mm tubes coated with the new high temperature phosphors have lumen maintenance characteristics similar to the 38 mm halophosphate-coated tube. 'Initial lumens', that is 100 hour lumens, are quoted throughout the world for fluorescent lamps, but in the UK 'lighting design lumens', a nominal value representing the average through-life output, are often used by lighting engineers when designing installations. This terminology is slowly disappearing and lumen maintenance curves are being adopted.

11.3.2 Life

The life of a fluorescent lamp normally ends when the emissive material on one or both electrodes becomes exhausted and fails to produce enough electrons to enable the lamp to strike.

When a lamp is running, a small amount of the emissive material is continuously lost from the electrodes, but when the lamp starts, particularly on switch-start circuits, a relatively large amount of emissive material is sputtered from the electrode and this shortens the life of the lamp. The rate of evaporation is also dependent on the gas-fill pressure and increases as the pressure is lowered, thus reducing lamp life. Typical gas pressure ranges for argon-filled 1200 mm and 1500 mm 38 mm diameter lamps are 260 Pa to 350 Pa and for krypton-filled 1200 mm and 1500 mm 26 mm diameter tubes are 160 Pa to 240 Pa.

Rated life is often quoted for fluorescent lamps and this is usually taken as the point at which a large installation would be relamped most economically. Quoted values are 7500 hours and at this point over 90% of the lamps would still be in operation giving over 80% of their initial light output. This concept is now being superseded with the availability of survival curves for specific lamp types, which take the form shown in Fig. 11.5.

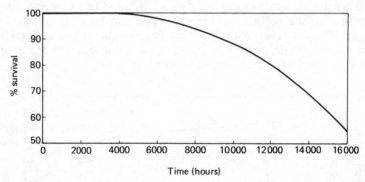

Fig. 11.5 Typical lamp survival curve

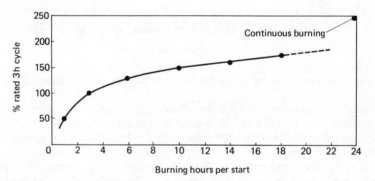

Fig. 11.6 Effect of switching on lamp life

Another factor which affects lamp life is the number of times the lamp is started. The previous values quoted are all based on the standard cycle of 8 switches per 24 hours or 3 burning hours per start. Figure 11.6 shows the effect of switching on lamp life and it can clearly be seen that the more the lamp is switched, the shorter is its life. (Also included is the expected life if the lamp is not switched at all.)

11.3.3 Colour appearance and colour rendering

Definitions of what we mean by colour appearance and colour rendering have already been given (Sects 3.1 and 3.5).

Fluorescent lamps are available commercially in over twelve shades of white and these have in the past been split up into two groups: the first group comprises lamps, such as white, warm white, and cool white, which give the highest efficacy, but have colour rendering indices R_a of the order of 50 to 60. The second group, often referred to as De luxe lamps, have lower efficacies, but higher colour rendering indices which may be as high as 95, as for artificial daylight. This old philosophy has however been upset with the introduction of lamps primarily in 26 mm diameter which use blends of the new narrow band red, green, and blue phosphors (Sect. 8.3.3) (called Polylux for Thorn manufactured lamps). These lamps have high efficacies, are up to 10% more efficient than the old high efficacy halophosphates, and have high colour rendering indices, of about 85.

Controlling the colour of fluorescent lamps in production and from batch to batch is therefore critical and international specifications are in existence which also quote allowable spreads in the accepted colour coordinates. These spreads, which are 5 m.p.c.d. (minimum perceptible colour differences) (Sect. 3.2.3) in any direction on the chromaticity point, are often larger than an individual manufacturer's normal accepted tolerances and this means that it is possible for lamps of different manufacturers of the same nominal colour to have different colour appearances.

Another problem is that fluorescent lamps are manufactured to operate at different powers even for lamps of the same length and consequently their operating temperatures differ. This changes the mercury vapour pressure in the lamp and hence the amount of ultraviolet and visible radiation such that the combined colour is different. This affects the colour appearance more than the colour rendering of the lamp and hence, if possible, it is advisable not to mix lamps of different loadings in the same installation. Theoretically, this problem could be overcome by using phosphor suspensions of slightly different colour, but with present production techniques this is impracticable.

Changes in ambient temperature, that is the temperature of the air around the lamp, can also change the lamp colour since this again changes the mercury pressure. Thus ventilated and unventilated luminaires using the same lamp type may have a different colour appearance.

The human eye is most sensitive to light at 555 nm in the yellow-green region of the spectrum (Sect. 1.3.1). Lamps producing this wavelength would have the highest efficacy, but would be quite unacceptable for general lighting because of their poor colour and colour rendering properties. Lamps are however now available which use a blend containing a yellow-emitting phosphor and have efficacies of up to 90 lm W^{-1}, but colour rendering indices of about 30.

The standard fluorescent lamps with the highest efficacy, such as warm white, white, and cool white, use single halophosphate phosphors. While producing acceptable 'white light' they are lacking in the red region of the spectrum and better colour rendering is often required. To achieve this several phosphors are blended together to improve the balance of radiation over the complete visible spectrum. These phosphors are less efficient than the standard halophosphate and emit their light in the less efficient regions of the spectrum, especially in the red, so the resultant overall efficacy is considerably less, but the colour rendering properties can be improved dramatically. In lamps of very high colour rendering, such as artificial daylight ($R_a = 95$), five phosphors are blended together.

Lamps using the new narrow band red, green, and blue phosphors (Sect. 8.3.3), which are all more efficient than the old phosphors, are all made by blending the three phosphors and the proportions of each colour used determines the final colour temperature. These lamps are usually defined by their colour temperature, and

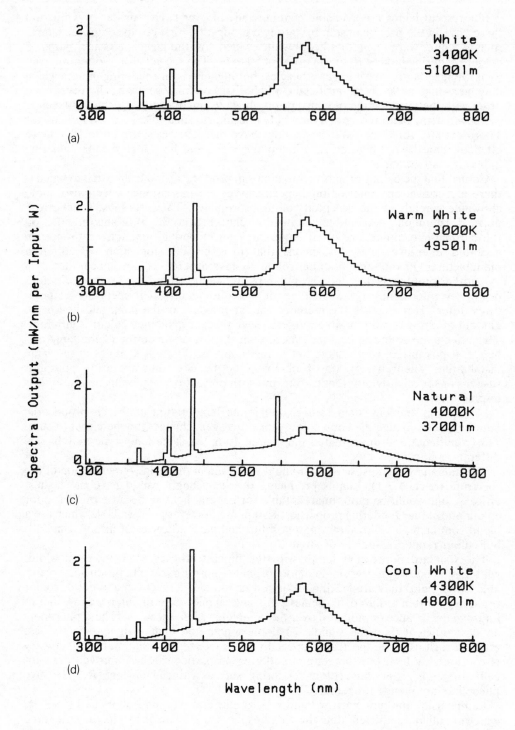

Fig. 11.7 Spectral characteristics of some 1500 mm lamps; all 65 W except Polylux, which is 58 W

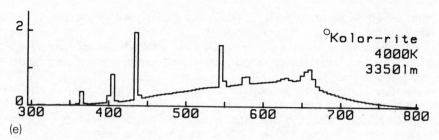

(e)

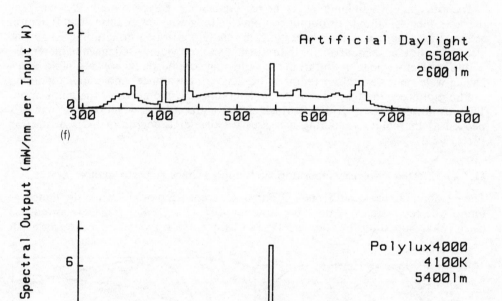

(f)

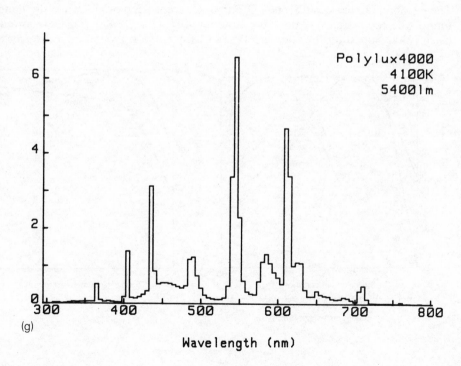

(g)

Wavelength (nm)

Fig. 11.7 *(cont.)*

rounded-off these are 3000 K, 3500 K, and 4000 K, which are equivalent to warm white, white, and cool white respectively.

The spectra of a range of standard, De luxe, and high temperature phosphor types, along with their initial lumen output, colour temperature, and colour rendering index are shown in Fig. 11.7.

Another cause of poor colour rendering from fluorescent lamps is the presence of the violet-blue mercury lines. It is possible to effect some reduction of these lines by a double coating of the bulb. The first coating is of magnesium arsenate, a red-emitting phosphor with a pale yellow body colour, and the second layer is a blend of phosphors. The first coating layer absorbs some of the near-ultraviolet and violet-blue lines, producing a lamp with good colour rendering properties. A similar correction may be obtained by a single coating including the arsenate phosphor.

The artificial daylight lamp meets the requirements of BS 950, Part 1 (BSI 1967) for the assessment of colour. Its output contains the long wavelength ultraviolet radiation essential for colour-matching operations normally performed in natural daylight, as well as for the true comparison of fluorescent dyes now widely used in white materials.

It can therefore be seen that from the wide range of phosphors now available lamps having wide ranges in colour temperature, colour appearance, and colour rendering can be produced, the final choice being determined by the needs of the application. There is however some evidence which suggests that a lower level of illuminance is needed as the colour rendering increases for the same degree of user satisfaction (Sect. 3.5.4).

11.3.4 Effect of ambient temperature and supply voltage on performance

The maximum light output from a 38 mm fluorescent lamp occurs when the temperature of the coolest part of the lamp is about 40 °C (Fig. 11.8a). This temperature is usually maintained on the standard type of lamp when it is running in free air at an

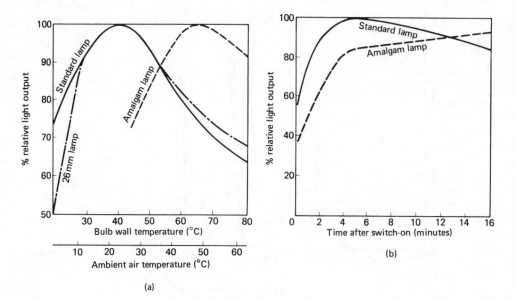

Fig. 11.8   Variation in light output with (a) temperature and (b) running time

ambient temperature of 25 °C. At this order of temperature the mercury vapour pressure is at an optimum for the generation of ultraviolet radiation at 253·7 nm. As the temperature of the lamp increases, the mercury vapour pressure increases and the lamp voltage decreases (Sect. 11.3.1). For smaller diameter tubes, as used for domestic applications, this optimum cool spot temperature increases since the amount of mercury self-absorption is reduced.

The effect of ambient temperature on lamp performance varies, depending on the type of circuit being used, but in general the new 26 mm tubes filled with krypton-based gases are more sensitive to changes in ambient temperature and, since at 0 °C their light output is already below 50% of optimum, they are not recommended for use in low ambient temperatures.

Similarly, the lamp characteristics of both standard and 26 mm lamps vary with the input supply voltage, the 26 mm krypton-filled tubes again being the most sensitive. The exact changes depend on the type of circuit used and manufacturers' technical data should be consulted where more detailed information is required.

11.4 Applications and special types

11.4.1 Standard and slimline types

Applications of these lamps are very similar, their prime uses being for commercial and industrial consumers. The new slimline tubes, apart from using less energy and being more efficient, have however enabled the fittings designers to construct smaller, neater, and yet optically as good, if not better, luminaires. The major problem is that, although interchangeable with standard tubes in 600 mm, 1200 mm, and 1500 mm sizes, they will only operate on switch-start or new electronic starterless circuits.

11.4.2 Special types

Reflector lamps The usual radially-symmetrical light distribution from a fluorescent lamp may be modified by including a reflecting surface in the lamp itself. The first reflecting coat usually consists of titanium dioxide and extends the length of the lamp and about 225° round the circumference. The whole tube is then coated with the phosphor layer on top of the reflecting layer, thus leaving the reflecting coat sandwiched between the glass and phosphor. Consequently, a certain amount of light control occurs in the lamp itself, the coating reflecting much of the incident light falling on it through the uncoated area.

These lamps are 10 to 15% less efficient than standard lamps, but have about 70% more light directed in the downward direction. They may be used with advantage in (a) dirty locations which are difficult to reach for cleaning purposes, (b) rooms with poor reflecting surfaces or with unfavourable proportions, (c) ceiling lighting where the ceiling has a poor reflecting surface, and (d) lighting installations where, due to space limitations, external reflectors are not practicable. A disadvantage may be the high brightness of the 'window' which can give rise to more glare than would the standard lamp.

Aperture lamps These are similar to reflector lamps except that the two layers, reflector and phosphor, coincide leaving a clear glass window of only 30° to 60°. This aperture runs the whole length of the lamp and has a luminance of about four times that of a standard lamp, although the total light output is less because the window is not coated with phosphor. These lamps give a narrow beam of light, which may be concentrated by the use of a lens or reflector to allow the light to be delivered to a small area. They may be used for lighting aircraft landing strips, bridge lighting, and sign lighting.

Lamps for high ambient temperatures   With the increased use of enclosed luminaires, many at ceiling height, large numbers of standard lamps are running at temperatures in excess of those which give the maximum light output. As much as 30% of the light can be lost in some cases (Sect. 11.3.4). Minimum bulb wall temperatures may be as high as 60 °C with ambient air temperatures of 35 °C.

To overcome this problem the mercury is combined with another metal, such as indium or bismuth, to form an amalgam (Vrenken 1976). The effect of this amalgam is to suppress the mercury vapour pressure for a given temperature so that it reaches optimum mercury vapour pressure at 60 °C instead of 40 °C (Fig. 11.8a). Practical lamps usually have a ring of indium mounted on the inner wall near one end and the mercury then amalgamates with the indium during initial operation. The crossover point for using amalgam lamps to give improved lumen output occurs at an ambient air temperature of about 36 °C. Amalgam lamps take considerably longer to attain equilibrium when switched on from cold and therefore indium is often placed on the electrode shield to form a secondary amalgam which initially warms up more quickly due to its proximity to the electrode. This improves the initial mercury vapour pressure in the lamp and decreases the lamp warm-up period to stability (Fig. 11.8b).

Lamps for low ambient temperatures   Similarly, if the ambient temperature is too low the lumen output falls (Fig. 11.8a) as the mercury vapour pressure is too low. In order to overcome this and maintain the bulb wall temperature as near to 40 °C as possible jacketed lamps may be used. These have a clear glass jacket with about 4 mm clearance of the lamp in all directions and thus increase the ambient temperature in the immediate vicinity of the lamp. The glass itself causes approximately a 2% drop in lumen output.

Such lamps are used in cold and windy conditions, such as refrigerator rooms, outdoor installations, tunnels, and subways. To improve starting under very cold conditions lower gas-fill pressures may be used, but these lamps have shorter lives and worse lumen maintenance than those of the standard lamps.

Circular lamps   The range of circular lamps available is rapidly changing as smaller and smaller versions of lower diameters are being introduced for use in domestic installations. They are more difficult to produce at high speeds and therefore they are more expensive than equivalent wattage standard lamps.

U-shaped lamps   A range of U-shaped lamps is made in ratings from 10 W to 65 W, the 40 W lamp being the most popular. These lamps fit inside a standard luminaire of the traditional 600 mm × 600 mm size. The 40 W lamp is made in two leg-spacing sizes measured between the centre points of each leg, 152 mm and 92 mm. It is possible to fit three of the 92 mm lamps in the 600 mm square luminaire, whereas with the larger size only two lamps are possible. Against this it is claimed that the lamps with the legs at wider spacings are cheaper and have a higher light output, also a lower weight owing to the use of thinner glass.

Germicidal lamps   The principal radiation which is generated in a low pressure mercury discharge has a wavelength of 253·7 nm, which prevents the growth of moulds and bacteria. The soda-lime glass used in the manufacture of normal fluorescent lamps absorbs this radiation, but if a special ultraviolet transmitting glass, fused silica or Vycor (96% silica), is used and this glass is not coated with phosphor, the radiation emitted from the lamp has germicidal properties. It is dangerous and can cause severe blistering of the skin and acute conjunctivitis. Therefore, these lamps should not be directly viewed when lit and over-exposure should be prevented (Sect. 1.4.3).

Erythemal lamps Radiation between the wavelengths of 290 nm and 320 nm is present in ordinary sunlight and is responsible for skin tanning and sunburn. Fluorescent 'sun lamps' used in solaria and sun beds have a special phosphor with an emission peak at about 300 nm and a band extending from 270 nm to 370 nm. A suitable glass to transmit this radiation is used. These lamps should be used only under medical supervision. They have been used to simulate outdoor sunlight conditions in under-cover installations (Sect. 1.4.3).

Ultraviolet lamps These are coated with a special phosphor which gives a peak output at about 370 nm. There is also a small amount of visible light from the discharge of the lamp added to the ultraviolet radiation. This visible light can be almost completely eliminated if the lamp is made in Wood's glass instead of soda-lime glass. Wood's glass contains oxides of nickel and cobalt and is of a dark purple-blue colour. It absorbs almost all visible radiation, but transmits the ultraviolet. Lamps made from this glass are often referred to as 'blacklamps'.

Lamps for horticultural purposes Many conditions are necessary for the growth of strong healthy plants, including correct soil conditions, humidity, temperature, and irradiation. Plants and seeds need light to grow and flower: red and blue radiations are particularly useful in photosynthesis, the conversion of water and carbon dioxide into carbohydrates by means of chlorophyll. Lamps are now available which emit mainly in the blue and red ranges of the spectrum. By limiting the green radiation in the lamp (largely reflected by chlorophyll), more power can be directed into the useful regions of the spectrum.

Lamps for printing Fluorescent lamps are used in various printing processes, such as making photocopies. In the diazo process the printing paper has a maximum sensitivity just below 400 nm and 'actinic blue' lamps are available which have an emission peak near this wavelength with a spread of from 300 nm to 500 nm. Other lamps, some of them aperture lamps, are available for printing processes which require maximum sensitivity at wavelengths in the visible spectrum. As for the other special purpose lamps, these are not made in the normal full range, but in suitable sizes for particular applications.

Coloured lamps A range of coloured lamps is available for decorative applications. Green and blue lamps are made simply with a suitable phosphor. If no phosphor provides an emission of the desired colour, a pigment coating is used between the phosphor and the glass wall, for example in red and gold lamps.

Cold electrode lamps Cold electrode fluorescent lamps emit light in the same way as do standard hot electrode lamps. These operate as normal glow discharges (Sect. 6.3.3) and their electrodes are uncoated hollow cylinders of nickel or iron. The cathode fall is high and to obtain reasonable efficacy for general lighting purposes the lamps must be made fairly long, say 3 m, with a diameter of 20 mm or 25 mm. About 2000 V is required for starting these lamps, and about 900 V to 1000 V for running. A leakage transformer is usually provided to start the lamp, the output falling to the lower running voltage when the lamp has lit (Fig. 18.12e). Lamps filled with neon, with or without phosphor, provide a variety of colours and are used in sign lighting.

The advantages of cold electrode lamps compared with the hot electrode types are:

(a) They have a very long life, usually 15 000 h or more, in consequence of their rugged electrodes and low current consumption.
(b) They start immediately, even under cold ambient conditions.
(c) Their life is unaffected by the number of starts.
(d) They may be dimmed to very low light output.

Their main disadvantage is that the luminous efficacy is only about two-thirds that of the hot electrode types because of the power loss at the electrodes.

11.4.3 Recent developments and future prospects

Recent years have seen the introduction of many new fluorescent lamps primarily aimed at the domestic market. These have been based on smaller diameter versions of the circline tube, the U-tube which has often been bent again to enclose it in another bulb so that it looks like an incandescent lamp, square lamps, spirals, and many other shapes. Sometimes these lamps come complete with gear and will just plug into an existing incandescent lamp socket. In parts of the world operating on 100/120 V supplies the problems involved in producing these small lamps are not so severe since the lamp volt drop required is only of the order of 50 V. However, in Europe and the UK, which operates off 220/240 V supplies, the lamp volt drop required is of the order of 100 V or losses in the ballast become excessive since the bulk of the supply voltage has to be dropped across the ballast. This means narrower tubes must be used to increase the voltage drop per unit length and longer tubes to obtain the required 100 V drop across the lamp. Narrower diameter tubes mean higher loadings per unit wall area and the standard halophosphate would give poor lumen maintenance at these loadings. Therefore, the new narrow band phosphors of higher efficacy, with the capability to withstand higher loadings and still give adequate lumen maintenance, are used. These new lamps, examples of which are shown in Fig. 11.9,

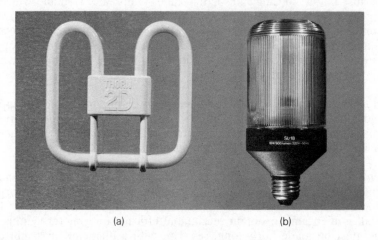

(a)   (b)

Fig. 11.9 (a) Thorn 2D lamp and (b) Philips SL lamp

have overall efficacies (including gear losses) of the order of 50 lumens per watt, about four times that of an incandescent lamp. Their use in domestic applications instead of GLS lamps would therefore lead to considerable energy savings, of the order of 70% per point which when multiplied throughout a home could mean considerable savings.

Regarding the future, other lamp types using the new high temperature phosphors will be developed which will be more efficient than our present lamps. They will probably be energy saving when compared to the lamps they are designed to replace and will almost certainly be operated at higher wall loadings. As the cost of energy increases, the fluorescent lamp is playing an important part in reducing energy costs and is likely to be one of the major light sources for many years to come.

Further reading

Amick C L, 1961, *Fluorescent lighting manual*, 3rd Edition (New York: McGraw-Hill)

Elenbaas W, 1971, *Fluorescent lamps*, 2nd Edition (London: Macmillan)

Elenbaas W, 1972, *Light sources* (London: Macmillan)

Jack A G and Vrenken L E, 1980, *IEE Proc.*, **127,** Part A, 149–157: Fluorescent lamps and low pressure sodium lamps

Penning F M, 1957, *Electric discharge in gases* (London: Macmillan)

Polman J, van Tongeren H and Verbeek T G, 1975, *Philips Tech. Rev.*, **35,** 321–330: Low pressure gas discharges

Waymouth J F, 1971, *Electric discharge lamps* (Cambridge, Mass: MIT Press)

12 Low pressure sodium lamps

The low pressure sodium discharge is basically very similar to the low pressure mercury discharge, i.e. there is a low pressure of a metal vapour in a rare gas. Since the melting point of sodium is higher than that of mercury the sodium arc tube temperature is higher and so, to conserve energy, it is insulated from its surroundings in an evacuated outer envelope. The resonance radiation produced is of a wavelength close to the peak of the eye sensitivity curve, making the low pressure sodium lamp the most efficient lamp available at present. However, because the radiation produced is monochromatic yellow, the use of this lamp is confined to locations which do not demand colour discrimination, hence its widespread use for streetlighting.

12.1 Design

The essential feature of the low pressure sodium lamp is a discharge in sodium vapour at a pressure of about $0 \cdot 1$ Pa plus a gas at a pressure of a few hundred Pa at an arc tube temperature of about 260 °C. To retain as much energy as possible the arc tube is mounted in an evacuated outer coated on the inside with an infrared reflecting film. Two basic lamp types are available at present: the single ended (SOX) lamp and the double ended linear (SLI) lamp (Fig. 12.1).

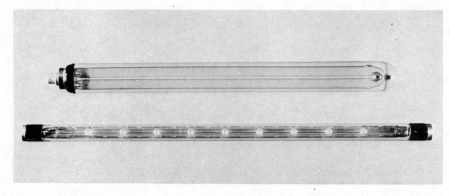

Fig. 12.1   135 W SOX and 140 W linear low pressure sodium lamps

12.1.1 Principles of operation

Sodium is an obvious choice as a lamp making material because the resonance D-line radiation at 589 nm falls near to the peak of the eye sensitivity curve. Resonance radiation is produced by the decay to the ground state of excited atoms from the first level of excitation at 2·1 eV. In a discharge of sodium the amount of D-line radiation produced is very temperature-sensitive. As the arc tube temperature is steadily increased, at constant current, the radiation output increases until a maximum is reached at about 260 °C, above which it falls. In addition to the sodium metal, an inert gas (mainly neon) is necessary to initiate and optimize the discharge (Sect. 6.3.3).

Atoms are excited and ionized by electron impact, the sodium ions so formed drift to the walls under the influence of the radial electric field, recombine, and neutral atoms diffuse back again into the discharge. As the current rises, an increased lack of neutral sodium atoms in the central region of the discharge develops, causing the efficacy to fall. The effect of this sodium depletion can be seen in the voltage waveform of a lamp on a 50 Hz supply (Fig. 12.2): as the current increases more gas is ionized to maintain conduction and the lamp voltage rises. The low pressure sodium discharge is unique in the extent to which this depletion process occurs and it has an important role in the design and performance of the lamp (Polman et al. 1975).

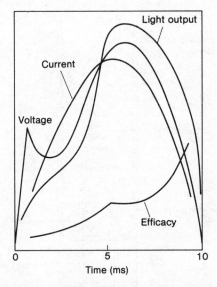

Fig. 12.2   Half-cycle performance of fully run-up low pressure sodium lamp on 50 Hz supply

Sodium atoms are also excited by the resonance radiation itself which is quickly re-radiated, so that radiation produced inside the discharge may be absorbed and re-radiated several times before escaping at the outside wall of the tube. The combined effect of the radiation trapping and the sodium depletion is that most of the useful light from the lamp is generated close to the arc tube wall.

12.1.2   Arc tube design

One of the first design requirements is a material which will contain the sodium metal and vapour at the required temperature without suffering any surface attack. To meet this requirement it is necessary to use tubing lined with a special ply-glass (Sect. 7.1). In order to maintain low current the arc volt drop needs to be high and therefore the tube needs to be quite long. To keep the overall length of the lamp manageable the arc tube is doubled back into a U-shape. Another approach, which aims at a high surface area and short sodium diffusion distance, is to modify the circular cross-sectional shape to that of a crescent or a cross (Fig. 12.3). One result of this is to increase the voltage and wattage gradient and thus for a given lamp wattage the arc length is considerably less than for a circular tube (Weston 1959).

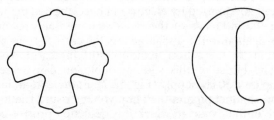

Fig. 12.3 Cross-sections of arc tubes for linear lamps

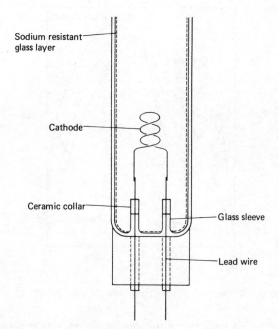

Fig. 12.4 Low pressure sodium lamp seal design

One other constraint on arc tube design is that of striking voltage. Since it can be kept low by having a short arc length and a large cross-sectional area a compromise is reached with the running requirements. Striking voltage can also be affected by the choice and pressure of filling gas and for this reason a small percentage of argon (about 1%) is added to the neon to form a Penning mixture (Sect. 6.3.3). The optimum pressure lies in the range 3–15 torr (400–2000 Pa).

The other important part of the arc tube is the cathode and its supporting system. Here, as with a fluorescent tube, an oxide-coated tungsten cathode is used but, because of the higher current and the requirement for cold starting, a more robust design of coil is adopted (Fig. 12.4). At the seals the lead wires are coated with a sleeving glass of high resistance. During operation the inside surface of the arc tube is negatively charged and attracts sodium ions; the sleeving glass surface is also at this negative potential, which is a few volts below that of the cathode lead wire and it must be of high resistance to prevent the electrolysis of sodium from the surface of the sleeve to the lead wire. The end of the sleeve is further protected by a ceramic collar.

12.1.3 Outer envelope design

The chief objective of the outer envelope is to keep the arc tube at the required temperature (260 °C) whilst maintaining a high transmission to the sodium D-lines. This is achieved in two ways. Firstly the space between the arc tube and outer bulb is evacuated to prevent heat loss by convection and secondly the inside of the outer bulb is coated with an infrared reflecting film (Groth and Kauer 1965).

The arc tube glass wall approximates to a black body (Sect. 6.3.1) and the radiated wavelength maximum for a body at 260 °C is about 5000 nm. The reflecting film is of indium oxide doped with tin, and of interference thickness set at such a level so as to give a transmission maximum to the D-lines. The level of tin dopant used gives the maximum reflectance at the required thickness of 300 nm (van Boort and Groth 1968). The optical characteristics of the coating are given in Fig. 12.5.

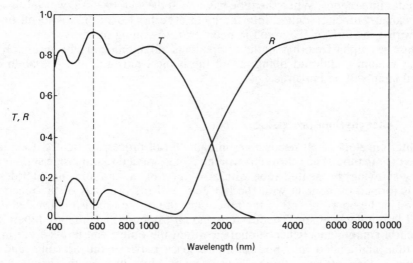

Fig. 12.5 Spectral characteristics of indium oxide film

The quality of the outer vacuum through the life of the lamp is maintained by a getter, in this case a layer of barium on the inside of the outer bulb near the cap, which absorbs gases given off while the lamp is in service.

12.2 Construction and manufacture

12.2.1 Arc tube

The arc tube glass is a two-ply glass (Sect. 7.1) which, in the case of SOX lamps, is first bent into a U-shape and an exhaust tube is joined to the arc tube on the crown of the bend. The tube is now ready to receive the cathode assemblies. The cathode lead wires are of Dumet (Sect. 7.4) and are first coated with a sleeving glass of high resistivity and of expansion between that of the wire and the arc tube. The cathode is of fine tungsten wire coiled round a supporting wire. After mounting on the lead wires an emitter is applied. This is a triple carbonate of barium, strontium, and calcium in powder form suspended in an organic solvent and is applied electrophoretically to give a tightly packed and carefully controlled deposit. The coated cathode is now sealed into the arc tube by carefully pinch-sealing the hot glass onto the cathode assemblies. The tube is now ready for exhausting.

All of these glassworking operations demand great care because of the nature of the soft ply-glass tubing and after each operation careful annealing is necessary to remove excessive strain.

12.2.2   Exhaust

The exhaust process takes the sealed tubulated tube and produces an evacuated arc tube containing sodium metal and filling gas ready for mounting into the outer envelope.

The tube is first evacuated and heated to outgas the glasswork. At the same time current is passed through the cathodes to heat them in order to convert the triple carbonates into oxides. When the tube has cooled the sodium dose, which is in a phial in the exhaust tube, is melted into the lamp. The final operation is to fill to about 8 torr with a mixture of 1% argon in neon prior to sealing off the tube.

It must be emphasized that all the components of the tube must be absolutely clean and the sodium metal and filling gas of the highest purity or the operation of the finished lamp will be impaired.

12.2.3   Outer envelope processing

The outer envelope itself needs a certain amount of processing before it is ready to receive the arc tube. The infrared reflecting film is applied to the inside surface of the tube by spraying the heated tube with a solution of indium and tin chlorides. The oxide is formed on contact with the hot glass and the products of the reaction are removed at the opposite end of the tube. One end of the tube is then sealed off and formed into a hemisphere. The arc tube mount assembly, i.e. the arc tube plus the mechanical components which support it within the outer, can now be put into the outer tube and sealed into position. The space between the arc tube and outer envelope is then evacuated to a high vacuum while heating the whole lamp to thoroughly outgas all the exposed surfaces. When the exhaust tube is sealed off the getter is fired by high frequency induction heating. Capping, ageing, and packing complete the sequence of operations.

Throughout the manufacturing process quality control plays a vital role and all fabricated parts are subject to a rigorous inspection.

12.3   Performance

By way of introduction it should be said that sodium lamps, in common with other discharge lamps, need to be operated in conjunction with a ballast of some sort. In practice this usually means a high reactance transformer or a choke (Sect. 18.4.1).

12.3.1 Electrical characteristics

The behaviour of the lamp in different circumstances is invariably governed by the arc tube temperature and therefore by the sodium vapour pressure.

Consider first the lamp during the running-up period. When first switched on the voltage across the lamp is due solely to the rare gas. After a few minutes the arc tube temperature rises and, as the sodium vapour pressure increases, the lamp volt drop rises and then falls as the lamp is fully run-up and there are sufficient sodium ions to carry most of the current. The total run-up time is usually of the order of 10–15 minutes. The exact operating point of the lamp is controlled by the circuit it is running on. However, if there is a drop in mains voltage the lamp current will fall causing the arc tube to cool slightly, so that the lamp volt drop will rise and the light output may remain steady or fall slightly. The converse follows from a rise in mains voltage.

12.3.2 Light output

The range of SOX lamps at present on the market is from 10 W to 180 W with light outputs of from 1000 lumens to 33 000 lumens and efficacies of 100 lm W^{-1} to 180 lm W^{-1}. The maximum theoretical efficacy from the sodium D-lines is 525 lm W^{-1}, but in a practical lamp there are many losses. Due to the wide spread of electron energies and the structure of the sodium atom there are many more possible excitation states and therefore many more spectral lines of radiation in addition to the D-lines. The D-lines are in fact a pair of lines at a wavelength of 589 nm. At the temperature and vapour pressure of a low pressure sodium lamp the intensities of the other spectral lines are considerably less than those of the D-lines (Fig. 12.6).

In a 90 W SOX lamp the light output is 30% of the input power, 5% is infrared radiation, the electrode losses amount to 22%, and other losses are 43%. Some losses, e.g. the electrode loss, are constant for a given lamp current so higher wattage lamps are more efficient than the low wattage ratings.

Two factors inhibit arc tube light output: one is the trapping of the resonance radiation and the other is the depletion of sodium atoms near the centre of the discharge at high current values. The former effect is overcome to some extent in the linear lamp design by increasing the surface area of the arc tube. In the U-shaped arc tube radiation from one leg is trapped in the other; in the linear lamp this cannot occur. The depletion effect can be reduced on alternating supplies by limiting the peak value of the current.

12.3.3 Life

The average life of the sodium lamp has been increased considerably over the years by improvements in lamp materials and processing techniques. A lamp can end its life with one obvious symptom: the arc fails to strike when switched on. This can result, for example, from loss of emission at the cathodes because of exhaustion of the emitter.

The sodium metal, its location, and temperature have a fundamental effect on the lamp as its life progresses. Sodium can migrate from one part of an arc tube to another under the influence of a temperature gradient or electric field. If there is movement of sodium to a cooler area then the lamp voltage drop and power slowly rise. Furthermore, the vapour pressure of sodium falls, causing more argon to be ionized and then trapped in the arc tube walls, which in turn causes an increase in striking voltage (Wheeldon 1959). Eventually, sodium is absorbed in the walls, even though they are made from resistant glass. These and similar changes bring about the end of useful life: the lamp still operates, but only inefficiently.

Lamp life can also be affected by environmental conditions (including vandalism). Lamps are designed to give good life for normal conditions of service. In the case of streetlighting installations many columns nowadays are of tubular metal (steel or aluminium) construction with heights of up to twelve metres and the lamp and fitting are subjected to varying degrees of vibration which both must be designed to withstand.

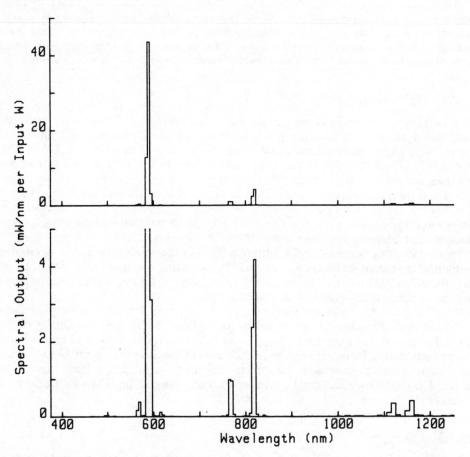

Fig. 12.6 Spectral power distribution of 90 W SOX lamps (same spectrum with different ordinate scales)

12.4 Applications

By far the most common application for low pressure sodium lamps is in streetlighting. This is one area where colour discrimination is not of paramount importance and the high efficacies of these lamps make them ideal for this purpose. In general the lower wattage lamps are used for side street lighting whilst the high wattage types are used on trunk routes and motorways (Sect. 28.4).

Other applications include area lighting, car parks, etc., floodlighting, and security lighting. Certain uses which require monochromatic radiation include the photographic industry for darkroom illumination and some photoprinting processes.

12.5 Future developments

Further activity in lamp development will revolve around ways to improve lamp efficacy still further. One possibility is the use of a modified outer reflecting film with a reflectance cut-off nearer to 800 nm. The lines in the infrared (Fig. 12.6) account for about 15% of the total radiated output, a modified film would reflect this radiation with a consequent improvement in efficacy.

Improvements in lamp performance can also be made by changing the ballast design and therefore the lamp running conditions. With traditional control gear on a 50 Hz supply the lamp current waveform is nearly sinusoidal and sodium depletion occurs around the peak value. However, if the peaks were removed and the shape was changed to a square wave, sodium depletion would be considerably reduced with a resultant improvement in efficacy. Another possibility would be to operate the lamp on a high frequency supply. Improvements of this kind can be achieved by the use of electronic techniques in ballast design (Sect. 18.2.3).

Further reading

Denneman J W, 1981, *IEE Proc.*, **128,** Part A, 397–414: Low pressure sodium discharge lamps
Elenbaas W, van Boort H J J and Spiessens R, 1969, *Illum. Eng.*, **64,** 94–98: Improvements in low pressure sodium vapour lamps
Jack A G and Vrenken L E, 1980, *IEE Proc.*, **127,** Part A, 149–157: Fluorescent lamps and low pressure sodium lamps

13 High pressure sodium lamps

Although employing the same element for light production the lamp described in this chapter is very different from the low pressure sodium lamp. The manufacture of the high pressure sodium lamp has only been possible since the development, about twenty-five years ago, of a specialized ceramic material that forms the arc tube body. Before the introduction of this material it had been impossible to successfully contain sodium vapour at high temperature and pressure within a light transmitting enclosure.

This light source has been commercially available for approximately fifteen years, which means that it is only in its infancy compared with some of the other discharge sources. However, in that relatively short time it has undergone a continuous development programme such that it has now become a lamp exhibiting very long life and high efficacy; only the low pressure sodium lamp can offer a higher efficacy. This excellent performance has meant that the lamp has gained world-wide acceptance for many exterior lighting applications, such as floodlighting and roadlighting and certain industrial interior lighting applications where good colour rendering is not of prime importance. Development still continues with a view to widening the field of application into the commercial interior environment and extending the use in exterior lighting.

13.1 Design

The high pressure sodium (SON) lamp consists essentially of a tubular ceramic arc tube containing metallic dose and a starting gas, which is sealed at each end with an electrically conductive closure that supports an electrode assembly. The arc tube is sealed into a glass or fused silica outer envelope that contains an inert atmosphere which protects the arc tube from oxidation and also provides thermal stability.

13.1.1 Principles of operation

In the low pressure sodium (SOX) lamp approximately 85% of the energy radiated is in the almost monochromatic sodium D-lines (Sect. 12.3.2). If the sodium vapour pressure is increased, from about 0·1 Pa in the SOX lamp, these resonance lines become strongly self-absorbed (Sect. 6.3.4) and the radiation efficacy falls. The lines become very strongly broadened until, at about 7000 Pa, the pressure in the SON lamp, they cover a substantial part of the visible spectrum. The radiation at the core of the lines is very much reduced by the self-absorption, and there are in effect two maxima separated by a dark region where the original D-lines were (Fig. 13.5) – a phenomenon known as self-reversal. (Note that this is unrelated to the doublet structure of the lines: this is much too fine to have any significant effect on self-reversal.) The radiation efficacy now rises to a second maximum (Light and

Lighting 1966), the broadening of the spectrum causes the colour of the discharge to become whiter and the colour rendering properties to improve significantly.

Discharges in all the alkali metals behave similarly (Schmidt 1963) and the important physical processes were soon understood (Cayless 1965). The positive column is a plasma with a temperature at the centre of about 4000 K and a wall temperature of about 1500 K. Most of the radiation is produced in the hot central region and most of the self-absorption occurs in the outer region, producing the characteristic double peak in the spectrum. More details of these processes can be found in Wharmby (1980).

In the SON lamp about 40% of the total radiant energy is contained in the broadened D-lines. Together with radiation from certain other lines, approximately 50% of the total radiant energy is produced in the visible region. The energy balance in a typical 400 W lamp is: visible radiation 100 W, infrared lines and continuum 100 W, electrode losses 20 W, and non-radiative losses in the column 180 W; there is negligible radiation in the ultraviolet. It should be noted that some 60 W is radiated in the infrared continuum from 800 nm to 2500 nm. The 10 W or so in the 568 nm line (Fig. 13.5) is important because it is close to the maximum eye sensitivity.

Nearly all SON lamps contain mercury and xenon as well as sodium. Xenon at a room temperature pressure of about 3000 Pa acts principally as a starting gas. Although argon, or neon–argon, would produce rather easier starting, xenon, with its lower thermal conductivity, provides the highest luminous efficacy (van Vliet and de Groot 1981). The sodium and mercury form an amalgam which, in a stable operating lamp, is formed in the coolest part of the arc tube, usually behind one or both electrodes, known as the 'cool spot'. There is more amalgam than necessary to maintain the required vapour densities in the arc, so the vapour pressures of sodium and mercury are those in equilibrium with the amalgam at the cool spot. The cool spot temperature and amalgam composition have a considerable influence on the electrical parameters, light output, and luminous efficacy of the lamp (Denbigh 1974). The values given to those two design variables are therefore chosen very carefully and controlled within tight tolerances. Any significant change in amalgam temperature or composition during the operating life of the lamp causes appreciable changes in all operating characteristics and could eventually lead to lamp instability due to excessively high lamp operating voltage. Typically, the vapour pressures for sodium and mercury in a lamp at the normal operating point are 7000 Pa and 60 000 Pa respectively. When the lamp is switched off the sodium and mercury vapours in the arc condense on the cooler surfaces of the arc tube, usually on or behind the electrodes, leaving only xenon in the arc space.

Mercury is present in the stabilized arc to act as a buffer gas (Sect. 6.3.3), with a minor contribution from the xenon, which has an operating pressure of approximately 20 000 Pa (Wharmby 1980). The buffer gas improves the luminous efficacy of the discharge by:

(a) Reducing the power lost both by thermal conduction and by the net outward diffusion of electrons and ions, thus allowing an increase in the radiated power by virtue of an increase in the arc core temperature.

(b) Increasing the arc field such that arc length can be reduced relative to that with pure sodium for the same arc voltage and thus allowing an increase in power per unit volume, which increases the arc temperature and radiated power.

The latter point also means that a more compact lamp can be produced with the consequent savings in material and processing costs.

Although both mercury and xenon play an important role in the efficient operation of the SON lamp, neither contributes any significant lines to the visible spectrum because their excitation energies are high compared with that of sodium; their effect on the visible spectrum is to alter the shape of the emitted D-lines (de Groot et al. 1975). It is possible for xenon to play a much greater part in the buffer gas with mercury by increasing substantially the xenon gas pressure (Jacobs and van Vliet 1980). The gain is a significant improvement in luminous efficacy compared to a lamp with a low fill pressure of xenon, but the penalty is more difficult starting (Sect. 13.4.4).

13.1.2   Design techniques

In order to formulate a lamp design the exact design targets must be clear. The main ones are:

(a)   Long life.
(b)   High luminous efficacy.
(c)   An acceptable colour appearance and colour rendering performance for the intended application.

Other criteria, such as compatibility with control gear and luminaire, ease of manufacture, etc., must also be borne in mind. It is quite possible that the most desirable value of each of the three main criteria cannot be achieved at the same time in one lamp and so the design finally chosen is necessarily a compromise.

During the development of the 400 W and 250 W SON lamps many exploratory designs were fabricated and tested in order to provide a background of information. From this a good understanding developed of the physical and chemical principles controlling the discharge and of the new materials or processing techniques used in this lamp.

Arc tube   Firstly, two key parameters need to be specified: lamp power and operating voltage. These are chosen after considering such lamp requirements as luminous flux, physical size, ballast type, and supply voltage. In order to complete the design work about nine parameters in all need to be specified (Denbigh 1978).

For the first stage experience from previous design work and lamp performance allows the designer to give values to one group of variables: electrode construction, weight and ratio of sodium to mercury in the amalgam, type and pressure of starting gas, and arc tube wall thickness. Each of these has a direct effect upon one or more of the three design targets; the most complex case is that of the amalgam where all three targets are closely related. The design approach described here assumes a low pressure of starting gas.

The second stage involves experimental work in order to determine the best values for amalgam temperature, arc length, and arc tube bore that will complete the design. It is possible to reduce the range of values that these three variables may take to cover only cases of practical interest. From prior experiments it is known that the amalgam temperature required for maximum efficacy is usually within the range 615 °C to 750 °C, depending on amalgam ratio and arc tube bore. The limits for arc length can be established by estimating the arc field for the current, amalgam composition and temperature, and probable region of arc tube bore that will be considered in the experiment. The range of arc tube bores to be used is derived from the estimate of arc length and the optimum arc tube wall loading of $20 \, \text{W cm}^{-2}$. It has been shown that wall loadings significantly in excess of this cause slow degradation of the arc tube material and hence premature failure. However, luminous efficacy increases with increasing wall loading and therefore this establishes that the above value should be used.

In the experimental work one technique that has been employed to make the task of assessment easier is the indium bath (Denbigh 1974). Here one end of the experimental arc tube is submerged in molten indium metal contained in an electrically heated alumina crucible. By varying the temperature of the molten metal it is possible to vary the temperature of the amalgam contained in the submerged end of the tube. The partial pressures of sodium and mercury can therefore be varied whilst the effect upon luminous efficacy, colour, and electrical characteristics of the discharge are monitored. From this the arc field for maximum efficacy is determined as a function of arc tube bore, current, and amalgam temperature. The observed fields are then used to calculate the arc lengths required at each bore to ensure maximum efficacy at the specified lamp operating voltage.

Data are available on colour from the experiment which must be considered before the final decision is taken on the arc tube design that best matches the original objectives. In general, the colour temperature increases with a reduction in arc tube bore or with an increase in arc power per unit length for any lamp design. In addition, an increase in colour temperature can be achieved by an increase in amalgam temperature for any amalgam composition.

The design technique described is not the only approach adopted by lamp manufacturers; at least two other methods have been used (de Groot et al. 1975, Collins and McVey 1975).

Outer envelope   It is essential that the arc tube is only operated within a protective environment in order to protect the electrical leadthroughs at each end of the arc tube; these are made of the metal niobium which reacts readily with oxygen or hydrogen at elevated temperatures. The environment can be either a vacuum or inert gas, such as argon, contained within a light transmitting outer jacket. A vacuum is usually preferred as this preserves the thermal energy of the arc tube significantly better than does a gas filling.

As can be seen in Fig. 13.1, the form of the outer envelope can be tubular clear or ellipsoidal coated, depending on the application. One important design feature is that the envelope temperature must be carefully controlled such that the material is not unduly stressed.

13.2   Construction and manufacture

13.2.1   Ceramic arc tube

The high pressure sodium lamp uses an arc tube body manufactured from a specialized optical ceramic, known as translucent polycrystalline alumina (PCA) (Sect. 7.2.1). The high reactivity of sodium vapour at the temperature and pressure encountered in this lamp makes the PCA a most vital component; all other glasses and fused silica would fail very rapidly if used as the arc tube. This material exhibits certain noteworthy characteristics:

(a)   A sharp melting point which means that it cannot be softened or worked.
(b)   A moderately high coefficient of expansion and adequate resistance to thermal shock.
(c)   It is crystalline in form with a good surface finish which is very important for obtaining the best luminous efficacy.
(d)   It is very hard and can only be cut successfully with diamond tools.

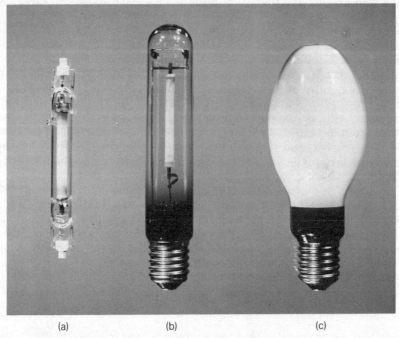

(a)   (b)   (c)

Fig. 13.1 The 250W SON lamp in three forms: (a) linear double ended in a fused silica envelope, (b) tubular clear, and (c) ellipsoidal coated in borosilicate glass envelope

The method of closing the ends of the arc tube during sealing and exhaust determines whether the arc tube body is left open ended or partially closed, as in the case of the 'monolithic' construction shown in Fig. 13.2a (Sect. 7.2.1; McVey 1980).

Arc tubes are produced for lamps in the range 1000 W to 50 W with bores between 11 mm and 4 mm and lengths between 180 mm and 40 mm respectively. The wall thickness is controlled to very close tolerances and is typically in the range 0·5 mm to 0·8 mm.

13.2.2 Arc tube assembly

The next stage in lamp making is to evacuate, dose, and seal the arc tube. Cleanliness and careful storage of components are essential features of the lamp making process and a great deal of effort is spent on this aspect. The main objectives of this part of the process are:

(a) To evacuate the enclosure of air and volatile contaminants.
(b) To contain the dose by a suitable seal.
(c) To provide electrodes for the arc.
(d) To provide an electrical leadthrough for the electrodes.

There are several ways in practice of achieving these objectives. The principal differences occur in the form of end seal and the type of electrical leadthrough, as shown in Fig. 13.2 which illustrates the four predominant types of end seal employed in lamp manufacture throughout the world.

As the alumina does not have a workable range the end seal has to be made by sealing a closing member to the end. The sealing material has to possess various

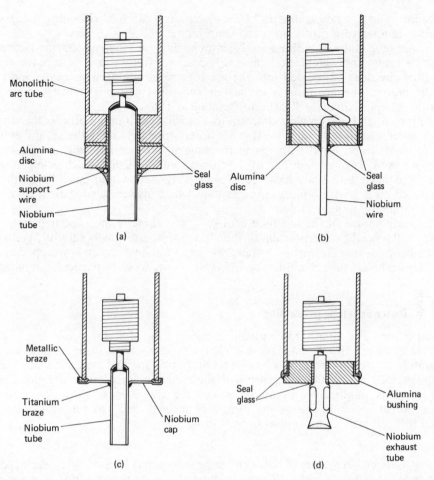

Monolithic arc tube
Alumina disc
Niobium support wire
Niobium tube
Seal glass
(a)

Alumina disc
Seal glass
Niobium wire
(b)

Metallic braze
Titanium braze
Niobium tube
Niobium cap
(c)

Seal glass
Alumina bushing
Niobium exhaust tube
(d)

Fig. 13.2 Four types of SON arc tube end seal

properties, e.g. high melting point (1200 °C to 1400 °C), resistance to attack from sodium, and reactivity with the other members in the seal. It can take the form of either a metal alloy containing metals such as titanium, vanadium, and zirconium, or a glass frit containing mainly oxides of calcium and aluminium. The completed seal has to be capable of withstanding thermal cycling up to temperatures of 700 °C, which is the normal end temperature during operation. The electrical leadthrough is usually in the form of a niobium tube, but a niobium wire (Fig. 13.2b) can be used. Niobium is employed because the coefficient of thermal expansion is a good match to that of alumina; it also resists attack by sodium, possesses good ductility, and has a high melting point. The sealing process must be performed in a high temperature furnace with an inert gas or vacuum atmosphere to protect the seal components.

The niobium leadthrough supports the electrode, which consists of a tungsten rod, the shank, carrying a coil of tungsten wire, the overwind. This is impregnated with an electron emissive material, usually a compound containing barium and calcium oxides. Tungsten is chosen for its high melting point and the emissive material is chosen to be stable at temperatures up to 1800 °C through many thousands of hours of operation. The size and geometry of the electrode is carefully chosen to achieve the required temperature profile for each lamp rating.

The arc tube is dosed with an amalgam of sodium and mercury having a carefully controlled ratio and weight. Sodium is very reactive with water vapour in the air and therefore the dose is inserted into the arc tube in an atmosphere of dry inert gas, usually argon. The arc tube is evacuated and filled with high purity xenon to a pressure of approximately 3000 Pa to facilitate starting.

The type of end seal employed determines at what point in the process the arc tube is evacuated and dosed. Some designs are dosed prior to making the second end seal and evacuated and filled with gas at the time of making the seal. An alternative approach is to dose through one of the tubular leadthroughs, which is left unsealed after both main end seals have been made; evacuation and gas filling are then performed on a separate piece of equipment which also makes the final closure by cold welding the niobium tube.

The temperature of the arc tube cool spot, and thereby the vapour pressures, is greatly influenced by the position of the electrode and so this is carefully controlled during lamp making. In certain instances a metal foil heat screen is wrapped around the ends of the arc tube to adjust the end temperature to suit a particular application.

13.2.3   Outer envelope processing

Mount frame   The mount frame usually takes the form of that shown in Fig. 13.1 and is made of either nickel, manganese–nickel, or nickel-plated iron. Its function is to accurately locate the arc tube within the outer envelope and give adequate support during periods of vibration or transit with the minimum obscuration of light. The arc tube expands significantly in operation, so the frame must allow for a flexible connection at one end. The mount frame is connected rigidly to a suitable glass stem which will conduct the maximum lamp starting current safely.

Outer envelopes   A variety of outer envelope shapes may be used, such as ellipsoidal, straight-sided tubular, and reflector. In general, the outer envelope is made from borosilicate glass to provide adequate resistance to thermal shock and low outgassing levels, but 70 W and 50 W lamps use cheaper soda-lime silicate glass.

Seal and exhaust   When the stem is sealed to the envelope a moulding is produced that accepts the cap termination. The sealed shape is then evacuated and baked to produce a high vacuum. This vacuum needs to be maintained through the life of the lamp to preserve the characteristics of the lamp and protect the metal components of the lamp from attack by outgassed contaminants. A getter of either barium or zirconium–aluminium alloy is provided to achieve this (Sect. 7.3.3).

13.2.4   Quality control

Production lamps are sampled according to a statistical sampling plan and tested to find if they meet acceptable quality levels for specific parameters. Certain parameters are determined by international specification, such as electrical characteristics, including starting voltage and lamp cap torsion test. Others are established within the manufacturing company, such as photometric performance and bulb coating quality.

13.3 Performance

13.3.1 Electrical characteristics

In common with most other discharge lamps the high pressure sodium lamp has a negative slope volt–ampere characteristic which means that it requires some current-limiting device connected in series. An inductive ballast is chosen as being the most suitable compared with resistance or capacitance, because it offers stable operation with relatively low losses.

The level of mains supply voltage influences the type of ballast used and also to some extent the operating voltage of the lamp. As supply voltages vary considerably around the world so practices vary and therefore the content of this section mainly applies to European practice.

Starting Since it is impractical to include an auxiliary starting probe within the arc tube the lamp must be ignited by a high voltage pulse. This is usually supplied by a separate electronic ignitor that is part of the control gear circuit (Sect. 18.4.2), but a switch mounted within the lamp and utilizing inductive collapse within the choke may also be used. The pulse width is only a few microseconds, but it is sufficient to cause adequate ionization within the gas to allow an arc to form. Electrical insulation within the control circuit, lamp holder, lamp cap, and lamp must be satisfactory to withstand the pulse voltage (typically 1·5 kV to 5·0 kV, depending on lamp rating).

Momentary interruption of the mains supply will cause the arc to extinguish. The electronic ignitor will commence to pulse immediately, but the lamp will not restart until the vapour pressures in the arc tube have fallen to such levels that the pulse can cause sodium atoms to ionize. This takes approximately 30 s to complete, which is a relatively short time compared with other high pressure discharges. In order to provide for instant hot restarting a very high pulse voltage (typically 20 kV) must be applied to the lamp which means that additional insulation is required and a new approach to lamp design (Sect. 13.4).

Run-up After the arc has been established the arc voltage is low, due to the low vapour pressures, so the power dissipated is also low (Fig. 13.3). The build-up to

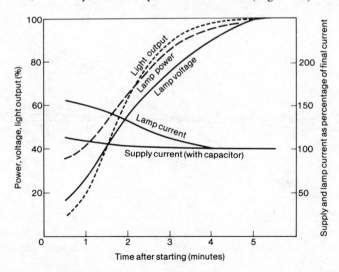

Fig. 13.3 Variation of SON lamp characteristics with mains current during run-up

operating vapour pressures requires several minutes and is closely related to lamp power and light output. International specifications deal with the lamp voltage run-up; an arc tube design optimized according to the technique previously described gives the correct power loading conditions to offer an acceptably quick run-up.

Stable operation   Under free-air burning conditions the lamp is designed to operate within certain limits for lamp voltage when operated from a specified ballast and supply voltage. These limits are established by international specification and take into account the sum total of the effects that can cause lamp voltage to vary during production (IEC 1980).

The nominal value of lamp voltage chosen for any lamp rating is determined mainly by three factors:

(a)   The reignition peak on the leading edge of the lamp voltage waveform is significantly higher than that found in the high pressure mercury lamp. This means that the high pressure sodium lamp is nearer to instability for the same r.m.s. lamp voltage and also that the lamp power factor is worse.

(b)   The high pressure sodium lamp has a rising lamp voltage characteristic through life (Sect. 13.3.3).

(c)   For good ballast efficiency a low lamp current is desirable.

(a) and (b) dictate a low r.m.s. lamp voltage whereas (c) requires the converse: the final choice is therefore a compromise. As lamp power is reduced the effect described in (a) becomes more pronounced and consequently the value of lamp voltage chosen has to be relatively lower.

Variations in the mains supply voltage have an exaggerated effect on lamp parameters as changes in lamp current produce changes in lamp voltage in the same sense due to the presence of the amalgam reservoir. Lamp power and light output can change significantly (Fig. 13.4) and ballast design has to limit these changes to reasonable proportions to preserve lamp life.

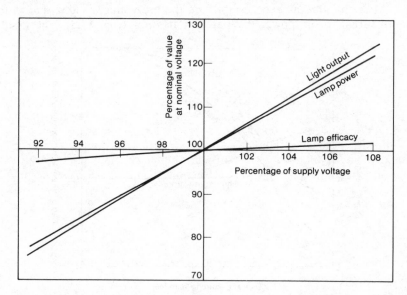

Fig. 13.4   Variation of SON lamp characteristics with supply voltage

The type of luminaire in which the lamp is operated can have a significant effect upon the electrical characteristics of the lamp. This is because radiation can be directed back into the lamp from the reflector and be absorbed by the arc tube. This in turn raises the temperature of the amalgam reservoir and thereby the lamp voltage. International specification provides guidance to luminaire manufacturers on the amount of voltage rise allowable in order to preserve good lamp life (IEC 1980).

13.3.2   Light output

The predominant feature of the spectrum of the high pressure sodium lamp is the self-reversal of the sodium D-lines (Fig. 13.5). This distribution of radiation over a limited range of wavelengths results in a lamp with high efficacy and a yellow-white appearance (correlated colour temperature 2000 K). Colour rendering can best be described as fair with a general colour rendering index R_a of 20.

The two spectra in Fig. 13.5 display the situation where mercury is acting as the buffer gas with xenon at low pressure as the starting gas. The ratio of sodium to mercury in the amalgam, at constant amalgam temperature, affects the shape of the spectrum to the extent that there is a particular ratio for maximum efficacy. Increasing the mercury vapour pressure by altering the ratio produces relatively more radiation in the red and if this trend is continued to very high percentages of mercury (say 90% by weight) a lamp with a pink appearance is produced with a reduced luminous efficacy (Denbigh 1974). Conversely, an amalgam with a high percentage of sodium, at a fixed amalgam temperature, produces a lamp with a yellow appearance and again a reduced luminous efficacy.

Increasing the sodium vapour pressure by increasing the amalgam temperature at a fixed ratio affects the spectrum (Fig. 13.5). If the sodium vapour pressure is above that necessary for maximum efficacy, more radiation is produced in the red and blue-green regions of the visible spectrum with a consequent whiter appearance to the light. However, a reduction in efficacy occurs due to the increased red radiation and the increase in the self-reversal width. It is possible to reach a compromise between loss of efficacy and whiter light to produce a lamp for special applications (Sect. 13.4).

The colour of the discharge is also affected by the power per unit length of arc. This parameter decreases with lamp current, and therefore in general the colour of the lower power lamps moves to the yellow compared with the 400 W lamp. This effect occurs because of a reduction in the arc temperature which results in a loss of radiation in the blue and green.

The luminous efficacy decreases with lamp power (Fig. 13.6) which is partly due to a substantial reduction in arc power loading; the data contained in the graph are for actual production and experimental lamps.

During the life of the lamp changes in the amalgam temperature and ratio can occur which are reflected in changes in sodium and mercury vapour pressures in the arc. These gradual effects produce shifts in colour which can produce either a whiter light, caused by an increase in amalgam temperature, or a pinker light, caused by sodium loss. In both cases the luminous efficacy also decreases.

13.3.3   Life

The life of the high pressure sodium lamp is very long. One method of describing lamp life is by means of a survival curve: this depicts the survival of a typical batch of lamps under normal burning conditions and would show, for example, that for a 400 W lamp 50% survival occurs at 24 000 h. The shape of the survival curve is altered

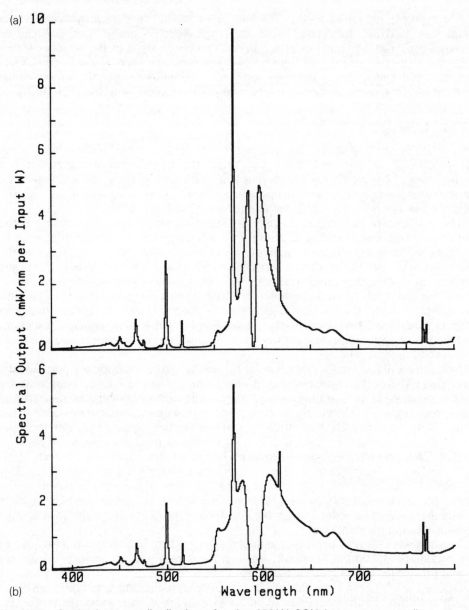

Fig. 13.5 Spectral power distributions for the 250W SON lamp at two sodium vapour pressures: (a) the standard lamp at 10^4 Pa and (b) the improved colour lamp at 4×10^4 Pa

by service conditions, such as excessive vibration caused by abnormal weather or very rapid switching cycles.

The major cause of ultimate failure is a rise in lamp voltage to the point where the supply cannot maintain the discharge. This can be caused by, for example:

(a) Sodium loss to the arc tube components.
(b) Increase in amalgam temperature caused by arc tube end-darkening or increase in electrode losses.

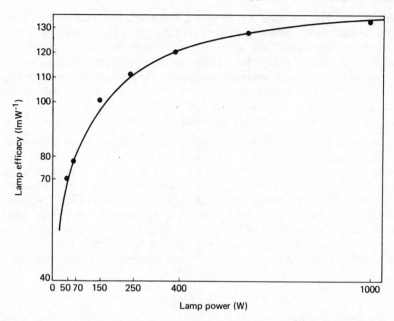

Fig. 13.6 Variation of SON lamp efficacy with lamp power showing values for actual lamp ratings

These effects occur at slow and different rates through life, so the survival curve takes a complex shape. The initial failures on the curve are due to random effects, such as outer envelope leaks and broken welds, before the end of life failures from the later part of the curve.

13.4 Applications and special types

13.4.1 Exterior lighting

Long life, high efficacy, and fair colour rendering have meant that the high pressure sodium lamp has been widely used for inner city roadlighting, side street lighting, precinct lighting, and floodlighting. In many schemes high pressure mercury, tungsten halogen, and incandescent lamps have been replaced by high pressure sodium because of the advantages of lower power consumption and longer life.

13.4.2 Interior lighting

For industrial interior applications where good colour rendering is not of prime importance high pressure sodium lighting has been used for similar reasons. A special form of the lamp is now being adopted for commercial interiors (Sect. 13.4.4).

13.4.3 Special types

Linear double ended This lamp (SON-TD) is very compact and offers good optical control of the light source. It is produced specifically to fit the same luminaire as that used for the linear tungsten halogen sources and is therefore double ended. Due to the high power loading on the outer envelope this is fabricated from fused silica and is tubular and clear. The arc tube is suspended within the outer envelope by spacers, so there is no mount frame, and end closure and electrical leadthrough are achieved by conventional pinch-sealing. The outer is filled with an inert gas filling to limit evaporation from the surface of the arc tube to the envelope. The lamp only operates satisfactorily when mounted inside the luminaire because the large lamp voltage rise caused by re-radiated energy (Sect. 13.3.1) is allowed for in the lamp design.

This lamp lends itself well to an instant hot restart version because the double ended configuration readily copes with the necessary high voltage.

Retrofit   It is possible to manufacture a high pressure sodium lamp that will start from mains supply voltage only – a 'retrofit' lamp. To effect this the arc tube has a gas filling of a Penning gas mixture (99% neon, 1% argon) and a third electrode as a starting aid wrapped around the arc tube. A severe penalty is paid in terms of loss of efficacy (approximately 20% reduction) due to the reduced radiation efficiency from the arc.

The lamp is intended to be compatible with high pressure mercury lamp control gear and therefore to ensure that the gear is not conducting current above its rating the voltage fall across the lamp must approach that of a HPMV lamp. This voltage is normally above that of a standard high pressure sodium lamp and therefore this type of lamp usually has a shorter life (de Neve 1976).

13.4.4   New developments

Improved colour rendering   As has been previously described (Sect. 13.3) it is possible to improve the colour appearance and colour rendering properties of the standard lamp at the expense of a loss in efficacy. An acceptable compromise produces a lamp with an R_a of 65 at a correlated colour temperature of 2200 K for a 15% reduction in efficacy. The lamp operates with a higher sodium vapour pressure (40 000 Pa) than normal and therefore the arc field is higher. So that the lamp has the same electrical characteristics as a standard lamp the arc length is reduced, which means that the arc tube bore has to be increased to return the arc tube wall loading to 20 W cm^{-2}.

High xenon pressure   Xenon can be used as the arc tube buffer gas (Sect. 13.1), either alone or with mercury vapour. The combination with mercury is preferred as this limits the amount of xenon that is required to about 40 000 Pa at room temperature and also the arc field is greater. The effect of the increase in the xenon operating pressure is to introduce some green radiation into the spectrum, which increases the luminous efficacy by about 15% compared with the standard lamp. The massive increase in xenon pressure creates starting problems: so that the lamp is compatible with existing control gear a starting aid has to be introduced adjacent to the arc tube wall. Several methods have now been devised for effecting this.

Further reading

Denbigh P L, 1978, *Ltg. Res. Technol.*, **10**, 28–31: Experimental approach to high pressure sodium lamp design

de Groot J J and van Vliet J A J M, 1975, *J. Phys. D.*, **8**, 651–662: The measurement and calculation of the temperature distribution and the spectrum of high pressure sodium arcs

de Groot J J, van Vliet J A J M and Wasznik J H, 1975, *Philips Tech. Rev.*, **35,** 334–342: The high pressure sodium lamp

McVey C I, 1980, *IEE Proc.*, **127,** Part A, 158–164: High pressure sodium lamp technology

van Vliet J A J M and de Groot J J, 1981, *IEE Proc.*, **128,** Part A, 415–441: High pressure sodium discharge lamps

Wharmby D O, 1980, *IEE Proc.*, **127,** Part A, 165–172: Scientific aspects of the high pressure sodium lamp

14 Mercury lamps

Mercury lamps as a general description covers a wide range of light sources from low pressure discharge devices of a few watts, providing a source of ultraviolet light, to very high pressure lamps of 1000 watts or more used for light projection.

The colour and efficacy of mercury lamps depend on the vapour density within the arc tube, although this can be modified by the use of phosphors or by incorporating inside the lamp a tungsten filament as the lamp ballast.

This chapter is primarily concerned with high pressure mercury types operating at a pressure of several atmospheres. In this country the main types are referred to as MBF lamps.

14.1 Design

14.1.1 Principles of operation

The operation of all discharge lamps is based on the collision processes between electrons, atoms, and ions within the discharge tube (Sect. 6.3.4). The lamp current is dependent on the ionization of atoms by electron collision, and excitation of atoms or molecules is necessary for the subsequent emission of the characteristic line spectrum. Light is also emitted as a continuous spectrum chiefly due to ion and electron recombination. The principal spectral lines of mercury are in the ultraviolet and the blue, green, and yellow regions (Fig. 6.4).

The effect of vapour pressure can be seen when a high pressure mercury lamp is running-up. When first switched on the voltage across the lamp is low, about 20 V (Fig. 14.4), and the discharge fills the tube and appears blue. At this stage the lamp is operating as a low pressure discharge, similar to that in a fluorescent tube, and the emitted radiation is strong in the 254 nm ultraviolet region. With time the lamp temperature rises, more mercury is evaporated, and the increased mercury pressure constricts the discharge to a narrow band along the arc tube axis. With further increase in mercury vapour pressure the radiated energy is concentrated progressively towards the spectral lines of longer wavelengths and a small proportion of continuous radiation is introduced so that the light becomes whiter. When fully run-up the MBF lamp operates at pressures from 2 atm to 10 atm, depending on lamp rating. At still higher pressures of 10 atm to 100 atm, reached in ME and MD type lamps, the spectral lines are progressively broadened and the continuous radiation increases relatively, resulting in improved quality.

Good accounts of mercury lamps are given in the books by Elenbaas (1951, 1965) and Waymouth (1971), and a recent review is that by ter Vrugt and Verwimp (1980).

14.1.2 General description

One of the earliest forms of mercury lamp was manufactured with an arc tube of borosilicate glass which limited the operating pressure to about 1 atm. This lamp, the

MA, was the forerunner of the common range known as MB lamps. These all have fused silica arc tubes which permit high temperature and pressure operation, resulting in increased efficacy. The range includes the clear bulb MB types and the phosphor-coated MBF, MBFR, and MBTF types.

MBF lamps   The construction of a 250 W MBF lamp is shown in Fig. 14.1a. The arc tube emits the greenish-white light typical of the mercury discharge, together with

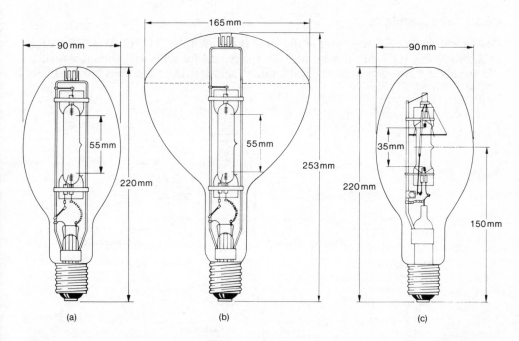

Fig. 14.1   Designs of 250 W mercury lamps: (a) MBF lamp, (b) MBFR lamp, and (c) MBTF lamp

some ultraviolet, but is deficient in the red end of the spectrum. The phosphor normally increases lamp efficacy by converting the ultraviolet into red light of 600 nm to 750 nm. The combined light from arc tube and phosphor is of a quality acceptable for street lighting, highway lighting, and some commercial exteriors.

MBFR lamps   A variation of the MBF lamp is the MBFR lamp which has a parabolic reflector shape (Fig. 14.1b). The envelope is coated internally with a fine titanium dioxide powder which has a reflectance of about 95% in the visible region. There is also a phosphor layer on top of this, but the front surface of the bulb is usually left clear. The polar distribution of a reflector lamp shows that about 90% of the light output is directed below the horizontal with the lamp operating in the cap-up position.

MBTF lamps   The lamp construction is shown in Fig. 14.1c. A filament is in series with the arc tube and is designed to control the lamp current and to cope with the long lamp life and the increased loading when the lamp is started and the volt drop across the arc tube is low. MBTF lamps operate without any additional control gear, but have a much lower overall efficacy than have the MBF types.

14.2   Construction and manufacture

This section describes the various parts of a typical MBF lamp as shown in Fig. 14.1a and discusses some of the considerations involved in manufacture.

14.2.1   The arc tube

The most important component of the lamp is the arc tube. The 125 W MBF arc tube is shown in Fig. 14.2 and this arrangement is typical for all types, although auxiliary electrodes at both ends are not uncommon if cold starting conditions are expected.

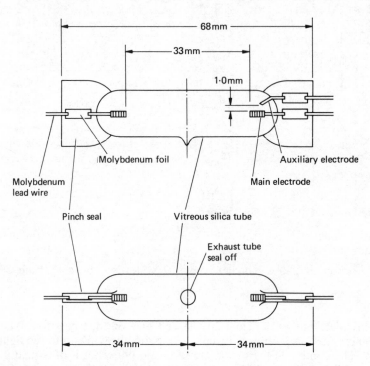

Fig. 14.2   The 125 W MBF arc tube

Body   This is manufactured from fused silica which can be operated at temperatures of up to 800 °C. In practice arc tube temperatures between 600 °C and 750 °C are experienced, depending on rating and operating position.

Seals   The high working temperature and low coefficient of expansion of fused silica makes it impossible to use methods employed in normal glass-to-metal seals where the expansion coefficients of glass and metal can be matched. The problem is overcome by using extremely thin molybdenum foil with feathered edges as described in Sect. 7.4.

The foil assembly is made by welding the components together as shown in Fig. 14.2. The structure is then inserted into the end of the silica tube which is heated to about 2000 °C and pinched onto the foil. The metal parts are protected from oxidization during this operation by a flow of inert gas.

Main electrodes and emitter The lamp lumen maintenance, starting, and life are all dependent to some extent on the quality of the main electrodes and the emitter they carry. The electrodes consist of a central shank, almost always of tungsten but occasionally of molybdenum. This carries a tungsten coil or braid or, possibly, a solid tungsten tip. Electrode tip temperature during operation is between 1500 °C and 1900 °C, with overwind temperatures of 1000 °C to 1400 °C.

The electrodes are generally impregnated with electron emissive materials by dipping in a slurry, usually of barium and strontium carbonates with thoria and other additives. This is retained in the spaces between the coils or braid. Excess material on the surface is removed as this would evaporate quickly onto the envelope and cause darkening. Dipped electrodes are then heated to a temperature of 2000 °C to 2200 °C in a reducing atmosphere, which reduces the carbonates to oxides. The mass of emitter picked up by each electrode must be adequate for the life of the lamp and amounts to a few milligrams. If the amount is too small, the lamp suffers from poor lumen maintenance due to tungsten evaporation caused by overheating of the electrodes as their emission declines.

Auxiliary or starting electrode This is simply a piece of molybdenum or tungsten wire positioned close to a main electrode, but connected to the opposite supply polarity through a resistor of 10 kΩ to 30 kΩ; it is essential for starting the lamp off normal mains supply (see Sect. 14.3.1).

14.2.2 Exhaust, filling, and mounting

After pinch-sealing, the arc tube is exhausted of air and filled with 2500–5000 Pa of argon, depending on rating, and an accurate dose of triple distilled mercury. The mercury dose varies with rating and typical doses are 18 mg for the 125 W MBF and 36 mg for the 250 W MBF. The control of mercury dose and argon pressure is critical: the former determines the voltage of the discharge tube and the latter, if too high, impedes starting, although higher argon pressures do improve lumen maintenance. The completed arc tube is then mounted onto a wire frame, normally of nickel-coated iron or nickel, which is attached to the glassware for sealing into the outer envelope (Fig. 14.1). Cleanliness of the mounted arc tube is essential and some form of cleaning is usual prior to sealing into the outer envelope.

14.2.3 The outer envelope

The most common form of outer envelope is an elliptical shape which is internally phosphor-coated. Wattages up to 125 W can use soda-lime glass envelopes, but the higher wattages are usually manufactured with borosilicate glass which can withstand higher operating temperatures and thermal shock. After sealing in the mounted arc tube, the envelope is exhausted and filled with nitrogen or an argon–nitrogen mixture to protect parts from oxidation and internal arcing. The filling pressure is important in order to run the discharge tube at the required temperature, and is of the order of 0·04 atm for wattages up to 125 W, but can be as high as 0·9 atm for higher wattages.

MBTF lamps usually have at least 0·6 atm of gas to prevent excess filament evaporation.

The phosphor coating is applied inside the envelope before sealing in. Methods of application include spraying, electrostatic coating, and a welling up and draining process. If solvents are used they are evaporated by directing an air flow into the coated envelope, and baking prior to sealing removes any binders. Europium-activated yttrium vanadate is currently in use (Sect. 8.4). Finally, lamps are capped and the lead wires soldered.

14.3   Performance

This section describes the electrical and light output performance of typical MB lamp types.

14.3.1   Electrical characteristics

All mercury lamps have a negative resistance characteristic and it is necessary to have some means of limiting the lamp current to the required value. The choice of control gear depends to some extent on the supply voltage, but in the UK and Europe it usually takes the form of a series choke with a capacitor across the mains for power factor correction (Sect. 18.4.3).

Starting and run-up   When first switched on the supply voltage appears across the main electrodes, but the gap is too large for the discharge to strike. The same voltage however appears across the relatively small gap between the auxiliary electrode and the adjacent main electrode and a localized discharge is initiated, limited by the series resistance. The low pressure argon filling is very important at this stage as it forms a Penning mixture with the mercury (Sect. 6.3.3) which ionizes at a lower voltage than does either of the single constituents. The local discharge expands and finally the discharge strikes between the main electrodes. The starting process is very dependent on ambient temperature as the mercury vapour pressure varies much more quickly with temperature than does the argon vapour pressure. This results in higher starting voltages at lower temperatures as shown in Fig. 14.3.

During the initial stages sputtering of the electrode may cause darkening of the discharge tube and result in loss of light output. Breakdown between the main electrodes establishes a diffused low pressure mercury discharge which originates from points on the overwinds. As the lamp warms up and the mercury pressure increases the discharge constricts and localizes onto the electrode tips. Figure 14.4 shows how the lamp characteristics vary during the run-up period.

Lamp restarting   The high operating pressure of several atmospheres makes immediate reignition impossible without special gear. A delay of three or four minutes is necessary to allow the mercury pressure and corresponding high breakdown voltage to fall to the required value before restriking is possible.

Supply voltage variation   Since the MB lamp operates with all the available mercury vaporized, pressure variation with temperature is small and the tube voltage remains sensibly constant with variations of supply volts. The current however is controlled by the choke, and Fig. 14.5a shows the change of lamp parameters with varying supply volts. The curves relate to stabilized conditions: a rapid reduction in supply voltage

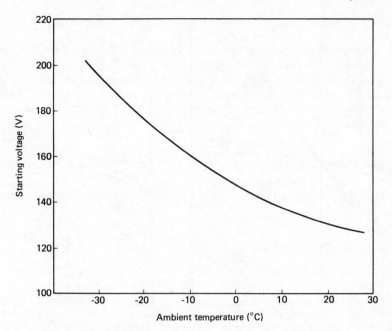

Fig. 14.3 Typical variation in starting voltage of MB lamps with ambient temperature

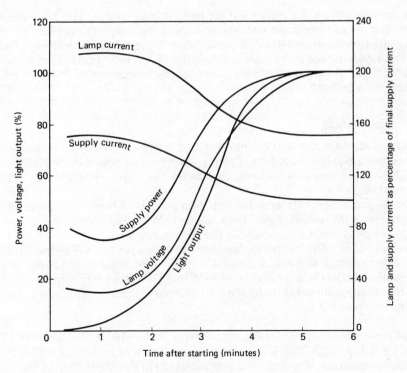

Fig. 14.4 Typical MB lamp run-up characteristics

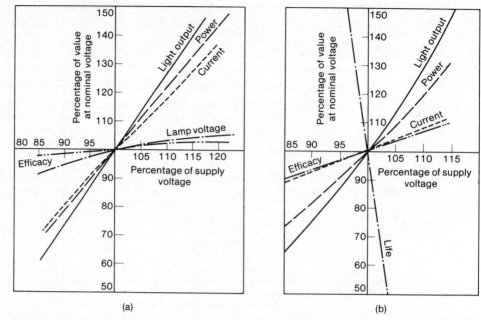

Fig. 14.5 Typical variation of lamp characteristics with supply voltage: (a) MBF lamp and (b) MBTF lamp

causes the current to fall initially and the lamp voltage to rise. The lamp voltage may then be too great for circuit stability and the lamp may extinguish. The effect of varying supply voltage on MBTF lamps is shown in Fig. 14.5b. The ability of a lamp to withstand rapid voltage reductions is primarily related to the ratio of lamp voltage to supply voltage. Figure 14.6 shows a typical relationship for a 400 W MB lamp operating on a 200/240 V supply.

14.3.2   Light output

Energy balance Of the 250 W consumed by a typical MB type lamp, only some 114 W is converted into radiation. The remainder is lost either at the electrodes or to non-radiative processes in the arc, and heats the outer envelope (ter Vrugt and Verwimp 1980).

In the case of a clear MB lamp the radiation consists of some 39 W ultraviolet, 39 W infrared, and 36 W visible light. Only some 13 W of the ultraviolet is transmitted through the glass envelope, mostly in the 365 nm region.

In the case of an MBF lamp the phosphor converts a further 8 W of the ultraviolet to visible light, but with the loss of some 4 W of the direct visible radiation, so that the total visible radiation is increased from 36 W to 40 W. Much more important, though, is that this additional light is in the red part of the spectrum, where there is little direct contribution from the arc.

Spectral power distribution Spectra of typical 250 W MB, MBF, and MBTF lamps are shown in Fig. 14.7. The MB lamp is clearly deficient in the red region and has a poor colour rendition. The improvement produced in the MBF lamp by the phosphor coating, in this example the europium-activated yttrium vanadate currently in use

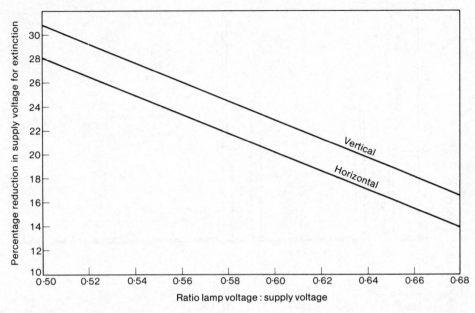

Fig. 14.6 Lamp extinction as a function of the ratio of lamp to supply voltage for the 400 W MBF lamp

(Sect. 8.4), is immediately apparent. There is a further improvement in the case of the MBTF lamp, but at the expense of a very much lower efficacy. Table 14.1 compares the three types. This includes the *red ratio*, a useful measure of 'colour correction' in these lamps. It is defined as the proportion of light transmitted by a red filter (Wratten 25).

Table 14.1 Light output and colour properties of typical 250 W mercury lamps

Lamp type	Efficacy (100 h) (lm W^{-1})	Colour rendering index (R_a)	Correlated colour temperature (K)	Red ratio (%)
MB	52	16	6000	1–2
MBF	54	48	3800	12
MBTF	20	52	3600	15

Efficacy The luminous efficacy of MBF lamps increases with wattage from about 40 lm W^{-1} at 50 W to 60 lm W^{-1} at 1 kW.

The efficacy of MBTF types is even lower than might be expected from the sharing of discharge and incandescent light because the ratio of the voltage across the filament to that across the arc has to be kept high to avoid extinguishing problems. Because the filament is a resistive ballast, the voltage across the arc tube is in phase with the supply and the arc only strikes on each half-cycle when the supply has reached a high enough value. As a result the lower efficacy filament consumes a relatively high proportion of the lamp wattage.

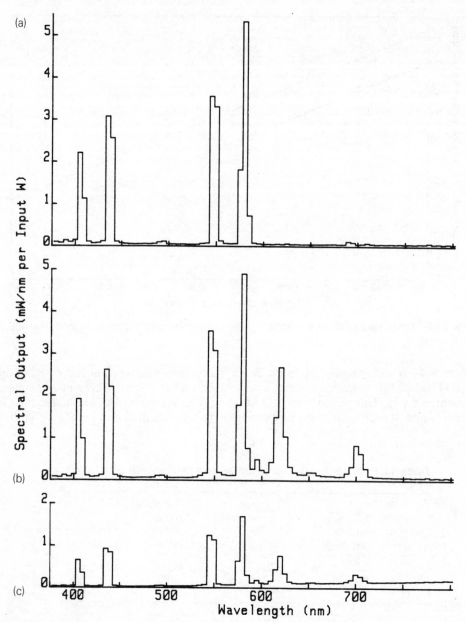

Fig. 14.7 Spectral power distributions of 250 W mercury lamps: (a) MB lamp, (b) MBF (°Kolorlux standard) lamp, and (c) MBTF lamp

Flicker   When lamps are operated on a.c. supplies there is a variation in light output every half-cycle, resulting in a 100 Hz pulsation with a 50 Hz supply. Normally this is imperceptible to the eye, but it may be visible in certain circumstances and can be important for some applications. One measure of this is the ratio of the area of the light output versus time curve which lies above the mean value to the total area beneath the curve. This is about 0·24 for MBF lamps, depending on the phosphor coating, and may be compared with 0·08 to 0·17 for fluorescent lamps and 0·03 for incandescent lamps.

Partial rectification of the lamp current can superimpose a 50 Hz modulation on the light output, to which the eye is much more sensitive. This can be controlled by careful electrode design and manufacture. To avoid perceptible flicker the difference in light output should not exceed a few per cent.

For critical applications flicker can be eliminated by operating the lamp on d.c. or from a rectified a.c. supply (Fig. 18.13d). An alternative is to operate from a high frequency supply.

14.3.3   Life

Failure of MB and MBF lamps is normally the result of loss of emission from the electrodes so that the arc fails to strike. MBTF lamps nearly always fail by the tungsten filament breaking.

Individual lamps may last for tens of thousands of hours, but at 2000 hours the lumen maintenance of MBF types is about 80% and of MBTF types about 75%. Because of this gradual loss of light output, it is desirable to replace lamps after some 8000 to 10 000 hours.

14.4   Special types and applications

14.4.1   Very high pressure lamps (ME and MD)

Air-cooled lamps   In lighting applications such as projection and theatre and studio lighting, and many industrial and commercial tasks, high intensity beams of light are required. To achieve these with relatively cheap optics it is necessary to make lamps of small size and high luminance. This results in almost spherical shaped arc tubes of relatively small size, designed to keep the temperature within safe limits. Such lamps are known as ME types and operate at mercury vapour pressures of above 30 atm. Typical applications are monochrome slide and film projectors, film printing projection microscopes, profile projection, and industrial inspection purposes. Lamps can be operated on a.c. or d.c. with appropriate control gear.

Figure 14.8 shows two typical lamp designs. The luminous efficacy is about 40 lm W^{-1} to 50 lm W^{-1} with rated life between 500 and 2000 hours, depending on rating and operating conditions. Since these lamps are used for projection the luminance of the discharge is important and is usually specified.

Water-cooled lamps   MD lamps are linear sources of high luminance operating at mercury vapour pressures in the 50 atm to 200 atm range. These require some additional means of cooling and Fig. 14.8c shows a typical arc tube and a completed lamp with water-cooled outer envelope. Uses include optical marking apparatus, profile projectors, and film projection. In the last case pulsed operation of the lamp can be employed to give an almost flickerless image without the use of a shutter. Luminous efficacy is about 60 lm W^{-1} and lamp life depends on the operating cycle, with 100 hours probably the maximum.

14.4.2   Long-wave ultraviolet production

High pressure types   These lamps are identical in construction to the MBF and MBT types, but employ a Wood's glass envelope which transmits a negligible amount of

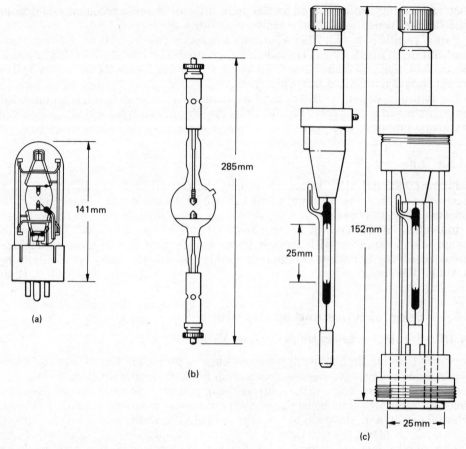

Fig. 14.8 Designs of some very high pressure mercury lamps: (a) 250 W ME lamp, (b) 1000 W ME lamp, and (c) 1000 W MD lamp

visible light while allowing most of the 365 nm ultraviolet to pass through. Lamp types are known as MBW or MBTW for the tungsten-ballasted version. They are used for bacteriological, micrological, and forensic investigations, and for detection methods using fluorescent pigments. They are also used for special effects in discotheques.

Low pressure types   These miniature lamps, known as M1 and M2, were originally developed for exciting fluorescent instrument panels. Present-day uses include time marking in recording camera equipment and wherever a small ultraviolet source is required as, for example, the light source in an insect trap. The M1 type operates on 24 V d.c. and the M2 type is designed for mains operation. Both require suitable control gear.

14.4.3   Erythemal applications

Bare silica arc tubes are used as sun lamps usually in series with a heater coil to give a combined source of ultraviolet and infrared radiations. The erythemal effectiveness curve peaks at 296·7 nm and silica arc tubes provide energy at this wavelength. It is essential that doped silica is used for this application to filter out potentially dangerous radiation produced in the shorter wavelength ultraviolet region.

14.4.4 Future developments

A De luxe range of MBF lamps has been established in the last few years with an increased proportion of red giving a colour rendition suitable for indoor applications. Future improvements may be dependent on phosphor development, but it is possible that lower power ratings will be developed as energy-saving alternatives to GLS lamps.

Further reading

Elenbaas W, 1951, *The high pressure mercury vapour discharge* (Amsterdam: North Holland)

Elenbaas W, 1965, *High pressure mercury vapour discharge lamps and their applications* (Eindhoven: Philips Technical Library)

ter Vrugt J W and Verwimp J K P, 1980, *IEE Proc.*, **127,** Part A, 173–180: High pressure mercury vapour lamps

Waymouth J F, 1971, *Electric discharge lamps* (Cambridge, Mass: MIT Press)

15 Metal halide lamps

At the start of the 1960s when high pressure mercury, low pressure sodium, and fluorescent tubes were well established, two new important discharge lamps were introduced – the high pressure sodium lamp (Chap. 13) and the metal halide lamp. During the last two decades the metal halide lamp has been greatly improved and developed in a variety of forms. These have found application in both interior lighting, using the conventional arc tube with an outer envelope or jacket, and specialized applications where an unjacketed design is frequently adopted. As well as covering the design principles and manufacture of metal halide lamps, the construction and characteristics of these two types of lamps are described in this chapter.

15.1 General considerations

15.1.1 Principles of operation

The few lines of visible radiation from a high pressure mercury discharge (MB) lamp are found in three main areas, i.e. 436 nm – blue, 546 nm – green, and 579 nm – yellow (Fig. 14.7). The absence of energy in other areas results in a lamp that is only moderately efficient ($\sim$52 lm W^{-1}) and which has poor colour rendition ($R_a \sim 50$). The high pressure sodium (SON) lamp is an example of how increased efficacy ($\sim$120 lm W^{-1}) can be achieved by using an element having a strong resonance line occurring in the visible region of the spectrum. However, neither sodium lamps nor lamps made using indium or thallium produce any improvement in colour rendition since the radiation from these elements occurs only over a limited wavelength range.

One method of improving the colour rendition of a mercury lamp is to include more than one metal within the discharge tube so that emission lines occur over a wide range of the visible spectrum. To maintain an efficient light source with an acceptable colour the proportioning of radiation from the various elements must be carefully controlled.

The properties which these metals must have for general improvements to efficacy and colour rendition are (a) the vapour pressure must be sufficiently high at the temperature of the arc tube wall to be excited into the discharge, (b) resonance lines within the visible part of the spectrum should have large oscillator strengths (Jack 1971), (c) non-resonance lines should have their lower excitation levels relatively near to ground level: the average excitation level being as low as possible in comparison with the average excitation of the mercury spectral lines (Jack 1971, Bauer 1964), and (d) the metals must not react with the arc tube material or its electrodes.

Silica-bodied discharge lamps available commercially may include elements such as dysprosium, gallium, indium, lithium, scandium, sodium, thallium, thorium, and thulium. Spectral enhancement however is not achieved merely by adding the metals to a mercury-containing arc tube. Although the core temperature of an arc of this type is of the order of 5700 °C, the coolest part of the silica body, behind the electrodes, may be only 700–800 °C. For many metals this is below their melting points, e.g. sodium m.p. = 1539 °C and dysprosium m.p. = 1407 °C, and so the low vapour pressure of the metal would make little contribution towards the spectral output of the lamp. A particular exception to this is the group of alkali metals, e.g. sodium m.p. = 97·8 °C and lithium m.p. = 108 °C. However, these react with silica and so would rapidly destroy the lamp. Sodium can be used in its metallic form if used in arc tubes of material other than silica, e.g. sodium resistant glass (SOX lamps) and translucent alumina (SON lamps).

It is now well established that the problems of low vapour pressure and reactivity can be overcome by using metals in the form of their halide salts – hence 'metal halide' lamps. The vapour pressure of the halide is generally higher than that of the metal itself and the reactivity in the case of the alkali metals is significantly less. The halide group includes fluorine, chlorine, bromine, and iodine but, because of the increasing reactivity of bromine, chlorine, and fluorine, the iodine compound is usually employed in most commercially available lamps. However, the use of fluorine in coated silica tungsten halogen lamps has recently been reported (Fitzpatrick 1979) and experimental sodium–tin chloride systems in silica-bodied lamps (Chalmers et al. 1975, Jack 1971) have also been described. Chlorides are used in some specialist lamps (e.g. CID lamps, see Sect. 15.4.1) having relatively short lives in comparison with lamps used for general lighting which are designed to last for over 6000 hours.

15.1.2   The halide cycle

When a metal halide lamp is first energized the output spectrum is initially that due to mercury vapour since the halides remain solidified on the relatively cool arc tube wall. As the arc tube wall temperature increases, the halides melt and vaporize. The vapour is carried into the hot region of the arc by diffusion and convection. The temperature of the arc causes dissociation of the halide compound into the halogen and metal atoms. The metal atoms are then excited in the high temperature arc core and produce their characteristic spectral emission (Sect. 6.3.4). The metal atoms continue to diffuse through the arc tube volume and, in the region of the relatively cool arc tube wall, metal and halogen atoms recombine to form the halide compound. This recombination process is particularly significant in the case of the chemically-active alkali metals in preventing attack of the silica wall. Compare the halogen cycle with tungsten as the volatile metal in tungsten halogen lamps (Sect. 10.1). A comprehensive review is given by Work (1981).

15.1.3   Manufacturing techniques

While the general fabrication of metal halide lamps is similar to that of MB lamps (Sect. 14.2), the characteristics of the halides demand certain differences in processing techniques.

Many of the halides used are deliquescent and so require handling in especially dry atmospheres in which water levels are held at better than 1 p.p.m. by volume. Water vapour or subsequent hydrogen released from 'wet' doses causes an increase in lamp striking voltage. The halide compounds must be kept free from surface contaminants and arc tube material needs to be of a higher purity grade of silica than that used for MB lamp manufacture. In particular hydroxyl levels need to be very low (less than 10 p.p.m.). In addition oxide emitters are excluded from the electrodes of metal halide lamps because of reaction of these compounds with the halogens. Instead use is made of thorium metal and/or thoriated tungsten electrode shanks to assist lamp starting.

Since the radiation characteristics of metal halide lamps are strongly dependent on the vapour pressure of the halides and consequently on the arc tube temperature, differences in the physical geometry of the arc tube are more critical than in MB lamps. In horizontally-operated lamps the position of the electrodes relative to the arc tube axis can significantly affect lamp performance (Odell and Preston 1980) by altering the concentricity of the arc core within the arc tube and hence the temperature profile over the arc tube. The key to producing uniform metal halide lamps can thus be summarized as: cleanliness, use of high purity components, and rigid geometric control.

15.2   Glass envelope lamps (MBI and MBIF)

These are made in several ratings with the 175 W, 250 W, 400 W, and 1 kW generally in elliptical outer envelopes and higher wattages (2 kW and 3 kW) in tubular envelopes. The designation MBI refers to a clear glass outer envelope and MBIF refers to a phosphor-coated envelope. The lower wattage lamps are providing a new stimulus to the indoor lighting of offices, supermarkets, and large stores where they offer improved colour quality and light output over conventional MBF and incandescent lamps. The metal halide lamp can also provide a useful, economically viable alternative to fluorescent tube lamps in design installations requiring compact sources of good colour and efficacy. The 1 kW lamp is used extensively for high bay (factory and warehouse) illumination and general outdoor floodlighting. The higher wattage ratings are used exclusively for general floodlighting. Notice that, although there has been a move to the more efficient high pressure sodium (SON) lamp for floodlighting, the metal halide lamp still has the advantage in its superior colour rendition properties.

Construction   The construction of a sodium–scandium lamp is shown in Fig. 15.1 with differences being shown in the arc tube mount from that of an MB lamp. The mount frame is split into two and the electrical connection to the electrode remote from the stem is made by a lead wire following the outer jacket contour. This construction reduces photoelectric currents which could otherwise lead to sodium loss by electrolysis through the arc tube wall with possible arc tube failure (Waymouth 1971). The thermal switch in the starting probe circuit has a similar purpose; when open it removes the potential difference between the starter probe and main electrode, thus preventing electrolysis in the pinch area of the arc tube body.

The silica arc tube is generally physically smaller than an MB lamp of the same wattage. This higher wall loading is essential to keep the wall temperature sufficiently high to vaporize the halides. The cool ends of the arc tube in the regions of the electrodes are usually coated with a heat-reflecting zirconium dioxide coating, thus preventing the halides from condensing onto the arc tube walls away from the main arc area. Other physical differences in arc tube construction can be seen in lamps designed for one specific mode of operation, e.g. horizontal-only burning. In horizontal operation the discharge forms an arch between the two electrodes. The middle section of the arc is therefore closer to the top of the discharge tube wall than to the bottom wall. Some manufacturers contour the discharge tube to accommodate this so that the arc is equidistant from the tube wall over the length of the discharge. Such lamp designs may require the lamp to be oriented in a particular plane of

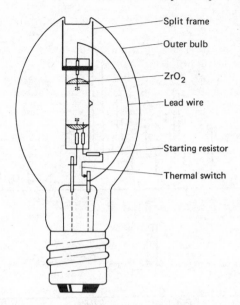

Split frame

Outer bulb

ZrO_2

Lead wire

Starting resistor

Thermal switch

Fig. 15.1   Construction of sodium–scandium MBI lamp

operation and so these lamps are provided with special locating caps and lamp holders.

In addition to the mercury vapour and halides the silica arc tubes usually contain argon (at a typical pressure of 660 Pa) to initiate the discharge. To reduce the voltage required to strike the lamps some manufacturers use a neon–argon mix. However, this has the disadvantage of making the lamp slightly less efficient.

As mentioned previously, the elliptical outer bulb can be either clear or phosphor-coated. The phosphor coating is nowadays usually yttrium vanadate as used in MBF lamps. However, since there is generally less ultraviolet radiation from metal halide lamps than from MB lamps, the spectral enhancement due to phosphor conversion (Sect. 14.2.3) is correspondingly less in these lamps. The phosphor coating serves mainly to diffuse the radiation from the arc tube, thereby effectively increasing the size of the point source, reducing glare, and making the design of luminaire optics less critical.

Characteristics   The spectra of a sodium–scandium lamp and a dysprosium–thallium lamp are shown in Figs 15.2a and 15.2b respectively. The improved spectral output from these lamps is readily identified in comparison with the spectrum of mercury lamps (Fig. 14.7). Both lamp types produce *line spectra* resulting from discrete electronic transitions within the excited metal atoms (Sect. 6.2).

A summary of 'typical performance' of metal halide lamps is shown in Table 15.1. In terms of luminous efficacy the metal halide lamps conveniently bridge the gap between the MB and SON lamp types. However, in terms of colour rendering index R_a they are far superior to both types. The values of correlated colour temperature CCT illustrate how the colour appearance of metal halide lamps may vary over a wide range even though the R_a values remain similar. Individual variations in colour appearance may be observed in a batch of lamps since the lamp is no longer a single system of mercury emission, but a complex one of several metals whose spectra cover

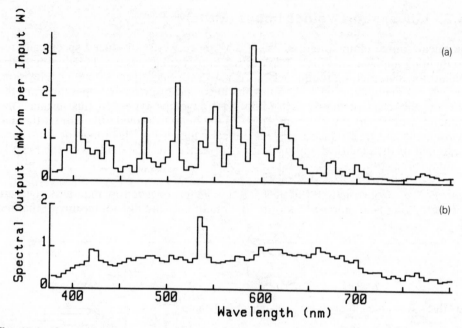

Fig. 15.2 Spectral power distributions of (a) sodium–scandium lamp and (b) dysprosium–thallium lamp

the whole visible wavelength region. It is often not appreciated that while a slight imbalance of the spectra of two or more nominally identical lamps may produce a visual difference in colour *appearance* between lamps, the general colour *rendering index* R_a can remain unaltered.

Electrically, metal halide lamps require a ballast, such as a series inductance (choke), to limit the lamp current. In comparison with MB lamps, the presence of iodine and the lack of any oxide emitter on the electrode result in these lamps requiring a higher starting voltage. This has resulted in the need for an additional starting aid in the lamp circuit, such as a high voltage pulse starter switch integral with the lamp, a starter switch positioned across the choke ballast, or the provision of a transformer winding to provide an adequate peak voltage.

Table 15.1 Summary of 'typical performance' of various glass envelope lamp types

Lamp type	Efficacy (lm W^{-1})	Colour rendering index (R_a)	Correlated colour temperature (K)
High pressure mercury (MB)	52	20	6000
High pressure mercury with phosphor coating (MBF)	58	48	3800
Sodium–scandium (MBI)	80	70	3800
Sodium–indium–thallium (HPI)	80	65	4000
Dysprosium–thallium (HQI)	75	85	6000
Tin	60–80	85	3000–6000
High pressure sodium (SON)	115	20	2000

15.3 Linear source silica lamps (MBIL)

The linear source lamps rated at 750 W and above were introduced specifically for floodlighting applications: the 1600 W rating in particular was developed to meet the demand for increased lighting levels associated with the advent of colour television. The general manufacturing techniques, halides, and principles of operation are the same for this class of lamps as for the glass envelope types. In this instance the luminaire itself forms the outer envelope of the lamp to provide the correct thermal environment and to produce excellent optical control. For this range of lamps any assessment of the electrical and optical performance must be made with the lamp in the luminaire.

Construction Constructional details for this lamp are given in Fig. 15.3. The arc tubes are long and narrow and are operated horizontally to ensure a thermal

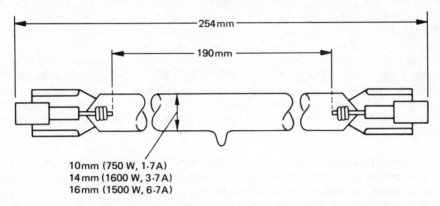

Fig. 15.3 Construction of linear MBIL lamp

equilibrium along their arc path. The arc tube bores of 10 mm, 14 mm, and 16 mm correspond to the increasing operating current of the 750 W 1·7 A, 1600 W 3·7 A, and 1500 W 6·7 A lamps. To minimize the effect of variation in colour across the arc the tubes are frosted and so the effective emission area is that of the arc tube outer surface.

Characteristics The optical performance of linear lamps is similar to that given for glass envelope lamps (Table 15.1), but the arc voltage is higher. The 750 W and 1600 W lamps require a high reactance transformer to ballast the lamps and to provide sufficient voltage to make the lamps self-starting. The 1500 W lamp is designed to operate from a series reactor circuit operating between phases of a 415 V 50 Hz supply. In this arrangement an ignitor is required in the circuit to switch on the lamp.

15.4 Compact source lamps

These lamps are used for numerous specialized applications normally associated with a lens or mirror optic. Depending on the optical system used, and the required intensity and beam spread, the arc brightness may be equally, if not more important than luminous efficacy. To achieve high source brightness the lamp should have a short arc gap and a high electric field; this normally means that lamps operate at a high pressure of mercury or other vapour (normally several atmospheres). Unlike compact source xenon lamps the fill pressure of a metal halide lamp when cold is less than atmospheric, so making it safer to handle.

15.4.1   Single ended lamps (CSI and CID)

The 400 W and 1 kW CSI (Compact Source Iodide) lamps were introduced in the late 1960s as high brightness sources for application in optical projector systems and spotlights. The introduction of colour television resulted in a requirement for higher illumination levels for stadium lighting than could be provided by existing tungsten halogen lamps. To fulfil this need the 1 kW lamp in a PAR 64 envelope (Aldworth 1975) was developed. The high axial intensity and the availability of spreader lenses have meant that this lamp has also found applications both in TV and location recording and more recently for solar simulation studies (Gillet 1977, Beeson 1978).

The demands of the film industry are even more stringent than those of colour TV, especially in regard to the spectral properties of the light source. Whereas the colour appearance of a television picture may be adjusted electrically, much less flexibility is available when filming. For location filming a light source with a colour temperature of 5500 K is appropriate to the daylight film stock. It was for this application that a new range of compact source lamps designated CID (Compact Iodide Daylight) was developed (Hall and Preston 1981). At present CID lamps cover the range 200 W to 2·5 kW.

Construction   The basic construction of CSI and CID lamps is very similar. The arc tube is fabricated from a high quality, low water content silica and a single pinch is used to position the tungsten electrodes. The filling for the arc tube consists of argon, mercury, and metal halides appropriate for the emission required, i.e. gallium, thallium, and sodium iodides for CSI lamps and tin and indium halides for CID lamps. The 1 kW lamp in its two unjacketed forms is shown in Fig. 15.4. The lamp mounted in the G22 bipin base is designed for switch-on using ignitor pulses of 7–10 kV which means that the lamp can only be switched on when the arc tube is cold. To achieve restrike of the lamp whilst it is still hot requires an ignitor pulse of 30 kV. To permit such a voltage to be used, without the possibility of arcing or tracking, the lamp is mounted on the G38 base. In addition the arc tube pinch is slotted and a mica preform inserted between the lamp leads. The 1 kW CSI and CID lamps are also produced in 200 mm diameter sealed beam envelopes. The use of an outer envelope which is filled with an inert gas means that the arc tube seal is protected from oxidation and this gives a corresponding increase in lamp life. As with the unjacketed lamps, both cold and hot restrike versions are available.

Characteristics   The higher power loading and consequent high arc tube temperatures associated with these compact source lamps result in the halide dose being completely evaporated during operation. The emission spectra for both types of lamp exhibit a combination of discrete lines (Sect. 6.2) and continuum (Sect. 6.3.4) throughout the visible region as illustrated in Figs 15.5a and 15.5b. This gives excellent colour rendering properties and a colour rendering index R_a greater than 80 for both types of lamp. It is noted that the tin halide dose used in the CID lamps has a relatively low melting point and high vapour pressure, which results in the emission spectrum being insensitive to power dissipation. This characteristic means that the

Fig. 15.4 Standard and hot restrike 1 kW CSI/CID lamps

emission spectrum is unchanged by fluctuations in mains voltage. Measurements show that the colour temperature of emission is relatively unchanged until the input power is reduced to less than 50% of its nominal value.

Despite their colour temperature, CID lamps radiate only 2% of the input power as ultraviolet radiation. This can be attributed to the absorption by the tin iodide vapour which acts as an effective filter. CSI lamps produce a high proportion of ultraviolet radiation (approximately 4% of the input power). For equal illumination intensity CSI lamps have a similar ultraviolet content to solar radiation. This property together with similar infrared radiation has resulted in the widespread use of these lamps for solar simulators.

One of the adverse characteristics which is common to all a.c.-operated discharge lamps is the fluctuation of light output at twice the supply frequency. This can give rise to beat effects when the lamps are used for TV recording or filming. In stadium applications this effect can be minimized by operating lamps from the separate phase of a 3-phase supply. However, more recently electronic gear has been developed which operates the lamp on a square-wave current. This virtually eliminates any light fluctuation from an individual lamp.

15.4.2. Double ended lamps (HMI)

HMI lamps were developed in Germany to meet the need created by the German Federal Television Service and were first established in service in Germany in 1969. Two ratings, 575 W and 1200 W, were introduced in 1969 and the range has now been extended to cover from 200 W to 4 kW. Although their initial application was for television lighting outside the studios, they are also now used for location lighting for films (Lemons 1978).

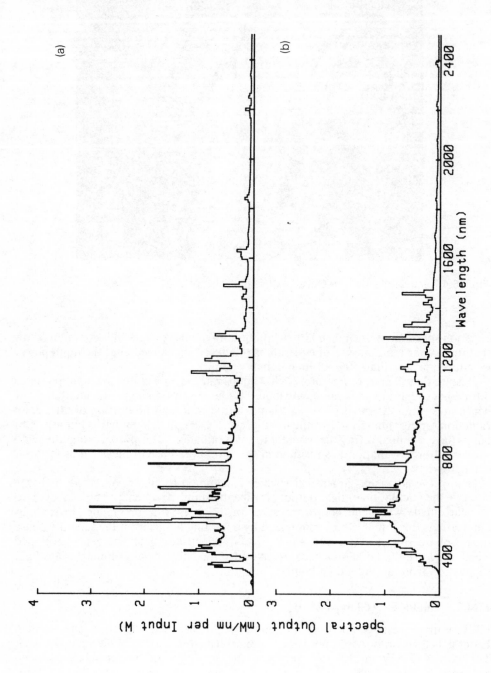

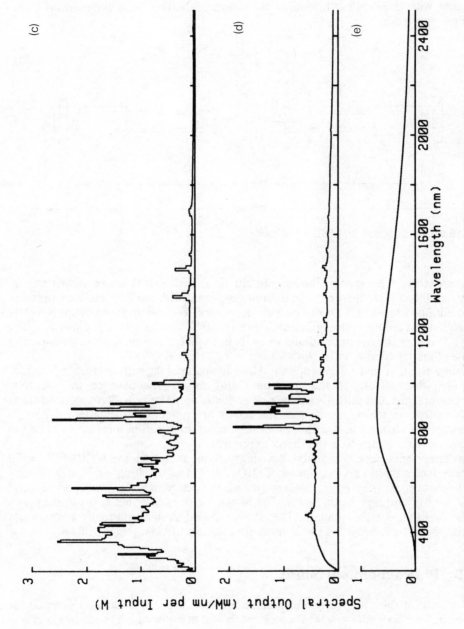

Fig. 15.5 Spectral power distributions of (a) CSI lamp, (b) CID lamp, (c) HMI lamp, (d) 1000 W XE xenon lamp, and (e) 1000 W K4 tungsten halogen lamp

Construction   The discharge tube consists of a thick walled, ellipsoidal silica body with axially mounted tungsten electrodes (Fig. 15.6). Long molybdenum foils in collapsed tubular appendages are used to minimize foil oxidation and still maintain a high temperature at the arc tube wall. The lamps are filled with mercury and argon together with the rare-earth iodides, dysprosium, thullium, and holmium to give a daylight spectrum.

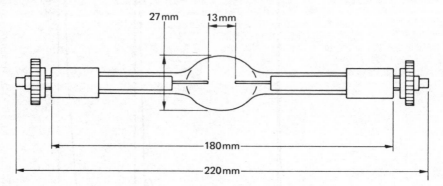

Fig. 15.6   Construction of 1200 W HMI lamp

Characteristics   The spectral energy distribution of the HMI lamps shown in Fig. 15.5c exhibits a high degree of continuum associated with the high mercury pressure and multiline emission from the rare-earth halides. The colour of emission is tightly controlled at a colour temperature of 5600 K ($\pm$ 400 K) and is centred below the black body. The high degree of continuum results in excellent colour rendering properties with a colour rendering index $R_a > 90$.

Unlike the CSI and CID lamps the HMI lamps operate with a saturated vapour pressure which results in the spectrum being more dependent on the arc tube temperature and consequently on the power dissipated. The radiation produced starts at about 220 nm which means that the lamps are practically ozone-free. They do however emit strongly in the ultraviolet region, so that caution must be exercised in the use of these lamps to avoid direct exposure.

The lamps have been designed to have high luminous efficacies (80–120 lm W^{-1}) and they produce a typical arc brightness of 1100 cd m^{-2}. This combination of high efficacy and brightness provides an excellent source for the design of lanterns to produce good beam control and high beam factor. The lamps are operated on a.c. supplies using a choke or other suitable ballast. The double ended design inherently permits hot restrike operation, provided the ignitors produce a sufficiently high voltage.

15.5 Photochemical lamps

The growth of the photocopy and graphic arts industry has stimulated demand for more efficient high energy light sources capable of providing high levels of violet and ultraviolet radiation. High pressure mercury lamps which are rich in radiation throughout the ultraviolet part of the spectrum (particularly at 365 nm) have provided a useful alternative to carbon arcs for photopolymer resist films and ultraviolet-curing inks. Further improvements have resulted from the development of metal halide lamps which utilize metals, e.g. magnesium, iron, and cobalt, specially chosen for their ultraviolet radiation characteristics (Beeson and Furmidge 1976, Gardner et al. 1975).

For application in platemaking and diazo-copying, metal halide lamps containing gallium iodide have been developed because of the intense radiation at 420 nm.

Although the majority of lamps used for photochemical applications are designed in the wattage range 1–5 kW, there has been a strong interest in a 400/800 W Graph-X lamp. This design incorporates a silica arc tube in a 200 mm sealed reflector envelope with a prismatic front lens, thus producing an intense beam of radiation over a defined working area (Beeson and Furmidge 1972).

The design of circuitry for metal halide lamps used in the photocopy and graphic arts industry is normally tailored to a specific exposure schedule. With all metal halide lamps, there is a delay from the lamp being switched on to attaining its full output. There is also a delay after a lamp has been switched off before it can be reignited. This has resulted in the equipment manufacturers resorting to forced cooling and lamp simmering schedules to improve lamp response. Further improvement can be expected in the future with the development of high voltage ignitors and hot restrike lamps.

15.6 Recent developments

Over the last fifteen years there has been intensive development of the metal halide lamp because it offers an efficacy gain over tungsten halogen lamps by a factor of three or more and still produces a light with excellent colour properties. With the increasing cost of energy, the quest for high lamp efficacy is of growing importance for both exterior and interior applications. Since the efficacy of a metal halide lamp has been found to decrease with decreasing power rating, the minimum rating commercially available for general illumination is about 200 W. This has obviously limited its application for interior use. However, recent investigations have resulted in a new design of metal halide lamps which can operate as low as 30 W and achieve 85 lm W^{-1} (Lake and Davenport 1980). This opens up the possibility of high pressure metal halide lamps finding wider application for interior use.

Other developments in metal halide lamp technology make use of ceramic arc tubes instead of the conventional silica. This would permit the use of other halide vapours and high arc tube temperatures with a consequent increase in efficacy at low powers (Brown et al. 1982). Looking further ahead are the possibilities of electrodeless lamps excited by a microwave source (Haugsjaa 1979). Although high efficacies at low power levels have been demonstrated experimentally, there are many difficulties associated with the generation and control of the microwave power.

Further reading

Drop P C, Fisher E, Oostvogels F and Wesselink G A, 1975, *Philips Tech. Rev.*, **35,** 347–353: Metal halide discharge lamps
Elenbaas W, 1972, *Light sources* (London: Macmillan)
Keeffe W M, 1980, *IEE Proc.*, **127,** Part A, 181–189: Recent progress in metal halide discharge lamp research
Waymouth J F, 1971, *Electric discharge lamps* (Cambridge, Mass: MIT Press)

Work D E, 1981, *Ltg. Res. Technol.*, **13,** 143–152: Chemistry of metal halide lamps: a review
van Heel A C S (Ed), 1967, *Advanced optical techniques*, Chapter 9: Modern light sources (Amsterdam: North Holland)

16 Neon, photoflash, and xenon lamps

Differing widely in their characteristics, all of these lamps provide instantaneous light output at switch-on.

Pure neon gas emits a red-orange glow and use is made of this as a visual indicator source; in long shaped tubes they are used for advertising purposes and at high loadings as a powerful source of red light for hazard warning beacons on tall structures.

Expendable photoflash lamps emit a large amount of light flux of controlled output for photographic purposes. Energy for these lamps is provided by the chemical combustion of a metal within an atmosphere of pure oxygen.

Xenon, like neon, is a pure gas, but under high current loading and pressure light of sunlight quality is emitted. Made in compact source forms, very high source brightnesses are obtained for optical purposes; high power linear source lamps of up to 65 kW have been applied to the lighting of city centres and sports stadia. The xenon flash tube today is inbuilt into cameras and other tubes are used for stroboscopic purposes. Pulsed xenon sources are applied to camera lighting for the exposure of printing plates used in the graphic arts field.

16.1 Neon lamps

16.1.1 Design

Most neon lamps operate with cold cathodes, indicator types having two closely spaced electrodes sealed within a soft glass envelope containing neon, at a pressure of about 8 torr, and other trace gases, providing a glow discharge at the negative electrode when a voltage is applied. On an a.c. voltage source each electrode is alternatively negative and positive to give the appearance of continuous glow at both electrodes. The electrodes are of pure nickel or iron and may be very thinly coated with an electron emitter.

Other neon lamps, with cold hollow cathodes of pure iron, have a long positive column and light is emitted from gas excitation producing the characteristic warm orange colour. These lamps can be many metres in length, of small bore (8 mm to 20 mm), and are more generally used in a shaped form for advertising or decorative purposes. Where a heated cathode is provided, increasing electron emission to support several amperes, the arc voltage becomes sufficiently low with a moderate length of arc tube that normal supply voltages can be used and efficacies of $10 \, \text{lm W}^{-1}$ to $15 \, \text{lm W}^{-1}$ are achieved.

16.1.2 Characteristics

In a closely spaced electrode system, where the negative glow emits light, a series resistance limits the lamp current, the discharge source having a negative glow characteristic. There is an optimum current for a particular size of electrode system and activated surface when the discharge is stable. Too low a current will give flickering of the discharge and a high current will give a bright stable discharge, but the life will be shorter and blackening of the envelope will occur. Lamp current is therefore specified to identify a standard or high brightness lamp being less than 1 mA or up to about 2·5 mA respectively. The standard brightness lamps emit about 0·06 lumens per mA and, with a current increase of about four times for a high brightness lamp, light output is increased by about ten times. Lamp life is very dependent on the current and normal brightness lamps have an average survival of 50 000 h which is reduced to about 5000 h for the high brightness loading. End of lamp life is not usually catastrophic, but occurs when the light output has fallen to an unacceptably low level. The striking voltage at which the neon indicator lamp glows is between 45 V a.c. and 65 V a.c. for standard brightness lamps and around 70 V a.c. to 100 V a.c. for the higher brightness ones. A small trace of argon gas or radioactive krypton in the neon is often used to lower this striking voltage. The light output of a neon lamp is mainly in the orange part of the spectrum between 570 nm and 750 nm, having a small infrared content between 820 nm and 880 nm.

Neon tubes with long positive columns having cold cathodes take currents of 50 mA to 100 mA and some 300 V is dropped across a pair of cathodes in providing the electron emission. The positive column has therefore to be made long, keeping the tube bore narrow to obtain a high voltage drop across it relative to the electrode losses in the interests of overall luminous efficacy which is around 3 lm W^{-1} to 7 lm W^{-1}. Much higher voltages are required to operate these tubes and high reactance type transformers provide voltages from 1·5 kV to 15 kV. Lamp life is long, achieving 20 000 h to 30 000 h.

Use of a hot cathode to increase the electron emission, reducing the voltage drop at the cathodes to about 15 V each, and to support a current of several amperes, results in a positive column of much reduced length and a lamp which can be operated from the normal supply mains. A lamp with these characteristics approaches a luminous efficacy of 15 lm W^{-1} with a life of 8000 h to 10 000 h.

16.1.3 Applications

The very small neon lamp is widely used as an indicator source and requires only a small resistor to limit the current, so unit cost is low (Fig. 16.1a). Fitted to electrical equipment it indicates that the supply is on, or fitted to a light switch it draws attention to the switch at night. As the lamp is voltage-sensitive it provides an indication of reaching a preset voltage, like the charged state of a capacitor. Electronic flash units for photography use this principle to indicate that the power supply is ready to trigger the xenon flash tube.

The largest type of neon lamp, often in a GLS shaped bulb with a 'beehive' cathode, operates at about 5 W, the current-limiting resistor being placed within the bayonet cap. It is used to provide a low light level of illumination, as may be required in a nursery at night. In display applications, instead of a 'beehive' coil, the wire is shaped to present letters, numerals, or other configurations in a glass tube. Another form of indicator lamp has a split circular plate mounted in a small bulb and dissipates about 0·5 W.

A more recent development is a lamp producing a flickering neon glow simulating a candle flame (Fig. 16.1b). A metal electrode is used, shaped in the form of a candle flame, and having a surface coating which not only provides a source of electron emission, but also contains material to generate a trace gas impurity. This results in

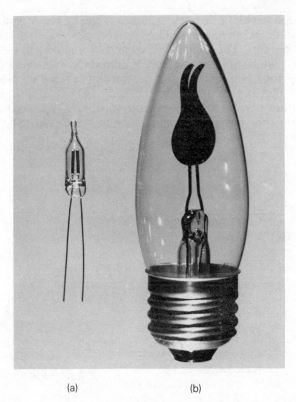

(a)   (b)

Fig. 16.1   (a) miniature neon lamp and (b) flickering neon candle

cathode spot movement producing random motion of the glow discharge, similar to that of a flickering candle flame.

The larger type neon lamps, either in long straight tubes for architectural lighting effects or suitably shaped to form letters, numerals, or signs, are to be seen in most city centres, often sequentially switched.

A design of hot cathode neon lamp, making use of some of the components from the linear sodium lamp, provides a lamp of 160 W in power with a luminous efficacy of about 15 lm W^{-1}. The characteristic neon glow is sufficiently close to signal red that it is used as an aircraft hazard warning beacon on tall structures. Used as a flashing beacon in a suitable lantern it has a range of up to 80 km on a clear night. Having a long lamp life it reduces expensive maintenance on tall structures.

16.2   Photoflash lamps

16.2.1   Design

A very fine tungsten or tungsten alloy filament (usually W–Re, Sect. 7.3.1) is mounted between a pair of contact wires. A primer paste, made from very fine particles of zirconium and magnesium and powerful oxidizing materials, is applied in accurately controlled quantities to the filament and tips of the contact wires. The filament assembly is sealed into a glass bulb or tube with a small moisture-sensitive spot applied to the inside glass wall for use as a leak detector. Finely shredded foil is introduced into the envelope in measured quantities. This is generally zirconium, replacing magnesium and aluminium which were formerly used; hafnium foil provides even higher light outputs. The lamp is heated and evacuated and sufficient oxygen to ensure complete combustion of the foil is introduced immediately prior to the completion of the final seal, usually at a pressure of several atmospheres. To avoid the possibility of bursting in operation the lamp is coated with a lacquer, which is usually a cellulose derivative in an organic solvent. A final coating of anti-static solution is applied to prevent inadvertent ignition by static electricity. Most lamps now made are capless.

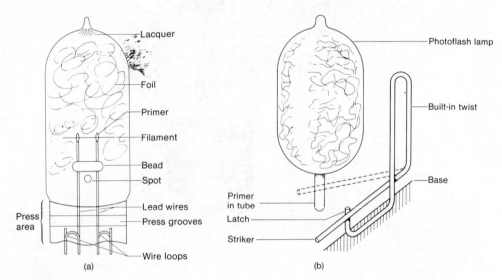

Fig. 16.2   (a) construction of AG1 photoflash lamp and (b) operation of torsion spring to fire lamp in Magicube

Figure 16.2a shows a typical design with base construction originating in the USA (Type AG1); the European capless design (Type 1) has a larger base.

16.2.2   Operation

To fire the lamp a current is passed through the contact wires to the filament, causing the primer paste to ignite and explode. Burning particles of primer are scattered throughout the interior of the lamp and the shredded foil ignites in several places simultaneously.

Figure 16.3 shows a typical photometric result from which the following essential parameters may be derived:

(a)   Time to peak (or half-peak): the time from initial closing of the firing circuit to the time at which the luminous flux reaches its maximum (or one-half of the maximum).

(b)   Effective duration: the time during which the luminous flux is more than one-half of the maximum value.

(c)   Peak light output: the maximum value of luminous flux.

(d)   Total light output: the total light emitted from start to completion of flash, or the integrated area under the curve measured in lumen seconds.

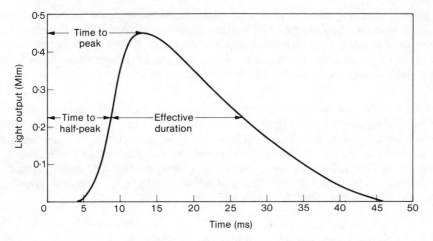

Fig. 16.3   Light output curve of AG1B or 1B lamp

To achieve an increase in total light output from a lamp of given volume an increase in combustible material and oxygen is necessary. A change in peak output, time to peak or half-peak, and effective duration can be achieved by altering the cross-sectional area of the foil strands: a lamp having twice as many strands as a standard lamp, but with the same weight and thickness of foil, will achieve a high peak output in a shorter time with a shorter effective duration. The 'dark time', or time lag between the closing of the firing circuit and the start of the flash, may be altered without changing the general shape of the time versus light output curve.

16.2.3   Photoflash range

A series of flashbulbs, cubes, or elongated arrays containing upward of ten bulbs with their own individual reflectors and matched to balance daylight colour and black and white films are available to meet the needs of both the professional and the amateur photographer.

Flash bulbs   Type 1B and AG1B are blue lacquered versions of the clear bulb type 1 and AG1 which are battery or battery–capacitor fired. They are of the capless type and are interchangeable by means of a socket adaptor.

Flash cubes   A plastic cube containing four precision reflectors and individual bulbs smaller than those in the type 1 or AG1 lamps and encased in a transparent plastic cover sealed to a base. These have been designed to fit cameras with a special socket providing automatic cube rotation as the film is advanced. They are normally fired from a battery–capacitor circuit.

Magicube   This cube, very similar in appearance to the flash cube, requires no battery or power source and eliminates failures associated with poor batteries or contacts. A torsion loaded spring, released through the shutter trigger mechanism, strikes a thin metal tube containing an anvil wire coated with a primer igniting the flash (Fig. 16.2b). The base is non-interchangeable, preventing the wrong type of flash cube being used.

Flip flash   An elongated flat container enclosing eight separate bulbs, each with its individual reflector and mounted on a specially designed circuit board. Energy from a piezoelectric crystal, built into the camera, fires the bulb and a heat-activated switch automatically connects the next bulb. When the top four bulbs have been used the unit is flipped over in readiness for the next four flashes.

Flash bar   This contains ten separate flashes per unit which are fired automatically in sequence. When five of the bulbs have been flashed the front of the flash bar is reversed for the other five flashes. These bulbs are electrically fired by the battery pack used in the 'Instant' picture cameras made by Polaroid. Hafnium foil filled, they provide a new standard in light output per unit volume. A lightly tinted blue transparent cover corrects the light output to daylight quality and gives added protection from bulbs which may shatter.

16.2.4   Light output classification and characteristics

Several types of flash bulb are required to synchronize the light flash because of the varied characteristics of camera shutters of the blade, iris, or focal plane type. Single speed cameras usually employ 'X' synchronization, whereas multispeed cameras usually have 'X' and 'M' synchronized shutters. With 'X' synchronization the camera shutter must be at least 80% open within 1 ms from the time of the initial closing of the firing circuit: class MF lamps may be used at shutter speeds up to $1/60$ s, or class M lamps at shutter speeds up to $1/30$ s. With 'M' synchronization a delay is incorporated so that the shutter must be fully open at $15 \, \text{ms} \pm 2 \, \text{ms}$ from the time of the initial closing of the firing circuit: class M or MF lamps may be used in this case at shutter speeds faster than $1/30$ s. Class FP and FP+ lamps are designed for use with cameras having focal plane shutters where a long flash duration is required, by using strands of foil with two or more different cross-sections which burn at different speeds. Table 16.1 shows the luminous flux–time characteristics in accordance with BS 5841 Part 1 (BSI 1980b).

Table 16.1   Flashbulb data

Class	Time to peak (ms)	Time to half-peak (ms)	Effective duration (ms)
MF	10 ± 3	8 ± 3	12 approx.
M	20 ± 5	15 ± 5	15 approx.
FP +		10 ± 4	25 min.
FP		15 ± 6	25 min.

Manufacturers issue guide numbers for the different lamp types or, for simple cameras, a working distance is given for an average indoor environment. Other simple cameras, such as the 'Polaroid', may have a built-in light intensity integrator to control the exposure where, for example, the light from a flash bulb supplements a daylight scene to fill shadows. The type with a clear lacquer coating has an approximate colour temperature of 3000 K, and to give a light equivalent to 5500 K to enable daylight type film to be used a blue dye is added to the lacquer.

16.3 Xenon lamps

16.3.1 Design

Xenon lamps consist of an arc of very high brightness burning between solid tungsten electrodes in a pressure of pure xenon contained in a fused silica envelope (Fig. 16.4). They may be designed to operate from a.c. or d.c. supplies and be of compact (XE) or linear (XB) form.

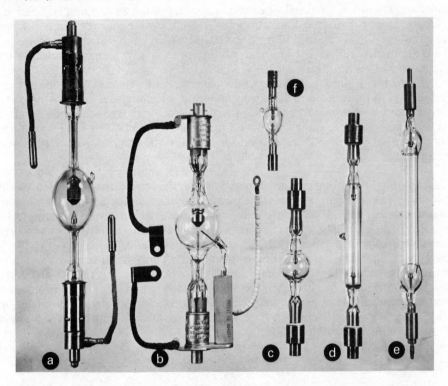

Fig. 16.4 Xenon lamp constructions: (a) 2500 W XE lamp, (b) 2000 W XE lamp, (c) 500 W XE lamp, (d) 1000 W XB lamp, (e) 1500 W XB lamp, and (f) 250 W XE lamp

Compact source xenon The arc of the compact source is a few millimetres in length, is electrode-stabilized, and is located at the centre of a relatively large bulb of approximately spherical shape. The shape of the electrode has a marked effect on the stability of the arc, and as 'pip-growth', leading to deformation of the electrodes, is more likely to occur with a fluctuating current, the lamps are usually designed to operate from a smoothed d.c. supply. Resulting from the short arc length, the lamp voltage is low and the current is high. The fused silica–molybdenum foil hermetic seals are described in Sect. 7.4; wider and thicker foils may be arranged to form an annular seal to carry currents of 100 A or more, some seals being shown on lamps in Fig. 16.4. Cold filling pressures up to 12 atm are commonly used. As a result there is a potential hazard from explosive failure of a lamp and suitable precautions are necessary.

Lamps are commercially available in ratings from 75 W to 6·5 kW in the compact source form. Ratings up to 500 W can be made to operate from a.c. with a shorter life than that of the equivalent d.c. form. Above 500 W, a reasonable life can be achieved only on d.c., which must be smooth with a ripple content less than 5% r.m.s. Other compact sources rated at 10 kW and 30 kW have been described in the literature.

Linear xenon   The linear form of xenon lamp has a wall-stabilized arc contained within a long, tubular, fused silica envelope. The lamp is of a simpler design than the compact source form, and since the assembly can be partially mechanized it is somewhat less costly to produce. Electrode shape does not have a serious effect on arc stability and the lamps are usually designed to operate from an a.c. supply. The longer arc length gives a higher voltage drop for a given power and the lamp current is correspondingly less. The cold filling pressure is usually 1 atm. Linear lamps are rated at 1 kW upwards, and are used most in ratings up to 20 kW. Larger types have been made up to 300 kW rating.

In both forms of the lamp, compact and linear, the permanent gas filling ensures that full light output is immediately available at switching on: there is no run-up period as there is with mercury lamps. A high voltage, high frequency pulse starter is used to initiate the arc, which requires a pulse order of 30 kV to 40 kV, although a lower voltage of 10 kV to 15 kV is used for lamps of the compact source type with a starting probe.

Pulsed xenon   The pulsed xenon lamp makes use of a long, narrow bore, fused silica tube and by passing high peak current pulses through the discharge a useful gain in luminous efficacy is achieved of the same mean power dissipation. Operating from a normal a.c. supply, light flashes occur at each half-cycle when the peak current approaches 70 A above a mean of 15 A. The arc tube is varied in length with a loading of 50 W cm^{-1}, the tube bore remaining substantially constant. It contains xenon at a cold pressure of 60–100 torr, being adjusted to provide a maximum arc voltage compatible with an ability to trigger the tube on each half-cycle. The lamp seals have to accommodate the high peak current and the electrodes follow very closely designs used in mercury vapour lamps, where a solid tungsten rod with helical overwinds supports an emissive coating.

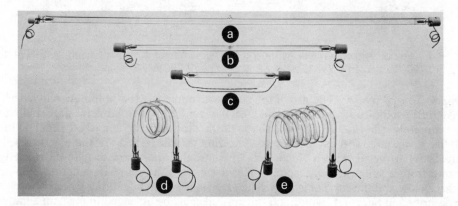

Fig. 16.5   Some linear and helical pulsed xenon lamps: (a) 3 kW, (b) 1·5 kW, (c) 750 W, (d) 4 kW, and (e) 8 kW

These lamps are either linear or coiled into a helix to provide a compact light source. Linear tubes are often used in a rectangular format operating two in series, or with smaller tubes four in series. To reduce electrode losses long tubes are also bent into a rectangular format. The lamps are fitted within reflector units with forced air cooling, which is important to obtain a good tube life. A range of lamps is shown in Fig. 16.5.

Xenon flash tubes Most flash tubes are fabricated from borosilicate glasses except for very high loadings when fused silica is used. The electrodes and seals must be designed to carry high peak currents which may be several thousands of amperes, the energy dissipation being limited by the crazing or melting of the surface of the arc tube. To maintain a high current density in the positive column, the tubes are of small diameter to constrict the arc. To form a more concentrated light source the tube is wound into a helix or other configuration without affecting performance significantly. The tube dimensions, gas filling pressure, electrode design, and emitter coatings all have a controlling influence on tube efficiency, flash duration, and life. Pure xenon provides a radiation quality suitable for most photographic applications in monochrome and daylight colour film, but for high speed photographic events, where motion is to be arrested, mixtures of argon and trace amounts of hydrogen provide light flashes of only microseconds in duration. The shorter arc gap lamps contain 1 atm to 2 atm of gas, while the linear or helical sources with a long positive column have pressures of 50 torr to 200 torr.

There are many and varied shapes, sizes, power ratings, and light output characteristics of xenon flash tubes. Power loadings vary widely, up to at least 10^4 J per flash.

16.3.2 Characteristics and performance

Compact source xenon The xenon lamp has a moderately high luminous efficacy (20 lm W^{-1} to 50 lm W^{-1}, depending on the type) and a usefully high luminance. In compact source lamps the usable areas of source approach the sun's luminance (2×10^9 cd m^{-2}), and in some lamps of 10 kW or above the cathode spot may exceed this value and reach 10^{10} cd m^{-2} in lamps with water-cooled electrodes. It is this combination of good colour appearance and rendering, reasonable luminous efficacy, and high luminance which makes the xenon lamp so outstanding.

In comparison with compact source mercury lamps the instant availability of full light output with xenon is a real practical advantage. Xenon provides a very powerful source of continuous ultraviolet radiation and, compared with a hydrogen discharge lamp or the efficient radiation of wavelength 253·7 nm from a low pressure mercury vapour lamp, its radiance and power rating are much higher. In the infrared region there is a pronounced peak at about 900 nm and a continuum up to 3000 nm which radiates about twice as much in proportion as in sunlight. Its radiance in comparison with an incandescent source or other infrared radiator is again high because of the power concentration in an arc gap of only a few millimetres.

A typical spectral power distribution is shown in Fig. 15.5d (p. 245) over the band 200–2500 nm, which may be compared with lamps such as the CSI PAR 64 (Fig. 15.5a), which provides a useful compromise at a lower overall and operating cost when simulating solar radiation.

Linear xenon The linear xenon has similar characteristics to the compact source xenon lamp, but current density is lower with reduced electrode losses relative to the longer positive arc column. Luminous efficacy is 15 lm W^{-1} for a 1 kW lamp to 35 lm W^{-1} for a 20 kW lamp. The spectral power distribution is similar to that of the compact source lamps.

Pulsed xenon   The lamp is started by a driving circuit (Fig. 16.6), producing in the pulse transformer a pulse of 10 kV to 15 kV which ionizes the xenon; energy stored in the capacitor is then released to produce a light flash whose duration is dependent on the inductance and capacitance of the circuit. On the next half-cycle of the supply voltage the capacitor is recharged and the pulse transformer again triggers the lamp. After a few seconds the trigger pulse can be stopped and the tube becomes self-operating, giving light pulses 100 times per second from the 50 Hz supply.

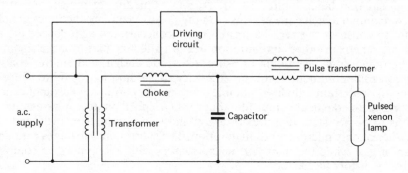

Fig. 16.6   Circuit for the operation of pulsed xenon lamps

Other circuits make use of triacs, where the voltage to the tube is switched on and off during the half-cycle to control lamp power, the lamp having been started initially by a voltage pulse.

Peak lamp currents vary between 20 A and 70 A and the pulse duration varies between 2 ms and 5 ms. The arc tube voltage and the volt–ampere characteristics vary and depend on peak current and duration, which are controlled by the circuit design. The open-circuit voltage provided by the circuit is normally about twice that of the lamp or the total of lamps used in series. Efficacy is about 25 lm W⁻¹ for a 1·5 kW linear type lamp and about 30 lm W⁻¹ for an 8 kW helical lamp.

Xenon flash tubes   The electrical energy to provide the flash power is obtained from energy stored in a capacitor. The flash tube connected across this only fires when the xenon gas is ionized by an external pulse of voltage of about 3·5–15 kV, which is applied to a wire wrapped around the tube wall or to an auxiliary electrode. Series pulse coils are also used.

Flash durations range from several microseconds to approximately 10 milliseconds. For short durations in the microsecond region short arc gaps are required, as are minimal values of the external resistance and the inductance of leads and capacitor. Operation at high voltage contributes to shortening of the flash duration. Longer flash durations may be obtained by including an inductance in the discharge circuit. The duration is then given approximately by

$$t = \pi \, (LC)^{1/2}$$

Most flash tubes have pure xenon as the filling gas and at the high current densities involved the characteristic broad continuum is produced. Higher operating voltages shift the spectrum towards the blue and low energy or under-loaded tubes fall off more at the red end of the spectrum.

At the ultraviolet end the nature of the envelope, or cover, determines the cut-off: approximately 180 nm for bare silica and 300 nm for glass tubes. In the infrared there are superimposed peaks in the 850 nm to 1000 nm region and the radiation ceases at approximately 2000 nm. The colour temperature of tubes for most photographic work falls into a range of 6000 K to 7500 K, although in some tubes, with xenon–hydrogen mixtures and an arc not confined by the tube walls, colour temperatures as high as 40 000 K may be reached. Fully-loaded tubes have an efficacy of 40 lm W^{-1}.

Tube life for single flash operation is generally stated at 5000 to 50 000 flashes, whereas for stroboscopic use the average life is given as 100 h to 200 h burning life. Life of a tube depends very much on the circuit and tube combination and, by suitable adjustments to these, most performance criteria can be satisfied.

16.3.3 Applications

Xenon compact source and linear xenon The major use of compact source xenon lamps, particularly in ratings of about 2 kW, is in cinema projectors and in lighthouses where, because of the small high luminance source, the large rotating optics are now replaced with elements of only 100 mm to 300 mm diameter. Larger lamps of 10 kW to 25 kW or more have uses in solar simulators, arc-imaging furnaces, and numerous specialized aids to scientific investigations. The smaller compact source lamps find many optical uses, while linear sources up to 6 kW rating are used for colour-matching and fadeometers. Higher power linear source lamps of up to 65 kW are applied to sports stadia and city centre lighting.

Certain disadvantages have limited the more widespread use of xenon lamps, mainly their cost and the bulky and heavy control gear. While the cost per lamp is high, lamp life is long compared with other projector sources and running costs are competitive. Precautions are necessary to safeguard against the high voltage starting pulse, the copious ultraviolet radiation, and the potential explosion hazard when using compact source lamps. Linear lamps are cheaper and for a given power the current is lower, a.c. operation is more applicable, and there is no explosion hazard. In practice, however, explosive failures of compact source types are rare.

Pulsed xenon As with other xenon discharges, full light output is obtained at once when a pulsed xenon lamp is switched on. With this characteristic and a reasonably high luminous efficacy, combined with daylight spectral quality, it is widely used for many applications in the graphic arts. Light output maintenance is good with a long life and, because it can be switched readily to make photographic exposures, the lamp is widely applied to copy-board lighting and printing down applications in colour and monochrome processes.

Xenon flash tubes The xenon flash tube with its very brief flash enables photographic recordings to be made with great clarity. It is also used for many scientific photographic studies in arresting motion with flashes of 1 microsecond in duration. Today, with increased film speeds, the more simple cameras have inbuilt electronic flash or they are fitted as an attachment to an ordinary camera.

Special circuits have been developed to operate xenon flash tubes repetitively and, again due to the short flash duration, they prove invaluable for high speed stroboscopic studies.

Further reading

Aldington J N, 1949, *Trans. IES*, **14,** No. 2, 19–51: The gas arc, a new light source

Aldington J N and Meadowcroft A J, 1948, *IEE Proc.*, **95,** Part II, 671–681: *The flash tube and its application*

Baum W A and Dunkelman L, 1950, *J. Opt. Soc. Amer.*, **40,** 782–786: Ultraviolet radiation of the high pressure xenon arc

Beeson E J G, Bocock W A, Castellain A P and Tuck F A, 1958, *British Kinematography*, **32,** No. 4, 59–71: The xenon lamp for film projection

Beeson E J G and Rhodes K M H, 1956, *J. Photog. Sci.*, **4,** 54–58: Some factors affecting the performance of low voltage flash tubes

Bourne H K, 1948, *Discharge lamps for photography and projection* (London: Chapman & Hall)

BSI, 1980, BS 5841: *Photographic flash equipment.* Part 1: *Definitions and requirements for luminous flux/time characteristics of expendable photoflash lamps*

Chesterman W D, Clegg D R, Peck G T and Meadowcroft A J, 1951, *IEE Proc.*, **98,** Part II, 619–634: A new power stroboscope for high speed flash photography

Edgerton E, 1970, *Electronic flash strobe* (New York: McGraw-Hill)

Rehmet M, 1980, *IEE Proc.*, **127,** Part A, 190–195: Xenon lamps

17 Electroluminescence

Electroluminescence is the emission of light caused by the interaction of an electric field with a suitable solid. Both electroluminescent panels and light emitting diodes (LEDs) will be considered. Light emitting films, a later development, which are similar to the panels in many ways, will also be described.

Electroluminescent panels employ microcrystalline powder phosphors based on II–VI compounds, such as zinc sulphide, whereas single crystal III–V compounds, such as gallium phosphide, form the basis of most LEDs. In general, electroluminescent panels operate at relatively high voltages, alternating or direct depending on the device, and at low current densities. LEDs are high current density devices and require d.c. supplies of about 2 V.

17.1 Electroluminescent panels

Electroluminescence in cells containing zinc sulphide powder phosphor was first reported by Destriau (1936), but it was not until the 1950s that electroluminescent panels became commercially available (Payne et al. 1950). Such a panel consists of a thin layer of electroluminescent phosphor embedded in a dielectric medium between two parallel, planar electrodes, one of which is transparent. When a voltage is applied across the electrodes, light is emitted. In most a.c. panels an additional white layer of high dielectric constant is interposed between the opaque electrode and the phosphor layer. This serves to concentrate the electric field across the phosphor grains, minimizes electrical breakdown across the cell, and reflects most of the light generated within the cell through the transparent electrode.

Several types of electroluminescent panel are available, some requiring an a.c. supply while others operate from a d.c. supply. Furthermore, a.c. panels can be made in either ceramic or organic forms.

17.1.1 Materials

The number of phosphors showing a significant electroluminescent effect is very limited and of these, zinc sulphide, usually activated by copper, is the most important. The a.c. phosphor is prepared by heating together highly purified zinc sulphide with a copper salt and the necessary fluxes. It is then washed to remove excess copper. For d.c. supply operation manganese is used instead of copper and, after firing, a layer of copper sulphide is chemically deposited onto the phosphor grains.

Zinc sulphide is a wide band gap material (3·6 eV) which is difficult to dope to significant conducting levels and the mechanism of light emission differs from that described for LEDs (Sect. 17.3.1). Under sinusoidal voltage excitation, the brightness waves show a ripple of twice the applied frequency above a constant background. The light is emitted from localized zones within the zinc sulphide crystals. These zones seem to be associated with linear inclusions of copper (I) sulphide impurity at crystal imperfections in the zinc sulphide lattice. Copper (I) sulphide, a narrow band gap (about 0·6 eV) material in which electrons are readily raised from the valence to conducting band, acts as a conducting needle within the insulating zinc sulphide lattice. When an alternating field is applied, holes are injected into the zinc sulphide from one end of the needle while electrons are injected from the other end. The electron density in the copper sulphide is maintained by thermal regeneration. The holes, because of their lower mobility and deeper traps, remain close to the point of injection. The electrons can travel further before trapping, but most combine radiatively with holes injected during the previous half-cycle. On field reversal the trapped electrons return to the tip of the needle from which they were injected, allowing additional electrons to be injected from the other end. Alternatively they can proceed directly to the recombination region through the bulk of the crystal without re-entering the conducting needles. This model (Fischer 1963) is one of several that have been proposed (Morehead 1967), but none has found universal acceptance and the true explanation may be found in a combination of two or three mechanisms.

17.1.2　Design and construction

a.c. ceramic panels　One of the first electroluminescent panels to appear on the market was of the a.c. ceramic type. The panel (Fig. 17.1a) is fabricated by fusing layers of specially formulated vitreous enamels onto a 0·6 mm steel substrate at successively decreasing temperatures. The ground coat consists of a white opaque enamel frit to which barium titanate is added in order to increase the dielectric constant of the layer. The phosphor, mixed with a transparent enamel frit, is applied next. A thin film of conducting tin oxide is formed in situ on top of the phosphor layer by spraying the surface while still hot with a solution of a tin salt. Finally, layers of transparent vitreous enamel are applied to seal the panel against moisture ingress. If an a.c. potential is applied between the steel substrate and tin oxide, light is emitted through the oxide film. The total thickness of the layers is less than 0·15 mm.

a.c. organic panels　The organic-on-glass panel is constructed on a sheet of transparent conducting glass, the conducting film being formed by spraying the hot glass surface with a tin salt solution. Layers of phosphor and of barium titanate or titania, both bonded in organic resins, are applied followed by an opaque back electrode of evaporated metal or conducting paint.

More common now is the plastic panel (Fig. 17.1b) in which the electroluminescent phosphor, dispersed in an organic binder, is sandwiched between electrodes of aluminium foil and conducting indium oxide powder. A layer of barium titanate in the same binder is incorporated between the phosphor coat and aluminium foil. Finally, leads are attached to the foil and conducting oxide and the whole construction is encapsulated in a plastic film.

d.c. panels　In the d.c. panel (Fig. 17.1c) a layer of d.c. electroluminescent phosphor dispersed in an organic binder is sandwiched between a sheet of highly conducting transparent glass and a film of an evaporated metal. After leads have been attached to the conducting glass anode and metal film cathode, a thick epoxy resin is applied to the back of the panel. This is separated from the metal film by a narrow gap containing a dry gas.

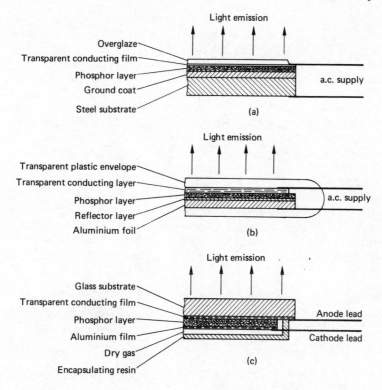

Fig. 17.1 Sections through electroluminescent panels: (a) a.c. ceramic, (b) a.c. plastic, and (c) d.c.

17.1.3 Characteristics

a.c. panels The colour of the emission from a panel depends on the phosphor employed, the most important being the green-emitting zinc sulphide activated by copper. Blue can be produced by a slight modification to the phosphor and yellow by the incorporation of manganese. Some very inefficient red phosphors are known, but colours in the yellow to red part of the spectrum are usually obtained by applying organic fluorescent paints to the surface of a green panel.

The luminance and current dissipation depend on the voltage and frequency applied. Initially, plastic panels are about four times as bright as ceramic panels (Fig. 17.2). In normal use the current density is low, being around $1 \cdot 5 \ \mu A \ mm^{-2}$ of panel area at 240 V 50 Hz, and the panel temperature remains within a few degrees of the ambient. At high frequency or voltage, the current rises considerably and the panel becomes hot.

Electroluminescent panels do not usually suffer catastrophic failure, but show a gradual decline in light output with time depending on the operating frequency. A measure of the life is the time taken for the luminance to decay to half of the initial value. For ceramic panels this varies from 6000 hours at 50 Hz to 2000 hours at 400 Hz and a few hours at 5 kHz. This half-life is much shorter for plastic panels, being for example little more than 1000 hours at 50 Hz (Ranby and Smith 1980).

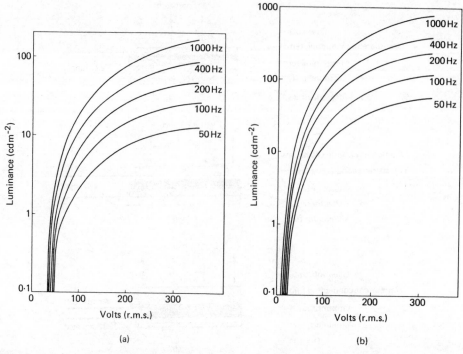

Fig. 17.2 Effect of frequency and voltage on the light output of green electroluminescent panels: (a) a.c. ceramic and (b) a.c. plastic

d.c. panels The most efficient d.c. phosphor is the yellow-emitting zinc sulphide activated by manganese and copper. Other colours have been reported using group II sulphides with rare-earth activators (Vecht 1973). When a voltage is applied to a freshly prepared panel, a high current flows. During the first few minutes it drops by an order of magnitude or more, coinciding with the emission of light which spreads gradually across the panel. This 'forming' process is irreversible for a given voltage and application of a higher voltage requires a new forming cycle. The luminance and electrical characteristics of a panel depend on its previous history, that is on the forming process and on the voltage applied. A typical luminance is $300 \, cd \, m^{-2}$ with a current dissipation of $50 \, \mu A \, mm^{-2}$.

For continuous operation a compromise between high luminosity and long life has to be made. The half-life of a $300 \, cd \, m^{-2}$ $100 \, V$ panel is about $1000 \, h$. The life of a panel can be extended by operation at constant power or by employing a pulsed voltage supply.

17.1.4 Applications

a.c. panels These give a diffuse uniform illumination at a low luminosity. No complicated control gear is needed and maximum luminosity is achieved within a few cycles of switching on. They are not bright enough to compete with the established methods such as incandescent or discharge lamps for general lighting, but their unique properties are valuable for many display applications. Thus a properly designed electroluminescent display can be more effective and considerably less bulky than an array of miniature filament lamps. The choice between ceramic and plastic panels depends on whether the high initial output of the plastic panel is more suitable than the longer life of the more robust ceramic type. Ceramic panels are also easier to make in complex shapes and do not deteriorate on storage.

Mass production methods have enabled electroluminescent panels to penetrate the domestic market with items such as luminous switch surrounds. Other current uses of electroluminescent panels include instrument lighting in locomotives, photographic darkroom lamps, and meter illumination in some London taxi cabs, while plastic panels are widely used in copying machines. In a lighting system devised for night-time military training a combination of large blue and green panels are suspended in a hanger simulating lighting levels from full moonlight to complete darkness. Electroluminescent panels are particularly useful in aviation applications, where a 400 Hz supply is readily available; the instrument display panel (Fig. 17.3) employs ceramic panels with an engraved opaque plastic overlay.

(a)   (b)

Fig. 17.3 'Plasteck' assembly incorporating a.c. ceramic electroluminescent panels: (a) in daylight (unenergized) and (b) in darkness (energized)

Future applications for all types of electroluminescent lighting, including panels or LEDs, are likely to be found in the automobile industry as electromechanical control and instrumentation are replaced by solid state circuitry. A display visible over a wide range of ambient lighting levels could be obtained by using an electroluminescent panel, driven by a d.c./a.c. inverter, to back-light a liquid crystal array.

d.c. panels As comparative newcomers, d.c. panels do not yet have the range of use demonstrated by the a.c. types. They cannot be operated directly from a mains supply and the rigid mode of construction limits both their flexibility and the range of shapes available compared with ceramic and plastic panels. However the high brightness of d.c. panels makes them an attractive proposition for dynamic or static displays visible in moderate ambient lighting levels. One projected use is for car instrumentation.

A variety of shapes and sizes of character on a panel can be arranged by etching the tin oxide film and by using photoetched insulating layers between the phosphor and conducting glass. Using such techniques dynamic displays in which as many as 1250 characters can be individually illuminated on a panel 175 mm × 175 mm in size have been prepared. Simpler constructions including static signs, bar-graphs, seven-segment digits, and 35-dot arrays have been produced.

17.1.5   Electroluminescent image storage devices

Image storage panel (ISP)   The ISP provides a simple method for obtaining an instant X-ray picture (Ranby and Ellerbeck 1971). The construction is similar to that of an organic a.c. electroluminescent panel, but with a zinc oxide layer interposed between the reflector layer and the opaque electrode. The high impedance of this layer is greatly reduced on brief exposure to X-rays and it only slowly returns to the high impedance state. Thus, if an X-ray opaque object is placed between the panel and the source of radiation during exposure to X-rays, an image is formed. The image can be viewed after irradiation by applying an a.c. potential across the panel and can be retained for up to an hour. After heating to remove the image, the panel is ready for re-use. 1000 or more exposures are possible.

The sensitivity of ISPs to X-rays is much lower than photographic film, which prevents their use for medical X-ray purposes. They have applications in industrial radiography, for example for checking the alignment of components in a sealed assembly and for the rapid inspection of suspect parcels and luggage.

Image retaining panel (IRP)   The construction of an IRP is very similar to that of an unglazed ceramic electroluminescent panel, but employs a special phosphor. If the panel is irradiated by X-rays or light while a potential of 50 V d.c. to 100 V d.c. is applied, the surface emits a yellow glow where it has been irradiated. The image is retained for 20 to 30 minutes and can be rapidly removed by reversing the voltage. Its sensitivity to X-rays is much lower than for an ISP and the main uses have been confined to the retention of light-induced images. For example IRPs are used in a marine radar system where the radar picture is stored and can be continuously updated (Harrison 1974).

17.2   Light emitting films

Since the early 1970s, when bright stable light emitting films were reported (Inoguchi et al. 1974), interest in electroluminescence has been revitalized. Like the panels previously described, light emitting films, also called thin film electroluminescent panels, are area electroluminescent light sources, but in which thin evaporated films are employed instead of powder layers. The phosphor film is usually zinc sulphide activated by manganese.

17.2.1   Design and construction

Successive layers are built up on a transparent, conducting, indium–tin oxide, glass substrate (Fig. 17.4a). Thin transparent layers of this kind can be produced by heating

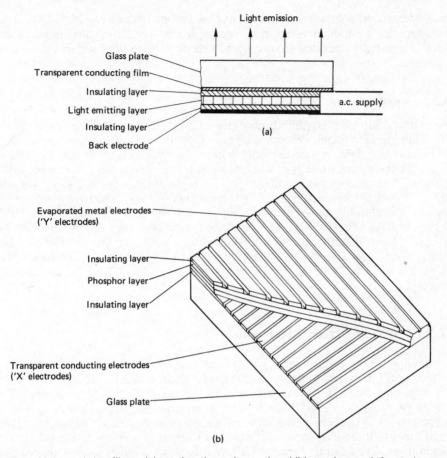

Fig. 17.4 Light emitting films: (a) section through panel and (b) matrix-type information panel

a source of the material in a very high vacuum and allowing the vaporized material to deposit on the heated substrate. The thickness of each layer can be accurately monitored and controlled. The most common construction consists of a 0·5 μm thick zinc sulphide (Mn) film sandwiched between 0·2 μm yttrium oxide insulating layers with an evaporated aluminium back electrode. The device is protected from humidity either by sealing a second glass sheet to the glass substrate or by sputtering an outer insulating layer of silicon nitride.

17.2.2 Characteristics

The colour emitted by a zinc sulphide (Mn) film is the characteristic yellow of manganese. Green or pink colours can be obtained by terbium or samarium activation, but at much reduced intensities. The outstanding feature of these yellow-emitting films is their high luminosity at moderate a.c. voltages. Thus $300 \, \text{cd m}^{-2}$ to $600 \, \text{cd m}^{-2}$ is easily attainable at 60 V to 80 V from a 400 Hz supply. The luminance rises rapidly as the voltage is increased and $3000 \, \text{cd m}^{-2}$ can be realized at 250 V, 5 kHz.

In common with other electroluminescent panels the light output slowly decays when operated at constant voltage. As a consequence of the steep luminance–voltage characteristic, a small increase in voltage will restore the original luminance and panels are initially operated from a slightly rising voltage until stability is eventually achieved.

17.2.3   Applications

The matrix-addressed graphic display (Fig. 17.4b) has been applied to all forms of electroluminescent panel. When a voltage is applied across one or more of the 'X' and 'Y' electrodes, light is emitted only where the elements intersect. In a simpler arrangement one electrode is divided into a number of separate strips to provide, for example, an alpha-numeric indicator. The high luminosity and steep non-linear brightness–voltage characteristic of light emitting films are particularly suited to such displays, and should enable them to compete with other established systems, such as plasma displays (Theis 1981). As a result of the transparency of light emitting films, the contrast can be enhanced by applying a black absorbing layer to the back of the panel. Hopes are high that realistically priced displays can be developed during the next few years. Both an alpha-numeric and a graphic display are already on the market.

17.3   Light emitting diodes

Although junction electroluminescence was first reported over seventy years ago (Round 1907), concerted efforts to develop LEDs date from 1962 when it was noted that a gallium arsenide junction biased in the forward direction was an efficient emitter of radiation. Electroluminescent p–n junctions are identical in electrical characteristics to conventional silicon and germanium diodes. However, when biased in the forward direction, some of the energy dissipated is converted into light rather than into resistive heating, hence the alternative description as semiconductor lamps.

17.3.1   Materials

The addition of selective impurity atoms to a crystalline semiconductor can produce an excess of free electrons in the conduction band. These are classified as n-type semiconductors. Using other impurities p-type material is formed in which there is an excess of holes, where a hole has a charge equal and opposite to that of an electron and a similar effective mass. In p-type material the electrons are the minority charge carriers and holes the majority carriers. The reverse is true for n-type material (Sect. 6.3.6).

   A number of techniques exist for preparing nearly perfect single crystals in which the conductivity changes from p-type in one part to n-type in another part within a narrow transition region. This is a p–n junction. If a forward bias direct voltage is applied across the junction, that is with the p-type side positive, holes flow into the n-type side and electrons into the p-type side. These injected minority carriers eventually recombine with the majority carriers. The excess energy of recombination may be dissipated as heat or as light. The simplest recombination process, which takes place in direct gap semiconductors, is the direct recombination of a free electron with a free hole where the emitted photon has an energy nearly equal to that of the energy gap. This is the highest energy photon that can normally be emitted from a semiconductor and indicates the minimum energy gap necessary for visible emission; for emission in the far red at 760 nm the corresponding energy gap is 1·63 eV.

By the controlled introduction of selected impurities into the lattice of a semiconductor, electronic states can be formed within the forbidden gap, giving rise to 'indirect gap' materials. In these recombination of charge carriers takes place via the levels in the forbidden gap and consequently the energy of the emitted photons is less than that of the band gap. This photon generation process is less efficient than by direct recombination, but unlike direct recombination the radiation is not attenuated within the semiconductor.

p–n junctions cannot easily be formed in the II–VI compounds used for electroluminescent panels (Peaker 1980). The requirements for an LED of a pure single crystal material which can be doped both p-type and n-type to give a p–n junction are satisfied by many of the semiconductor III–V compounds. Some of the most important commercially available LEDs are based on gallium arsenide and gallium phosphide. The former has a direct band gap of 1·49 eV and is an efficient infrared electroluminescent emitter. Gallium phosphide has an indirect gap of 2·25 eV. They form a continuous solid solution over the entire arsenic–phosphorus range and the alloy composition can be tailored to give intermediate band gaps between the extremes. Suitable dopants are necessary in the phosphorus-rich alloys which have an indirect band gap.

17.3.2   Design and construction

A flow diagram giving an indication of the processes involved in the fabrication of LEDs is shown in Fig. 17.5. Single crystal material is produced, in the form of a rod, by slowly withdrawing a seed crystal of gallium phosphide or gallium arsenide from a saturated melt. Gallium phosphide can also be produced by growth from a solution. Epitaxial layers, in which the p–n junctions are formed, are grown on to chips sliced from the rod. In an epitaxial layer the atoms are arranged in exactly the same way as in the substrate. During liquid phase epitaxy, the compound is allowed to crystallize on the substrate from a saturated solution in a metal of low melting point. This method is used for gallium phosphide devices. The first layer is grown n-type followed by a layer of p-type material. Oxygen or nitrogen is also incorporated into the lattice, depending on whether red or green emission is required. For gallium arsenide phosphide devices the epitaxial layers are grown by vapour phase deposition onto gallium phosphide or gallium arsenide wafers. Zinc and arsenic are subsequently introduced by vapour diffusion to give p-type material and produce a p–n junction about 3 μm below the surface. Contacts to the n-type and p-type sides are formed by metal evaporation and photolithographic techniques before the wafers are scribed and divided into dice. Finally the dice are mounted on suitable bases, lead wires are attached, and the chip is encapsulated in a tinted or diffusing epoxy resin dome (Fig. 17.6a). The resin increases the light output from the chip by reducing the reflection at the semiconductor surface. It also physically protects the device and the dome shape determines the radial distribution of the emission.

17.3.3   Characteristics

LEDs have electrical characteristics similar to those of a normal rectifying diode. A forward drop of 2 V at a current of 10 mA is typical. It is necessary to limit the forward current in order to avoid undue temperature rise in the device by using a limiting series resistor or by operating from a current source.

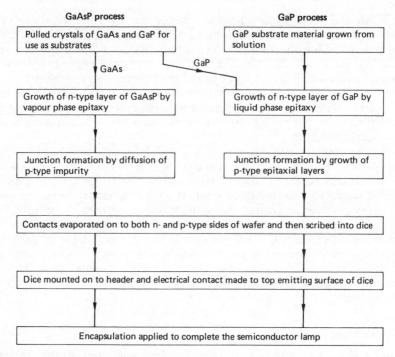

Fig. 17.5 Process chart for the fabrication of LEDs

Fig. 17.6 Light emitting diodes: (a) a single gallium arsenide phosphide lamp and (b) a five-character 7 × 5 array

A range of colours is available (Table 17.1). The intensity of the emission depends on the current density and LEDs are virtually point sources of high intensity radiation. For comparison the luminance of a commercial red LED is 3500 cd m^{-2}, whereas that for a representative fluorescent lamp is 5000 cd m^{-2}. The life of the device is very long, normally quoted values being in excess of 100 000 hours.

17.3.4 Applications

Indicator lamps LEDs, because of their long life, mechanical robustness, and low current consumption, are extensively used as indicator lamps. By altering the

Table 17.1 Characteristics of commercial LEDs

LED	Colour	Peak emission wavelength (nm)	Best luminous efficacy (lm W^{-1})
GaP : Zn, O	Red	699	3·00
GaP : N	Green	570	4·20
GaP : NN	Yellow	590	0·45
GaAs$_{0.6}$ P$_{0.4}$	Red	649	0·38
GaAs$_{0.35}$ P$_{0.65}$: N	Orange	632	0·95
GaAs$_{0.15}$ P$_{0.85}$: N	Yellow	589	0·90

geometry of the dome, wide or narrow viewing angles are possible and, by mounting two LEDs in one package, bi-colour indicators can be produced. Current-limiting devices are necessary either within the lamp package or in the associated circuit. The drive requirements are compatible with integrated circuitry. Thus LEDs can be mounted directly on to printed circuit boards as circuit status and fault indicators.

Display For small numeric displays found in pocket calculators with characters 3 mm high or less seven p-type segments are produced monolithically on a single semiconductor slice with a common cathode. For larger displays hybrid constructions are used with bar segments or square dice in reflector housings. To produce alpha-numerics 7 × 5 arrays of square dice are mounted on a ceramic substrate (Fig. 17.6b). Each row and column is connected to a common pin. Characters are obtained by sequentially addressing the appropriate diodes.

Thus LEDs, able to operate from low voltage d.c. supplies using conventional microcircuitry, have found wide use for small- and medium-sized displays. For larger displays the current requirements become unacceptably large and, coupled with increased material costs (Dean 1981), there is strong competition from other sources, such as plasma and electroluminescent panels. For applications like wrist watches where battery power is limited an LED display is only energized when required. Here competition from liquid crystal displays where the power drain is much lower is intense.

Further reading

Bergh A A and Dean P J, 1976, *Light-emitting diodes* (Oxford: The University Press)

Henisch H K, 1962, *Electroluminescence* (Oxford: Pergamon Press)

Pankove J I (Ed), 1977, *Topics in applied physics*, **17**, Electroluminescence (Berlin: Springer-Verlag)

Thornton P R, 1967, *The physics of electroluminescent devices* (London: E & F N Spon Ltd)

Vecht A, Werring N J, Ellis R and Smith P J F, 1973, *IEEE Proc.*, **61**, 902–907: Direct-current electroluminescence in zinc sulphide: state of the art

Williams E W and Hall R, 1978, *Luminescence and the light emitting diode* (Oxford: Pergamon Press)

Williams F (Ed), 1981, *J. Luminescence*, **23**, 1–235: Workshop on the physics of electroluminescence

Williams F (Ed), 1981, *J. Luminescence*, **24/25**, 827–928: Applications and device-related mechanisms, *Proc. 1981 Int. Conf. on Luminescence*, Section XIII

Part III
Luminaires and circuits

18 Electrical and electronic circuits

A lamp circuit connects and controls the electrical supply to the lamp so that electrical energy can be efficiently converted into useful visible radiated energy. In previous chapters the physical processes leading to the production of light in gas and vapour discharges have been explained and various lamps using this principle have been described. This chapter considers further the electrical characteristics of the discharge and practical methods used to start and stabilize the different lamps on mains voltage supplies. Recent developments using electronic devices for starting and controlling lamps are illustrated. Specialized systems for transport and emergency lighting are examined, as are dimming circuits and some features of electrical installation design.

18.1 Electrical characteristics of lamps

Incandescent filament lamps can be connected directly to a suitable electrical power supply, but all fluorescent and discharge lamps require suitable circuits and control gear or ballast components for starting and operation. The electrical characteristics and the behaviour of such lamps are complex and depend on the type of circuit, the supply source, the design of the ballast components, and sometimes the operating conditions.

18.1.1 Lamp starting and run-up

Starting voltage   The process of starting current flow through a gas or vapour has been explained in Chap. 6 where it was noted that a voltage higher than the normal lamp operating voltage is usually required. If the supply voltage is insufficient then additional starting voltage may be generated by transformers, starting devices, semi-resonant circuits, or pulse-producing components. The voltage required for lamp starting may depend on the external temperature, humidity, and any electric fields. In the case of lamps without preheated cathodes the starting circuit has to provide sufficient energy to enable the transition from glow to arc discharge (Sect. 6.3.4) to be made rapidly. Until electron emission from both cathodes is established, some lamps may rectify for a few cycles before fully starting.

Starting aids   To make economical circuits it is often necessary to reduce the required lamp starting voltage by means of starting aids. One or more of the following may be used:

(a)   Preheating of the cathodes to produce electron emission.
(b)   A starting conductor placed on or near to the surface of the discharge tube to produce an electric field.

(c)   An auxiliary starting electrode placed inside the discharge tube close to one of
      the main electrodes to produce a local glow discharge.
(d)   Superimposed high voltage pulses to assist breakdown and reduce the r.m.s.
      starting voltage required from the circuit.
(e)   Radioactive materials inside the discharge tube to assist ionization and starting.

Lamp run-up   A discharge lamp containing metallic vapour requires a short period to
warm up before full vapour pressure is reached, during which time the electrical
characteristics of the lamp change. The time of run-up depends on the lamp, the
circuit, and the ballast. Fluorescent lamps stabilize in a very short time and give full
light output almost immediately after starting. High pressure lamps require a few
minutes run-up, during which time the lamp current drops and the lamp voltage
increases. Low pressure sodium lamps require about 15 minutes, with the lamp
current increasing slightly as the lamp voltage falls. Discharge lamps containing only
rare gas require no run-up time and the electrical characteristics do not change after
starting. To ensure satisfactory run-up the margin between the sustaining voltage from
the circuit and the instantaneous lamp voltage must be sufficiently great throughout
the a.c. cycle.

18.1.2   Lamp running and stability

Current runaway   Figure 18.1 shows schematically the relationship between the
voltage across and the current through a self-sustaining gas discharge as the current is
slowly increased from a low value. In the arc discharge region the characteristic has a
negative slope due to the cumulative effect of electron–atom collisions producing
ionization: it is in this region that most discharge lamps operate. To prevent current
runaway and ensure stable operation from a constant voltage power supply the
negative characteristic must be counterbalanced by a circuit element or component

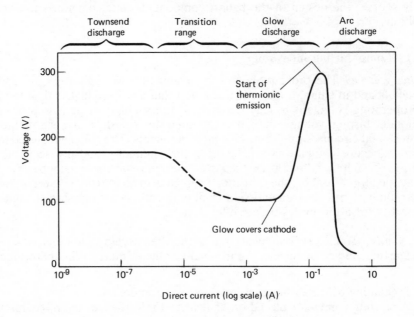

Fig. 18.1   Static volt–ampere characteristic of a gas discharge

having a positive characteristic (Waymouth 1972). This element is called a stabilizer or ballast.

Alternating current operation   When operated on an alternating supply, the electrical properties of a gas or vapour discharge depend on the frequency and the type of ballast. The effective impedance of the lamp is approximately equivalent to a non-linear resistance and an inductance in series (Zwikker 1953). A sudden increase in current does not immediately affect the gas conductivity and a short time is required before it reaches equilibrium at a new increased value. On 50 Hz supplies the impedance of the lamp is changing continuously throughout a cycle and this results in non-sinusoidal voltage and current waveforms and the generation of harmonics. In the case of a fluorescent lamp, as the frequency increases beyond about 1000 Hz the ionization state can no longer follow the rapid changes of lamp current, which results in a near-constant plasma density and an almost constant effective impedance throughout the cycle. The dynamic lamp voltage–current characteristic (Fig. 18.2)

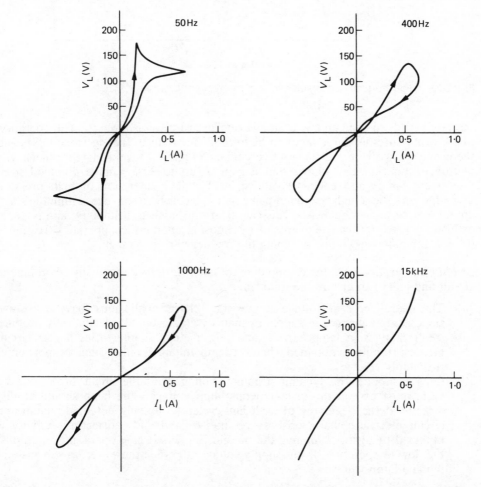

Fig. 18.2   Dynamic volt–ampere characteristics of a fluorescent lamp operated at various frequencies on a choke ballast

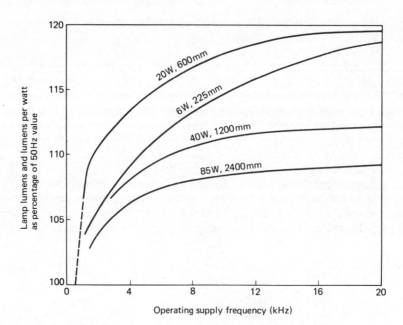

Fig. 18.3   High frequency characteristics of fluorescent lamps

therefore tends to become linear and waveform distortion is reduced. The operation of a low pressure discharge lamp on high frequency reduces the electrode losses and there may be a slight gain in positive column radiation. Overall lamp efficiency is improved and Fig. 18.3 shows that a gain of up to 20% can be obtained from fluorescent lamps at frequencies above 20 kHz. The operation of high pressure discharge lamps at a high frequency can result in 'acoustic resonance' within the small arc tube at certain frequencies. This causes arc turbulence, instability, and possible extinction. The effect can be overcome by choosing a non-critical operating frequency or by continually varying or sweeping the frequency over a range.

Stability and extinction   Stable lamp operation is determined mainly by designing the circuit and ballast to ensure the following:

(a)   The overall current–voltage steady state characteristic must have a positive slope. Large changes in supply or mains voltage should, ideally, only produce small changes in lamp current and power. In a simple series ballast circuit greatest stability is obtained when the lamp voltage is only a small proportion of the supply voltage.

(b)   On a.c. supplies the dynamic sustaining voltage from the circuit throughout the cycle must exceed the instantaneous lamp voltage. The lamp should readily reignite at the beginning of each half-cycle. As already noted, the lamp and circuit electrical characteristics are inter-related and satisfactory stability is obtained by again examining the margin (under extreme operating conditions, e.g. low temperature or low supply voltage) between the waveforms of sustaining and lamp voltages.

All practical discharge lamps can only withstand a limited drop in supply voltage before operation becomes unstable and extinction occurs. The ballast and circuit must be designed so that momentary or prolonged reductions of supply voltage of up to 15% do not cause lamp extinction.

18.1.3 Lamp restart and failure

Restart If a low pressure discharge lamp is switched off, restarting and full light output can be obtained quickly. The time to restart the lamp depends on the starting device (Sect. 18.3). If a high pressure discharge lamp is switched off, the vapour pressure caused by the high lamp temperature prevents immediate restriking on normal circuits and a period of several minutes is required for the lamp to cool and restart. A further period of time is then required for the lamp to run up and reach full light output. The problem of hot restarting can be overcome by the use of special circuits which generate a very high starting voltage (Sect. 18.4), or by using a secondary incandescent lamp which automatically operates until the discharge lamp restarts after cooling. Figure 18.4 shows a simple maintained lighting circuit using a single relay; the actual run-up and restart times depend on the type of lamp involved and its ambient temperature.

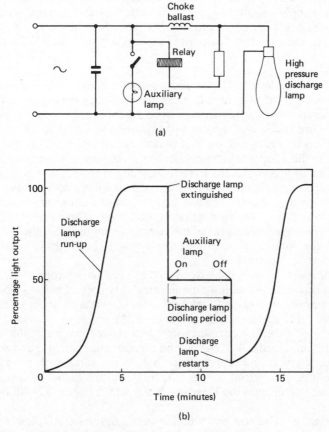

Fig. 18.4 (a) maintained lighting circuit for a high pressure discharge lamp using an auxiliary filament lamp and (b) typical light output versus time characteristic

Lamp failure   When, after a long life, the lamp eventually fails to operate, a higher than normal current may flow through some circuit components. Electron emission may be lost from one cathode and the lamp may then function as a partial rectifier.

To prevent problems of overheating due to lamp failure, the circuit and its components may be designed to ensure a safe handling of an excess alternating or rectified current. Alternatively, protective devices can be used which sense current or temperature and automatically cut off the circuit during the failed lamp condition.

18.2   Ballasts

18.2.1   Conventional ballasts

The prime function of a ballast is to prevent current runaway and to operate the lamp at its correct electrical characteristics. The ballast should be efficient, simple, ensure proper lamp starting, have no adverse effect on lamp life, and ensure stable lamp run-up and operation.

Resistor ballasts   A simple series-connected resistor can be sometimes used as a ballast, but the waste of power results in low overall efficiency. The use of a resistor on an alternating supply produces greater distortion of the current waveform since a delay in reignition causes near-zero current periods at the start of each half-cycle (Fig. 18.5a). An incandescent filament is used as a ballast for MBTF mercury lamps (Chap. 14).

Choke or inductor ballasts   The series-connected choke ballast produces a phase displacement of 55 to 65 electrical degrees between supply voltage and lamp current and this enables more sustaining voltage to be available at the start of every half-cycle. Operation is more stable and the current distortion is low (Fig. 18.5b).

The power loss in a choke is low and overall circuit efficiency is usually 80 to 90%. Losses occur in the copper winding due to coil resistance, increasing with temperature, and in the iron core due to hysteresis, eddy currents, and gap fringing losses. Like many engineering products, the design of a choke is a compromise between size, shape, performance, and cost. The size and weight of a choke are largely determined by its volt–ampere rating: high power lamps operating at high current requiring larger chokes. Very often the dimensions of the choke are limited from the outset by the size and shape of the luminaire, as for example when chokes have to be mounted in shallow reflectors or channels.

A choke ballast (Fig. 18.6) consists of a coil of enamelled copper wire, wound on a plastic bobbin or a former, with a high permeability core of silicon–iron laminations, and usually enclosed in a sheet steel case. The laminations are insulated from each other to reduce eddy current losses in the core. An air gap is provided in the core to obtain satisfactory electrical characteristics and reduce magnetic flux saturation. To improve insulation, electrical strength, and thermal conductivity, and to reduce noise level, it is necessary to impregnate the choke with varnish or resin or a bitumen mixture. Core flux density and copper current density, together with surface area and thermal transfer, determine the temperature at which the choke will operate.

Ballast temperature   The coil and winding insulating materials slowly deteriorate at an increasing rate as their temperature is increased. The permitted rated operating temperature of the ballast winding (t_w) is based on a ten-year expected life and is

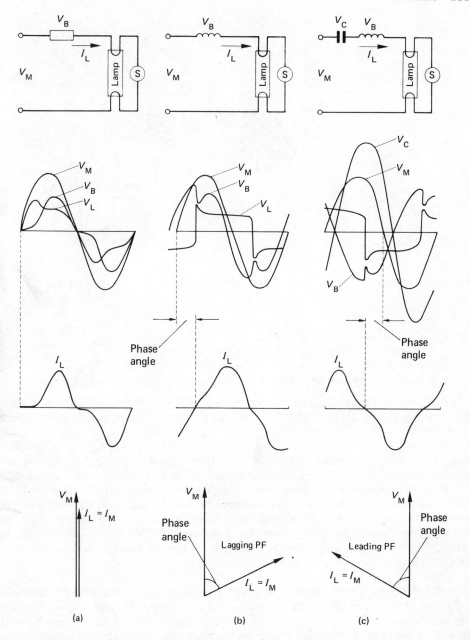

Fig. 18.5 Series ballast circuits for fluorescent lamps on a 50 Hz supply: (a) resistor ballast, (b) choke ballast, and (c) choke–capacitor ballast

estimated from accelerated endurance tests (BSI 1981a) carried out for 30 to 60 days. The relationship between temperature and life is

$$L = Ke^{D/T}$$

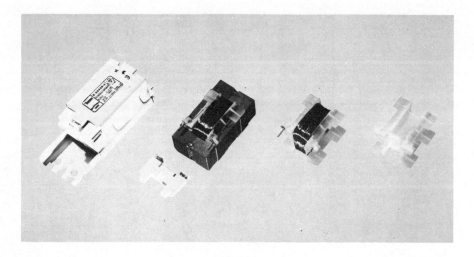

Fig. 18.6   Construction of 36/40 W fluorescent lamp choke

where L = life of the insulation system,
   T = absolute temperature of the insulation,
   D = constant which depends on the insulation materials,
   K = constant which depends on the units chosen and the materials.

If $1/T$ is plotted against $\log L$, a straight-line relationship is formed between life and temperature. In Fig. 18.7 are shown the graphs for three ballasts with different classes of insulation.

Noise   Any electromagnetic device such as a transformer or choke operating on a.c. is inherently noisy, to a degree depending on its size and design. The ballast waveforms contain harmonic components ranging from 100 Hz to 3000 Hz or more, so that noise may vary from a low pitched hum to a high pitched rustle. Noise can be generated in several ways – by cyclic magnetostrictive changes in the dimension of the core, by vibration of the core, and by stray magnetic fields causing vibration of the ballast case or steel housing of the luminaire – and all these aspects need to be considered during design if noise is to be minimized.

Capacitor ballasts   On 50 Hz to 60 Hz supplies capacitors are unsuitable ballasts since the inrush of energy to charge the capacitor at the beginning of every half-cycle causes harmful heavy peak current pulses of short duration through the lamp. A small resistor in series with a capacitor can produce an acceptable current waveshape to operate short fluorescent lamps of large diameter from a 240 V supply. On high frequency supplies the rapid current fluctuations do not occur and simple capacitor ballasts can then be used.

Choke–capacitor ballasts   A choke in series with a capacitor (Fig. 18.5c) provides a ballast arrangement having a number of useful features. If the capacitive reactance is arranged to be about twice the inductive reactance, a high sustaining voltage can be obtained with a good current waveform. The circuit enables lamps with high lamp

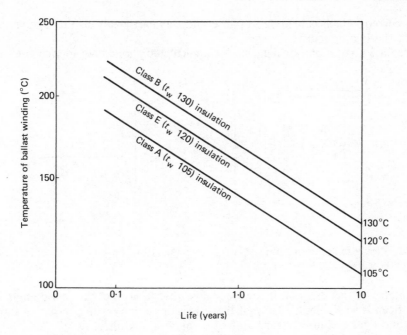

Fig. 18.7 Life of ballasts

voltages to be operated. It has a near-constant current characteristic and is thus less sensitive to variations in supply voltage.

Leakage-reactance transformer ballasts Normal a.c. supply voltages may not be sufficient to start and operate certain types of lamp, in which case a transformer will be required to step up the voltage. The inductive ballast impedance required to stabilize the lamp can often be incorporated in the transformer design by deliberately introducing leakage reactance. Such a device is known as a 'stray-field' or 'leakage-reactance' transformer. The mutual magnetic flux linking primary and secondary windings is deliberately reduced by introducing a shunt leakage path so that only a limited amount of electrical energy is delivered to the lamp load. This type of ballast usually has autotransformer connection.

18.2.2 Power factor correction

Power factor is defined for any waveshape as the ratio $\text{watts}/(\text{volts}_{\text{r.m.s.}} \times \text{amps}_{\text{r.m.s.}})$. A low value of power factor is undesirable for the following reasons:

(a) It unnecessarily increases the kVA demand from the supply.
(b) The useful load that can be handled by cables, wiring accessories, and distribution equipment is reduced.
(c) Special tariffs and penalties may be imposed on the consumer taking a load with a low lagging power factor.

All lamp circuits using chokes or leakage-reactance transformer ballasts have a low lagging power factor, usually between 0·3 and 0·5. This can be corrected quite simply by connecting a suitable capacitor in shunt across the mains a.c. supply. The capacitor takes a current which is leading in phase and this partly cancels the lagging current taken by the lamp circuit.

Figure 18.8 gives a phasor diagram for a corrected choke ballast circuit. Using the

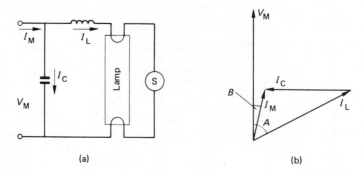

(a)   (b)

Fig. 18.8 Power factor correction: (a) corrected choke ballast circuit and (b) phasor diagram of the circuit shown in (a)

trigonometry of this diagram it can be shown that to correct the phase angle of the current from A to B, when a lamp of W watts is operating on an alternating supply of V volts and f Hz, requires a capacitor of C microfarads where

$$C = \frac{W(\tan A - \tan B)10^6}{2\pi f V^2}$$

In the UK it is usual to correct lamp circuits to give a power factor of at least 0·85, but circuits below 30 W rating are often uncorrected. A typical correction from 0·5 to 0·85 gives a 40% reduction in supply current.

Distortion of the waveforms of supply voltage and lamp circuit current has an important effect on the power factor obtainable. Harmonic components in a distorted load current waveform are not reduced by adding a capacitor current. The percentage harmonic content of the supply current actually increases because of the reduction in the fundamental.

Capacitors consist essentially of two electrically conducting plates or electrodes separated by a thin dielectric insulating material having high permittivity. To form compact capacitors the electrodes and dielectric are rolled up into a cylinder and usually sealed into a metal or plastic case having two connections. Several forms of construction are used, some being impregnated with suitable materials to improve dielectric strength and permittivity. It is important to ensure that capacitors are not operated above rated temperature or voltage, otherwise life will be shortened. Power losses in mains voltage capacitors are very small and vary between 0·2 W μF^{-1} for paper capacitors to 0·05 W μF^{-1} for plastic film types. To reduce danger from electric shock, capacitors are fitted with discharge resistors so that the terminal voltage is reduced to less than 50 V within a minute of switching off.

18.2.3 Electronic ballasts

Using modern semiconductors it is possible to make electronic ballasts operating from the mains supply for many fluorescent and discharge lamps. These generally operate in the range of 20 kHz to 100 kHz and may have the following features:

(a) Improved circuit efficiency, i.e. reduced ballast loss.
(b) Reduction in weight, particularly for larger lamp sizes.
(c) Improved luminous efficacy for many lamp types (Fig. 18.3).
(d) Absence of flicker.
(e) Elimination of audible ballast noise.
(f) Elimination of supply current harmonics and provision of unity power factor without use of a correction capacitor.
(g) Facility for accurate control of lamp power or current.
(h) Reduced run-up time and restart time for high pressure lamps.
(i) Better controlled starting and operating conditions leading to improved lamp life.

Figure 18.9 shows the outline of a number of different circuits, only the more complex of which achieve most of the features listed above: at present these circuits

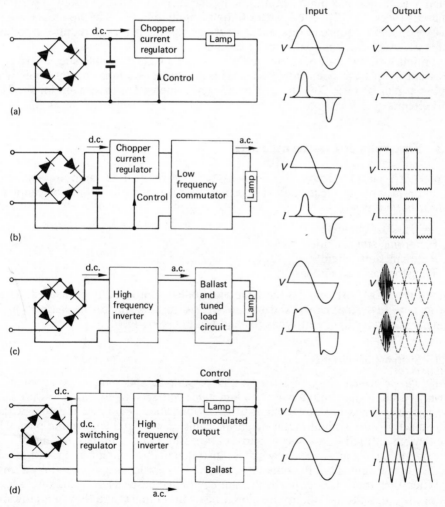

Fig. 18.9 Electronic ballast circuits: (a) d.c. chopper regulator, (b) d.c. chopper and commutator, (c) h.f. inverter modulated output, and (d) switching regulator and controlled inverter

are expensive, containing a large number of passive and active components. To offset their higher cost they can readily include additional energy management features, such as remote switching, dimming, and photocell control (Sects 20.3.3 and 21.2.4).

Circuit (a) uses a chopper regulator to operate the lamp on controlled d.c. and is limited to certain lamp types. Due to the input rectifier and filter capacitor, the input current waveform is distorted. Circuit (b) is an improvement on (a) and uses a commutating circuit to supply the lamp with controlled a.c. Again the input current waveform is unsatisfactory. Circuit (c) comprises a high frequency inverter operating from an unsmoothed d.c. supply. The lamp current is modulated at 50 Hz and little improvement in lamp efficiency is obtained. The input current waveform is distorted, but can be improved with a large additional filter. Circuit (d) uses a switching regulator to supply smoothed d.c. to the input of a high frequency inverter. The regulator can be designed to give a sinewave input current and unity power factor and its d.c. output may be fixed or varied in response to control signals. The inverter frequency is chosen to obtain optimum lamp performance and to avoid any critical resonances (Sect. 18.1.2). The inverter output is unmodulated. The frequency can be fixed or varied in response to internal control signals. The lamp still requires a ballast, but this becomes small and efficient at high frequencies.

To optimize the overall performance of electronic ballast circuits special types of fluorescent lamp have been introduced (Hirschmann 1981) and present equipment achieves a gain of over 20% in circuit efficacy compared with conventional 50 Hz ballast circuits.

18.3   Fluorescent lamp circuits

As noted in Sects 11.1.2 and 11.1.3, many types of fluorescent lamp are available, with different types of electrode. The available circuits for this variety of lamps fall into four basic types:

(a)   Switch-start circuits.
(b)   Electronic-start circuits.
(c)   Resonant-start circuits.
(d)   Transformer-start circuits.

In circuit types (a), (b), and (c) the lamp electrodes are invariably preheated, as are some in type (d). An earthed starting aid or a strip adjacent to the lamp to assist starting is necessary in circuit types (b) and (c) and some in (d).

18.3.1   Switch-start circuits

A glow starter switch (Fig. 18.10) is a cheap, simple, and reliable component. It consists of a small glass bulb having two bimetallic contacts, filled with a low pressure noble gas or gas mixture plus tritium to assist ionization, mounted together with a small capacitor into a small metal or plastic canister with two connecting pins. The starter switch is fitted into a socket and can be easily removed for replacement.

The operation of a glow starter switch is illustrated in three circuits in Fig. 18.11a, b, and c. Before switching on, the bimetal contacts of the switch are separated by a small gap. When the circuit is energized, the supply voltage is sufficient to initiate a glow discharge through the gas filling: this slowly heats the contacts and they bend towards each other. When the contacts touch after one or two seconds, a series circuit is made through the ballast and lamp cathodes and a relatively heavy (preheat) current rapidly

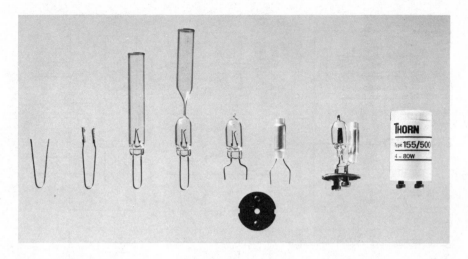

Fig. 18.10 Construction of glow discharge starter switch

warms the cathode coils for a time T_H. When the bimetal contacts touch, the glow discharge is extinguished since there is no voltage between the contacts. The contacts now begin to cool and after a short interval they spring apart and open the circuit. Since the circuit is inductive, a voltage pulse of between 600 V and 1500 V, depending on lamp type, is produced across the ends of the lamp for about a millisecond. This pulse rapidly ionizes the gas and vapour filling of the fluorescent lamp and a current flow starts between opposite lamp electrodes. The voltage between the ends of the lamp in the running condition is not sufficient to reignite the glow in the switch. If the switch were to open near the zero part of the alternating current cycle, a very small voltage pulse would be produced, in which case the switch would automatically reclose and make a second attempt to start the lamp.

Sometimes, when a lamp fails at the end of life, the cathodes remain intact, but with insufficient emission to maintain the arc current. Under these conditions the normal glow starter continuously attempts to start the lamp, causing flashing and blinking, and the starter itself may fail unless the lamp is replaced.

18.3.2 Electronic-start circuits

A unidirectional starter using a thyristor can be substituted for a glow starter switch in a choke-ballasted circuit: its operation is shown in Fig. 18.11d. If the thyristor is triggered every cycle into conduction by a fixed gate pulse V_t then the lamp cathodes are preheated with a constant unidirectional current and at the same time a constant unidirectional lamp starting voltage is generated. After a very short time the lamp starts and the trigger circuit is arranged to cut off. The disadvantage of this simple circuit is that on lamp failure the heavy continuous preheat current may burn out the ballast.

In the unidirectional starter shown in Fig. 18.11e a progressive trigger V_{pt} is generated to turn the thyristor into conduction so that the preheat current slowly reduces until the lamp starts (Graham and Pegg 1978). On lamp failure the trigger signal slowly changes so that after about two seconds the preheat current is reduced

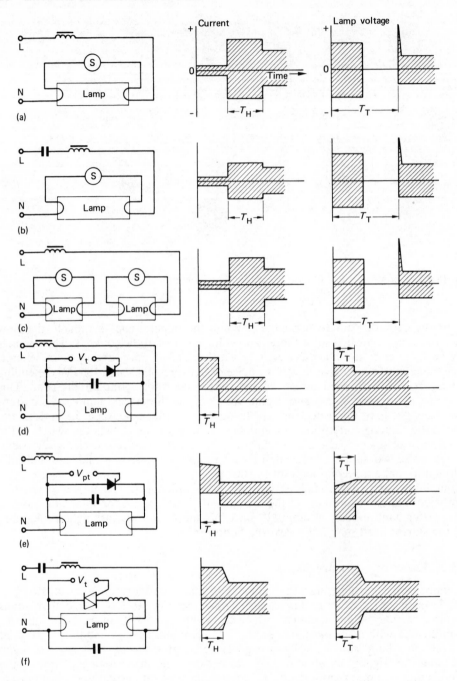

Fig. 18.11 Starter circuits for fluorescent lamps (T_H = cathode preheat time, T_T = total time to start lamp): (a) glow starter, choke ballast, (b) glow starter, choke–capacitor ballast, (c) glow starter, choke ballast, twin series lamps, (d) electronic starter, unidirectional fixed trigger, (e) electronic starter, unidirectional progressive trigger, and (f) electronic starter, bidirectional

automatically to a very low value. This type of starter only makes one attempt to start with no blinking, but is not suitable for 2400 mm lamps.

A bidirectional starter using a triac (Fig. 18.11f) can be used as a fast-acting switch to generate high frequency oscillations which provide both cathode preheat current and a high lamp starting voltage. This type of starter is used mainly for 2400 mm lamps in circuits with either choke or choke–capacitor ballasts. The starter contains a special device which cuts out its operation if the lamp fails to start after a few seconds.

18.3.3 Resonant-start circuits

The necessary preheat current and lamp starting voltage can be obtained from circuits using resonant combinations of inductance and capacitance. Such circuits require neither a starter switch nor power factor correction.

In the twin choke circuit of Fig. 18.12a resonance between one choke and the capacitor produces a high voltage for starting, the second choke being used as a ballast. Cathode preheat current is obtained from auxiliary windings on the first choke.

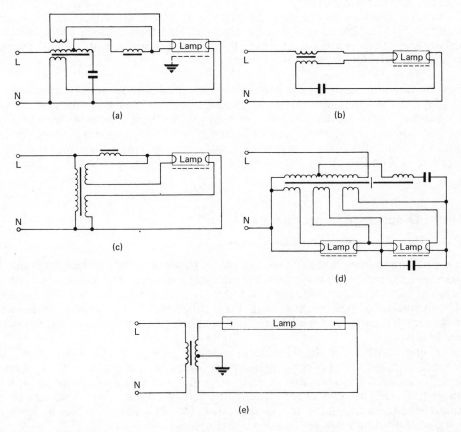

Fig. 18.12 Starterless circuits for fluorescent lamps: (a) resonant-start circuit for 2400 mm lamp, (b) semi-resonant-start circuit for 1200–1800 mm lamps, (c) quickstart circuit, (d) twin lamp rapid-start circuit, and (e) high voltage leakage-reactance transformer circuit for cold cathode lamp

Figure 18.12b shows the 'semi-resonant-start' (SRS) circuit; it has a single choke ballast with an additional overwinding in opposition to the main winding. Both windings are connected in a series circuit with the two lamp electrodes and a capacitor. When the circuit is switched on, the cathodes are preheated by a current through the series circuit; the voltage across the lamp, being the vector sum of capacitor and overwinding voltages, is usually higher than the supply voltage. When the lamp has started, the main winding acts as a ballast to stabilize the lamp and the overwinding carries a capacitive current which improves the overall power factor.

18.3.4   Transformer-start circuits

It is necessary to distinguish here between those circuits where the cathodes are preheated, such as the 'quickstart' and 'rapid-start' circuits, and those where a cold start takes place, such as the 'instant-start' circuit.

Cathode preheating can be obtained from various circuits using transformers which are separate from or form part of the ballast. In the quickstart circuit of Fig. 18.12c a small transformer provides independent heating for the lamp cathodes. The rapid-start circuit of Fig. 18.12d, using a leakage-reactance transformer and a series capacitor ballast, is most commonly used to operate two lamps in series, with a small capacitor connected across one lamp to assist starting.

Cold starting is possible for lamp types with electrodes designed to permit starting without preheat – the 'instant-start' lamp type has given its name to the (IS) cathode designation. There is a second group of lamps with cylindrical electrodes which run cold as well as starting cold – cold cathode lamps. A typical circuit is shown in Fig. 18.12e in which the leakage-reactance transformer generates a starting voltage of between 1 kV and 10 kV for the cold cathode lamp operating at 50 mA to 120 mA.

18.4   Discharge lamp circuits

18.4.1   Low pressure sodium lamp circuits

Low pressure sodium lamps (Chap. 12) are cold started, using voltages generated by leakage-reactance autotransformers or electronic ignitors. The transformer circuit shown in Fig. 18.13a provides 460 V to 650 V for starting. As a result of the low ratio of lamp voltage to open-circuit voltage, these circuits have a low lagging power factor of between 0·3 and 0·4 which is corrected by connecting a large capacitor across the supply input.

An ignitor circuit for the 35 W lamp is shown in Fig. 18.14a. On starting, the thyristor is triggered to generate high voltage pulses every cycle by switching a small capacitor in series with the choke ballast. After the lamp has started the thyristor is no longer triggered into conduction. The ignitor circuit enables a much smaller choke ballast to be used, together with a smaller power factor capacitor. Further benefits are that circuit efficiency is much improved and cost is lower.

Lamp voltage often increases through life with a corresponding increase in power consumption. Operation at the correct current is very important to obtain optimum tube wall temperature and lamp efficacy. With an electronic ballast a square-wave shape current can be obtained which gives an improved lamp efficacy.

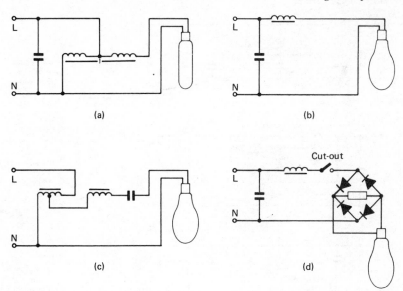

Fig. 18.13 Discharge lamp circuits: (a) low pressure sodium (SOX) lamp circuit with leakage-reactance autotransformer ballast, (b) high pressure mercury (MBF) lamp circuit with choke ballast, (c) high pressure mercury (MBF) lamp and metal halide (MBI) lamp circuit with peaking transformer–capacitor ballast, and (d) high pressure mercury (MBF) lamp circuit with bridge rectifier and choke ballast

18.4.2 High pressure sodium lamp circuits

During the operation of high pressure sodium lamps, part of the sodium amalgam (Sect. 13.1.1) is vaporized and part remains liquid in the coolest spot within the arc tube. The vapour pressure in the arc tube depends on the temperature of the cold spot and this in turn controls the lamp arc voltage. The arc voltage may be increased by thermal radiation from the optical system of the surrounding luminaire, and it also increases slowly through lamp life. Under these circumstances the lamp current and power depend critically on the ballast parameters, which must be specified to within close tolerances if stable and satisfactory operation is to result (Van Vliet and De Groot 1981).

In Europe these lamps are operated on choke ballasts similar to those for mercury lamps and designed so that the arc voltage is about half the mains supply voltage. In the USA special magnetic regulator ballasts have been used to give satisfactory operation with wide changes of arc and supply voltage. However, all high pressure sodium lamps require special circuit arrangements for starting. The usual method is to generate a high pulse voltage by using an electronic ignitor. Lamp starting depends on pulse height, waveshape, width, polarity, position, and repetition rate (IEC 1980).

Figure 18.14b shows one type of circuit which uses a thyristor to discharge the energy stored in a small capacitor into part of the choke ballast winding. The pulse is increased by the turns ratio of the winding and appears across the lamp as a very short pulse having a 3 kV to 4 kV peak. Circuits of this type may give continuous pulses every half-cycle or intermittent pulses every few seconds. Figure 18.14c shows a circuit with a separate pulse transformer which is connected in parallel with the lamp. This also uses a thyristor to discharge a capacitor to generate repetitive and very short

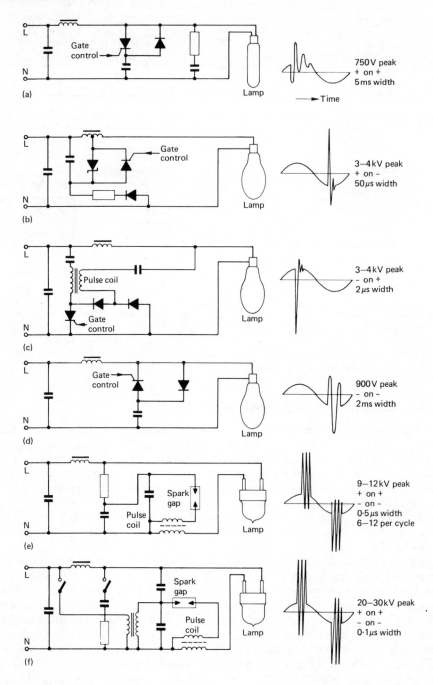

Fig. 18.14   Ignitor circuits for discharge lamps: (a) SOX lamp ignitor (35 W), (b) SON lamp ignitor (ballast pulse generation), (c) SON lamp ignitor (parallel pulse coil generation), (d) MBI lamp ignitor (high energy pulse), (e) CSI lamp cold-start ignitor (automatic-start), and (f) CSI lamp hot restart ignitor.

pulses of high voltage. Pulse voltages may be reduced by the capacitive loading of the connecting cables between ignitor and lamp and so limits are necessary for the length of these cables. Immediate hot restarting of some double ended lamps is possible if ignitors with extra-high voltage pulses are used.

18.4.3 Mercury lamp circuits

The most common mercury lamps (Chap. 14) are the high pressure lamps, such as type MB or MBF which have lamp voltages between 95 V and 145 V. They have built-in starting electrodes and are usually designed to start and operate on a 220/240 V supply using a choke ballast (BSI 1971b). The circuit shown in Fig. 18.13b is simple, efficient, and of low cost. The lamp starting voltage increases at low temperature.

In the USA autoregulator ballasts are often used with a peaking leakage-reactance transformer (Fig. 18.13c), providing multivoltage operation with good control of lamp power. They are more costly and less efficient than are the simple choke ballasts.

Flicker of 100 Hz can be troublesome in certain applications. It can be eliminated by running the lamp on d.c., using a bridge rectifier circuit as shown in Fig. 18.13d. The cut-out prevents overheating due to rectifier failure and the small resistor reduces overvoltage transients.

Very high pressure lamps, such as type ME or MD, have short arc lengths and low arc voltages. Some lamp types require starting components in addition to the ballast and are operated on a.c. or d.c. circuits. When used on a d.c. supply, the lamp electrodes should be connected to the correct polarity.

18.4.4 Metal halide lamp circuits

The various versions of metal halide lamps (Chap. 15) contain different mixtures of metal halides. Their electrical characteristics have some similarity to the corresponding mercury lamps, except that increased voltages are required for starting and run-up. Electrical starting and operating requirements are not yet standardized and so lamps and circuits are not always compatible.

The most common type of metal halide lamp, type MBI, has a silica envelope and is usually started with an electronic ignitor. The circuit shown in Fig. 18.14d uses a thyristor to generate high energy pulses of long duration once every cycle. In the USA the starting voltage is generated by 'peaking' ballast circuits, as for a mercury lamp (Fig. 18.13c).

The linear metal halide lamp, type MBIL, has a higher arc voltage than has the MBI, which makes it suitable for phase-to-phase operation on 380 V to 440 V a.c. supplies. It uses a choke ballast in conjunction with an electronic ignitor for starting, the circuit being similar to that shown in Fig. 18.14b for the SON lamp.

Compact source metal halide lamps, types CSI, CID, and HMI, have high filling pressures and require extra-high voltages for starting. Figure 18.14e shows a circuit for cold starting: the series-connected pulse transformer generates up to 12 kV from a spark gap generator. Operation of the pulse starter can be manual or automatic. Figure 18.14f shows a circuit for hot restarting such lamps, and again a high frequency burst of pulse voltages is generated every half-cycle by a spark gap generator. Special high voltage insulation is required for the 30 kV peak and the ignitor must be mounted very near to the lamp.

18.5   Transport and emergency lighting systems

Transport and emergency lighting share a common feature: they both operate from sources of stored energy and high efficiency is therefore important. Various incandescent lamps are used, but the inverter–fluorescent lamp combination is around five times more efficient and is the preferred choice for many applications.

18.5.1   Inverters

The function of an inverter is to provide a sufficiently high alternating voltage to start and operate a lamp from a low d.c. voltage, usually provided by a battery. All inverters use transistors or other switching devices to repeatedly connect and disconnect the primary winding of a transformer with the d.c. source, a higher voltage output winding supplying the lamp. To reduce the size of the inverter, to avoid problems with acoustic noise, and to take advantage of the higher fluorescent lamp efficiency at high frequency (Fig. 18.3) inverters usually operate above 20 kHz. Voltages to control the switching transistors are commonly obtained from feedback windings on the transformer.

Preheat type fluorescent lamps may be started very many times without electrode damage or end-blackening if the lamp voltage is withheld until the cathodes have been heated. In practice, however, the majority of inverters apply both cathode voltage and lamp voltage simultaneously. If such an inverter is designed to start the lamp at minimum battery voltage and ambient temperature, the applied lamp voltage will be high under normal conditions and the lamp is liable to start without the benefit of cathode heating. The number of lamp starts before end-blackening occurs is then drastically reduced: this effectively determines the life of the lamp. Where inverter driven fluorescent lamps must be switched on and off at frequent intervals, for example over the entrance to a bus, then special multistart circuits are used to ensure that the lamp cathodes are preheated before the lamp is allowed to start.

Figure 18.15 shows a simple blocking oscillator circuit. Its operation is very dependent on uncontrolled parameters, such as transistor current gain, transistor storage time, and the saturation characteristics of the transformer. In a more complex form it is used for some small lamp non-maintained emergency lighting inverters, but its very 'peaky' waveforms cause short lamp life. It is not suitable for maintained

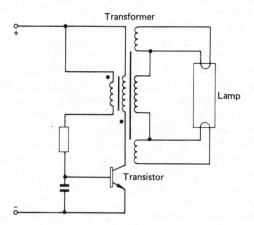

Fig. 18.15   Simple blocking oscillator

operation or for transport applications. In this circuit energy is stored in the transformer when the transistor is on and is discharged into the lamp circuit when the transistor switches off. Since the circuit does not turn on again until all the stored energy has been discharged, no separate lamp ballast is required.

Figure 18.16 shows a transport inverter used by British Rail for coach lighting with twin 20 W lamps. The output transformer has leakage reactance to ballast the lamps.

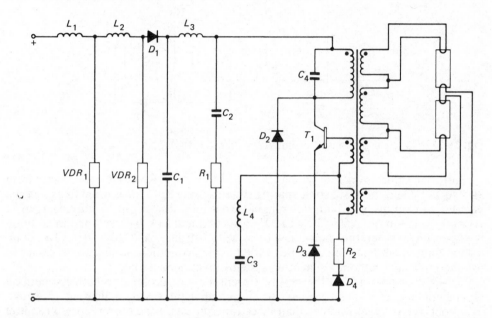

Fig. 18.16 Class-C sinewave inverter with leakage-reactance ballast

When the transistor T_1 switches on, choke L_3 controls the inrush current to the tuning capacitor C_4. The discharge of the bias capacitor C_3 determines the length of time T_1 remains on. The various filter components on the input protect the transistor from supply transients.

Figure 18.17 shows a class-D circuit (Baxandall 1959) using two transistors which are alternately switched at zero voltage into half of the primary winding. L_1 reduces the ripple current from the battery and ensures constant current feed. In the arrangement shown the lamp is ballasted by C_1 which also acts as the tuning capacitor. Before the lamp starts, the inverter runs at a high frequency which reduces when the lamp is operating. Cathode preheating is supplied via capacitors C_2 and C_3 so that maximum heating current is obtained before starting and this reduces when the lamp is operating. This circuit has an efficiency of up to 90% and is used for both transport and emergency lighting applications. For small lamp non-maintained emergency lighting where only a limited number of lamp starts is required the cathode heating may be omitted to save battery power.

18.5.2 Transport lighting

Fluorescent lamps are used in road and rail vehicles, ships, and aircraft. Inverters are generally designed to operate one or two lamps, the bulk inverter now being obsolete.

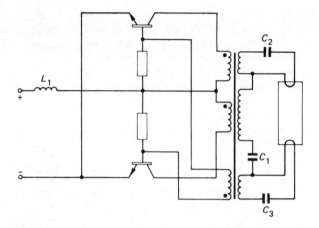

Fig. 18.17   Basic class-D sinewave inverter with capacitor ballast

Most road vehicles operate with a 12 V or 24 V battery. Railways use voltages from 24 V to 110 V and there are some marine systems using 220 V. It is usual to expect the inverter to operate with batteries ranging from fully discharged to fully charged, a possible variation of ±25% (18 V to 30 V for a nominal 24 V battery), and in addition the operating temperature range may be as wide as from −20 °C to +60 °C. To obtain a good fluorescent lamp life over this wide range of conditions it may be necessary to use the multistart cathode preheating systems mentioned earlier.

Transients and surges on the supply present a major problem to battery-operated equipment and can cause damage to the components used in lighting inverters. Transient overvoltages of more than three times normal have been reported (Knittel 1979). Stringent tests to ensure that equipment will withstand high energy, high voltage transients have been incorporated into various specifications (IEC 1974, British Railways Board 1976). Also, transport lighting inverters must not produce radiated or conducted interference capable of upsetting other electronic equipment in the vehicle. To limit the effect of these transients and to reduce any conducted radio interference it is necessary to include filter components in the supply leads, those in Fig. 18.16 showing the precautions necessary to meet the requirements of British Rail.

18.5.3   Emergency lighting

When planning an emergency lighting installation, the designer has to make a number of decisions about the type of system he will use, as discussed in Sect. 21.4. He has to choose between fluorescent and tungsten lamps, between maintained and non-maintained operations, between battery-powered and motor-generator systems, and between self-contained and central battery systems (Bedocs 1980). Typical circuits for some of the most popular options are outlined below. ·

Non-maintained battery-powered systems   In the system shown in Fig. 18.18a the battery is being charged while the mains supply is present. In the event of a mains failure the changeover switch connects the battery to the lamp. It is very common for the changeover device to be an electronic switch rather than a mechanical one and this would almost certainly be the case if an inverter were used. This simple system can be a self-contained one, with all the components described located inside the luminaire.

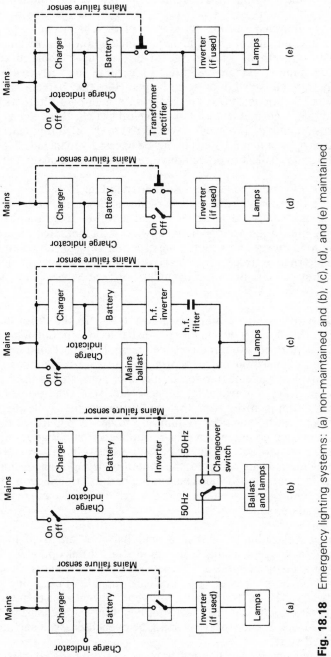

Fig. 18.18 Emergency lighting systems: (a) non-maintained and (b), (c), (d), and (e) maintained

Alternatively, the battery and charger may be mounted separately and sized to feed a number of luminaires. Or, yet again, the inverter may also be housed centrally and made large enough to feed all the lamps. In this case its frequency will almost certainly be standard 50 Hz and a normal 50 Hz ballast will connect it to the lamp.

Maintained battery-powered systems   A system of the changeover type is shown in Fig. 18.18b. Once again, all components may be included within the luminaire or the charger and battery, with or without the inverter, may be housed centrally and designed to feed a number of lamps. Figure 18.18c shows an alternative system of this type particularly suited to small fluorescent lamps. Here the charger–battery–inverter circuit is permanently connected to the lamp via a high-pass filter, with the mains supply connected via a normal ballast and an on–off switch. If the mains supply fails, the inverter turns on and feeds power directly through the high frequency filter to the lamp. For some designs of mains ballast it may be necessary to include a low-pass filter in series with the mains ballast to prevent inverter power being dissipated in it instead of the lamp.

A 'floating' type of maintained system is outlined in Fig. 18.18d, where the inverter is used to operate the lamp in both the emergency and normal mode. If this is to be successful, the inverter must be so designed that it will both start and run the lamp without impairing life. In the arrangement shown the charger circuit must be capable of supplying full load power and maintaining accurate voltage control to float-charge the battery. An alternative circuit with a less costly charger is shown in Fig. 18.18e. As in some of the previous circuits, if an incandescent lamp is used the inverter is not required.

Motor-generator systems   One example is shown in Fig. 18.19a. With such a system, even if starting of the motor is automatic, it is usual to incorporate a back-up system operating from a battery–inverter and capable of supplying part load for long enough to ensure that the combustion engine starts and runs up correctly. Figure 18.19b shows an alternative arrangement whereby the a.c. generator is used at all times. When normal mains supply is available, the generator is driven by an electric motor. Should the mains fail, it is driven from the combustion engine. A flywheel is fitted to maintain the output as the engine is running up to speed. Figure 18.19c shows yet another system in which emergency power is obtained from a battery driving a d.c. motor and an a.c. generator set. When the normal mains voltage is available, the roles of the motor and generator are reversed, the generator acting as an a.c. motor to drive the d.c. machine as a generator which charges the battery. Connection to the ballasts and lamps is via a semiconductor 'static switch' which operates almost instantaneously on the loss of the mains supply.

Batteries   Both nickel–cadmium and lead–acid batteries are used for emergency lighting supplies. Each type is available in a number of forms optimized for different performance characteristics (Barak 1980): provided the right cell is chosen and then properly maintained, both types of vented cell are capable of providing good service for at least ten years. The lead–acid battery is generally cheaper than the equivalent nickel–cadmium battery, but it is electrically far less robust. Care must be taken to see that the battery is properly charged; it must not be over-discharged and must never be left in a discharged state.

For self-contained emergency lighting applications fully sealed versions of both nickel–cadmium and lead–acid cells are available (Barak 1980, General Electric Co USA 1979 and 1975). Intrinsically unable to provide the same long life as the vented

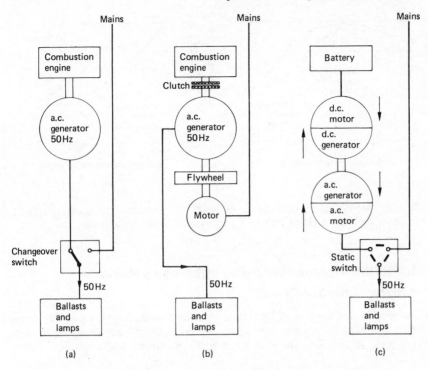

Fig. 18.19 Emergency lighting systems using rotating machines

cell, in practice their lives are further reduced by their operating condition inside the heated environment of the luminaire. This is particularly true of the lead–acid cell and therefore nickel–cadmium sealed cells with polypropylene separators are used almost exclusively for self-contained application.

In addition to the direct effects of elevated temperature, cell life depends on the charge current applied to the cell in its fully charged state. If, as is usual, charge current is not reduced as the cell becomes charged then the continuous charge current results in oxidation and breakdown of the separator material. It is therefore desirable that only sufficient charge current to recharge the cell in 24 hours is supplied (Fig. 18.20a). There is no consensus of opinion on the relative importance of overcharge current and temperature on the life of the cell, but the curve shown in Fig. 18.20b may be regarded as typical.

Another important factor which must be taken into account is a cell's ability to accept a deep discharge and possible reverse charge. The weakest cell in a battery will discharge first and, unless adequate precautions are taken to prevent it, the discharge of the remaining cells will reverse-charge the weakest cell. In this case the cell will almost certainly vent and release some gas. This in itself may be acceptable, but it is essential that the cell's safety vent is automatically resealable. Cells with non-resealable vents will dry out and the cell will become open-circuit in a matter of weeks. It is thus essential, when designing for sealed cells, to measure charge currents and cell temperatures within the luminaire under working conditions. Indeed, the current UK specification (ICEL 1978) requires certificates, from the luminaire manufacturer and the battery manufacturer, to the effect that the cells are expected to have a life of four years under the operating conditions of current and temperature.

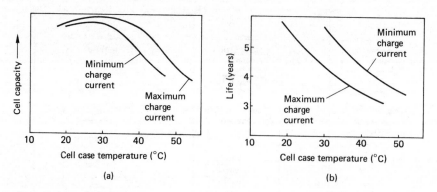

Fig. 18.20   Characteristics of batteries for emergency lighting: (a) cell capacity as a function of cell temperature and (b) life of battery as a function of cell temperature

18.6   Installation and control of lighting systems

18.6.1   Lighting system installation

For the successful installation of lighting equipment consideration has to be given to some particular electrical characteristics of lighting circuits, not least those involving discharge lamps, in deciding the ratings of fuses, switches, and cabling.

Inrush currents   An incandescent filament lamp has a cold resistance which is only about 8% of its hot operating resistance. The maximum inrush current occurs when the lamp is switched on at the a.c. voltage peak and this may have a peak value of about 20 times the normal r.m.s. current. The time taken for the current to drop to a steady value depends on the thermal time constant of the filament and varies from a few milliseconds to several seconds. In discharge lamp circuits using power factor correction a large momentary inrush current flows after switch-on until the capacitor is charged. Again, the maximum circuit current occurs when the capacitor is switched on at a.c. voltage peak, its value depending on the resistance and inductance in the circuit and the supply impedance. A 5 μF capacitor switched on to a 240 V a.c. supply will take a momentary peak current of between 50 A and 100 A for about 25 μs. In switch-start fluorescent lamp circuits using choke or choke–capacitor ballasts the maximum ballast inrush current occurs when the starter contacts close at zero a.c. voltage. The inrush current lasts for about 10 ms and has a value of up to six times the normal. Some discharge lamps may act as partial rectifiers for a few cycles during starting, during which time a current of two or three times the normal will be taken from the mains supply.

Fusing   In determining the correct fuse rating for lamp circuits allowance must be made for both the inrush current and the starting and run-up current. The current rating of fuses and circuit breakers must always be higher than the steady state operating current. The 'up-rating' factor recommended varies from four for individual lamp circuits to 1·5 for multilamp installations. Guidance on the selection of fuse ratings is available from lamp manufacturers (e.g. Thorn Lighting 1979).

Overvoltage transients during switching off   When lamp circuits with inductive or transformer ballasts are switched off, high voltage transients may be generated across the connecting wiring and the switch. The actual voltage developed depends on many factors, but it is attenuated by any parallel capacitance. It is usually only necessary to consider special protection against these if the wiring is of mineral insulated cable and is used with circuits which do not include power factor correction. Suitable protection is arranged by connecting voltage-dependent resistors across each lamp circuit to absorb the transient switching voltages.

Harmonic currents   All fluorescent and discharge lamps generate harmonic currents, i.e. components of frequencies which are multiples of the fundamental supply frequency, as a consequence of the lamp current having a non-sinusoidal waveshape (Sect. 18.1). The harmonic content may vary between 5 and 30% of the fundamental, depending on the type of lamp and ballast. Limits are specified in BS 2818 (BSI 1981a) and BS 4782 (BSI 1971b).

In a four-wire star-connected system with a balanced load the fundamental frequency currents will cancel in the neutral, but harmonic currents with a multiple of three times the fundamental are additive in the neutral. It is therefore necessary to use a neutral cable having the same cross-sectional area as the line cables and also to apply a different 'correction factor' (IEE 1981) for bunched cables.

Earth leakage currents   Earth leakage circuit breakers are frequently installed to give fault protection against leakage currents which may cause a fire or electric shock hazard. It must be noted that most lighting equipment produces a small inherent earth leakage current which needs to be taken into account if 'nuisance tripping' is to be avoided. Also, there is an obvious advantage in separating power and lighting circuits using such circuit breakers so that an earth fault on one piece of equipment does not plunge the whole installation into darkness.

Radio frequency interference   Fluorescent and discharge lamps, particularly towards the end of their life, generate radio signals which may interfere with radio and television reception. The r.f. interference signal is modulated at twice the power supply frequency and so causes a low pitched hum in the loudspeaker. Lamps generate interference over a wide frequency range, 100 kHz to 10 MHz, which covers the long, medium, and short wave broadcasting bands.

Interference may reach a receiver by several routes:

(a)   Direct radiation from the lamp to the aerial.
(b)   Conduction along the mains wiring to the receiver.
(c)   Conduction along the wiring and subsequent radiation to the aerial.
(d)   Radiation to, conduction along, and then re-radiation from wiring not directly connected to the lamp.

In practice most interference is caused by route (c) and is reduced by the fitting of small suppression capacitors into starter switches or other control gear components. In troublesome cases interference can be reduced by fitting r.f. line filters or possibly by the repositioning of aerials.

18.6.2   Lighting system control

The degree of control called-for in most lighting systems is satisfied by an on–off switch. In some cases a simple manual switch suffices, but in others (Sects 21.2.4, 21.4, 28.4, and 28.5) some form of remote and/or automatic on–off switch is needed. There are also applications where a continuously-variable level of lighting is required – not least in the theatre (Chap. 25), but increasingly in residential and commercial lighting (Chap. 22).

Present-day dimmers use phase-control circuits with SCR thyristors or triacs to vary the conducting period of each half-cycle of lamp current and hence reduce the light output. Typical voltage and current waveforms are shown in Fig. 18.21. Electronic dimmers of this type have high efficiency (98%) and a single unit can control several kilowatts of lighting. Professional dimmers for stage and television are normally controlled by a low voltage d.c. signal and include suitable filters, interference suppressors, and overload protection. On simple dimmers a manually-operated potentiometer is used to vary the gate signal of the SCR. Automatic dimming is obtained from electronic timer circuits and can be initiated from external signals or sensors. For stage and television complex versatile control systems have been developed (Sect. 25.3).

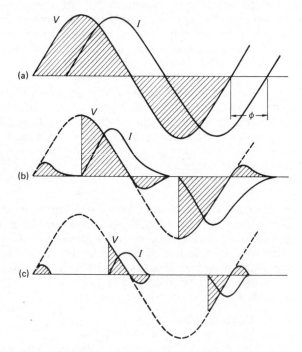

Fig. 18.21 Phase-controlled dimmer waveforms (fluorescent lamp): (a) lamp full on, (b) lamp partly dimmed, and (c) lamp dimmed

Filament lamps All standard lamps can be dimmed on equipment of the correct voltage rating. In the case of certain high efficiency tungsten halogen lamps prolonged operation at low brightness may impair the regeneration cycle and the full expected lamp life may not be obtained. When incandescent lamps are dimmed their light output drops much faster than does the power consumption (Fig. 18.22). There is also a reduction in colour temperature since the filament is cooler when the lamp is dimmed, but lamp life is extended.

Discharge lamps Mercury lamps can be dimmed over a very limited range. Other discharge lamps are generally unsuitable for dimming because of the changes in

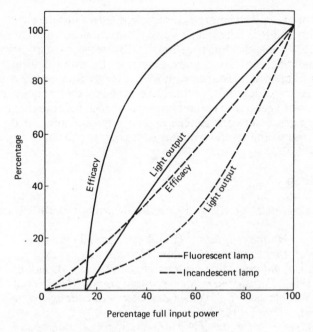

Fig. 18.22 Dimming characteristic of lamps

vapour pressure, colour, temperature, and cathode operation which occur when current is reduced.

Fluorescent lamps Normal choke or choke–capacitor ballast circuits, without power factor correction, can be dimmed down to about half the normal current, but starting or restarting may be difficult at this level. Using special ballast circuits it is possible to dim many argon-filled lamps down to 1% of their normal light output and obtain satisfactory restarting at any intermediate level. As can be seen in Fig. 18.22, a partially-dimmed fluorescent lamp may have a slightly higher efficacy than an undimmed one.

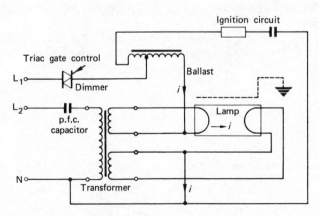

Fig. 18.23 Fluorescent lamp dimming circuit

At low levels of arc current there is insufficient current to provide 'self-heating' of the lamp cathodes and it is necessary to provide continuous cathode heating from an external source. The circuit shown in Fig. 18.23 uses a current-fed transformer to supply cathode heating, and has the advantage that the voltage adjusts automatically to suit either high or low resistance cathodes. For good dimming it is necessary to provide additional reignition aids, such as an earthed metal fitting near the lamp, and to generate pulse voltages at the commencement of each half-cycle of lamp current. A small resistor–capacitor network generates a ringing oscillation in the choke ballast which is transferred to the lamp terminals with correct phasing.

Further reading

Bedford B D and Hoft R G, 1964, *Principles of inverter circuits* (New York: John Wiley)

Elenbaas W, 1971, *Fluorescent lamps* (London: Macmillan)

Elenbaas W, 1972, *Light sources* (London: Macmillan)

Francis V J, 1948, *Fundamentals of discharge tube circuits* (London: Methuen)

Grossner N R, 1967, *Transformers for electronic circuits* (New York: McGraw-Hill)

Kusko A and Wroblewski T, 1969, *Computer aided design of magnetic circuits* (Cambridge, Mass: MIT Press)

LIF, 1978, *Guidance notes on the radio interference suppression of fluorescent luminaires* (London: Lighting Industry Federation)

LIF, 1980, *Fact finder No. 2: Dimming guidance note* (London: Lighting Industry Federation)

Macfadyen K A, 1953, *Small transformers and inductors* (London: Chapman & Hall)

Matsch L W, 1964, *Capacitors, magnetic circuits and transformers* (Englewood-Cliffs, New Jersey: Prentice-Hall)

McLyman W T, 1979, *Transformer and inductor design handbook* (New York: Marcel Dekker)

Roddam T, 1963, *Transistor inverters and converters* (London: Iliffe)

Skilling H H, 1965, *Electrical engineering circuits*, 2nd Edition (New York: John Wiley)

Snelling E C, 1969, *Soft ferrites: properties and applications* (London: Newnes-Butterworth)

van Eldik P F and Cornelius P, 1962, *A.C. devices with iron cores* (London: Cleaver-Hume)

Waymouth J F, 1971, *Electric discharge lamps* (Cambridge, Mass: MIT Press)

Welsby V G, 1960, *Theory and design of inductance coils* (London: McDonald)

19 Luminaire design and manufacture

Whether a luminaire is primarily decorative or primarily functional, differences in the design process are simply matters of emphasis. This chapter, written by a designer, examines firstly the objectives, the disciplines, and the procedures associated with the birth pangs of a new product. An essential element in successful design is a full appreciation of possible materials and production processes which could be used, and a section of this chapter is devoted to materials and manufacturing methods, touching therein on some of the principles underlying optical design. Also implicit in the design process is the matter of luminaire specifications, in which safety looms large: a broad summary is given of the necessary safety requirements and how these can be tested in prototype or production luminaires. The chapter concludes with some case studies of actual designs.

19.1 Design objectives

The design of any successful product which necessitates the integration of several disciplines must involve a balance of the separate requirements of those disciplines. Thus the design of luminaires, which combine mechanical, optical, aesthetic, economic, and safety requirements, must be a team activity where no undue favour is shown to one requirement at the expense of another. The person who is at the centre of the collection of information, and who must maintain the balance of this input, is the product designer. Whether the product is for domestic use, where a high visual quality is vital, or for an industrial application, where resistance to corrosive atmospheres is of great importance, it is the designer who will collate expert advice and determine priorities.

The design of any product is thus a summation and balance of various requirements, realized in materials appropriate to the available plant and processes, and presented to the user as a total package. The total visual impact of the product, its packaging, and its literature cannot be over-emphasized. For when the technical and financial specifications of different products are closely similar, a potential customer is more likely to be attracted towards the one which has the best all-round appearance of a professionally executed design. Good appearance and a positive impact become the expression of the function and quality of the product, suggesting how it is likely to perform.

19.1.1 Design disciplines and programme

Design disciplines can be categorized under four main headings:

(a) Industrial design: the visualization of a design suitable for the most efficient means of manufacture at the lowest cost consistent with quality and market expectancy.

(b) Optical design: the means of modifying or redirecting the light from the source into a controlled pattern in the most efficient way.

(c) Mechanical design: the combination of both industrial and optical design requirements into a practical, workable solution.

(d) Technical design: the understanding of materials, processes, production methods, and limitations which will be used to accomplish (c).

It is important in approaching problem-solving for the designer to proceed in a logical fashion, the programme in Fig. 19.1 giving an indication of the normal steps

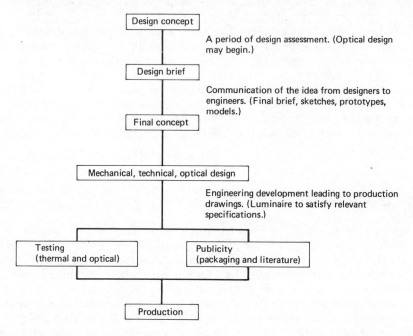

Fig. 19.1   Luminaire design programme

which are followed. However, since the act of design has by its very nature a degree of intuitive judgement, it is not always possible to follow a clearly-defined design programme. Very often, the stages towards the end of the programme will be happening concurrently, while in the early formulation stages the work tends to proceed from step to step, the time intervals being dependent on the rate at which information can be gathered to enable a firm design brief to be formulated.

19.1.2   Design concept and brief

It is essential that the designer has a clear idea of the intended function or reason for the new luminaire, if the project is to proceed with the minimum waste of time or resources. It may be helpful here to examine briefly the major stimuli to the development of a new luminaire.

The most important stimulus for a design is the development which arises from a new light source demanding a new solution to maximize the use of the available light. The old Sunflood (an updated version is illustrated in Fig. 19.2) was a specific development for the new linear tungsten halogen lamp: since its original inception some fifteen years ago this type of luminaire has become a 'product norm', found in the catalogues of most manufacturers.

Fig. 19.2 Sunflood for linear tungsten halogen lamp

Another stimulus to new design is a clear marketing need. An example of this is the development of integrated ceiling systems (Sect. 20.3.2), where the combination of the separate services of lighting, ceiling, and air conditioning were combined to offer specifiers a more convenient way of obtaining the necessary components: in this case from one supplier instead of three.

A somewhat similar situation to the marketing need is where a recurring special requirement by different customers suggests that it would be sensible to develop a standard product.

A further obvious spur to product development is the clear need to produce something which competes directly with a competitor's offer: a situation which, apart from minor deviations in style, materials, or production methods, involves very little true design work.

Finally, although in most companies product design is usually a corporate effort to a mutually-agreed programme, there does arise from time to time a successful product which is based purely and simply on the intuition of an individual designer.

One, or possibly more, of the stimuli outlined above leads to the formal recording of a design brief, a document which states the requirements and conditions of the design project. It is both useful and necessary at the outset of any design to specify the design requirements of the product and the extent of responsibility of the designer. Since a brief is drawn up at the commencement of work, it cannot specify accurately every detail of the final product. Some factors, such as optical and thermal performance, will be to some extent unknown until a considerable part of the work is done. For this reason the initial specification in a brief must allow for some variation as the work proceeds.

Typically a design brief will contain four main sections:

(a) Objective: the objective defines the general parameters of the product to enable a logical design method to be applied.
(b) Technical specification: photometric requirements, environmental conditions, lamp, and control gear to be used. At the brief stage it is particularly important that the technical information available is assessed and studied in order to evaluate the degree of risk in producing an incorrect design.
(c) Standards: home and export markets. All luminaires may be required to comply with the relevant standards (Sect. 19.3.1).
(d) Marketing specification: target costs, quantities, and construction. Production and design methods are largely dictated by the cost and quantity requirements: if the quantity is small, emphasis must be on methods which are less specialized and which carry a lower investment than methods used for larger scale manufacture.

Following the establishment of a design brief comes the development and engineering of the luminaire. At this stage co-operation with production engineers becomes essential. In parallel with the later stages of the designers' work the following activities are necessary from the production standpoint:

(a) Consultation on the possible production methods and materials.
(b) Initial considerations of tooling requirements.
(c) Initial costing.
(d) Production planning.
(e) Tool design and manufacture.
(f) Carton design.
(g) Final costs.
(h) Production samples.

19.2   Materials and production processes

The choice of materials for a luminaire is generally dictated by functional requirements, such as the working environment and the degree of optical control required. Secondly, there are visual requirements. Thirdly, there are matters of production: an analysis of the manufacturing plant which is already available and the cost of plant and processes which would enable new materials to be used.

19.2.1   Luminaire bodies

Sheet metal   Sheet steel is the most common material used in luminaire production due largely to its formability, combined with its mechanical strength, cost, and adaptability to manufacturing methods. The steel can be supplied either in standard size sheets, which are cut into blanks of the required size by means of a manually-operated power guillotine, or in non-standard sizes ordered specifically for maximum utilization. An alternative method of producing blanks is from coils which are up to 1·5 m wide. The coils are slit by shearing wheels and rollers into narrow strips and recoiled on to mandrels. These slit coils are then fed into a powered automatic shearing machine which crops the steel to length.

Although it is possible to pierce holes in a section after it has been formed, it is usually more practical to carry out this operation in the flat stage before forming. The cut blanks are fed manually into a power press, known as a 'brake press' because it is possible for the operator to stop the action of the press at any point during its operating stroke. There are two distinct types of tooling which can be used in the press for piercing operations: a one-piece purpose-made piercing tool which is the full length of the blank to be pierced, or a tooling system, such as the well-known 'Redman' type, consisting of a series of standard tools, one for each hole or group of holes, which is set up in the press to a template and operated simultaneously by the upper member of the press. Tools of this latter type can be broken down and repositioned to allow for modifications, or even a different design of luminaire.

The most common method of producing the required section from the flat pierced blank is to form each bend or group of bends separately with a succession of operations. The blank is fed manually into a brake press set up with a standard vee block and blade, the vee block being fixed to the bed of the machine and the blade to the upper moving member. By adjusting the stroke of the press, the desired angle of bend is formed. A more advanced method is the cold rolled forming process in which the pierced blank is fed through a series of powered rollers, which together with a system of guides form it into the required section.

This process only becomes an economical proposition when long, uninterrupted production runs can be guaranteed, as the set-up time and the cost of the tooling is high. However, if volume justifies it, it is possible to link the piercing and roll forming operations, by automatic transfer, enabling sections to be produced on one line starting as coiled strip and leaving as a complete, but unpainted, section (Fig. 19.3).

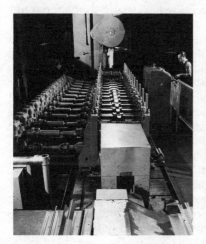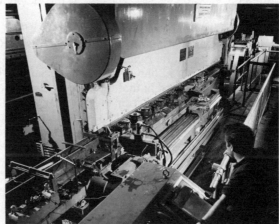

Fig. 19.3   Luminaire metal forming

Ancillary steel components can be joined to steel formed sections either before finishing, using welding or pressure processes, or after finishing, using nuts and bolts, self-tapping screws, industrial adhesives, etc.

Since unprotected steel deteriorates very quickly, a protective finish is important. Of the many finishing processes available, stoved-enamel painting is the most economical method of protecting large areas. Before the metalwork can be painted it has to be subjected to a chemical process which removes any oil from its surface and gives a thin coating of iron phosphate: phosphating can be done by either spraying or dipping.

As soon as possible after phosphating, the metalwork is painted, either with a hand spray gun or an electrostatic spray system. With electrostatic spraying the metalwork is suspended from a continuous conveyor which carries the components round a spinning disc, the disc travelling up and down a predetermined stroke to suit the size of components. Paint is fed on to the spinning disc to be sprayed off by centrifugal force: it is charged to a positive potential of 90 kV and attracted to the metalwork which is at earth potential. This gives a 50% saving in paint when compared with conventional hand spraying and ensures an even coating without runs.

On leaving the spray booth the metalwork continues on the conveyor for a short distance to give time for the solvent in the paint to evaporate before entering the stoving oven. The configuration of the conveyor system inside the oven is arranged to give a period of 30 to 35 minutes for stoving to be completed.

Developments and improvements of finishes using either wet-sprayed paint or powdered paint have rendered the vitreous-enamelling process largely redundant, the latter process now being limited to luminaires to be installed in highly corrosive atmospheres or in areas where maintenance is a problem. A protective finish can also be achieved by the well-established process of plating, but this is relatively expensive and is generally confined to small parts, such as screws, nuts, and bolts. Plating is generally zinc-based, but when the protective medium has also a decorative role, chrome plating is commonly used. For areas where protection is of the utmost importance, and appearance is not, hot dip galvanizing should be considered: it is eminently suitable where exposure to the elements is the norm, such as the mounting stirrups for floodlights.

Aluminium alloy castings   Floodlights and street lanterns present the designer with problems of structural rigidity and strength, together with positive sealing against the ingress of moisture. The problems associated with corrosion-resistant and exterior luminaires are related in that they are both exposed to similar adverse conditions, but because of market requirements exterior luminaires need to be more robust and frequently need to withstand far greater temperatures because they house more compact discharge lamps. The materials most commonly used for the manufacture of exterior luminaires are aluminium alloys, and because most lanterns are comparatively compact in design they lend themselves to the technique of casting.

The casting method adopted is dependent on the size and quantity requirements, but generally the choice is limited to two processes: gravity or pressure die-casting. Both processes employ metal split moulds, often referred to as dies, into which the molten alloy is cast; the basic difference is the method employed to force the molten metal into the mould. Gravity die-casting relies on the pressure from a head of metal above the cavity; whilst in pressure die-casting the molten metal is injected into the die at high pressure. The latter method of casting gives a greater degree of precision and allows thinner sections to be produced, but because more expensive dies are necessary it is an uneconomic process unless long production runs are required.

The grade of aluminium alloy usually selected is LM6. This has good corrosion resistance, high ductility, and is suitable for all shapes of die castings, including those with thin sections. The alloys LM2 and LM24, for example, have less critical die-casting characteristics than those of LM6, but offer less protection against corrosion. For most outdoor applications castings in LM6 would be given a paint finish only when needed for aesthetic reasons.

It should be noted that corrosion will occur, due to electrochemical reaction, wherever aluminium is in contact with a dissimilar metal, such as brass, nickel, copper, or phosphor-bronze. This means that all non-aluminium accessories, such as support brackets and screws, should be plated with a metal of an intermediate potential, a cadmium-plated finish being common for steel accessories, or be separated from the aluminium by a non-metallic barrier.

Plastic materials Plastic has long enjoyed a traditional application as a housing for certain luminaire types which are exposed to corrosive atmospheres. The choice of a specific plastic material depends on the properties required, on quantity–cost factors, and on the manufacturing processes available. Plastics technology, both of materials and production processes, is developing rapidly and all that can be given here is a brief synopsis of the major types of materials and the most common manufacturing processes used in the lighting industry.

Plastic materials fall into two main groups, thermo-plastic and thermo-setting materials. Thermo-plastic materials can be softened to a pliable mass by heating and then shaped to a desired form, which is retained on cooling: this softening process can be repeated a number of times without significantly changing the material. Thermo-setting materials are produced by the application of heat to certain polymers, normally with applied pressure: this curing process results in an irreversible chemical change taking place and further heating will not re-plasticize the material. Both types of material have applications in luminaire construction.

Thermo-set materials are used mainly for such accessories as ceiling galleries, terminal blocks, and lampholders, moulded in urea or phenolic, where material stability in thermally-stressed conditions or non-flamability is important. One very important thermo-setting material used for luminaire bodies is glass reinforced polyester (GRP). This is an epoxy or polyester pre-impregnated glass fibre material, usually supplied in the form of a sheet moulding compound (SMC). Mouldings made of GRP are light in weight and have excellent impact strength and rigidity as well as good corrosion resistance.

Thermo-plastic materials used for luminaire body components include acrylonitrile butadiene styrene (ABS), acrylic, nylon, polybutylene terephthalate (PBT), polycarbonate, polypropylene, polystyrene, and polyvinyl chloride (PVC). Such materials are being constantly modified and developed to satisfy design needs and a close liaison with material suppliers is necessary. For example, PBT, with a high thermal stability, has long been attractive to the luminaire designer, but very expensive. The recent change, from the material being formulated only in laboratory quantities to becoming one produced in volume, has resulted in it now being economically viable for both accessories and major components.

Injection moulding of thermo-plastic materials is a production technique used increasingly in the manufacture of luminaires and electrical accessories. Generally the thermo-plastic material is heated to plasticity in a cylinder and forced by a ram through channels into a split mould, which is prevented from opening by external clamping pressure; the article is then allowed to solidify before the mould opens. The high cost of the moulds usually limits the process to components requiring relatively large production runs, but the process can be economically viable for smaller quantities when the only alternative production methods involve a large amount of hand fabrication. The process produces finished parts with thin walls with a high standard of moulded detail and surface finish.

Compression moulding is the usual technique for thermo-setting materials. The moulding compound, in either a powder state or in the form of heated pellets, is placed in a split mould which is closed at high pressure and heated. The material hardens and may be removed without waiting for the mould to cool. This process is used for the production of electrical accessories and for GRP luminaire bodies using a sheet rather than powder or pellets.

19.2.2   Light controllers

Reflectors   The upper part of Table 19.1 lists the reflector materials most commonly used in luminaires. Two kinds of reflectance are distinguished: regular reflectance, which includes only the light that is reflected in accordance with the laws of optical reflection, and diffuse reflectance, which includes all the reflected light.

Table 19.1   Optical properties of materials

Material	Finish	Diffuse reflectance (%)	Regular reflectance (normal incidence) (%)	Transmittance (normal incidence) (%)	Refractive index	Critical angle (°)
Aluminium commercial grade	Anodized and polished	0	70			
Aluminium super-purity	Anodized and polished	0	80			
Aluminized glass or plastic	Specular	0	94			
Chromium	Plate quality	0	65			
Stainless steel	Polished		60			
Steel	White paint glossy	up to 75	5			
Flint glass 3 mm	Polished	0	8	92	1·62	38
Soda glass 3 mm	Polished	0	8	92	1·52	41
Clear acrylic 3 mm	Polished	0	8	92	1·49	42
Opal acrylic 3 mm	Polished	10–15	4	50–80		
Polystyrene 3 mm	Polished	0	8	92	1·60	39
Polyvinyl chloride (PVC) 3 mm	Polished	0	8	88	1·52	41
Polycarbonate (LS) 3 mm	Polished	0	8	88	1·58	39
Cellulose acetate butyrate (LS) 3 mm	Polished	0	8	85	1·47	43

The most popular specularly reflecting material is aluminium. This has taken the place of silvered glass because it is lighter, not fragile, and easier to form. To obtain the best specularity, enabling a sharp image to be formed, the aluminium has to be polished: mechanically, chemically, electrolytically, or by a combination of these. High reflectances can be obtained with super-purity aluminium, but this material is soft and expensive. Both disadvantages can be overcome by cladding commercial grade aluminium with a thin layer of super-purity aluminium. Glass surfaces which have been aluminized give a high reflectance, but this process is seldom used except on lamp envelopes. Aluminized plastic with a protective coat of lacquer is used for some indoor luminaires, but the process tends to be expensive. Chromium plate and stainless steel, although of good specularity, have low reflectance and are not used for reflectors.

The use of the specular parabolic reflector to produce a narrow beam of light has been illustrated in Sect. 1.5.1 for a point source. The effect of the finite sizes of practical sources and reflectors is to produce a beam which, for a given source flux, is wider and less intense. Figure 19.4a shows the theoretical intensity distribution for a parabolic trough mirror with a tubular source at its focus, the source having a diameter of the same order as the focal length of the mirror.

Ignoring the imperfections of the mirror, the peak intensity is equal to the luminance of the source multiplied by the projected area of the mirror: this implies an amplification of the intensity of the bare source equal to w/d, where w is the width of the mirror mouth and d is the diameter of the source. The critical angles in the theoretical distribution of Fig. 19.4a are identified in Fig. 19.4c. When viewed at angles less than θ, the mirror is fully flashed (Sect. 1.5.1); at greater angles, such as θ_2, the mirror is only partially flashed and the flashed area is proportional to LM. At angles above θ_3 only the light from the source is seen, and above θ_4 this is progressively obscured by the mirror itself. Figure 19.4b shows the practical distribution resulting and what happens if the lamp is defocused by moving it closer to the mirror.

Imperfections in the shaping of specular reflectors, for example deviations from a perfect parabola, together with the imperfect symmetry of practical light sources, often result in beam patterns with marked striations – small peaks or troughs in an otherwise smooth intensity distribution. Two common ways of reducing this are firstly the use of patterned reflectors, dimpling for example, and secondly the replacement of a smooth contour by a series of facets, but these techniques are only suitable when fairly wide beams are to be generated.

White paint on metal provides diffuse reflection. For ease of cleaning the paints used are usually glossy, but the specular component due to gloss is of no practical significance in designing optical systems.

Refractors and diffusers Refracting systems utilizing prisms or lenses are generally used in systems where several beams are needed from one source, as in beacons. They are also used in street lanterns where only two beams are required, but where there is a need to keep the lantern narrow. Sheets of refracting prisms (prismatic controllers) are also used in general purpose indoor luminaires for fluorescent lamps: these give less stringent glare control than where reflectors are used, but are capable of giving higher light output ratios, and their more lively appearance is preferred by some.

The lower part of Table 19.1 gives the optical characteristics of materials used for refractors and diffusers. The values of transmittance given are for normal incidence of a parallel beam; for diffuse incidence (as from a sky of uniform luminance) the values are somewhat lower, for example 85% rather than 92% for clear acrylic. The absorptance, a measure of the light loss in the material, is equal to the sum of the transmittance and reflectance subtracted from unity. In selecting a material for optical control not only must the optical properties be taken into account, but also the suitability of the materials as regards strength, durability, resistance to heat and ultraviolet radiation, and ease of manufacture of the final product.

Glass may be found in outdoor luminaires, having cast-in prisms or lenses or used to form a plain protective face. It offers the advantages of low cost and a high percentage

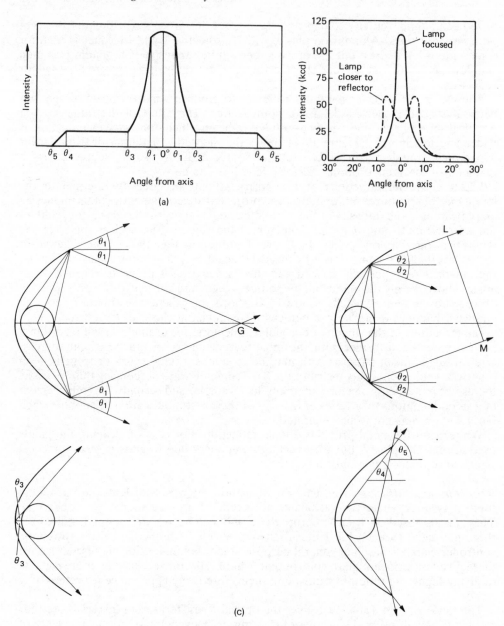

Fig. 19.4   Parabolic trough reflector: (a) theoretical intensity distribution, (b) practical intensity distribution, and (c) critical angles in theoretical distribution

of light transmission. Obviously glass should only be considered for use in installations where there is little likelihood of physical damage. This basic weakness of glass has resulted in an increased use of plastics, particularly acrylic and polycarbonate. Acrylic has a transmission equal to that of glass and a good resistance to physical damage and to chemical attack. Grades of impact-resistant acrylic are available which bring this material close to the resistance offered by polycarbonate, with a clear cost-benefit. Polycarbonate is generally reserved for applications where physical damage is highly probable, such as low level lighting and vandal-prone areas: it has excellent impact resistance, but its light transmission and rate of ultraviolet degradation are worse than for acrylic.

Although polycarbonate is used indoors, where impact resistance is important, the plastic controllers most commonly found indoors are of polystyrene or acrylic. Either of these can be formed, extruded, cemented, welded, or injection-moulded. Acrylic is somewhat more expensive, but has slightly better mechanical properties than has polystyrene. In addition, it is available in an opal form for applications where light is to be generally diffused rather than redirected by refraction. Polystyrene is the plastic generally adopted for the manufacture of diffusers or refractors for fluorescent luminaires intended for use in normal atmospheres. General purpose polystyrene is an unsuitable material because of its rapid ultraviolet degradation and its mechanical properties: both limitations can be overcome by employing ultraviolet-stabilized or toughened grades, which still result in a low-priced material, albeit with a reduced transmittance.

A refractor unit is normally made up of a series of linear prisms, two faces of each being working faces and one the return face. It is common to design the bank of prisms so that one set of faces forms a smooth surface, the angles of the other working faces being chosen so as to deviate rays of light from the source into the desired direction (Sect. 1.5.2). The return face is set parallel to the path of a ray which emerges in the beam. A prism bank will thus appear fully flashed when viewed from the direction of the desired beam. Use is sometimes made of reflecting prisms (Sect. 1.2.3) when a very wide prism bank is required. Due to the finite size of the light source, partial flashing occurs at angles near to the beam, just as with the parabolic specular reflector described earlier. Imperfections arise from the rounding of the tips and the troughs in a prism bank, so full flashing is never 100%.

A more complete treatment of refractor design than can be given here, and a source reference for all aspects of luminaire optical design, is to be found in Bean and Simons (1968).

19.2.3 Electrical components

Wiring The internal wiring, or flying leads in the case of portable luminaires, must be of such a quality so as to remain electrically safe during the working life of a luminaire. Internal wiring can be either solid core conductor or flexible multistrand, whereas external wiring is inevitably flexible. A wide range of insulating materials are available with different working temperatures. Among the most common insulators are PVC (105 °C), EVA (140 °C), silicone rubber (170 °C to 200 °C), and PTFE (250 °C). Double insulated wiring is generally PVC on PVC.

Control gear The principles of operation of ballasts have been covered in Chap. 18, but the prime concerns of the luminaire designer are the questions of physical size and the management of the generated heat. By intelligent positioning of the ballast the problems of heat generation can be minimized. A piece of control gear in close proximity to external metalwork will dissipate heat more readily than when it is thermally insulated from the outside, as for example when mounted inside a GRP body. To a large extent the positioning of a ballast in the luminaire housing is dictated by requirements outlined in national standards, by the proximity of other internal components, and by the mounting attitude of the completed luminaire.

19.3   Specifications and testing

19.3.1   Specifications

Specifications are laid down to govern the design and construction of luminaires so that they conform to agreed requirements of safety, reliability, durability, performance, and ease of maintenance. Of these five it is safety which predominates, the dominant objective of specifications being to provide protection for the consumer and his premises when luminaires are installed. Although a considerable amount of recent legislation in the UK has been directed at consumer protection and equipment safety, there is no general requirement here for a luminaire manufacturer to obtain an approval certificate before putting a product onto the market, unlike the situation in some countries.

To encourage manufacturers to produce only quality products the British Standards Institution has introduced its safety mark (Fig. 19.5). When this symbol appears on a

Fig. 19.5   BSI safety mark

particular luminaire the customer can be assured that the product meets the luminaire specification BS 4533 (BSI 1981b), which means in turn that it satisfies the relevant UK and EEC regulations regarding safety of electrical equipment. Inspectors from BSI not only have samples of the product tested, but also visit the production and testing facilities of the manufacturer in order to be satisfied about quality control. The latest version of the British luminaire specification, BS 4533, is firmly based on the luminaire specification of the International Electrotechnical Commission IEC 598 (IEC 1979). Despite the existence of this international document there is as yet no international safety mark, only equivalents of the BSI mark used by similar national standardizing bodies, e.g. VDE in Germany, DEMCO in Denmark, etc., each with its own national idiosyncrasies. Even within the smaller international grouping of the EEC the long-promised E mark is still awaited.

Mechanical requirements   The actual constructional requirements of luminaires are laid down by specifying such things as the minimum mechanical strength of the components to ensure reasonable durability in handling and in use and the strength of the suspension used to mount the luminaire. Metal components must be adequately protected against corrosion and attention must be paid to dissimilar metals in contact that could cause electrolytic action in the presence of moisture and thereby cause the onset of more serious corrosion.

Enclosure requirements   Luminaires for street lighting and other outdoor uses must satisfy very rigorous weatherproofing requirements and indoor luminaires for some special applications must provide protection against the entry of water or dust. The requirements depend on the IP classification of the luminaire, outlined in Sect. 24.2.2.

Electrical requirements   Luminaires are classified according to the method of protection they employ to protect the user from electric shock. A luminaire having basic insulation in which all the metalwork is connected to an earth terminal, for connection to the earthing system of the premises power supply, is said to be Class I. Protection can be given for a luminaire to be operated on a two-wire lighting circuit by the use of double insulation, and this would be deemed a Class II luminaire. The original Class 0 luminaire, unearthed and with only single insulation, is not acceptable in the UK.

The electrical wiring of a luminaire is of importance for safe operation; specifications include such things as the types of insulated cable that can be used, the minimum size of cables, the method of connection to the supply, and the protection against damage and chafing where the supply cable passes through apertures in the body. Another important factor specified is the minimum distance that must be maintained between live parts and adjacent earthed metalwork: creepage distances, which are measured along surfaces, and clearances, which are measured in straight lines through the air.

The various electrical components, such as ballasts, lampholders, and capacitors, have their own relevant specifications and should comply with these in order to be incorporated in a luminaire that is to satisfy BS 4533.

Thermal requirements   One of the main problems in the design of a luminaire is limiting the temperatures which will occur during operation, and to this end BS 4533 is quite specific on the maximum temperatures that can be permitted at various points and on various materials. A concise table is included that covers such things as the maximum temperature of windings, capacitors, painted surfaces, wiring insulation, and the various materials used in the construction of the luminaire and its components. These temperature limits must be achieved when the luminaire is mounted in a draught-free enclosure and operated at 100 to 110% of the rated voltage (depending on the specific test and lamp type). In the case of luminaires designed for use on combustible ceiling surfaces it must be shown that even under abnormal fault conditions the temperature of the mounting surface does not become excessive.

Thermal endurance must also be proved, by subjecting luminaires to on–off switching cycles for seven days in an ambient 10°C above the rated ambient temperature and with an overvoltage of 5 or 10%.

Marking requirements   Another important factor governed by specification is the marking that must be applied to permit ready identification of the manufacturer, supply voltage, rated wattage, classification, rated maximum ambient temperature, etc. – essential data for the installer and maintenance engineer. The marking must be durable and the manner in which it is applied is itself subject to a test.

Optical requirements   Since luminaire specifications are primarily concerned with safety, photometric requirements are rare. One exception is in Section 103.1 of BS 4533 where the intensity distributions of road lighting lanterns are specified – a subject discussed in Sect. 28.4. Another is in Section 102.22 of BS 4533 where there is the requirement that an emergency lighting luminaire shall provide the rated lumen output 5 s after being switched on, and also that photometric data be provided to show the effect of battery performance both over a specified emergency period and over the quoted life of the battery.

19.3.2 Testing

Before a new design is passed to the production department a thorough testing programme must be carried out. Some of the tests are made many times during the development of a luminaire, particularly if it is for outdoor applications. It is necessary at an early stage to make a detailed appraisal of a prototype sample and thus provide the data for subsequent modifications throughout later stages of development. At the final design stage a complete formal test programme is carried out to the relevant specification. Virtually all the requirements of BS 4533 are covered by an associated test and the test procedures are clearly laid down.

Mechanical tests   The various components of a luminaire must be able to withstand the mechanical forces encountered in service. For example, screws which are used during installation or servicing, and the mounting arrangements for outdoor luminaires, are subjected to tests appropriate to the torques and forces occurring in practice.

Luminaires must be reasonably proof against impact damage. Even indoors luminaires can be damaged by accidental blows and those used outdoors are often subject to vandalism. It is particularly important that covers for live parts are robust, but the weakest part of a luminaire is usually the bowl or diffuser covering the lamp chamber. For many years a pendulum impact hammer was used to test mechanical strength, but a spring-operated impact hammer (Fig. 19.6) is the norm today.

Fig. 19.6 Impact hammer

Materials and finishes are normally assessed by small samples, but an additional check is made on the complete luminaire during long-term environmental tests, covering hardness as well as resistance to scratching, staining, and corrosion.

Enclosure tests   The apparatus used for the rain-proof testing is shown in Fig. 19.7. A semicircular tubular hoop is fitted with many fine jets through which water is directed at the luminaire to simulate rain. The hoop oscillates 60° either side of the vertical and the luminaire is rotated in the horizontal plane, thereby ensuring that every relevant part is sprayed with water. The luminaire is switched on and operated for an hour before the rain begins. It is thus in a hot condition when the cold rain arrives and is therefore subjected to thermal shock, a condition which will occur during normal

Fig. 19.7   Rain test

service. This is a particularly important part of the test when external parts are made from glass or a similar material. The rain continues for ten minutes with the luminaire energized, after which the luminaire is switched off, and the rain continues for another ten minutes. During this second period the luminaire is cooled by the rain and the air pressure within it falls, providing an effective check on the ability of the luminaire to 'breathe' without drawing in water.

Luminaires which are required to be dust-proof or dust-tight are tested in a special cabinet in which a fine dust, such as talcum powder, is agitated by means of a blower so that the air surrounding the luminaire is heavily laden with dust particles. During this test, which may last for between two and eight hours, a partial vacuum is maintained inside the luminaire to encourage the ingress of dust through any seals. At the end of the test there must be no dust within a luminaire classified as dust-tight and for dust-proof luminaires the dust which has entered must not cause any danger or impair efficient operation.

Electrical tests   A safety requirement is that no live parts should be able to be accidentally touched, and this is checked by using a standard test finger (Fig. 19.8). Luminaires must also satisfy requirements such as minimum creepage distances across the surfaces of insulating materials and minimum clearance distances between live parts and between live parts and earth or touchable metal parts. Luminaires must also pass high voltage flash tests and insulation resistance tests after several days in humid conditions.

Thermal tests   Luminaire temperatures are usually measured in a standard draught-free room. The luminaire is fitted with many fine wire thermocouples and it is then operated under specified conditions until the temperatures indicated by these thermocouples are stable. In the case of fluorescent or discharge lamp luminaires with built-in ballasts the operating temperature of the ballast winding is determined by the change in resistance of the winding.

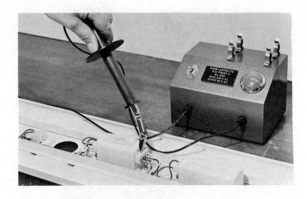

Fig. 19.8 Electrical test finger

During the thermal measurements the luminaire is usually mounted in the most unfavourable position which it is likely to encounter in use, for example a fluorescent luminaire for indoor use would be mounted on the underside of a large sheet of block-board to simulate ceiling mounted conditions.

In addition to the measurements in thermal test enclosures, luminaires are subjected to long-term environmental tests. Street lighting and other outdoor luminaires are mounted outdoors so that the effect of the elements may be observed. Some of them are operated almost continuously with only short off periods to accelerate any thermal effects, while others are operated on their normal switching cycle or by photoelectric cells to simulate street lighting conditions.

Photometric tests　The light distribution characteristics of a road lighting lantern are obtained using a polar photometer as described in Sect. 4.4.3. The measurement of the light output of an emergency lighting luminaire involves the use of an integrating enclosure of the type described in Sect. 4.4.2, but because of the low value of light output smaller enclosures than normal are used, frequently with extra-sensitive cells.

19.4　Examples of design

19.4.1　CSI floodlight

A lantern utilizing the 1 kW compact source iodide lamp (Sect. 15.4.1) in a sealed beam PAR 64 envelope had been in service for several years, during which time two deficiencies had become apparent: lamp changing was not an easy task and there were undesirable constraints on the mounting attitude. An opportune time to design a new lantern to overcome these deficiencies occurred with the development of two new lamps, both in the same general form as the original. One lamp was a hot restrike version of the original CSI lamp, the second a compact iodide daylight (CID) lamp, specifically developed for film and television lighting, with a 5500 K colour temperature suitable for daylight film stock.

Although the hot restrike lamp had the same general format as the standard lamp (Fig. 15.4), the electrical characteristics were somewhat different, a very high starting voltage being necessary and consequently the lantern required increased 'creepage' protection, as evidenced by the wider pin spacing on the base. The design problems were further aggravated by the use of a dichroic reflecting surface for the PAR envelope, a further consequence of the high starting voltage – this was liable to result in a higher thermal build-up in the floodlight. These factors dictated a change in the volume and in the material of the lantern body in order that electrical safety could be guaranteed and the heat dissipation improved.

The designer was able to justify producing the whole body in cast aluminium (Fig. 19.9) instead of spun aluminium, with a cast 'bezel' to hold the front glass. The use of

Fig. 19.9 CSI/CID floodlight

a more substantial material for the body permitted a higher class of protection against the ingress of moisture to be achieved and also gave an opportunity of improving the method of securing the alternative front glasses, used as outlined in Sect. 26.2.1 to provide different light distributions.

Another feature that the more substantial body material enabled the designer to incorporate was the choice of mounting positions. This acknowledged the diametrically-opposed relamping procedures preferred in stadia and in studios. In the former, with all the unpleasant aspects of maintenance at the top of a tower (Sect. 26.2.2), the servicing of lanterns from the back is preferred. In filming a rigidly mounted body is preferred with an easily removable front to permit filter, front glass, and lamp changes.

Both normal and hot restrike versions of the new floodlight are outwardly identical, the differences being internal, consisting of the starting circuit, the lampholder, and the heat baffle. The ignitors are contained in a separate cast metal box mounted behind the lamp housing. The unit has been designed to be interchangeable with the earlier versions on existing towers without any modification to either fixing arrangements or wiring.

19.4.2   Master track and Master spot

This new simple track system and spotlight range was based on market feedback from existing products over the years, giving the designer a clear idea of the critical safety and economic constraints necessary to produce a potentially high production volume product.

Market research had indicated the mass market requirement to be for a single circuit track. The track design was approached from the standpoint of obtaining the necessary electrical clearance and creepage within the smallest section possible, thus minimizing the cost of high value raw materials. To a large extent the size of a minimal track section is dictated by the requirements laid down in BS 4522 Section 2.6 (BSI 1979b). The only detail which is not specified is the position of the earth strip. In the case of Master track the designer placed the earth contact so that the top central extruded section was clear for screw mounting direct to the wall or ceiling surface.

With a single circuit track, mains connector boxes could be designed which were simple, safe, and easy to both install and rewire. Switched luminaire adaptors were not found to be a major requirement and a very limited range of accessories and attachments would meet the majority of customer applications. Adaptors and accessories were therefore designed so that standard sub-components could be used.

There were obvious benefits in reconsidering the design of spotlights and interior floodlights to be used on this track at the same time as designing the track. The range would cover both the conventional and the new reflector spotlamps (Sect. 9.2). As anticipated, high volume production of some units enabled the designer to consider sophisticated tooling and a broad choice of possible materials. The final choice was one of the new generation of heat-stable plastics (Sect. 19.2.1) giving sufficient thermal stability for any of the proposed lamp types to be incorporated. A series of luminaire bodies were designed, with suspension posts housing the wiring, to enable each to be used with several lamp types. Light control, if not provided in the lamp, was achieved by reflectors which clipped into moulded details in the body. Where fashion dictated it, or where product volume did not justify a high tooling commitment, polished aluminium (Fig. 19.10) replaced the moulded plastic body.

19.4.3   Luminaires for 2D

A prime example of the way a new light source acts as a stimulus for luminaire design has been the advent of the energy-saving 2D fluorescent lamp (Sect. 11.4.3). The unique flat square format, allied to its cool running characteristics, offered the possibility of very shallow and small enclosures. Apart from the possibilities of its use in elegantly slim table lamps, reading lamps, and pendant luminaires in the home, there were innumerable applications where a shallow square opal tablet would prove useful, e.g. for underneath wall cupboards in a kitchen, as the basic element for a hotel corridor luminaire, or as an illuminated number plate beside the house door.

Such wide applications made a highly-tooled opal acrylic enclosure for 2D lamps a good commercial base for the introduction of a new range of luminaires into a market where a rapid introduction would be important. Behind the lamp, or alongside it if a slim unit were to be achieved, would be the necessary ballast. The housing of this and the base mounting for the lamp and the opal could utilize a variety of plastic mouldings or metal pressings, depending on the application.

Fig. 19.10   Master track/spot

Figure 19.11 shows one example of the first generation of 2D luminaires, known as the 'Wedge', designed for outdoor use. The version illustrated in Fig. 19.11a is a single unit: it can either be wall mounted or be mounted on the top of a high or low pole, thus serving to light entrances, paths, or drives. A modified end pressing permits the use of two Wedges back-to-back for pole mounting (Fig. 19.11b). The unit will operate down to −10 °C, with the opal enclosure gasketed to provide the necessary degree of rain-proofing.

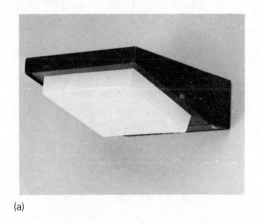

(a)

(b)

Fig. 19.11   2D Wedge: (a) single and (b) twin

Further reading

Bean A R and Simons R H, 1968, *Lighting fittings performance and design* (Oxford: Pergamon)

Part IV
Interior lighting

20 The interior environment

The essential purpose of a building is to modify the natural climate over a specific area in order that various human activities can be carried out efficiently and comfortably. Electric lighting, the concern of the second half of this book, is just one of several building services which are used, together with the basic building structure, to produce a satisfactory interior environment. Nowadays, lighting design takes into account several interactions between lighting, other services, and the building structure. This chapter, after considering the non-visual criteria that make for a satisfactory environment, considers three points of interaction – the window, the suspended ceiling, and the mechanical services system – firstly as isolated elements and secondly when featuring in co-ordinated design.

20.1 The well-tempered environment

20.1.1 Visual phenomena

The visual environment, in which lighting plays a part, is more immediately apparent to most people than is either the thermal or the aural aspect of the environment, at least until they have to work in it.

As has been shown in Chap. 2, the visual sense is a very powerful one and a very complex one. Equally complex would be any set of criteria purporting to define a satisfactory visual environment. Within such a set would be found lighting criteria, pointers to some of which have been outlined in Chap. 2. These pointers are more frequently limits of acceptability than specific targets. So when the basics of interior lighting design are spelt out in Chap. 21 it will be found that constraints to prevent an ill-tempered visual environment are at least as numerous as criteria to encourage a well-tempered one.

20.1.2 Acoustics

Sound is a form of energy, produced by a vibrating source and propagated through any elastic medium, which stimulates the sensation of hearing. The essentials of a good interior environment in acoustical terms are that the occupants of the interior should be able to hear the sources of sound they wish to hear, while being isolated from other, intruding, sounds. Apart from auditoria, which have very specific acoustic requirements, the dominant acoustic factor influencing satisfaction with the interior environment tends to be the degree of control of unwanted sound – noise.

Vibrational energy to which the human ear responds ranges roughly from 20 Hz to 20 kHz, the maximum response being in the region 3 kHz to 5 kHz, falling away at higher and lower frequencies. The presence of sound can be detected by a cyclic increase and decrease in atmospheric pressure, so one way of defining the quantity of sound would be the r.m.s. value of this alternating pressure (measured in pascals). Since there is a power flow associated with this pressure disturbance, the power density or intensity ($W m^{-2}$) could also be used. In fact the quantity of sound is expressed in decibels, where the intensity or pressure (I or p) is expressed on a logarithmic scale with respect to a reference value (I_0 or p_0) near the threshold of human hearing.

$$\text{sound level (decibels)} = 10 \log_{10}\left(\frac{I}{I_0}\right) = 20 \log_{10}\left(\frac{p}{p_0}\right) \text{ dB}$$

The threshold values, I_0 and p_0, are $10^{-12} W m^{-2}$ and $2 \times 10^{-5} Pa$ respectively: the range of hearing extends from here to a threshold of pain at I and p values of about $1 W m^{-2}$ and $20 Pa$ respectively. Thus, sound levels experienced in practice range from 0 dB to 120 dB.

Noise criteria In industrial environments, where considerable noise is associated with the industrial processes taking place, noise limits used to be set with respect to the potential damage to the human hearing mechanism. Short exposure to sound levels of 140–150 dB upwards is dangerous, as is prolonged exposure to 80–90 dB unless the noise is predominantly low frequency (under 500 Hz). Nowadays, noise limits are set at lower levels, showing more consideration for human comfort.

In commercial buildings noise criteria based on the average sound level in the three octave bands 600 Hz to 4800 Hz were used in the past in the belief that this measure gave a good indication of speech interference. Nowadays, for offices and for a wide section of other interiors, the use of noise criteria (NC) or noise rating (NR) curves is preferred. Either of these, the first favoured in the USA and the second in Europe, produce safer criteria for speech interference. They can also provide criteria for annoyance, given certain corrections for different types of sound.

Some criteria and NR curves are shown in Fig. 20.1. The noise limit for a private office is stated there to be NR 40: this requires that the spectrum of ambient sound, when plotted on the graph, should lie entirely below the curve NR 40 for the noise climate to be acceptable. In the case of dwellings (living room or bedroom) the appropriate NR criterion requires correcting, depending on the nature of the noise and the zoning of the dwelling, before comparing the spectrum with a NR curve.

A steady ambient noise level considerably lower than the appropriate NR specification may prove to be as unacceptable as one which is higher, because of the effect of one sound on another (known as 'masking'). A steady low level ambient noise may reduce to imperceptability, or at least to acceptability, the occasional distracting short-period sound. Equally, it might reduce speech sounds to unintelligibility and thereby provide a degree of privacy in an interior occupied by several people. For all this, it is rare to find a minimum noise level being specified for a working interior.

Sound propagation Sound is propagated through any elastic medium – which excludes only a vacuum – but how much sound is transmitted and how much is absorbed in travelling through an element of a building depends on the nature of the element.

The dominant characteristic influencing the sound transmission loss between two spaces in a building is the mass per unit area of the intervening medium. Webb (1976) has found that this 'mass law' of sound insulation can be expressed approximately by taking $(14 \cdot 5 \log_{10} M + 10)$ dB as the mean sound transmission loss introduced by a dividing element of mass M kg m^{-2}, for M in the range 1 to 500. This expression shows

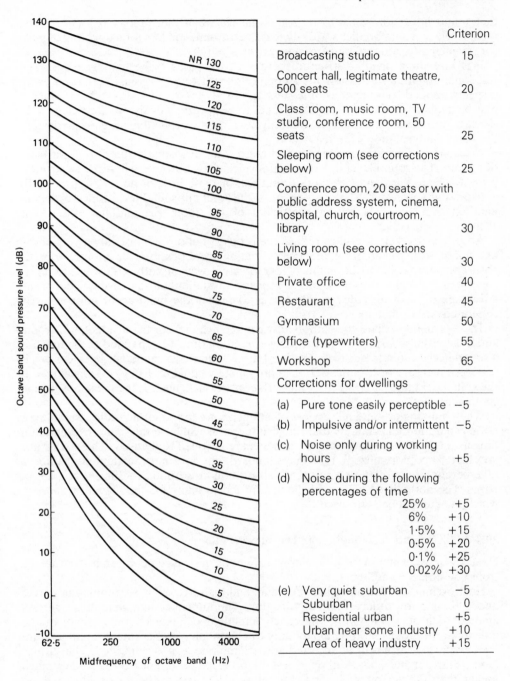

	Criterion
Broadcasting studio	15
Concert hall, legitimate theatre, 500 seats	20
Class room, music room, TV studio, conference room, 50 seats	25
Sleeping room (see corrections below)	25
Conference room, 20 seats or with public address system, cinema, hospital, church, courtroom, library	30
Living room (see corrections below)	30
Private office	40
Restaurant	45
Gymnasium	50
Office (typewriters)	55
Workshop	65

Corrections for dwellings

(a)	Pure tone easily perceptible	−5
(b)	Impulsive and/or intermittent	−5
(c)	Noise only during working hours	+5
(d)	Noise during the following percentages of time	
	25%	+5
	6%	+10
	1·5%	+15
	0·5%	+20
	0·1%	+25
	0·02%	+30
(e)	Very quiet suburban	−5
	Suburban	0
	Residential urban	+5
	Urban near some industry	+10
	Area of heavy industry	+15

Fig. 20.1 Noise rating curves with tables of criteria and corrections

that sound insulation tends to be somewhat less than that predicted by acoustical theory, which would predict a 6 dB increase in transmission loss for a doubling of mass (or, incidentally, a doubling of frequency).

It is rare for a dividing structure between two spaces to be homogeneous. The fractional sound transmission of a composite structure of areas A_1 and A_2 with respective sound transmissions of T_1 and T_2 is $(T_1A_1 + T_2A_2)/(A_1 + A_2)$, from which it may be deduced that sound insulation tends to be governed by the weakest element in the structure. Thus, for example, a relatively narrow surrounding air gap can destroy the potential insulation of a heavy door.

A second factor in the propagation of noise is the acoustical nature of the surfaces of a room. The sound level in a room into which noise obtrudes will increase strongly if the walls are hard and reverberant, but will increase little or not at all if the walls are soft and absorbent. The component of the resultant sound level which is dependent on the mean absorption coefficient of the room (α) and its area (A) is $10\log(1 - \alpha)/\alpha A$ dB.

Absorbers are very useful to reduce the propagation of fan noise down ventilation ducts, but with the limit of practical variation in α possible for rooms, acoustic absorption turns out to be a much less effective way of cutting down externally-generated noise in a room than is acoustic insulation of the room. The prime advantage of 'acoustic' tiles in interiors is to reduce the build-up of noise actually generated within that space.

There is an immediate correlation between the liveliness or the deadness of a room and its acoustic absorption. The term 'reverberation time' (T_r), defined as the time for a sound in the room to decay by 60 dB after the source of a sound has been cut off, is used as a measure of liveliness. T_r is approximately equal to $0.16\,V/\alpha A$ s, where V is the volume of the room (m³), A is the surface area (m²), and α is the mean absorption coefficient.

When building or building services components are tested for acoustic insulation or noise generation it is unlikely that the testing spaces will have the same reverberation time as the spaces in which the components are destined to be used. The test results are therefore 'normalized' to some standard interior, most commonly either a reverberation time of 1 s or a reference absorption (absorption coefficient × area) of 10 m². The normalized values are later adjusted to allow for the actual interiors in which the components are used.

20.1.3   Temperature, humidity, and air movement

Heat, the most common form of energy, cannot be destroyed but it can be transferred from one object to another.

Heat exchanges take place between man and his surroundings, stimulating nerves under his skin to produce thermal sensation. The human system generates a certain amount of heat at all times, the exact amount depending on the activity of the individual. In order that the human body can maintain constant internal temperature the metabolic heat has to be rejected at the same rate as it is generated. The surface temperature of the body, although less than the blood temperature, is very much higher than the surrounding air temperature. Heat can therefore be liberated via the skin to the ambient air at rates depending on the temperature difference, the insulation value of clothing, and the rate of air movement around the body surface.

Veins and capillaries near the surface of the skin expand and contract according to the stimulus received by the nerves. If the blood temperature drops, indicating excessive loss of body heat, the capillaries will contract, allowing less blood to flow to the skin. The skin temperature will then drop, reducing the rate of heat loss. If the losses continue from the skin, involuntary shivering or 'goose-pimples' occur to induce activity and generate more heat. If in hot conditions the body cannot shed heat fast enough, the internal temperature rises and heat rejection turns to sweating, the released moisture eventually being evaporated. Rapid body cooling can take place in this way, but its effectiveness depends on both the humidity and rate of movement of air around the body. If the body cannot reject heat at the same rate that it is generated, heat exhaustion or heat stroke eventually takes place.

Radiant heat has a great effect on skin temperature. With large areas of heat-radiating surfaces, comfortable conditions can be maintained at low air temperatures since they can supply sufficient heat to keep skin temperature at comfort level. Equally, large areas of heat-absorbing surfaces, such as cold windows, can cause discomfort even in moderate ambient temperatures.

Clothing has a major effect on the regulation of body heat gain or loss: it functions as insulation and offers protection against loss or gain.

Comfort criteria   The factors which influence thermal comfort or discomfort are air temperature, room surface temperatures, fresh air level, air movement, and humidity. For each of these five there is a range of values for comfort: it is not generally possible to compensate for shortcomings in one by careful attention to another.

Air temperature should lie between 18 °C and 22 °C. The upper value tends to be enjoyed by women and is also appropriate for people over 40 years. The lower limit is used where heating is by radiant means and the work carried out is not sedentary. The gradation of air temperature vertically between head and toe should not exceed 3 °C, and differences between the temperature of adjacent rooms or between incoming air and room air need to be limited to 10 °C. The average temperature of the walls should not be more than 3 °C lower than that of the air to avoid the sensation of stuffiness, and should preferably be higher.

Fresh air should be supplied at a minimum rate of about $5 \, \mathrm{l\,s^{-1}}$ per occupant of the room. This rate of change is normally sufficient to prevent high concentrations of contaminants, but in crowded or smoky areas the rate should be doubled.

There should be adequate air movement, variable rather than uniform. A general movement of $0 \cdot 1 \, \mathrm{m\,s^{-1}}$ is acceptable, increasing up to $0 \cdot 25 \, \mathrm{m\,s^{-1}}$ to achieve a sense of freshness, but with no higher velocities in the occupied zone, otherwise there will be complaints of draughts.

The relative humidity should be between 40 and 70%. High humidity produces a feeling of chill at low air temperature and oppressiveness at high air temperatures, while low humidity causes a sensation of dryness and allows a significant build-up of static electricity on many objects.

Much of the success in providing thermal comfort indoors will depend on the shaping, siting, and orientation of the building and on the insulation and fenestration of its walls and roofs. It is the building structure which provides the coarse adjustment of the external climate, with the fine control being achieved by the mechanical services.

20.1.4   Energy considerations

The acknowledgement that the availability of fossil fuel is decreasing rapidly has led to an increasing concern world-wide about the sensible use of energy. It has been estimated that about one-half of the energy consumed in the UK is currently used in producing acceptable environments in and around buildings – mainly in heating.

These facts, coupled with the increasing cost of energy, have resulted in energy conservation techniques being taken very seriously in recent years in the designing of buildings and of building services.

A logical approach to the problem of energy conservation is to adopt energy targets for all environmental services installed in buildings. These may be set in terms of energy demand or energy consumption.

Energy demand targets determine the design of the building envelope and the equipment in it. They are readily applied to new buildings and allow a balance to be made at the design stage between one factor and another to yield an economic and viable solution. This method also encourages the exploitation of new techniques.

Energy consumption targets govern mainly the use of the building and its services. They may be achieved by rationing or costing, but frequently factors beyond the user's control upset the situation, for example a change in the climatic conditions or the building use. Despite this problem, energy consumption targets do encourage the user to balance large energy-consuming equipment, to use automatic controls, and to implement good housekeeping.

The CIBS (1977c) has introduced the first part of a four-part Building Energy Code to guide the designers of buildings and their services towards energy-consciousness. The documents contain energy targets as well as methods for estimating and controlling energy consumption: they emphasize the importance of choosing efficient equipment and operation programmes, in addition to which they highlight the roles played by integrated lighting and air conditioning systems, the co-ordination of daylighting with the electric lighting, and the switching and control of lighting systems to save energy.

20.2   Elements of environmental significance

20.2.1   Windows and daylight penetration

The sun is the basic source of our natural light. At the earth's surface daylight consists of two components. One component is that coming directly from the sun, referred to as sunlight. In the course of passing through the earth's atmosphere some sunlight is always scattered (particularly the shorter wavelengths, giving a blue appearance) and this reaches us from the whole vault of sky. In the presence of clouds the direct sunlight is also diffused. The sum total of the diffused and the scattered light is the second component of our daylight and is referred to as skylight.

The quality of daylight received and the relative size of the sun and sky components depend on the position of the sun and atmospheric conditions. Hunt (1979) has analysed meteorological data in this country over a ten-year period and produced figures of the availability, by the hour and by the month, of daylight and its components, recording horizontal illuminances of up to 125 kilolux. Daylight has a correlated colour temperature in the range 4000 K to 100 000 K: the upper values corresponding to clear blue sky and the lower values to direct sunlight.

Daylight factor   The daylight inside a building varies from moment to moment and from point to point. The variation with time follows a similar pattern to that out of doors: with a densely overcast sky the patterns are identical. The fundamental measure of the quantity of daylight at a point indoors, the *daylight factor*, is the ratio of the daylight illuminance (usually horizontal) at the point to the horizontal illuminance simultaneously existing under an obstructed overcast sky: it is usually expressed as a percentage rather than as a fraction.

Daylight at a point is composed of light coming through the windows, directly from the sky and reflected from objects outside, together with inter-reflected light from the walls and ceiling of the room. In a sidelit room the light through the window produces most of the high daylight factors near the window wall, while the inter-reflected daylight is responsible for most of the low daylight factors far away from the windows. The variation of daylight over the room can be described by plotting daylight factor contours. A CIBS/IES technical report on daytime lighting (CIBS 1972) gives a summary of methods of producing such contours.

An indication of the general subjective adequacy of the daylighting provided in a room is given by the average daylight factor. For a sidelit room this can be evaluated from the expression $\tau A_g \theta / A_t (1 - \bar{\rho})\%$, where A_g and A_t are respectively the area of window glass and all room surfaces (ceiling, floor, walls, and windows), τ is the transmittance of the window glass, $\bar{\rho}$ is the average (area-weighted) room surface reflectance, and θ is the angle subtended in the vertical plane normal to the window wall by the sky visible from the centre of the window.

Broadly speaking, an average daylight factor of 5% gives a room a cheerful appearance, whereas in rooms with under 2% the daylight will normally be judged inadequate. However, the BSI is producing a *Draft for development – Basic data for the design of buildings – Daylight* to succeed an earlier daylight code, which gives a schedule of recommendations for average daylight factors for a variety of interiors, working and recreational. These are given for situations described as 'full daylighting' and 'supplemented daylighting' (a topic considered in Sect. 20.3.3).

In addition to average daylight factors, the BSI schedule recommends that the minimum daylight factor in a sidelit working interior should not be less than 0·3 of the average and it includes recommendations on the minimum window area (for the sake of the view) and on the maximum values of daylight glare. This emphasizes the point that the intelligent design of windows involves much more than providing an adequate penetration of illumination. Such matters as the flow of light and the view out are discussed by Lynes (1968) in his monograph on daylighting principles.

20.2.2 Suspended ceilings

The prime role of the suspended ceiling was originally to conceal unsightly services, such as pipes, cables, ducts, and untidy structural elements. It has proved to be an asset in connection with the thermal environment as well as the visual one. In an air conditioned building the void between the suspended ceiling and the structural ceiling is almost certain to be used as the manifold termination of either the air supply or, more commonly, the exhaust system.

In acoustic terms the suspended ceiling can be an asset or a liability. Its asset is that unlike the structural ceiling, where strength is important, the dominant material of a suspended ceiling can be selected to provide a suitable degree of sound absorption for the interior and, since most absorbing materials are fragile and liable to damage, the ceiling is a good place to locate them. The liability of the suspended ceiling is in the all too common situation where space is partitioned below a suspended ceiling with inadequate sound insulation properties: the physically separated areas then become one acoustically. Lightweight (say, under $20\,kg\,m^{-2}$) single-skin ceilings are unlikely to give adequate insulation in quiet environments, as are heavier or multilayer ceilings with ill-fitting components or ill-designed air supply/extract units.

A suspended ceiling is made up of hangers, a grid, and infill panels. The hangers are steel wires, rods, or straps, normally fixed directly to the structural ceiling and giving a ceiling suspension depth of between 100 mm and 1500 mm. There are three main types of grid system, illustrated in Fig. 20.2. In the simplest, the exposed tee system, infill panels, luminaires, air diffusers, etc. all lie directly on the main tees. The concealed

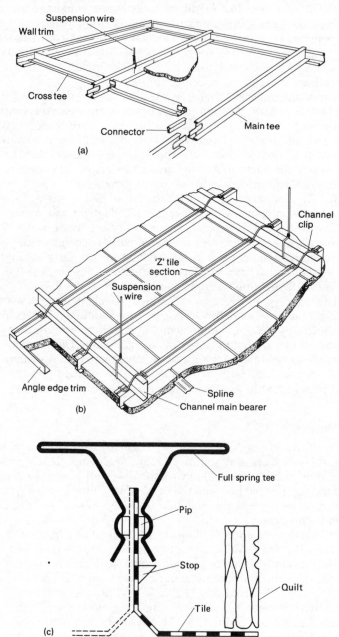

Fig. 20.2 Suspended ceilings: (a) exposed tee, (b) concealed fix, and (c) spring tee

fix system needs more careful planning and erection since all the ceiling components are needed simultaneously. In the spring tee system, like the exposed tee, there is no problem in installing or removing individual panels or components.

There are infill panels of many different materials: the choice may be made on visual, acoustic, and/or air-tightness grounds. Fibre boards and tiles can provide a high degree of sound absorption, but with a mass per unit area of about 4 kg m^{-2} they offer little sound insulation: they commonly require a PVC or foil backing to make them air-tight. Cast plaster tiles, much heavier at about 15 kg m^{-2}, provide good sound insulation, but little absorption: when perforated and backed with mineral or glasswool their sound absorption improves, but with an increase in air-leakage. Pressed-metal trays, usually painted zinc-coated steel or aluminium, are lighter than plaster tiles and can also be plain or perforated.

Suspended ceilings may feature translucent panels or louvres, with lamps above them: they are then usually called luminous ceilings. Whether formed of films stretched over a frame or as self-supporting vacuum-formed shapes, the panels are very light, typically 2–3 kg m^{-2}, and have no acoustic significance. They tend to be used on exposed tee grids for ease of maintenance and access because the cavity must be kept highly reflective and the panels clean if they are to form an efficient lighting system.

20.2.3 Heating, ventilating, and air conditioning systems

Although the envelope of a building protects the occupants from the extremes of the external climate, additional plant is inevitable if the comfort conditions quoted in Sect. 20.1.3 are to be provided in the UK. Heating will most likely be needed in winter and forced ventilation will be required in all but the shallowest of buildings. If, in addition, cooling is required in part of a building or for part of the year, an air conditioning plant becomes necessary.

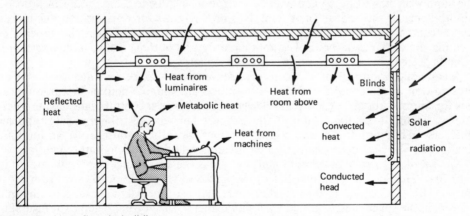

Fig. 20.3 Heat flow in buildings

Figure 20.3 indicates the different sources of heat gains in a room, with the biggest contribution likely to be due to natural radiation from the sun and sky. In addition to radiation transmitted directly through the window glass, there is a heat gain due to the natural radiation which has been absorbed by the opaque surfaces of a building. The size of this heat gain depends on the external climate and on the orientation and nature of the building structure: calculation methods are described in guides produced by the CIBS (1971). Other gains are from people (100–150 W per person), lighting (10–40 W m^{-2}), and other electrical equipment (up to 30 W m^{-2} in non-industrial locations).

There is a heat gain or loss by conduction through the room boundary surfaces, depending on the relative temperatures on either side of the boundaries and the thermal transmittance of the boundaries. Additionally, forced ventilation and natural ventilation, deliberate or accidental, produce an infiltration heat load which also is a net loss or gain, depending on the temperatures inside and out.

Taking the winter situation, when the room temperature is set to comfort conditions, the conduction and infiltration heat losses are likely to exceed the heat gains, and the necessary balance has to be provided by a heating system.

The simplest form of thermal conditioning in this country is a heating system operated locally or centrally, the source of fuel being electricity, coal, gas, or oil. Heat is generated in boilers, carried by hot water or steam and distributed by pipes to radiators where the heat is transferred to the space by radiation and convection. The usual place to site radiators is under windows where the highest heat losses will normally occur and where they combat the discomfort arising from cold windows. During the summer the heating is switched off and, if needed, cooling is introduced by partial opening of windows.

Natural ventilation can only be induced into relatively small areas; in deeper buildings forced ventilation is required. Forced ventilation may be produced locally or centrally, a local plant usually consisting of a fan unit sited on an outside wall or a roof. A central plant consists of a fan taking in fresh air which is distributed by ducts to the various areas where it is diffused into the room. Forced ventilation can provide some cooling, but its effectiveness largely depends on the outside air temperature and humidity.

Air conditioning   It is not uncommon to find buildings where summer cooling loads are much greater than could be supplied by a simple ventilation system. In such cases the supply air has to be cooled well below room or outside temperature in order to absorb some of the heat in the room. This process calls for refrigeration, which is a major component of an air conditioning plant. Air conditioning is the process of treating the air so as to control, simultaneously and automatically, its temperature, humidity, cleanliness, distribution, and movement.

An air conditioning plant may consist of self-contained package units installed in an outside wall of the conditioned space, but these are suitable neither for large spaces nor for internal rooms. A more usual system consists of a central plant having filter, cooler, heater, humidifier supply, and exhaust fan with distribution ducts and air diffusers. In addition to diffusing the air into the space, the air diffusers or air terminal devices may be active in mixing air or providing additional temperature control.

The simplest form of air conditioning system is the single duct system illustrated in Fig. 20.4. Exhaust air is drawn out of the space to be conditioned, and fresh air is mixed with it. The air is then heated or cooled, to an extent defined by thermal sensors in the space, and returned via a single duct to the air supply units (diffusers) in the space. In this single duct system the air supplied at each outlet is constant in volume, but variable in temperature. There is an alternative (VAV) single duct system in which the air supply temperature is held constant and the volume of air is varied. There are also dual-duct systems, where terminal mixing units are supplied from the central plant with hot and cold air in separate ducts. Finally, there are various types of systems involving the circulation around a building of small volumes of hot or cold water instead of large volumes of air, the air to be conditioned being drawn over water coils for a temperature change.

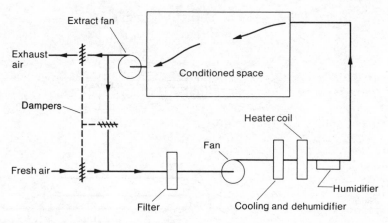

Fig. 20.4 Single duct air conditioning system

Air diffusion The success of an air conditioning system is judged at least as much by the way the supply air is diffused into space as by its temperature and humidity. The significant part of space is the 'occupied zone' – from floor level to 1·8 m above it – and within this zone there has to be sufficient air movement to prevent stagnation, yet not so much movement that draughts are caused. The location of air terminal diffusers (ATDs) and their discharge characteristics are therefore critical.

Supply air leaves an ATD at speed and pulls room air into its train. As this mixing (entrainment) takes place, the velocity of the air stream falls. The most useful performance characteristic of an ATD is the three-dimensional surface contour joining points where the air velocity has fallen to 0·25 m s^{-1} – the maximum subjectively-acceptable air movement. For a ceiling mounted ATD this surface is succinctly described by the three parameters of throw, spread, and drop, which are effectively defined in Fig. 20.5. Due to the way a supply air stream tends to cling to flat surfaces near an ATD (the Coanda effect) the presence of the ceiling gives this ATD a long throw and a shallow drop.

Air diffusion design consists of the intelligent manoeuvring of the location and/or the shapes of ATD discharge envelopes on building plans to guarantee the avoidance of stagnation and draughts. Additionally, exhaust points need to be located so that no short-circuiting of the supply air can take place.

20.3 Co-ordinated design features

20.3.1 Air-handling luminaires

As stated in Sect. 20.2.3, one of the thermal loads imposed on a building is generated by the lighting equipment. An illuminance of 750 lux in a deep plan building implies an electrical load somewhere between 20 W m^{-2} and 40 W m^{-2}, depending on the efficacy of the light sources and luminaires employed. This loading represents nearly half the total electrical energy used in commercial buildings; all this energy finally appears as a heat gain, and becomes a cooling load on any air conditioning plant.

In a fluorescent tube luminaire this heat increases the ambient temperature in the lamp compartment with a consequent rise in the tube wall temperature and a resulting loss of light output, about 1% per °C rise.

These two problems can be reduced by the use of air-handling luminaires, designed

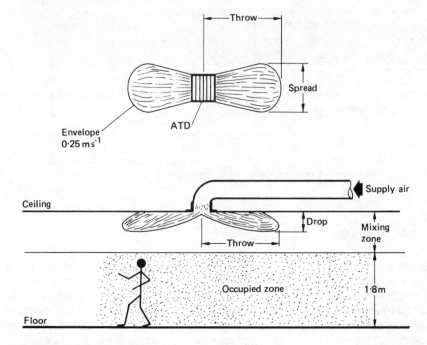

Fig. 20.5 Discharge characteristics of air terminal diffusers

to permit the forced air in the return air path of a ventilation or air conditioning plant to flow through them. This provides an efficient removal of much of the heat generated by the lamps and gear, energy removed at its source and potentially re-usable.

Air-handling luminaires are often no different to normal types except for air slots in the body. They are designed to integrate with most available types of ceiling. The housing or body is generally fabricated from sheet steel, finished with high reflectance stove enamel. The two main types of optical systems in use today are the low brightness batwing reflector and the enclosed prismatic controller type, illustrated with their air paths shown in Fig. 20.6.

The reflector type offers a distinct advantage in that the shape of the reflector profile and the location of the return air slots above the lamps can be designed to control the direction and velocity of the air flow to ensure that maximum heat transfer takes place. At the same time the air flow scavenges dirt and dust from the reflector and lamp surfaces, reducing depreciation dramatically. Heat pick-up efficiencies are of the order of 65–75%.

In the enclosed type of luminaire the air flow path is not so easily controlled, but it has the advantage that the plastic lens will absorb most of the infrared energy emitted which can then be picked up by the air stream. To minimize dirt entry dust traps are often included in the design of the inlet slots. 80–85% heat pick-up efficiencies can be achieved.

A typical set of air-handling characteristics is reproduced in Fig. 20.7. These data are for a recessed luminaire designed for use in a plenum-exhaust air conditioning system – one in which the ceiling void acts as a large exhaust manifold. The pressure drop across such a luminaire should not be allowed to exceed 20 Pa, otherwise the

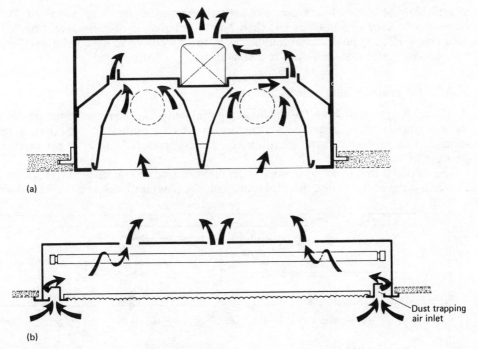

(a)

(b)

Dust trapping
air inlet

Fig. 20.6 Air-handling luminaires: (a) louvred reflector and (b) enclosed prismatic

air-leakage through weaknesses in the ceiling become more than the 10–20% which can be tolerated in most schemes.

Additionally, two sets of acoustic characteristics are often produced for air-handling luminaires. One of these is the level of noise generation at different air flow rates, commonly given as NR numbers. The other is the degree of sound insulation which would be found across a very heavy ceiling with the luminaire inserted, sometimes described as the 'crosstalk attenuation', expressed in dB. The design of the air path

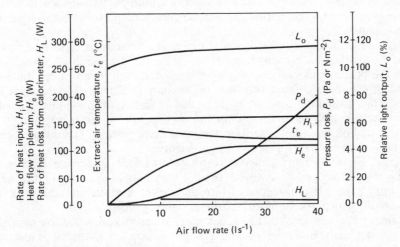

Fig. 20.7 Typical data for an air-handling luminaire

affects both of these, but a smooth path encountering no sharp edges or loose components, with air velocities less than $2\,\mathrm{m\,s^{-1}}$, is necessary if noise levels are to be kept below NR 25. Fluorescent luminaires to this specification have been developed with crosstalk attenuation values reaching 35 dB.

20.3.2 Integrated ceiling systems

A natural progression from the air-handling luminaire has been the development of the integrated ceiling system – a structure in which lighting, air diffusion, sound control, fire protection, and partitioning are co-ordinated. It is a pre-designed package of solutions.

The essential feature of a modular integrated ceiling system of the type shown in Fig. 20.8 is the grid. Ideally, this grid represents the planning module size and contains

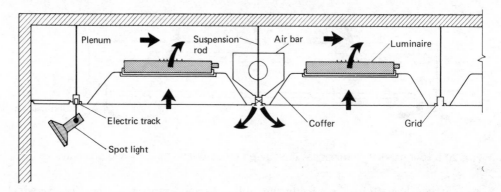

Fig. 20.8 Section of integrated ceiling system

all the necessary environmental service elements. The grid consists of twin tee, 'H' or top-hat sections, usually 50 mm to 100 mm wide and cut to modular lengths of 1200 mm, 1500 mm, or 1800 mm. The grid forms a square or rectangular frame and is designed to support the weight of a number of additional items, such as air diffusers, luminaires, electric track, sprinklers, smoke detectors, partitions, and signs as well as the infill panels.

Supply air diffusers may be modular or linear. A modular diffuser drops into the grid and consists of a plenum box with a spigot for flexible duct connection. In its mouth the box contains an air controller shaped so that it can direct the air flow in specific directions. A linear diffuser, or air bar, is usually 10 m to 20 m long and formed either from steel covered with thermal insulation or from mineral or glass fibre boards: these boards have aluminium foil on one side to act as a vapour seal and a neoprene seal on the other side to minimize fibre migration. The ducts, clipped onto the grid, can be end- or top-fed through spigots.

Exhaust air is normally collected through air-handling luminaires. For modular systems the luminaires have to be small enough to fit into either the grid width or an infill panel. It is possible to introduce electric track into the grid, single or multi-circuit, which can support additional lighting units.

For fire protection, smoke or heat detectors are used, connected to a central control system and ideally mounted on the grid for maximum coverage. However, their location has to be governed by the discharge patterns of the ATDs since smoke or heat could be diverted away from the detectors. Sprinklers are used for controlling a fire: since they must maintain their position the system is fitted to the structural ceiling with the heads projecting through the suspended grid at junctions of modules.

Infill panels usually consist of preformed coffer units of phenolic resin bonded mineral felt, glass reinforced gypsum/plastic, or metal. Cut and assembled flat mineral fibre boards are also used. The one-piece coffers are ideal for supporting luminaires and are easy to remove for changes in the lighting or the room layout. The panels are finished in matt white, plain or textured, and are made airtight for plenum-exhaust systems.

Modular ceilings must readily accept demountable partitions, usually consisting of sandwiched panels, stud panels, or frame and panel. They are normally supported by jacking bolts on the floor and are stabilized by a head channel fitted to or offered by the grid, the channels being filled with a rubber gasket to allow for compression during jacking. These demountable partitions range from 50 mm to 100 mm in thickness with sound insulation values of 25 dB to 40 dB.

When planning an integrated ceiling system the designer needs to know the operation and performance characteristics not only of each component, but also of the assembled system. They not only offer savings in design time, installation time, and materials, but are also easy to service.

20.3.3 Natural and electric lighting

PSALI Frequently, the occupants of interior spaces in a working interior with side windows believe their working light is inadequate despite having electric lighting providing the recommended illuminance for the task in hand. This happens when either the workers involved can see a large area of unobstructed sky or when there is a rapid gradient of daylight factor between them and the window wall – neither of which would occur with a well-designed window system.

The problem is one of brightness balance, and the solution suggested by Hopkinson and Longmore (1959) was PSALI – permanent supplementary artificial lighting in interiors – exemplified by Fig. 20.9a, where by day less electric lighting is on in the outer zone (A off) and more in the interior zone (C on). Theoretically, even if rarely in practice, the interior lighting in such a scheme would illuminate vertical surfaces particularly well, because the object of the exercise is brightness-enhancement.

Switch/dim systems Interest in PSALI sagged in the 1960s and 1970s, but surfaced again in the early 1980s in a rather different form as an energy conservation measure, exemplified by Fig. 20.9b. On the assumption that there has been intelligent window design, there is no need for a supplementary row of luminaires in the interior, but the remaining four rows are on separate circuits. Near to the window, under row A, daylight illuminance would be adequate for the task in hand for most of the day. Under row B, with a lower daylight factor, electric light would be needed for longer. It may be that under D electric light would be necessary all day.

Three levels of sophistication can be recognized. The lowest is to provide manual switches and hope that individuals will switch their respective rows on and off as needed. Studies at the Building Research Establishment (Crisp 1978) showed that switch-on will occur, but switch-off will not. The next level of sophistication is to have a photocell monitor the variation of daylight outdoors and automatically switch on or off the appropriate rows, knowing the daylight factor variation across the room. As opposed to this on–off open-loop system, the third level is a dimming closed-loop system, where photocells monitor the illumination on sample tasks across the room

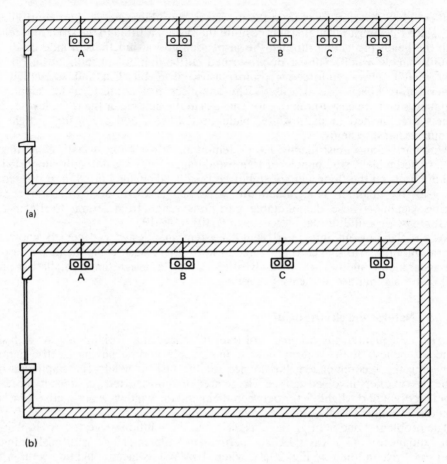

Fig. 20.9 Lighting arrangements: (a) for PSALI (B and C on by day, A and B on by night) and (b) for switch/dim systems

and dim up and down appropriate banks of luminaires to maintain a specified working lighting level. Of these, the on–off system is the least popular subjectively, the manual switching is the cheapest, and the third system saves the most power.

Further reading

Bedford T, 1964, *Basic principles of ventilation and heating*, 2nd Edition (London: H K Lewis)

Boje A, 1971, *Open plan offices* (London: Business Books)

Croome D J, 1977, *Noise, buildings and people* (Oxford: Pergamon Press)

Day B F, Ford R D and Lord P, 1969, *Building acoustics* (London: Applied Science)

Harris C M, 1957, *Handbook of noise control* (New York: McGraw-Hill)

Hopkinson R G, Petherbridge P and Longmore J, 1966, *Daylighting* (London: Heineman)

Jones W P, 1973, *Air conditioning engineering* (London: Edward Arnold)

Kell J R and Martin P L, 1971, *Heating and air conditioning of buildings*, 5th Edition (London: The Architectural Press)

Kinzey B Y and Sharp H M, 1963, *Environmental technologies in architecture* (Englewood Cliffs, New Jersey: Prentice-Hall)

Markus T A and Morris E N, 1980, *Buildings, climate and energy* (London: Pitman)

McIntyre D A, 1980, *Indoor climate* (London: Applied Science)

Parkin P H and Humphreys H R, 1969, *Acoustics, noise and buildings* (London: Faber & Faber)

Pilkington Brothers Ltd, 1969, *Windows and environment* (Newton-le-Willows, Lancs: McCorquodale & Co)

Taylor R, 1970, *Noise* (London: Penguin Books)

21 Interior lighting design

Lighting is an art as well as a science, which implies that there are no hard and fast rules of design. Nor will there be one ideal or optimum solution to a particular lighting problem. More often than not, the lighting designer finds himself with a set of conflicting requirements to which priorities have to be allocated before a satisfactory compromise can be found.

This chapter can therefore do little more than give general guidance: firstly on the requirements of lighting, secondly on some of the critical decisions which need to be made during the process, and thirdly on the relevant calculation procedures. It should be read in conjunction with the four chapters which follow, and with the CIBS/IES Code for Interior Lighting (CIBS 1977a).

21.1 Lighting objectives and criteria

Figure 21.1 gives a flowchart showing a sequence of steps in planning a lighting scheme, the first stage of which is the important one of establishing the design objectives. Ignore this step and the result is design by default.

21.1.1 Lighting design objectives

The lighting objectives can be considered under three broad headings:

(a) Safety and health.
(b) Performance.
(c) Appearance and comfort.

Safety and health Interior lighting should enable the occupants to see sufficiently well to work and move about in safety, both under normal conditions and in the event of an emergency involving a power failure. The lighting must not create conditions which are injurious to people's health, requiring, for example, the elimination of harmful radiation, the prevention of eye strain, and the control of glare.

Performance The type of work which takes place and the characteristics of the workforce together define the nature and variety of the visual tasks in an interior. The quantity and quality of the lighting required to achieve satisfactory visual conditions depends on these tasks, ideally analysed in terms of size, contrast, duration, age of observer, colour discrimination, complexity, etc.

Appearance and comfort The way in which a space is illuminated can affect its character and the appearance of objects within it (Sect. 2.4). Where the creation of

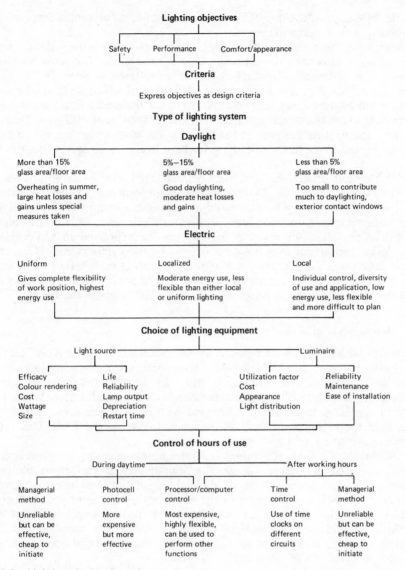

Fig. 21.1 Lighting design flowchart

mood or atmosphere is predominant this must be the prime lighting objective, but some consideration should be given to this factor in all designs.

The designer should attempt to weight these objectives according to their relative importance. Quite clearly, safety objectives must never be ignored or mitigated. For sustained working environments, such as offices and factories, performance will normally rank more important than appearance. In general interiors with few sustained visual tasks for the majority of occupants, for example banks, shops, transport termini, etc., the balance between performance and appearance may be fairly even. In interiors devoted to relaxation and leisure with no primary visual tasks, such as discotheques, churches, domestic dwellings, and so on, appearance is usually more important than performance.

In addition to these lighting objectives, other design objectives should be considered, which usually take the form of physical constraints. The most obvious and most important of these is financial, a subject considered in Sect. 21.2.1, but it is desirable at this stage of the design to establish at least which method of economic assessment will be used at a later stage. Allied to the financial constraints is the need for the system to use the minimum amount of energy consistent with good design: this may involve the lighting designer in fundamental decisions about the use of daylight (Sect. 20.3.3), but more likely will affect his later decisions on system control (Sect. 21.2.4).

Once the lighting objectives have been defined, they must be expressed wherever possible in terms of realizable physical parameters to form a design specification. Not all the design objectives can be expressed as measurable quantities: for example the need to make an environment appear 'prestigious', 'efficient', or 'vibrant' cannot be quantified. Also, although many objectives can be expressed in physical terms, suitable design techniques may not exist or may be too cumbersome. Here, experience and judgement must replace calculation. Quantitative criteria can be cited in respect of illuminance, uniformity, and glare, and to some extent in respect of the spatial distribution of light on room surfaces and objects within the room.

21.1.2   Illuminance, uniformity, and glare

Illuminance   Such statutory instruments as the *Health and Safety at Work Act* (HMG 1974) and the *Factories Act* (HMG 1961) require that the lighting at places of work shall be both sufficient and suitable. Sufficiency is normally taken to imply an adequate quantity of light (illuminance) both on work tasks and in areas where people circulate. Legislation is normally concerned with what is adequate, which is less onerous than the recommendations in documents, such as the CIBS/IES Lighting Code, which are concerned with good practice.

The schedule in the Code recommends service illuminances for interiors according to the tasks involved, where the service illuminance is the mean illuminance throughout the maintenance cycle of the lighting system and averaged over the relevant area. The relevant area may be the whole of the interior or just that occupied by the tasks and their immediate surround. In the latter case the service illuminance of the general surround areas of a working environment should be based upon tasks that are carried out in these areas, but should not be less than one-third of the highest task illuminance or problems of adaptation will arise.

Illuminances should be increased if reflectances or contrasts in the tasks are unusually low, if errors would have serious consequences either in terms of cost or danger, or if the building is windowless and the standard service illuminance is less than 500 lux. Where eye protection is worn, or tasks must be viewed through transparent screens, the contrast of the task may well be reduced and, in such circumstances, the illuminance on the task should be increased in an attempt to compensate. Also, if the most onerous visual tasks are to be carried out by occupants with poor sight or an average age that is higher than normal, say over 50 years, then the designer would be justified in increasing the illuminance. Conversely, the illuminance may be decreased if the duration of the task is unusually short. The service illuminance should not be less than 750 lux for industrial processes involving critical colour matching.

The illuminance recommendations apply to the tasks themselves, which may be complex in both shape and position. This can cause major difficulties in both prediction and measurement. It is commonly assumed that the illuminance on the task will be the same as the illuminance on a plane at the same angle and position as the task. This is good enough for most practical purposes, but is, nevertheless, an assumption and its validity should always be questioned. It frequently happens that the location of the tasks is not precisely known, in which case a horizontal plane at workstation height is usually taken. Where vertical tasks are involved, but their orientation is not known, then mean vertical (i.e. cylindrical) illuminance may be used.

In addition to providing sufficient light for tasks to be carried out, the occupants must also feel that there is enough light. Experiments have shown that the correlation between average horizontal illuminance and observers' assessments of how well lit the room appears is poor. Conflicting evidence has suggested that scalar illuminance, cylindrical illuminance, or the geometric mean of cylindrical and horizontal illuminance are all possible correlates. Scalar illuminance is used in the Code as a criterion for circulation areas.

Uniformity of illuminance is important for three reasons. Firstly, excessive variations in illuminance mean that some parts receive less illumination than is desirable, whilst others receive more than is necessary. Secondly, the luminance of the immediate surround to a visual task can affect visual performance and comfort. Thirdly, excessively uneven lighting is liable to be judged subjectively as unsatisfactory. The Code recommends that the uniformity of illuminance, measured as the ratio of the minimum illuminance to the average illuminance *over the task area*, should not be less than 0·8. This is not to say that the horizontal illumination *over the room* should be perfectly uniform. Although such lighting would ensure that the relevant visual tasks could be carried out anywhere in the space, it implies a considerable wastage of energy in providing task lighting levels in non-critical areas. Uniform lighting is, on the whole, uninteresting; when correctly applied, non-uniformity can create interest and is frequently preferred.

Glare As has been explained in Chap. 2, excessively bright areas in the visual field can, separately or simultaneously, impair visual performance (disability glare) or cause visual discomfort (discomfort glare). Lighting systems in most working interiors are unlikely to cause significant disability glare, but a degree of discomfort glare is probable.

Discomfort glare systems for interior lighting fall into two groups: those defining luminance limits for acceptable luminaires and those evaluating discomfort glare indices for installations. As explained in Sects 2.4.1 and 5.5.1, the system used in the UK is one of the second group. The degree of discomfort glare which can be tolerated decreases as the task difficulty increases, and the UK system specifies an upper limit for the glare index for different situations, selected through experience and practice to represent a standard of visual comfort acceptable to most people. Limiting glare indices are specified in the range from 13 to 28 in steps of 3 units. No difference should be ascribed to alternative lighting schemes where the glare indices differ by only one or two units, and there is little merit in attempting to achieve a glare index lower than that required.

21.1.3 Room surfaces

It is rare for lighting designers to be in control of the selection of room surfaces, which is unfortunate when the characteristics of these surfaces affect glare, modelling, and lighting system efficiency as well as the appearance of the room. When the opportunity does arise to select colours, inexperienced designers may find it best to consider first how light or dark the colours should be (Munsell value), then select the hue (i.e. which colour), and then the saturation (Munsell chroma). Subdued colours are often chosen where a restful or dignified atmosphere is required, whilst strong colours and high contrasts are normally used to create lively and exciting effects. The colour appearance of a surface is a function of the surface itself and the illuminant, so the type of light source used will affect the appearance of the room surfaces. When trying to assess the effect that a particular light source will have on coloured surfaces, there is no substitute for a practical test.

The recommendations of the CIBS/IES Lighting Code on the reflectance of the major room surfaces are shown in Fig. 21.2. To achieve a ceiling cavity reflectance of

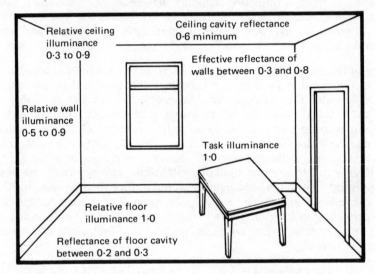

Fig. 21.2 Recommended room reflectances and illuminance ratios

0·6 is fairly easy with a flat ceiling, but it may be difficult, if not impossible, when luminaires are suspended a long way beneath the ceiling. The upper limit of 0·8 for effective wall reflectance is also difficult to realize in practice, and floor cavity reflectances within the recommended range (0·2 to 0·3) are seldom achieved. In installations using luminaires with little or no upward light, the ceiling is illuminated by inter-reflected light. When the room index is large, most of this inter-reflection is from the floor, which may produce problems. A highly-coloured carpet gives rise to a highly-coloured ceiling: variations in floor cavity reflectance give rise to an uneven ceiling appearance.

The reflectances of tasks and their background deserve consideration. If the outline of the task is the prime consideration then good contrast with the background is essential. Where detail within the task is more important then the contrast between the task and its background should be low to avoid adaptation problems, the luminance of the immediate background to a task being no less than one-third of the task luminance. In most cases the characteristics of the visual task are fixed and the easiest way to ensure that the background has a satisfactory luminance is to vary its reflectance.

Luminance and illuminance distributions The relative brightnesses of the major surfaces have a significant effect on the appearance of a room. Brightness depends on luminance (Sect. 2.2.2), but since surface reflectances are recommended it is possible to cover this aspect of appearance by recommending illuminance ratios.

The recommendations in Fig. 21.2 are only guidelines. They will produce acceptable results in most situations, but there are many reasons why a designer may wish to deviate from them. Bright walls make a room seem larger and perhaps more spacious. Dark walls make it seem smaller and possibly cramped. Bright ceilings and dark walls give the impression of formality and tension, whilst the reverse, bright walls and dark ceilings, create an informal and relaxed or sociable atmosphere. These are not hard and fast rules, but are well-supported by experiments and experience.

21.1.4 Directional effects

Any object in a room is surrounded by a luminous field, made up of luminaires and illuminated surfaces, and its appearance will be dictated by the way this field interacts with the characteristics of the object. What might be described as directional effects involve texture, modelling, shadows and veiling reflections.

Surface texture is best revealed by light at glancing angles, and is subdued by light from the front. Surface imperfections can be revealed by directing light at low angles to the surface or be hidden by frontal lighting. In many situations, certainly where critical inspection is involved, it is best to determine the most suitable direction by experiment.

Modelling is the ability of the lighting to reveal solid form. It is harsh and unpleasant if the difference between highlights and shadows is too great or the dominant direction of lighting is unnatural; it is weak, flat, and lifeless if the differences are too small. Between these two extremes is an acceptable range of modelling to suit different applications.

Dramatic modelling may be provided to emphasize particular objects in display lighting, whereas in most spaces the lighting must provide satisfactory modelling of the human occupants. Moderately strong modelling is desirable for formal or distant communication; weaker modelling for informal or close communication. This directional quality of lighting can be adequately described by the vector/scalar ratio (Sect. 2.4.3). A scale of acceptable vector/scalar ratios is given in Fig. 21.3.

Shadows may be cast over the area of a visual task, reducing the illuminance, causing adaptation problems, and producing disturbance or distraction. To avoid excessive shadowing in industry, where high machines or racks are often closely spaced, it is often necessary to space luminaires less far apart than would be needed to satisfy illuminance and uniformity requirements.

The visibility of detail within a task depends on its contrast and will be impaired if the lighting system degrades the contrast. This can happen if images of bright sources, such as luminaires or windows, are reflected within the surface of the task. The contrast rendering factor (*CRF*) is a measure of the degradation of contrast that is caused by veiling reflections. As explained in Chap. 2, *CRF* is the ratio of the measured contrast in the task to the contrast that would be obtained if the same task were in an integrating sphere – a reference lighting situation. The *CRF* varies considerably with the task, with the relative positions of task and luminaires, and with the direction of view. Its influence on visual performance is significant: a 10% improvement in *CRF* at 500 lux being equivalent to a doubling of illuminance. It has also been found to correlate with the subjective assessment of the visual quality of a lighting installation.

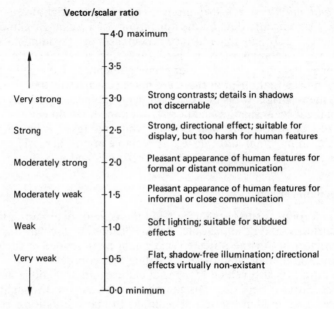

Fig. 21.3   Vector/scalar ratio and modelling

21.2   Design decisions

Once the objectives and criteria have been established, the designer can begin to make design decisions. There can be no rigid design sequence, since the priority of each decision will be determined by its influence on other decisions and its importance in meeting the objectives. However, at all stages of the design, capital costs and running costs need to be scrutinized, so it is appropriate to examine first of all in this section the evaluation of costs.

21.2.1   Costs

The methods of financial assessment employed by the designer must be acceptable to the client. This can be difficult when grants, tax benefits, tariffs, accounting methods, and other factors vary. The designer needs to satisfy himself and others on two matters – firstly that a new lighting scheme is justified and secondly that the proposed scheme is a sound economic proposition.

A new scheme may be justified because the building is new or because the existing scheme is no longer acceptable for its intended purpose; otherwise it may be necessary to decide whether it is better to retain existing equipment or replace it with a new scheme.

Scheme economics are difficult to judge in absolute terms, so comparisons are often used. They can be against an existing scheme or between alternative new designs, but for a comparison to be meaningful the two schemes must be of equitable standard. There are many methods of scheme comparison ranging from simple annual cost methods to the more complex discounted cash flow methods. For all of them the costs of owning and operating an installation are needed. These can be divided conveniently as follows:

Capital costs:
  Luminaires and associated equipment
  Installation and wiring

Operating costs:
  Fixed annual costs
    Electricity supply (maximum demand charge, etc.)
  Running costs
    Electricity consumed (kWh)
    Replacement lamps
    Relamping labour
  Maintenance costs
    Cleaning luminaires/lamps
    Repairing equipment

In the annual cost method the capital costs are transposed into a series of equal annual costs over an assumed lifetime for the installation. These can then be added to the annual operating costs to arrive at a total annual cost. The scheme with the lowest total annual cost is then considered to offer the best investment. This method is crude, but is a useful tool with which to compare schemes.

Where a proposed scheme is to be compared with an existing scheme, or one with a lower capital cost, a simple payback analysis can be used. The extra capital outlay of the proposal is compared to the cumulative savings in annual running costs. After a certain period the total savings will be equal to, and will therefore pay for, the extra capital investment. This period is the payback time, and will normally be unacceptable if greater than three or four years, unless other non-financial benefits are considered important. A realistic assessment must be made, when analysing payback, of the maintenance and repair costs for an existing installation, particularly towards and beyond the end of its nominal life.

The most realistic method of cost analysis is to itemize the anticipated expenditure on a year-by-year basis, enabling the effect of grants, tax concessions, and inflation to be allowed for. The cost of money needs to be included: if capital is expended then either it must have been borrowed or, if already available, it could have been invested elsewhere. In the latter case interest has been lost; in the former it must be paid. It is sometimes sufficient in a year-by-year analysis to add together the various items of expenditure and arrive at an overall figure. However, this makes no allowance for changes in the worth of money with time. This can be done by translating all costs to a fixed point in time, normally the present time. If, in year n, the costs are F and the (fractional) interest rate is i then the present worth P is given by

$$P = F/(1 + i)^n$$

Electricity tariffs   Each Area Electricity Board in the UK has its own tariffs for different classes of consumer, but the most common commercial and industrial systems are two-part tariffs and maximum demand tariffs.

The two-part tariff consists of a single rate per kWh of electricity supplied plus a standing charge, usually payable monthly or quarterly, based upon some measure of the maximum power demand. In the maximum demand tariff a maximum demand charge is levied for each kVA (or kW with a power factor adjustment) of annual or monthly maximum connected load. This may be at a higher rate in the winter months. A service capacity charge for each kVA or kW of installed load may also be levied. In addition to charges for the size of the connected load, a charge is made for each kWh of electricity consumed, which may be at one flat rate or at separate rates by day and night.

Control of the lighting load profile by switching or dimming, so that unnecessary lighting is not used, will reduce the amount of electricity consumed. In addition to this, and sometimes of more financial significance, maximum demand charges can be reduced by shedding lighting load at times of peak demand, which often occur around the middle of the day when adequate daylight may be available.

21.2.2   Choice of lighting system

Uniform or general lighting   Lighting systems which provide an approximately uniform illuminance on the horizontal working plane over the entire area are called general or uniform lighting systems. As in Fig. 21.4a, the luminaires are arranged in a regular layout, giving a tidy appearance to the installation. General lighting is simple to plan and install and requires no co-ordination with task locations, which may not be known or which may change. The greatest advantage of such a system is that it permits complete flexibility of task location. Its major disadvantage is that energy is wasted illuminating the whole area to the level needed only for the most critical tasks.

Localized lighting   Localized lighting systems (Fig. 21.4b) employ an arrangement of luminaires related to the position of tasks and workstations. They provide the required service illuminance on work-areas together with a lower level of general illumination for the space. By careful luminaire positioning, good light utilization is achieved with few problems from shadows, veiling reflections, and discomfort glare. Localized systems normally consume less energy than do general systems, unless a high proportion of the area is occupied by workstations.

Local lighting   Local lighting provides illumination only over the small area occupied by the task and its immediate surroundings (Fig. 21.4c). A general lighting system is installed to provide sufficient ambient illumination for circulation and non-critical tasks, so the local lighting system simply supplements the general lighting to achieve the necessary service illuminance on tasks. The system is sometimes referred to as task-ambient lighting. It is a very efficient system, particularly when high standards of task illuminance are required.

Local lighting is commonly provided by luminaires mounted on the workstation, providing a very flexible room layout. Such local units must be positioned carefully to minimize shadows, veiling reflections, and glare: there is therefore much to be said against making the units adjustable by their lay users. They offer some personal control of lighting, which is often a popular feature in a large open office.

21.2.3   Choice of lamp and luminaire

The choice of lamp affects the range of luminaires available, and vice versa, so one cannot be considered without reference to the other.

Choice of lamp   The designer should compile a list of suitable lamps by rejecting those which do not satisfy the design objectives. The availability of suitable luminaires can then be checked and the economics of the combinations assessed.

Lamps must have satisfactory colour rendering properties. Visual tasks requiring accurate perception of colour are less common than is generally believed, but there are many merchandizing situations where good colour rendering is desirable. The

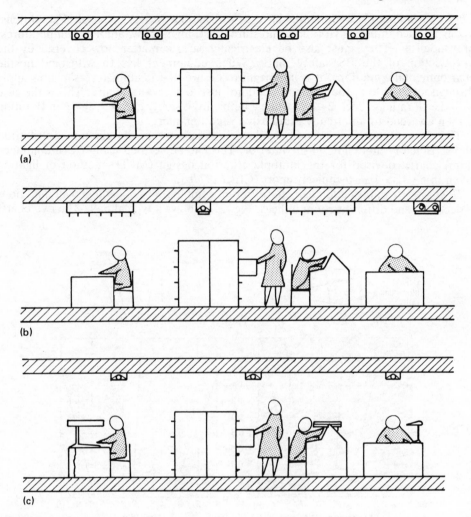

Fig. 21.4   Lighting systems: (a) general, (b) localized, and (c) local

suitability of a lamp for a particular application is best decided by experimental test. A warm colour appearance tends to be preferred for informal situations, at lower illuminances, and in cold environments, whilst a cool appearance tends to be preferred for formal situations, at higher illuminances, and in hot environments. It is normally undesirable to illuminate visibly adjacent areas with sources of significantly different colour appearance.

The run-up time of many high pressure discharge lamps is too long for applications requiring rapid provision of illumination, unless auxiliary tungsten or fluorescent lamps are provided.

Lamp life and lumen maintenance must be considered in conjunction with the maintenance policy for sensible economic calculations, and it needs to be remembered that standardization of lamp types and sizes within a particular site can simplify maintenance.

Choice of luminaire   Luminaires have to withstand a variety of physical conditions, involving such things as vibration, moisture, dust, high or low ambient temperatures, or vandalism. They must also be electrically safe, a matter now covered by the introduction of the BS safety mark. When equipment has to withstand hostile environmental conditions, it is important to ensure that manufacturers' claims apply throughout the life of the luminaire and not just to a new luminaire. This is the case with the IP ratings (Sect. 24.2.2) when a luminaire is safety marked, since an IP rating is then awarded to an already arduously-tested luminaire.

The chosen luminaire should provide both a satisfactory illumination distribution and satisfactory modelling in the interior. This can be verified using *IR* (illuminance ratio) charts, devised for the multiple criterion design (MCD) method of lighting given in a CIBS/IES technical report (CIBS 1977b).

IR charts are published in pairs for different combinations of ceiling, wall, and floor reflectance and different room indices: Fig. 21.5 shows a typical pair. The two charts

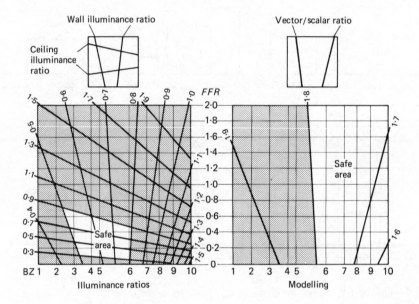

Fig. 21.5 Illuminance ratio (*IR*) charts

are identical except for the loci plotted onto them. The left-hand chart has lines of constant wall/task and ceiling/task illuminance ratios and the right-hand chart has lines of constant vector/scalar ratio. Regions outside the general recommendations of the Lighting Code are shaded.

The charts can be used in two ways. Real luminaires can be plotted onto the charts, according to their BZ number (Sect. 5.5.2) and flux fraction ratio *FFR* (up/down), and suitable ones can be identified. Alternatively, the range of BZ and *FFR* values for luminaires which will provide the desired appearance and modelling can be determined. Sometimes it is impossible to simultaneously achieve the desired illuminance ratios and vector/scalar ratios, and a compromise must be found. The charts illustrate that for most cases a proportion of upward light is necessary from luminaires to achieve the desired appearance. If the wall/task illuminance ratio is too low then wall-washing luminaires or closer spacing at the walls may be the answer. Having used *IR* charts to identify several acceptable luminaires, the final decision about which luminaire to use can be based on cost, efficiency, glare control, or other factors, and may have to be left to a later stage in the design process.

21.2.4 System management

A lighting system should not only be well designed, but also be managed and operated effectively and efficiently. Good system management implies (a) maintaining the system in good order and (b) controlling its use to conserve money and energy. Both of these components of management must be considered in the design. The maintenance policy will affect the number of luminaires needed to achieve the service illuminance, and the degree of control required will determine the circuits in which they will operate.

Maintenance A lighting system needs to be serviced, i.e. failed lamps replaced, equipment faults rectified, and lamps and luminaires cleaned.

Lamp replacement may be done individually when a lamp is seen to have failed (spot replacement) or all the lamps in an installation may be replaced periodically (group replacement). The latter is frequently the cheaper option, firstly because of the high labour cost of a multiplicity of spot replacements and secondly because the output of most lamps falls continuously with burning time, giving a low efficacy ahead of actual failure. The optimum time for bulk replacement can be determined from the lumen maintenance and mortality curves for the particular type of lamp, coupled with a knowledge of labour, lamp, and electricity costs. Bulk replacement will be cheaper if it coincides with one of the periodic cleanings of the installation.

Even without the lumen depreciation of lamps throughout replacement periods, dirt accumulating on the surfaces of lamps, on the reflecting and transmitting portions of luminaires, and to some extent on room surfaces, combine to ensure that the initial performance of a lighting installation will not be realized throughout the life of the installation. The degree of dirtiness depends on the type of premises and the general cleanliness of its location. The effect of the dirt on the transfer of light from the lamps to the working surface depends mainly on the type of luminaire used. The total influence of all this on the maintenance of lighting levels depends on the cleaning interval in the maintenance schedule. As with the interval for bulk lamp replacement, it is possible to determine economically the optimum cleaning interval for an installation.

Reproduced in Tables 21.1 and 21.2 are data derived from a CIBS/IES technical report (CIBS 1967a) which enable a 'maintenance factor' to be predicted for an installation with a particular cleaning interval. This factor is nowadays looked on as the product of two other factors, one for luminaire dirt depreciation (*LDD*) and one for room surface dirt depreciation (*RDD*). Each of these factors is the ratio of the actual service illuminance (Sect. 21.1.2) to the value of illuminance in the absence of dirt. Even in an immaculately clean environment, the time-averaged illuminance will always be less than the initial illuminance because of two factors connected with the lamps. One of these is the lamp failure factor (*LFF*), consequent on all failed lamps not being replaced immediately: its value is dependent on maintenance policy. The other factor is the lamp lumen depreciation (*LLD*): this factor has until recently been taken into account in lighting design by using in calculations the 'lighting design lumens' for lamps – values representative of through-life output. Nowadays, with the

Table 21.1 Classification of rooms and luminaires for maintenance

Premises	Location	Room category (X = Particularly clean, Y = Average, Z = Particularly dirty)	Bare lamp batten	Open ventilated reflector	Dust-tight, dust-proof, or reflector lamp	Open non-ventilated reflector, enclosed diffuser	Open base diffuser or louvre	Recessed diffuser or louvre, diffusing or louvred luminous ceiling	Indirect cornice
Offices, shops and stores, hospitals, clean laboratories and factories, schools, etc.	All air conditioned buildings	X	A	A	A	A/B	A/B	A	B
	Clean country area	X	A/B	A/B	A/B	B	B	A/B	C/D
	City or town outskirts	Y	B	B	B	C	B/C	B	E
	City or town centre	Y	B/C	B/C	B/C	C/D	C	B/C	F/G
	Dirty industrial area	Y	C	C	B/C	D	C/D	C	G
Factories, laboratories, manufacturing areas, machine shops, etc.	All air conditioned buildings	X	A/B	A	A	C	B/C	B	B/C
	Clean country area	Y	B	A/B	B	C/D	C	B/C	D/E
	City or town outskirts	Y	B/C	B	B	D	C/D	C	F
	City or town centre	Y	C	B/C	B/C	D/E	D	C/D	G
	Dirty industrial area	Z	C/D	C	C	E	D/E	D	H
Steelworks, foundries, welding shops, mines, etc.	All air conditioned buildings	X	B	A/B	A/B	D	C/D	C	—
	Clean country area	Y	C	B/C	B	D/E	D	C/D	—
	City or town outskirts	Y	C/D	C	B/C	E	D/E	D	—
	City or town centre	Z	D	C/D	B/C	E/F	E	D/E	—
	Dirty industrial area	Z	D/E	D	C	F	E/F	E	—

Table 21.2 Maintenance factors (product of luminaire and room surface dirt depreciation factors)

Luminaire category	Room category	Months per cleaning									
		1	2	3	4	5	6	8	9	12	18
A	X	—	—	—	—	—	—	0·94	—	0·92	0·90
A	Y	—	—	—	—	—	—	0·92	—	0·90	0·88
B	X	—	—	—	—	—	0·88	—	0·86	0·85	—
B	Y	—	—	—	—	—	0·87	—	0·85	0·83	—
C	X	—	—	—	—	0·84	—	0·81	—	0·79	—
C	Y	—	—	—	—	0·83	—	0·80	—	0·78	—
C	Z	—	—	—	—	0·82	—	0·78	—	0·76	—
D	X	—	—	—	0·82	—	0·79	—	0·75	—	—
D	Y	—	—	—	0·81	—	0·77	—	0·73	—	—
D	Z	—	—	—	0·79	—	0·75	—	0·71	—	—
E	Y	—	—	0·78	—	0·73	—	0·68	—	—	—
E	Z	—	—	0·77	—	0·72	—	0·67	—	—	—
F	Y	—	0·77	—	0·71	—	0·67	—	—	—	—
F	Z	—	0·76	—	0·70	—	0·66	—	—	—	—
G	Y	—	0·73	0·69	0·66	—	—	—	—	—	—
G	Z	—	0·72	0·68	0·65	—	—	—	—	—	—
H	Z	0·75	0·68	0·63	—	—	—	—	—	—	—

use of a variety of sources with different depreciation rates, it is recommended that 'initial lumens' are used, together with a realistic *LLD* factor.

A light loss factor (*LLF*) is used in the calculation of how many luminaires are needed in an installation to produce a specified service illuminance. This is the product of the four factors referred to in the previous paragraph (*LDD*, *RDD*, *LFF*, and *LLD*), each of them representing a specific cause of light loss, but all recoverable by cleaning or relamping. A further factor is sometimes included in *LFF* to allow for unrecoverable losses, such as any progressive degradation of luminaire finishes, and for practical differences between the lamp output in the installation and in the test laboratory because of differences in temperature, auxiliary gear, or supplies.

Control   A lighting system must be designed and managed to permit good control of energy use, both during the working day and outside working hours. For satisfactory control the lighting circuits must be sufficiently flexible to allow unwanted lights to be turned off, without inconvenience to others.

Methods of control fall into three broad categories:

(a)   Manual control.
(b)   Automatic control (non-intelligent).
(c)   Processor control (intelligent).

Manual methods rely upon individuals and appointed members of staff controlling the lighting system. These methods tend to be inexpensive to implement, but are less effective than automatic methods. To be effective the lighting system must be well laid out to permit flexible switching of individual luminaires or banks of luminaires. The switch panels must be sensibly located and clearly marked (a mimic diagram can be very helpful). An education programme, to ensure staff awareness, is essential and this can be reinforced with posters or labels on the switch panels.

One of the main disadvantages with manual methods is that whilst occupants may be aware that natural lighting is insufficient and will turn on lights, there is nothing to prompt them to turn off lights if the natural lighting becomes adequate. An imposed switch-off (particularly at lunch-time) can be effective, for if natural lighting is sufficient the luminaires may not be turned back on. In addition, a considerable amount of energy is often wasted after working hours when the lights are left on. The full lighting system may be on when cleaners are in the building, and the provision of special cleaners' circuits in which only some of the lighting is switched on can save money. Time clocks provide a convenient method of ensuring that unwanted lighting is not operated outside working hours.

Automatic control systems can utilize inexpensive time clocks or photocells to switch (or dim) banks of lights. As indicated in Sect. 20.3.3, photocells can monitor the level of useful daylight and turn off luminaires in rows adjacent to the windows when daylight levels are high. Whether or not the payback time for such a system is acceptable will depend on the proportion of the working year for which the required illuminance can be provided by natural light, and hence save energy costs.

Automatic systems must normally have some degree of manual override to cater for unexpected circumstances, and a time-lag must normally be built into the system to prevent premature switch-off. The presence of occupants can be signalled by proximity detectors utilizing radar, acoustic, or infrared techniques.

Computer-based control systems are becoming increasingly popular. These rely upon dedicated computers or processors to control the building services and operate the building at maximum efficiency. Information from transducers and sensors about the state of the building is used by a program to control the various services, such as lifts, fire alarms, lighting, air conditioning, and other equipment. Although such systems are expensive, this is offset by the wide variety of services that can be controlled at optimum efficiency.

21.3   Design calculations

21.3.1   Average illuminance

The average illuminance produced by a lighting installation, or the number of luminaires required to achieve a specific average illuminance, can be calculated by means of utilization factors, a *UF* being the ratio of the total flux received by a particular surface to the total lamp flux of the installation.

The average illuminance $E(S)$ over a reference surface S can be calculated from the 'lumen method' formula

$$E(S) = \frac{F \times n \times N \times LLF \times UF(S)}{\text{area of surface S}}$$

where F is the initial bare lamp flux,
n is the number of lamps per luminaire,
N is the number of luminaires,
LLF is the total light loss factor,
$UF(S)$ is the utilization factor for the reference surface S.

Utilization factors can be determined for any surface or layout of luminaires, but, in practice, are only calculated for general lighting systems with regular arrays of luminaires and for three main room surfaces. As indicated in Sect 5.3.3, the first of these surfaces, the C surface, is an imaginary horizontal plane at the level of the luminaires having a reflectance equal to that of the ceiling cavity. The second surface, the F surface, is a horizontal plane at normal working height which is often assumed to be 0·85 m above the floor. The third surface, the W surface, consists of all the walls between the C and F planes.

The method of calculating utilization factors is outlined in Sect. 5.3.3 and detailed in a CIBS technical memorandum (CIBS 1980b). Although utilization factors can be calculated by the lighting designer, most manufacturers publish utilization factors for standard conditions for their luminaires. The standard method of presentation is shown in the upper half of Table 21.3. To use this table it is necessary to know the room index and the reflectances of the three standard surfaces.

Room index is a measure of the angular size of the room, and is the ratio of the sum of the areas of the F and C surfaces to the area of the W surface. For rectangular rooms the room index is given by

$$RI = \frac{L \times W}{(L + W)H}$$

where L is the length of the room,
        W is the width of the room,
        H is the height of the luminaire plane above the horizontal reference plane.

If the room is re-entrant in shape, for example L-shaped, then it must be divided into two or more non-re-entrant sections which can be treated separately.

Effective reflectances are needed for the wall surface, the ceiling cavity, and the floor cavity. The wall surface will generally consist of a series of areas A_1 to A_n of different reflectances R_1 to R_n respectively. The effective reflectance of a composite surface is the area-weighted average R_a, given by

$$R_a = \sum_{k=1}^{n} R_k A_k \bigg/ \sum_{k=1}^{n} A_k$$

In the case of either cavity the effective reflectance depends on both the reflectance of the cavity surfaces and the relative depth of the cavity. The CIBS technical memorandum gives an accurate table of effective reflectances R_e, but an approximate value is given by

$$R_e = \frac{CI \times R_a}{CI + 2(1 - R_a)}$$

where R_a is the area-weighted average reflectance of the surfaces of the cavity and CI is the cavity index, a similar measure to room index, defined as

$$CI = \frac{L \times W}{(L + W)d}$$

where d is the depth of the cavity.

Spacing to height ratio, the spacing between luminaires divided by their height above the horizontal reference plane, affects the uniformity of illuminance on that plane. When the *UF* tables are determined, for a nominal spacing to height ratio *SHR NOM* as indicated in Sect. 5.3.3, the maximum spacing to height ratio *SHR MAX* of the luminaire is also calculated, and is a value which should not be exceeded if the uniformity is to be acceptable.

Table 21.3　Utilization factor and initial glare index tables

| Utilization factors (*UF*[F]) | | | | | | | | | | | | | SHR NOM = 2·00 |

Room reflectances · Room index

C	W	F	0·75	1·00	1·25	1·50	2·00	2·50	3·00	4·00	5·00
0·70	0·50	0·20	0·44	0·55	0·59	0·63	0·68	0·72	0·74	0·77	0·80
	0·30		0·38	0·49	0·54	0·58	0·64	0·68	0·70	0·74	0·77
	0·10		0·34	0·45	0·50	0·54	0·60	0·64	0·67	0·71	0·74
0·50	0·50	0·20	0·40	0·50	0·54	0·57	0·61	0·64	0·66	0·69	0·71
	0·30		0·35	0·46	0·49	0·53	0·58	0·61	0·63	0·66	0·69
	0·10		0·31	0·42	0·46	0·49	0·55	0·58	0·61	0·64	0·67
0·30	0·50	0·20	0·36	0·45	0·48	0·51	0·55	0·57	0·59	0·61	0·63
	0·30		0·32	0·42	0·45	0·48	0·52	0·55	0·57	0·59	0·61
	0·10		0·29	0·39	0·42	0·45	0·50	0·53	0·55	0·58	0·60
0·00	0·00	0·00	0·25	0·34	0·36	0·39	0·42	0·44	0·46	0·48	0·49
BZ class			4	3	3	3	4	4	4	4	4

Glare indices

Ceiling reflectance	0·70	0·70	0·50	0·50	0·30	0·70	0·70	0·50	0·50	0·30
Wall reflectance	0·50	0·30	0·50	0·30	0·30	0·50	0·30	0·50	0·30	0·30
Floor reflectance	0·14	0·14	0·14	0·14	0·14	0·14	0·14	0·14	0·14	0·14

Room dimension

X	Y	Viewed crosswise					Viewed endwise				
2H	2H	7·0	8·4	8·0	9·5	10·8	6·8	8·2	7·8	9·2	10·5
	3H	8·9	10·2	10·0	11·3	12·6	8·6	9·8	9·6	10·9	12·2
	4H	9·9	11·1	10·9	12·2	13·5	9·4	10·6	10·4	11·7	13·0
	6H	11·0	12·1	12·0	13·2	14·5	10·3	11·4	11·3	12·5	13·8
	8H	11·6	12·6	12·6	13·7	15·1	10·7	11·8	11·7	12·9	14·2
	12H	12·2	13·2	13·2	14·3	15·7	11·1	12·1	12·1	13·2	14·6
4H	2H	7·7	8·9	8·7	10·0	11·3	7·5	8·7	8·5	9·8	11·1
	3H	10·0	11·0	11·0	12·1	13·5	9·6	10·6	10·7	11·7	13·1
	4H	11·2	12·1	12·2	13·2	14·6	10·6	11·6	11·7	12·7	14·1
	6H	12·5	13·4	13·6	14·5	15·9	11·8	12·6	12·8	13·7	15·1
	8H	13·3	14·0	14·4	15·2	16·6	12·3	13·1	13·4	14·2	15·7
	12H	14·0	14·8	15·1	15·9	17·3	12·8	13·5	13·9	14·7	16·1
8H	4H	11·8	12·6	12·9	13·7	15·2	11·4	12·2	12·5	13·3	14·7
	6H	13·5	14·2	14·6	15·3	16·8	12·8	13·5	13·9	14·6	16·1
	8H	14·4	15·0	15·5	16·1	17·6	13·5	14·1	14·6	15·2	16·7
	12H	15·4	16·0	16·6	17·1	18·6	14·2	14·8	15·4	15·9	17·4
12H	4H	12·0	12·7	13·1	13·8	15·3	11·6	12·3	12·7	13·5	14·9
	6H	13·7	14·3	14·9	15·5	17·0	13·1	13·7	14·3	14·9	16·4
	8H	14·8	15·3	16·0	16·5	18·0	14·0	14·5	15·1	15·7	17·2
	12H	15·7	16·2	16·8	17·3	18·8	14·6	15·0	15·7	16·2	17·7

Conversion terms:

Luminaire length (mm)	1500	1800
Wattage (W)	1 × 65	1 × 75
Conversion factor (*UF*)	1·00	1·00
Glare indices conversion	0·63	0·00

For linear luminaires with conventional distributions *SHR MAX* may be supplemented by *SHR MAX TR*, the maximum transverse spacing to height ratio. (But note that *SHR MAX TR* must not be used in isolation.) The axial spacing to height ratio *SHR AX* should not exceed *SHR MAX* and the transverse spacing to height ratio *SHR TR* should not exceed *SHR MAX TR*. In addition, the product of *SHR AX* and *SHR TR* must not exceed *SHR MAX* squared. Thus

$$SHR\ AX \times SHR\ TR \leqslant (SHR\ MAX)^2$$

$$SHR\ AX \leqslant SHR\ MAX$$

$$SHR\ TR \leqslant SHR\ MAX\ TR$$

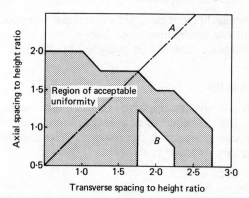

Fig. 21.6 Acceptable axial and transverse spacing to height ratios for a batwing luminaire

For some luminaires, notably those with distinctly disymmetric distributions, extra spacing to height ratio information may be necessary. The best form of this information is to provide a graph of acceptable *SHR* combinations in the axial and transverse directions as in Fig. 21.6.

Calculation procedure The following sequence of calculations should be performed when calculating the number of luminaires necessary to achieve a given average illuminance:

(a) Calculate the room index *RI*, the floor cavity index *CI*(F), and the ceiling cavity index *CI*(C).
(b) Calculate the effective reflectances of the ceiling cavity, walls, and floor cavity. Remember to include the effect of desks or machines in the latter.
(c) Determine the *UF*(F) value from the table for the luminaire, using the room index from (a) and the effective reflectances from (b).
(d) Apply any necessary correction to the *UF*(F) value for lamp type, using conversion factors given in the table.
(e) Determine *LLD* and *LFF* from the lamp lumen maintenance and lamp mortality curves respectively, based upon the expected relamping policy. Determine the product of *LDD* and *RDD* from Tables 21.1 and 21.2.
(f) Calculate the total light loss factor (*LLF*) by multiplying together the four factors from (e) with any factor representing unrecoverable losses/practical differences.
(g) Insert the appropriate values into the lumen method formula

$$N = \frac{E \times L \times W}{F \times n \times LLF \times UF(\text{F})}$$

to obtain the number of luminaires required.

(h) Determine a suitable layout. If necessary, allow for the effect of non-standard perimeter spacing, using the method given in the CIBS technical memorandum (CIBS 1980b), recalculate the number of luminaires with a modified *UF*(F), and determine a modified layout.

(i) Check that the geometric mean *SHR* of the layout is within the range of the *UF* table, i.e.

$$\sqrt{(SHR \ AX \times SHR \ TR)} = SHR \ NOM \pm 0{\cdot}5$$

(j) Check that the proposed layout does not exceed the maximum spacing to height ratios, using one of the techniques given above.

(k) Calculate the illuminance that will be achieved by the final layout.

21.3.2   Illuminance at a point

When local or localized systems are employed or when unusual layouts or unconventional distributions are used, calculations of average illuminance can be inadequate or meaningless. In such circumstances it is necessary to calculate the illuminance at all points of interest, using one of three tools:

(a) Basic photometric data.
(b) Pre-calculated aids, such as isolux diagrams.
(c) A computer program.

The use of basic photometric data has been described in Chap. 5. Hand calculations, when used with discretion, can yield much information about the required solution, but become tedious in quantity.

Isolux diagrams, where contours of equal illuminance on a specified plane are plotted, offer a faster method of carrying out the same calculations. For local and localized lighting systems they can provide considerable guidance on the location of luminaires, but isolux diagrams are not always available.

When a computer is available with suitable programs, illuminance values can be calculated easily. Although some limited design programs do exist, most progra simulate the illuminance pattern produced by a chosen layout of luminaires. However, the ease with which computers can be used often results in abuse. The quality of the results is only as good as the quality of the thought that went into the design; the accuracy of the final result is no greater than the accuracy of the data supplied, despite the impression of precision given by the printout.

At the planning stage it is often better to obtain illuminance plots for individual luminaires or groups of luminaires than to attempt to simulate the complete installation. The performance of an individual luminaire or group can be analysed to assist with the selection of the best layout. When the layout has been established it can be simulated on the computer.

The format of output data is important. If the information is insufficiently detailed then important features may be overlooked. More commonly, if the data is too detailed it becomes too complex to interpret. Tabulated illuminance values provide a considerable amount of detail, but are difficult to assess. Graphic methods, such as contour maps or boundary maps, are much easier to understand, and are preferable, but require more sophisticated software and hardware than do conventional printouts.

21.3.3 Discomfort glare

The glare index system for predicting the degree of discomfort glare in an installation is detailed in a CIBS/IES technical report (CIBS 1967b), shortly to be replaced by a CIBS technical memorandum.

One method of using the system, a simple one mentioned in Sect 5.5.2, involves using the BZ classification of the luminaires. This is now known to be inaccurate, and cannot be recommended for anything but approximate calculations (i.e. ± 6 units of glare index).

Another method requires the use of a suitable computer, a program based on the Building Research Establishment formula cited in Chaps 2 and 5, and detailed photometric data for the luminaires used. The advantage of this method is that any layout of luminaires and any viewing position can be considered. However, the expense of developing or buying the software makes it an unlikely method for most lighting designers.

The third, and most practical method, is the use of tables, produced and supplied by the manufacturer of the luminaires used. Such a table appears in the lower half of Table 21.3. The values in it are labelled *initial* glare indices, because they will almost inevitably require to be corrected to allow for differences between the real installation and the standard installation on which the tables are based.

The geometrical characteristics of different installations are, for the purpose of glare, expressed as functions of one particular dimension H, the height of the luminaires above seated eye level, where the latter is taken to be 1·2 m above the floor. It will be noted from Table 21.3 that the room dimensions in the glare table are expressed as multiples of this quantity H. The horizontal dimensions X and Y have specific meanings related to an observer in the room, X being the room dimension perpendicular to his line of sight and Y being the parallel one, with the observer located in the worst possible glare position, in the middle of one wall. In the standard installation $H = 3·05$ m, the spacing to height ratio of the luminaires is 1·0, and the downward flux from each luminaire is 1000 lm. Correction factors are usually needed for the downward flux per luminaire and for the H value of the installation. The corrections are given in graphical form in the CIBS/IES report, but can be expressed mathematically as values to be added to the initial glare index.

$$\text{downward flux correction} = 6\log_{10}(F_{\text{d}}/1000)$$

where F_{d} is the actual luminaire downward lumens.

$$\text{height correction} = 4\log_{10}H - 1·94$$

where H is the actual luminaire height above a 1·2 m eye level. Any correction term for luminaire length is usually incorporated in the manufacturer's data, as at the foot of Table 21.3.

The example given in Table 21.3 is for a linear luminaire, where different indices are shown for luminaires viewed crosswise and endwise. An intelligent lighting design procedure examines the effect of running the luminaires in two different directions and selects the one which minimizes the higher of two glare indices, one with X as the shorter wall and one with X as the longer wall.

21.4 Emergency lighting

The *Fire Precautions Act* (HMG 1971) and the *Health and Safety at Work Act* (HMG 1974) make it obligatory to provide adequate means of escape in all places of work and public resort in the UK. Emergency lighting is an essential part of this requirement: BS 5266 (BSI 1975b) lays down minimum standards for the design, implementation, and certification of such installations.

Escape lighting   This type of emergency lighting is provided to ensure the safe and effective evacuation of the building. It must:

(a)   Indicate clearly and unambiguously the escape routes.
(b)   Illuminate the escape routes to allow safe movement towards and out of the exits.
(c)   Ensure that fire alarm call points and fire equipment provided along the escape route can be readily located.

Standby lighting   Some building areas cannot be evacuated immediately in the event of an emergency or power failure because life would be put at risk, for example a hospital operating theatre or chemical plants where shut-down procedures must be used. In these circumstances the activities must be allowed to take place and standby lighting is required. The level of standby lighting will depend upon the nature of the activities, their duration, and the associated risk, but the provision of 5 to 25% of the standard service illuminance is common.

Standby lighting can be regarded as a special form of conventional lighting and be dealt with accordingly, but escape lighting requires different treatment and is the major concern of BS 5266. Like most British Standards, this is not a legal document, but it can acquire legal status by being adopted as part of the local bye-laws. Although most local authorities quote BS 5266, many modify the conditions, for example by insisting on higher illuminances. It is left to the enforcing authority to decide for what duration emergency lighting shall be required to operate: this is normally longer than the time needed for an orderly evacuation, for the sake of rescue services – typically one, two, or three hours.

Marking the escape route   All exits and emergency exits must have exit or emergency exit signs. Where direct sight of an exit is not possible or there could be doubt as to the direction, then direction signs with an appropriate arrow and the words exit or emergency exit are required: the idea of this is to direct someone who is unfamiliar with the building to the exit. All signs must be illuminated at all reasonable times so that they are legible.

Illuminating the route   The emergency lighting must reach its required level 5 seconds after failure of the main lighting system. If the occupants are familiar with the building this time can be increased to 15 seconds at the discretion of the local authority. The minimum illuminance along the centreline of the escape route must be 0·2 lux or more. In an open area, such as a hall or open plan office, this applies to all areas where people may tread on their way to the exits. The ratio of the maximum illuminance to the minimum illuminance along the centreline of the escape route should not exceed 40:1. Once again, in open areas, this applies to all parts of the floor where people may tread on their way to the exits.

Glare   Luminaires should not cause disability glare and should therefore be mounted at least 2 m above floor level: they should not be too high or they may become obscured by smoke.

Exits and changes of direction Luminaires should be located near each exit and emergency exit door, and at points where it is necessary to emphasize the position of potential hazards, such as changes of direction, changes of floor level, and staircases.

Fire equipment Fire fighting equipment and fire alarm call points along the escape route must be adequately illuminated at all reasonable times.

Lifts and escalators Although these may not be used in the event of fire they should be illuminated. Emergency lighting is required in each lift car in which people can travel. Escalators must be illuminated to the same standard as the escape route to prevent accidents.

Toilets and control rooms In toilets of over $8\,m^2$ gross area, emergency lighting should be installed to provide a minimum of $0.2\,lux$. Emergency lighting luminaires are required in all control rooms and plant rooms.

Types of systems There are two main types of supply for emergency lighting (Sect. 18.5.3):

(a) Generators.
(b) Batteries.

Few generators will run up to provide the required illuminance within 5 or 15 seconds, in which case they must either be running continuously or be backed up with an auxiliary battery system. Generators require considerable capital investment and are difficult to justify except for standby use.

A battery system can be one of two types: either a central system, where the batteries are in banks at one or more locations, or a self-contained system, where each individual luminaire has its own battery.

Central systems have battery rooms or cubicles in which the charger, batteries, and switching devices are located. Modern systems tend to have several cubicles to improve system integrity in the event of fire damage to one cubicle.

Self-contained luminaires are self-powered and operate independently in an emergency. Thus, although an individual luminaire may be destroyed in a fire, the other luminaires will be unaffected. The fact that each luminaire is an independent unit means that maintenance must be thorough. For most applications self-contained luminaires must operate for a period of 1 hour to 3 hours. Most designers base their designs on the safer 3-hour standard irrespective of the requirements of the enforcing authority.

Self-contained luminaires can have three modes of operation:

(a) Maintained: in this mode the lamp is on all the time. Under normal conditions it is powered directly or indirectly by the mains. Under emergency conditions it uses its own battery supply.
(b) Non-maintained: here the lamp is off when mains power is available to charge the batteries. Upon failure the lamp is energized from the battery pack.
(c) Sustained: this is a hybrid of the previous two modes. A lamp is provided which operates from the mains supply under normal conditions. Under emergency conditions a second lamp, powered from the battery pack, takes over. Sustained luminaires are often used for exit signs.

Although self-contained luminaires are the easiest and most flexible to install, maintenance and testing must be thorough if operation in the event of an emergency is to be guaranteed. Maintained systems continuously demonstrate the integrity of the lamp, but the lamp is continually ageing and an operating lamp says nothing about the state of the battery or charger circuits. In non-maintained and sustained systems the lamps do not age, but only regular testing will reveal faults.

Luminaire data   Figure 21.7 shows a typical page of photometric data for an emergency lighting luminaire. It states how far apart luminaires can be spaced along an escape route while providing a minimum 0·2 lux, and at what distance away from the end of a single luminaire the illuminance falls to 0·2 lux. These values are given for various mounting heights, as are the average illuminance and the uniformity. The data in Fig. 21.7 are based upon set conditions of 25 °C and 87 lm for the 300 mm 8 W fluorescent lamp. This lumen output is the emergency lighting design lumens and is considerably lower than the normal lighting design figure of 420 lm, because the worst combination of conditions must be planned for.

Planning   When planning an emergency lighting system the following sequence is recommended:

(a)   Define the exits and emergency exits.
(b)   Mark the escape routes.
(c)   Identify any problem areas, for example areas that will contain people unfamiliar with the building, toilets over 8 m², plant rooms, escalators, etc.
(d)   Mark location of exit signs. These can be self-illuminated or illuminated by emergency lighting units nearby. Mark these onto the plan.
(e)   Where direction signs are required mark these and provide necessary lighting.
(f)   Identify the area of the escape route illuminated by the lighting needed for the signs.
(g)   Add extra luminaires to complete the lighting of the escape route, paying particular attention to stairs and other hazards. Remember to allow for shadows caused by obstructions or bends in the route.
(h)   Add extra luminaires to satisfy the problem areas identified in (c) above. Make sure that the lighting outside the building is also adequate for safe evacuation.
(i)   Check that all fire alarm call points and fire equipment have been adequately dealt with.

Testing   The local inspector will normally require a written guarantee that the installation conforms to the appropriate standards. Drawings of the system must be provided and retained on the premises (this also applies to modifications).

All self-contained luminaires and internally-illuminated signs must be tested for a brief period once a month. Twice a year the battery system must be used in a simulated mains failure for a period of at least 1 hour. The charging system must also be checked. The system must be operated to its full duration (normally 3 hours) at least once every 3 years.

These testing requirements call for a sensible wiring system with adequate provision for testing. Luminaires are available with switches fitted in the supply leads. These may be simple key-operated switches or even magnetically-operated reed switches operated by a magnet attached to the outside of the luminaire. There are also systems which will respond to infrared or ultrasonic signals from a hand-held remote controller. It is possible to include, within the luminaire, circuits which will automatically switch to the emergency mode at timed intervals and which will record the result of the test as a go–no-go signal on an indicator lamp. These electronic systems will usually revert automatically to the normal charge after a nominal test period.

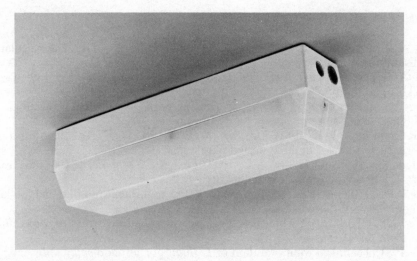

The data are for the centreline of the escape route and are based on the following:
(a) Luminaires are ceiling mounted on the centreline of the escape route.
(b) A minimum illuminance of 0·20 lux.
(c) Corrected lamp output of 87 lumens†.
(d) An ambient temperature of 25 °C.

Mounting height (metres)	Maximum spacing (metres) End	Between	Average illuminance (lux)	Maximum intensity 70–90 degree zone (cd) Actual	Limit	Uniformity ratio (max/min) (Limit 40 : 1)	Notes
Transverse							
2	3·8	9·6	1·09	6·8	1930	15 : 1	
3	4·1	10·8	0·64	6·8	700	6·7 : 1	
4	4·2	11·5	0·45	6·8	330	3·8 : 1	
5	4·0	11·8	0·35	6·8	180	2·4 : 1	
6	3·6	11·9	0·28	6·8	110	1·7 : 1	
7	2·6	11·5	0·25	6·8	80	1·2 : 1	
8	This luminaire is not suitable for mounting at this height or above						
Axial							
2	3·2	8·0	1·12	3·3	1930	15 : 1	
3	3·6	9·2	0·64	3·3	700	6·7 : 1	
4	3·7	10·1	0·44	3·3	330	3·8 : 1	
5	3·6	10·4	0·38	3·3	180	2·4 : 1	
6	3·1	10·4	0·28	3·3	110	1·7 : 1	
7	2·2	10·1	0·24	3·3	80	1·2 : 1	
8	This luminaire is not suitable for mounting at this height or above						

†Corrected for *BLF* (ballast lumen factor), *F*5 or *F*-end (5 second or end of life factor), and a maintenance factor of 0·90.

Fig. 21.7 Typical page of photometric data for an emergency lighting luminaire

Further reading

Bean A R and Bell R I, 1976, *Ltg. Res. Technol.*, **8**, 200–210: The calculation of utilisation factors

Bean A R and Hopkins A G, 1980, *Ltg. Res. Technol.*, **12**, 135–139: Task and background lighting

Bedocs L and Simons R H, 1972, *Ltg. Res. Technol.*, **4**, 80–89: The accuracy of the IES glare index system

Bell R I and Page R K, 1981, *Ltg. Res. Technol.*, **13**, 49–57: The need for a unified approach to interior lighting design parameters

Bellchambers H E and Godby A C, 1972, *Ltg. Res. Technol.*, **4**, 104–106: Illumination, colour rendering and visual clarity

Boyce P R, 1970, *Ltg. Res. Technol.*, **2**, 74–94: The influence of illumination level on prolonged work performance

CIBS, 1968, CIBS/IES Technical Report No. 11: *The calculation of direct illumination from linear sources*

CIBS, 1981, Technical Memorandum 6: *Lighting for visual display units*

CIE, 1975, Publication No. 29 (TC-4.1): *Guide on interior lighting*

CIE, 1981, Publication No. 19/2 (TC-3.1): *An analytical model for describing the influence of lighting parameters upon visual performance* (2 volumes)

Crisp V H C, 1978, *Ltg. Res. Technol.*, **10**, 69–82: The light switch in buildings

Cuttle C, 1971, *Ltg. Res. Technol.*, **3**, 171–189: Lighting parameters and the flow of light

de Boer J B and Fischer D, 1978, *Interior lighting* (Holland: Philips Technical Library)

Hunt D R G, 1979, *Ltg. Res. Technol.*, **11**, 9–23: Improved daylight data for predicting energy savings from photoelectric controls

IES, 1981, *Lighting handbook*, 6th Edition (New York: Illuminating Eng. Soc.) (2 volumes)

Lynes J A (Ed), 1978, *Developments in lighting*, **1** (London: Applied Science)

Lynes J A, 1978, *Ltg. Res. Technol.*, **10**, 156–160: Prescriptive appraisals

Lynes J A, 1980, *Ltg. Res. Technol.*, **12**, 181–185: Limiting ratios of luminance and illuminance

22 Lighting for commercial and public buildings

This is the first of four chapters concerned with the lighting of specific types of interior. There are some common threads in the lighting practice for the commercial and public buildings found in this chapter – offices, hotels and catering establishments, teaching establishments and libraries, hospitals and health care buildings, and churches – but there are important differences, not least are the differences in the freedom of action given to the lighting designer as a consequence of who his client is. In the UK the lighting of schools is very much subject to the rules of the Department of Education and Science, and the lighting of hospitals to specifications used by the Department of Health and Social Services. There are also differences in the weighting to be given to lighting for function and lighting for effect in the various interiors. In no case should no weight be given to one of these, but it would be facile to pretend that the architectural features of a health centre corridor are as important to be revealed as the nave of Gloucester Cathedral.

22.1 Offices

The dictionary defines the office as a room or set of rooms in which business, professional duties, clerical work, etc., are carried out. It fails to mention the fact that offices are for people and that a high proportion of all working people are employed in offices of one kind or another. The standards of design and levels of efficiency achieved within these areas therefore have a profound effect on the gross national product.

The office is presently undergoing perhaps its most significant stage of development in the increased use of electronic instrumentation, such as word processors, electronic calculators, micro-film systems, and visual display units, all with their own special lighting needs. Although these changes are blurring the distinction between general offices and business machine rooms, they are examined separately here, as are private offices and drawing offices.

The provision of lighting in all offices in the UK is subject to legislation under the *Offices, Shops and Railway Premises Act* (HMG 1963), and such premises are not exempt from the requirements of the *Health and Safety at Work Act* (HMG 1974). The provision of sufficient and suitable lighting may well be equated with satisfying the minimum requirements of the CIBS/IES Code for Interior Lighting (CIBS 1977a) – those for offices being given in Table 22.1 – but meeting these illuminance and glare limits is no guarantee of a satisfactory visual office environment. As has been indicated in Chap. 21, all the inter-related factors contributing to a satisfactory visual condition must be considered by the lighting designer.

Table 22.1   CIBS/IES recommendations (1977) for offices

	Standard service illuminance (lux)	Position of measurement	Limiting glare index
General offices with mainly clerical tasks and occasional typing	500	Desk	19
Deep plan general offices	750	Desk	19
Business machine and typing offices	750	Copy	19
Filing rooms	300	File label	19
Conference rooms	750	Table	16
Computer rooms	500	Working plane	19
Drawing offices drawing boards	750	Board	16
Reference tables	500	Table	16
Print room	300	Table	19

22.1.1   General offices

The visual tasks in general offices are quite diversified, ranging from those which are spasmodic and easy to those which are continuous and exacting. Unfortunately, the more exacting work is frequently undertaken by the more experienced worker, who is older and therefore has a reduced visual performance capability. Most office occupations involve the reading of type, either printed or type-written: the severity of the visual task depends on the type size and its clarity and on the reflectances of the type and paper on which the message appears. Management can ease the visual tasks of their employees by paying attention to the choice of type and typewriter, by ensuring that staff are not regularly required to read poor carbon copies, and by choosing papers of appropriate reflectance and colour.

Many office tasks have a number of areas of interest. For example the typist needs to look at the original copy, the typewriter keys, and the script in the machine. Generally it is the original copy which receives the most attention, and some typists prefer to have this on an inclined plane. Specular reflections from typewriter keys and the surfaces of office machinery should be avoided whenever possible.

The vast majority of existing offices have general lighting schemes with ceiling mounted luminaires arranged to give an overall coverage to the total office area. Such installations will usually have been designed without reference to the actual task to be carried out in the lit space, but have the advantage of enabling the user to rearrange his workstations at will, without reference to the lighting layout.

A marked trend in the early 1980s has been the recognition by enlightened architects, developers, and users that lighting energy should be used in these areas more effectively. This has been achieved by utilizing energy-conscious luminaires in localized or local lighting systems (Sect. 21.2.2) to ensure that task lighting levels are provided on tasks and circulation lighting levels elsewhere.

22.1.2 Business machine and computer offices

The advent of electromechanical data processing in the late 1950s led to the rapid development of machine systems relying on the production of punch cards for the storing and processing of information. The transfer of information from printed form to punch card is achieved by clerical operators, usually in large segregated offices. In most machines the arduous visual tasks are in the vertical plane. Since this equipment is usually fairly large, the layout of the room is unlikely to be changed, so the lighting designer has an opportunity to provide the high vertical illuminances of 750 lux at the points where they are needed, with minimum shadowing.

These electromechanical units are rapidly being replaced by all-electronic devices. The information for processing is now being passed into computers by operators seated at terminals, a terminal consisting of a typewriter keyboard and a visual display monitor. The visual task remains that of reading information and transferring it to the keyboard, but the punched card is replaced by a self-luminous display screen, a feature which requires little or no direct light and in the glazed front of which veiling reflections become an immediate disabling factor.

The most widely-accepted lighting system to meet these new requirements consists of individual or continuous lines of recessed low brightness luminaires, located so that the workers are facing in the direction of the axis of the luminaires. Reflected glare is reduced below that from a conventional luminaire, and the 'batwing' distribution (Fig. 22.1) enables a greater spacing to mounting height ratio to be used while maintaining a uniform 500 lux on the horizontal. This design approach, based on luminaires with a markedly disymmetric distribution, does place restrictions on the orientation of the workstations.

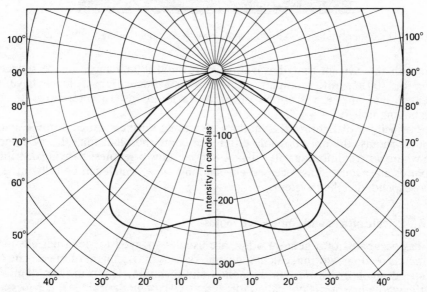

Fig. 22.1   Intensity distribution of batwing luminaire

Recently, indirect lighting systems have been used with considerable success, given a ceiling with a reasonably high reflectance (Fig. 22.2). The large area of lit ceiling with a low luminance results in the complete absence of veiling reflections. It has been

Fig. 22.2　Uplighting installation in conjunction with a visual display workstation

found with this system that the average horizontal illuminance can be reduced to 300 lux or 400 lux with complete worker satisfaction. Light sources have been concealed into the top sections of office furniture as an alternative to being free-standing uplights.

The principles of lighting the modern electronic business office apply equally to computer rooms, the only possible difference being the older main-frame computer room where air conditioning will still be essential. Low brightness batwing distribution luminaires are available as recessed air-handling units, which can be fully integrated into a suspended ceiling system.

22.1.3　Private offices and conference rooms

Whereas occupants of a general office are usually engaged for long periods in such activities as reading, writing, calculating, and typing, the occupant of the private office may spend much of his time in discussion and dictation. Uniformity of illuminance over the whole interior is not called for: it may well be undesirable. It is necessary to light the desk area to a minimum illuminance of 500 lux; if the office is close to a general office having 1000 lux then a level of 600 lux or 700 lux should be considered to prevent a sense of deprivation. This may be provided by special lighting features. The lighting of the general surroundings, giving scope for an imaginative treatment, should provide a comfortable but stimulating atmosphere. It should be remembered that the predominant sightline is likely to be nearer the horizontal than for a worker in a general office.

The principles of lighting for private offices also apply to conference rooms. Whilst it is often necessary to make notes at the conference table, much of the time is taken up with discussion and an evenly-lit room rarely helps to create an appropriate atmosphere. The area of the table should be lit to 500 lux with equipment which will offer the minimum of specular reflections in the surface of the table. Care must be exercised if downlights fitted with concentrating tungsten reflector lamps are located directly above the heads of seated people. Even a short exposure to the concentrated radiant heat from a powerful reflector lamp is most uncomfortable and will do nothing for the creation of an appropriate atmosphere. The designer should bear in mind the widespread use of visual aids in conference rooms. Provision should be made to illuminate blackboards and display screens as appropriate, and if slides or films or television monitors are to be viewed, dimming facilities should be provided for the general lighting.

22.1.4   Drawing offices

The most exacting visual tasks in offices are usually to be found in a drawing office. Critical detail must be seen with precision and contrasts are often poor, as for example when pencil lines have to be seen through tracing paper or cloth. Further difficulties arise through shadows thrown by the various drawing instruments used. Reflected glare is an everpresent danger when a large proportion of the worker's visual field may be filled with a surface of high reflectance: a matt backing medium of about 40% reflectance is advisable to reduce this effect.

The preferred lighting installation for a drawing office has always been a topic of controversy, particularly the choice between a modest general installation supplemented by local lighting and a generous general lighting scheme. Draughtsmen often prefer the former, since this usually gives the individual control over at least the direction of light on his work, and psychologically some feeling of privacy. However, the local light used by one draughtsman is liable to become a source of glare to another, so it is not uncommon to introduce some constraints on the permissible range of movement of local board lighting units. If total general lighting is to be used, it has to be remembered that drawing boards may be set at any angle between the horizontal and the vertical. The provision of shadow-free lighting, with a flow down the board, is the prime requirement: ideally this will be provided by a large-area source to reduce reflected highlights in the drawing paper. The luminous ceiling, or the indirect uplights referred to in Sect. 22.1.2, satisfy these requirements. If direct ceiling mounted luminaires are to be used, lines running parallel to the horizontal axis of the drawing board are to be preferred.

22.2   Hotels and catering establishments

22.2.1   Hotels

Hotels have many differing areas, each with its own particular lighting requirements and needing differing techniques, but the final result must be aimed at creating the correct atmosphere and attractive ambience, welcoming the visitor and making him feel 'at home'. The need for correct lighting may not be so readily accepted behind the scenes, in areas unpenetrated by visitors, but a well-run and efficient concern requires that all members of staff, doing whatever job, should have adequate lighting to enable them to carry out their tasks with efficiency and safety. The recommendations of the CIBS/IES Lighting Code for hotels are given in Table 22.2.

Table 22.2　CIBS/IES recommendations (1977) for hotels

	Standard service illuminance (lux)	Position of measurement	Limiting glare index
Entrance halls			
general	75 scalar	1·2 m above floor	19
reception, cashier	300	Desk	19
Public rooms			
bars, coffee bars	150	Table	—
dining rooms, grill rooms, and restaurants			
general	100	Table	—
cash desks	300	Desk	—
lounges	100 scalar	1·2 m above floor	16
writing rooms	150	Table	19
cloakrooms	150	Floor	—
Bedrooms			
general	50	Floor	—
bedhead	150	Bed	—
Bathrooms	100	Floor	—
Service areas			
kitchens			
food stores	150	Floor	—
working areas	500	Working surface	22
baggage rooms	100	Floor	—
laundries	300	Working plane	—
cellars	150	Floor	—

Entrance halls　These are for many people their first contact with the hotel and should reflect the attitude of the concern as a whole. The entrance hall, generally in use 24 hours a day, has to appear bright and cheerful to those entering from daylight. By night these lighting levels may appear excessive, so some form of switching may be desirable, with scalar illuminances down to the region of 75–100 lux.

Any lighting design must be in sympathy with the interior decor. A traditional entrance may be lit with a combination of crystal chandeliers and indirect fluorescent lighting to give both sparkle and practical working light. For a modern hotel a common approach is the use of a luminous ceiling made from decorative louvres with either tungsten spotlights or fluorescent tubes above.

Upon entry the guest should be able to recognize immediately the reception desk and the porters' lodge. This is usually achieved by highlighting these areas, provided the interior designer has enabled them to be a focal point of the interior decor, otherwise strategically-placed illuminated signs are called for. These desks are working areas, so a suitable illuminance of 300 lux is recommended, typically using downlighters or spotlights in keeping with the general decor.

Lounges often form an extension to the foyer or entrance hall and therefore the lighting design should reflect the style adopted there. General overhead lighting to give sufficient light for casual reading or writing throughout a lounge could well prove harsh and unrestful. So a lower level of general lighting, together with supplementary lighting from either wall brackets, table, or floor lamps is preferable. If television viewing is to take place in the space, care is needed to prevent distracting reflections of luminaires appearing on the screen. Pelmet or cornice lighting is particularly useful in this situation. Dimmer control, to permit a different level of lighting by day and by night, could be advantageous.

Reception suites Such rooms in hotels have the most diverse use, ranging from conferences to banquets, from committees to exhibitions. Ideally, the lighting design should be flexible enough to accommodate these diverse needs, but this is unlikely to be achieved without considerable compromise. The most satisfactory approach is to provide an economically feasible range of lighting units which, by switching and dimming, enable the pattern to be varied to suit the needs of the occasion. In practice this means that a mixture of decorative and functional lighting will be employed, for example chandeliers and downlighters. In positioning pendant fittings it is important that the sight lines for projectors and other AV equipment are not interrupted. Whether or not a stage is included, the versatility of lighting control is important. In the case of cabaret or dances the performers or the band will need highlighting whilst the remainder of the room is lit to fairly low levels. Specialist stage lighting equipment with its facility for beam shaping and colour changing should always be used in preference to commercial spotlights.

Dining rooms The dining room in most hotels has to undergo a transformation between breakfast and dinner time. The brisk business-like requirement for breakfast time has to give way to the soft 'linger a while' atmosphere. This may be accomplished by the change from downlights (Fig. 22.3) to a softer form of illumination as provided by table lamps or even chandeliers. Wall or curtain lighting is likely to be needed to supplement either form of main lighting.

Corridors, stairs, and lifts The provision of adequate lighting (75–100 lux) in all of these areas is usually a 24 hours-a-day exercise. These long burning hours need to be considered when selecting the light source if a major maintenance problem is not to be encountered. It has to be remembered that tungsten lamps have a continuous life of only six weeks or so. The choice of a discharge lamp, particularly the fluorescent tube, makes better economic sense. Its long life, coupled with low heat output, extends luminaire maintenance periods and reduces the required frequency for decoration.

In new buildings, or when major renovation of older premises is being undertaken, it is usually possible to make provision for the installation of recessed fluorescent lighting set into a purpose-made slot in the suspended ceiling. This can take the form of a continuous slot adjacent to one side wall, providing inconspicuous wall washing for the length of the corridor. Where a renovation requires the continued use of existing filament lighting points, the small compact 2D lamp (Sect. 11.4.3) is an ideal replacement for the tungsten lamp, from the considerations of maintenance, energy use, and cost.

Coupled with the provision of adequate normal lighting on corridors and stairs, there is the need for escape lighting in accordance with the *Fire Precautions Act* (HMG 1971). The design of this type of emergency lighting has been outlined in Sect. 21.4.

Bedrooms The prime requirement of general lighting in a hotel bedroom is to meet

Fig. 22.3   Hotel dining room lit with downlights only

the needs of the guest on his first entry into the room, and is often satisfied by a centrally mounted tungsten luminaire. Local lighting is then provided at the bedhead and commonly over dressing tables, wash basins, mirrors, and desks. These are generally tungsten lamps in decorative fittings, either free-standing or wall mounted, except for pelmet lighting over desks and curtains where fluorescent lamps are more common. The colour appearance of any fluorescent lamp should be warm so as to blend with the tungsten general lighting. Provision is normally made for the remote switching of all room lights from the bedside. The provision of local lighting over a wash basin or in a bathroom must take into account the added requirement of resistance to water and steam. It is often the practice here to install a combined light and shaver socket luminaire.

22.2.2   Restaurants, pubs, and clubs

Restaurants of the specialist type will often go far beyond the standards of a hotel dining room (Sect. 22.2.1) to establish an appropriate atmosphere in support of its specialist cuisine, e.g. Indian, Greek, Chinese, etc. However, in those having both a daytime and evening trade it is not uncommon, as in hotels, to provide a means of varying the mood to suit the time of day – not least by changing the quality and the quantity of lighting by switching and/or dimming. As the layout of tables is likely to be constant, the positioning of lighting equipment can be planned with downlights and/or decorative pendants on rise and fall suspensions directly over each table. The addition of individual candle lamps to each table will help create a soft and romantic ambience. Even in specialist restaurants attention must be paid to the provision of adequate illumination over serving points and waiter stations; it may also be necessary to provide auxiliary lighting to enable cleaners to carry out their essential business.

There are other types of restaurant, not least the 'fast food' multiples, having both eat-on-the-premises and take-away facilities. Individual and distinctive house styles have developed and branches of these multiples are easily recognized by their standard decor and fitments. This, coupled with a limited standard range of dishes on offer, gives to the operator economy in operation. In all of these outlets the lighting design must be tailored to suit the decor and any attempt to just provide light without integration will almost certainly result in an unsatisfactory appearance: fast food restaurants will usually require sparkle and glitter as part of their image. In the main the decor will be light and colourful and will be lit using a mixture of concealed fluorescent tubes together with tungsten spotlights.

Pubs and clubs A pub is a place where people meet in convivial relaxing surroundings to drink and talk. The variations in the interior design of pubs are wide, but there is one general rule for lighting – it must be in keeping with the decor. A centuries-old coaching inn full of copper and brass ornaments will require a completely different lighting design to a modern city centre pub, but in both cases a balance has to be struck between the creation of the relaxing atmosphere and the provision of adequate illumination at the focal points of the room, such as the bar, the darts board, and the card table.

General lighting is often provided by low powered wall brackets and multiway pendants supplemented by curtain lighting, and spot-lit pictures or objects creating an attractive mixture of light, shade, and colour. A more subdued lighting is provided in lounge and cocktail bars than in a public bar, where higher levels allow for the playing of games, such as darts and billiards. In the serving area of the bar adequate provision must be made in the vicinity of the till, glass washing machines, and food serving areas to ensure satisfactory standards of operation. The bar fitments usually allow the concealment of fluorescent tubes which back-light the bottles and glasses, give an attractive appearance, and provide a focal point in the room (Fig. 22.4).

The only extra provision necessary for clubs is where there is a dance floor or a stage for cabaret, in which case professional stage lighting equipment together with appropriate controls should be provided (Chap. 25).

22.3 Teaching establishments and libraries

22.3.1 Classrooms and lecture rooms

The Education (School Premises) Regulations (HMG 1981), which covers all elements of school design, makes reference to the Department of Education and Science Design Note No. 17: *Guidelines for Environmental Design and Fuel Conservation in Educational Buildings* (DES 1981). These guidelines in turn make recommendations for the standards to be achieved in the design of educational buildings. Primarily intended for new buildings, they do however provide a design brief for the improvement of existing buildings.

The recommendations place particular emphasis on the utilization of daylight in the provision of the bulk of the light needed during the typical 7-hour school day. Where the window design and building orientation allow for a minimum daylight factor of 2%, electric lighting will only be required for some 400 hours during a school year to

Fig. 22.4   Bar counter with decorative and functional concealed lighting

maintain the minimum recommended illuminance of 150 lux. The lowest level of maintained illuminance, whether daylight or electric light, at any point on the working plane should not be less than 150 lux and, where fluorescent lighting is employed, the general illuminance should not be less than 300 lux. Coupled with this is the requirement for a limiting glare index of 19 for the electric light with due regard being paid to the control of sky glare. In primary schools, where hours of use are short, the lighting can be by means of tungsten lamps and a recommended minimum level of 150 lux is acceptable for the majority of tasks and activities. In upper schools, colleges, and universities, where either the pupils are older or the tasks more onerous, minimum illuminances of 300 lux are applicable and, indeed, where the correct balance has to be struck between daylight and electric light, levels in excess of 350 lux may be justified.

The reliance on horizontal illuminance only as a yard stick for good design will not necessarily produce a satisfactory balance of vertical to horizontal illuminances. Any design which produces a ratio of between 0·5 and 0·8 vertical to horizontal illuminance will help maintain the daylight quality of the space, as well as generally improving the seeing ability of the occupants. This increase in vertical illuminance must not be achieved at the expense of glare control and the limiting index of 19 applies. Where the main view is across the space towards the chalkboard, this glare index should be reduced to 16. The lighting of chalkboards will generally be by means of angle reflector fittings and care must be exercised to establish the correct offset for the luminaire to achieve reasonable uniformity and avoid unwanted reflections. The CIBS/IES Lighting Code recommends a vertical illuminance of 500 lux for chalkboards.

This Code also gives recommendations for the lighting of specialized teaching spaces, which are summarized in Table 22.3. In addition to the Code, the IES has produced a lighting guide to lecture theatres (CIBS 1973).

Table 22.3 CIBS/IES recommendations (1977) for schools

	Standard service illuminance (lux)	Position of measurement	Limiting glare index
Assembly halls			
general	300	Working plane	19
platform and stage	Special lighting		
Teaching spaces			
general	300	Working plane	19
general where also used for further education	500	Working plane	19
chalkboard	500	Vertical plane	—
Lecture theatres			
general	300	Desk	16
chalkboard	500	Vertical plane	—
demonstration benches	500	Bench	16
Needlework rooms	500	Working plane	19
Art rooms	500	Easel	19
Laboratories	500	Bench	19
Workshops	300	Working plane	19
Dining spaces	150	Table	22
Gymnasia	300	Floor	—
Music practice rooms	300	Music	19

22.3.2 Libraries

The recommendations for illuminance values in the various areas of either reference or lending libraries are given in the CIBS/IES Lighting Code, as are the recommended limiting glare indices (Table 22.4). This advice is expanded in a technical report on library lighting (CIBS 1966).

Table 22.4 CIBS/IES recommendations (1977) for libraries

	Standard service illuminance (lux)	Position of measurement	Limiting glare index
Shelves, book stacks	150	Vertical at floor level	19
Reading tables	300	Table	19
Reading rooms			
newspapers and magazines	300	Desk	19
reference libraries	500	Desk	19
Counters	500	Desk	19
Cataloguing and sorting	500	Desk	19
Binding	500	Desk	19
Closed book stores	100	Vertical at floor level	—

On the basis of economics the fluorescent tube is usually the most appropriate light source for general lighting. While the use of high efficiency tubes would seem to be the most suitable choice on cost grounds, their colour rendering may not be completely satisfactory; de luxe lamps, whilst having lower luminous efficacies, will provide a more pleasing and comfortable environment. The only possible disadvantage in the use of fluorescent tubes is the noise level produced by the control gear. This could be a nuisance in the reading room of a reference library, which usually will have a low general noise level, but if good quality luminaires are employed and care is taken that the luminaires are not mounted directly on to a surface that will act as a resonator, no trouble should be experienced.

The design of the lighting within any new library interior will almost certainly meet with a ceiling height of between 2·75 m and 5 m and the size of luminaires for fluorescent tubes will preclude the use of suspended units if a satisfactory visual appearance is to be achieved. Surface or recessed luminaires are to be preferred, but care must be taken in their selection to avoid excessive luminance contrast with the ceiling. A general diffusing luminaire will produce an evenly-distributed and subjectively flat lighting condition (Fig. 22.5), but if some additional local lighting is provided for certain areas, perhaps by means of tungsten spotlights directed on to notice and display boards, and with highlighting of the counters, a satisfactory interior luminance pattern can result.

Fig. 22.5 School library with air-handling recessed luminaires

Bookstacks The addition of special lighting on bookcases has a two-fold effect. Firstly it increases the luminosity of the bookcase front and hence adds to the visual appearance of the interior and secondly, if correctly designed, it adds to the visibility of the book titles on display. The main problems in bookstack lighting are getting light to the lower shelves and dealing with the obstruction caused by the borrowers: no perfect solution exists, but several methods are currently used to overcome the problems. One solution to the first problem is a change in the form of the stack: if the lower shelves are inclined outwards an immediate improvement in the visibility of the lower shelves becomes evident. Whether or not this is done, the most suitable solution to both problems is to use fluorescent tubes incorporated into a canopy affixed to the top of the stack. Ideally the lamps should be used in conjunction with reflectors designed to direct as much light to the lower shelves as possible. ⊁

22.4 Hospitals and health care buildings

22.4.1 Public areas

Entrance halls, involving waiting areas, reception, and enquiry desks, have no specific lighting requirements from a medical point of view except that a sense of well-being should be promoted in the visitor, who may be in an anxious frame of mind and rather apprehensive. The design techniques follow those in Sect. 22.2.1, remembering, of course, that the reception staff will probably be carrying out a clerical function and will need appropriate task lighting standards.

The lighting for general circulation around hospitals and clinics, often through a maze of corridors and stairs, requires attention to be paid firstly to the adequate illumination of direction signs and secondly to the provision of general lighting. Continuous lines of luminaires, positioned along one side of a corridor, are preferred to luminaires on the centreline. Transversely mounted luminaires should not be used in any corridor where patients are likely to be conveyed on trolleys as the visual disturbance of moving under alternating high and low brightness patterns is undesirable.

Provision must be made in all public areas for emergency lighting (Sect. 21.4), where reference should be made to DHSS Memorandum HTM 11: *Emergency Electrical Services* (DHSS 1974) as well as to BS 5266 (BSI 1975b).

22.4.2 Wards

Over many years ward units have developed from the large multi-bedded Nightingale types to the compact four-, five-, or six-bedded wards of present-day design, but the lighting of any ward unit must satisfy the dual requirements of both the patient and the nursing staff throughout the day and night.

Modern small wards are generally situated on the outside of the buildings with the beds parallel to the main window wall (Fig. 22.6). The major daytime lighting is natural light, providing maxima ranging from 40 lux to 50 lux at the back of the room on a dull day to over 25 000 lux near the window on a sunny day. There will be periods during which it will be necessary to supplement the daylight with electric lighting.

The duties of the nursing staff include the general observation of the patient's state, taking readings of blood pressure and temperature, and marking charts and records. For these tasks an average illuminance is advisable of between 30 lux and 50 lux at the patient's head and not less than 100 lux in the central space between the bed footrails. Experience has shown that these illuminances will simultaneously satisfy the visual needs of patients who are awake without causing disturbance to those who wish to sleep. Fluorescent lamps are entirely acceptable, provided that approved clinical colour rendering types are used, °Kolor-rite and Trucolor 37 currently being acceptable to the DHSS.

The lighting guide on hospitals prepared by the CIBS (CIBS 1979a) recognizes three methods of providing general ward lighting, all involving luminaires mounted along the centreline of a ward. *Suspended luminaires*, unsuitable for low ceilings,

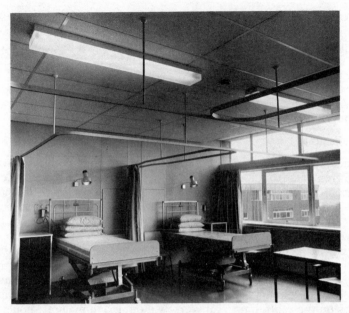

Fig. 22.6 Typical hospital ward with general fluorescent and local bedhead lights

should be mounted between 2·7 m and 3·5 m above the floor at a spacing of between 3·5 m and 3·8 m. The luminaires should emit between 40 and 70% of their light upwards, with an average luminance in the direction of the bedhead not exceeding 1000 cd m⁻². *Ceiling mounted luminaires* (Fig. 22.6), for ceilings below 3 m, should be spaced at about 2·2 m or 3 m (twin lamps), give between 15 and 30% of upward light, and have a luminance limit of 1800 cd m⁻². *Recessed/semi-recessed luminaires* are not suitable alone in multi-bedded wards, but need to be used in conjunction with wall mounted bedhead luminaires. Both ceiling and wall units should be spaced similarly to the beds at about 2·2 m, with critical luminances below 700 cd m⁻².

Reading lights may incorporate either fluorescent or, more usually, tungsten lamps. The positioning and design of any reading light must be such that a minimum illuminance of 150 lux is provided at the bedhead, while not causing glare to other patients in the ward. Mechanical stops are commonly incorporated to limit movement and thereby restrict the luminance towards adjacent or opposite patients to 700 cd m⁻².

All wards need some low level lighting for the hours of darkness to enable nursing staff to monitor patients without disturbing those who are sleeping. Illuminances of 0·1 lux at the bedhead and 3 lux to 5 lux within the circulation space are recommended. This light is commonly provided by 5 W to 8 W tungsten lamps set into the general lighting units, screened to limit the critical luminance to 30 cd m⁻².

Where a nursing station is integral or adjacent to a ward the service illuminance during the day of 300 lux should be reduced to between 30 lux and 100 lux at night, and the luminance of any part of the station should be limited to 10 cd m⁻².

22.4.3 Operating theatres

Operating theatres are areas having the most critical visual tasks. General lighting is usually provided from fully-recessed fluorescent luminaires, which are sealed against the ingress of dust from the ceiling void, can be easily cleaned, and use lamps with clinical quality colour rendering. Local lighting on the operating table is provided by a very specialized luminaire capable of providing shadow-free illumination in the operating cavity by means of a multi-lamp and multi-faceted reflection system.

Whilst the illuminance on the operating table may be in the region of 10 000 lux to 50 000 lux on a selective and variable basis, it is usual to provide a background illuminance of 400 lux to 500 lux. This will be sufficient for the theatre staff to carry out ancillary tasks, such as the operation of life support apparatus. Clinical quality colour rendering should be maintained not only throughout the operating theatre, but also in the anaesthetic and recovery rooms.

In operating theatre suites, as in delivery rooms and intensive care units, the emergency lighting provided is Grade A, i.e. lighting of the level and quality equal, or nearly equal, to that provided by normal lighting, which calls for the use of a generator set plus an auxiliary battery for during the generator run-up.

22.5 Churches

The provision of a lighting system in any ecclesiastical building has to be a careful blend of art and science. It should provide sufficient illuminance for the visual tasks being carried out and yet should unobtrusively complement or enhance the appearance of the interior. It is this mixture which can provide the interior of a great cathedral with an added dimension of grandeur or mystery.

The greatest examples of medieval architecture are to be found in some of our ancient cathedrals with their shape and form receiving subtle revelation as a result of the penetration of daylight. The shaft of light from the sun, streaming through stained glass windows, has all the drama of the theatre in it: the successful artificial lighting of cathedrals, by yesterday's flame sources or today's electric lamps, inevitably owes something to the theatre also.

Attempts have been made in recent years to reproduce, using electric light, the day-lit appearance of an interior (Fig. 22.7): several of these interiors have been churches or cathedrals. The apparent brightness method of design, first proposed by Waldram (1954), permits an orderly calculation of the lighting needed to produce any proposed visual effect, this effect being specified by allotting relative brightness values to each surface in the interior, in arbitrary units. Using apparent brightness scales, the reflectances of the surfaces, and inter-reflection calculations, it is possible to determine the relative direct illuminance needed on each major surface. Absolute illuminances follow from some requirements related to visual tasks, for example the provision of 100 lux in the body of a church, rising at the focal points of the interior to between 150 lux and 200 lux. (With the average age of churchgoers now tending to be over 50 years, there is an argument for higher illuminances than this on hymn and prayer books.)

In churches used only for a few hours weekly tungsten lamps still find favour. This is partly because of their low cost, their small size, and the fact that no auxiliary gear is necessary to run them. However, they are very expensive sources to run, particularly when a real cost is allocated for access to lamps for replacement and cleaning. In buildings where large numbers of visitors, pilgrims, or tourists are present each day and the lighting is required to operate for extended periods, consideration must be given to the use of discharge lamps with their long life characteristics and low power consumption.

Many churches are now being used for activities other than religious ceremony. It is

Fig. 22.7   The nave of a cathedral lit using the apparent brightness concept

becoming increasingly common for orchestral concerts and plays to be enacted in the nave of many of the large city centre churches. Here, special theatre and concert hall lighting will be necessary. This equipment may be installed on a temporary basis or may form part of the standard installation. In either case the ability to control the general lighting by means of dimmers will be an advantage, so provision should be considered at an early stage of design as this requirement may dictate the light source selected.

No hard and fast guidelines can be laid down for church lighting, since the sacred, secular, and aesthetic needs for no two churches are the same. However, a successful scheme will not only satisfy the visual needs of the worshipper and emphasize the liturgical practice of the religious community, but it will also show to full advantage the architectural merits of the building.

Further reading

Church of England, 1981, *Lighting and wiring of churches* (London: CIO Publishing)
Dept of Health and Social Services, 1977, DHSS Memo HTM 7: *Electrical services supply and distribution* (London: HMSO)
Electricity Council, *Better office lighting*
Electricity Council, *Lighting for hotels and restaurants*

23 Lighting for display

The connection between boutiques and supermarkets on the one hand and art galleries and museums on the other is that items are on display, and the displays are not peripheral to the prime activity taking place – they are central. Although the general ambience in these interiors may differ greatly, there is the common requirement that objects on display will be recognized readily and be shown to advantage. The core of this chapter is therefore concerned with local lighting techniques for counters, showcases, gondolas, shop windows, and wall displays. Local lighting is usually accompanied by general lighting, and these together affect the ambience of an interior, so a section of this chapter is devoted to the different general lighting techniques for selling and exhibition spaces. Included in a section dealing with the principles of lighting in these areas is a note on the problems of conservation in art galleries and museums.

23.1 Principles

Objects which are displayed for either selling or for appreciation must be presented so that their form, colour, and size can be readily recognized. In many shops, certainly self-service types, customers are permitted to handle the goods so that their appraisal is both tangible and visual. In a museum or art gallery visitors are hardly ever allowed to touch the exhibits, so texture, shape, and colour can only be revealed by the lighting. With solid objects it is the direction of the lighting and not the quantity that most controls revealing power (Sect. 2.4.3).

In shops the lighting is required to draw the customer's attention to the goods, help him to appraise them, and provide an atmosphere conducive to sales. The method will vary according to the types of goods displayed, the form of trading, the design of the shop, and the class of customers expected. It is usually necessary to provide ambient general lighting and not rely solely on 'spill' light from displays to illuminate the rest of the interior, otherwise flexibility in the disposition of the displays is impaired.

In museums and art galleries a pleasant relaxing ambience is required so that the displays can be studied at leisure. The general ambient lighting must be complementary to the function of the interior: it is most effective if the source of this lighting is not obvious. However, a dominant consideration in both local and general lighting here is that of conservation.

Conservation This subject is comprehensively discussed in the CIBS Lighting Guide to Museums and Art Galleries (CIBS 1980a). Vandalism apart, valuable and perhaps unique materials can be damaged by electromagnetic radiation, biological attack, excessive humidity, air pollution, and to some extent heat. Even slight damage to materials or colours may produce changes in the overall appearance of objects such that confusion may arise in art scholarship.

Radiation is the most widespread cause of trouble. Any radiation (infrared, visible, or ultraviolet) which is absorbed by an object is liable to cause damage, at a rate depending largely on the chemical constitution of the object. Ultraviolet radiation is the most dangerous because it is more likely to cause photochemical changes in organic materials. As the wavelength of radiation increases, so its destructive effect falls, because the absorption of radiation now promotes chemical changes only indirectly by heating. High humidity accelerates these reactions and should therefore be an additional matter of concern in museums and art galleries.

The admission of daylight into an art gallery (or a shop window display) will, over a period of time, cause excessive fading in certain materials due to the ultraviolet present. Fluorescent tubes and high pressure discharge lamps also produce ultraviolet radiation, in varying degrees according to the colour selected. Since electric lighting is generally found in smaller quantities than daylight, most conservation effort has been directed towards the provision of ultraviolet filters for windows and skylights rather than for electric lighting units. However, the recommended service illuminances on objects in museums and art galleries in the CIBS/IES Code for Interior Lighting (CIBS 1977a), reproduced in Table 23.1, are entirely related to the sensitivity to light of different materials.

Table 23.1   CIBS/IES recommendations (1977) for museums and art galleries

	Standard service illuminance (lux)	Position of measurement	Limiting glare index
General			
exhibits insensitive to light	300	Display	16
light-sensitive exhibits	150	Display	16
specially light-sensitive exhibits	50	Display	16
Ancillary areas			
entrances, corridors, staircases, offices, workshops, etc.	Need to ensure correct adaptation sequences		

Colour rendering   As has been indicated in Chap. 3, the spectral distribution of the illuminant is critical when a faithful rendering of the colour of an object becomes important: a condition which certainly applies to paintings and fabrics. The colour rendering properties of different light sources, defined in Sect. 3.5 and specified in the various chapters of Part II of this book, result in a few types of lamps being completely unsuitable for shops or exhibitions. When specifying which are the most suitable, other factors will also need to be considered, at least for local lighting: size, light distribution, heat output, and ultraviolet output.

Lamps   The major advantages of filament lamps for display are that they are compact, they operate without control gear, and they provide a full spectrum of light (albeit weak in the blue and strong in the red). Their disadvantages are a low efficacy, a short life, and a considerable production of heat. Of the different types of filament lamps described in Chaps 9 and 10, the most effective types for display purposes are those with very compact filaments, such as the low voltage and tungsten halogen types, which permit good light control from built-in or external reflectors.

Fluorescent lamps are used for general lighting and for local lighting where strong emphasis is not required. In the latter case, where space is often at a premium, the recently-developed 26 mm diameter tubes (Sect. 11.1.3) are proving particularly useful, with the triphosphor colours (Sect. 8.3.3) in areas where good colour rendering is essential.

Of the high pressure discharge lamps, some use is made of metal halide, de luxe mercury, and sodium types for general lighting, but it is advisable, certainly with the last of these, to check out the colour demands of the particular selling and exhibition spaces to be lit.

Equipment Display lighting equipment, whether lamps with reflective coatings or luminaires consisting of lamps with external parabolic reflectors, must be capable of being pointed in any direction. It is not good practice to feed the electrical supply wires through the swivelling device, since the cable may be pinched: most well-designed spotlights have the cable taken separately through the back of the lamp housing.

Fig. 23.1 Boutique lighting technique used in small specialist shops

The use of a track system (Fig. 23.1) allows equipment to be moved about a display area at will, achieving lighting effects which are not possible with fixed lighting equipment. It is recommended, particularly in display cabinets and windows, that vertical lines of track should be installed as well as horizontal ones whenever possible.

A very important factor in the choice of luminaires for shops, whether for local or general lighting, is ease of maintenance. Except where specialist maintenance firms are contracted to clean and relamp at regular intervals, cleaning staff are nearly always unskilled and luminaires which cannot be serviced easily by one man should be generally avoided.

23.2   Creating the ambience

The basic recommendations for shop lighting in the CIBS/IES Lighting Code, reproduced in Table 23.2, suggest that 500 lux is required on displays and counters – very different from the 50 lux, 150 lux, or 300 lux recommended on displays in art

Table 23.2   CIBS/IES recommendations (1977) for shops

	Standard service illuminance (lux)	Position of measurement	Limiting glare index
Conventional with counters	500	Counters – horizontal	19
Conventional with wall displays	500	Display – vertical	19
Self-service	500 ⎱	Vertical on displayed	⎰ 19
Supermarkets	500 ⎰	merchandise	⎱ 22
Hypermarkets	500	Vertical on displayed merchandise	22
	1000	Horizontal on working plane	22
Showrooms			
car	500	Vertical on cars	19
general	500	Merchandise	19
Covered shopping precincts and arcades			
main circulation spaces	100–200 or 100 scalar	Floor	22

galleries and museums. However, the lighting levels on displays are not necessarily related to the general lighting level, particularly when a sense of drama is to be created: the interplay of the two levels has a significant influence on the atmosphere.

Considered from the viewpoint of both the ambience and the lighting techniques involved, individual shops fall into the three categories of boutiques and small specialist shops, department stores and large specialist shops, and self-service stores and supermarkets.

Boutiques and small specialist shops. Lighting here is at the point of sale and on displays, spill lighting providing the necessary lighting for circulation, as in Fig. 23.1. Lighting wall displays from open-topped canopies makes the shop look wider and provides some indirect lighting to soften shadows in gangways and aisles. The rear part of the shop should be given special lighting treatment to draw customers well into the shop, making full use of the floor area. Since the position of the counters is usually fixed, downlighters can be arranged over them, eliminating the need for internal lighting and the possible resultant heat build-up inside. This also ensures that goods taken out of the counter and put on the top of it are even better lit than they were before, but care must be taken to align the downlighters with the front edge of the counter to avoid annoying reflections in the glass.

Department stores and large specialist shops, normally with high ceilings (4 m to 5 m), are usually lit by an array of suspended or ceiling mounted luminaires unrelated to the counters and displays. The choice of luminaires is little different from that for an office, but a higher glare index is acceptable. For all that, the glare of an array of diffusing luminaires over a very large selling floor can be rather overpowering, and vaulted or coffered ceilings, integrating the luminaires within their construction, are becoming very popular. Such systems are not only efficient, but also give a pleasant appearance to the ceiling plane and do not distract the attention of the customers from the goods on display.

On plain flat ceilings the monotony of the general lighting can be reduced by arranging the luminaires in square, triangular, or polygonal formations, with down-lighters at the luminaire junctions. Alternatively, suspended ceiling modules can be used, carrying concealed lamps for general lighting above and possibly spotlights for display below (Fig. 23.2). More commonly, effective display lighting is not possible

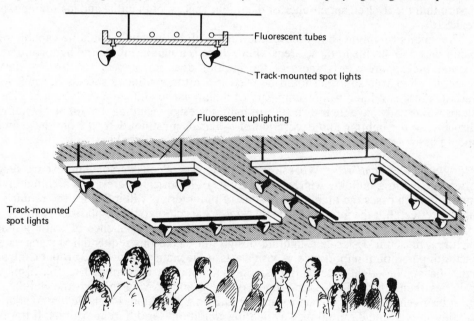

Fig. 23.2   Suspended ceiling module lighting for departmental stores

from the ceiling level because of the length of the throw, so the majority of the stores use internally-lighted counters, often arranged around lighted shelves or showcases enclosing what is virtually a supplementary stock-room. Where displays are not self-lit, the general lighting luminaires must have a light distribution providing good vertical components of illumination. Lighted canopies are often provided on island displays and almost always on wall shelves or displays.

Supermarkets and self-selection stores are lit by rows of bare fluorescent tubes. If these are oriented end-on to the check-out positions and in line with the gondolas, there is good lighting on the goods on the gondola shelves; if sited above the gangways, maintenance is facilitated. However, some supermarket companies prefer to run the lines of fluorescent tubes across the rows of gondolas, to give more flexibility in repositioning their displays. Although enclosed luminaires are sometimes used, it is claimed that bare tubes give a busy, bustling appearance to the shop, discourage loitering, and suggest a 'no nonsense' place where money is not wasted on frills. Bare tubes reduce maintenance to an absolute minimum, and the tubes need only to be wiped occasionally between replacement periods. Supplementary lighting is often provided in freezer cabinets, because of light obstruction, and on meat and cheese counters, to enhance the appearance of the food. Special lighting treatment may also be given to new or unusual selling activities, such as a bakery, a fresh fish counter, etc.

Shopping centres are concentrated shopping facilities offering customers under one roof a wide variety of merchandising outlets. Access to the stores and shops is through a series of malls and squares, often air conditioned, with trees, plants, waterfalls, fountains, etc., all contributing to a pleasant visual environment. Such interiors offer a challenge to the lighting designer who needs to work closely with the architect to ensure that the desired appearance of the public spaces, both initial and maintained, is realized.

The ambient lighting should be in the region of 200 lux, but should be capable of being raised to 400 lux in those areas where there is a significant natural light content, so that the apparent brightness of the interior does not appear too low by day. Long-life discharge sources should be used, since the continued success of interiors such as these is related to the simplicity of maintenance and lamp replacement. The shops will usually have their own style of lighting design including that for any window displays, so the lighting and decoration of the malls must not detract from these and should assist would-be customers to find the shop they are seeking.

Museums and art galleries   Works of art and objects of considerable interest are very often housed in a building which itself may be of historical interest and architectural merit. In such cases the architectural style of the interiors will influence the required lighting effect, but the interior must still act as a backcloth to the displays and exhibits.

In any museum interior the visitor is presented with a sequence of static visual pictures: museum design and lighting design must take this sequential viewing as a factor of paramount importance. A visit starts at the main entrance and proper control must be applied right from this position and not only be confined to the display galleries themselves. The visitor, upon entering and moving through the building, must be given time and satisfactory ambient lighting conditions to enable him to adapt continuously to the different display lighting conditions for different exhibits. If this is done, no dissatisfaction will be experienced with the relatively low illuminances required for any light-sensitive objects. The lighting of the exhibits and their backgrounds must be carefully adjusted so that the objects on display are seen to full advantage. Instead of a formal layout with regular rows of pictures or showcases along the walls, there is a tendency nowadays to exhibit objects in easily assimilated groups on free-standing movable screens or in island showcases, requiring several of the local lighting techniques described below.

23.3   Local display lighting

23.3.1   Shop windows

The shop window is the main link between the shopkeeper and the public and is more important than any other part of the shop. There are many ways in which goods are displayed, ranging from a complete catalogue of the wares available to ideas of luxury where only a few items are exhibited. Most supermarkets, motor car dealers, and specialist stores make use of open-backed windows which allow a view of the shop interior over or through the display. In these cases, and where windows are glazed on more than one side (multi-aspect), special care has to be taken that light sources do not cause glare to the customers. Lighting design techniques are many and the one adopted will depend on the location of the shop, on management policies, and on the class of customer, as well as on the size and shape of the windows.

Single-aspect windows One side only is glazed and there is no problem in screening the lighting equipment behind baffles (Fig. 23.3a). Although tungsten lamps and

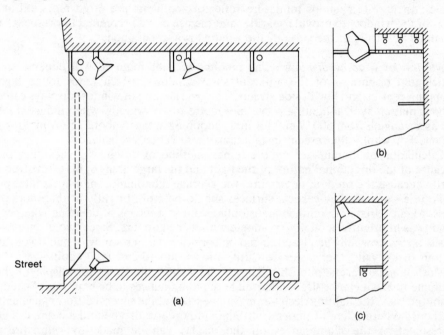

Fig. 23.3 Shop window lighting: (a) single-aspect window, (b) multiple-aspect window, and (c) shallow window

white fluorescent tubes are most commonly used, strongly coloured sources can be used for effect, providing they do not intermix. For maximum efficiency all lamps without integral reflectors should be used with external reflectors. Filament spotlights may be mounted on trunking or track systems to give flexibility to the installation when the display is changed. Low voltage tungsten lighting provides very effective highlighting in a display.

Double-aspect windows These occur in the majority of shops which have a window to one side of the entrance or two windows flanking it. Windows with little depth on one aspect are usually lit by two or more rows of fluorescent tubes mounted behind a pelmet and supplemented by tungsten spotlights, very much as for the single-aspect window. Where both aspects are extensive, the use of cross baffles or louvres becomes essential, Fig. 23.3b showing a very popular technique.

Island and open-back windows Island windows are usually found in the entrance arcade of departmental stores and are best lit by highly-concentrating spotlights arranged to avoid glare to the viewer. If general background lighting is needed, fluorescent tubes can be used, screened from view by pelmets or louvres. Lighting equipment in open-backed windows can constitute a glare source when seen from inside the shop, so the methods used for island windows apply again here.

Very shallow windows   Jewellers and confectioners commonly display their goods on shelves mounted very close to the window glass or in shallow window-showcases. Both types of window are difficult to light from the top only. Extra lamps mounted under the shelves are sometimes effective, and miniature fluorescent tubes can be used (Fig. 23.3c). In jewellers' shops miniature reflector spotlights are often mounted at the sides of the window to provide sparkle, and the use of well-screened fluorescent tubes mounted vertically at the sides of the window is also common.

Brightness of window displays   The amount of light required will depend on the anticipated brightness of the adjacent shop windows, which tends to be high in shopping centres and low in side streets. The overheating of window displays can be a serious matter, typical lighting power per metre run of window when tungsten lamps are used ranging from $600\,\mathrm{W\,m^{-1}}$ for main shopping areas to about $150\,\mathrm{W\,m^{-1}}$ for side streets. For wholly fluorescent installations these values are halved.

Calculation of illuminance by the lumen method of design is misleading, partly because of the directional nature of the light and the large areas of glass involved and partly because the method determines the average illuminance on a horizontal plane while in a shop window vertical surfaces should be more brightly lit than horizontal ones. Mean horizontal illuminance is only useful as a means of deciding whether the window is lit brightly enough to compete with its neighbours. Since two or more sides of a shop window may be glazed, it can be considered as a room with one, two, three, or four black walls, thus a very low utilization factor (0.2 or less) applies.

Most manufacturers publish 'light in the beam' diagrams for display lighting equipment which can be used to calculate the illuminances to be expected. When this is not the case, the lighting designer may have to combine several different calculation methods. Where a line of fluorescent luminaires is installed behind a pelmet, a good assessment of the illuminances on the display can be made by estimating the proportion of the total lamp lumens cast in that direction, using a scale drawing. It is important to note that while the illuminance at points opposite the middle of a tube will be roughly proportional to the inverse of the distance from it, those opposite the ends will be more nearly proportional to the inverse of the square of that distance.

23.3.2   Counter and showcase lighting

Exhibitors use a variety of methods for the housing of their displays, with a full range of cabinetry in such forms as flat top counters, lectern designs, wall units, and free-standing islands. Where glass is used to protect the displays, the lighting presents problems of both conservation and ventilation as well as having to cope with internal and external reflections.

The objects displayed should be brighter than their general surroundings and the ambient lighting should not interfere with their visibility. Although glazed showcases can be illuminated externally by narrow beam spotlights, difficulties can arise from reflections in the glass and reflections of an observer, as well as from reflections of the spotlights. The usual technique is therefore to use internal lighting in the showcase, either fluorescent tubes or low wattage tungsten lamps in metal reflectors, the reflectors obstructing the source from direct view. Fluorescent tubes, or even low wattage high pressure discharge lamps, have the advantage over tungsten lamps for internal lighting in that they have a lower heat content. However, most of them have a higher ultraviolet content, which needs to be filtered out if the objects are more sensitive to radiation than to heat. All light sources and their control gear generate some heat and therefore internally-lit showcases must be ventilated, naturally or forced, whatever the source used.

Figure 23.4a shows the normal method of mounting a lamp in a counter showcase, on the customer's side of the counter. This gives a good distribution of light, but if the

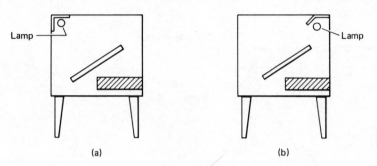

(a)   (b)

Fig. 23.4 Methods of lighting a counter showcase

design of the showcase is of slender framing it may be preferable to mount the lamps at the back of the showcase, as in Fig. 23.4b. If a discharge lamp is used, the necessary control gear is mounted in a ventilated drawer, shown shaded in the figure. Wall showcases and shelf displays are usually lit from the top, sometimes with additional individual lighting, as in the shallow window illustrated in Fig. 23.3c.

Certain objects respond to special lighting. For example, blown or engraved glass is best seen against a softly-lit and lightly-textured neutral-coloured background; low quality moulded glass looks better when light is passed through it from below. The qualities of cut glass are readily revealed by strong top lighting, with the cut glass mounted on a dark matt plinth. Silverware and jewellery should be shown under compact sources, so that facets glitter in reflecting the high luminance of the lamps. Modelling as well as highlights has a marked effect on the appearance of displayed merchandise. Goods with a strongly textured surface, such as deep-pile carpets, knitwear, and some furnishing fabrics, need strong directional lighting to bring out their qualities.

The techniques used for lighting showcases can be extended to gondolas, although it is more common practice to use fluorescent tubes mounted in canopies and on the underside of shelving. The facia of the canopy can contain a legend, indicating the contents, which can be back-lit but must not be too bright otherwise its visibility will be impaired. If no lamps are used on the underside of shelving, the canopy tubes will need to have reflectors designed to direct as much light as possible to the lower shelves.

23.3.3 Murals, pictures, and tapestries

Wall lighting, to display murals, pictures, or tapestries, usually involves fluorescent tubes and reflectors concealed behind baffles. These are mounted either in a cavity at the edge of a floating ceiling or in a purpose-built pelmet system. Incandescent wall washers can be used, but if filament lamps are to be used it is preferable to employ tungsten halogen lamps in projectors, which can provide a controlled light distribution. A limited variation of 3:1 in illuminance over the displayed item is sometimes required, but variations of up to 10:1 are usually found quite satisfactory.

Figure 23.5 shows a wall lighting unit. The offset distance needs to be considered carefully. With short offsets the texture of the display wall will be emphasized, but deep frames and shelves will cast unwanted long shadows. By increasing the offset distance a more even illumination can be achieved, but specular reflections from any

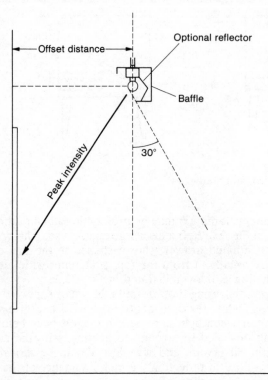

Fig. 23.5   Unit for lighting murals, pictures, or tapestries

glazing or glossy surfaces become more apparent to the observer. A visual cut-off to the source is generally achieved by the lower edge of the reflector, which should never be greater than 30° from the downward vertical. Where such lighting systems are suspended they can afford a degree of indirect lighting on the ceiling, thus avoiding undue contrast between well-lit walls and dark ceilings. If a pelmet lighting unit of the type shown in Fig. 23.5 is mounted on the wall and directed across the ceiling, it becomes a cornice lighting unit, and is very effective for the lighting of ceiling murals or for displaying elegant mouldings. The appropriate depth below the ceiling, like the offset distance for a pelmet unit, involves compromising the spread of light across the ceiling with the degree of modelling produced, and depends on the feature to be displayed.

Further reading

Electricity Council, *Lighting for retailers*

24 Lighting for industrial buildings

The lighting of industrial areas covers a multitude of different visual tasks, requiring different lighting solutions and different lighting equipment. The task is not always on a horizontal plane and in many industrial situations local lighting is needed to compensate for the shadowing of general lighting. Some tasks require illuminance from a particular direction, others for very accurate colour rendering. There are areas in industry where the luminaires must survive a very hostile environment, others, for example explosive areas, where only very specialized luminaires may be used. This chapter is concerned with the lighting equipment developed particularly for industrial use and the lighting design techniques enabling the equipment to be used effectively.

24.1 Principles

The service illuminances recommended for many industrial processes are found in the general schedule of the CIBS/IES Code for Interior Lighting (CIBS 1977a). In addition to this value in lux, the position of measurement is given, the limiting glare index is specified, and a list of acceptable light sources is given. A part of the schedule relating to machine shops is reproduced in Table 24.1.

Table 24.1 CIBS/IES recommendations (1977) for machine and fitting shops

	Standard service illuminance (lux)	Position of measurement	Limiting glare index
Casual work	200	Working plane	25
Rough bench and machine work	300	Working plane	25
Medium bench and machine work, ordinary automatic machines, rough grinding, medium buffing and polishing	500	Working plane	22
Fine bench and machine work, fine automatic machines, medium grinding, fine buffing and polishing	1000	Working plane	22

The working plane in such a schedule is defined as the horizontal, vertical, or inclined plane in which the visual task lies, which can be at any height. In the case of fabrication shops the working plane may rise during course of construction: with a capstan it could be in a vertical and horizontal plane at one time. On a warehouse rack the label could be at floor level or at the top of the rack, but always on the vertical plane. With large machine manufacture, a man could be working inside a cylindrical enclosure, the working plane being the interior surface of the cylinder. It is certainly wrong to assume the working plane to be horizontal and 0·85 m above the floor (Sect. 21.3.1) without having verified the task.

Shadowing is more pronounced in the industrial building than in its commercial counterpart due to the presence of machinery and racking: people themselves frequently cast shadows onto their own work and that of their neighbours. This phenomenon is becoming more apparent with the increasing use of high pressure discharge lamps, in low height buildings as well as in high bay areas. When fluorescent lamps were in universal use for all but the highest industrial buildings, the shadow problem was not acute because many low powered luminaires were used. Now, however, low wattage discharge luminaires are available for use at low mounting heights and wide spacings.

The shadow problem implies that the designer needs to do more than use the lumen method of design: he must check his results by some form of point-by-point calculation if the task obstructions are specified. Where bench work is performed in an interior, the light must fall on to the task from at least two luminaires to soften the shadow effect.

Despite the range of industrial processes given in the Code schedule, not all tasks are covered. A series of general descriptions of work, with examples, is therefore provided, with standard service illuminances alongside. This table, reproduced in Table 24.2, also shows conditions under which the standard illuminance should be increased or decreased from that given in the schedule.

24.2   Equipment

24.2.1   Light sources

The most fundamental change in industrial lighting in the last ten years has been in the light sources used. Prior to the 1970s colour corrected high pressure mercury lamps were inevitably used for mounting heights above 6 m and fluorescent lamps below 6 m. Now, because of its high efficacy, the high pressure sodium lamp is easily the most popular light source for new installations at the higher mounting height and it is being used with ever-increasing frequency at lower heights.

Table 24.3 lists all the different types of light source used in industrial buildings today: for each type the range of power available is shown, together with the range of circuit efficacy and the colour rendering classification (Group 1, $R_a \geqslant 85$; Group 2, $70 \leqslant R_a < 85$; Group 3, $R_a < 70$).

GLS incandescent and tungsten halogen lamps are used primarily for local lighting or for emergency use because of their compact size and instant switching facility. The colour of the light is pleasing to most people, although there is a heavy bias towards red.

Fluorescent lamps have been used for most general lighting applications in low mounting height situations, miniature tubes for local lighting applications. With a large number of sources contributing to the illuminance at any one point, there is little shadowing and it is possible to tolerate a proportion of failed lamps in the installation. Improved colour and polyphosphor fluorescent lamps are required where an industrial process calls for a high degree of colour discrimination, for example in paint or wallpaper or dyestuff manufacture, accident repairs to motor vehicles, matching thread to material in garment manufacture, and colour printing.

Mercury lamps have now become the second choice high pressure source to sodium,

Table 24.2 CIBS/IES recommendations (1977) for different task groups, with modifying factors

Task group and typical task or interior	Standard service illuminance (lux)	Are reflectances or contrasts unusually low?	Will errors have serious consequences?	Is task of short duration?	Is area windowless?	Final service illuminance (lux)
Storage areas and plant rooms with no continuous work	150					150
Casual work	200				NO → 200 / YES ↗	200
Rough work, rough machining and assembly	300	NO — 300 / YES ↗	NO — 300 / YES ↗	NO — 300 / YES ↗	NO — 300 / YES ↗	300
Routine work, offices, control rooms, medium machining and assembly	500	NO — 500 / YES ↗	NO — 500 / YES ↗	NO — 500 / YES ↗	NO — 500 / YES ↗	500
Demanding work, deep-plan, drawing or business machine offices, inspection of medium machining	750	NO — 750 / YES ↗	NO — 750 / YES ↗	NO — 750 / YES ↗		750
Fine work, colour discrimination, textile processing, fine machining and assembly	1000	NO — 1000 / YES ↗	NO — 1000 / YES ↗	NO — 1000 / YES ↗		1000
Very fine work, hand engraving, inspection of fine machining or assembly	1500	NO — 1500 / YES ↗	NO — 1500 / YES ↗	NO — 1500 / YES ↗		1500
Minute work, inspection of very fine assembly	3000	NO — 3000 / YES ↗	NO — 3000 / YES ↗	NO — 3000 / YES ↗		3000

Using local lighting, if necessary supplemented by use of optical aids.

Table 24.3   Lamps for industrial lighting

Lamp type	Range of lamp power (W)	Range of circuit efficacy (lm W⁻¹)	CIE colour rendering group
GLS incandescent	15–1500	8–19	1
Mains voltage tungsten halogen	150–2000	16–22	1
Low voltage tungsten halogen	10–100	20–22	1
High efficacy fluorescent	4–125	10–65	3
Improved colour fluorescent	15–125	20–40	1
Polyphosphor fluorescent	18–58	50–69	1
Mercury	50–1000	29–52	3
Tungsten-ballasted mercury	100–500	12–23	3
Metal halide	250–3500	55–76	2
High pressure sodium	50–1000	60–110	3

except where copper and brass are worked or where there is some psychological resistance to the warm colour of sodium. Tungsten-ballasted mercury lamps have been used, and are still to be found, as low budget plug-in replacements for tungsten lamps, used primarily in circulation areas where they could be fitted into existing luminaires.

Metal halide lamps can be used in industrial areas where colour is important without being critical. They provide a cool white light which is more popular in some situations than is that of the warmer high pressure sodium lamps.

High pressure sodium lamps have the highest circuit efficacy. Some initial consumer resistance was experienced to the golden white light, particularly when this was seen simultaneously with light from other sources. This resistance commonly disappeared when a complete installation using the new source was experienced. With both mercury and sodium high pressure lamps, reflector versions are available for particularly dirty environments.

Temperature effects   There can be a considerable difference in temperature at roof and floor level in a high bay area, and the performance of light sources is affected by their ambient temperature. Fluorescent lamps are far more temperature-sensitive than are other light sources (Sect. 11.3.4) and if they are used at high or low temperatures the consequent reduction of illumination will have to be allowed for in lighting design. High pressure discharge lamps (mercury, metal halide, and sodium lamps) all have a greater tolerance to high temperatures than do fluorescent lamps, and the limiting thermal factors in industrial lighting then tend to be the permitted temperatures of the luminaire materials and the electrical wiring. At very low temperatures fluorescent lamps can be used in suitably designed luminaires, high pressure sodium is very effective as it requires very little protection from the atmosphere, and both mercury and metal halide lamps can be used, but may be sluggish in starting.

Stroboscopic effect   The light output from any lamp running on an alternating supply is not constant, but has a 100 Hz component. It is a very large component in the case of discharge lamps, particularly those without a phosphor coating. This pulsating light can cause rotating or reciprocating machinery to appear to be running at speeds other than their actual speed, or even appear to be stationary. Complaints of this stroboscopic effect are most common in machine shops, the degree of the effect depending on the lamp type, the speed of motion, and the construction and colours of the moving parts. The connection of adjacent luminaires to different electrical phases solves the problem with fluorescent lighting, but not with wide-spaced high pressure discharge luminaires, where the illumination at most places is from one luminaire only. The use of local tungsten lighting over machines will normally swamp out the worst of the effects. Any trials of lighting installations to study stroboscopic effects should be carried out with daylight excluded, as the steady natural light reduces the effect.

24.2.2 Luminaires

The functions of a luminaire are to offer physical protection to a light source and to direct the luminous flux from that source into the desired distribution pattern. It has to provide the necessary glare control, be able to withstand specified inhospitable environments, and comply with appropriate safety standards. The shape and size of the luminaire will depend on its light source and also on the type of area in which it is to be used.

Most fluorescent units for industrial workshop environments consist of a spine housing the control gear, and a white-painted reflector, often slotted to enable convection currents to reduce the settling of dust on the lamp. Such a unit would have a total light output ratio of 80 to 85%, some 10% of it being upward. A lower proportion of upward light is provided than in most commercial luminaires, because of the lower reflectances of industrial roofs compared with commercial ceilings. Where a higher degree of light control is required, as for example in electronic assembly, prismatic controllers or specular reflectors may be employed.

(a)   (b)

Fig. 24.1 High bay luminaires: (a) for clear or elliptical lamp and (b) for reflector lamp

Luminaires for high pressure discharge lamps fall into the three groups of high bay, low bay, and directional luminaires.

High bay luminaires are suitable for mounting heights of over 6 m. Since the unit is designed for high mounting positions, the depth of the luminaire is not too critical, so the control gear is commonly mounted vertically above the lamp. By controlling the spacing between components, the unit can be designed to operate in ambient temperatures up to 45–50 °C without detrimental effects to control gear or wiring. There are two versions, as shown in Fig. 24.1, one for a clear or elliptical lamp and the other for a reflector lamp. Light output ratios are between 80 and 95%, 20% or less of it upwards, with a symmetrical light distribution and lamp power normally in the range 250 W to 1000 W.

Low bay luminaires are suitable for mounting heights down to 3 m and have light distributions with a much wider spread than those of high bay luminaires in order to prove economic. It is not unusual to be able to space these units at as much as twice their mounting height. Designed for the minimum depth, the low bay luminaire has its lamp mounted horizontally, with the control gear alongside, as shown in Fig. 24.2a. Such a unit is used in general workshops and in assembly plants with a normal atmosphere, where a standard paint finish proves quite satisfactory. Light output ratios lie between 75 and 85%, all the light downward with an asymmetric distribution, the range of lamp power being typically 150 W to 400 W.

Directional luminaires are used where a regular array of high bay luminaires would not be accessible in practice for reasons of safety or because of obstructions. Directional projectors, mounted on side walls or fixed on walkways, can then be employed. The most common type of directional luminaire is the exterior floodlight, illustrated in Fig. 24.2b, which normally has a wide double asymmetrical distribution (Fig. 26.3c) and employs lamps with powers ranging from 150 W to 1000 W. Such units may also be used to supplement overhead lighting when it is required to increase vertical plane illumination or to compensate for obstruction shadowing.

Any luminaire, regardless of light source and intended mounting, must be suitable for the environment in which it is to operate. As with other electrical equipment installed in factories, the *Electrical Regulations* (IEE 1981) and the *Health and Safety at Work Act* (HMG 1974) require that any possible danger to safety should be recognized and the necessary action taken to ensure adequate protection of the workforce, placing considerable responsibility on the user and the installer.

In the first part of the British Standard specification for luminaires, BS 4533 (BSI 1981b), luminaires are classified in three ways: firstly according to the type of protection against electric shock, secondly according to the degree of protection against the ingress of dust and moisture, and thirdly according to the material of the supporting surface for which the luminaire is designed. The second of these classifications is the most important for industrial (and outdoor) lighting. It uses the International Protection (IP) Code for electrical equipment.

The IP number, classifying a luminaire, has two digits, the first numeral defining the smallest size of foreign body which can enter the enclosure, the second the most potent form of liquid assault which the luminaire can repel (Table 24.4). Of the 63 theoretically-possible classifications, eight are sufficiently common to be allocated one of the symbols shown in Fig. 24.3, which can be marked on the luminaire.

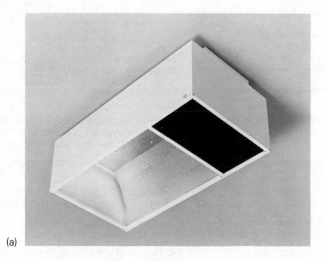

(a)

(b)

Fig. 24.2 Industrial luminaires: (a) low bay and (b) directional

Another important classification system for industrial lighting is the zoning of hazardous areas where there is a risk of explosion because of the presence of flammable gases or vapours. Zone 0 is an area where an explosive gas/air mixture is present continuously or for long periods, Zone 1 is an area where it is likely to occur in normal operation, and Zone 2 is an area where it is not likely to occur or if it does it will exist for only a short time.

As with other electrical equipment for use in a potentially explosive atmosphere, special forms of luminaire are manufactured giving different degrees of protection against inadvertent ignition for the various zones. Such luminaires are designated and marked Ex 'e', Ex 'N', etc. where the 'e', 'N', etc. categorizes the type of protection

Table 24.4 IP classification of luminaires

| First characteristic numeral | Degree of protection | |
	Short description	Brief details of objects which will be 'excluded' from the enclosure
0	Non-protected	No special protection
1	Protected against solid objects greater than 50 mm	A large surface of the body, such as a hand (but no protection against deliberate access). Solid objects exceeding 50 mm in diameter
2	Protected against solid objects greater than 12 mm	Fingers or similar objects not exceeding 80 mm in length. Solid objects exceeding 12 mm in diameter
3	Protected against solid objects greater than 2·5 mm	Tools, wires, etc., of diameter or thickness greater than 2·5 mm. Solid objects exceeding 2·5 mm in diameter
4	Protected against solid objects greater than 1·0 mm	Wires or strips of thickness greater than 1·0 mm. Solid objects exceeding 1·0 mm in diameter
5	Dust-protected	Ingress of dust is not totally prevented, but dust does not enter in sufficient quantity to interfere with satisfactory operation of the equipment
6	Dust-tight	No ingress of dust

| Second characteristic numeral | Degree of protection | |
	Short description	Details of the type of protection provided by the enclosure
0	Non-protected	No special protection
1	Protected against dripping water	Dripping water (vertically falling drops) shall have no harmful effect
2	Protected against dripping water when tilted up to 15°	Vertically dripping water shall have no harmful effect when the enclosure is tilted at any angle up to 15° from its normal position
3	Protected against spraying water	Water falling as a spray at an angle up to 60° from the vertical shall have no harmful effect
4	Protected against splashing water	Water splashed against the enclosure from any direction shall have no harmful effect
5	Protected against water jets	Water projected by a nozzle against the enclosure from any direction shall have no harmful effect
6	Protected against heavy seas	Water from heavy seas or water projected in powerful jets shall not enter the enclosure in harmful quantities
7	Protected against the effects of immersion	Ingress of water in a harmful quantity shall not be possible when the enclosure is immersed in water under defined conditions of pressure and time
8	Protected against submersion	The equipment is suitable for continuous submersion in water under conditions which shall be specified by the manufacturer. *Note:* normally this will mean that the equipment is hermetically sealed. However with certain types of equipment it can mean that water can enter, but only in such a manner that it produces no harmful effects

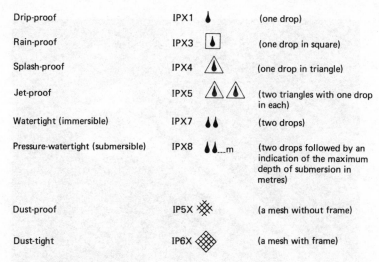

Drip-proof	IPX1	(one drop)
Rain-proof	IPX3	(one drop in square)
Splash-proof	IPX4	(one drop in triangle)
Jet-proof	IPX5	(two triangles with one drop in each)
Watertight (immersible)	IPX7	(two drops)
Pressure-watertight (submersible)	IPX8 ...m	(two drops followed by an indication of the maximum depth of submersion in metres)
Dust-proof	IP5X	(a mesh without frame)
Dust-tight	IP6X	(a mesh with frame)

Fig. 24.3 IP classification symbols

provided. Depending on the ignition temperature of the particular flammable material liable to be present, the surface temperature of the luminaire must be limited. To this end luminaires are also classified and marked $(T_1, T_2, \ldots, T_6)$ according to their maximum surface temperature in a 40 °C ambient. Full details of the Ex and T luminaire classifications are given in the first part of a British code of practice, BS 5345 (BSI 1976f), which deals with the selection, installation, and maintenance of all electrical equipment for hazardous areas. A CIBS lighting guide for hazardous and hostile environments is under preparation to replace the obsolete CIBS/IES Technical Report No. 1 on this subject.

Figure 24.4 illustrates typical luminaires designed for use in Zone 1 and Zone 2.

24.3 General lighting design

It has been pointed out in Sect. 24.1 that lighting design starts with an analysis of the tasks to be lit. This analysis should not be forgotten once it has been decided what illuminances and maximum glare indices are to be realized, particularly when considering which type of luminaire will fulfil the design requirements.

To illustrate this, consider a warehouse with 2–3 m wide gangways and racking some 8 m high. The critical visual task here may be anywhere on the rack surface, so the aim should be to provide an even illumination over this entire vertical surface. Two alternative schemes are continuous 2400 mm 100 W twin fluorescent trough reflector luminaires or 250 W high pressure sodium low bay luminaires spaced at 12·5 m. The light flux per metre length of gangway is the same, as is the illuminance on a vertical plane at ground level, but higher up the racks the illumination from the high pressure sodium scheme becomes very patchy. The driver of a stacker truck, when looking upwards, would find the glare from a row of fluorescent trough luminaires less than that from the discontinuous and brighter sodium luminaires. The low output continuous fluorescent scheme is more suitable for this job even though it may have a higher capital cost.

When overhead cranes are used in an industrial interior lit by high bay luminaires, the bulk of the crane may at some positions totally obscure a row of discharge

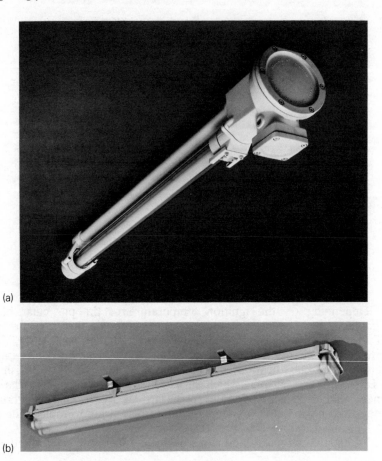

Fig. 24.4   Luminaires for hazardous areas: (a) Zone 1 and (b) Zone 2

luminaires causing deep shadowing. If this is likely to occur then additional lighting equipment should be mounted on the underside of the crane to compensate for this.

Also with high pressure luminaires, the powerful specular reflection on newly-finished metalwork must be considered: the brighter the light source, the higher will be the brightness of the reflections. The use of louvres over the luminaires will assist in reducing this problem, but the positioning of luminaires with respect to the task is most important.

One of the most arduous visual tasks in industry is electronic assembly, where operators may have to read the colour coding on resistors and small markings on other components. The operators are generally in lines facing the same direction, which simplifies the lighting installation. Rows of fluorescent luminaires with low brightness reflectors running in the same direction as the operators' line of view create the best visibility with the minimum veiling reflections from the solder joints, but optical aids may still be needed.

When designing industrial installations, the matter of maintenance is most important. Many industrial processes are automatic and continuous and cannot be stopped during the normal working day. If a fault develops on lighting equipment above these machines, remedial work may have to be done out of normal hours, which is both expensive and inconvenient. Access from an overhead crane may be acceptable during working hours providing the crane does not have to be in motion with personnel on board. Alternatively, key luminaires can be installed with a plug and socket and hoist arrangements, enabling the units to be brought to ground for repairs. Since routine maintenance is required at all lighting points, it is sensible to plan for access to luminaires at the design stage. Cleaning of luminaires is necessary periodically, as is relamping, and the lighting designer will have allowed for some light loss factor in his design (Sect. 21.3.1) related to cleaning and relamping frequency. It is rare in industrial areas for bulk replacement to work out more expensive than spot replacement.

An essential part of the lighting design for an industrial building is the provision of emergency lighting (Sect. 21.4). A point of significance in the factory environment is that emergency lighting luminaires in a given location must have no less protection, in terms of IP classification, than the standard luminaires in that area. A further point arises from the widespread use of high pressure lamps for general lighting. A momentary dip in the mains supply voltage may cause these lamps to be extinguished and to remain out for some time: under a minute with sodium, but several minutes with mercury or metal halide. Whatever the escape and standby lighting arrangements, it is a useful anti-panic measure to ensure that there are some tungsten filament or fluorescent lamps or lighting units operating in otherwise purely high pressure lighting installations.

24.4   Inspection lighting

It is normal to carry out the inspection of products under a higher lighting level than that under which the products are made. However, more important than the level of lighting for inspecting finished work is the type of lighting. This must be designed to highlight defects in the product, and it is therefore necessary for the lighting designer to know what features the inspector is looking for.

As an example of the highlighting of defects, consider scratches on polished metal. The irregularities in the surface reflect light in a different manner from the main surface and may be detected in two ways. Light may be directed onto the surface from the direction of the observer: reflected light from the scratches shows up light on a dark background. Alternatively, a large-area source may direct light towards the observer, when the opposite effect is created: blemishes appear dark against the bright background.

Accurate inspection or matching of colour is a common problem: BS 950 (BSI 1967) specifies the performance of light sources for accurate colour appraisal in industrial inspection and manufacture. Fluorescent lamps complying with this specification are available, but their efficacy is low and therefore, for economic reasons, they tend to be used in booths (Fig. 24.5a) rather than for general lighting. The recommended illuminance for colour assessment is 1000 lux and the surface of the booths should have a neutral matt finish. The colour properties of other light sources can assist with other inspection problems. For example the monochromatic light provided by low pressure sodium lamps or specialized mercury lamps can be used to check the flatness of precision finished surfaces. The reflections from the test surface are allowed to interfere with light reflected from an optical flat, setting up bands or fringes which are observed through the optical flat. The number and contour of these bands indicate the errors in the test surface.

Colour contrast can be used in inspection processes, for example a coloured dye can

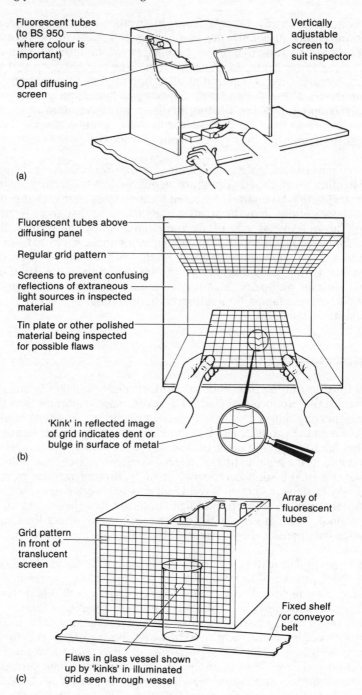

Fluorescent tubes
(to BS 950
where colour is
important)

Vertically
adjustable
screen to
suit inspector

Opal diffusing
screen

(a)

Fluorescent tubes above
diffusing panel

Regular grid pattern

Screens to prevent confusing
reflections of extraneous
light sources in inspected
material

Tin plate or other polished
material being inspected
for possible flaws

'Kink' in reflected image
of grid indicates dent or
bulge in surface of metal

(b)

Grid pattern
in front of
translucent
screen

Array of
fluorescent
tubes

Fixed shelf
or conveyor
belt

Flaws in glass vessel shown
up by 'kinks' in illuminated
grid seen through vessel

(c)

Fig. 24.5 Inspection lighting: (a) colour-matching booth, (b) imperfections in polished surfaces, and (c) imperfections in transparent objects

be applied to a surface in which scribe marks are to be seen. Under light of a colour which is absorbed by the dye, but reflected by the base material, the contrast is enhanced further.

Lighting having radiation predominantly in the ultraviolet region can be used to make fluorescent or phosphorescent objects visible. For example fluorescent tracers are often added to engine coolant fluids when an examination is to be made for possible leaks, signs of the tracer showing up under an ultraviolet lamp. Crack detection in castings and the inspection of certain types of welding operations are carried out using this technique.

A less sophisticated method than the use of monochromatic light to detect irregularities in polished surfaces is the use of a large uniform source. The inspector views a reflection of the source in the object: any irregularities will show up as a deviation in the uniformity of brightness. Improved detectability occurs if a grid pattern is superimposed on the source (Fig. 24.5b). This technique is also used for flaws in transparent materials (Fig. 24.5c).

Shape and edge defects in flat opaque objects show up well by viewing the objects in silhouette against a large-area source. This is a favoured technique in the clothing industry, where garments are passed over an illuminated table.

Small-area sources are also used for inspection, usually tungsten or tungsten halogen lamps, illuminating materials at a glancing angle to show up surface irregularities. The shadow pattern is an exaggerated version of the irregularity pattern, and is therefore easier to see. Using their versatile little local lighting units, this technique is employed by the operators of many workshop machines, and explains why a pure general lighting scheme for workshops, however efficient and tidy and shadow-free, is so often regarded by the operators as inadequate.

Further reading

Frier J P and Gazley Frier M E, 1980, *Industrial lighting systems* (New York: McGraw-Hill)

Pritchard D C (Ed), 1982, *Developments in lighting*, **2**, *Industrial* (London: Applied Science)

25 Lighting for entertainment

The lighting criteria for stage and studio, outside television broadcasts, and disco-theques are less quantitative than for any of the other lighting applications featured in Parts IV and V of this book: this is not to say that there is no technology involved in satisfying the requirements of lighting for entertainment. After a brief consideration of the lighting objectives and principles, this chapter concerns itself with the available lighting and control equipment for various applications. It concludes with some typical lighting layouts for the small theatre, where so often the provision of electrical supply and equipment mounting facilities has been a sad legacy of the work of an architect or electrical contractor, rather than a specialist consultant.

25.1 Lighting objectives and principles

Stage   The stage lighting designer works with the director and production designer to complement the dramatic or entertainment effect which the director intends to convey to his audience. The intensity of lighting (overall and within specific areas of the stage), the direction of lighting, and the colour will all be controlled to produce the required effect. Levels of illuminance are neither specified nor measured, the designer using his experience and flair to determine the levels necessary. He balances lighter and darker areas of the stage to create the 'picture' which he requires.

Studio   Film and television cameras do not have the same latitude as the human eye. The studio lighting designer must control variations of intensity and colour within limits imposed by the camera system which will only work satisfactorily between specified maximum and minimum illuminance limits, and the designer must ensure that these limits are observed.

Recently-developed camera systems are able to operate satisfactorily at much lower levels of illuminance than traditional film cameras, but still require the entire scene to be lit within narrow limits of diversity. The colour appearance of the light source has to be carefully controlled, either to balance the characteristics of the film or to maintain acceptable rendering of neutral-colour surfaces with video cameras.

Outside broadcasts   The prime concern of the outside broadcast lighting designer is usually to provide sufficient illuminance to enable the camera system to operate when the size of the area to be illuminated is very large. Although a picture quality lower than studio standard is acceptable for most events, the distance between camera and scene makes it necessary to use long focus lenses and range extenders, which in turn require higher levels of illuminance. For good quality pictures it is necessary to provide about 1000 lux measured on a plane normal to the camera lens. The uniformity of illuminance over the scene must be controlled so that the maximum to minimum illuminance is within a ratio of 5:1 and any variations in illuminance must occur gradually. Although the broadcast authorities specify illuminance requirements normal to the camera, it is necessary to provide some back-lighting to prevent 'flat' pictures. The backlight illuminance would ideally equal the value of the front lighting and should certainly not be less than half of it.

Discotheques　The primary objective of discotheque lighting is to provide an exciting visual atmosphere capable of variation so that the lighting effect can reflect the atmosphere of the music. Saturated coloured lighting, controlled by sound-stimulated dimming and switching, coupled with flashing lamps and strobes, provides most of the lighting and is commonly used in conjunction with lasers and revolving spotlights.

There are few, if any, rules for general lighting practice. Each design is created to meet the needs of the particular venue. There is a vast range of specialist equipment available to the designer and one could be forgiven for believing that the objective is simply to use as much equipment as the financial budget will allow.

25.2　Lighting equipment

25.2.1　Lamps

Filament lamps　The low cost, the simplicity of operation, and the totally predictable colour performance of incandescent filament lamps make these the most widely used light source.

Although simple GLS lamps (Chap. 9) are used for some flood lanterns, most stage and studio lanterns are designed for use with Class T and Class CP tungsten halogen lamps (Sect. 10.3.4). These have compact, precisely-located filaments which permit their light to be accurately controlled by the optical system of the lantern. Some smaller luminaires are designed to use Class M tungsten halogen lamps, which are very suitable for the small scale stage where regular maintenance is not possible. Linear tungsten halogen lamps, Class K and Class P, are used in wide beam flood lanterns for stage use and in soft lights for studio use. The tungsten halogen cycle ensures an extended life, a high efficiency, and a consistent colour temperature. Some studio lamps incorporate dual filaments, allowing the lamp to be operated at 50 or 100% light output without the change of colour temperature which occurs with dimming. Sealed beam reflector envelopes are used with tungsten halogen lamps embodied within them. The front lens of the sealed beam unit can be clear, stippled, or prismatic providing variation of beam shape. This arrangement allows the use of very simple lanterns which do not require any optical control devices.

Discharge lamps　The high efficiency of discharge lamps makes them an attractive option, especially for studio and outside broadcast use. However the fact that the lamps cannot be dimmed by simple electronic dimmers, together with the problems of colour performance consistency and both run-up and restrike times, inhibits the use of most discharge lamps for stage and studio work.

One discharge lamp used with some regularity for stage lighting is the compact source iodide lamp (Sect. 15.4.1). It is used in follow spots, with mechanical dimmers and shutters, and also for special effects projectors in studios. The sealed beam version of the lamp is widely used for outside broadcasts.

25.2.2   Lanterns

Flood lanterns   The simplest form of stage and studio lantern consists of a GLS lamp in the range 100 W to 1000 W with a simple specular reflector. Lanterns for the smaller lamp ratings, up to 200 W, are usually arranged in groups, known as battens, which are connected electrically to three or four separate circuits so that adjacent lamps can be fitted with different colour filters to enable colour mixing to be achieved. Sealed beam PAR 38 lamps are also used in battens, obviating the need for any reflector in the lantern.

Batten type flood lanterns have largely been superseded for both stage and studio lighting by asymmetric reflector lanterns using horizontal linear tungsten halogen

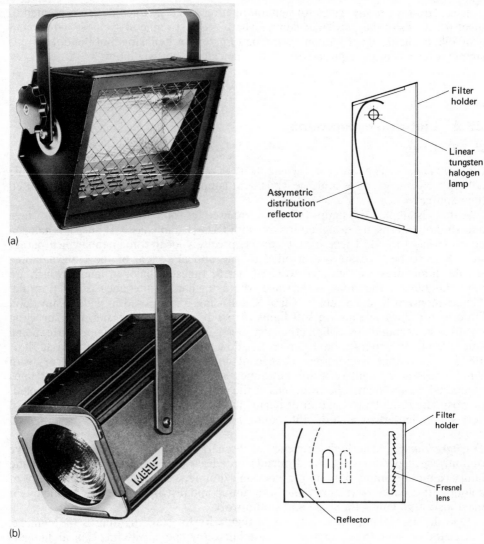

(a)

(b)

Fig. 25.1   Typical stage and studio lanterns: (a) flood lantern, (b) soft edge beam spotlight, (c) dual-purpose spot/flood, and (d) profile spotlight

lamps rated at 500 W to 2000 W. Asymmetric reflectors with linear lamps have accurate optical control, allowing lanterns to provide an even lighting of cycloramas and backcloths from close offset. Colour filters in this type of lantern are operated at high temperature and it is essential that high temperature rated filters are used. A typical asymmetric reflector flood lantern is shown in Fig. 25.1a.

Soft edge beam spotlights Figure 25.1b illustrates a typical arrangement for this type of lantern. The lamp and spherical specular reflector are capable of adjustment along the axis of the Fresnel or 'pebble' convex lens. With the lamp and reflector moved close to the lens a wide beam angle is produced which narrows progressively as the distance between lamp and lens is increased. Typical lanterns enable the beam angle to be adjusted between about 15° and 65°. The Fresnel lens comprises a number of annular prisms. The 'pebble' convex lens is based on a conventional plano-convex lens, the plane surface of which is covered by a large number of very small convex lenses or 'pebbles'. These very small lenses ensure a soft edge beam free from striations. Additional control of the beam is achieved by external adjustable masks,

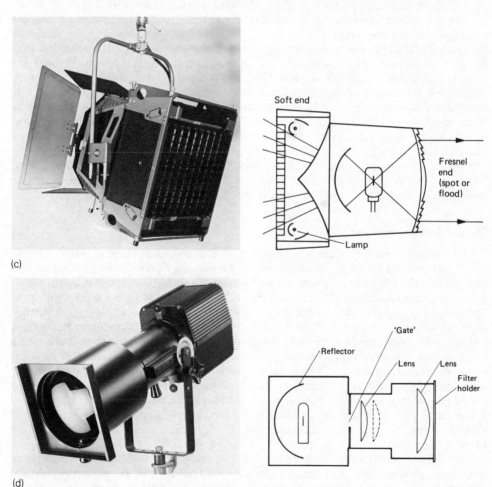

(c)

(d)

Fig. 25.1 *(cont.)*

known as barn doors, which can be adjusted and rotated to provide some control of the beam shape and to cut off 'spill' light.

For stage use soft edge beam spotlights are available for a lamp range of 300 W to 2000 W. Larger lanterns for lamps up to 10 kW are used in television studios and up to 20 kW in film studios. For studio use the dual-purpose lantern illustrated in Fig. 25.1c has been developed. One side of the lantern is a Fresnel lens soft edge beam spotlight for use with a dual-filament 2·5 kW + 2·5 kW lamp and the other side of the lantern is a flood, or soft light, fitted with two pairs of 1·25 kW linear tungsten halogen lamps.

Tungsten halogen lamps in sealed beam pressed glass reflectors also provide soft edge beam spotlights. Three beam angles are available, using different front lenses on the sealed beam envelope. Asymmetric beams are produced, the asymmetry of which is more pronounced in the wide angle type. The lamp can be rotated in the lantern to alter the orientation of the beam.

Profile spotlights   This type of lantern has a focusable 'gate' which can be adjusted to produce any desired beam shape by adjustable shutters or by shaped cut-outs, usually produced by etching patterns in discs of stainless steel, and called 'gobos' (Sect. 25.2.4). Iris diaphragms can be also inserted into the gate and adjusted to provide a continuously-variable circular beam.

Figure 25.1d shows the typical arrangement of a profile lantern. The lamp filament is located at the focus of an ellipsoidal reflector and the light, after passing through the gate, is focused by the objective lens. The image of the gate can be 'hard' or 'soft' focused by movement of the objective lens. Most profile spot lanterns for stage use now incorporate two independently adjustable lenses allowing for adjustment of the beam width as well as the focus. A further adjustment of the beam width is obtained by varying the size and curvature of the lenses, and typical lantern systems employ a range of lens tubes capable of use with a common lamphouse and gate assembly.

Profile lanterns are available for compact filament tungsten halogen lamps from 300 W to 2000 W. Compact source iodide and HMI lamps are also used in profile spots, especially for follow spots and for special effects projection.

25.2.3   Lantern accessories

A wide range of lantern rigging accessories is available. For stage use lanterns are usually suspended by hook clamps from 48 mm diameter alloy tube. For permanent installations the tube can be prewired and fitted with socket outlets. Adjustable floor mounting stands and tripods are available enabling lanterns to be supported up to about 3·5 m above floor level. All stage lanterns are made with a suspension stirrup, allowing vertical adjustment of the lantern, arranged for a 12 mm diameter fixing bolt. For use with floor stands a spigot is fitted over this bolt. For television studio use a range of suspension components based on the TV standard 28 mm diameter spigot is manufactured. Lanterns are fitted with flexible heat-resisting supply cable, usually about one metre long. It is normal practice in stage use for this to be fitted with a 15 A round pin plug top, although 5 A plugs are used for some small installations. Plug and socket arrangements between the lantern and the (usually dimmer-controlled) supply should not incorporate fuse links, excessive load in these cables being protected by fuses at the supply.

Each lantern needs to be adjusted for pan, tilt, and focus to suit the requirements of individual productions. For stage applications this is usually a totally manual operation and it is essential that safe means of reaching every lantern in an installation is provided. Manual focusing and adjustment is obviously very time-consuming and many attempts have been made to provide remote control systems, but the systems available to date are expensive to purchase and install and have so far found little application in the theatre. In television studios, where adjustment is required more often, remote lantern adjustment devices become more economic. Radio transmitter control devices, which enable the focusing operator to control the dimmers from the lantern location, are used for some studios and large stages.

Colour media   Colour is an important part of the lighting design, particularly in the theatre, and accurate colour correction is important for film studios. Unfortunately there is no agreed standard for colour filters and each of the many specialist manufacturers produces an individual range of colours, making a total range of several hundred. The filters are made of thin sheets of acetate or polycarbonate material. Modern lanterns and lamps require colour filters to operate at high temperatures and so acetate materials are being superseded. All stage and studio lanterns make provision for the fitting of filters and it is a simple matter to cut the sheets to size to fit individual lanterns.

25.2.4   Special effects equipment

Many productions require special projected effects. Mention has already been made of cut-out shaped masks or gobos used in the 'gate' of profile lanterns. A wide range of gobos is available to project simple stationary images, such as windows, clouds, trees, and foliage. Manufacture of gobos is simple and inexpensive, making it possible to prepare 'specials' to suit the specific requirements of a production. There is also available a range of moving effects used in conjunction with special effects projectors. The required effect is painted or photographically transferred onto a glass disc which is focused by a lens system. When the disc is rotated by a small motor the projected effect moves. Standard discs are available for the effects regularly required, such as clouds, rain, snow, and flames. Special discs can be produced, but are relatively expensive. Other equipment makes use of reciprocating slides and break-up glasses to represent underwater and sea-wave effects. Stroboscopes are used to freeze or distort movement, lightning effects are produced by pulsing photoflood lamps, and lasers are used to create special trace patterns for light entertainment and 'pop' concerts. A specialist range of projectors using tungsten halogen lamps rated from 2000 W to 10 000 W is made for use with painted or photographic slides for the projection of 'scenery'. It is essential that slides for scenic and some effects projection are very carefully prepared so that the projected image does not appear distorted. Slides for scenic projection are usually 18 cm × 18 cm or 24 cm × 24 cm: smaller sizes are unlikely to transmit sufficient light to produce satisfactory images.

25.3   Control equipment

The ability to control the light output of individual lanterns or groups of lanterns is fundamental to all stage and studio installations. For film studios the control may be quite simple, for example the ability to switch dual-filament lamps to half or full light output. The limitations of colour film make dimming less important for film studios than for television studios and the stage.

Most television studios and all theatres need control equipment capable of varying light output smoothly from maximum to zero. The simplest form of control is a variable resistance in series with the lantern or group of lanterns and control systems based on resistance dimmers are still in use. Complicated mechanical and electromechanical devices were used to enable small numbers of operators to control systems employing up to as many as 200 resistance dimmers either simultaneously or in groups. Autotransformers, saturable reactors, and thyratron valves have also been used. These simplify the physical problems of controlling large numbers of dimmers, but all these devices are load conscious, making it necessary to balance the load on each dimmer so that the dimming rate is consistent.

The advent of the semiconductor has revolutionized lighting control systems and nearly all systems now employ thyristor dimmers. Variable loads can be accommodated over a very wide range, for example a dimmer capable of a maximum load of 5000 W will also control a single 100 W lamp. Furthermore the power loss in the dimmer is reduced to insignificant levels. Thyristor dimmers are usually produced in modular form, suitable for maximum loads of 1 kW to 5 kW, and are built into racks enclosing from 5 to 30 modules. The thyristor dimmer controls the lighting load and is itself controlled by varying the d.c. voltage applied to the 'trigger'. The required control voltage is usually of the order of 12 V and the control current for each dimmer is only a few mA.

The control voltage for the dimmers is provided by the lighting control desk, which may be situated at any convenient point which gives a good view of the stage or studio. The desk can be remote from the dimmers themselves, control being effected through low load multicore control cables between the desk and the dimmer rack. Control desks may be either manually-controlled or may incorporate electronic memory control.

Manual systems　The simplest form of manual-control system incorporates a fader (Sect. 18.6.2) to vary the control voltage to each dimmer. Faders should be of the linear type and need a graduated scale so that the position of the control lever can be recorded and repeated when required. If the system involves more than five dimmers a master control will be required so that the individual dimmers are controlled in a group by the master. Most systems have duplicated or triplicated controls so that a second or third scene can be set up whilst the first scene is being played. Each series of faders is known as a preset and each preset is controlled by a master fader.

In some systems the individual faders can be allocated to alternative sub-master controls by a two- or three-position selection switch associated with the fader. Thus each preset can be under the control of two or three sub-masters and the sub-masters then be controlled by a grand master. The operation of sub-masters and/or grand masters allows groups of faders to be brought up or down together and the simultaneous operation of two masters, one increasing and one decreasing, provides a cross-fade from one preset to another. In the event that two faders controlling the same dimmer are both above zero setting the fader having the higher setting will take precedence. During cross-fades individual dimmers may fade to levels lower than their setting in either preset, causing a 'dip' during the cross-fade. Some manual systems now incorporate 'dipless' cross-fade controls which overcome this problem.

As an alternative to selector switches for allocating faders to sub-masters some larger systems incorporate a pin matrix. The matrix consists of a panel of sockets into which miniature contact pins can be inserted. Each column of sockets in the panel represents the dimmers and each row of sockets represents a sub-master fader. Contact pins are inserted at the intersection of the dimmers and sub-masters in the matrix, causing sub-master control of the dimmers to be allocated to the matrix sub-master. Thus any dimmer or group of dimmers can be allocated to any sub-master. Typical arrangements use a matrix with 10 or 20 sub-master rows.

Very complex manual-control systems can be made, but the useful complexity is limited by the dexterity of the operator. Figure 25.2a shows a typical manual-control desk. If a system involves such complex operation that it cannot be accurately used by the operator then a memory system should be used.

(a)   (b)

Fig. 25.2   Control desks: (a) manual and (b) memory

Memory systems   The availability of computers and microprocessors has made it possible to provide control desks capable of single-man operation for systems employing up to 500 dimmers and having control facilities which would be impossible with a manual system. The basis of all such control systems is a memory facility whereby the setting required for each dimmer for each scene can be recorded and recalled when required.

Individual faders for each dimmer are replaced by decimal coded push buttons, similar to a calculator keyboard, which are used to select individual dimmers or groups of dimmers: in association with command keys these also allocate dimmer levels. When the complete setting required for a scene has been achieved it is transferred to the system memory bank, leaving the complete system available to set up the next scene. The settings can be recalled from the memory bank in any desired order. The change from one memory to the next may be made gradually or instantaneously. Figure 25.2b shows a memory control desk.

All memory systems incorporate these basic facilities, but an enormous range of additional facilities can also be specified, such as mimic diagrams showing dimmers in use for the recalled memory, visual display units showing the state of each dimmer and/or memory, automatic timers to control the rate of change from one memory to the next, and recording disc facilities to store the memories for complete productions.

In purchasing a memory system it is essential to analyse carefully the purposes to which the system will be put, to avoid the cost of sophisticated facilities which will never be used. However, two features are always desirable: some means of displaying the dimmer settings in the recalled memory and a manual back-up facility to allow limited use of the system in the event of an electronic breakdown.

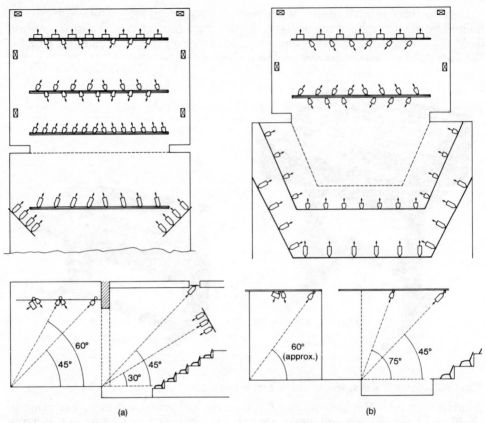

Fig. 25.3 Typical stage lighting layouts: (a) proscenium stage, (b) thrust stage, and (c) open stage. These would use 500 W lanterns for proscenium or stage widths of 6–8 m or 1000 W lanterns for widths of 8–10 m

Audio-stimulated control   Systems which allow groups of dimmers to be automatically controlled in response to audio signals are commonplace today. Typically, an audio signal – usually musical – is divided into three or four frequency bands by a controller which then drives the dimmers in accordance with the incidence and volume of sound in each band. Thus the lighting will change in keeping with changes in the music.

More complex systems, based on this simple sound-to-light facility, are available to enable audio signals to provide a number of special lighting effects, some using plug-in cartridges to produce a non-repetitive sequence of dimming and switching actions, time-programmed or manually-operated.

Colour controls   The remote operation of colour change devices can reduce the number of lanterns required for a production. Two basic systems are available using either a colour wheel or colour filters held in semaphore arms. Both systems allow for five colour options. Control is by multicore cables from a control unit which allows a second set of colours to be selected whilst the first set is in use. A master control then switches all the colour change units simultaneously. An alternative to the use of multicore cables, which are expensive and cumbersome, is to multiplex the control signals.

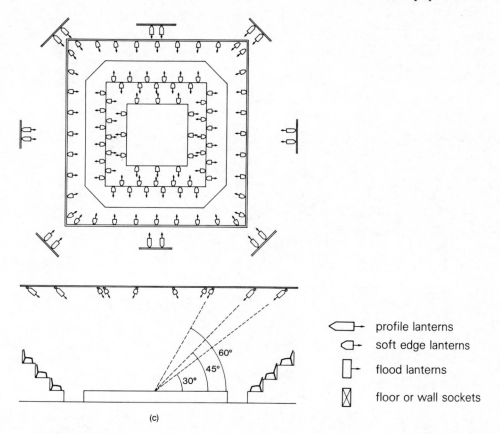

profile lanterns

soft edge lanterns

flood lanterns

floor or wall sockets

(c)

Fig. 25.3 *(cont.)*

25.4 Layouts

The design of the technical systems for large theatres and for studios will always be entrusted to specialist consultants. In the case of small theatres, however, this design is often part of the work of the architect, electrical services consultant, or electrical installation contractor.

In Fig. 25.3 are shown layouts which will satisfy the basic requirements for (a) a conventional proscenium stage, (b) a thrust stage, and (c) an open stage presentation.

Further reading

Bentham F, 1976, *The art of stage lighting*, 2nd Edition (London: Pitman)

Gillespie Williams R, 1958, *The technique of stage lighting*, 2nd Edition (London: Pitman)

Pilbrow R, 1971, *Stage lighting* (London: Studio Vista)

Part V
Exterior lighting

26 Exterior lighting design

Lighting is installed out of doors for many different reasons. One of these is the safe movement of vehicular traffic: the subjects of road lighting and navigational lighting are treated separately in Chaps 28 and 29. Most other exterior lighting installations are given the one general label of floodlighting, although they serve a wide range of needs, such as to deter thieves or vandals, to attract tourists, to ensure safe pedestrian movement around a refinery, and to allow the extended use of sports facilities. Associated with these different purposes are different lighting design criteria, and also different techniques to satisfy them, as will be seen in Chap. 27, but there are some common threads in floodlighting design, not least the available equipment and the design calculations. It is to these matters and some commonality in criteria that this chapter is devoted.

26.1 Lighting objectives and criteria

Objectives   The three broad lighting design objectives of safety, performance, and appearance cited for interior lighting (Sect. 21.1) apply also to exterior lighting. Safety and security are the prime concern of the majority of installations out of doors, for example the detection of obstructions by pedestrians or the detection of an attacker or an intruder by a guard. Industrial floodlighting is installed in order that visual tasks can be carried out after dark, and so is sports lighting. Most building floodlighting schemes have a commercial purpose (including tourism), and some are just for fun, but the important design objective is to provide an enhanced appearance.

However, in translating these objectives into lighting criteria there are two dramatic departures from the interior lighting situation. Firstly, since the visual size of the details to be seen are generally much larger (with the single exception of certain sports activities), lower levels of lighting tend to suffice out of doors. Secondly, whereas most of these details lie on a horizontal plane indoors, the lighting of vertical surfaces tends to be more important outdoors.

Illuminance and uniformity   Table 26.1 shows the ranges of average illuminance regarded as satisfactory for various area floodlighting applications, together with the plane on which it is recommended that this illuminance should be provided. In many area lighting installations there should be limits on the diversity of illumination provided: Table 26.2 suggests, for various applications, limiting values for two alternative measures of overall uniformity – the ratio of maximum to minimum illuminance over the critical plane and the average to minimum ratio – and also the 'gradient' or maximum rate of change of illuminance with distance.

It is obviously necessary to limit the number of points for which the illuminance is calculated in order to predict the average illuminance and its uniformity. Figure 26.1a

Table 26.1   Illuminance ranges recommended for exterior lighting

Illuminance range (lux)	Critical plane	Application
1–10	Horizontal	Amenity General storage areas
	Vertical	Security Casual sport training
10–50	Horizontal	Stock and cargo handling Non-critical working areas Car parks
50–100	Horizontal	Critical working areas Sports practice Playgrounds
	Vertical	Aircraft service areas Advertising – unlit roads
100–500	Horizontal	Club and tournament sports Sales areas
	Vertical	Advertising – lit roads Spectator sports
500–1000	Vertical	International sports and lighting for colour TV

suggests upper and lower limits for the number of points which provides a satisfactory compromise between accuracy and excessive effort for rectangular areas of different size. A number of points which is a multiple of two numbers (preferably odd) should be selected, the points corresponding to the centres of small grid squares making up the rectangular area (Fig. 26.1b). If data is needed on the illuminance gradient at the boundaries, the calculation grid should be extended to include the points on the dotted lines in Fig. 26.1b. These points should not be included in the calculation of the average value of illuminance for the area. A single value at each grid point suffices when horizontal illuminance is being considered, but this is not so for vertical

Table 26.2   Uniformity recommendations for exterior lighting

Application	Uniformity of illuminance in critical plane of measurement		Minimum distance over which 20% change in illuminance occurs (metres)
	max : min	av : min	
Non-critical areas: parks, gardens, amenity lighting	50 : 1	—	—
Working areas Most building facades Sports training areas	20 : 1	10 : 1	2
Even lighting of plain light-coloured surfaces Spectator sports areas	10 : 1	5 : 1	3
Filming and television	3 : 1	1·5 : 1	4

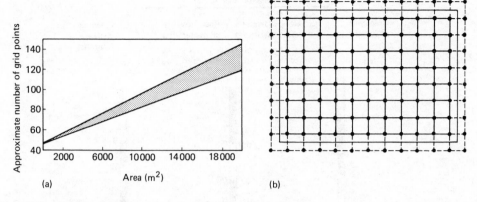

Fig. 26.1   Grid for illuminance and uniformity calculations

illuminance. It is then usual to evaluate the illuminance on each of the four vertical sides of a cube placed at each grid point. To compare with the criteria, the average value and the uniformity of the north-facing cube faces, the west-facing faces, etc. should be considered separately.

Atmospheric losses   An important factor which affects illuminances in outdoor installations is the atmospheric loss caused by air-borne moisture and solid particles. The loss varies with the time of day, the season, and the location. It also varies with the mounting height and the length of throw, so it must be taken into account in designing the lighting for large areas, such as football pitches. Calculations should be based on the performance on a clear night, as the effects of other weather conditions are too variable to be taken into account. A typical loss of illuminance on a clear night in an urban football installation using four 30 m to 45 m towers, can be as much as 20 to 30%.

Maintenance   Over and above an allowance for atmospheric loss, a maintenance factor should be included in floodlighting design calculations to allow for a loss of light due to dirt between cleaning intervals. Figure 26.2 gives a nomogram to find the appropriate maintenance factor: the use of the nomogram is exemplified by an 18-month cleaning cycle in a 'fairly clean' environment, pointing to a factor of 0·6 or 0·7, depending on the 'cleaning characteristics'. In high illuminance installations the extra cost of towers, cabling, and floodlights to provide 20 or 30% more light to allow for dirt accumulation can be very great: it is much better to look for a maintenance factor of between 0·9 and 1·0 by choosing floodlights with good cleaning characteristics and accepting short cleaning cycles.

Glare   Disability and discomfort glare arise in floodlighting, but the assumptions in calculating discomfort glare in interiors (Sects 5.5.1 and 21.3.3) or either type of glare in street lighting (Sect. 28.3.1) do not apply to area floodlighting, with its irregular array of sources, viewable from many different points inside and outside the illuminated area. At present, there is no generally-accepted method of glare determination in floodlighting. Nevertheless, from the practical point of view, the factors affecting glare and the measures that can be taken to control it are fairly well known. In particular, glare increases as floodlights move closer to the centre of an observer's

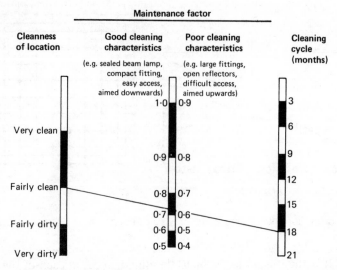

Fig. 26.2 Nomogram for determining the maintenance factor of an outdoor installation

field of view, also as the illuminance on the observer's eye increases, and as the brightness of the background to the floodlights decreases.

For an observer within a floodlit area glare will be reduced by increasing the floodlight mounting height, by aiming the peak intensity of the floodlights at angles below 70° to the downward vertical, and by ensuring that the luminance of the area and its surrounds is as high as possible: some compromise is needed on the first two points or the ratio of vertical to horizontal illuminance will become too low and reduce visibility. The most important single factor to control glare to observers outside the floodlit area is to limit the intensities outside the actual beam of the floodlight. For observers both within and outside the illuminated area the location and aiming of floodlights should not coincide with important directions of view.

26.2 Floodlighting equipment

26.2.1 Floodlights – optical characteristics

From the point of view of the general pattern of light distribution, floodlights fall into three basic groups. These are identified by the general shape of the isocandela contours (Sect. 4.4.4) on a graph with the angles from the beam axis in the vertical (V) and horizontal (H) planes as coordinates. Figure 26.3 shows the general shapes of the three groups, which can be described as symmetrical, asymmetrical, and double asymmetrical.

Within each of these patterns there can be varying degrees of spread of the light. This is described by some angular measurement of the *beam*, the beam being defined as embracing all directions where the intensity of the floodlight exceeds 0·1 of the maximum intensity. The *beam angle*, indicating spread, is the angular extent of the beam in the vertical and horizontal planes. For a symmetrical floodlight one figure suffices, e.g. 60° (or 2 × 30°, implying 30° on either side of the axis). For an asymmetrical distribution two values are required, e.g. horizontal 100° and vertical 40°. For a double asymmetrical pattern three values are required, e.g. horizontal 100°,

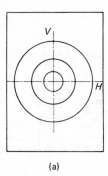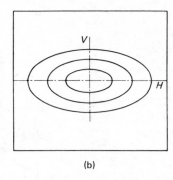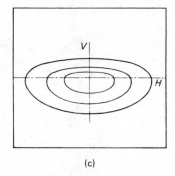

| (a) | (b) | (c) |

Fig. 26.3 Light distribution patterns of floodlights: (a) symmetrical, (b) asymmetrical, and (c) double asymmetrical

vertical above peak 20°, and vertical below peak 40° (or horizontal 2 × 50°, vertical 20° + 40°).

In addition to the beam angle, which is concerned with the $0.1I_{max}$ contour, the relevant angles of two other contours are frequently quoted: the $0.5I_{max}$ contour to indicate the 'peakiness' of the light within the beam and the $0.01I_{max}$ contour to indicate where the effective 'cut-off' of light takes place. Additional data to cover the optical characteristics of floodlights are the *peak intensity*, usually evaluated in candelas per thousand lamp lumens, and the *beam factor*, which states what fraction of the lamp lumens are emitted in the beam.

In Table 26.3 are summarized the optical characteristics of a number of floodlights, using different lamp types and different methods of optical control. Projectors with narrow beams inevitably use light sources of small size mounted in specular reflectors. Projectors with wide beams use either sources with a large diffusing outer bulb or matt reflectors or prismatic glass spreaders.

Most reflector profiles are based on the parabola, which theoretically produces a parallel beam of light (Sect. 1.5.1). This never occurs in practice because no source is infinitesimally small and no reflector has a perfectly specular reflectance, in addition to which there are inevitable tolerances in the reflector profile and the lamp mounting position. Axially-symmetric parabolic reflectors are used for most symmetrical floodlights and parabolic trough reflectors, with linear lamps, for most asymmetrical floodlights. Double asymmetrical floodlights frequently use compound trough reflectors, the profiles being made up of a series of parabolas of different focal lengths. However, imperfections in specular reflector profiles and non-uniformities of source luminance do give rise to striations in floodlight beams, i.e. local marked irregularities in intensity and/or colour. Partly as a consequence of this undesirable feature, and partly because of some advantages in production processes, faceted reflectors are becoming quite popular alternatives nowadays to the smooth parabolas used hitherto.

Three further elements of light control feature in some floodlights. Firstly, auxiliary reflectors, mounted in front of the lamp, are used to direct otherwise uncontrolled forward flux from the lamp back onto the main reflector to improve the beam factor and reduce spill light. Secondly, and with much less efficacy than auxiliary reflectors, external elements, such as louvres, hoods, and spill rings, are used to reduce stray light: their presence tends to reduce the peak intensity and to modify the beam pattern. Thirdly, alternative front glasses consisting of moulded lenses or stippled diffusers may be used to enable a variety of distribution patterns to be derived from one basic narrow beam floodlight.

Table 26.3 Floodlight photometric data

Symmetrical floodlights

Lamp type, power: lumen output	Optical control method	Beam angle (to 0·1 peak)	Angle to 0·5 peak	Cut-off angle (to 0·01 peak)	Beam factor	Peak intensity (cd klm^{-1})
GLS 1500 W: 26 klm	Specular reflector	25	9	180	0·38	8600
MBI 1000 W: 78 klm	Diffuse reflector	38	15	180	0·47	5000
	Specular reflector	20	6	180	0·32	13700
SON 1000 W: 100 klm	Diffuse reflector	30	12	180	0·39	6100
	Specular reflector	78	36	180	0·43	980
TH 300/500 W: 5/8·5 klm	Diffuse reflector	83	40	180	0·48	900
	Specular reflector	6	9	40	0·43	19280

Asymmetrical floodlights

Lamp type, power: lumen output	Optical control method	Beam angle (to 0·1 peak)		Angle to 0·5 peak		Cut-off angle (to 0·01 peak)		Beam factor	Peak intensity (cd klm^{-1})
		Hor.	Vert.	Hor.	Vert.	Hor.	Vert.		
TH 300/500 W: 5/8·5 klm	Prismatic glass	32	20	24	12	98	98	0·39	5400
SOX 135 W: 21·5 klm	Specular reflector	140	102	92	34	160	150	0·40	425

Double asymmetrical floodlights

Lamp type, power: lumen output	Optical control method	Beam angle (to 0·1 peak)			Angle to 0·5 peak			Cut-off angle (to 0·01 peak)			Beam factor	Peak intensity (cd klm^{-1})
		Hor.	Vert. above peak	Vert. below peak	Hor.	Vert. above peak	Vert. below peak	Hor.	Vert. above peak	Vert. below peak		
TH 1500 W: 33 klm	Specular reflector	98	19	29	62	7	8	120	54	57	0·62	2044
SON TD 400 W: 42 klm	Diffuse reflector	104	37	45	70	20	30	118	55	55	0·55	600
	Specular reflector	100	34	37	78	8	10	120	46	55	0·53	1090
	Diffuse reflector	100	38	42	72	14	20	104	50	56	0·50	640
MBIL 1500 W: 110 klm	Specular reflector	92	11·5	50	58	3	7	110	72	68	0·44	1450
	Dimpled reflector	98	30	58	60	5	26	160	80	80	0·41	646

26.2.2 Floodlights – mechanical characteristics

The classification of luminaires identifying the degree of protection against ingress of water and dust (Sect. 24.2.2) is as important in exterior lighting as in industrial lighting, the majority of floodlights having ratings between IP 23 and IP 54. However, there are other mechanical design considerations of importance in floodlighting systems, i.e. those affecting their installation, their aiming, and their maintenance, which depend on the particular application. For example the built-in features of a low wattage unit to be used for lighting features in a garden will be quite different to those provided on a high wattage narrow beam discharge projector intended to light railway sidings from a height of 30 m. Both types will probably be fully enclosed, but a linear tungsten halogen floodlight designed for general area lighting at low to medium mounting heights can be of an open design so long as such a unit is only directed downwards.

Floodlights may be mounted on the ground and directed upwards, or mounted on a wall, or mounted singly on columns or in groups on masts or towers. The design of the mounting stirrups or spigots must take this diversity of use into account and it is often more economic to design a number of mounting accessories, which are used as required, rather than designing alternative mounting facilities into each standard unit. For floodlights providing a wide angle distribution accurate aiming is not necessary, but with long range projectors aiming to an accuracy of $\pm 0.5°$ may be essential. In these cases the floodlight body should be balanced within its stirrup, with facilities for locking the floodlight firmly into position once it is aimed. It is also important that once an installation is aimed, relamping and cleaning should be possible without disturbing the orientation of the unit. Where accurate aiming is necessary then the angular markings provided on many standard floodlights are totally inadequate and a special aiming device must be used to set up the floodlighting system.

Ease of access to the lamp, the reflector, and the front glass for relamping and cleaning is another important consideration. Rear access is usually the most convenient method for floodlights mounted on towers or mast headframes, but in other situations front access is often preferable. Conditions for a maintenance man at the top of a column or on a tower headframe can be very unpleasant: either cold, wet, and windy or, in the tropics, unbearably hot, humid, and dusty. All bolts, screws, and nuts should be captive, fixings should not be prone to seize up, removable components should be retained by chains or cords, and the need for tools which are easily dropped or which cannot be held in a gloved hand should be avoided. Most maintenance men have only two hands and usually one of these is used for holding on!

26.2.3 Columns, masts, and towers

The decision whether to use columns or towers for area floodlighting is governed by a number of factors. At heights of up to 12 m there is a strong case for the use of columns; between 12 m and 30 m the choice depends on the quantity of equipment to be supported; above 30 m towers or heavy duty masts are used.

Columns Until comparatively recently the majority of lighting columns were made of concrete or steel, but aluminium has the advantages of lighter weight and a natural resistance to corrosion, even in atmospheres heavily laden with salt or chemicals. Aluminium, steel, and concrete columns are generally available in 8 m, 10 m, and 12 m heights, with provision being made to accommodate control gear, mounted on a wooden base-board, in a locked compartment at the bottom of the column. The foot of a metal column is coated internally and externally with bitumen over the whole of the planted depth and to 50 mm above ground level.

Masts   Masts are commonly available in heights up to 30 m and are used extensively in large areas, such as docks and lorry parks. The lanterns are mounted on a cradle with special raising and lowering gear consisting of a system of steel cables carried inside the mast and controlled by a portable winch at ground level. Shorter masts up to 16 m high, which hinge down for maintenance, are also available. There are also very large steel masts up to 50 m high, with floodlighting equipment mounted on a headframe, accessed by means of an internal ladder.

Towers   A lattice tower may be an economic alternative to a single mast, its aesthetic disadvantage being compensated by its ability to carry a greater number of floodlights and by the versatility of the various types of head platforms. Towers of up to 24 m height with a narrow base and standing on a single foundation are available and may be erected in fairly confined spaces without the use of cranes or heavy equipment. Towers which are extensively prefabricated look better than those assembled on site, but this may sometimes be outweighed by practical convenience, particularly that of access. Heavier towers of up to 45 m are normally of bolted construction using angle or tube. The width of the tower at the base requires separate foundation blocks for each leg.

Control gear housing   Control gear is mounted as close as is practicable to its lamp: in the floodlight itself or in the base compartment of a column. Large tower and mast installations usually require the provision of a locked, weatherproof, ventilated cubicle in which all the gear is housed, normally at the base of the tower. Open racks can be used in areas protected from the weather and where there is no public access. In a control gear cubicle heat-sensitive components, such as capacitors and switches, are mounted as low as possible, air vents at the base should be equivalent to between 50 and 60% of the plan area, and a slot at least 15 mm wide should be provided all round the top.

26.2.4 Costs

The methods of financial assessment for interior lighting projects (Sect. 21.2.1) are generally applicable to exterior lighting, but with a major possible addition to capital costs due to the installation of columns, masts, or towers. Also, in determining the annual running costs there are considerable differences in the periods of time during which different types of exterior installations are in use, typical hours of use being given in Table 26.4.

In comparing alternative lamp/lantern combinations for floodlighting it is useful to evaluate, as the common base, the total annual cost per thousand beam lumens, rather than repeatedly working out complete designs to satisfy illuminance and uniformity requirements. Some experience is needed when doing this: the lamp/lantern combinations being compared should have lumen outputs related to the illuminance to be provided or there would be a danger of overspacing and consequently a poor uniformity.

Table 26.4 Annual use of exterior lighting installations

Type of installation	Number of days used p.a.	Average hours of use per day	Total hours of use p.a.
Street lighting			
main street	365	11	4000
side street	365	6	2000
Industrial area floodlighting			
security lighting	365	11	4000
prestige lighting	365	6	2000
working areas	150	2	300†
Decorative floodlighting, commercial and municipal			
all the year round	365	6	2000
summer only	200	6	1200
Sports			
professional	25	4	100
amateur (municipal)	300	6	1800
private	125	4	500

† Assuming no shift work is involved.

26.3 Design and calculation techniques

The designs of many decorative floodlighting schemes rely for success on a combination of aesthetic appreciation, experience, intuition, and flair: some useful guidance is provided in Chap. 27. However, the majority of exterior lighting installations, certainly for the floodlighting of functional areas, succeed by satisfying the various lighting criteria outlined in Sect. 26.1, following a design process normally consisting of three stages:

(a) A practical assessment is made of where to locate the floodlights, the type of light distribution required, and the light source characteristics which suit the particular application.
(b) A 'lumen calculation' is carried out to establish the number and loading of the lamps to achieve the required average illuminance.
(c) When necessary, 'point-by-point calculations' are performed to determine the aiming pattern of the floodlights for the required uniformity.

The third stage may necessitate modifications to the preliminary calculations, and is the stage when the use of a computer becomes invaluable for large and complex installations.

26.3.1 Layout and mounting height

The major problem at the initial stage of designing a floodlighting installation is that there are so many possible variables. Unlike interior lighting, where the boundaries of the space are clearly defined by walls and ceiling and floor, floodlighting equipment can be placed within the area to be lit or located on towers well outside the area. The height of the towers and their distance outside the area will have to be considered because, until such matters are decided, it is impossible to tell what beam distributions

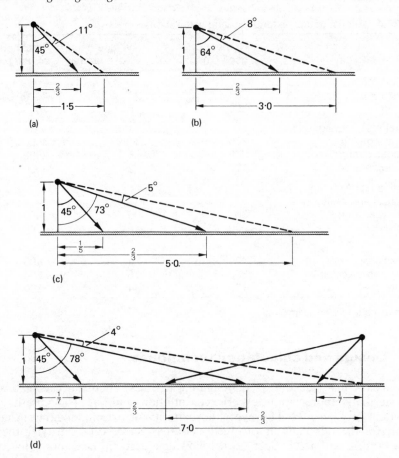

Fig. 26.4   Aiming of floodlights for the following area depth to mounting height ratios: (a) 1·5, (b) 3·0, (c) 5·0, and (d) 7·0

are required or how the floodlights should be aimed. The best advice for anyone embarking on a design problem is to start by studying, preferably in situ, the characteristics and limitations of the site. With areas of regular shape and with set dimensions, such as sports areas, standard pole layouts may be available to guide the designer, but this is rarely the case with industrial and commercial areas.

It is generally true to say that the higher the mounting height, the smaller is the number of columns, masts, and towers required. As a result a high mounting height generally achieves the most effective and efficient floodlighting at the lowest installation cost, but the relationship between mounting height H and the depth of the area to be lit D is important.

If an open area is to be lit from one side, the ratio D/H should not be greater than 5. If, however, there are obstructions within the area, such as in a stock yard, then the ratio should be reduced to 3 or even 2 with extensive obstructions. When lighting from two or more directions, the ratio can be increased to 7, but should be reduced to 4 if there are obstructions.

In the initial design the peak intensity of the floodlight is usually directed to a point some $\frac{2}{3}$ of the way across the depth of the area (Fig. 26.4), the resultant geometry defining the vertical beam spread required from the floodlight to illuminate the full depth of the area. Floodlights using trough reflectors are available with double asymmetric distributions providing vertical beam spreads suitable for different D/H ratios, but such floodlights have wide horizontal distributions. Where D/H exceeds 3 it is often necessary to use a supplementary floodlight with a wide vertical beam angle aimed at a lower elevation to fill in the area close to the base of the tower or pole. If floodlights with symmetrical distributions are used to illuminate very large spaces, the lighting of the various zones ranging from the most distant to those at the base of the tower is provided by a series of projectors: those aimed at high elevations have narrow beam angles and are followed by floodlights with progressively wider beam angles aimed at lower elevations.

Spacing The spacing between columns, when areas are to be lit from one or two sides, may be dictated by site limitations. Given no constraints, the spacing to height ratio *SHR* is determined primarily by the horizontal beam spread of the floodlights, selected in the first place because of their vertical beam characteristics.

Values of *SHR* in the range 1·5 to 2·0 are commonly used with asymmetrical floodlights: values over 3 are unlikely to provide acceptable uniformity. Where higher *SHR* values prove to be necessary because of site constraints, some floodlights may have to be aimed at points which do not lie on a transverse line from their column or a more complex aiming pattern of symmetrical floodlights may have to be used. It will be necessary to check the consequences of the aiming pattern on both illuminance and uniformity by a point-by-point calculation.

26.3.2 Lumen calculations

For their lumen calculations exterior lighting designers use a formula very similar to that used by interior lighting designers and quoted in Sect. 21.3.1. The formula is

$$E = \frac{N \times L \times MF \times AL \times UF}{A}$$

where *E* is the average illuminance (lux),
   N is the number of lamps used in the installation,
   L is the lighting design lamp lumens (the product of initial lumens and lamp lumen depreciation factor),
   MF is the maintenance factor (Sect. 26.1),
   AL is the factor to represent atmospheric absorption losses (Sect. 26.1),
   UF is the utilization factor of the floodlights used,
   A is the area (m²) to be lit.

Utilization factor The utilization factor of a floodlight, a measure of the proportion of the bare lamp flux which reaches the area to be lit, is considered to be made up of two factors. One of these is the beam factor *BF* (Sect. 26.2.1), a characteristic of the floodlight itself. The other is the waste light factor *WL*, a measure of how much of the beam reaches the area to be lit, and which is therefore a characteristic of the installation design. Taking these two factors together, $UF = BF \times WL$.

If the average utilization factor of the floodlights were known, as well as the lamp type, the number of floodlight locations, and the average illuminance required over the area, then the lumen formula above would enable the number of lighting design lumens needed at each location to be evaluated. This would then determine the lamp loading and the number of floodlights.

In a first rough assessment of a scheme it is common practice to take $UF = 0.3$: this value will inevitably be low for asymmetric projectors and high for very wide angle projectors. A better estimate is obtained by multiplying the beam factor of the type of floodlight to be used by an estimate of the waste light factor. This is likely to be somewhere in the range of 0.5 to 0.9: the lower value for a long narrow site or one with an irregular shape and the upper value for a large site or one where the beam angles of the chosen floodlight relate well to the angles subtended by the site at the chosen floodlight locations. The estimate is made by sketching the general shape of the various beams on the plan of the area to be lit and evaluating what fraction of the beams are actually intercepted by the area.

Zonal flux diagram   If they are available for the range of floodlights being considered, zonal flux diagrams provide a more accurate and yet easy way of determining utilization factors for floodlighting schemes. As has been explained in Sect. 5.2.7, a particular system of angular scaling (Fig. 5.11) is used for floodlight photometric data, firstly for plotting isocandela contours and secondly for evaluating zonal flux values.

The right-hand side of Fig. 26.5 is the zonal flux diagram for one-half of a 400 W SON TD floodlight. The figure in a particular grid square evaluates the flux emitted per thousand lamp lumens in the zone defined by the two pairs of vertical and

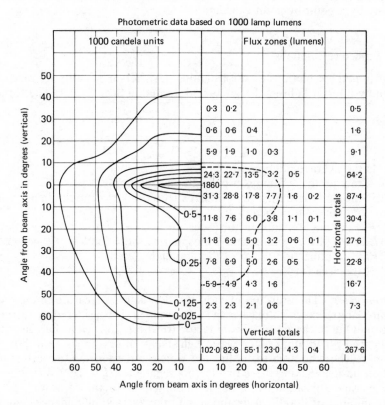

Fig. 26.5   Zonal flux and isocandela diagrams for floodlighting

horizontal angles forming the grid square. The total flux emitted by the floodlight is equal to twice the sum of all the flux values shown, indicating that in this particular floodlight only $2 \times 267 \cdot 6/1000 = 0 \cdot 535$ of the bare lamp flux escapes from the floodlight. The dotted line is the isocandela contour for $0 \cdot 1$ of the peak intensity, thus identifying the beam. An area to be illuminated can be expressed in V–H angular units and drawn out as an overlay, which can be moved up and down the $H = 0$ line to account for elevational adjustments of the floodlight. For azimuth adjustments redrawn overlays are required. The use of the diagram is best illustrated by an example.

Figure 26.6a shows a 60 m × 50 m cargo handling area which requires an average horizontal illuminance of 50 lux. 400 W SON TD floodlights are being considered, on

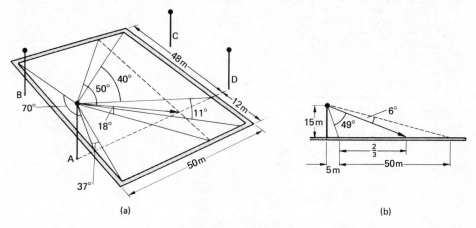

Fig. 26.6   Four-pole installation for lighting cargo handling area

15 m poles located 5 m outside the area, two poles spaced at 36 m on either side of the area. As indicated in Fig. 26.6b, the normal $\frac{2}{3}$ aiming point is selected for all floodlights.

With this symmetrical layout, all floodlights will have the same *UF*, and so one floodlight on pole A will be considered. The overlay to be prepared requires two areas to be plotted on it, that to the right of pole A and that to the left, shown in Fig. 26.7 as solid and dotted lines respectively. The aiming point plots on the V–H grid as $(0, 0)$. The area boundaries parallel to AB plot as horizontal lines $V = 49°$ below and 6° above the aiming point. The horizontal angles of the four corners, and also of the two points on the side boundaries in line with the aiming point, are shown in Fig. 26.6a. The side boundaries actually plot as curves, but are each approximated by two straight lines.

The total flux (per 1000 lamp lumens) intercepted by the actual area is determined by adding all the zonal flux values within the area as plotted on the zonal flux diagram, estimating the contribution from part-zones. Figure 26.7 shows this value to be $372 \cdot 3$, implying a *UF* of $372 \cdot 3/1000 = 0 \cdot 37$.

Rearranging the lumen formula gives $N = (E \times A)/(L \times MF \times AL \times UF)$. With $E = 50$, $AL = 1 \cdot 0$, $MF = 0 \cdot 8$, and $L = 42\,000$, N becomes $12 \cdot 07$. This layout, using 3 floodlights on each pole, will therefore produce the required average illuminance. Whether it is satisfactory from the point of view of uniformity requires a point-by-point calculation check.

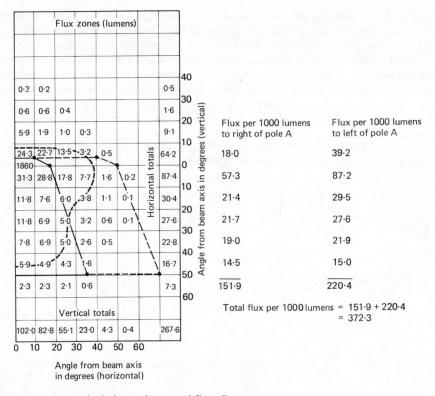

Fig. 26.7   Lumen calculation using zonal flux diagram

26.3.3   Point-by-point calculations

To examine the uniformity of a proposed floodlighting scheme requires illuminances to be calculated at specific points. The inverse square and cosine laws of illumination (Sect. 1.4.5) lead to the expression $E = (I \cos \theta)/r^2$ for the illuminance on a surface due to a source of intensity I cd at a distance r m away when the light falls at an angle of θ to the normal to the surface. In floodlighting the effective source intensity is the photometric value multiplied by the maintenance factor and by the atmospheric light loss factor.

Illumination diagram   For some exterior luminaires, primarily those with a fixed mounting attitude, illumination diagrams may be available. One form of these, shown in Fig. 26.8, evaluates the illuminance at the centre of each square of a grid with a spacing equal to one-quarter of the luminaire mounting height when that height is 8 m. For different mounting heights a table of conversion factors is given. An alternative to the matrix of illuminance values is to plot on the grid a series of equi-illuminance contours. In this form the illumination diagram is usually given the title of an *isolux* diagram. Such diagrams could be produced for floodlights, but since a different diagram would be needed for every aiming angle, this is not a practical proposition.

Isocandela diagram   For floodlighting it is usual to resort to the inverse square and cosine law formula. The most useful form of intensity data is one using the *V–H*

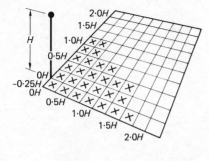

2·0H	4·0	4·0	4·0	4·0	3·5	3·0	2·5	2·0	1·5
	6·5	6·0	5·5	5·5	5·0	4·0	3·0	2·0	1·5
1·5H	9·0	9·0	8·0	7·0	6·5	5·0	3·5	2·5	1·5
	13·0	12·5	11·0	9·5	8·5	6·0	4·0	2·5	1·5
1·0H	20·5	19·0	17·0	13·0	10·0	7·0	4·0	2·5	1·5
	28·0	27·0	24·0	16·5	12·5	6·5	4·5	2·5	1·5
0·5H	37·0	33·0	28·0	17·5	12·0	6·5	4·5	2·5	1·5
	37·5	35·5	27·0	17·5	11·0	6·0	4·0	2·0	1·5
0H	38·5	34·5	24·0	15·0	9·5	5·5	3·5	2·0	1·0
-0·25H	31·0	27·0	19·0	12·0	7·5	4·0	2·5	1·5	1·0

0H   0·5H   1·0H   1·5H   2·0H

Value of horizontal illuminance
at centre of grid square

Mounting height (H) in metres	Conversion factor
5	2·56
6	1·78
7	1·31
8	1·00
9	0·79
10	0·64
11	0·58
12	0·45
14	0·33

Fig. 26.8 Illumination diagram

coordinate system, such as the isocandela contours on the left-hand side of Fig. 26.5. This accompanies the zonal flux diagram deliberately to facilitate a point-by-point calculation after a lumen calculation.

The use of this diagram can be illustrated by calculating the illuminance at one corner of the cargo handling area examined previously. This is likely to be the minimum illuminance, and so the ratio of the average 50 lux to this value is one uniformity measure likely to need checking. The illuminance at a corner is the sum of the illuminances provided by each lantern. For each lantern the coordinates of the corner have to be identified and the intensity in that direction interpolated from the isocandela contours. Since identical lanterns with the same aiming angle are used, the exercise can be carried out on one diagram.

In Fig. 26.9 the coordinates of the corner nearest to pole A with respect to the lanterns on each pole are identified by the appropriate pole letter A, B, C, or D. The interpolated intensity of each lantern, in candelas per 1000 lumens, is tabulated, together with the appropriate $\cos \theta$ term. The illuminance expression $(I\cos\theta)/r^2$ can be rewritten $E_H = (I\cos^3\theta)/H^2$, where E_H is the horizontal illuminance due to a source mounted H m above the horizontal. With a maintenance factor of 0·8, an atmospheric absorption factor of 1·0, a bare lamp lighting design lumens of 42 klm, and 3 lanterns on each pole, the illuminance at the corner is given by

$$E_H = \frac{42 \times 0\cdot8 \times 1\cdot0 \times 3}{15^2}\, \Sigma(I\cos^3\theta)$$

$$= 0\cdot448\Sigma(I\cos^3\theta)$$

$$= 0\cdot448 \times 31\cdot2$$

$$= 14\cdot0\,\text{lux}$$

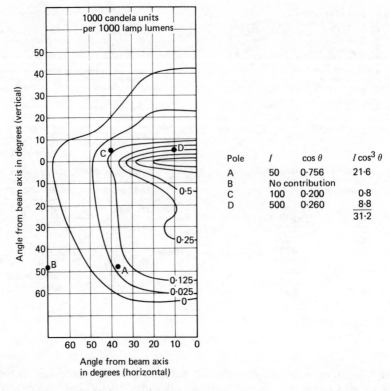

Pole	I	$\cos \theta$	$I \cos^3 \theta$
A	50	0·756	21·6
B	No contribution		
C	100	0·200	0·8
D	500	0·260	8·8
			31·2

Fig. 26.9   Point-by-point calculation using isocandela diagram

The ratio of average to minimum illuminance is therefore 3·6, which satisfies the criterion value in Table 26.2.

Computers   For the majority of floodlighting problems the use of a computer is difficult to justify, but on the more complex projects where many repetitive calculations must be carried out to ascertain the diversity of illuminance on the horizontal, vertical, or inclined planes, the machine can be valuable. However, the computer can only act as a design aid in the limited sense that the final printout of the results can tell the planner quickly and accurately whether the design works or not.

It is usual in these cases to define an *XY* grid covering the area. The steps in *X* and *Y* can be selected to give either a coarse or fine grid, depending on the requirements. The positions of the floodlights are then defined in terms of *X*, *Y*, and *Z* for altitude. Floodlight aiming can be noted either in degrees of elevation and azimuth or by using the *X* and *Y* coordinates of the point at which the peak intensity reaches the area. The photometric performance of the floodlights is then entered in the form of an angular grid. The intensity values between grid points are handled in the program either by curve fitting or by straight-line interpolation.

It is also necessary to define the format for printout presentation. This can either be tabulated in the form of a chosen grid or a line plotter can be used to produce isolux diagrams. By introducing standard formulae into the program the printout can be in terms of horizontal, vertical, inclined-plane, vector, scalar, mean cylindrical, or any other form of illuminance for the whole or part of the specified grid.

The possibilities of the use of computers are endless and no doubt in the future the computer will be used in the initial design stages, but it will never knowingly make a building look beautiful nor replace the designer's intuition. What it can do is calculate with great efficiency and so produce more information on a single project than its master can assimilate in a lifetime.

Further reading

Cox K T O, 1972, *Ltg. Res. Technol.*, **4,** 236–242: Value for money – exterior lighting

Heard F W, Stone F H S and Jewess B W, 1976, *Ltg. Res. Technol.*, **8,** 151–156: Effect of atmospheric attenuation on exterior lighting design

Lyons S L, 1980, Exterior lighting for industry and security (London: Applied Science)

Thorn Lighting, 1974, *Outdoor lighting handbook* (Epping, Essex: Gower Press)

27 Floodlighting

Floodlighting is a term which has never had a precise definition, but with the passage of time is now accepted as meaning the lighting of an object or an area out of doors so that it becomes brighter than its surroundings. The objectives are many and varied: to provide security, to allow work to carry on after dark, to model a feature such as a statue, to enable sporting events to be seen by spectators or to be televised, to advertise, or to enhance the appearance of a scene or a building for pleasure. Whereas the previous chapter concerned itself with the lighting criteria, the available equipment, and the design calculations for this wide range of objectives, this chapter surveys the different practical lighting techniques used to achieve them.

27.1 Sign lighting

The quantity of light required from floodlights to illuminate signs will depend on four things: the size of the sign, the distance from which it is viewed, the contrasts of various parts of the sign with each other, and the ambient lighting conditions. A small sign, or one to be viewed from a distance, will need more light than will a large one or one to be read at close quarters, if it is to be readily noticed. When the sign message has the maximum contrast with its background, the amount of light required is a minimum. A sign in a city centre where there is a high ambient illuminance from shop windows, street lights, and other nearby illuminated signs will require a substantially higher luminance than will the same sign in a suburban area. The illuminance ranges for advertising signs in Table 26.1 give general guidance, but should be used with discretion.

Most signs are viewed from below, so floodlights for externally-lit signs should be mounted on brackets from the top of the sign rather than from the bottom, to prevent obstruction. Alternatively, on some sites the floodlights could be mounted on the ground. Many signs have a specular surface, so floodlight locations must be chosen so that direct reflections of the illuminating sources do not prevent the sign being read. Also, since it is rarely possible for the light from generally-available commercial floodlights to be confined to the sign, care should be taken to ensure that spill light beyond the sign does not cause annoyance. To allow for variations in light distributions from one floodlight to another it is advantageous to provide for directional adjustment in the fixing arrangements. To obtain a reasonable uniformity of illuminance along the length of a sign, luminaires bracketed from above should be spaced laterally at between 2·5 and 3 times the bracket length, provided that asymmetric wide angle floodlights are used. If units are overspaced, a scalloping effect will be created. The bracket length should be no less than one-quarter of the sign height. Under these conditions, a very approximate method of calculating the illuminance on a floodlit sign is to take one-third of the total luminous flux of all the lamps and divide this by the area of the sign in square metres to give the illuminance in lux.

Interior-lit signs, sometimes described as self-luminous signs, require a reasonable uniformity of luminance. To achieve this the lamps within should not be spaced further apart than the distance between the front panel and the lamps. The interior should be painted matt white, which often has a higher diffuse reflectance than gloss paint. A very approximate method of calculating the luminance of a self-luminous sign is to take one-sixth of the total enclosed lamp lumens and divide this by the area of the sign in square metres to give the luminance in candelas per square metre.

UK Local Authorities frequently have bye-laws covering the luminance of advertising signs to ensure they do not cause glare. It is therefore advisable to obtain clearance from the Local Authority for a proposed sign before proceeding. There are also recommended limits on the luminance of road traffic signs (Sect. 29.2).

27.2   Lighting of vehicle parks

It is rare for detailed calculations to be carried out to assess the number of floodlights required for a car park, whether municipal or commercial. The simple method of assuming that some 30% of the lamp flux will fall onto the area ($UF = 0.3$, as suggested in Sect. 26.3.2) is usual when an illuminance of between 20 lux and 50 lux is to be provided. Allied to this, a simple but adequate way to determine the disposition of floodlights around the perimeter of an area is to assume that wide angle floodlights will provide useful illuminance over a depth of area equal to three times the height at which they are mounted, and that the lateral spacing between floodlights should also equal about three times the mounting height.

The chosen height will often have to be a compromise. It needs to be high enough to ensure that floodlights are well above parked vehicles, which throw increasing lengths of shadow with increasing distance from the floodlight positions, and to minimize glare to drivers using the car park. At the same time the height must be related sensibly to the height of nearby buildings: it may well be limited by Local Authority bye-laws.

If the method given above for determining the disposition of equipment indicates that pole heights are going to be excessive, the alternative is to use post-top luminaires having a symmetrical light distribution on shorter columns arranged in a regular array at a spacing to height ratio of 3 or 4. A 30% utilance of lamp flux may be assumed to calculate the average illuminance.

Lorry parks are most satisfactorily lit from the perimeter of the area to reduce the risk of damage to poles and floodlights caused by bad driving. If this is not practical, crash barriers should enclose island-sited columns. The inherent height and bulk of lorries require that perimeter floodlights should be mounted at least 12 m from the ground to ensure some reduction of shadowing, which will be far greater than in a car park. At these heights the number of columns can be minimized, each supporting a number of floodlights, if necessary trained in different directions. Where island-sited positions are used, it is usual to mount floodlights on free-standing single columns at heights of 30 m or more (Fig. 27.1). Such columns are usually fitted with headframes that can be lowered for maintenance of the luminaires, but hinged columns of ever-increasing heights are being marketed.

Fig. 27.1   Manufacturer's finished car pound

Multistorey and underground car parks   Luminaires used in these locations need to be capable of operation in semi-exposed weather conditions and need to be robust. These requirements imply enclosed luminaires, usually using high pressure discharge or fluorescent lamps. Glass fibre reinforced plastic or aluminium luminaires, with acrylic or polycarbonate gasketed enclosures, will stand up most satisfactorily to the climatic conditions and corrosive atmosphere created by vehicle exhausts. If sheet steel luminaires are to be used, they should have suitable protective finishes. In underground car parks Local Authorities' bye-laws may require Zone 2 luminaires (Sect. 24.2.2) to be used, a point which needs checking before a scheme is planned.

The installation should be designed to indicate clearly the correct routes along each level, and the way from one level to the next. A luminaire should be sited at each route intersection so that at these points the illuminance will be above the average 30 lux to which the whole complex has been lit. A strict uniformity of illuminance is not required along the routes between intersections because traffic will be moving slowly, or should be: a diversity of 30 to 1 is acceptable. An increased illuminance of 50 lux should also be provided at the entrances and exits, since at these points the visual task is more severe.

27.3   Industrial floodlighting

Outdoor industrial complexes, whether quarries, tank farms, stock yards, or shipping wharves, have two common lighting problems: the multiplicity of shadows caused by the nature of the site and the processes being carried out.

Surfaces on which work is being carried out will be at varying angles, making a precise specification of illuminance level impossible. Average horizontal illuminance would seem worthless in the absence of any average horizontal surface (Fig. 27.2). A vertical value? Cylindrical or scalar illuminance? At what points? Some starting-point

Fig. 27.2 Petroleum cracking plant

for design has to be found. As indicated in the illuminance ranges specified in Table 26.1, or in the relevant CIBS/IES report (CIBS 1969), the usual approach is to calculate for an appropriate horizontal illuminance at ground level over the entire site, assuming no obstructions. With a knowledge of the probable obstructions, floodlights should be mounted so as to project light from as high as is practical and from above probable obstructions to minimize shadows. The number of floodlight positions should be as many as is practicable so that light at any point comes from a multiplicity of directions softening such shadows as may arise. In very obstructed areas additional local lighting may be necessary.

Quarries and open cast mines present problems related to dimensions. In the former case the site often increases in horizontal distance; in the latter the depth progressively increases. As a floodlight installation will probably be permanent, it is useful to plan for the ultimate distance or depth when these can be established, advising that a progressively increasing number of units be brought into operation as work proceeds. As distances increase, there will be a progressively greater overlap of the distribution of adjacent floodlights and at the same time a decrease in the illuminance due to the inverse square law. It is therefore desirable to submit sequential re-aiming plans to cater for changing depths and distances so that the user can redirect floodlights from time to time.

Tank farms can be lit in two ways. If the tanks are arranged in a regular array, high mounted floodlights can be sited on the perimeter of the farm, and therefore outside the hazardous area, projecting light between the tanks. Where this is not possible, the only recourse is to provide local lighting units where visual tasks demand it (Fig. 27.2), for example on access ladders, walkways, valves, gauges, etc., and rely on spill light and reflected light for general background lighting. Any local lighting units within the complex will certainly need to be flameproof. Reference will be needed to the Petroleum Industries' code of practice (Inst. Pet. 1965) and to BS 5345 (BSI 1976f) to select the particular form of luminaire (Ex and T classifications, Sect. 24.2.2).

Stock yards imply the storage of large objects and the frequent movement of such goods. Transporter lorries may enter the yard and use will inevitably be made of cranes or fork-lift trucks. If sufficient general lighting is provided to allow the safe movement of personnel around the yard, the necessary task lighting for the movement of goods is most acceptably provided by projectors on the crane jib or on the fork-lift or, if gantry cranes are involved, by floodlights mounted on the crane girderwork and directed downwards. In the case of cranes, where vibration is likely to occur, discharge lamps are more resilient than filament lamps, but where stock is identified by colour coding, low pressure sodium lamps should not be used. For fork-lift trucks low wattage tungsten halogen lamps in sealed beam units offer the best solution.

Building sites present a special problem in the UK, where low voltages of 110 V or below are mandatory for lighting equipment. This means the use of discharge lamps is excluded, because few such lamps will strike at these voltages, so tungsten halogen lamps are almost always used. Since the duration of operation is usually short and the treatment afforded to the units tends to result in a short life-span, the high electrical running cost can be accepted. A thorough treatment of the lighting of building and civil engineering sites is provided in a CIBS/IES lighting guide (CIBS 1975a).

Docks   The lighting of wharves needs to be effected from some distance back from the edge so that the working area where loading and unloading are carried out remains unobstructed (Fig. 27.3). Such an arrangement, normally using discharge lamp floodlights, may cast a shadow on the deck of moored vessels when the tide is low. Reliance will then have to be placed on deck lighting on board, and on crane jib floodlights. Floodlights on board ship and on the dock side must be resistant to the saline marine atmosphere: diecast aluminium, copper, stainless steel, or plastics are suitable materials. On board ship tungsten halogen floodlights are most frequently used.

In comparison with the lighting of wharves it may be thought that the lighting of a dry dock is a simple matter. Here is a deep rectangular hole, which could be lit by cross-projecting light from floodlights mounted along each side. However, lighting is really needed when the dry dock is substantially full of ship, frequently leaving little space between the dock wall and the vessel, the latter having a lower surface curving away from the vertical side to a horizontal bottom resting on the stocks.

The only really satisfactory way of providing light on the sides and bottom of a vessel is to recess wide angle floodlights into the sides of the dock at successive levels, the units being capable of complete submersion. The alternative is to site floodlights at each end of the dock directing light between the ship's side and the dock, cross-projecting from each end, but this will not light under the keel, so temporary supplementary lighting units will be required. The CIBS has published a specific lighting guide for ship building and ship repair (CIBS 1979b).

Fig. 27.3   Hamburg docks

27.4   Security lighting

Security lighting requires that intruders shall be detected, either directly by the human eye or indirectly via a closed-circuit television system. In either case vertical illuminance is the most relevant quantitative criterion, and this does not need to be very high since the human or electronic system is operating in dim ambient conditions and the degree of detail to be detected is quite coarse.

The least sophisticated form of security lighting is that for unattended sites, such as manufacturers' storage areas (Fig. 27.1) and lorry parks, lit to discourage vandalism. They are subject to irregular inspections by police or security guards, and the lighting merely allows for the detection of unauthorized movement. Such lighting calls for high efficacy units, having a long life and mounted as high as possible to obtain the maximum coverage and to minimize interference or mechanical damage.

On an attended site, with a gatehouse at the entrance, floodlights should be positioned so that the whole field of view from within the building is adequately illuminated. Lighting inside the gatehouse should be localized and preferably dimmable, with shielded luminaires permitting no reflections in the windows which would interfere with a clear view of the exterior.

Some or all of the security lighting at some establishments is normally off, but linked to an alarm system requiring the lighting to be activated instantaneously so that a visual assessment of the situation may be made. In these circumstances only tungsten halogen lamps are used.

It is an advantage on most attended sites to mount floodlights fairly low with considerable glare from the viewpoint of the intruder or the potential intruder. At the same time the siting of floodlights must allow for security staff to move about behind the light sources, inconspicuously and with their ability to see unimpaired.

If there is a risk that rifle or small arms fire may be used to extinguish floodlights, considerable protection can be effected by directing the floodlights into the site and using aluminium plastic foil stretched over wooden frames as easily-replacable reflectors to redirect the light outwards.

Where closed-circuit television surveillance is employed, advice should be sought from the camera manufacturer as to the illuminance level of visible light or the wattage of infrared radiation required. Care must be taken to ensure that there is no lens flare from badly-sited luminaires which would render the system inoperative.

In prisons or detention centres security is a matter of preventing the inmates leaving and at the same time making it difficult for accomplices outside to assist in any escape. Floodlighting of the boundary area is the prime lighting requirement. In the case of a double chain-link fence the space between the fences should be lit from floodlights mounted inside the inner fence. In the case of a high wall the area immediately inside the wall, and the area outside if this is patrolled, is commonly lit by groups of floodlights mounted on the perimeter wall.

27.5   Sports lighting

There is only one floodlighting application where absolute levels of illuminance are commonly greater than those required in most interiors. This is in the lighting of large areas for spectator sports. In a stadium, spectators may need to see relatively small detail and fast movement at distances of 150 m or more. To achieve this the illuminance will need to be higher than that strictly dictated by the visual needs of the players. Where sports are televised, the demands of the camera system may dictate an even higher illuminance which is in excess of the minimum visual requirements of the most distant spectator.

Televised and spectator events apart, many sports can be played at lighting levels comparable with, or even less than, those provided in commercial or industrial interiors. The level to be recommended depends firstly on the size and speed of the critical object, which obviously vary from sport to sport, and secondly (for many sports) on the standard of play or competition. In accordance with the proposals of international sporting authorities the CIBS/IES lighting guide to sports (CIBS 1974) recognizes three standards of competition: national and international, club and county, and recreational. Adherence to the recommendations results in a team finding comparable lighting conditions for both 'home' and 'away' fixtures.

There are a number of sports played on standard sized areas, for example tennis, football, rugby, etc., for which there are well-established methods of lighting, some with readily-available standard layouts of pole-mounted floodlights (Thorn Lighting 1974). Floodlights are aimed across the main direction of play, with the poles sited sufficiently far back from the sides of the area to ensure that players will not collide with them and to ensure that the near sidelines are adequately lit. For economic reasons the number of poles is kept to a minimum, commensurate with providing reasonable uniformity, which frequently means large lumen packages at each position. This increases the probability of glare, so floodlights are mounted as high as is practical, certainly no lower than 8 m for single tennis courts, and as high as 50 m for football or cricket.

Television   For spectator sports in large stadia where television coverage is provided the lighting requirements relating to the camera take priority (CIBS 1974). For any sporting event there are seldom less than three fixed cameras, and frequently this number is supplemented by other fixed or mobile hand-held cameras. For games such as football, rugby, and ice-hockey cameras are limited to one side of the arena and behind the goals, so that cutting between the cameras does not produce an apparent change in the direction of play for the television viewer. For athletics and cricket, on the other hand, cameras are disposed around the complete area.

The lighting criterion for colour television uses the illuminance on a plane normal to the camera position: the average value of this over the field of play should lie between 800 lux and 1400 lux. This results in pictures ranging in quality from acceptable to excellent, even with the use of long focal length lenses. No matter how many cameras are used it is usual to identify one main camera position, and the illuminance value normal to this camera is calculated: its position is usually on the transverse centreline of the arena and 5 m or more above pitch level. If a symmetrical floodlighting layout is used, this will ensure adequate lighting levels for all other camera positions. For sports where the cameras are located only on one side of the arena it is acceptable to reduce the backlight component, but by no more than 50%. This economy, however, is only achieved at the cost of some reduction in picture quality and spectator viewing conditions.

27.6 Building floodlighting

Of all exterior lighting applications, the decorative floodlighting of buildings is unique in three ways. Firstly, it is possible to use too much light: buildings which have been beaten into a luminous pulp are at the very least visually unsatisfying and frequently downright uncomfortable. Secondly, the characteristics of the surface of the building are as important as those of the illuminant. Thirdly, areas of shadow make as useful a contribution to the final effect as do illuminated areas.

The CIBS/IES lighting guide to the outdoor environment (CIBS 1975b) recommends a series of average illuminances for building floodlighting. These range from 15 lux to 450 lux, depending on the ambient lighting conditions and the reflectance of the building materials, and have the objective of producing an acceptable level of overall building brightness. Uniformity criteria for building floodlighting are to be found in Table 26.2.

It is not only the lightness of the building surface which is important, but also the degree of specularity. Highly specular surfaces, such as glass, gold leaf, aluminium, stainless steel, mosaic, glazed bricks, and tiles, may present particular difficulties when floodlighting buildings. In daylight, with the main source of light above the building, specular reflections are projected downwards towards an observer and these materials appear to sparkle and shine. When floodlights are installed at ground level, the direction of light is reversed and any specular reflections are directed skywards: to the observer the building looks dull and lifeless.

Whatever the reflection characteristics of a building surface, the absence of a large diffuse sky and the general reversal of the direction of incident light mean that floodlighting cannot duplicate the daytime appearance of a building. Although the daytime view of a building with the sun at a low altitude may suggest a floodlighting pattern, the best installations are those which exploit the differences between day and night rather than attempt to minimize them, not least in making effective use of shadow and possibly colour.

A coherent flow of light across a facade is desirable, implying one general aiming orientation for the main floodlights. This direction should not coincide with the most common viewing direction for the building, since no shadows will then be visible and the scene will appear flat (Fig. 27.4). The main floodlighting should be done from a

(a)

(b)

Fig. 27.4 Buckingham Palace: (a) viewed from behind the main floodlights and (b) viewed from the front

substantially different angle, and it is well worth examining the different shadow patterns cast by the architectural features of the facade when alternative angles are used.

Completeness of floodlighting is important in that the whole building should be revealed, including the return walls to the main facade, the roof, and the full height of any chimney stacks. The main floodlighting units usually need supplementing, not only to guarantee completeness, but sometimes to avoid the 'floating' appearance which can arise from the base of the building being shadowed or underlit. It is important that floodlighting equipment is shielded from view by being installed behind existing or purposely-introduced features. The overall effect of a scheme is spoiled if the lighting units are silhouetted against the floodlit scene.

Coloured light can be used in other ways to produce a deliberately garish effect or festival atmosphere. A colour contrast between, for example, the facade and a side wall of a building emphasizes the depth of the structure. Artists use blue colours to simulate shadow and a similar technique has proved successful in floodlighting, using tungsten or sodium light to suggest a sunlit area with mercury light suggesting shadowed areas.

Some of the calculation techniques of Chap. 26 are very relevant to building floodlighting, and the photometric characteristics of floodlights are still important, but no better advice can be offered to someone undertaking building floodlighting for the first time than this: take a floodlight outside, point it at something, walk around, look at the varying pattern of light and shade, and never let that visual experience be overruled by illuminating engineering theory.

Further reading

Baker J E and Lyons S L, *Ltg. Res. Technol.*, **10,** 11–18: Lighting for the security of premises

Boyce P R, 1979, *Ltg. Res. Technol.*, **11,** 78–84: The effect of fence luminance on the detection of potential intruders

Davies I F, Jackson M G A and Rogers B C, 1972, *Ltg. Res. Technol.*, **4,** 181–201: Lighting techniques and associated equipment for outdoor colour television with particular reference to football stadium lighting

Electricity Council, *Lighting for productivity and amenity*

Electricity Council, *Lighting for outdoor work and storage*

Electricity Council, 1976, *Essentials of security lighting*

Frier J P and Gazley Frier M E, 1980, *Industrial lighting systems* (New York: McGraw-Hill)

Holmes A D V, 1972, *Ltg. Res. Technol.*, **4,** 202–214: A review of current railway lighting practice in Great Britain

Lyons S L, 1972, *Ltg. Res. Technol.*, **4,** 67–79: Electric lighting for building sites and construction

Lyons S L, 1980, *Exterior lighting for industry and security* (London: Applied Science)

28 Road lighting

With such a large proportion of the general public using the highway after dark as pedestrians, drivers, and passengers, and with vehicle speeds that can be around 30 metres per second, it is of paramount importance that the road user's visual perception gives sufficient information to ensure his safety. In order to meet the visual needs of the road user after dark, and of the driver in particular, some overall illumination of the immediate environment is necessary. Relying on navigational lighting as do ships at sea would be totally unsatisfactory with all the hazards that can occur in the road situation. Two systems of lighting are in use: road lighting, provided by luminaires mounted on columns behind the kerb, and headlighting, provided from the vehicle itself. Of these, only road lighting can provide the conditions necessary to enable the driver safely to maintain speeds at night similar to those in use by day. The greater part of this chapter is therefore devoted to road lighting, and the lesser part to vehicle headlight systems.

28.1 Justification

Accidents In the UK the accident rate at night, weighted for distance travelled, is about 80% higher than by day. For fatal accidents the risk at night is over three times that by day. The cost to the nation of a road accident is considerable, for example in 1980 the cost of a fatality was estimated at £133 800 in terms of lost earning power, insurance, pensions to dependents, etc., quite exclusive of the pain and suffering involved.

It has been shown in several studies that the effect of installing good road lighting is to reduce night-time accidents by about 30% (Fisher 1977). The most recent study of this type involved the collection of lighting data from nearly 100 single carriageway urban roads under dry conditions (Green and Hargroves 1979). A mobile laboratory continuously recorded values of road surface luminance and illuminance, uniformity, glare, and surrounding luminance. Representative values of each variable were derived for each road and related to the corresponding accident figures. The strongest relationship found (Fig. 28.1) was that for average road surface luminance $\bar{L}$: over the range $0.5\,\mathrm{cd\,m^{-2}}$ to $2.0\,\mathrm{cd\,m^{-2}}$ it is estimated that an increase of $1\,\mathrm{cd\,m^{-2}}$ is associated with a 35% decrease in night accidents compared with those by day (Scott 1980).

Savings to the nation resulting from accident reduction are generally sufficient to cover the cost of improved lighting together with the increase in operating costs. It is therefore usually accepted that roads in built-up areas must have a road lighting system. On rural roads and motorways the cost-benefit may be greater, but because of the great expense of lighting the whole of a road network a priority system must be introduced. In the UK justification for capital expenditure on road lighting is based on balancing the cost of a new installation against the savings of 30% of the accidents at

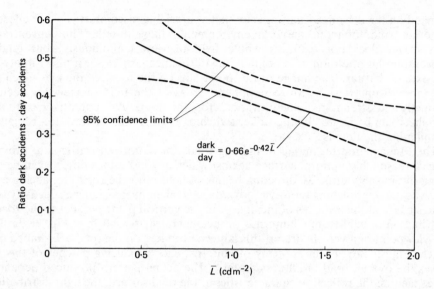

Fig. 28.1 Best fitting relationship between road surface luminance and the ratio of accidents by night and day

night over the previous three years. Dividing the annual saving by the capital cost gives the Merit Rating on which priority is allocated.

While installing and improving road lighting gives considerable benefits, reductions in lighting, such as occurred during the emergency period of the 1973–4 winter, result in increased accident costs which far outweigh any apparent saving in energy (Austin 1976).

Crime   Historically, the main reason for the introduction of street lighting, in large towns in particular, was to reduce the high crime rate. Although there are no national statistics available, it is still generally acknowledged that public lighting is one of the best deterrents to crime.

Some quantitative evidence became available following the reductions in public lighting during the winter of 1973–4 (Austin 1976), and several towns reported substantial increases in crime, particularly burglaries and theft, during this period compared with the same period the previous year. Also, in areas where lighting cuts were made, the authorities received many more complaints about their public lighting, particularly from the parents of young children and from older people afraid to go out in the dark. This underlines the sense of comfort and security that is imparted by good public lighting.

28.2 Principles

A vehicle driver must be able to stop within his seeing distance and be able to see the run of the road ahead. He needs to be able to respond to hazards, such as pedestrians stepping off the kerb, and generally have a sense of security resulting from an adequate supply of visual information. This information should not make such a demand on the driver's visual capacity that appreciable discomfort is experienced; on the other hand, too monotonous an environment is liable to reduce his concentration.

A driver does not scan his whole field of view continuously, but tends to concentrate his attention on a point about 100 m ahead, or closer if his visibility does not extend that far. The image of this point falls on the fovea of the eye which gives the most distinct vision. More peripheral areas of the field of view are seen less distinctly and 'stream' radially outwards across the retina. Any potential hazard in the periphery can be fixated by the driver switching his direction of view accordingly and assimilating the details.

The fundamental technique in lighting roads for motorized traffic is to provide a bright, reasonably uniform surface against which any hazardous objects can be seen, primarily in silhouette. By directing beams of light onto the road at glancing angles towards the approaching motorist, advantage is taken of the higher reflectivity of the road surface at these angles of incidence. In the vertical plane parallel to the road the distribution of light from a lantern is of the general shape shown in Fig. 28.2a. From the viewpoint of a vehicle driver, this lantern produces on the road a T-shaped bright patch (Fig. 28.2b). From an array of lanterns, each producing patches of this type, arises the overall road brightness pattern. The actual pattern produced depends on three factors: the reflection characteristics of the road surface, the light distribution of the lanterns, and the geometrical layout of lanterns/columns (their 'arrangement').

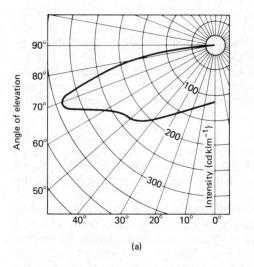

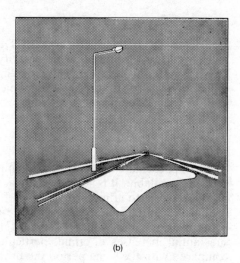

(a)   (b)

Fig. 28.2   Road lighting lantern: (a) intensity distribution in vertical plane parallel to road; (b) bright patch on road from single lantern

28.2.1   Road surface reflection

The reflection characteristics of a road surface are such that the luminance can be related to the illuminance by a factor called the luminance coefficient (Sect. 5.4.2). There is generally an increase in this factor when the incident light falls on the surface at a near-glancing angle from the opposite direction to the direction of view. This effect is known as quasi-specular reflection, and its precise nature depends on the surface concerned. In the UK most traffic route surfaces are of the hot rolled asphalt variety with the aggregate varying according to the area of the country and the locally-available stone. On secondary roads surface dressings are more common. In neither case, unfortunately, has the lighting engineer any voice in the selection of the surface despite its significant effect on the quality of road lighting.

The rougher and the more harsh the surface, then the shorter, the wider, and the lower the luminance of the tail of the T-shaped patch extending towards the driver, and the wider its head. Conversely, the smoother and the more polished the surface, the longer, the narrower, and the higher the luminance of the tail, and the narrower the head of the patch. On a wet road the tail becomes more of a streak and the head non-existent. If the road is particularly shiny and/or badly drained, with surface flooding occurring, then the road behaves like a mirror, the luminance of small areas of the surface being directly related to the luminance of the lanterns themselves.

28.2.2   Lantern distribution

The greater the beam intensity projected along the road at high angles to the downward vertical, the longer will be the tail of the bright patch towards the driver. If more light is thrown across the road then the head of the patch will be wider. It is necessary to limit the high angle light towards the driver because of glare: the degree of this limitation determines the degree of cut-off of the lantern distribution.

A so-called 'semi-cut-off' (SCO) light distribution is the most common one used in the UK. 'Cut-off' (CO) lighting, having a lower beam angle, is used on some UK motorways and trunk roads where a lower level of glare is desirable, sometimes on undulating roads where SCO lanterns might cause troublesome glare, and quite frequently on roundabouts. The current UK code of practice for road lighting (Sect. 28.4) requires CO lanterns to be spaced 30% closer than SCO lanterns, thus penalizing CO lanterns economically, unfairly so in the view of some authorities (Sarteel 1976).

28.2.3   Lantern/column arrangement

On most single carriageways in the UK lanterns are staggered, i.e. placed alternately on one side of the road and then on the other. The SCO distribution is eminently suitable, because as the luminance of the head of the patch from one lantern falls off towards the far side of the road, it is supplemented by the tail from the next lantern beyond it. Up to a certain road width the bright patches comfortably cover the whole width of road when lanterns are placed above or near the kerb. On a level curve of small radius (less than about $80 \times$ mounting height) the staggered arrangement is replaced by a single-side arrangement with the lanterns on the outside of the curve. On sharp bends it may be necessary to reduce the spacing as well.

On wider roads a staggered arrangement may suffice with the bracket length increased to give a moderate overhang, but if this is carried too far dark areas may be left near the kerbs. Equally, the mounting height can be increased, but with the widest roads it is necessary to resort to an opposite arrangement.

On narrow roads a single-side arrangement is frequently satisfactory; this may be used on wider roads to avoid overhead telephone wires or trees, in which case long brackets and cut-off lanterns should be used.

On dual carriageways, with central reservations up to 5 m wide, the most common arrangement in the UK is to use twin lanterns on columns on the central reservation. This is much preferred to an opposite arrangement on the outside of the carriageways in view of the considerable savings in columns, cables, and electricity supply services. However, with very wide dual carriageways a staggered combination of opposite and central lanterns may be necessary. Central catenary systems are becoming more common. Although requiring fewer columns, the overall cost of installation is greater than for a conventional system. Catenary lighting gives a high luminance uniformity, low glare, reveals the run of the road very clearly, and tends to be preferred aesthetically, certainly by night.

28.3   International recommendations

Technical Committee 4.6 (Road Lighting) of the International Commission on Illumination has prepared recommendations for the lighting of roads for motorized traffic (CIE 1977a). These recommendations are advisory, not mandatory, and are prepared in order to provide a common basis for the drafting of national specifications and codes of practice for road lighting.

28.3.1   Quality criteria

The performance of an installation is assessed on the basis of five characteristics, utilizing photometric quantities, which are considered to be of major importance:

(a)   The average luminance of the road surface $\bar{L}$ (cd m^{-2}). The area over which the average is taken covers a section between two lanterns in the same row, the nearest lantern being at a distance of 60 m from the observer. The lateral position of the observer is one-quarter of the carriageway width from the near-side kerb.

(b)   The overall uniformity U_o of the road surface luminance. This is defined as $L_{min}/\bar{L}$, where L_{min} is the minimum local luminance within the standard area used for $\bar{L}$ and viewed from the same position.

(c)   The longitudinal uniformity U_l. This relates to visual comfort and is defined as the lowest ratio of the minimum to the maximum local luminance along the centreline of any driving lane within the standard area, seen from an observation point on the relevant centreline.

(d)   Disability glare, threshold increment TI (%). Direct light from the lanterns into a driver's eyes increases the minimum contrast (Sect. 2.3) he can detect on the road ahead. The percentage increase in this contrast threshold is calculated by relating the 'equivalent veiling luminance' L_v, produced at the observer's eye by the lanterns, to the average road luminance $\bar{L}$. The contribution of a single lantern to L_v is a function of the vertical illuminance the lantern gives at the observer's eye E_v and the angular separation of the lantern from his line of sight $\theta°$. The total L_v is given by $10\Sigma(E_v/\theta^2)$ cd m^{-2} and the corresponding TI is then approximately $65L_v/\bar{L}^{0.8}$%, where Σ implies the summation of the contributions of all lanterns in the field of view, with an assumed cut-off due to the car roof at 20° above the horizontal (CIE 1976b).

(e)   Discomfort glare control mark G. A scale of G ranging from 1 to 9 indicates the subjective impression of the limitation of discomfort experienced from an array of lanterns. $G = 1$ implies that the glare is 'unbearable', 3 that it is 'disturbing', 5 is 'just admissable', 7 is 'satisfactory', and 9 is 'unnoticeable'. Glare impression has been found to be dependent on several photometric and geometric parameters,

Table 28.1 CIE road lighting quality criteria

Type of traffic	Class of road	Surrounds	Luminance level	Uniformity ratios		Glare restriction	
			Average maintained road surface luminance ($\bar{L}$ cd m^{-2})	Overall uniformity ratio (U_o)	Longitudinal uniformity ratio (U_l)	Glare control mark (G)	Threshold increment ($TI\%$)
Heavy and high speed	Motorway	Any	2	0·4	0·7	6	10
	Trunk or major	Bright	2	0·4	0·7	5	10
		Dark	1	0·4	0·7	6	10
Heavy/mixed and moderate speed	Ring or radial	Bright	2	0·4	0·5	5	20
		Dark	1	0·4	0·5	6	10
Fairly heavy/mixed and moderate/slow speed with pedestrians present	Trunk or commercial shopping	Bright	2	0·4	0·5	4	20
Mixed and limited speed	Collector or local	Bright	1	0·4	0·5	4	20
		Dark	0·5	0·4	0·5	5	20

and with this particular scale the following empirical relationship (CIE 1976b) applies

$$G = 13\cdot84 - 3\cdot31 \log I_{80} + 1\cdot3[\log(I_{80}/I_{88})]^{0\cdot5}$$
$$-0\cdot08 \log(I_{80}/I_{88}) + 1\cdot29 \log F + 0\cdot97 \log \bar{L}$$
$$+ 4\cdot41 \log h' - 1\cdot46 \log p$$

where I_{80} and I_{88} are the lantern intensities (cd) at 80° and 88° respectively to the downward vertical in the vertical plane parallel to the road axis, F is the flashed area (m²) of the lantern projected at 76° to the downward vertical in the vertical plane parallel to the road axis, $\bar{L}$ is the average road surface luminance (cd m⁻²), h' is the height of the lanterns above eye level (m), and p is the number of lanterns per km of road length.

For various types of road, with different ambient brightnesses, the CIE recommends limiting values for these five criteria: minimum values for $\bar{L}$, U_o, U_l, and G and a maximum value for *TI*. These recommendations are shown in Table 28.1, and apply only to road surfaces under dry conditions.

On wet roads it is necessary to accept a lower value of overall uniformity, 0·15 being suggested in a recent technical report concerned with the problems of designing for wet conditions (CIE 1979b). In practice the deterioration of uniformity in the wet can be reduced by using rough road surfaces and by using light distributions with a strong transverse component.

28.3.2   Road luminance calculations by computer

All the road lighting quality criteria involve local or average values of road surface luminance. With an array of lanterns involved, each having a markedly asymmetrical light distribution, and with the road reflectance varying with the direction of incident light and the viewing direction, it is not surprising that a computer is normally called upon to perform the necessary luminance calculations. The CIE has developed the necessary programs for both straight and curved roads (CIE 1976a).

Tables of both lantern intensity (*I*-tables) and road reflectance (*r*-tables) are used as input to the programs, together with the dimensions of the actual installation. Four standard *r*-tables represent, with reasonable accuracy, the gamut of practical road surfaces in dry conditions. The surface designated R3 most closely resembles the reflective characteristics of the average British road. A further series of standard *r*-tables, designated W1–4, has been produced for wet roads, but little experience has yet been gained in designing lighting schemes for wet conditions.

Each program uses the formula in Eq. 5.23 (Sect. 5.4.2) to evaluate the luminance at each intersection of a grid over the standard area of road, interpolating from the *I*- and *r*-tables provided. A printout for a straight section of the installation shown in Fig. 28.3 is reproduced in Table 28.2. *R* and *S* define distances, respectively perpendicular to and parallel to the road axis, from a reference point (O on Fig. 28.3).

28.3.3   Luminance yield and utilization factor

If only the average luminance $\bar{L}$ of a road lighting installation needs to be predicted, use can be made of luminance yield curves, introduced in Sect. 5.4.2. It is appropriate at the same time to consider utilization factor curves, introduced in Sect. 5.2.6, which enable the average illuminance $\bar{E}$ to be calculated. As will be seen in Sect. 28.3.4,

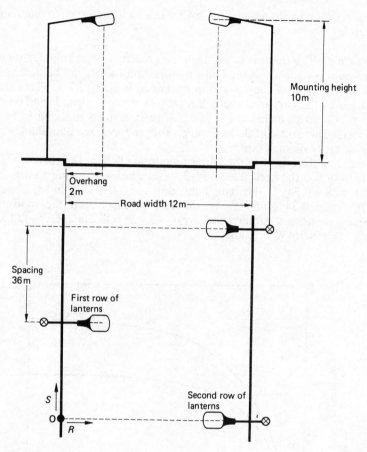

Fig. 28.3 Staggered arrangement of road lanterns

Table 28.2 Output from CIE luminance design program (luminance distribution in cd m^{-2}).
Observer position: $R = 3 \cdot 00$, $S = -60 \cdot 00$

R \ S	0·0	4·8	9·6	14·4	19·2	24·0	28·8	33·6	38·4	43·2	48·0	52·8	57·6	62·4	67·2
0·60	1·01	1·19	1·39	1·52	1·72	1·71	1·42	0·97	0·86	0·89	0·87	0·81	0·82	0·89	0·99
1·80	1·50	1·74	1·91	2·01	2·16	2·04	1·65	1·13	1·01	1·07	1·06	1·02	1·06	1·18	1·33
3·00	1·66	1·87	2·00	2·08	2·21	2·08	1·75	1·28	1·19	1·19	1·17	1·16	1·22	1·33	1·44
4·20	1·39	1·54	1·65	1·74	1·89	1·83	1·68	1·36	1·30	1·26	1·25	1·23	1·34	1·37	1·34
5·40	1·31	1·34	1·39	1·47	1·62	1·61	1·63	1·43	1·47	1·43	1·43	1·40	1·52	1·43	1·29
6·60	1·27	1·26	1·31	1·36	1·44	1·56	1·66	1·59	1·68	1·73	1·80	1·75	1·78	1·59	1·37
7·80	1·20	1·06	1·08	1·14	1·23	1·40	1·53	1·71	1·91	2·01	2·09	2·08	2·06	1·78	1·39
9·00	1·09	0·93	0·91	0·92	0·95	1·04	1·15	1·40	1·70	1·88	2·08	2·15	2·17	1·85	1·36
10·20	0·92	0·83	0·81	0·77	0·74	0·76	0·82	0·98	1·22	1·41	1·68	1·87	2·00	1·76	1·24
11·40	0·80	0·75	0·71	0·64	0·59	0·58	0·63	0·74	0·88	1·00	1·17	1·38	1·57	1·46	1·08

Quality characteristics:
Average luminance = 1·38 cd m^{-2}
Overall uniformity = 0·42
Longitudinal uniformity = 0·52
Veiling luminance = 0·53 cd m^{-2}

Threshold increment = 22·16%
Colour constant = 0·00
Flashed area of luminaire = 0·08 m^2
Discomfort glare, $G = 3 \cdot 77$

there are parts of the world where illuminance design is preferred to luminance design for road lighting.

Utilization factor   The fraction of the lamp flux reaching an infinite length of straight road from a lantern, known as the lantern utilization factor, can be determined from the isocandela diagram of the lantern as explained in Sect. 5.2.6. This calculation is normally made by the lantern manufacturer for a series of strips of road on either side of the lantern, the strips increasing in width. Curves of the type shown in Fig. 28.4 are then produced. The user can deduce very easily the average illuminance of a given road lit by an array of such lanterns.

For example, with respect to the lantern mounting height, the road in Fig. 28.3 has a B/H ratio of 0·2 on the kerb side and 1·0 on the road side, giving a utilization factor $UF = 0·06 + 0·28 = 0·34$. If the bare lamp output is 25·5 klm and the maintenance factor is 0·8 then $0·34 \times 0·8 \times 25·5 = 6·94$ klm of flux reach the road from each lantern. Since there is a lantern for every $12 \times 36 = 432$ m² of road, the average illuminance $\bar{E} = 6940/432 = 16$ lux.

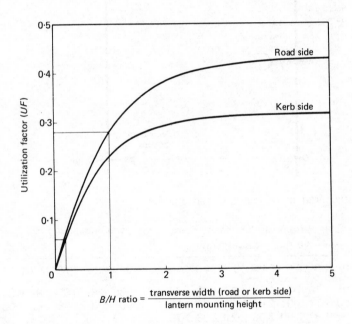

Fig. 28.4   Utilization factor

Luminance yield   A similar treatment to that for the utilization factor characteristic enables luminance yield curves of the type shown in Fig. 28.5 to be obtained (Sect. 5.4.2). There are notable differences between η_L and UF. Firstly, a separate set of characteristics is required for each road surface: those in Fig. 28.5 are for the R3 standard road. Secondly, since luminance varies with observer position, curves are needed for different viewpoints.

In the example installation of Fig. 28.3 luminance yield has to be determined with the observer 3 m in from the kerb: it has to be evaluated for each row of lanterns. For the first row of lanterns interpolation between B and C for the observer 1 m to the

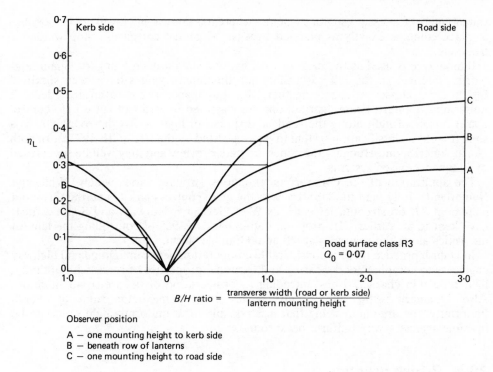

Fig. 28.5 Luminance yield

road side gives $\eta_L = 0\cdot10$ for $B/H = 0\cdot2$ on the kerb side and $\eta_L = 0\cdot30$ for $B/H = 1\cdot0$ on the road side. For the second row of lanterns interpolation between B and C for the observer 7 m to the road side gives the comparable values of $0\cdot07$ and $0\cdot36$. Rearranging Eq. 5.24 (Sect. 5.4.2) gives $\bar{L} = \eta_L F Q_0 / WS$. The total $\eta_L = 0\cdot83$, $F = 25\,500$, $Q_0 = 0\cdot07$, $W = 12$, and S (between lanterns in a row) $= 72$. Allowing for a maintenance factor of $0\cdot8$, $\bar{L} = 1\cdot37\,\mathrm{cd}\,\mathrm{m}^{-2}$.

28.3.4 National standards

Most countries incorporate to some extent the CIE recommendations in their own national standards or codes of practice, but local variations, particularly with regard to installation design, are of considerable interest.

The French code adopts the CIE recommended luminance levels for the various classes of road, but gives two design methods for their achievement. One is the CIE method using computer calculations, with the proviso that illuminance calculations must also be included. Luminance data cannot be accepted as a basis for contractual agreement because of the difficulty in checking it. The second design method uses a ratio R, defined as average illuminance/average luminance, where R is given for various road surfaces. Thus, for a required road luminance the necessary illuminance is evaluated and the appropriate installation layout derived using utilization factors. Some control over uniformity is provided by limiting the spacing to mounting height ratio. It is not a precise method, but is very useful (a) in obtaining approximate lantern spacings for important projects before turning to the computer for exact values and (b) for less prestigious schemes where it is known that it will not be possible to place columns exactly as planned because of garage entrances, shop windows, trees, etc.

Illuminance is used as the basis of road lighting standards in Hungary, Spain, and North America. In the last case minimum illuminance values have been specified for different classes of road, together with illuminance ratios to ensure adequate uniformity. Lantern beam distributions are classified in terms of cut-off (to control glare), throw of light along the road, and spread of light across the road. This is a similar lantern classification system to one suggested by the CIE (CIE 1977b). In both North America and Hungary the codes are under review and may well be superseded by luminance-based systems.

The application of the CIE recommendations on glare varies widely. While the Netherlands, Italy, and the USSR accept the glare control mark *G* and the threshold increment *TI*, other countries, such as West Germany, Norway, and South Africa, have kept to an earlier CIE proposal dating back to 1965 of controlling the lantern intensities along the road axis at 80° and 90° in elevation.

In Danish practice there is considerable co-operation between lighting and highway engineers to combine good wearing and frictional properties of roads with optimum light reflection characteristics, including a consideration of the wet road situation. Also, Denmark is the only country to lay down a maximum value of overall uniformity, the argument being that it is possible for a uniformly light object to be invisible against a very uniform background.

28.4 British practice

Current road lighting practice in the UK provides yet another variation of national standards, in this case by using a 'recipe' system of installation design. In the various parts of the relevant British Standard, BS 5489 (BSI 1973), appear tables of the type shown in Table 28.3. Column spacings are specified for various arrangements, mounting heights, road widths, and for two standardized lantern types (SCO and CO). The public lighting engineer, knowing the width of the road to be lit and having decided on the lantern type, mounting height, and arrangement, needs only to refer to this table to read off the spacing which should then give a satisfactory road lighting performance.

Table 28.3 Extract from code of road lighting practice BS 5489

			Effective width (m)								
			5	6	7	8	9	10	11	12	13
Arrangement	Type	Height (m)	Design spacing (m)								
Staggered	CO	10		30	30	28	25	22	20	18	17
		12				36	35	32	29	26	24
	SCO	10				40	40	36	33	30	28
		12						48	47	43	40
Twin central on dual carriageway	CO	10				33	31	28			
		12						40	37	34	
	SCO	10				44	41				
		12						53	49		

The standardization of lantern types is a key element in this recipe system. BS 4533 Section 103.1 (BSI 1981c) puts constraints on the light distribution of acceptable lanterns. The location of the peak intensity is restricted to a few degrees around 75° in elevation for the SCO lantern and around 65° for the CO, maximum and minimum peak intensities being prescribed in both cases. Glare is controlled by restricting the intensity at the horizontal and in the upper part of the beam. The shape of the beam is further constrained at a lower angle of elevation. In addition, maximum and minimum values are specified for intensities at angles up to 30° from the downward vertical. All the controlling intensities in BS 4533 are evaluated in terms of the total light output of the lamps used in a lantern (cd klm^{-1}), and BS 5489 specifies minimum values for the total lower hemispherical lantern flux for different mounting heights, for example values of flux of 20, 12, 7, 3·5, and 2 klm for heights of 12, 10, 8, 6, and 5 m respectively.

Historically, this recipe system has provided a satisfactory average standard of road lighting in the UK, and recent measurements of over 100 single carriageway roads (Hargroves 1981) have produced a median value of road surface luminance of 1 cd m^{-2}. However, the range of measured luminance and uniformity values has demonstrated a fundamental inconsistency of the system in that both substandard and extravagant lighting can result. At the same time the tight specifications of lantern photometrics and column spacing have had an inhibitory effect on the application of new lamp and lantern technology. As a consequence of these drawbacks a fundamental revision of the code of practice has been proposed (Simons 1980) which brings in CIE luminance design without the need for the public lighting engineer to have access to a computer.

Traffic route lighting in the UK (Part 2 of BS 5489) uses lanterns at mounting heights of 10 m or 12 m, with low pressure sodium lamps of 135 W at 10 m height predominating, despite their monochromatic light. The high pressure sodium lamp, 150/250/400 W, hitherto used only in town centres and other areas demanding improved colour rendering, has now become a viable alternative to the low pressure source for all major roads because of its long life expectancy. Most systems operate from dusk to dawn, implying about 4000 hours of use a year. Programmed time-switch control is now less common than photocell control, partly for maintenance reasons and partly because of the photocell's ability to respond to meteorological conditions. Remote override switches, responding to infrared or ultrasonic signals operated by police patrols, are being introduced on some motorways.

Minor roads (Part 3 of BS 5489). Some district distributor roads in urban areas, although not classified as major traffic routes, carry considerable peaks of traffic and are usually lit by lanterns at 8 m height, utilizing 90 W low pressure or 150 W high pressure sodium lamps. On quieter access roads and on residential roads 5 m or 6 m columns are the norm, with lanterns using 18/35/55 W SOX, 70 W SON, or 80/125 W MBF lamps. These installations should harmonize with their surroundings and be attractive as well as useful by night.

Discontinuities, such as junctions and roundabouts, require that attention be paid to the siting of specific lanterns: recommended layouts are given in Parts 4 and 5 of BS 5489. In Parts 6, 8, and 9 are the peculiar requirements of elevated roads and bridges, roads in the vicinity of airfields and railways and canals, and roads in city centres. Part 7 is concerned with underpasses and bridged roads, which involve something of the special techniques required for the lighting of tunnels.

28.5 Tunnel lighting

The lighting of tunnels presents quite different problems to those encountered in normal road lighting: the chief problem is not the night-time lighting, but the lighting by day. A driver entering a long tunnel, possibly at high speed, must maintain his visual capability while moving from daylight into the tunnel itself. Well into the tunnel, average road surface luminances of 10–$20\,\mathrm{cd\,m^{-2}}$ for urban tunnels and 5–$10\,\mathrm{cd\,m^{-2}}$ for rural tunnels are recommended, but much higher luminances are needed in the first few hundred metres of the tunnel if it is not to give the approaching driver the appearance of a 'black hole'.

The level and the extent of the necessary supplementary lighting depend on the average luminance of the tunnel surroundings seen by the driver on his approach (the access zone luminance) and on the maximum permitted vehicle speed. It has been found by experiment that to ensure satisfactory visibility, the luminance of the immediate tunnel interior (the threshold zone luminance) should be one-tenth of the access zone luminance as determined for an approaching driver at a distance of $100\,\mathrm{m}$ (Schreuder 1964).

Access zone luminances can reach $8000\,\mathrm{cd\,m^{-2}}$ in summer, calling for a threshold zone road luminance of $800\,\mathrm{cd\,m^{-2}}$. This is a very high level of lighting and is not usually considered economic. The international recommendations (CIE 1973b) therefore concede that a threshold/access ratio of $1/15$ is acceptable, possibly in conjunction with a speed limit. In practice it is possible to reduce the luminance in the access zone, and therefore in the threshold zone, in several ways: by providing dark carriageway surfaces, cutting walls, and tunnel facades; by the planting of trees; or by screening the daylight from the entrance.

The length of the threshold zone should take into account the safe stopping distance. It is therefore dependent on the speed of the traffic, for example $200\,\mathrm{m}$ for speeds up to $100\,\mathrm{km\,h^{-1}}$.

In order that drivers adapt smoothly while travelling from the access zone, through the threshold zone, and into the interior, further transition zones of lighting are provided beyond the threshold. The ratio of the luminance in the threshold zone to that in the first transition zone should not exceed 3:1 and this ratio also applies between successive transition zones and finally the interior. Supplementary lighting in the exit zone at the end of the tunnel is not usually considered necessary because the eye adapts far more quickly to higher luminances than to lower ones.

When the level of daylight varies, particularly at dusk and dawn, the lighting in the tunnel must be adjusted accordingly. This can be achieved by continuous dimming, but more usually is achieved by switching. No one zone should change in one switching operation by more than a factor of 3, and this means that it may be necessary in well-lit high speed tunnels to incorporate as many as six switching levels.

In most tunnels in the UK two rows of fluorescent lamps run the whole length of the tunnel. These provide all the required lighting for the interior by day; at night half the lamps are switched off. In the threshold and transition zones by day the fluorescent luminaires are supplemented by high or low pressure sodium lanterns. The use of continuous rows of fluorescent luminaires avoids the unpleasant flicker effects which drivers can experience with discontinuous units. These effects arise as a result of either the individual luminaires themselves or their reflections moving into and out of the driver's field of vision. Flicker frequencies between 2·5 and 15 per second are particularly to be avoided, except in short doses. Particular attention has to be paid to the spacing of both the complete and partially switched lighting system in the threshold and transition zones in relation to the traffic speed.

Where a tunnel is less than 100 m long and the exit is visible from some distance before the entrance, which applies to most underpasses, it may be unnecessary to provide lighting. If it is provided, it should be at a constant level throughout.

28.6 Vehicle headlight systems

The earliest headlights on vehicles were simple projector units, but with the rapid increase in motor traffic in the 1920s the problem of glare from oncoming vehicles and the need for some form of dipping beam became obvious. Initially the reflectors were dipped mechanically, but very soon the twin filament system was introduced. The main or driving beam in such a system is provided by a transverse filament mounted at the focus of a parabolic reflector. For the dipped or meeting beam two different arrangements are in use.

In one arrangement, the so-called Anglo-American or AA beam, a second transverse filament is positioned off-axis so that the light is reflected principally towards the near side. A small shield intercepts direct light from the filament and a front glass lens refines the reflected light distribution to satisfy the appropriate specification, which is Parts 3 and 4 of BS AU40 in the UK (BSI 1966b, c). The other arrangement, the European or E beam, employs a second filament mounted axially in front of the reflector focus with a shield positioned underneath to intercept light which would otherwise be reflected upwards, the resultant light distribution complying with EEC regulations (EEC 1965).

The actual beam patterns produced by these two systems (Sect. 9.3.1) differ mainly in the sharpness of the cut-off between the higher values of intensity directed below the horizontal and the lower intensities directed upwards, the latter being responsible for most of the glare to oncoming drivers. The peak intensity is directed along the near-side kerb and is somewhat greater in the AA beam than in the E beam, but since intensities in the glare zone differ in about the same proportion the overall performance of the two systems might be expected to be similar. Many comparisons, both simulated and on site, have been carried out over the years: the situation is best summarized by the results of a series of recognition distance measurements made in controlled trials in 1968–9 (Yerrell 1976). On unlit roads, either straight or with right-hand curves, the E beam reveals off-side objects significantly better, but for near-side objects on left-hand curves and at the tops of hills the AA beam is superior. One disadvantage of the E beam is that when a car pitches, other road users are liable to experience a flashing effect as the sharp cut-off moves up and down across their line of sight, counterbalancing the advantage that the E beam produces less discomfort glare.

The ultimate test of any meeting-beam headlight is its performance on the road in normal use. Roadside checks of headlight intensities around the horizontal in several European countries have shown up a wide spread in values (Yerrell 1971), due not so much to imperfections in optical design as to incorrect aiming and poor maintenance on the vehicle, and several proposals have been made for improving this situation. Self-levelling headlamp systems to compensate for changes in vehicle attitude have been devised, but probably the most widely discussed concept is that of polarized lighting. Most of the technical problems have been overcome, but there is little possibility of its introduction in the near future mainly because it requires the co-operation of all road users. More promising in this respect are headlamps with variable beam distributions. One such arrangement, the 'Autosensa' (Hicks 1970), senses the position of oncoming headlamps and triggers an electromechanical shutter to obscure that part of a high intensity projector beam which would otherwise glare the other driver. The remaining unobscured light gives a considerable increase in seeing distance during the passing situation. To date this system has proved to be too expensive.

In this chapter road and vehicle lighting have been considered separately, but in many cases they are in use together. As the law stands at the present time in the UK, headlights must be used on all roads where the road lighting is inadequate. The decision on what is adequate is left to the individual driver, with the result that headlights are frequently in use on well-lit roads. The mechanisms of revealing hazardous objects by fixed road lighting and by headlighting are different, most objects showing up as darker than their background in the former case and brighter in the latter. In a well-lit street the visibility of many objects is therefore reduced when headlights are used, firstly because the two mechanisms are working against each other and secondly because of the additional glare of opposing headlights. The one argument in favour is that vehicles with headlights are rendered more conspicuous, certainly more than those showing only small sidelights, which may well be appreciated by pedestrians. However, the real solution to the lighting of vehicles in well-lit streets is the use of a 'town beam' (CIE 1976c) composed of marker lights of intensity between 50 cd and 100 cd having areas similar to those of current headlights.

Further reading

Boyce P R, 1981, *Human factors in lighting* (London: Applied Science)
van Bommel W J M and de Boer J B, 1980, *Road lighting* (London: Macmillan)
Yerrell J S, 1976, *Ltg. Res. Technol.*, **8,** 69–79: Vehicle headlights

29 Navigation lighting

The importance of lighting in assisting safe night-time driving has been explained in Chap. 28, and attention has been paid to the role of road lighting as a guidance aid to the driver. Light sources and optical systems are used in many other ways to provide guidance to drivers: navigation lighting is an essential element in ensuring safe traffic movement, whether on road, by rail, at sea, or in the air. Much transport is international, and so most recommendations for signalling systems are specified internationally in order to avoid confusion. Signs, signals, and all other forms of navigation lighting have the prime objectives of increasing safety and facilitating the rapid movement of traffic.

29.1 Signs and signals

Flashing lights are used to enhance 'conspicuity' and have become widely used either to draw attention to obstructions, such as roadworks, hazards at sea, and high buildings, or to identify moving vehicles or aircraft. Flashing lights have been the subject of considerable research because what is perceived owes much to the response of the eye, its adaptation, and the various inter-related effects of intensity, repetition rate, duration, and colour. The two fundamental relationships defining the effective intensity of flashing lights have been discussed in Sect. 2.2.3: these are Bloch's law for very brief flashes, and the more generally-applicable one for navigation lighting, the Blondel–Rey law.

Coloured signal lights and coloured non-self-luminous signs are used to ensure the proper guidance and control of the various forms of transport. Signals usually utilize incandescent sources (sometimes oil lamps) and are defined by different restricted areas on the CIE chromaticity diagram (Chap. 3). The essential requirement is not so much to control colours as to avoid confusion between similar colours. The permitted variation in a colour will therefore differ according to the number of colours in the system, for example if white and yellow are used as independent signals, a smaller tolerance for white would be specified than in a system where white did not have to be distinguished from yellow. There are also grades of red and green of different precision whose use varies with the type of transport concerned. This subject is codified in BS 1376 (BSI 1974): in Fig. 29.1 are shown the specified restricted colour limits. The CIE has produced internationally-agreed recommendations for signal colours (CIE 1975) for national authorities to incorporate in their regulations. A further publication (CIE 1978b) extends these to give a similar guide for non-self-luminous signs.

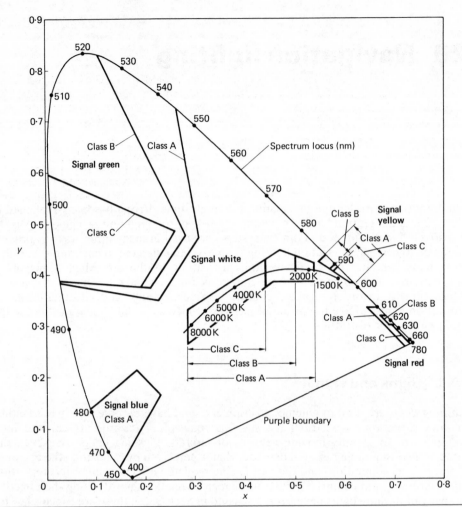

Colour	Red	Yellow	Green	Blue	White
Application	Class				
Aircraft	A	B	A	A	B
Airfields (general)	A	B	A	A	B
Airfields (high recognition)	C	B	B	A	B
Lighthouses	A	A	A	A	A†
Railway signals (day colour lights)	C‡	B	C	—	C§
Railway signals (semaphore)	C	C	C	—	—
Road traffic lights	B	A	C	—	—
Ship's lights	B + C	—	B	—	A†

† The acceptable area for white lights of class A extends appreciably towards the yellow boundary of the CIE chromaticity diagram in order to include the light from oil lamps as these are still used in some signalling systems, and thus also includes light from high pressure sodium sources. The colour of both these lights is, however, undesirably yellow for signalling purposes because there is a risk of its being confused with a true yellow light. Accordingly, it is recommended that wherever possible a white light which is as yellowish as this should be avoided and that a class B white light should be employed instead.
‡ Restricted to y not greater than 0·295 for high intensity red signals.
§ Restricted to between $x = 0·330$ and 0·420 and known as 'lunar white'.

Fig. 29.1 British Standard signal colours

29.2   Road traffic

The visual task of the car driver, and the assistance provided by fixed road lighting and by vehicle headlights, have been discussed in Chap. 28, but there is the need for additional information to the driver beyond the visual guidance derived from the road lighting, his headlights, and the identification and marker lights on other vehicles. Route direction information must be clearly visible, particularly when the increasing traffic volume on our roads is making more complex the driver's visual task in guiding the vehicle. There is also the need to present the driver with clear traffic regulation information, i.e. traffic lights, statutory road signs, pedestrian crossings, lane diversions, hazard warnings, etc. In urban environments with a high ambient lighting from shop windows and advertising signs the luminance of road signs and signals needs to be correspondingly high and needs to be located so as to avoid confusion with other light sources. A recent CIE document (CIE 1980) is concerned with matters which influence the road user in his perception of road traffic signals.

Road signs   Both internally- and externally-illuminated signs are used: the former usually employ fluorescent lamps with colour temperatures in the region of 4000 K and the latter can often use high pressure mercury lamps. Generally at least two lamps are employed to ensure a 'fail-safe' source of illuminance. The lighting of a road sign has to be such as to render the sign readily visible, but without giving rise to unacceptable glare. It should be evenly illuminated and must provide for clear daytime viewing. Chapter 11 of the *Traffic Signs Manual* (DOE 1967) describes the recommended lighting of signs: for signs illuminated externally a mean luminance of at least $34\,cd\,m^{-2}$, with the maximum luminance not exceeding $342\,cd\,m^{-2}$ and the ratio of maximum to minimum luminance not exceeding 10:1.

Part-time and variable legend signs have in recent years become a feature of motorway information systems. In view of the high speed of motorway traffic the sign has to be conspicuous at 500 m and the inscription legible between 200 m and 20 m in clear weather over the widest range of ambient light levels. The legend is formed from a matrix of 13×11 50 mm units, each unit, when operating, having an intensity of 13 cd at up to 0·1 rad from its optical axis. In one form the matrix consists of individual 24 V 2·8 W lamps, each located at the focus of a parabolic reflector, with a black tube and lens to control it. In another form a single 24 V 70 W tungsten halogen lamp is used for each possible legend at the common end of a number of 1 mm fibre optic light guides. Four amber or red 125 mm diameter lanterns are located at each corner, with intensities of 800 cd (amber) and 400 cd (red) at up to 0·085 rad from the optical axis. The upper and lower pairs of lanterns flash alternately when a speed restriction or other instruction is displayed on the indicator matrix, which is featureless when unactivated. Such signals are installed at 1·5 km or 3 km intervals in rural areas and are used before and during the area of restriction, with a white octagon crossed by a white diagonal line without flashing lights to signal the end of the restriction. An enhanced information sign with increased graphic representation of the nature of the hazard is now being evaluated.

Traffic lights comprise three lanterns in a vertical configuration of red, amber, and green. They are operated in a sequence of red, red and amber, green, and then amber before repeating the cycle. Where used at pedestrian crossings a modified sequence involving flashing the amber is employed. The usual traffic lights use rough service mains voltage 65 W lamps, housed in simple parabolic reflectors. A prismatic front glass is made from the correct colour materials and is designed to eliminate 'phantom' effects. Phantom is the term which describes the effect of the signal reflecting some external light (sunlight in particular) and making the signal appear to be operating.

The British Standard for traffic signals BS 505 (BSI 1971a) recommends that some signals have two intensities, one for night use and one for use during the day, to allow for the different ambient light conditions. The night intensity recommended is between 1/5 and 1/12 of the day intensity, depending on the particular conditions. Peak intensities of 475 cd for red and green signals and 950 cd for amber are required, these values being increased to 800 cd and 1600 cd respectively when the speed of approach can be in excess of 80 km h^{-1}.

Since 1971, tungsten halogen lamps (Chap. 10) have been used for all new traffic light units, special lamp designs having been developed to achieve a quarter of a million switchings, equivalent to a six-month duty cycle.

Illuminated bollards are usually used to indicate traffic islands and utilize fluorescent lamps to illuminate translucent panels which may carry direction arrows or legends.

Belisha beacons were one of the earliest flashing road signs to be put into general use at pedestrian crossings. Experimental evidence obtained by the Road Research Laboratory in 1953 showed that amber beacons flashing at 60 times per minute were the most conspicuous. The conspicuity of beacons is not as great as it was, due to the rapid growth of adjacent lighting, so there is a tendency for the luminance of the beacons to be increased and for the crossings to be floodlit.

Hazard warning lights, usually amber in colour and flashing at a rate of approximately 40 times per minute, are generally associated with marking temporary hazards, such as road works, accidents, or where road diversions are in force.

29.3   Rail traffic

Railway signals   In the UK all railways must satisfy certain governmental requirements, but good signalling practice has been developed by the Institution of Railway Signal Engineers (Pope 1975). Signals form the link between a central control system on the one hand and the locomotive driver on the other. The purpose of a signal is to give a clear, unambiguous message which informs the driver of the state of the 'road' ahead and, at junctions, the direction in which he will travel.

Mechanical signals are largely of the semaphore arm type (with coloured indications for use at night), operated in conjunction with a telegraph system linked to conventional signal boxes. As with other forms of transport, the running speed of trains has increased, to 200 km h^{-1} with the introduction of the high speed train, and the advanced passenger train aims to raise this to 240 km h^{-1}. Signalling systems must therefore be suited to these demands.

Colour light signals display their aspects by means of illuminated red, yellow, or green lights. Low voltage lamps are used, having twin filaments at 90°: these cross at the focus of the optical system, and there is an automatic changeover from the main filament to the auxiliary low wattage one in the event of premature failure. There are two principal systems in use: one using a separate lens for each aspect, the other a searchlight type with one colourless lens system and an electrically-operated filter. Both types display the same aspects so far as the driver is concerned, with a visibility of 1 km or more in clear conditions. Multi-aspect signals have permitted the closure of many intermediate signal boxes. In addition to these main signals there is a series of subsidiary signals, ground signals and repeating signals which are variously externally- and internally-lit. Whilst the primary purpose of signals is for safety they can also contribute towards increased line capacity.

Locomotives were in the past required to have four front lights (white) arranged to indicate the type of train that the locomotive was pulling. The present system is that trains must carry an indicator board which must be illuminated at night and also in tunnels or fog by day. The 'head code' on the board consists of a figure indicating the type of train, a letter denoting its destination and two numbers which may identify the train. At the rear of the train only one red light is necessary (which may be oil or electric).

29.4 Maritime traffic

International Regulations for the Prevention of Collisions at Sea, prepared by the Inter-Governmental Maritime Consultative Organization (IMCO 1973), details navigation lighting requirements for all types of water-borne vessels. In the UK guidance is found in the *Admiralty Manual of Navigation* (Navy Department 1971).

Ships at sea The regulations state that power driven vessels less than 50 m long, when under way, should have a white light on the mast, red and green lights on the port and starboard sides respectively, and a white light at the stern. The growth in size of vessels, particularly of oil tankers, has increased the danger and actual occurrence of collision at sea, with a consequent increased risk of explosion and pollution. An international conference in 1972 on the prevention of collisions at sea has led to the requirement in the UK that luminaires used as navigation lights must be certified by the Marine Division of the Department of Trade.

Vertical and horizontal beam spreads are specified and, from the relationship of these various lights, approaching vessels can infer a ship's relative course. The intensity of light emitted and required range of visibility are specified in the regulations. Certain dispensations are permitted, for example small craft may have the navigation lights combined into one unit using only one lamp, to reduce power requirements.

The main reasons for displaying navigation lights can be summarized as the need to reveal:

(a) The presence of a vessel.
(b) Whether the vessel is under way or at anchor.
(c) The relative course of the vessel.
(d) The type, size, and mode of propulsion of the vessel, for example sailing vessel or power driven vessel, more or less than 50 m in length.
(e) Hazards, such as a fishing vessel at work, a vessel engaged in mine-sweeping, a vessel restricted in ability to manoeuvre.

This information is used to determine if a risk of collision exists, and to assess what avoiding action should be taken if necessary.

There are many other forms of lighting used on vessels and on static structures, such as oil rigs. The luminaires chosen should have a high IP classification (Sect. 24.2.2) and be made of materials immune to salt-water corrosion. Vibration is also a problem on vessels and rigs, requiring a rugged lamp construction. Additionally, tankers and rigs will require proof luminaires consistent with the zonal classification (Sect. 24.2.2) of the cargo they carry.

Lighthouses are used to provide a visible signal to shipping over a long range, the maximum range being limited by the height of the light and the curvature of the earth. The intensity of signal for a required range can be calculated, using the Blondel–Rey law (Sect. 2.2.3). The colour and flashing characteristics are unique to each lighthouse so that each can be identified by its particular signal. Although the prismatic lens has not changed much in the past century, the light source has progressed from the incandescent mantle to the filament lamp and on to the xenon discharge lamp. The intensity may vary from 10 cd for a small harbour light to as much as 10 Mcd for a larger lens.

The mariner likes to see a 'loom' of light over the horizon, requiring that some part of the beam is emitted above the horizontal and into the sky. A downward component is also useful for the benefit of small craft in foggy conditions close under the lighthouse. However, the principal objective of a lighthouse optic is to collect as much light flux as practicable from a reliable light source and direct it into a horizontal beam of high intensity which is then mechanically swept around a shallow zone at the horizon. Normally the flashing lights from lighthouses are produced by means of revolving screens or by revolving the entire optical system (where a narrow beam is produced) or by shutters. A lamp of small size and very high luminance combined with long life is needed for a lighthouse, these lamp characteristics enabling the associated optics to produce the very intense narrow beam normally required. An automatic means of changing failed lamps and advancing a replacement is part of the associated equipment. A 3·5 kW incandescent lamp with a cruciform or bunch filament is a commonly used light source, but 2 kW compact source xenon lamps have been used.

For UK waters Trinity House has the responsibility for the provision of navigation marks and the operation of lighthouses. It is a member of the International Association of Lighthouse Authorities which publishes recommendations on navigation aids (IALA 1970).

Buoys are normally used to mark navigable channels and wrecks, shallows, or other hazards and employ flashing lights. Reliability is an important factor in that servicing may only be carried out annually. Buoys are not necessarily used to establish precise locations by mariners, as movements caused by dragging or breaking their moorings could arise.

29.5   Air traffic

Aircraft in flight have a variety of sophisticated radar and radio guidance and communication systems, but they are still required to maintain navigation lights, derived in essence from those used at sea. In particular a red light is used on the port wing tip, a corresponding green to starboard, and a white rear-facing light on the tail. In the absence of anti-collision lights these are made to flash at a frequency of 40 per minute, but usually additional red anti-collision lights are employed, flashing at between 40 and 100 per minute. Proposals to limit this to between 60 and 90 per minute have been made with an optimum of 75 ± 10. The effective intensity of these lights is usually of the order of 200 cd, making identification by fast aircraft in flight a difficult visual task. The use of high intensity xenon discharge tubes, with a coding to indicate the direction of the aircraft (e.g. double flash forward, single flash aft) have been introduced, with the effective intensity increased to 400 cd. Special consideration during the supersonic phase of flight has also been mooted using a white flashing light (cf. red for subsonic speeds), although Concorde was fitted with red lights to comply with existing regulations. Forward-facing white lights with a controlled narrow beam are used during landing.

Hazard warning beacons Just as the speed of aircraft has steadily increased, so too have the heights of buildings, chimneys, and communication towers. High intensity hazard beacons were developed in the late 1960s and early 1970s using a 160 W neon lamp, with an effective intensity of not less than 2000 cd of red light, which is far greater than could be achieved by the use of filtered white light, with a flash rate between 120 and 180 per minute and a flash duration of 0·1 s. The luminaire and light source have had to be designed for operation in extreme environmental and atmospheric conditions, as well as being highly reliable due to the difficulty of access.

Airfield lighting To obtain a Government licence an aerodrome must comply with conditions laid down by the Civil Aviation Authority in its publication *Licensing of Aerodromes* (CAA 1978), Chapter 6 being concerned with the performance of the lighting units to be used. From the time the pilot first sees the airfield until he safely disembarks he will be helped by nine types of lighting units. In order of usage these are:

(a)   Airport location beacons are often morse flashing lights mounted on the roof of a central building in the airport. They use conventional incandescent lamps (500/1000 W) housed in parabolic reflectors and are green.

(b)   Approach lights are arranged to give a pattern of lights leading into the runway. 300 W PAR 56 lamps have been used, but now 200 W tungsten halogen lamps are more commonly employed.

(c)   Visual Approach Slope Indicator (VASI) units define the correct angle of approach to the runway. A VASI unit emits white light in the upper half of its beam and red light in the lower half. Units are laid out to form two bars as shown in Fig. 29.2a: the pilot sees only white bars if he is too high, only red bars if he is too low, and a combination of red and white bars if he is approaching correctly. A development of this, the Precision Approach Path Indicator (PAPI) system, uses VASI units with a rapid red-to-white transition, laid out in a single bar as shown in Fig. 29.2b. The different setting angle for each of the four units gives the pilot an indication of how much he is deviating from the glide path. It also enables the signal to be read until the aircraft is nearer to touchdown than with a traditional VASI system. 200 W tungsten halogen lamps are the usual sources for these units.

(d)   Threshold lights mark the threshold of the runway and are seen by the pilot as he approaches touchdown. They are either surface mounted or recessed luminaires using 200 W tungsten halogen lamps with glass prismatic lenses and green filters.

(e)   Touchdown zone lights mark the immediate area of landing. They are recessed into the runway, use 200 W tungsten halogen lamps, and are white and red.

(f)   Runway centreline lights are recessed into the runway centreline at up to 30 m intervals. They use 100/200 W tungsten halogen lamps and are white.

(g)   Runway edge lights are either surface mounted or recessed into the runway, using tungsten halogen lamps (100/200 W) housed in glass prismatic lenses and placed at up to 60 m intervals in lines at each side of the runway, and are also normally white.

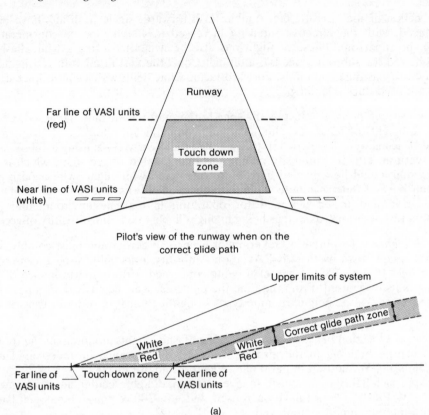

Fig. 29.2   Airfield approach: (a) traditional VASI system and (b) PAPI system

(h) Taxiway lights guide the pilot to the disembarkation area after landing. They are either surface mounted (side) or recessed into the taxiway (centreline) or both. They use 45 W to 100 W lamps and are green (centreline) or blue (side).

(i) Apron floodlights used for the disembarkation area. They have a tightly-controlled cut-off to avoid glare to pilots in approaching aircraft. Metal halide or high pressure sodium are usually preferred due to their high efficacy and long lamp life.

Further reading

Bellion W E and Holmes J G, 1978, *Light measurement in industry SPIE*, **146,** 35–43: On site photometry of lighthouses (Washington: Soc. Photo-Opt. Instru. Eng.)

BSI, 1949, BS 942: *Formulae for the calculation of intensities of lighthouse beams*

Dept of Trade, 1971, *Survey of lights on signalling equipment – instructions for the guidance of surveyors* (London: HMSO)

Grundy J T and Weston R F, 1966, *Electrical Times*, **7,** April: Hazards to aircraft, warning beacon

Hargroves J A and Hargroves R A, 1971, Supplement to vision research No. 2: *Bibliography of work on flashing lights (1711–1969)* (Oxford: Pergamon)

Hymers R T, 1981, *Lighting J.*, **23,** 8–11: VASI or PAPI (London: THORN EMI Lighting)

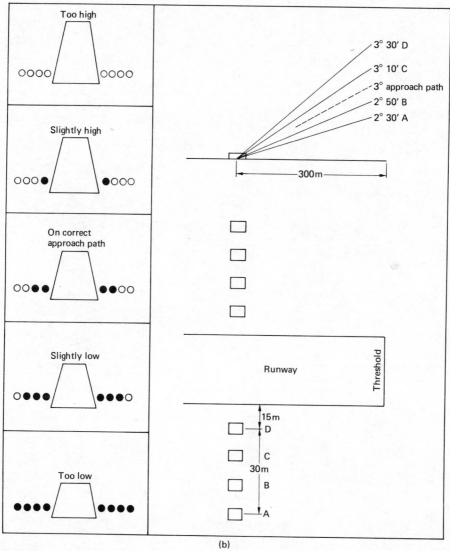

(b)

Fig. 29.2(b)

ICAO, 1976, *Aerodrome design manual – Part 4: Visual aids* (Cheltenham: International Civil Aviation Organization)

International Symposium, 1971, *The perception and application of flashing lights* (London: Adam Hilger)

Masaki H, Kawai S, Inagaki J and Ichikawa V, 1980, CIE Publication No. 50, *Proc. 19th Session*, 389–392: Composite effect of multiple coloured sources

Obara K, Ikeda K and Nakayama M, 1980, CIE Publication No. 50, *Proc. 19th Session*, 392–398: Visual appearance of a sequence of signal lights

Poole P H, 1973, *Lt. & Ltg.*, **66**, 258–261: Motorway communication system

Rumsey G R, 1978, *Light measurement in industry SPIE*, **146**, 44–48: Photometry and colour measurements of ships' navigation lights (Washington: Soc. Photo-Opt. Instru. Eng.)

Appendix I Lamp data

This appendix includes selected data on typical lamps to illustrate the comparative performance of the various types. It makes no attempt at completeness, nor at providing definitive values: for these, and for information on other lamp types, manufacturers' literature should be consulted.

The following points should be noted:

All dimensions are in mm.
CCT – typical correlated colour temperature.
R_a – typical general colour rendering index.
Initial lumens – light output at start of life, after 100 h in the case of discharge lamps and fluorescent tubes.
Lighting design lumens – nominal light output for lighting design purposes, representing the average through-life output.

For many design purposes the provision of lighting design lumens and average life data for discharge lamps and fluorescent tubes are inadequate. A better guide to life performance is given by survival curves of the type shown in Fig. A.1, which are now provided by many manufacturers. This composite curve and the accompanying table give a general indication of the relative performance of the principal lamp types.

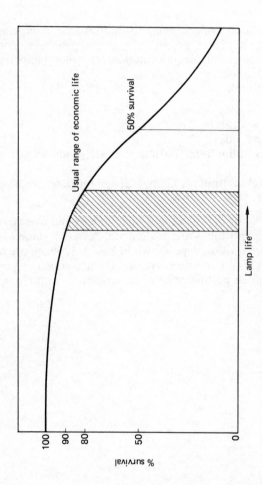

	Fluorescent tubes	Low pressure sodium	High pressure sodium	Mercury	Mercury–tungsten	Metal halide
90% survival (h)	8000	8000	12000	12000	7000	6000
Maintenance (%)	85	85	85	70	75	70
50% survival (h)	12000	12000	30000	20000	10000	12000
Maintenance (%)	75	80	80	55	70	60

Fig. A.1 Typical survival curve, survival values, and lumen maintenance figures for discharge lamps and fluorescent tubes

General lighting service incandescent filament lamps

(a)   240 V – design life 1000 h

Rating (watts)	Lumens Initial	Lighting design	Class	Bulb finish	Cap	Bulb diameter
40	420	400	Coiled coil	Internally frosted	B22/25 × 26	61
60	710	675				61
100	1360	1290				61
150	2180	2070				69
40	340	320	Single coil	Internally frosted	B22/25 × 26	61
60	610	575				61
100	1230	1160				61
150	2060	1950				81
200	2880	2730	Single coil		E27/27	81
300	4550	4300			E40/45	111·5
500	8200	7700				111·5

(b)   240 V – design life 2000 h

Rating (watts)	Lumens Initial	Lighting design	Class	Bulb finish	Cap	Bulb diameter
40	375	355	Coiled coil	Internally frosted	B22/25 × 26	61
60	630	595				61
100	1220	1160				61
150	1960	1860				69

Tungsten halogen lamps

240 V – linear floodlight

Rating (watts)	Lumens	Average life (h)	Operating position	Cap	Maximum dimensions Length	Diameter
150	2100	4000	U	R7s	78	12
200	3100	4000	U	R7s	118	12
300	5000	2000	U	R7s	118	12
500	9500	2000	H	R7s	118	12
750	15000	2000	H	R7s	189	12
1000	21000	2000	H	R7s	189	12
1000	21000	2000	H	R7s	254	12
1500	33000	2000	H	R7s	254	12
2000	44000	2000	H	R7s	331	12

Note:
U = universal; H = horizontal ±4°

Fluorescent lamps

(a) Standard lamps in 38 mm and 16 mm diameter tubes

Rating (watts)	Length	Plus white	White	Warm white	Natural	Cool white	°Kolor-rite	De luxe warm white	De luxe natural	North light colour matching	Artificial daylight
CCT		3600	3400	3000	4000	4300	4000	3000	3600	6500	6500
R_a		74	56	54	85	64	92	79	92	94	95
125	2400	9000	9500	9400	7150	9000	6300	6800	5500	6000	4800
		8400	**8900**	**8800**	**6500**	**8500**	**5700**	**6200**	**4800**	**5600**	**3800**
85	2400	7000	7350	7250	5500	7000	4800	5300	4300	4500	—
		6500	**6850**	**6750**	**5000**	**6500**	**4400**	**4700**	**3800**	**4100**	—
75	1800	5800	6050	5950	4400	5750	3900	4200	3400	3600	3000
		5500	**5750**	**5650**	**4000**	**5450**	**3500**	**3800**	**2900**	**3200**	**2400**
65	1500	4800	5100	4950	3700	4800	3350	3500	2900	3000	2600
		4500	**4750**	**4600**	**3400**	**4450**	**3000**	**3200**	**2500**	**2700**	**2100**
40	1200	2900	3050	2950	2300	2900	2000	2150	1750	1900	1500
		2700	**2800**	**2700**	**2100**	**2650**	**1800**	**1950**	**1500**	**1700**	**1200**
20	600	1150	1225	1200	900	1150	850	850	700	800	650
		1050	**1100**	**1100**	**800**	**1050**	**750**	**750**	**600**	**700**	**500**
13	525†		850	850		800					
			750	**750**		**700**					
8	300†		480	480		400					
			420	**420**		**360**					
6	225†		300	290		275					
			250	**250**		**240**					
4	150†		130								
			100								

†16 mm diameter tubes; all others in 38 mm diameter tubes

(b) Slimline lamps in 24 mm diameter tubes and others

Rating (watts)	Length	CCT / R_a	With halophosphate phosphor coatings			With narrow-band polyphosphor coatings			2D
			Pluslux 3000 (warm)	3500 (white)	4000 (cool)	Polylux 3000 (warm)	3500 (white)	4000 (cool)	
		CCT	3100	3600	4300	3000	3400	4100	2800
		R_a	51	54	58	85	85	85	82
100‡	2400‡		8400 / **7900**	8500 / **8000**	8100 / **7600**	9400 / **8900**	9400 / **8900**	9400 / **8900**	— / —
70	1800		5950 / **5600**	6050 / **5700**	5750 / **5400**	6550 / **6300**	6550 / **6300**	6550 / **6300**	— / —
58	1500		4950 / **4550**	5100 / **4700**	4800 / **4400**	5400 / **5100**	5400 / **5100**	5400 / **5100**	— / —
36	1200		2950 / **2700**	3050 / **2800**	2900 / **2650**	3450 / **3200**	3450 / **3200**	3450 / **3200**	— / —
18	600		1200 / **1100**	1225 / **1100**	1150 / **1050**	1450 / **1325**	1450 / **1325**	1450 / **1325**	— / —
40	525U		2825 / **2550**	2875 / **2575**	— / —	— / —	3250 / **3000**	— / —	— / —
16	2D		— / —	— / —	— / —	— / —	— / —	— / —	1050 / **925**

‡ 38 mm diameter tube; others in 24 mm diameter tubes (except 2D)

Key:
Initial lumens
Lighting design lumens

Sodium lamps

(a)   High pressure sodium lamps – SON. $CCT = 2100$ K, $R_a = 25$

Rating (watts)	Type of envelope	Lumens Initial	Lighting design	Operating volts	Cap	Maximum dimensions Overall length	Diameter
50	Elliptical	3500	3100	85	E27	154	71
70	Elliptical	5800	5300	90	E27	154	71
70	Tubular	6000	5500	90	E27	154	39
150	Elliptical	15500	15000	100	E40	227	91
150	Tubular	16000	15500	100	E40	210	47
250	Elliptical	26500	25500	100	E40	227	91
250	Tubular	28000	27000	100	E40	257	47
400	Elliptical	46000	45000	105	E40	286	122
400	Tubular	48000	47000	100	E40	285	47
1000	Elliptical	120000	110000	110	E40	410	167

(b)   De luxe high pressure sodium lamps – SON DL. $CCT = 2300$ K, $R_a = 70$

Rating (watts)	Lumens Initial	Lighting design	Operating volts	Cap	Maximum dimensions Overall length	Diameter
150	13000	12500	100	E40	227	91
250	23000	22000	100	E40	227	91

(c)   Linear high pressure sodium lamps – SON TD

Rating (watts)	Lumens Initial	Lighting design	Operating volts	Cap	Maximum dimensions Overall length	Diameter
250	26000	25000	100	RX7s	189	24
400	48000	46000	105	RX7s	254	24

(d)   Low pressure sodium lamps – SOX

Rating (watts)	Lumens Initial	Lighting design	Operating volts	Cap	Maximum dimensions Overall length	Diameter
18	1800	1750	56	BC	210	53
35	4390	4300	70	BC	311	53
55	7650	7500	107	BC	425	53
90	12750	12500	112	BC	528	67
135	22000	21500	164	BC	775	67

Mercury lamps

(a)　Phosphor-coated mercury lamps – MBF. $CCT = 4350$ K, $R_a = 45$

Rating (watts)	Lumens		Operating volts	Cap	Maximum dimensions	
	Initial	Lighting design			Overall length	Diameter
50	2000	1900	95	E27	129	56
80	3850	3650	115	E27	154	71
125	6300	5800	125	E27	175	76
250	13500	12500	130	E40	227	91
400	23000	21500	135	E40	286	122
700	42000	38000	140	E40	328	143
1000	62000	58000	145	E40	410	167

(b)　Mercury–tungsten lamps – MBTF. $CCT = 3600$ K, $R_a = 48$

Rating (watts)	Lumens		Supply volts	Cap	Maximum dimensions	
	Initial	Lighting design			Overall length	Diameter
160	2900	2560	240–250	B22 or E27	175	76
250	5500	4840	240–250	E40	227	91
500	12500	11500	240–250	E40	286	122

Metal halide lamps

(a)　Metal halide lamps – MBI and MBIF. $CCT = 3700$ K, $R_a = 78$

Rating (watts)	Lumens		Operating volts	Cap	Maximum dimensions	
	Initial	Lighting design			Overall length	Diameter
250†	19000	16000	100	E40	227	91
400‡	29000	24000	120	E40	286	122
1000‡	92000	85000	250	E40	410	167

†Coated, ‡clear or coated

(b)　Linear metal halide lamps – MBIL. $CCT = 4500$ K

Rating (watts)	Lumens		Supply volts (a.c.)	Operating volts	Cap	Maximum dimensions	
	Initial	Lighting design				Overall length	Diameter
750	67000	58500	200–250	500	RX7s	256	13·3
1500	120000	110000	380–415	250	RX7s	256	20·1
1600	135000	115000	200–250	450	RX7s	256	17·7

(c)   Compact source metal halide lamps – CSI. $CCT = 3800–4000\,K$, $R_a = 80$

Rating (watts)	Type	Lumens		Operating volts	Cap	Maximum dimensions	
		Initial	Lighting design			Overall length	Width
400	Standard	32000	27000	100	2-pin	55	30
1000	Standard or hot restrike	90000	81000	70–85	G22, G38	115	51
1000	Sealed beam, standard, or hot restrike	Peak initial beam candle power 1500000		70–85	G38	175	205

(d)   Compact source iodide daylight lamps – CID. $CCT = 5500\,K$, $R_a = 85$

Rating (watts)	Type	Lumens		Operating volts	Cap	Maximum dimensions	
		Initial	Lighting design			Overall length	Width
200	Standard	14000	12600	70	GY9·5	57	22
1000	Standard or hot restrike	70000	63000	70–85	G22, G38	115	51
2500	Hot restrike	200000	180000	95	G38	175	51
1000	Sealed beam, standard, or hot restrike	Peak initial beam candle power 850000		70–85	G38	175	205

Appendix II Glossary

This appendix gives brief definitions of technical terms and units more particularly used in the science and technology of lighting and light sources. It makes no attempt to be a complete compendium of the more generally used terms which appear in the book, nor does it define, for example, the various kinds of lamp, circuit, design technique, etc.: for information on these the index should be consulted.

Further definitions and, in some cases, more detailed information, may be found in the *International Lighting Vocabulary* of the Commission Internationale de l'Éclairage (CIE 1970).

Where appropriate, the usual symbol is given in parentheses after the definition.

ABSORPTANCE (absorption factor/coefficient) Ratio of absorbed flux to incident flux (radiant, luminous, or acoustic). (α)

ACHROMATIC STIMULUS A stimulus that, under the prevailing conditions of adaptation, gives rise to a perceived colour devoid of hue.

ADAPTATION The process by which the state of the visual system is modified by previous and present exposure to stimuli that have various luminances and spectral power distributions.

APOSTILB Non-SI unit of luminance, equal to $1/\pi\,\mathrm{cd\,m^{-2}}$; the luminance of a uniform diffuser having an exitance of $1\,\mathrm{lm\,m^{-2}}$. (asb)

APPARENT BRIGHTNESS *see* LUMINOSITY.

ASPECT FACTOR That part of the illuminance equation for a line source relating to the angle subtended by the source at the point considered and to the intensity distribution of the source. (*AF* or *af*)

ATMOSPHERE, STANDARD Non-SI unit of pressure equal to 101 325 Pa or 760 torr. (atm)

ATMOSPHERIC ABSORPTION Attenuation of illuminance caused by absorption and scattering (diffusion) of light in air by solid particles or liquid droplets or both.

AZIMUTH ANGLE An angle measured in the horizontal plane relative to a fixed direction.

BAR Non-SI unit of pressure, equal to 10^5 Pa; approximately 750 torr. (bar)

BEAM ANGLE The beam width or spread of light from a projector, defined as the angle over which the luminous intensity is not less than a specified percentage, usually 10 or 50%, of the peak intensity; also called FIELD ANGLE.

BEAM FACTOR The proportion of luminous flux from a projector contained within the beam angle.

BLACK BODY   *see* FULL RADIATOR.

BREWSTER ANGLE   Angle of incidence of light at which it becomes linearly polarized by specular reflection.

CANDELA   Unit of luminous intensity, equal to $1\,\mathrm{lm}\,\mathrm{sr}^{-1}$. (cd)

CAVITY INDEX   A term, indicating angular size, used in determining the effective reflectances of room surfaces for interior lighting design: defined for a cavity of length L, width W, and depth d as $LW/d(L + W)$. (*CI*)

CELSIUS   Correct name of the temperature scale commonly called centigrade. The scale unit is the degree celsius. (°C) *See also* KELVIN.

CHROMA   Subjective estimate of the amount of pure chromatic colour present in the sample observed judged in proportion to the average brightness of its surroundings. Quantitative parameter in the Munsell system.

CHROMATIC ADAPTATION   Adaptation to the visual effects of stimuli that differ in spectral power distribution.

CHROMATICITY   Colour quality of a stimulus defined by coordinates on a plane diagram; or by the combination of dominant wavelength and purity.

CHROMATICITY DIAGRAM   Plane diagram showing the result of mixtures of colour stimuli, each chromaticity being represented unambiguously by a single point on the diagram.

CHROMINANCE   Product of luminance and a chromaticity difference; used in colour television to express a colorimetric difference.

COLOUR ATLAS   Collection of colour samples arranged according to specified rules.

COLOUR RENDERING INDEX   Applied to a light source. A measure of the degree to which measured colours of objects conform to those of the same objects under a reference illuminant, suitable allowance having been made for the state of chromatic adaptation. (*R*)

COLOUR SOLID   That part of a colour space that is occupied by surface colours.

COLOUR SPACE   Geometric representation of colours in space, usually of three dimensions.

COLOUR TEMPERATURE   Temperature of a full radiator which emits radiation of the same chromaticity as the radiator considered. (Often used incorrectly as an abbreviation for correlated colour temperature.)

CONTINUOUS SPECTRUM (CONTINUUM)   A spectrum with an uninterrupted distribution of power over a wide wavelength range.

CONTRAST   Subjective estimate of a difference in luminosity. *See also* LUMINANCE CONTRAST.

CONTRAST RENDERING FACTOR   The ratio of the luminance contrast of a task under a given lighting system to that under reference sphere illumination. (*CRF*)

CONTRAST SENSITIVITY   Reciprocal of the minimum perceptible contrast.

CORRELATED COLOUR TEMPERATURE   The colour temperature corresponding to the point on the full radiator locus which is nearest to the point representing the chromaticity of the illuminant considered on a (u, v) uniform-chromaticity-scale diagram. (*CCT*)

CRITICAL ANGLE   The angle of incidence at which the path of a ray changes abruptly from transmission to total reflection.

DAYLIGHT FACTOR   Ratio of total illuminance at a point in a building, usually on a horizontal plane, received directly and indirectly from the sky, to the illuminance of a horizontal plane exposed to an unobstructed hemisphere of the same sky. Direct sunlight is excluded in both measurements.

DECIBEL   Dimensionless unit denoting a logarithmic expression of two powers (electric or acoustic); 10 times the logarithm to base 10 of the power ratio.

DOMINANT WAVELENGTH   Wavelength of a monochromatic light stimulus which, combined with an achromatic stimulus, gives a colour match with the stimulus considered. (λ_d)

EFFICACY, LUMINOUS   Of radiation, the quotient of the luminous flux by the radiant flux, in lumens per watt. (K or $K(\lambda)$ for monochromatic radiation.)
   Of a source, the quotient of the luminous flux by the power consumed, in lumens per watt. (η_v)

EFFICIENCY, LUMINOUS   Ratio of the radiant flux, weighted according to $V(\lambda)$, to the corresponding radiant flux. (V)

EFFICIENCY, RADIANT   Ratio of the radiant flux to the power consumed. (η_e)

EFFICIENCY, SPECTRAL LUMINOUS   Ratio of the radiant flux at wavelength λ_m to that at λ such that they produce equal luminous sensations; λ_m being the wavelength at which the luminous effect is a maximum. ($V(\lambda)$)

ELECTRON-VOLT   Non-SI unit of energy, equal to $1 \cdot 6021 \times 10^{-19}$ J, acquired by an electron moving through a potential difference of 1 volt. (eV)

EMISSIVITY   Ratio of thermal radiant exitance of a solid to that of a full radiator at the same temperature. (ε)

EQUIVALENT REFERENCE ILLUMINANCE   The illuminance which would produce, under reference sphere illumination, the same task visibility as is found under a given lighting system. Also known as EQUIVALENT SPHERE ILLUMINANCE. (*ERI* or *ESI*, as appropriate)

E-VITON   Non-SI unit of erythemal radiant flux, producing the same effect as 10 μW at a wavelength of 297 nm; in watts.

EXITANCE, LUMINOUS   Luminous flux leaving a surface element divided by the area of the element; in lumens per square metre. (M_v)

EXITANCE, RADIANT   As above, for radiant flux; in watts per square metre. (M_e)

FARAD   Unit of electric capacitance, equal to 1 coulomb per volt. (F)

FIELD ANGLE   *See* BEAM ANGLE.

FINSEN   Non-SI unit of erythemal dose rate, of equal effect to an irradiance of $0 \cdot 1$ W m^{-2} at a wavelength of 297 nm; 1 E-viton cm^{-2}.

FLUX FRACTION RATIO   The ratio of the upward flux to the downward flux from a luminaire or from an installation of luminaires. (*FFR*)

FLUX, LUMINOUS   Radiant flux weighted according to the spectral luminous efficiency function; in lumens. (Φ_v or Φ)

FLUX, RADIANT   Power emitted, transferred, or received as radiation; in watts. (Φ_e)

FOOT-CANDLE   Non-SI unit of illuminance, equal to 10·76 lux; an illuminance of 1 lumen per square foot.

FOOT-LAMBERT   Non-SI unit of luminance, equal to 3·426 cd m^{-2}; the luminance of a uniform diffuser emitting 1 lumen per square foot. (ft L)

FORM-FACTOR   Applied to uniform diffusers, equal to the proportion of luminous flux leaving surface S_a which is received by surface S_b. (f_{ab})

FULL RADIATOR   A thermal radiator obeying Planck's radiation law and having the maximum possible radiant exitance at all wavelengths for a given temperature; also called a BLACK BODY to emphasize its absorption of all incident radiation.

FULL RADIATOR LOCUS   The curve on a chromaticity diagram representing the colour of the radiation from a full radiator as a function of its temperature.

GLARE CONTROL MARK   Number indicating the degree of control of discomfort glare experienced from a road lighting installation. (G)

GLARE INDEX   Number indicating the degree of discomfort glare experienced from an interior lighting installation. (GI)

GUIDE NUMBER   Number assigned to a photoflash lamp as a guide to correct photographic exposure; the product of subject distance and lens stop number.

HARMONIC   Sinusoidal component of a complex repetitive wave, with a frequency which is an exact multiple of the fundamental repetition frequency.

HERTZ   Unit of frequency equal to the number of cycles per second. (Hz)

HUE   Subjective attribute of a colour stimulus distinguished by names like blue, green, red.

ILLUMINANCE   Luminous flux on a surface element divided by the area of the element; in lumens per square metre or lux. (E_v or E)

ILLUMINATION   The process of lighting.

ILLUMINATION VECTOR   A vector whose component perpendicular to a small plane surface in space is equal in magnitude to the difference in illuminance on opposite sides of the surface for all orientations of the surface.

IRRADIANCE   Radiant flux on a surface element divided by the area of the element; in watts per square metre. (E_e)

JOULE   Unit of energy, equal to the work done when the point of application of a force of 1 newton moves through a distance of 1 metre in the direction of the force. (J)

KELVIN   Unit of thermodynamic temperature; measure of temperature above absolute zero ($-273·15$ °C). As a measure of temperature difference one kelvin is equal to one degree celsius. (K)

LAMBERT   Non-SI unit of luminance equal to $10^4/\pi$ cd m^{-2}; the luminance of a uniform diffuser emitting 1 lm cm^{-2}.

LIGHT LOSS FACTOR   Ratio of the mean illuminance on a working plane after a period of use of the lighting installation to the initial mean illuminance (strictly after 100 hours of use). Unlike 'maintenance factor', this term takes into account the lumen depreciation of the lamps during the period of use and, possibly, the effect of failed lamps not being replaced. (*LLF*)

LIGHT OUTPUT RATIO   Ratio of the light output of a luminaire to the sum of the light outputs of the lamps it contains. (*LOR*)
   May be divided into upward and downward components. (*ULOR, DLOR*)

LIGHTING DESIGN LUMENS   Nominal light output from a lamp for lighting design purposes, representing the average through-life output.

LIGHTING EFFECTIVENESS FACTOR   The ratio of the equivalent reference illuminance to the actual illuminance. (*LEF*)

LIGHTNESS   Subjective estimate of the proportion of light diffusely reflected by a body.

LINE SPECTRUM   A spectrum in which the power is concentrated at one or more narrow wavelength bands, appearing as bright lines when observed through a spectroscope.

LUMEN   Unit of luminous flux; the luminous flux associated with a radiant flux of $1/683$ W at a wavelength of 555 nm in air. (lm)

LUMEN SECOND   Unit of quantity of light. (lm s)

LUMINANCE   Flow of light in a given direction, at a point on the surface of a source or a receptor, or at a point in space through which the light passes, defined as the limit of the quotient of the luminous flux passing through an element of surface at the point within an elementary cone containing the direction, divided by the projected area of the surface element perpendicular to the direction and the solid angle of the cone. In lumens per square metre per steradian, or candelas per square metre. (L_v or L)

LUMINANCE COEFFICIENT   Ratio of the luminance of an element of surface to the illuminance on it for given angles of viewing and incident light. (q)

LUMINANCE COEFFICIENT, REDUCED   The product of the luminance coefficient and the cube of the cosine of the angle of incidence of the light. (r)

LUMINANCE CONTRAST   The luminance difference between a task detail and its background, expressed as a proportion of the background luminance. Sometimes known as CONTRAST. (C)

LUMINANCE FACTOR   Ratio of luminance of a body to that of a perfect reflecting diffuser identically illuminated.

LUMINANCE YIELD   A measure of the effectiveness of a road lighting lantern in giving luminance to a road surface. (η_L)

LUMINOSITY   Subjective estimate of how bright an area looks; also known as APPARENT BRIGHTNESS.

LUMINOUS INTENSITY   Quotient of the luminous flux leaving a source in an element of solid angle, by the solid angle; in lumens per steradian or candelas. (I_v or I)

LUX   Unit of illuminance, produced by a uniform luminous flux of one lumen on a surface of one square metre. (lx)

MAINTENANCE   Of a lamp, the gradual deterioration of light output with operating time. Usually expressed as a percentage of initial lumens after a stated time, or as a continuous curve.

MAINTENANCE FACTOR   Ratio of the mean illuminance on a working plane provided by a lighting installation in an average condition of dirtiness to the mean illuminance when it is clean. (*MF*)

MEAN CYLINDRICAL ILLUMINANCE   Mean illuminance on the curved surface of a small cylinder with its axis vertical and located at the point considered. (E_c)

METAMERISM   The phenomenon in which spectrally different colour stimuli appear to match under certain viewing conditions, but fail to match for other observers or illuminants.

MONOCHROMATIC STIMULUS   A light stimulus consisting of a very small range of wavelengths that can be described by a single wavelength.

MUTUAL EXCHANGE COEFFICIENT   Quotient of the flux (radiant or luminous) which one surface sends to another surface, by the exitance of the first surface; in square metres. (*g*)

NANOMETRE   Unit of length, equal to 10^{-9} metre; convenient for specifying wavelengths of light. (nm)

NEWTON   Unit of force; the force producing an acceleration of $1 \, \text{m s}^{-2}$ in a mass of 1 kg. (N)

NORMAL TO CAMERA ILLUMINANCE   The illuminance on a plane surface on the extended axis of a camera lens and at right angles to it; a term commonly used in the lighting of sports arenas for television cameras.

OFFSET DISTANCE   In building floodlighting the distance of the floodlight from the base of the building.
   In area floodlighting the distance from the boundary of the area to the base of the column or tower.

PASCAL   Unit of pressure, equal to $1 \, \text{N m}^{-2}$. One standard atmosphere equals 101 325 pascals. (Pa)

PHOTON   A quantum of electromagnetic radiation having an energy equal to the frequency multiplied by Planck's constant. For a wavelength λ m the energy of a photon is equal to $1 \cdot 986 \times 10^{-25}/\lambda \, \text{J}$ or, for λ nm, $1240/\lambda \, \text{eV}$.

PLANCKIAN RADIATOR   *see* FULL RADIATOR.

PLANCK'S CONSTANT   A fundamental physical constant equal to $6 \cdot 626 \times 10^{-34} \, \text{J s}$; relates photon energy to frequency; *see* PHOTON. (*h*)

POWER FACTOR   In an electric circuit, equal to the ratio of the power in watts to the product of the r.m.s. values of voltage and current; for sinusoidal waveforms also equal to the cosine of the angle of phase difference between voltage and current.

PRIMARIES   The colours of reference colour stimuli by whose additive mixture nearly all other colours may be produced.

PURITY Measure of the proportions of the amounts of the monochromatic and specified achromatic light stimuli that, when additively mixed, match the colour stimulus. The proportions can be measured in different ways yielding either COLORIMETRIC PURITY (p_c) or EXCITATION PURITY (p_e).

PURKINJE PHENOMENON The shift in maximum eye sensitivity toward the blue end of the spectrum at low light levels.

QUANTUM The smallest discrete quantity of energy exchanged in a physical process.

RADIANCE Flow of radiant energy in a given direction, at a point on the surface of a source or a receptor, or at a point in space through which the light passes, defined as the limit of the quotient of the radiant flux passing through an element of surface at the point within an elementary cone containing the direction, divided by the projected area of the surface element perpendicular to the direction and the solid angle of the cone. In watts per square metre per steradian. (L_e)

RATED LIFE The declared effective life of a lamp; either the average life or the life at which replacement becomes economically advantageous.

RECEPTORS Those parts of the visual mechanism that are capable of reacting to a light or colour stimulus.

REFERENCE COLOUR STIMULI The stimuli on which a trichromatic system is based. *See* PRIMARIES.

REFLECTANCE (REFLECTION FACTOR) Ratio of reflected flux to incident flux (radiant or luminous). (ρ)

REFRACTIVE INDEX Ratio of velocity of electromagnetic waves in vacuum to the phase velocity of waves of the wavelength considered in the medium. (n)

RELATIVE CONTRAST SENSITIVITY Contrast sensitivity expressed as a percentage of the contrast sensitivity at a luminance of $100\,\text{cd}\,\text{m}^{-2}$. (RCS)

RELATIVE HUMIDITY The ratio, expressed as a percentage, of the partial pressure of water vapour in an atmosphere to the saturated vapour pressure of water at the same temperature.

ROOM INDEX A term related to room geometry defined as $LW/H_m(L + W)$ for a room of length L, width W, and mounting height H_m of the luminaires above the working plane. (RI)

ROOT MEAN SQUARE The square root of the mean of the squares of successive ordinates of a wave through one complete cycle. (r.m.s.)

SATURATION Subjective estimate of the amount of pure chromatic colour present in the sample observed judged in proportion to its brightness. Compare CHROMA.

SCALAR ILLUMINANCE (mean spherical illuminance) Mean illuminance on the surface of a small sphere located at the point considered. (E_s)

SOLID ANGLE Subtended by an area at a point and equal to the quotient of the projected area on a sphere, centred on the point, by the square of the radius of the sphere; unit is the steradian. (ω)

SPACING TO HEIGHT RATIO Ratio of the spacing between the centres of adjacent luminaires to their height above the working plane. (SHR)

SPECTRAL DISTRIBUTION   Manner in which radiant flux or other quantity varies with wavelength (or frequency) over the spectrum.

SPECTRAL LUMINANCE FACTOR   Ratio of the spectral luminance of the object to that of a perfect reflecting or transmitting diffuser identically illuminated. (β_λ)

SPECTRAL REFLECTANCE   Ratio of the reflected spectral radiant or luminous flux to the incident spectral flux. (ρ_λ)

SPECTRAL TRANSMITTANCE   Ratio of the transmitted spectral radiant or luminous flux to the incident spectral flux. (τ_λ)

SPECTRUM LOCUS   The locus in a chromaticity diagram that represents monochromatic stimuli.

STERADIAN   Unit of solid angle; $1/4\pi$ of a complete sphere. (sr)

STILB   Non-SI unit of luminance, equal to 10^4 cd m^{-2} or 1 cd cm^{-2}. (sb)

STRIATION   Non-uniformity in the intensity distribution of a light source caused by irregularities in its associated light controlling elements.

THRESHOLD CONTRAST   The value of luminance contrast when the task detail is just visible. ($\check{C}$)

TORR   Non-SI unit of pressure, equal to 133·322 Pa. Almost exactly the pressure produced by a 1 mm column of mercury at the earth's surface. (torr)

TRANSMITTANCE (TRANSMISSION FACTOR)   Ratio of transmitted flux to incident flux (radiant or luminous). (τ)

UNIFORM-CHROMATICITY-SCALE DIAGRAM; UCS DIAGRAM   Chromaticity diagram in which the coordinate scales are chosen with the intention of making equal intervals represent as nearly as possible equal steps of discrimination for colours of the same luminance at all parts of the diagram.

UNIFORMITY   The variation of illuminance or luminance usually expressed as a ratio of maximum to minimum or average to minimum.

UTILIZATION FACTOR   Ratio of the luminous flux falling on the working plane to the total flux emitted by the lamps in the luminaires. (UF)

VALUE   Subjective estimate of lightness on a black-to-white scale. Quantitative parameter in the Munsell system.

VECTOR/SCALAR RATIO   The ratio of the magnitude of the illumination vector to the scalar illuminance.

VISIBILITY LEVEL   The ratio of the luminance contrast of a given task to its threshold contrast. (VL)

VISUAL ACUITY   Reciprocal of the angular separation, in minutes of arc, between two points or lines just separable by the eye.

WATT   Unit of power; 1 joule per second. (W)

WAVE NUMBER   Reciprocal of wavelength: in number of waves per metre (or, in most tabulations, waves per cm). (σ)

ZONE FACTOR   Factor by which the mean luminous intensity over a zone of given angular width is multiplied to determine the luminous flux in the zone; equal to the solid angle containing the zone.

References

Aldworth R C, 1975, *JSMPTE*, **84,** 70–76: The development and application of metal halide lamps for color filming and television

Antezak S M, Getzendiner A E and Riggert M C, 1973, *US Patent No. 3 764 286*

Armstrong B H and Nicholls R W, 1972, *Emission, absorption and transfer of radiation in heated atmospheres* (Oxford: Pergamon)

Austin B R, 1976, *Pub. Ltg.*, **41,** 67–70: Public lighting – the deadly reckoning

Barak M, 1980, *Electrochemical power sources* (London: Peregrinus)

Bartleson C J, 1979a, *Col. Res. Appln*, **4,** 119–138: Changes in color appearance with variations in chromatic adaptation

Bartleson C J, 1979b, *Col. Res. Appln*, **4,** 143–155: Predicting corresponding colors with changes in adaptation

Bauer A, 1964, *Lichttechnik*, **16,** 118–120: Hochdruckentladungslampen mit metall-halogenidzusätzen

Baxandall P J, 1959, *IEE Proc.*, **106B,** Supplement 16, 748–758: Transistor sinewave *LC* oscillators

Bean A R and Simons R H, 1968, *Lighting fittings performance and design* (Oxford: Pergamon)

Bedocs L, 1980, *IEE Conf. Publn No. 186*, 65–70: Emergency lighting

Beeson E J G, 1978, *Ltg. Res. Technol.*, **10,** 164–166: The CSI lamp as a source of radiation for solar simulation

Beeson E J G and Furmidge K F, 1972, *Ltg. Res. Technol.*, **4,** 250–253: A high performance graphic arts lamp

Beeson E J G and Furmidge K F, 1976, *Prof. Printer*, **20,** 4–6: Ultraviolet generation, its application and utilisation to ultraviolet ink cure systems

Beiser A, 1967, *Concepts of modern physics* (New York: McGraw-Hill, Kogakusa)

Bellchambers H E and Godby A C, 1972, *Ltg. Res. Technol.*, **4,** 104–106: Illumination, colour rendering and visual clarity

Blackwell H R, 1970, *Illum. Eng.*, **65,** 267–291: Development of procedures and instruments for visual task evaluation

Born M, 1957, *Atomic physics*, 6th Edition (London: Blackie)

Born M and Wolf E, 1975, *Principles of optics* (Oxford: Pergamon)

Boyce P R, 1978, *Ltg. Res. Technol.*, **10,** 179–183: Is equivalent sphere illumination the future?

Boyce P R and Lynes J A, 1976, CIE Publication No. 36, *Proc. 18th Session, London*, 290–297: Illuminance, colour rendering index and colour discrimination index

Brett J, Fontana R, Walsh P, Spura S, Parascandola L, Thouret W and Thorington L, 1981, *J. Illum. Eng. Soc.*, **10,** 214–218: Development of high energy-conserving incandescent lamps

British Railways Board, 1976, *Specification RIA 13: Electronic equipment*

Brown J A C, 1970, *Social psychology of industry* (London: Penguin)

Brown K E, Chalmers A G and Wharmby D O, 1982, *J. Illum. Eng. Soc.*, **11,** 106–114: Tin sodium halide lamps in ceramic envelopes

BSI, 1952, BS 1875: *Bi-pin lampholders for tubular fluorescent lamps for use in circuits, the declared voltage of which does not exceed 250 volts*

—— 1962, BS 555: *Tungsten filament miscellaneous electric lamps*

—— 1963, BS 52: *Bayonet lamp-caps, lampholders and BC adaptors (lampholder plugs) for voltages not exceeding 250 volts*

—— 1966a, BS 841: *Lamp caps and lampholders for architectural lamps*

—— 1966b, AU40: *Motor vehicle lighting and signalling equipment.* Part 3: *Headlamps with prefocused filament lamps*

—— 1966c, AU40: *Motor vehicle lighting and signalling equipment.* Part 4a: *Sealed beam headlamps*

—— 1967, BS 950: *Artificial daylight for the assessment of colour.* Part I: *Illuminant for colour matching and colour appraisal*

—— 1968, BS 667: *Portable photoelectric photometers*

—— 1970, BS 941: *Filament lamps for road vehicles*

—— 1971a, BS 505: *Road traffic signals*

—— 1971b, BS 4782: *Ballasts for high pressure mercury vapour and low pressure sodium vapour discharge lamps*

—— 1973, BS 5489: *Code of practice for road lighting* (9 separate parts)

—— 1974, BS 1376: *Colours of light signals*

—— 1975a, BS 5225: *Photometric data for luminaires.* Part 1: *Photometric measurements*

—— 1975b, BS 5266: *Emergency lighting.* Part 1: *Code of practice for the emergency lighting of premises other than cinemas and certain other specified premises used for entertainment*

—— 1976a, BS 161: *Specification for tungsten filament lamps for general service (batch testing)*

—— 1976b, BS 4900: *Specification for vitreous enamel colours for building purposes*

—— 1976c, BS 4901: *Specification for plastics colours for building purposes*

—— 1976d, BS 4902: *Specification for sheet and tile flooring colours for building purposes*

—— 1976e, BS 5252: *Framework for colour co-ordination for building purposes*

—— 1976f, BS 5345: *Code of practice for the selection, installation and maintenance of electrical apparatus for use in potentially explosive atmospheres.* Part 1: *Basic requirements for all parts of the code*

—— 1978, BS 5042: *Specification for lampholders and starterholders.* Part 2: *Edison screw lampholders*

—— 1979a, BS 1853: *Tubular fluorescent lamps for general lighting service.* Part 1: *Specification for internationally specified lamps.* Part 2: *Specification for lamps used in the UK not included in Part 1*

—— 1979b, BS 4533: *Luminaires.* Part 2, Section 2.6: *Detail requirements, Electrical supply track systems for luminaires*

—— 1980a, BS 5971: *Safety and interchangeability of tungsten filament lamps for domestic and similar general lighting purposes.* Part 1: *Specification for safety and interchangeability*

—— 1980b, BS 5841: *Photographic flash equipment.* Part 1: *Definitions and requirements for luminous flux/time characteristics of expendable photoflash lamps*

—— 1981a, BS 2818: *Specification for ballasts for tubular fluorescent lamps*

—— 1981b, BS 4533: *Luminaires.* Part 101: *Specification for general requirements and tests*

BSI 1981c, BS 4533: *Luminaires*. Section 103.1: *Specification for light distribution from road-lighting lanterns*

—— 1981d, BS 4800: *Specification for paint colours for building purposes*

Burgraff A J and Van Velzen H C, 1969, *J. Amer. Ceram. Soc.*, **52**, 238–242: Glasses resistant to sodium vapor at temperatures to 700 °C

Butters J N, 1971, *Holography and its technology* (London: Peregrinus)

Cayless M A, 1963, *Brit. J. Appl. Phys.*, **14**, 863–869: Theory of the positive column in mercury rare-gas discharges

Cayless M A, 1965, *Proc. 7th Int. Conf. on Phenomena in Ionized Gases* (Beograd: Gradevinska Knjiga Publishing House), **1**, 651–654: Resonance radiation from high-pressure alkali-metal vapour discharges

CIBA-GEIGY Ltd, 1973, CIBA-GEIGY Review No. 1, 2–40: *White*

CIBS, 1966, CIBS/IES Technical Report No. 8: *Lighting of libraries*

—— 1967a, CIBS/IES Technical Report No. 9: *Depreciation and maintenance of interior lighting*

—— 1967b, CIBS/IES Technical Report No. 10: *Evaluation of discomfort glare: the IES glare index system for artificial lighting installations*

—— 1968, CIBS/IES Technical Report No. 11: *The calculation of direct illumination from linear sources*

—— 1969, CIBS/IES Technical Report No. 13: *Industrial area floodlighting*

—— 1971, CIBS Guide, Volume A: *Design data* (10 separate parts)

—— 1972, CIBS/IES Technical Report No. 4: *Daytime lighting in buildings*

—— 1973, CIBS/IES Lighting Guide: *Lecture theatres*

—— 1974, CIBS/IES Lighting Guide: *Sports*

—— 1975a, CIBS/IES Lighting Guide: *Building and civil engineering sites*

—— 1975b, CIBS/IES Lighting Guide: *The outdoor environment*

—— 1977a, CIBS/IES Code for Interior Lighting   (New edition 1983)

—— 1977b, CIBS/IES Technical Report No. 15: *Multiple criteria design: a design method for interior electric lighting installations*

—— 1977c, CIBS Building Energy Code. Part 1: *Energy conserving design*

—— 1979a, CIBS Lighting Guide: *Hospitals and health care buildings*

—— 1979b, CIBS Lighting Guide: *Shipbuilding and ship repair*

—— 1980a, CIBS Lighting Guide: *Museums and art galleries*

—— 1980b, CIBS Technical Memorandum 5: *The calculation and use of utilisation factors*

Chalmers A G, Wharmby D O and Whittaker F L, 1975, *Ltg. Res. Technol.*, **7**, 11–18: Comparison of high-pressure discharges in mercury and the halides of aluminium, tin and lead

Chandrasekhar S, 1960, *Radiative transfer* (New York: Dover Publications)

Cherrington B E, 1979, *Gaseous electronics and gas lasers* (Oxford: Pergamon)

CIE, 1970, Publication No. 17 (E-1.1): *International lighting vocabulary*

—— 1971, Publication No. 15 (E-1.3.1): *Colorimetry*

—— 1972a, Supplement No. 1 to Publn No. 15: *Special metamerism index: change in illuminant*

—— 1972b, Publication No. 19 (TC-3.1): *A unified framework of methods for evaluating visual performance aspects of lighting*

—— 1973a, Publication No. 24 (TC-2.4): *Photometry of indoor type luminaires with tubular fluorescent lamps*

—— 1973b, Publication No. 26 (TC-4.6): *International recommendations for tunnel lighting*

—— 1973c, Publication No. 27 (TC-2.4): *Photometry of luminaires for street lighting*

CIE, 1974, Publication No. 13.2 (TC-3.2): *Method of measuring and specifying colour rendering properties of light sources*
—— 1975, Publication No. 2.2 (TC-1.6): *Colours of light signals*
—— 1976a, Publication No. 30 (TC-4.6): *Calculation and measurement of luminance and illuminance in road lighting*   (Now superseded by Publication No. 30.2, 1982)
—— 1976b, Publication No. 31 (TC-4.6): *Glare and uniformity in road lighting installations*
—— 1976c, CIE Bulletin 30, 6–7: *CIE statement on vehicle front lighting used on urban traffic routes*
—— 1977a, Publication No. 12.2 (TC-4.6): *Recommendations for the lighting of roads for motorized traffic*
—— 1977b, Publication No. 34 (TC-4.6): *Road lighting lantern and installation data – photometrics, classification and performance*
—— 1977c, Publication No. 38 (TC-2.3): *Radiometric and photometric characteristics of materials and their measurement*
—— 1978a, Supplement No. 2 to Publn No. 15: *Recommendation on uniform color spaces – color-difference equations, psychometric color terms*
—— 1978b, Publication No. 39 (TC-1.6): *Surface colours for visual signalling*
—— 1979a, Publication No. 43 (TC-2.4): *Photometry of floodlights*
—— 1979b, Publication No. 47 (TC-4.6): *Road lighting for wet conditions*
—— 1980, Publication No. 48 (TC-1.6): *Light signals for road traffic control*
—— 1981a, Publication No. 19/2 (TC-3.1): *An analytical model for describing the influence of lighting parameters upon visual performance.* Volume 1: *Technical foundations.* Volume 2: *Summary and application guidelines*
—— 1981b, Publication No. 51 (TC-1.3): *A method for assessing the quality of daylight simulators for colorimetry*
Civil Aviation Authority, 1978, CAP 168: *Licensing of aerodromes*, Chapter 6: Aerodrome lighting
Coaton J R, 1969, *Ltg. Res. Technol.*, **1**, 98–103: *The optimum operating gas pressure for incandescent tungsten filament lamps*
Coaton J R, 1970a, *IEE Proc.*, **117**, 1953–1959: *Modern tungsten-halogen lamp technology*
Coaton J R, 1970b, MSc thesis: *Transport processes in gasfilled filament lamps* (Loughborough University of Technology)
Coaton J R, 1971, *Ltg. Res. Technol.*, **3**, 163–164: Calculation of power loss to the gasfilling of incandescent lamps
Cobine J D, 1958, *Gaseous conductors* (New York: Dover Publications)
Coble R L, 1957, *US Patent No. 3 026 210*
Collins B R and McVey C I, 1975, *US Patent No. 3 906 272*
Coolidge W D, 1909, *GB Patent No. 23 499*
Corney A, 1977, *Atomic and laser spectroscopy* (Oxford: The University Press)
Cotton H, 1960, *Principles of illumination* (London: Chapman & Hall)
Crisp V H C, 1978, *Ltg. Res. Technol.*, **10**, 69–82: The light switch in buildings
Curie D, 1963, *Luminescence in crystals* (London: Methuen)
Cuttle C, 1971, *Ltg. Res. Technol.*, **3**, 171–189: Lighting patterns and the flow of light
Dean P J, 1981, *J. Luminescence*, **23**, 17–53: Comparisons and contrasts between light emitting diodes and high field electroluminescent devices
de Groot J J and van Vliet J A J M, 1975, *J. Phys. D.*, **8**, 651–662: The measurement and calculation of the temperature distribution and the spectrum of high-pressure sodium arcs

de Groot J J, van Vliet J A J M and Waszink J H, 1975, *Philips Tech. Rev.*, **35**, 334–342: The high pressure sodium lamp

Denbigh P L, 1974, *Ltg. Res. Technol.*, **6**, 62–68: Effect of sodium/mercury ratio and amalgam temperature on the efficacy of 400 W high-pressure sodium lamps

Denbigh P L, 1978, *Ltg. Res. Technol.*, **10**, 28–31: Experimental approach to high-pressure sodium lamp design

de Neve G, 1976, *Ltg. Res. Technol.*, **8**, 157–161: High pressure sodium lamps to replace MBF lamps in existing installations

Denneman J W, 1981, *IEE Proc.*, **128**, Part A, 397–414: Low pressure sodium discharge lamps

Dept of Education and Science, 1981, DES Design Note 17: *Guidelines for environmental design and fuel conservation in educational buildings*, 2nd Edition (London: HMSO)

Dept of Health and Social Services, 1974, DHSS memo HTM 11: *Emergency electrical service* (London: HMSO)

Dept of the Environment, 1967, *Traffic signs manual*, Chapter 11: Illumination of signs (London: HMSO)

Destriau G, 1936, *J. Chim. Phys.*, **33**, 587–625: Influence de la taille des cristaux phosphorescents sur le rayon d'action des particules alpha

Dettingmeijer J H, Dittmer G, Klopfer A and Schröder J, 1975, *Philips Tech. Rev.*, **35**, 302–306: Research on incandescent lamps. Part III: Regenerative cycles in tungsten halogen lamps

De Vos J C, 1954, *Physica*, **20**, 690–714: A new determination of the emissivity of tungsten ribbon

Dexter D L, 1953, *J. Chem. Phys.*, **21**, 836–850: A theory of sensitised luminescence in solids

Ditchburn R W, 1973, *Eye movements and visual perception* (Oxford: The University Press)

Ditchburn R W, 1976, *Light* (London: Academic Press)

Dushman S, 1949, *Scientific foundations of vacuum technique*, and subsequent editions (New York: Wiley)

Eardley G, Jones B F, Mottram D A J and Wharmby D O, 1979, *J. Phys. D.*, **12**, 1101–1115: A simple model of metal-halide arcs

ECE, 1958a, UN Geneva Agreement Regulation Nos. 1, 2, 5, 8, 20, 31, 37: *Agreement concerning the adoption of uniform conditions of approval and reciprocal recognition of approval for motor vehicle equipment and parts*

—— 1958b, UN Geneva Agreement Regulation No. 37: *Uniform provisions concerning the approval of incandescent filament lamps to be used in approved lights of power driven vehicles and of their trailers* (E/ECE/324-E/ECE/TRANS/505 Revl. Addendum 36)

EEC, 1965, European Economic Community Regulation E/ECE 324 No. 20 (1976): *H4 headlamps*

—— 1976, *Official Journal of the European Communities*, **19**, 96–121: Council directive 76/761/EEC

Elenbaas W, 1951, *The high pressure mercury vapour discharge* (Amsterdam: North Holland)

Elenbaas W, 1965, *High pressure mercury vapour discharge lamps and their applications* (Eindhoven: Philips Technical Library)

Evans D T, Hing P, and Marshall R, 1976, *GB Patent No. 1 571 084*

Fincham W H A and Freeman M H, 1980, *Optics* (London: Butterworths)

494   References

Fischer A G, 1963, *J. Electrochem. Soc.*, **110**, 733–748: Electroluminescent lines in ZnS powder particles

Fischer D, 1981, *Licht-Forschung*, **3**, 25–31: Ein vereinfachtes System zur Bewertung von Kontrastwiedergabe bei der Bürobeleuchtung

Fisher A J, 1977, *Australian Road Res.*, **7**, 3–16: Road lighting as an accident counter-measure

Fisher E, Fitzgerald J, Lechner W and Lems W, 1975, *Philips Tech. Rev.*, **35**, 296–302: Research on incandescent lamps. Part II: Transport and burn-out in incandescent lamps

Fitzpatrick J R and Rees J M, 1979, *Ltg. Res. Technol.*, **11**, 85–89: Progress towards a practical fluorine lamp

Gardner P J, Morris J C, Watson W R, Silver H G and Scholz J A, 1975, *J. Illum. Eng. Soc.*, **5**, 45–49: A new metal halide ultraviolet curing source

General Electric Co USA, 1975, GET-3148: *Nickel cadmium battery application handbook* (Gainsville: GE)

—— 1979, BBD-OEM-237: *The sealed lead acid battery handbook* (Gainsville: GE)

Gershun A, 1936, *The light field* (Moscow). English translation by Moon P and Timoshenko G T, 1939, *Math. Phys.*, **18**, 50–151

Geszti T and Gaal I, 1974, *Acta Tech. Acad. Sci. Hung.*, **78**, 479–488: On the theory of the halogen lamp. Part II: Gas-controlled axial transport (in Hungarian)

Geutler G, 1974, *Farbe*, **23**, 191–235: Zur Farbmessung nach dem Dreibereichsverfahren

Gibson J J, 1968, *The senses considered as perceptual systems* (London: Allen and Unwin)

Gillet W B, 1977, *UK Section Int. Solar Energy Soc. Conf. C11*: Solar simulators and indoor testing

Goldberg D (Ed), 1966, *Luminescence of inorganic solids* (London: Academic Press)

Gooch C H (Ed), 1969, *Gallium arsenide lasers* (New York: Wiley-Interscience)

Graham K and Pegg J C, 1978, *Lighting J.*, **19**, 26–28: Vivatron 5 electronic starter for fluorescent lamps

Green J and Hargroves R A, 1979, *Ltg. Res. Technol.*, **11**, 197–203: A mobile laboratory for dynamic road lighting measurement

Griem H R, 1964, *Plasma spectroscopy* (New York: McGraw-Hill)

Groth R and Kauer E, 1965, *Philips Tech. Rev.*, **26**, 105–111: Thermal insulation of sodium lamps

Grum F, Saunders S B and MacAdam D L, 1978, *Col. Res. Appln*, **3**, 17–22: Concept of correlated color temperature

Guild J, 1932, *Phil. Trans. Roy. Soc.*, **230A**, 149–187: The colorimetric properties of the spectrum

Halberstadt A, Letchford J, Thorp R and Swain R, 1980, *GB Patent Applications Nos. 80 004 025 and 80 301 645*

Hall R and Preston B, 1981, *JSMPTE*, **90**, 678–685: High-power single-ended discharge lamps for film lighting

Hargroves R A, 1981, *Ltg. Res. Technol.*, **13**, 130–136: Road lighting – as calculated and as in service

Harrison A, 1974, *Radio Electron. Eng.*, **44**, 537–544: A novel radar situation display

Haugsjaa P O, 1979, *US Patent No. 4 070 603*

Hawkins F S, 1965, *Trans. Illum. Eng. Soc.*, **30**, 7–17: Glass for modern electric lamps

Henderson S T, 1977, *Daylight and its spectrum*, 2nd Edition (Bristol: Adam Hilger)

Henderson S T and Ranby P W, 1951, *J. Electrochem. Soc.*, **98**, 479–482: Barium titanium phosphate: a new phosphor

Henderson S T, Ranby P W and Halstead M B, 1959, *J. Electrochem. Soc.*, **106,** 27–34: Activation of ZnS and (Zn, Cd) S phosphors by gold and other elements

Hewitt H, Bridgers D J and Simons R H, 1965, *Trans. Illum. Eng. Soc.*, **30,** 91–116: Lighting and the environment

Hicks H V, 1970, *Automotive Eng. Congress, Detroit*: A fresh approach to an idea for seeing at night (Soc. of Automotive Engineers)

Hirschmann W, 1981, *Power Conversion Int. Proc.*, 451–466: Electronic ballasts for modern fluorescent lamps with SIPMOS transistors

HMG, 1961, *The factories act*

—— 1963, *Offices, shops and railway premises act*. Section 8: *Lighting*

—— 1971, *Fire precautions act*

—— 1974, *Health and safety at work etc. act*

—— 1981, SI 909: *The education (school premises) regulations*

Hopkinson R G, 1963, *Architectural physics: lighting* (London: HMSO)

Hopkinson R G and Longmore J, 1959, *Trans. Illum. Eng. Soc.*, **24,** 121–148: The permanent supplementary artificial lighting of interiors

Hoyaux M F, 1968, *Arc physics* (Berlin: Springer-Verlag)

Hunt D R G, 1979, *Availability of daylight* (Watford: Building Research Establishment)

Hurvich L M and Jameson D, 1966, *The perception of brightness* (Boston: Allyn & Bacon)

IALA, 1970, *International dictionary of aids to marine navigation*, Chapter 2: Visual aids (Paris: Int. Assoc. of Lighthouse Authorities)

ICEL, 1978, ICEL 1001: *The construction and performance of battery-operated emergency lighting equipment* (BEAMA)

IEC, 1969, Publication No. 161: *Lamp caps and holders together with gauges for the control of interchangeability and safety*

—— 1973, Publication No. 64: *Tungsten filament lamps for general service*

—— 1974, Publication No. 458: *Transistorized ballasts for fluorescent lamps*

—— 1979, Publication No. 598: *Luminaires*. Part 1: *General requirements and tests*

—— 1980, Publication No. 662: *High pressure sodium vapour lamps*

IEE, 1981, *Regulations for electrical installations*, 15th Edition (London: Institution of Electrical Engineers)

IMCO, 1973, *Final act of the international conference on revision of the international regulations for preventing collisions at sea 1972* (London: HMSO)

Inoguchi J, Takeda M, Kakihara Y, Nakata Y and Yoshida M, 1974, *SID Int. Symp. 1974, Digest of technical papers*, 84–85: Stable high brightness thin film electroluminescent panels (California: Soc. for Information Display)

Institute of Petroleum, 1965, *Electrical safety code, Part 1*

Jack A G, 1971, *10th Int. Conf. on Phenomena in Ionized Gases, Invited paper*, 205–220: High pressure gas discharges as intense non-coherent light sources (Oxford: Donald Parsons)

Jacobs C A J and van Vliet J A J M, 1980, *Philips Tech. Rev.*, **39,** 211–215: A new generation of high-pressure sodium lamps

Jay P A, 1968, *Trans. Illum. Eng. Soc.*, **33,** 47–71: Inter-relationship of the design criteria for lighting installations

Judd D B, 1961, Special Technical Publication 297: *A five-attribute system of describing visual appearance* (Philadelphia: Amer. Soc. for Testing Materials)

Judd D B, MacAdam D L and Wyszecki G, 1964, *J. Opt. Soc. Amer.*, **54,** 1031–1040: Spectral distribution of typical daylight as a function of correlated color temperature

Keitz H A E, 1971, *Light calculations and measurements*, 2nd Edition (London: Macmillan)

Kenty C, 1950, *J. Appl. Phys.*, **21**, 1309–1318: Production of 2537 radiation and the role of metastable atoms in an argon–mercury discharge

Kingery W D, Bowen H K and Uhlmann D R, 1976, *Introduction to ceramics* (New York: Wiley)

Kohl W H, 1972, *Handbook of materials and techniques for vacuum tubes* (New York: Reinhold)

Knittel W, 1979, IEE Publication 181, *2nd Conf. on Automotive Electronics*, 205–210: Environmental requirements for automotive electronics

Lake W H and Davenport J M, 1982, *J. Illum. Eng. Soc.*, **11**, 66–73: Low wattage metal halide lamps

Langmuir I, 1913, *AIEE Proc.*, **32**, 1894: Tungsten lamps of high-efficiency. Part I: Blackening of tungsten lamps and methods of preventing it. Reprinted in Suits C G (Ed), 1962, *The collected works of Irving Langmuir*, Volume 2, 176–202 (Oxford: Pergamon)

Langmuir I, 1962, *The collected works of Irving Langmuir*, Volume 2, Suits C G (Ed) (Oxford: Pergamon)

Legrand Y, 1968, *Light, colour and vision*, 2nd Edition (London: Chapman & Hall)

Lemons T M, 1978, *Ltg. Des. Appln*, **8**, August, 32–37: HMI lamps

Lengyel B A, 1971, *Lasers* (New York: Wiley-Interscience)

Leverenz H W, 1936, *US Patent No. 2 118 091*

Levine A K and Palilla F C, 1966, *Proc. Int. Conf. on Luminescence*, **2**, 2050–2057: YVO_4-Eu, a new red color-correction phosphor for high pressure mercury vapor lamps (Budapest: Akademiai Kiado)

Light and Lighting, 1966, *Lt. & Ltg.*, **59**, 166–175: Recent developments in discharge lamps

Lipson S G and Lipson H, 1969, *Optical physics* (Cambridge: The University Press)

Lochte-Holtgreven W (Ed), 1968, *Plasma diagnostics* (Amsterdam: North-Holland)

Luckiesh M, 1946, *Applications of germicidal, erythemal and infrared energy* (New York: Van Nostrand)

Lynes J A, 1968, *Principles of natural lighting* (London: Elsevier)

Lynes J A, 1971, *Ltg. Res. Technol.*, **3**, 24–42: Lightness, colour and constancy in lighting design

Lynes J A, 1979, *Ltg. Res. Technol.*, **11**, 67–77: Lighting for texture

Lynes J A, 1982, *Ltg. Res. Technol.*, **14**, 1–18: Designing for contrast rendition

Lynes J A, Burt W, Jackson G K and Cuttle C, 1966, *Trans. Illum. Eng. Soc.*, **31**, 65–91: The flow of light into buildings

MacAdam D L, 1937, *J. Opt. Soc. Amer.*, **27**, 294–299: Projective transformations of ICI color specifications

MacAdam D L, 1942, *J. Opt. Soc. Amer.*, **32**, 247–274: Visual sensitivities to color differences in daylight

MacAdam D L, 1956, *J. Opt. Soc. Amer.*, **46**, 500–513: Chromatic adaptation

Marsden A M, 1970, *Ltg. Res. Technol.*, **2**, 10–16: Brightness–luminance relationships in an interior

McCartney E J, 1976, *Optics of the atmosphere* (New York: Wiley)

McDonald R, 1982a, *J. Oil & Colour Chem. Ass.*, **65** (2), 43–53: A review of the relationship between visual and instrumental assessment of colour difference, Part 1

McDonald R, 1982b, *J. Oil & Colour Chem. Ass.*, **65** (3), 93–106: A review of the relationship between visual and instrumental assessment of colour difference, Part 2

McKeag A H and Ranby P W, 1942, *GB Patent No. 578 192*

McKeag A H and Randall J T, 1936, *GB Patent No. 480356*

McSparron D, Mohan K, Raybold R, Saunders R and Zalewski E, 1970, NBS Technical Note 559: *Spectroradiometry and conventional photometry: an interlaboratory comparison* (Washington: National Bureau of Standards)

McVey C I, 1980, *IEE Proc.*, **127**, Part A, 158–164: High pressure sodium lamp technology

Mitchell A G C and Zemansky M W, 1934, *Resonance radiation and excited atoms* (Cambridge: The University Press). Reprinted 1971

Moon D M and Koo R C, 1971, *Metall. Trans.*, **2**, 2115–2122: Mechanism and kinetics of bubble formation in doped tungsten

Morehead F F, 1967, *Physics and chemistry of II–VI compounds*, Chapter 12 of *Electroluminescence*, Aven M and Prener J S (Eds) (Amsterdam: North-Holland)

Navy Dept, 1971, *Admiralty manual of navigation* (London: HMSO)

Nickerson D, 1976, *Color Res. Appln*, **1**, 69–77: History of the Munsell color system, company and foundation. II: Its scientific application

Odell E C and Preston B, 1980, *CIBS Nat. Ltg. Conf. Paper CD*, 1–5: Aspects of colour and lumen control in sodium/scandium metal halide lamps

Ostrovsky Y I, Butusov M M and Ostrovskaya G V, 1980, *Interferometry by holography* (Berlin: Springer-Verlag)

Palmer D A, 1972, *J. Opt. Soc. Amer.*, **62**, 828–830: Tetrachromatic matches

Parrish J A, Anderson R R, Urbach F and Pitts D, 1978, *UV-A, biological effects of ultraviolet radiation with emphasis on human responses to longwave ultraviolet* (New York: Wiley)

Parrott M A, 1974, *Ltg. Res. Technol.*, **6**, 19–23: Translucent ceramics as lamp envelopes

Partridge J H, 1949, *Glass to metal seals* (Sheffield: Soc. of Glass Technology)

Payne E C, Mayer E C and Jerome C W, 1950, *Illum. Eng.*, **45**, 688–693: A new method of producing light

Peaker A R, 1980, *IEE Proc.*, **127**, Part A, 202–210: Light emitting diodes

Peelan J G J, 1976, *Philips Tech. Rev.*, **36**, 47–52: Light transmission of sintered alumina

Phillips R O and Prokhovnik S J, 1960, *IES Monograph No. 3*, 1–17: The new approach to inter-reflections

Polman J, van Tongeren H and Verbeek T G, 1975, *Philips Tech. Rev.*, **35**, 321–330: Low pressure gas discharges

Pope R, 1975, *Signalling the layout – British railways practice* (Reading: Inst. of Railway Signal Engineers)

Ranby P W and Ellerbeck R P, 1971, *J. Photogr. Sci.*, **19**, 77–82: A new type of image storage panel

Ranby P W and Smith D W, 1980, *IEE Proc.*, **127**, Part A, 196–201: Electroluminescent panel devices

Rees J M, 1970, *Ltg. Res. Technol.*, **2**, 257–260: Bromophosphonitrile lamps

Rhodes W H, 1978, *US Patent No. 4115134*

Richtmyer F K, Kennard E H and Cooper J W, 1969, *Introduction to modern physics* (New York: McGraw-Hill)

Round H J, 1907, *Electrical World*, **19**, 309: A note on carborundum

Sarteel F, 1976, CIE Publication No. 36, *Proc. 18th Session 1975*, 646–657: Les implications économiques du contrôle de l'éblouissement en éclairage public

Schmidt K, 1963, *Proc. 6th Int. Conf. on Phenomena in Ionized Gases* (*Paris: SERMA*), **3**, 323–330: Radiation characteristics of 'high pressure' alkali metal discharges

Schreuder D A, 1964, *The lighting of vehicular traffic tunnels* (Eindhoven: Philips Technical Library)

Schröder J, 1964, *Philips Tech. Rev.*, **25**, 359–364: Chemical transport reactions at very high temperatures using fluorine

Scott P P, 1980, TRRL Report LR 929: *The relationship between road lighting quality and accident frequency* (Crowthorne, Berks: Transport and Road Research Laboratory)

Scribner E A, 1881, *US Patent No. 254 780*

Siegel R and Howell J R, 1972, *Thermal radiation and heat transfer* (New York: McGraw-Hill, Kogakuska)

Simons R H, 1980, *APLE Public Ltg. Conf.*, pp. M1–M15: A basis for a new road lighting code of practice

Smith R A, 1964, *Semiconductors* (Cambridge: The University Press)

Snavely B B, 1969, *IEEE Proc.*, **57**, 1374–1390: Flashlamp-excited organic dye lasers

Sobel'man I I, 1969, *Introduction to the theory of atomic spectra* (Oxford: Pergamon)

Speranskaya N I, 1959, *Optics and Spectroscopy*, **7**, 424–428: Determination of spectrum color coordinates for twenty-seven normal observers

Stevens S S, 1975, *Psychophysics: Introduction to its perceptual, neural and social prospects* (New York: Wiley)

Stiles W S and Burch J M, 1959, *Optica Acta*, **6**, 1–26: NPL color-matching investigation: final report (1958)

Stitch M L (Ed), 1979, *Laser handbook*, Volume 3 (Amsterdam: North-Holland)

Studer F J and Cusano D A, 1953, *J. Opt. Soc. Amer.*, **43**, 522–525: Titanium dioxide films as selective reflectors of the near infrared

Summer W, 1962, *Ultraviolet and infrared engineering* (New York: Interscience Publishers)

Svet D Y, 1965, *Thermal radiation* (New York: Consultants Bureau)

ter Vrugt J W and Verwimp J K P, 1980, *IEE Proc.*, **127**, Part A, 173–180: High pressure mercury vapour lamps

Theis D, 1981, *J. Luminescence*, **23**, 191–207: Application of thin film electroluminescent devices

Thorn Lighting Ltd, 1974, *Outdoor lighting handbook*

—— 1979, *Technical handbook*

Thorne A P, 1974, *Spectrophysics* (London: Chapman & Hall)

Thornton P R, 1967, *The physics of electroluminescent devices* (London: E & F Spon)

Thornton W A, 1971, *J. Opt. Soc. Amer.*, **61**, 1155–1163: Luminosity and color-rendering capability of white light

Tooley F V, 1971, *Handbook of glass manufacture*, Volume 1 (New York: Ogden Publishing Co)

Tyco Laboratories, 1970, *GB Patent No. 1 205 544*

van Boort H J J and Groth R, 1968, *Philips Tech. Rev.*, **29**, 17–18: Low pressure sodium lamps with indium oxide filter

van Vliet J A J M and de Groot J J, 1981, *IEE Proc.*, **128**, Part A, 415–441: High-pressure sodium discharge lamps

van Zeggeren F and Storey S H, 1970, *The computation of chemical equilibria* (Cambridge: The University Press)

Vecht A, 1973, *J. Luminescence*, **7**, 213–227: DC electroluminescence in zinc sulphide and related compounds

Verstegen J M P J, 1974, *Ltg. Res. Technol.*, **6**, 31–32: New class of phosphors for 'de luxe' fluorescent lamps

Volf M B, 1961, *Technical glasses* (London: Pitman)

von Engel A, 1965, *Ionised gases* (Oxford: The University Press)

von Kries J, 1902, Festschrift der Albrecht-Ludwigs-Universität, 145–158: *Chromatic adaptation*. Reproduced in translation in MacAdam D L (Ed), 1970, *Sources of color science*, 109–119 (Cambridge, Mass: MIT Press)

Vrenken L E, 1976, *Ltg. Res. Technol.*, **8,** 211–218: New fluorescent lamps for interior lighting

Vrenken L E, 1978, *Ltg. Res. Technol.*, **10,** 161–163: Fluorescent lamps with very high luminous efficiency

Waldram J M, 1954, *Trans. Illum. Eng. Soc.*, **19,** 95–133: Studies in interior lighting

Waymouth J F, 1971, *Electric discharge lamps* (Cambridge, Mass: MIT Press)

Waymouth J F, 1972, *J. Illum. Eng. Soc.*, **2,** 43–49: Current runaway in fluorescent lamps

Webb J D, 1976, *Noise control in industry* (Sudbury, Suffolk: Sound Research Laboratories)

Weston R F, 1959, *Electrical Times*, **135,** 719–722: High output sodium lamps

Wharmby D O, 1980, *IEE Proc.*, **127,** Part A, 165–172: Scientific aspects of the high-pressure sodium lamp

Wheeldon J W, 1959, *Brit. J. Appl. Phys.*, **10,** 295–298: Absorption of sodium and argon by glass

Williams E W and Hall R, 1978, *Luminescence and the light emitting diode* (Oxford: Pergamon)

Winch G T, 1951, *Instrument Practice*, January, 137–144: The physical-eye photometer, colorimeter and spectrophotometer

Work D E, 1981, *Ltg. Res. Technol.*, **13,** 143–152: Chemistry of metal halide lamps: a review

Wright W D, 1928–9, *Trans. Opt. Soc.*, **30,** 141–164: A redetermination of the trichromatic coefficients of the spectral colours

Wright W D, 1929–30, *Trans. Opt. Soc.*, **31,** 201–218: A redetermination of the mixture curves of the spectrum

Wright W D, 1941, *Proc. Phys. Soc.*, **53,** 93–113: The sensitivity of the eye to small colour differences

Wright W D, 1943, *J. Opt. Soc. Amer.*, **33,** 632–636: Graphical representation of small colour differences

Yerrell J S, 1971, TRRL Report LR 383: *Headlight intensities in Europe and Britain* (Crowthorne, Berks: Transport and Road Research Laboratory)

Yerrell J S, 1976, *Ltg. Res. Technol.*, **8,** 69–79: Vehicle headlights

Zemansky M W, 1957, *Heat and thermodynamics*, 2nd Edition (New York: McGraw-Hill)

Zubler E G and Mosby F A, 1959, *Illum. Eng.*, **54,** 734–740: An iodine incandescent lamp with virtually 100 per cent lumen maintenance

Zwikker C, 1953, *Philips Tech. Rev.*, **15,** 161–188: The equivalent circuit of a gas discharge lamp

Author index

Subject index